THE
AUTO
BOOK

BOOKS AND INSTRUCTIONAL MATERIALS

BY WILLIAM H. CROUSE AND *DONALD L. ANGLIN

Automotive Air Conditioning*
  Workbook for Automotive Air Conditioning*
Automotive Chassis and Body*
  Workbook for Automotive Chassis and Body*
Automotive Electrical Equipment*
  Workbook for Automotive Electrical Equipment*
Automotive Emission Control*
  Workbook for Automotive Emission Control*
Automotive Engines*
  Workbook for Automotive Engines*
Automotive Fuel, Lubricating, and Cooling Systems*
  Workbook for Automotive Fuel, Lubricating, and
    Cooling Systems*
Automotive Tools, Fasteners, and Measurements—A
  Text-Workbook*
Automotive Transmissions and Power Trains*
  Workbook for Automotive Transmissions and
    Power Trains*
  Transparencies for Automatic-Transmissions
    Hydraulic Circuits*
Automotive Tuneup*
  Workbook for Automotive Tuneup*
Automotive Service Business: Operation and
  Management
Automotive Engine Design
Workbook for Automotive Service and Trouble
  Diagnosis
Automotive Mechanics
  Study Guide for Automotive Mechanics*
  Testbook for Automotive Mechanics*
  Workbook for Automotive Mechanics*
  Automotive Engines—Sound Filmstrip Program
    Set 1 and Set 2
    Preview-Review Exercises
  Automotive Room Chart Series

Automotive Electrical Equipment Charts
Automotive Engines Charts
Automotive Fuel Systems Charts
Automotive Emissions Controls Charts
Automotive Engines Cooling Systems, Heating,
  and Air Conditioning Charts
Automotive Suspension, Steering, and Tires
  Charts
Automotive Transmissions and Power Trains
  Charts
Automotive Brakes Charts
Automotive Troubleshooting Cards
Motor Vehicle Inspection*
  Workbook for Motor Vehicle Inspection*
The Auto Book*
  Auto Shop Workbook*
  Auto Study Guide*
  Auto Test Book*
Pocket Automotive Dictionary*
General Power Mechanics (with Robert Worthington
  and Morton Margules*)
Small Engines: Operation and Maintenance
  Workbook for Small Engines: Operation and
    Maintenance

AUTOMOTIVE TRANSPARENCIES

BY WILLIAM H. CROUSE AND JAY D. HELSEL

Automotive Air Conditioning
Automotive Brakes
Automotive Electrical Systems
Automotive Emission Control
Automotive Engine Systems
Automotive Transmissions and Power Trains
Automotive Steering Systems
Automotive Suspension Systems
Engines and Fuel Systems

ABOUT THE AUTHORS

WILLIAM H. CROUSE

Behind William H. Crouse's clear technical writing is a background of sound mechanical engineering training as well as a variety of practical industrial experience. He has worked in General Motors plants and as Director of Field Education in the Delco-Remy Division of General Motors Corporation.

He has written a number of technical manuals for the Armed Forces and served as editor of technical books for the McGraw-Hill Book Company. He has contributed numerous articles to automotive and engineering magazines and has written many books about science and technology.

William H. Crouse's outstanding work in the automotive field has earned for him membership in the Society of Automotive Engineers and the American Society of Engineering Education.

DONALD L. ANGLIN

Trained in the automotive and diesel service field, Donald L. Anglin has worked both as a mechanic and as a service manager. He has taught automotive courses in high school, trade schools, community colleges, and universities. He has also worked as curriculum supervisor and school administrator for an automotive trade school. Interested in all types of vehicle performance, he has served as a racing-car mechanic and as a consultant to truck fleets on maintenance problems.

Mr. Anglin's work in the automotive service field has earned for him membership in the American Society of Mechanical Engineers and the Society of Automotive Engineers.

THE AUTO BOOK

SECOND EDITION

WILLIAM H. CROUSE
DONALD L. ANGLIN

Gregg Division

McGraw-Hill Book Company

New York	Düsseldorf	Paris
St. Louis	Johannesburg	São Paulo
Dallas	London	Singapore
San Francisco	Madrid	Sydney
Auckland	Mexico	Tokyo
Bogotá	Montreal	Toronto
	New Delhi	
	Panama	

Library of Congress Cataloging in Publication Data

Crouse, William Harry, (date)
  The auto book.

  Includes index.
  SUMMARY: Describes the various parts of the
automobile, how they function, and how they can be
repaired. Includes the latest developments in
the automotive field.
  1. Automobiles—Maintenance and repair.
2. Automobiles—Maintenance and repair—Vocational
guidance. [1. Automobiles—Maintenance and
repair. 2. Automobiles—Maintenance and repair—Vocational
guidance. 3. Vocational guidance]
I. Anglin, Donald L., joint author. II. Title.
TL152.C68 1979   629.28′7   78-10481
ISBN 0-07-014560-1

THE AUTO BOOK, SECOND EDITION

1 2 3 4 5 6 7 8 9 0 VHVH 7 8 5 4 3 2 1 0 9 8

The editors for this book were D. Eugene Gilmore and Alice V. Manning, the art and design coordinator was Tracy Glasner, the designer was Jerry Wilke, the cover designer was Jack Weaver, the art supervisor was George T. Resch, and the production supervisor was Kathleen Morrissey. It was set in Century Schoolbook by Progressive Typographers.
Printed and bound by Von Hoffman Press, Inc.

PREFACE

Since the first edition of *The Auto Book* was published, much has occurred in the fields of automotive design, production, and service. The new pollution, safety, and gasoline-mileage standards mandated by Washington, as well as the free-wheeling competition of foreign-made vehicles, has brought forth a veritable flood of new developments and devices. Five years ago none of us in the automotive service field had heard of phase 2 or three-way catalytic converters; electronic spark-advance and air-fuel-ratio controls; or electronic control of automatic transmissions, automatic load levelers, exhaust gas recirculation, antilock braking, and other electronically controlled devices. Today, the tide of electronic controls is rushing in, sweeping before it the old mechanical controls we have all been so familiar with.

Servicing procedures and testing equipment have also changed drastically. Electronic testers have become commonplace in the service shop. If an electronic module does not test up to specifications, you replace it. Contrast the adjustment procedures for the old-time voltage regulator with the modern nonadjustable regulator, or the electronic ignition system with the older contact-point ignition system, which required periodic point adjustment and replacement.

In this new edition of *The Auto Book,* we have attempted to cover all the latest developments in the automotive field, working on the manuscript right up to press time. It thus becomes the most up-to-date book in the fast-moving field of automotive science and service.

We have not forgotten, however, the basic aim of the book, along with its related materials, also updated: to provide a comprehensive, integrated, and flexible teaching program for students of automotive mechanics.

These related materials include the *Auto Study Guide*, the *Auto Shop Workbook*, the *Auto Test Book*, the *Automotive Transparencies*, and the *Auto Instructor's Guide*.

During the many months that this edition of *The Auto Book* was in preparation, the authors had the assistance and counsel of many, many people—educators, automotive-service experts, automotive engineers, researchers, and artists. It would be impossible to acknowledge them all on this page, but special thanks must go to the following: Mr. Donald W. Patten, Lou Salvadore, and John M. Steck, who took time out from busy schedules to attend the master planning sessions for the new edition of the book; and Frank C. Derato and Ronald G. Dreucci, who spent many hours reviewing the manuscript and offering many suggestions for improving it.

William H. Crouse
Donald L. Anglin

NOTE TO THE INSTRUCTOR

The Auto Book is but one part of a comprehensive and integrated cluster of teaching materials for students of automotive mechanics. As mentioned in the Preface, *The Auto Book* program correlates with the recommendations of the Motor Vehicle Manufacturers Association–American Vocational Association Industry Planning Council and incorporates guidelines for automotive mechanic certification, state plans for vocational education, and recommendations for automotive trade preapprenticeship and apprenticeship training. The program has been designed to fit every type of teaching situation. The *Auto Instructor's Guide* explains in detail how to fit the various parts of the program to any teaching situation.

The Auto Book program consists of:

- The textbook—*The Auto Book* (TAB).
- The *Auto Study Guide*, correlated with TAB. This is a true study guide. It states the objective of each chapter, outlines the chapter, provides numerous checkpoints and tests to evaluate the students' comprehension, lists the key words that students must know, and provides reinforcement of difficult concepts.
- The *Auto Shop Workbook*, correlated with *The Auto Book*. This workbook features step-by-step instructions on how to perform all the basic auto shop jobs. The instructions follow the latest recommendations of automobile and equipment manufacturers. The *Auto Shop Workbook* includes ample tests to check the students' comprehension of their shop activities as well as an individual progress chart so that the students can keep track of how they are progressing.
- The *Auto Test Book* for *The Auto Book*. This test book permits the students to check their progress throughout the program.
- The *Automotive Transparencies*. This series consists of nine transparency books. The transparencies are used with an overhead projector to provide visual reinforcement of automotive fundamentals.
- The *Auto Instructor's Guide*. This guide describes the various ways all or any part of the program can be used and tells how the program can be tailored to fit any teaching situation.

All parts of the cluster of materials that compose *The Auto Book* program were tested to assure the level of readability and to verify that the content is comprehensible by the students. You can therefore utilize them with the confidence that they will do the job they were designed to do.

NOTE TO THE STUDENT

This book—*The Auto Book*—was designed with you, the student, in mind. It covers all the fundamentals of automobile construction, operation, maintenance, and servicing. By the time you have finished this book and the related automotive shop work, you will be ready to enter the world of automotive service as a wage earner. This means that now, as you do your job of studying and working in the school shop, you are getting ready for a good job in the automotive service business. Various special teaching materials have been developed to help you. These materials consist of a study guide, a shop workbook, a test book, and transparencies. If you use any of these in your automotive mechanics course, your instructor will tell you when and how to use them.

Here are some hints on how to study. Studying is usually hard for everyone, but if you follow the suggestions listed below, you will find studying much easier. You will also make good progress in your automotive mechanics course.

1. The first thing to do when you pick up your textbook to study your assignment is to turn the pages one by one. Look at the pictures. Read the numbered section headings. Study each section heading carefully. This will give you an idea of what the assignment is about.
2. If you are starting a new chapter in the textbook, read the introductory paragraph and the objectives. These tell you more about what you are going to study in the chapter.
3. Read the first section in your assignment. Then read the first section again slowly and carefully to make sure you understand it.
4. Continue studying the pages assigned to you. Read each section carefully. When you come to a "Check Up on Yourself," try to answer the questions. If you can answer them, it means you are doing a good job of studying. If a question stumps you, go back and reread the section that will give you the right answer.
5. If you come to a sentence that you don't understand, read it aloud. Think about it. If this does not help, write the sentence on a piece of paper. When you have a chance, ask your instructor to explain the sentence to you.
6. Don't hesitate to admit that something puzzles you. Everybody gets stuck once in a while. Your instructor is there to help you understand.
7. Don't worry about not getting everything the first time you read it. Most good students read and reread their lessons several times. That is the way to make it stick! Reread it!
8. If you feel yourself getting sleepy, or if your attention begins to wander—wake up! Wake up this way: Get up. Stretch. Put cold water on your face. Have a cup of coffee or a soft drink. Then get back to work.

CONTENTS

Part Eight   Auto Air-Conditioning Systems   569

Glossary   590

Index   620

PART ONE
AUTO SHOP FUNDAMENTALS

This is your introduction to the automobile and to the tools you will use in your automotive shopwork. You will learn how to work safely in the shop so that you can protect yourself and fellow workers from injury. We also describe the two systems of measurement used in the shop: the United States Customary System (USCS) and the metric system. You will learn how to use various measuring tools such as rules and micrometers. You will also learn about the different types of fasteners used to hold together automotive parts such as screws, bolts, nuts, and rivets. We concentrate heavily on the tools you will be using, including hammers, screwdrivers, and wrenches. When you finish Part One of this book, you will have the background information you need to begin your shopwork. There are seven chapters in Part One:

CHAPTER ONE
YOU AND THE AUTOMOBILE

After studying this chapter, you should be able to:

1. List the various types of service businesses.
2. Describe the types of service jobs in dealerships and other service businesses.
3. Explain the purpose of the pictures in the book and describe the types used.

The Auto Book tells you about automobiles. It tells you how automobiles run, how to tell when something is wrong, and how to fix troubles that may occur. As you study this book and perform the related shop-work on automobiles, you will learn what you need to know to be a success in the automotive service business. In the pages that follow, we describe many kinds of jobs that are available to you in the automotive service business.

1-1 THE AUTOMOTIVE SERVICE BUSINESS

The automotive business is big—one of the biggest businesses in the world. One of every six persons working in the United States is employed in the transportation field (Fig. 1-1). That amounts to more than 14 million people! There are hundreds of thousands of good, well-paying jobs in the automotive business. And the automotive service business offers some of the best jobs.

The automotive service business includes:

- Dealerships, where the cars are sold and serviced
- Service stations, where the cars get gasoline and oil and related products and services
- Tire and battery dealers
- Independent garages
- Specialty shops, where front-end alignment, transmission, body, tuneup, engine rebuilding, and air conditioning work are handled
- Fleet garages, where truck and bus lines have their own service shops
- Parts stores, where automotive parts are sold
- Automotive machine shops, where certain automotive parts are reconditioned

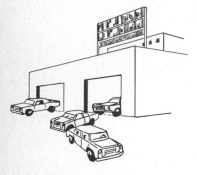

Fig. 1-1
One out of every six persons working in the United States is employed in the transportation field.

1-2 JOBS IN AUTOMOTIVE SERVICE

More than 133 million cars, trucks, and buses are rolling on our highways. There are millions more off-the-road vehicles, such as farm machines, power mowers, dune buggies, motorcycles, and so on. It takes a lot of people to service all these vehicles. More than a million men and women are working in the automotive service business right now. But tens of thousands more women and men are needed! For example, there is a serious shortage of automotive mechanics.

It is up to you to study this book and learn what is in it so that you can get one of these good jobs.

Let's take a look at some of these jobs in the automotive service business.

1-3 JOBS IN SERVICE STATIONS

There are more than 180,000 service, or gasoline, stations in the United States (Fig. 1-2). Their basic job is to supply the fuel, oil, and lubricants needed to keep automobiles going. Many service stations also wash and wax cars, repair tires, balance wheels, adjust brakes, do front-end alignment work, and so on. In addition, most service stations sell TBA. "TBA" stands for tires, batteries, and accessories (such as shock absorbers, seat covers, light bulbs, and car wax).

Fig. 1-2
There are more than 180,000 service stations in the United States.

1-4 JOBS IN AUTOMOTIVE-DEALER SHOPS

There are about 24,000 new-car dealers in the United States. Every one of these dealers has a service shop. Some of the shops are fairly small, employing only a few automotive mechanics. Others are large and employ 100 or more automotive mechanics and other service people. These shops have people who can usually do just about everything required to service and repair cars. They can

- Diagnose car troubles
- Repair engines
- Repair transmissions
- Service drive shafts, differentials, and axles
- Repair and replace steering-system parts
- Repair and replace brake-system parts
- Repair and replace suspension parts, such as springs, ball joints, shock absorbers, and so on
- Service air conditioners, heaters, and radios
- Handle body and glass work, including collision repair and painting

This is quite a list. It shows you the many opportunities that are available in the service department of an automobile dealership.

1-5 JOBS IN INDEPENDENT GARAGES

There are about 90,000 independent garages, both large and small, in the United States. The large garages do all the jobs that are done in the dealer service shops. There are many more independent garages than there are dealer service shops because after a while, some people do not go back to their new-car dealers for automotive service. They go to an independent garage when their car needs servicing. Also, many owners of used cars have no dealer contact. They may prefer to go to an independent garage.

1-6 JOBS IN SPECIALTY SHOPS

Thousands of specialty shops provide backup service for service stations, dealer shops, and independent garages. Some specialty shops have the special machinery needed for such major reconditioning jobs as grinding crankshafts and camshafts; boring engine blocks; overhauling automatic transmissions, carburetors, and alternators; and so on.

The jobs in specialty shops vary greatly. But, as a rule, people who work in these shops are very well paid because they have a high degree of training and skill.

1-7 JOBS IN FLEET GARAGES

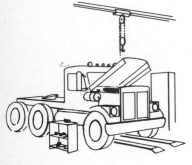

Fig. 1-3
Buses and trucks usually are maintained in fleet garages.

A fleet of trucks or buses usually requires a sizable service shop to keep them running (Fig. 1-3). A truck or bus is much more complicated and expensive than an automobile. Therefore the equipment required to service trucks and buses is more complicated and requires more skill to operate than the equipment required to service cars. Therefore, the service technician in the fleet garage must be *highly trained* and a *very careful mechanic*. The technician cannot afford to make a mistake. Think what would happen if the service mechanic slipped up and, as a result, a truck loaded with frozen food broke down. The food could thaw and spoil, costing the truck owner thousands of dollars. So it is easy to understand why a fleet operator demands the very best automotive mechanics available. And they are paid very well.

1-8 JOBS IN PARTS STORES

The parts dealer sells automotive parts to anyone who wants to buy them and keeps a supply of service parts on hand. Working for a parts dealer is a lot like working in a retail store. You must know the merchandise—automotive parts—and you must know where everything is located in the stockroom. There are hundreds of thousands of different automotive parts, so it is a big job to keep track of them all. This is where training as an automotive mechanic is useful. If you know automobiles, you know automotive parts.

Of course, the typical parts dealer does not stock *all* these parts. Only fast-moving parts are kept on hand. These are the parts that most often require replacement. Distributor contact points, spark plugs, and oil filters are examples of fast-moving parts.

When a parts dealer gets an order for a part that is not in stock, it is ordered from a warehouse or, sometimes, from the car factory. In any case, the dealer can probably get nearly any automotive part within a few hours or days at most.

1-9 SUCCESS IN THE AUTOMOTIVE SERVICE BUSINESS

When you get your job in the automotive service business, you will become a member of the business community. This means you will have steady work and a steady income. There are well-paying jobs in the automotive service business, and there is always the chance for advancement—the chance to move up to a better job. How far you go and how much money you make are largely up to you! Your progress depends on how much you study, how well you learn about automobiles, and how well you do your shopwork. You've already made a very good start toward a good future in the automotive service business by reading *The Auto Book.*

CHECK UP ON YOURSELF

You have already made a good start toward a career in the automotive service business. After you have completed your automotive course and have done the related shopwork, you should be able to troubleshoot and fix any car having trouble. Now check up on yourself to make sure that what you have read is sticking with you. If you don't get the right answers to the questions the first time, reread the past few pages. The answers and the sections from which they come are given below.

1. How many people in the United States work in the transportation field?
2. How many cars, trucks, and buses are running in the United States?
3. What does "TBA" stand for?
4. Why does a mechanic working in a fleet garage get top pay?

ANSWERS
1. About 14 million people (Sec. 1-1). 2. About 133 million (Sec. 1-2). 3. Tires, batteries, and accessories (Sec. 1-3). 4. Because the technician works with very expensive and complicated equipment and must be a top-grade mechanic (Sec. 1-7).

COMPONENTS OF THE AUTOMOBILE

1-10 AUTOMOTIVE COMPONENTS
The automobile is made up of four components:

1. Engine, or source of power, which makes the car go.
2. Chassis, or support for the engine and the wheels, which includes the steering and braking systems. The chassis also includes the engine.
3. Power train, which carries the power from the engine to the car wheels. The power train includes the transmission, the drive shaft, the differential, and the wheel axles.
4. Car body, which fits over and around all the other components. To these components can be added the car heater, air conditioner, lights, radio, and other parts which make driving more pleasant. These other parts are called *accessories*.

PICTURES IN *THE AUTO BOOK*

1-11 THE PICTURES
Before we talk about the components of the automobile, let's look at the different kinds of pictures, or illustrations, you will find in this book. Don't try to understand them right now. We are explaining the different kinds of illustrations so that you can use them to learn about automobiles.

Many of the pictures in the book are *external*, or *outside, views*. For example, Fig. 1-4 is an external view of a car.

Many of the illustrations have been prepared especially for you in a sectional view. Figure 1-5 is a sectional view of an engine. It is called a *sectional view* because the engine shown has been cut or sliced in two to show you what the inside looks like. By comparison, Fig. 1-6 shows an apple that has been cut in two. The picture is a sectional view of the apple, which shows you what the inside looks like.

Fig. 1-4
This picture of a car is an example of an external, or outside, view. (*Chrysler Corporation*)

Another kind of picture is a cutaway view (Fig. 1-7). It is called a *cutaway view* because part of the engine has been cut away, rather than sliced in two as in Fig. 1-5.

Another kind of picture that shows the inside parts of a component is an exploded view, which is shown in Fig. 1-8. Look at this picture for a moment. Notice how the parts of the gear housing are laid out in the exact order in which they go into the component. You can see why it is called an *exploded view*. Everything has been "blown out" of the gear housing in a well-arranged "explosion." You can use this picture when you are putting together the parts of the component shown.

One other kind of picture you will see is a *phantom view*. Figure 1-9 is a phantom view of an automobile. Here the artist has drawn some of the parts as though you could see through them. The purpose is to show you where the various parts are located and how they are put together.

The last type of illustration that we want to point out to you is the line drawing (Fig. 1-10). Often it tells you a story simply by looking at it. When a line drawing breaks up a complicated series of parts or ac-

Fig. 1-5
Sectional view from the end of an engine. (*Chrysler Corporation*)

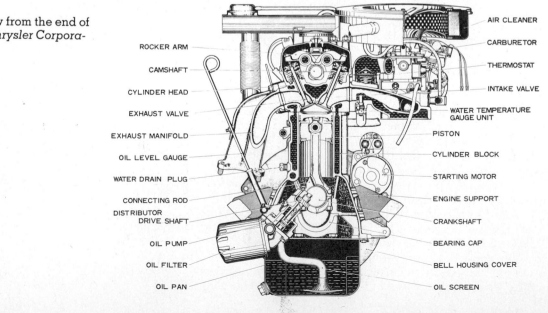

ROCKER ARM

CAMSHAFT

CYLINDER HEAD

EXHAUST VALVE

EXHAUST MANIFOLD

OIL LEVEL GAUGE

WATER DRAIN PLUG

CONNECTING ROD

DISTRIBUTOR DRIVE SHAFT

OIL PUMP

OIL FILTER

OIL PAN

AIR CLEANER

CARBURETOR

THERMOSTAT

INTAKE VALVE

WATER TEMPERATURE GAUGE UNIT

PISTON

CYLINDER BLOCK

STARTING MOTOR

ENGINE SUPPORT

CRANKSHAFT

BEARING CAP

BELL HOUSING COVER

OIL SCREEN

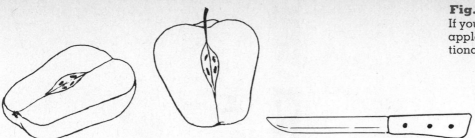

tions into blocks, it is called a *block diagram*. Figure 1-10, for example, is a block diagram of the high-energy ignition system. When the line drawing shows you accurately in complete detail the connections and values of even the smallest part in an assembly, then that type of line drawing is called a *schematic*. You will see it frequently in electrical work.

Just remember this: These pictures are in the book to help you understand what the automobile and its components are all about. Once you understand how the parts go together, you can understand how they work. And that makes it easier to understand how to fix the components when something goes wrong.

CHECK UP ON YOURSELF
Read the questions that follow and answer them carefully. Then check your answers with the correct answers given below.

1. What are the four components of the automobile?
2. What are five types of pictures used in this book?

ANSWERS
1. The engine, chassis, power train, and body (Sec. 1-11). 2. External, sectional, cutaway, exploded, and phantom (Sec. 1-12).

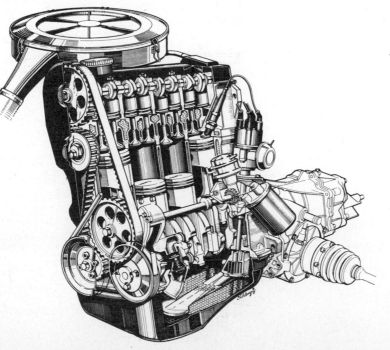

Fig. 1-7
A cutaway view of a four-cylinder engine. (*Volkswagen of America, Inc.*)

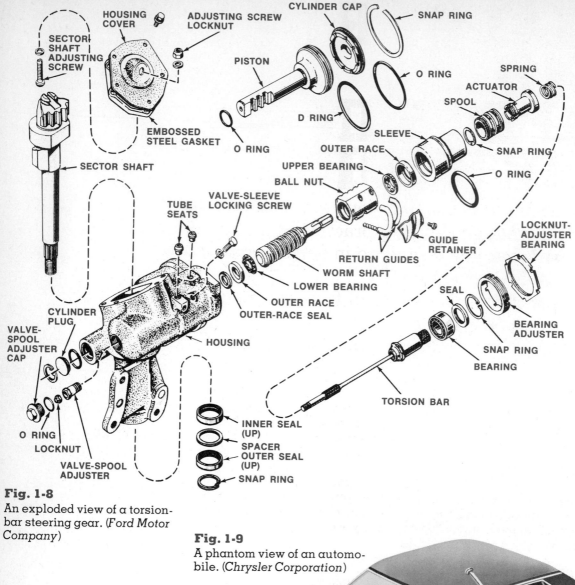

Fig. 1-8
An exploded view of a torsion-bar steering gear. (*Ford Motor Company*)

Fig. 1-9
A phantom view of an automobile. (*Chrysler Corporation*)

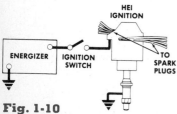

Fig. 1-10
A simple line drawing. (*Delco-Remy Division of General Motors Corporation*)

CHAPTER TWO SAFETY IN THE SHOP

After studying this chapter, you should be able to:
1. Explain what good safety practice in the shop means.
2. Explain what you should do in an emergency.
3. Discuss fire prevention.
4. Describe the various types of fire extinguishers and the fires they are to be used on.
5. List the safety guidelines you should follow in the shop.

Shopwork is varied and interesting. The shop is where all the automotive service jobs are done. These jobs include grinding valves, replacing bearings, honing engine cylinders, checking and correcting wheel alignment, and so forth. These and many other jobs are discussed in later chapters of this book.

Before you start working in the shop, you should know about safety. Safety in the shop means protecting yourself and your fellow workers from possible danger or injury. In this chapter, you will learn how to protect yourself and others by safely working with and handling tools.

2-1 SAFETY IS YOUR JOB
Yes, safety is your job. When working in the shop, you are being "safe" if you are protecting your eyes, your fingers, your hands—yourself— from danger at all times. And, just as important, safety means looking out for the safety of those around you.

In Sec. 2-6 there are safety guidelines that you should follow when you work in the shop. These guidelines are based on common sense. If you pay attention to the guidelines, you can prevent accidents. Remember, safety is *your* job.

2-2 LAYOUT OF THE SHOP
The first thing to do when you start working in the shop is to find out where everything is located. This includes the different machine tools as well as the car lifts and the work areas. Many shops mark off work areas with painted lines on the floor (Fig. 2-1). The lines guide customers and workers away from danger zones in which machinery is

Fig. 2-1
Typical shop layout. (*Motor Vehicle Manufacturers Association*)

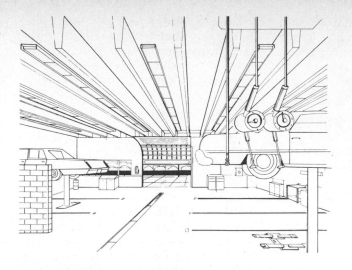

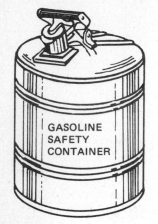

Fig. 2-2
Store gasoline and all flammable liquids in approved safety containers.

Fig. 2-3
Never store gasoline or other flammable liquids in glass bottles, jars, or jugs. If the container should break, a disastrous explosion and fire could result.

operating. The lines also remind workers to keep their tools and equipment within the work areas.

Notice the warning signs posted around the shop. These signs are there to remind you about safety. Read them carefully and follow the instructions at all times. Failure to follow instructions is the most common cause of accidents in the shop.

2-3 EMERGENCIES

If there is an accident and someone gets hurt, notify your instructor at once! Your instructor will know what to do—call the school nurse, a doctor, or an ambulance. If there is a fire, get help at once.

2-4 FIRE PREVENTION

Gasoline is such a familiar item in the shop that people often forget that it can be extremely dangerous. A spark or lighted match in a closed place filled with gasoline vapor can cause an explosion. Even the spark from a light switch can set off gasoline vapors. There have been cases in which employees washed the floor of a service bay with gasoline—with the doors closed—and then turned off the lights. The spark from the light switch set off a terrible explosion of gasoline vapor that not only destroyed the shop, but also injured or killed the employees.

Remember that it is also dangerous and against the law to pour gasoline down floor drains. Gasoline can form vapors in the sewer line, and these vapors could be set off by a lighted match or cigarette thrown down a drain.

To prevent explosions, keep the doors open or the ventilator system going if there is gasoline vapor around. Wipe up spilled gasoline at once and put the rags outside to dry. *Never* light or smoke cigarettes around gasoline. If you are working on a car with leaky carburetor, fuel line, or pump, catch the leaking gasoline in a container or with rags. Then put the rags outside as soon as possible. Fix the leak right away. Be very careful to avoid sparks around the car. Store gasoline in an approved safety container (Fig. 2-2). Never, *never*, keep gasoline in a glass jug. The jug could break and cause a terrible explosion or fire (Fig. 2-3).

Oily rags are another possible source of fire, because the oil on the rags might cause so much heat to develop that the rags could ignite spontaneously, or catch fire. This is called *spontaneous combustion,* and it results from a chemical action that produces heat and fire. Oily rags and waste should be put into special closed metal containers where they can do no harm (Fig. 2-4).

2-5 FIRE EXTINGUISHERS

Note the location of the fire extinguishers in the shop. Make sure you know how to use them. Figure 2-5 shows different types of fires and the kinds of fire extinguishers used to fight them. Ask your instructor about fire extinguishers if you have any questions.

2-6 TAKING CARE OF YOURSELF IN THE SHOP

Some people say, "Accidents will happen!" Safety experts do not agree. They say, "Accidents are *caused*"—caused by carelessness, by inattention to the job at hand, by the use of damaged or incorrect tools, and sometimes by just plain stupidity. To keep accidents from happening, follow these simple safety guidelines:

1. Work quietly and give the job your undivided attention.
2. Keep your tools and equipment under control.
3. Keep jack handles out of the way. After using a creeper, prop it against the wall with the wheels out (so that the wheels will not mark the wall). See Fig. 2-6. Or push the creeper under the car being worked on (Fig. 2-7).
4. Never indulge in horseplay or other foolish activities. You could cause someone to get seriously hurt.
5. Don't put sharp objects, such as screwdrivers, in your pocket. You could cut yourself or get stabbed. Or you could ruin the upholstery in a car.
6. Make sure your clothes are suitable for the job. Dangling sleeves or ties can get caught in machinery and cause serious injuries. Do not wear sandals or open-toe shoes. Wear full leather shoes with nonskid rubber heels and soles. Steel-toe safety shoes are best for shopwork.
7. Wipe excess oil and grease off your hands and tools so that you can get a good grip on tools or parts.
8. If you spill oil or grease, or any liquid, on the floor, clean it up so that no one will slip and fall.
9. Never use compressed air to blow dirt from your clothes. Never point a compressed-air hose at another person. Flying particles could injure an eye.
10. Always wear goggles or a face shield on *any* job where there is danger from flying particles (Fig. 2-8).
11. Watch out for flying sparks from the grinding wheel or when you are welding. The sparks can set your clothes on fire.
12. To protect your eyes, wear goggles when using chemicals, such as solvents. If you get a chemical in your eyes, wash it out with water at once (Fig. 2-9). See the school nurse or a doctor as soon as possible.
13. When using a shop jack, make sure it is centered so that it won't slip. And never, *never,* jack up a car while someone is working under it! People have been killed when the jack

Fig. 2-4
Safety can for the storage of oily rags.

slipped and the car fell down on them! Always place safety stands under a car before going under it (Fig. 2-10).

14. Always use the right tool for the job. The wrong tool could damage the part being worked on and could also cause you to get hurt.

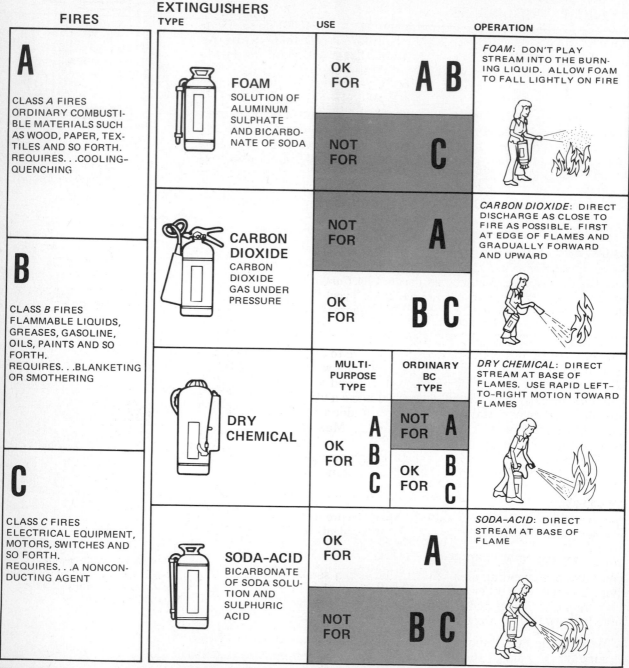

Fig. 2-5
Chart showing types of fire extinguishers and the classification of fires. (*Ford Motor Company*)

Fig. 2-6
When jacking up a car, always finish with the handle pointing up so that no one can trip over it. When creepers are not in use, stand them up against the wall, wheels out, where no one can stumble over them.

Fig. 2-7
After using a creeper, shove it under the car being worked on.

CAUTION

Never run an engine in a closed garage that does not have a ventilating system. The exhaust gases contain carbon monoxide. *Carbon monoxide* is a colorless, odorless, tasteless, poisonous gas that can kill you! Enough carbon monoxide to kill you can accumulate in a closed one-car garage in only three minutes.

2-7 DRIVING CARS IN THE SHOP

Cars have to be moved in the shop. They have to be brought in for service, and they may have to be moved from one work area to another. When the job is finished, they have to be moved out of the work area. You must be extremely careful when you drive a car in the shop. Make sure the way is clear. Make sure no one is under a nearby car. The person might suddenly stick out an arm or leg. Make sure there are no tools on the floor that you could run over.

When you take a car out on the street for a road test, *fasten your seat belt* even if you're going only a short distance.

CAUTION

You should always fasten your seat belt when you are in a moving car. Use it whether you are the driver or a passenger. In accidents, seat belts save lives.

CHECK UP ON YOURSELF

You have been reading about how to develop a safety attitude in the shop. You will find other safety precautions in the chapters dealing with shop tools. Now find out how well you understand what you have just studied by answering the following questions.

1. What is the first thing you should do if there is an accident in the shop?
2. Why should you never use gasoline when the garage doors are closed?

Fig. 2-8
Always wear safety glasses, goggles, or a face shield when using a bench grinder. (*Ford Motor Company*)

Fig. 2-10
Always use safety stands, properly located, to hold the car safely.

Fig. 2-9
If solvent or some other chemical splashes in your eye, immediately wash your eye with water.

3. How can oily rags be dangerous?
4. What is wrong with operating a car in a shop when the doors are closed?
5. What is the first precaution to observe when you are using a grinding wheel?

ANSWERS
1. Notify your instructor immediately if there is an accident (Sec. 2-3).
2. Gasoline vapor may accumulate and cause a terrible explosion (Sec. 2-4).
3. They can catch fire, or ignite spontaneously (Sec. 2-4). **4.** Enough carbon monoxide to kill you can accumulate in only a few minutes (Sec. 2-6). **5.** Wear goggles to protect your eyes (Sec. 2-6).

CHAPTER THREE
SHOPWORK AND SHOP MANUALS

After studying this chapter, you should be able to:

1. List the six steps in any service job and explain what each means.
2. Explain and describe the various sources of automotive service information and specifications.

In the shop there are many jobs to be done. Jobs on engines, for example, include installing new piston rings, grinding valves, and replacing bearings. Then there are the jobs that have to be done on the suspension system, the transmission, the brake system, and the steering system.

Although there is a tremendous variety of jobs to be done in the shop, all these jobs can be done in a few basically simple steps. Believe it or not, every job requires no more than six steps. These are shown in Fig. 3-1. They are measuring, disassembling, machining, installing new parts, reassembling, and making adjustments. Many jobs require fewer than six steps.

3-1 MEASURING

Before you can begin work on a car, you have to find out what is wrong with it. Begin by measuring. When you listen to a rough engine, you are measuring. Yes, you are measuring the sounds of a faulty engine against the sounds of a good engine as you know them. When you check the oil in an engine, you are measuring its level in the crankcase. When you use electric meters to check the output of an alternator, you are measuring. When you check engine vacuum or compression, you are measuring engine performance. The results of your measurements tell you what kind of job you have to do.

Linear measurements are another type of measurement. *Linear measurements* are measurements that are taken in a straight *line,* such as inches, fractions of an inch, or centimeters [cm] and millimeters [mm]. (These are units in the metric system, which we cover in Chap. 4.) For example, when you measure valve-stem clearance, contact point opening, or engine-cylinder diameter, you are taking a linear measurement.

SIX STEPS TO SHOPWORK
1. MEASURING
2. DISASSEMBLY
3. MACHINING
4. INSTALLING NEW PARTS
5. REASSEMBLY
6. ADJUSTMENTS

Fig. 3-1
The six steps used in shopwork.

3-2 DISASSEMBLY

Sometimes the measurements show that something is wrong. You then have to *disassemble,* or take apart, the component to get at the trouble. Suppose, for example, that your measurements show that engine valves are not doing their job. You have to take the cylinder head off the engine in order to get to the valves and fix them.

3-3 MACHINING

Sometimes the job requires you to remove metal from a part. Using a machine to remove metal is called *machining.* Suppose you find valve trouble. This could require grinding the valves and the valve seats. Or you might find that the engine cylinders require machining. Special machines—called *power tools*—are required to do these jobs.

3-4 INSTALLING NEW PARTS

You may find that old parts are so worn out that they must be thrown away and new parts must be installed. Sometimes new parts have to be fitted with power tools.

3-5 REASSEMBLY

After you have fixed the trouble, you have to put the parts back together. This is called *reassembly.* In other words, you have to reassemble all the parts to make the component operate again.

3-6 ADJUSTMENTS

As an automobile is operated, parts naturally wear. Thus, various adjustments are required. Also, some adjustments are necessary after reassembly. Let's take a valve job as an example. After you have finished grinding the valves and valve seats, you must put the engine back together. Then you have to measure the valve action and make adjustments so that the valve movements will be within specifications.

3-7 SPECIFICATIONS

In the shop you will often hear the word "specification," or "spec." The specs give you the right measurements for the car you are working on. The car manufacturer sets the specs. You can find the specs in the car shop manual. After a valve job, for example, you have to adjust valve clearances "to spec" on some engines.

3-8 THE SIX STEPS

Not every job requires all six steps. Sometimes you may only make some adjustments. Other times you may replace a part without making any adjustments. But remember, every job you do in the auto shop requires no more than six steps to complete.

CHECK UP ON YOURSELF

Do you understand what you have just studied about shopwork?
Find out by answering these questions. The answers follow the questions.

1. What are the six steps in automotive service jobs?
2. What are linear measurements?
3. Why is machining necessary?
4. Who sets the specifications?

ANSWERS

1. Measuring, disassembling, machining, installing new parts, reassembling, and making adjustments (Secs. 3-1 to 3-6). **2.** Measurements that can be taken in a straight line (Sec. 3-1). **3.** To remove metal (Sec. 3-3). **4.** The car manufacturer (Sec. 3-7).

3-9 SHOP MANUALS

Every automobile manufacturer issues shop manuals for its cars. These manuals—also called *service manuals*—are published every year when the new models come out. The manuals cover all service procedures, provide the specs, name the special tools needed for different jobs, and explain how to fix all kinds of car trouble on the new models.

Figure 3-2 shows an automobile manufacturer's shop manual for one model year. Note that this manual is almost 2 inches [50 mm] thick. It contains all the servicing procedures that might be required. The student in Fig. 3-3 is checking up on how to service engine valves. The manual gives the various steps of the procedure.

This book, plus the accompanying Workbook and the shopwork that you get in your automotive course, will give you all the fundamentals you need right now. Later, when you are working in a garage or a dealer's shop, you will be able to look up information in the shop manuals for the cars you service. But to understand the shop manuals, you have to know the fundamentals. And that's what you get in *The Auto Book* and the Workbook—the fundamentals.

3-10 AUTO REPAIR MANUALS

Repair manuals covering almost all cars are published by the Chilton Book Company, Motor, and other companies (Fig. 3-4). Any of these manuals can be used by auto mechanics to find the specs and the service procedures for the cars built in the United States in the past seven years. These manuals come out every year. You will find one or more of these manuals in almost every service shop of almost every dealership and garage and in many service stations as well.

3-11 OTHER SOURCES OF INFORMATION

Many automotive service magazines contain information on servicing various cars. Often they help explain how to do hard jobs, how to take service shortcuts, and how to become a better and better-paid auto mechanic.

Testing-equipment manufacturers provide operating instructions or manuals on how to use their equipment. Parts makers, such as manufacturers of pistons, piston rings, and bearings, also provide booklets that are very helpful to the automotive mechanic.

3-12 SPECIALIZED TEXTBOOKS

There are a number of specialized textbooks that cover in detail the various components of the automobile such as engines, electrical equipment, transmissions, and brakes. For example, McGraw-Hill publishes the *Automotive Technology Series,* which includes such books as

- *Automotive Air Conditioning*
- *Automotive Body Repair and Refinishing*
- *Automotive Chassis and Body*

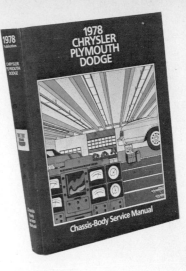

Fig. 3-2
Service manuals, issued each year by the car manufacturers, supply specifications and details of servicing procedures for their cars. (*Chrysler Corporation*)

Fig. 3-3
When you need some specific information on a car, look it up in the manufacturer's service manual.

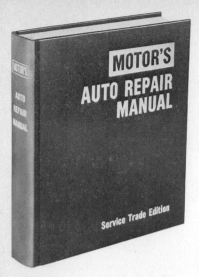

Fig. 3-4

An auto repair manual such as this supplies you with the specifications and highlights of servicing all cars made in recent years in the United States. (*The Hearst Corporation*)

- *Automotive Electrical Equipment*
- *Automotive Emission Control*
- *Automotive Engines*
- *Automotive Fuel, Lubricating, and Cooling Systems*
- *Automotive Transmissions and Power Trains*
- *Automotive Tuneup*

If you want to dig deeper into any of these subjects, refer to the book covering the parts which especially interested you. These specialized books cover the basics of construction, operation, troubleshooting, and servicing, in great detail.

There is also the McGraw-Hill *Automotive Technician's Handbook,* which is a reference book covering all aspects of automotive service.

CHECK UP ON YOURSELF

Let's find out how well you understand what you have studied about shop manuals. Answer the following questions.

1. How often do car manufacturers issue shop manuals?
2. What does this book—*The Auto Book*—give you that you can't find in the car shop manuals?
3. In addition to the car manufacturers' shop manuals, what are other sources of information on servicing cars?

ANSWERS

1. Every year (Sec. 3-9). **2.** *The Auto Book* gives you the fundamentals (Secs. 3-9 to 3-11). **3.** Chilton and Motor auto repair manuals, service magazines, and other similar publications (Secs. 3-10 to 3-12).

CHAPTER FOUR
SYSTEMS OF MEASUREMENT

After studying this chapter, you should be able to:

1. Describe the two basic systems of measurement used in the United States.
2. List the basic units of measurement in each system.
3. Explain what kilo, deci, centi, and milli mean.
4. Explain how to convert measurements from one system into the other system.

4-1 WHY SHOULD WE LEARN THE METRIC SYSTEM?

Most people brought up in the United States are familiar with U.S. Customary System (USCS) measurements. These are inches, feet, miles, pints, quarts, gallons, and so on. But the United States is the only major country in the world still using this system. All other major countries use the metric system. Cars, motorcycles, and machinery imported into the United States are dimensioned in the metric system. All measurements, all nuts and bolts, are measured in metric units—meters, centimeters, millimeters, liters, and so on. The United States is also switching to the metric system. Some automobiles manufactured in the United States are already metric. In the near future, all automobiles and other machines made in this country will be built to metric measurements. The metric system is easy to learn and logical. It is based on multiples of 10. A meter [m], for example, which is 3.281 feet, is 100 centimeters [cm] or 1000 millimeters [mm]. (In this book, we give the USCS measurement first, followed by the metric equivalent in brackets: 1 inch [25.4 mm].)

4-2 THE USCS MEASUREMENTS

Measurements in the USC System include

Length	
	12 inches = 1 foot (ft)
	3 feet = 1 yard (yd)
	5280 feet = 1 mile (mi)

Liquid or Volume	16 fluid ounces (fl oz) = 1 pint (pt)
	2 pints = 1 quart (qt)
	4 quarts = 1 gallon (gal)
Weight	16 ounces (oz) = 1 pound (lb)
	2000 pounds = 1 ton

Notice how many different numbers there are and the different units of measurement. Yet these are only a few of the many numbers and names in the USC system.

4-3 METRIC SYSTEM

The metric system is based on multiples of 10, the same as our money system. Ten cents is one dime, and 10 dimes is one dollar. In the same way, 10 millimeters [mm] is 1 centimeter [cm], 10 centimeters is 1 decimeter [dm], and 10 decimeters is 1 meter [m] (Fig. 4-1). Note that "meter" is part of every word. This is because the meter is the unit of length in the metric system. As Fig. 4-1 shows, 1 m is 39.37 inches.

The first part of the words, the prefix, is the multiplication factor:

- Kilo means 1000 (one thousand)
- Deci means 0.10 (one-tenth)
- Centi means 0.01 (one-hundredth)
- Milli means 0.001 (one-thousandth)

Therefore 1 kilometer [km] is 1000 meters (which equals 0.62 mile). Table 4-1 relates USCS measurements with metric measurements.

The metric unit of mass or weight is the *gram* [g] (Fig. 4-2). It is the mass of 1 cubic centimeter [cc] of water at its temperature of maximum density. A cubic centimeter is a cube that measures 1 cm [1/100 m] on each side (Fig. 4-3).

The metric unit of liquid measurement is the *liter* [L]. It is the volume of a cube that measures 10 cm or 1 dm [1/10 m] on a side (Fig. 4-4). The liter is slightly larger than a quart, as shown in Fig. 4-2.

Fig. 4.1
The meter is the metric unit of length. (*General Motors Corporation*)

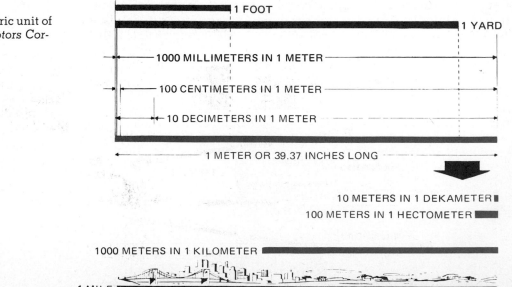

1 FOOT

1 YARD

1000 MILLIMETERS IN 1 METER

100 CENTIMETERS IN 1 METER

10 DECIMETERS IN 1 METER

1 METER OR 39.37 INCHES LONG

10 METERS IN 1 DEKAMETER

100 METERS IN 1 HECTOMETER

1000 METERS IN 1 KILOMETER

1 MILE

TABLE 4-1

LENGTH

1 in (inch)	= 25.4 mm (millimeters)	or 0.0254 m (meter)
1 cm (centimeter)	= 0.390 in	or 0.03281 ft (foot)
1 mm	= 0.039 in	or 0.003281 ft
1 ft	= 304.8 mm	or 0.3048 m
1 mi (mile)	= 1.609 km (kilometers)	or 1609 m
1 km	= 0.62 mi	or 3281 ft

VOLUME/CAPACITY

1 in³ (cubic inch)	= 16.39 cc (cubic centimeters)	or 0.01 liter
1 cc	= 0.061 in³	or 0.001 liter
1 liter	= 61.02 in³	or 1.057 qt (quarts)
1 gal (gallon)	= 4 qt	or 3.780 liters

WEIGHT

1 kg (kilogram)	= 2.2 lb (pounds)	= 35.2 oz (ounces)
1 lb	= 454 g (grams)	= 0.454 kg

**Here are the metric measurements,
taken from the complete metric-system table,
that you will work with most often.**

LENGTH

1 km	= 1000 m	= 100,000 cm
1 m	= 100 cm	= 1000 mm (millimeters)

VOLUME/CAPACITY

1 kL (kiloliter)	= 1000 liters	= 100,000 cL (centiliters)
	= 1000 cc	= 1000 mL (milliliters)

WEIGHT

1 kg	= 1000 g	= 100,000 cg (centigrams)

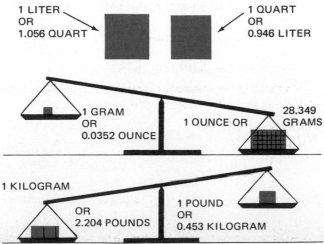

Fig. 4-2
The gram is the metric unit of mass or weight. The liter is the metric unit of fluid capacity or volume. (*General Motors Corporation*)

21

Fig. 4-3
A cubic centimeter is a cube measuring 1 centimeter on a side.

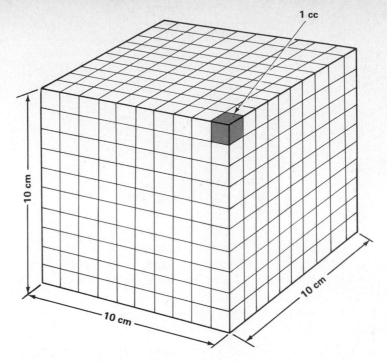

1 cc

10 cm

10 cm

10 cm

Fig. 4-4
A liter is 1000 cc.

Now you can see how simple the metric system is. Everything—length, weight or mass, and volume—is related in multiples of 10. Contrast that with the many different units for the USC system, as shown in Fig. 4-5.

4-4 USING THE METRIC SYSTEM

As you will learn in the following chapter, you can take measurements of length, weight or mass, and volume in either the USCS or the metric

Fig. 4-5
Three metric units replace many different USCS units.

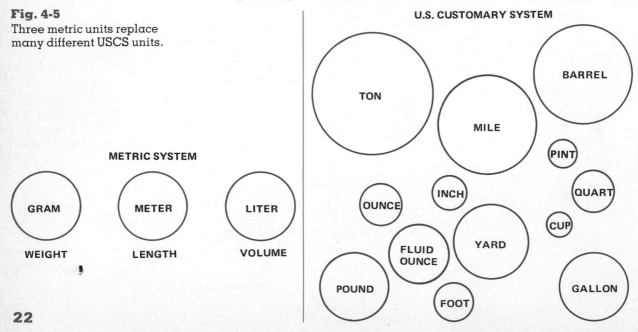

U.S. CUSTOMARY SYSTEM

METRIC SYSTEM

GRAM
WEIGHT

METER
LENGTH

LITER
VOLUME

TON

MILE

BARREL

PINT

INCH

QUART

OUNCE

CUP

FLUID OUNCE

YARD

POUND

FOOT

GALLON

22

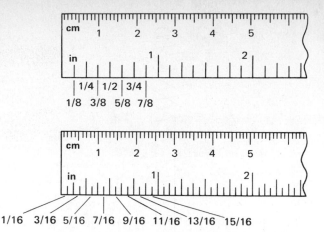

Fig. 4-6
Rule, or steel scale, marked in both inches (United States Customary System) and centimeters (metric system).

system. You can buy rules with both systems of measurement on them (Fig. 4-6). To work on all domestic and imported cars, you need two sets of wrenches and sockets—a USCS set for most of the domestic cars and a metric set for the imports and other cars. We cover this in detail in later chapters on mechanics' tools.

CHECK UP ON YOURSELF

This chapter is very short, but it is very important. You must know how to take measurements in both the USC and the metric system when you are in the shop. You should also know how to change USCS measurements to metric measurements, such as inches to millimeters. Now check up on yourself by answering the questions below. If you miss a question, go back and study the section that covers it. The answers follow the questions.

1. Why should you learn about the metric system?
2. What are some of the measurements of length in the USC system?
3. What are some of the measurements of length in the metric system?
4. Why is the metric system compared to our money system?
5. What are some of the measurements of volume in the USC system?
6. What is the basic unit of liquid measurement in the metric system?
7. What are some of the measurements of weight in the USC system?
8. What is the basic unit of weight in the metric system?
9. Refer to the conversion table (Table 4-1) and find the following: How many millimeters are there in 1 inch? How many kilometers are there in 1 mile? How many liters are there in 1 gallon? How many pounds make 1 kilogram [kg]?

ANSWERS

1. Because the metric system is beginning to replace our USC system of measurement (Sec. 4-1). **2.** Inch, foot, yard, mile (Sec. 4-2). **3.** Millimeter, centimeter, meter, kilometer (Sec. 4-3). **4.** Because both deal in multiples of 10 (Sec. 4-3). **5.** Ounce, pint, quart, gallon (Sec. 4-2). **6.** Liter (Sec. 4-3). **7.** Ounce, pound, ton (Sec. 4-3). **8.** Gram (Sec. 4-3). **9.** 1 inch = 25.4 mm; 1 mile = 1.61 km; 1 gallon = 3.78 L; 2.2 pounds = 1 kg.

CHAPTER FIVE MEASURING TOOLS

After studying this chapter, you should be able to:

1. Describe the various measuring tools discussed in the chapter and explain how each is used.
2. Explain how to read the USCS micrometer and how to convert decimal readings into fractions of an inch.
3. Explain how to use the metric micrometer.
4. Explain how to use and read the vernier caliper.

5-1 RULES

Rules, or steel scales (Fig. 5-1), are marked off in inches and fractions of an inch. Dual-dimensioned rules, shown in Fig. 5-2, are also marked off in centimeters. Figure 5-3 shows how to take various measurements with a rule.

5-2 CALIPERS

The calipers (Fig. 5-4) has two legs which can be spread more or less to take measurements. There are two types: inside calipers and outside calipers (Figs. 5-4 and 5-5). To measure a shaft diameter with outside calipers (Fig. 5-4), adjust the thumb nut so that the two legs just slide over the shaft. Then use a rule to measure the distance between the legs (Fig. 5-6). Inside calipers can be used to measure the diameter of a hole (Figs. 5-5 and 5-7).

5-3 FEELER GAUGES

Feeler gauges (Fig. 5-8) are strips or blades of hardened steel or other metal. They are ground or rolled with great accuracy so that they are the exact thickness stamped on the blade. Many feeler gauges are dual-dimensioned. For example, the 3 on the first blade in Fig. 5-8 means that it is 0.003 inch, or 0.08 mm, thick.

Some feeler gauges are stepped. That is, the tip of the blade is thinner than the rest of the blade (Fig. 5-9). The thinnest gauge, shown in Fig. 5-9, is 0.004 inch [0.10 mm] at the tip and 0.006 inch [0.15 mm] thick over the rest of the blade.

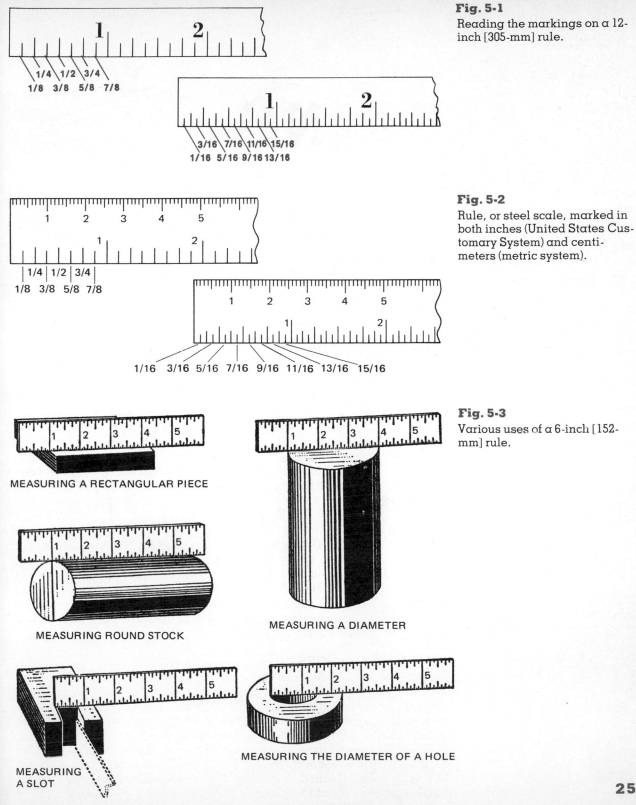

Fig. 5-1
Reading the markings on a 12-inch [305-mm] rule.

Fig. 5-2
Rule, or steel scale, marked in both inches (United States Customary System) and centimeters (metric system).

Fig. 5-3
Various uses of a 6-inch [152-mm] rule.

MEASURING A RECTANGULAR PIECE

MEASURING ROUND STOCK

MEASURING A DIAMETER

MEASURING A SLOT

MEASURING THE DIAMETER OF A HOLE

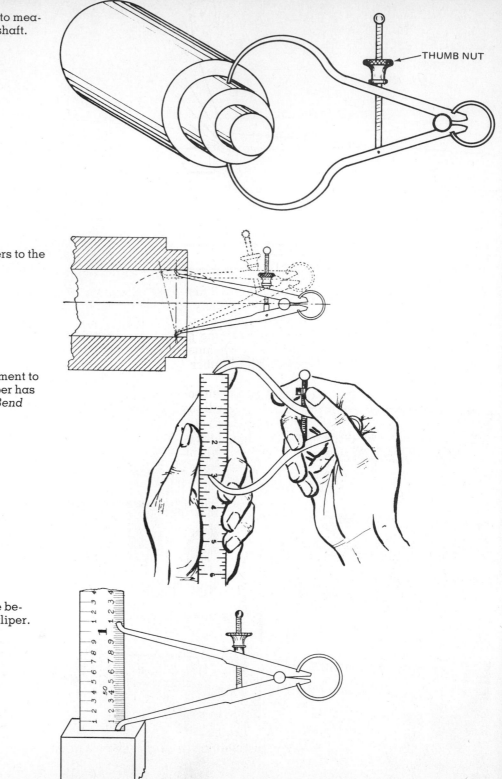

Fig. 5-4
Using outside calipers to measure the diameter of a shaft.

THUMB NUT

Fig. 5-5
Adjusting inside calipers to the size of a hole.

Fig. 5-6
Checking the measurement to which the outside caliper has been adjusted. (*South Bend Lathe Works*)

Fig. 5-7
Measuring the distance between the legs of the caliper.

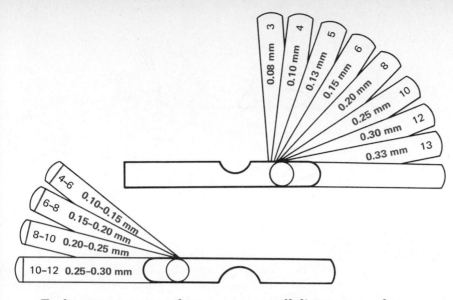

Fig. 5-8
Set of feeler gauges.

Fig. 5-9
Set of stepped feeler gauges.

Feeler gauges are used to measure small distances, or clearances, between objects that cannot be measured in any other way. For example, Fig. 5-10 shows a feeler gauge being used to check the clearance between the side of a piston ring and the ring groove in a piston. To determine the clearance, feeler gauges of various thicknesses are tried until one is found that fits snugly. The number on that gauge is the clearance.

The stepped feeler gauge is easy to use on some jobs where an adjustment is made. When the specifications call for a clearance of 0.005 inch [0.13 mm], select the 0.004–0.006-inch [0.01–0.15-mm] gauge. The clearance is adjusted so that the 0.004-inch [0.10-mm] tip fits, but the 0.006-inch [0.15-mm] part does not fit. This means the clearance is 0.005 inch [0.13 mm]. Stepped feeler gauges are often called *go no-go* gauges.

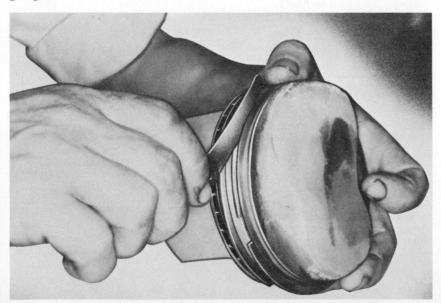

Fig. 5-11
Set of wire feeler gauges.

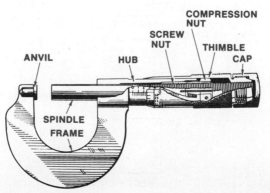

5-4 WIRE FEELER GAUGES

Wire feeler gauges (Fig. 5-11) are made of accurately drawn wire. They are used for measurements such as spark-plug gaps and contact point openings.

5-5 MICROMETERS

There are two types of micrometers: the outside micrometer and the inside micrometer. The outside micrometer (Fig. 5-12), commonly called the "mike," is a tool that can measure the thickness and diameter of solid objects in thousandths of an inch. *It is a precision instrument, and it must be treated with care!* Study Fig. 5-12 carefully; identify the thimble, hub, spindle, frame, and anvil. Note in the cutaway view of the mike (Fig. 5-12) that there are screw threads and a screw nut inside the thimble. By turning the thimble, you move the spindle toward or away from the anvil. Here's how to use the micrometer, or mike.

Suppose you want to measure the diameter of a rod. Hold the rod between the end of the spindle and the anvil, as shown in Fig. 5-13. Turn the thimble gently to move the end of the spindle toward the rod. The rod should be touched lightly on one side of the anvil and on the other side by the end of the spindle. Never turn the spindle tight against anything, for you can ruin the mike. Turn the thimble only until the spindle touches. Then back off the thimble a little if you are going to store the mike.

The mike in Fig. 5-13 has a small knob on the end of the thimble called a *ratchet stop*. When the spindle approaches the object being measured, turn the ratchet stop instead of the thimble. Then, when the spindle comes into contact with the object, the ratchet continues to turn without putting any pressure on the object. When you use the ratchet stop, you cannot damage the mike by turning the thimble too tightly.

Fig. 5-12
Outside micrometer.

CAUTION

Never try to measure a part that is moving—a shaft that is turning, for example. The mike might jam on the shaft, be whirled around, and break. You could be seriously injured by the mike or flying particles.

5-6 READING THE MIKE

After you have adjusted the mike, you have to read the mike to find out the diameter of the rod. To do this, you take two readings and add them. The markings on the mike in the USC system are in thousandths of an inch, that is, in decimals. There are metric micrometers also. These are discussed later.

First look at the markings on the hub. See Fig. 5-14. Note that the hub is marked off with numbers that run from 0 to 9. Each of these numbers means one-tenth, or 0.1 inch. The 2 that is exposed in Fig. 5-14 indicates two-tenths, or 0.2 inch. Note that there are also markings between the numbers. Each of these markings means twenty-five thousandths of an inch, or 0.025 inch.

Note also that there are markings on the end of the thimble. The numbers are marked in thousandths of an inch. There are 25 of these markings, one for each thousandth. Every time the thimble is turned one revolution, it moves exactly 0.025 inch. When the thimble is turned four times, it moves 0.100 inch (4 × 0.025 = 0.100).

Look at Fig. 5-14 again. The 2 and one of the markings next to the 2 are exposed on the hub. This means the distance between the spindle and the anvil is 0.2 inch plus 0.025 inch. However, something must be added to this number to get the actual distance. Note that the thimble has been turned back almost one complete revolution from the 0.225 mark on the hub. It has, in fact, been turned back 0.024 inch. So 0.024 inch must be added to 0.225 inch to get the actual setting, which is 0.249 inch.

Remember: Add the reading on the hub to the reading on the thimble to get the actual measurement. Other mike settings are shown in Fig. 5-15.

5-7 DECIMAL EQUIVALENTS

The table of decimal equivalents (Fig. 5-16) helps you to change the decimals you read on the mike to fractions. For example, if you got a

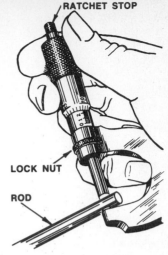

Fig. 5-13
Using an outside micrometer to measure the diameter of a rod.

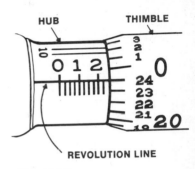

Fig. 5-14
Hub and thimble marking on a micrometer.

Fig. 5-15
Reading a micrometer.

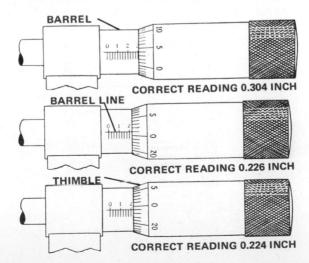

CORRECT READING 0.304 INCH

CORRECT READING 0.226 INCH

CORRECT READING 0.224 INCH

Fig. 5-16
Decimal equivalents.

$\frac{1}{64}$	.0156	$\frac{17}{64}$	.2656	$\frac{33}{64}$	.5156	$\frac{49}{64}$	.7656
$\frac{1}{32}$	.0312	$\frac{9}{32}$	.2812	$\frac{17}{32}$	.5312	$\frac{25}{32}$	.7812
$\frac{3}{64}$	.0468	$\frac{19}{64}$	.2969	$\frac{35}{64}$	.5469	$\frac{51}{64}$	.7969
$\frac{1}{16}$	.0625	$\frac{5}{16}$	.3125	$\frac{9}{16}$	.5625	$\frac{13}{16}$	.8125
$\frac{5}{64}$	.0781	$\frac{21}{64}$	.3281	$\frac{37}{64}$	.5781	$\frac{53}{64}$	.8281
$\frac{3}{32}$	.0937	$\frac{11}{32}$	.3437	$\frac{19}{32}$	.5937	$\frac{27}{32}$	.8437
$\frac{7}{64}$	.1094	$\frac{23}{64}$	.3594	$\frac{39}{64}$	.6094	$\frac{55}{64}$	.8594
$\frac{1}{8}$	.125	$\frac{3}{8}$	.375	$\frac{5}{8}$	.625	$\frac{7}{8}$	.875
$\frac{9}{64}$	.1406	$\frac{25}{64}$	.3906	$\frac{41}{64}$	.6406	$\frac{57}{64}$	.8906
$\frac{5}{32}$	.1562	$\frac{13}{32}$	.4062	$\frac{21}{32}$	.6562	$\frac{29}{32}$	.9062
$\frac{11}{64}$	.1719	$\frac{27}{64}$	.4219	$\frac{43}{64}$	.6719	$\frac{59}{64}$	.9219
$\frac{3}{16}$	.1875	$\frac{7}{16}$	.4375	$\frac{11}{16}$	.6875	$\frac{15}{16}$	.9375
$\frac{13}{64}$	.2031	$\frac{29}{64}$	.4531	$\frac{45}{64}$	.7031	$\frac{61}{64}$	.9531
$\frac{7}{32}$	.2187	$\frac{15}{32}$	.4687	$\frac{23}{32}$	.7187	$\frac{31}{32}$	.9687
$\frac{15}{64}$	.2344	$\frac{31}{64}$	.4844	$\frac{47}{64}$	.7344	$\frac{63}{64}$	.9843
$\frac{1}{4}$	.25	$\frac{1}{2}$	.5	$\frac{3}{4}$	.75	1	1.0

reading of 0.25, you would look at the table and see that this is $\frac{1}{4}$. A reading of 0.5625 is $\frac{9}{16}$ inch. Many mikes carry a table of decimal equivalents either on the frame or on the thimble.

5-8 METRIC MICROMETER

With the metric micrometer, there is no need to change measurements between fractions and decimals. You read the measurements directly in millimeters and hundredths of a millimeter [0.01 mm], as shown in Fig. 5-17. The barrel is marked off in millimeters above the line and half-millimeters below the line. The thimble is marked off in divisions of 0.01 mm. To read the mike in Fig. 5-17, add the reading on the barrel [11 mm] to the reading on the thimble [0.45 mm] to get the total, 11.45 mm. As you can see, reading a metric mike is easier than reading a USCS mike. Some metric mikes are even easier to read than the one shown in Fig. 5-17. They are called *digital micrometers* (Fig. 5-18). A counter on the mike shows directly the measurement to which the mike is adjusted.

Fig. 5-17
Metric micrometer. (*Volkswagen of America, Inc.*)

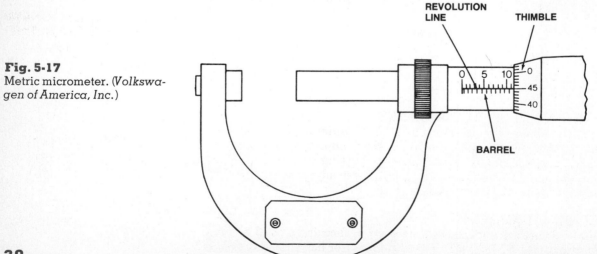

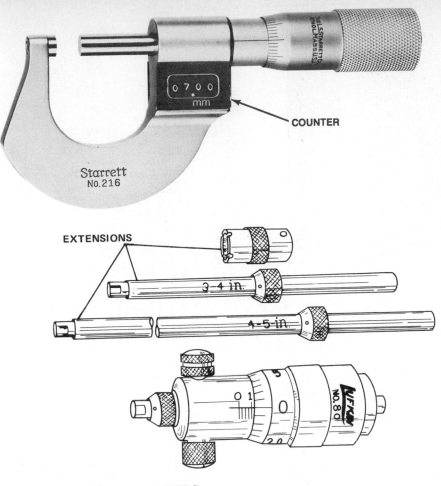

Fig. 5-18
Digital micrometer that reads in the metric system. (*The L.S. Starrett Company*)

EXTENSIONS

Fig. 5-19
Inside micrometer with extensions. (*Lufkin*)

5-9 INSIDE MICROMETERS

Inside micrometers (Fig. 5-19) can be used to take direct measurements of inside diameters, such as the bore of a cylinder (Fig. 5-20). Extensions, shown in Fig. 5-19, can be added to measure larger distances.

NOTE

An outside micrometer and a telescope gauge can be used to measure inside diameters, as shown in Fig. 5-21. The telescope gauge is adjusted to the diameter, and then the outside mike is used to measure the gauge.

5-10 MICROMETER ADJUSTMENTS

Much of the precision equipment used in the automotive shops has micrometer adjustments. The machines have adjusting knobs or dials similar to the micrometer that move the cutting or grinding edges of the machines in thousandths of an inch. These adjustments are read in the same way as the mike adjustments.

5-11 DIAL INDICATORS

The dial indicator is a gauge that uses a dial face and a needle to register measurements (Fig. 5-22). The dial indicator has a movable contact arm. When the arm is moved, the needle rotates on the dial face to

Fig. 5-20
Using an inside micrometer to measure the diameter, or bore, of a cylinder.

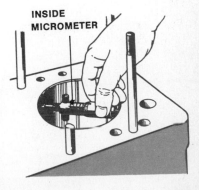

INSIDE MICROMETER

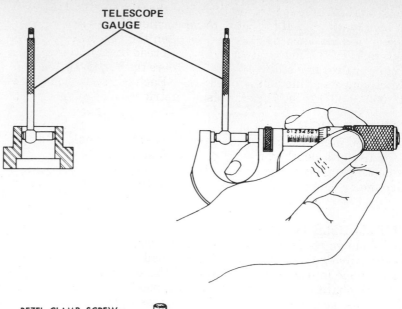

Fig. 5-21

Using a micrometer and telescope gauge to measure the diameter of a small cylinder. (*The L.S. Starrett Company*)

TELESCOPE GAUGE

Fig. 5-22

Dial indicator. (*Ford Motor Company*)

Fig. 5-23

Using a dial indicator to detect wear in an engine cylinder. (*Pontiac Motor Division of General Motors Corporation*)

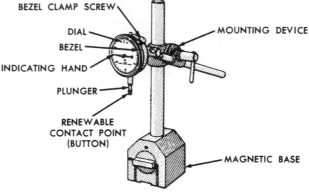

BEZEL CLAMP SCREW

DIAL

BEZEL

INDICATING HAND

PLUNGER

RENEWABLE CONTACT POINT (BUTTON)

MOUNTING DEVICE

MAGNETIC BASE

show movements in thousandths of an inch. The dial indicator is used to measure end play in shafts or gears, movement of contact points, cylinder wear in engine blocks, and so on. Figure 5-23 shows a cylinder-bore gauge being used to measure the taper of a cylinder. The cylinder-bore gauge is a dial indicator fastened in a special frame. As the dial indicator is moved up and down, any difference in the diameter will cause the needle to move. Differences in the cylinder diameter at various points indicate cylinder wear.

To use the dial indicator to find the actual diameter of a cylinder, insert the indicator in the cylinder and note the position of the needle. Then remove the dial indicator and use a micrometer, as shown in Fig. 5-24. You must adjust the mike until the needle is in the same position as it was in the cylinder. Then read the setting of the mike to get the actual dimension in thousandths of an inch.

5-12 VERNIER CALIPER

Ordinary calipers (Fig. 5-4) are not very accurate and do not give a direct reading of the measurement taken. Because of this, they are seldom used in the shop today. The vernier caliper does give a direct reading, however (Fig. 5-25). To read it, add the number of inches on the fixed scale on the frame to the number of tenths that are seen between the last inch marking and the zero on the vernier scale. Then you add the number of 0.025-inch marks seen between the last tenth reading and the zero on the vernier scale. Finally, you read the number of lines from zero on the reverse scale to the point where the line on the vernier scale exactly meets a line on the fixed scale. Each of these lines represents 1/1000 (0.001) inch. There is also a metric vernier caliper.

5-13 DEPTH GAUGE

Sometimes you must accurately measure the depth of a hole. This requires the use of a depth gauge. Figure 5-26 shows three types. The vernier depth gauge is more accurate than the steel-rule depth gauge. The micrometer depth gauge is more accurate than the vernier depth gauge.

5-14 SMALL-HOLE GAUGE

The small-hole gauge is used to measure the diameter of small holes such as the valve-guide hole in a cylinder head. Figure 5-27 shows a small-hole gauge in use. It is adjusted until the split ball just slides in the hole with slight drag. Then the distance between the two sides of the split ball is measured with a micrometer, as shown in Fig. 5-27.

CHECK UP ON YOURSELF

You have read about the various measuring tools that the automotive mechanic uses. Now find out how well you understand measuring tools by answering the questions that follow.

1. What is another name for the rule?
2. What is a dual-dimensioned rule?
3. What are the two types of caliper?
4. What is a stepped feeler gauge?
5. What are the two types of micrometer?

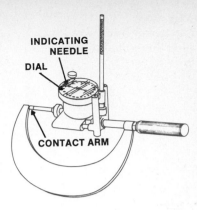

Fig. 5-24
A dial indicator and micrometer can be used to measure the diameter, or bore, of a cylinder. Once the reading is taken with the dial indicator, the dial is set to zero and the reading is measured with the micrometer. (*Pontiac Motor Division of General Motors Corporation*)

Fig. 5-25
Vernier caliper. (*The L.S. Starrett Company*)

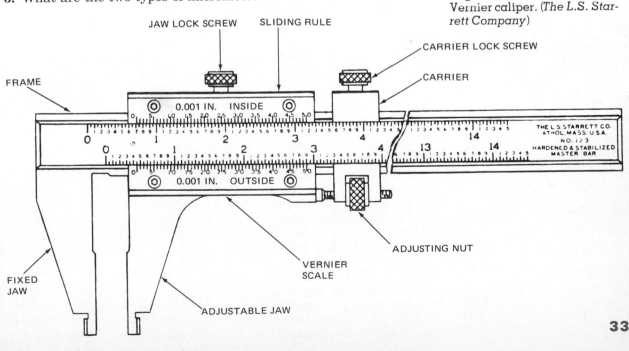

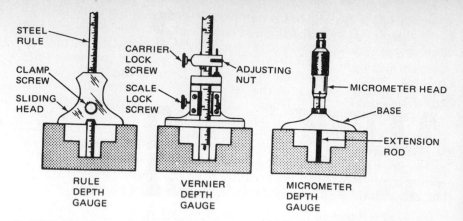

Fig. 5-26
Using depth gauges to measure the depths of holes.

STEEL RULE

CARRIER LOCK SCREW

ADJUSTING NUT

CLAMP SCREW

SCALE LOCK SCREW

SLIDING HEAD

MICROMETER HEAD

BASE

EXTENSION ROD

RULE DEPTH GAUGE

VERNIER DEPTH GAUGE

MICROMETER DEPTH GAUGE

6. Which is the simpler micrometer to read, USCS or metric?

7. When you turn a dial indicator around in an engine cylinder, what are you checking?

8. What is the depth gauge for?

9. What is the purpose of the small-hole gauge?

ANSWERS

1. Scale or steel scale (Sec. 5-1). **2.** A rule with both metric and USCS units (Sec. 5-1). **3.** Inside and outside (Sec. 5-2). **4.** Feeler gauge with the tip thinner than the rest of the blade (Sec. 5-3). **5.** Inside and outside, or USCS and metric (Secs. 5-5 and 5-8). **6.** Metric, because you do not have to deal with fractions and decimals (Sec. 5-8). **7.** Variations in diameter (Sec. 5-11). **8.** To measure the depth of holes (Sec. 5-13). **9.** To measure the diameter of small holes (Sec. 5-14).

Fig. 5-27
Using a small-hole gauge to measure the size of a hole.

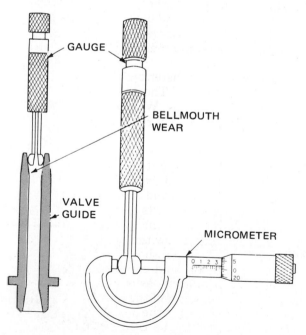

GAUGE

BELLMOUTH WEAR

VALVE GUIDE

MICROMETER

CHAPTER SIX
AUTOMOTIVE FASTENERS

After studying this chapter, you should be able to:

1. Discuss screw threads and explain pitch, series, and classes.
2. Explain how bolts and screws are marked to indicate their strength.
3. Explain how metric threads differ from USCS threads.
4. List and describe the various types of nuts, screws, and bolts.
5. List and describe the various types of locking devices.

A great variety of fasteners hold car parts together. "Fastener" is the name given to any device that holds parts together. The most common examples of fasteners are the screw, the nut and bolt, and the stud and nut (Fig. 6-1). Other types of fasteners include cotter pins, snap rings, splines, and rivets. We will discuss these and many other fasteners in this chapter.

There are also permanent methods of fastening used in automotive assembly, such as welding and soldering. The car frame is welded together. Also, the car body is welded together. Welding and soldering are specialized jobs often done in the auto body repair shop.

6-1 THREADS

Before we talk about screws, bolts, studs, and nuts, let's find out about threads in the USC system. Screws, bolts, and studs all have external threads, that is, threads on the outside. Nuts and threaded holes have threads on the inside. As you know, nuts and bolts come in many sizes, from very small to very large. Large nuts and bolts have *coarse* threads, which means that there are only a few threads per inch. You can count the number of threads on a bolt, as shown in Fig. 6-2. You measure 1 inch from the end of the bolt and count the number of threads. There are also other measurements, as shown in Fig. 6-2. These include the length of the bolt, diameter of the bolt, length of the thread, and size of the wrench required to turn the head. Figure 6-3 is a table showing how threads are classified in the USC system.

6-2 PITCH

Pitch is the number of threads per inch (Fig. 6-2). In addition to using a ruler to count the number of threads per inch, you can also use a thread

Fig. 6-1
Screw, bolt, and stud. Top shows the attaching parts separated, but aligned for assembly. Bottom shows the parts together, in sectional view.

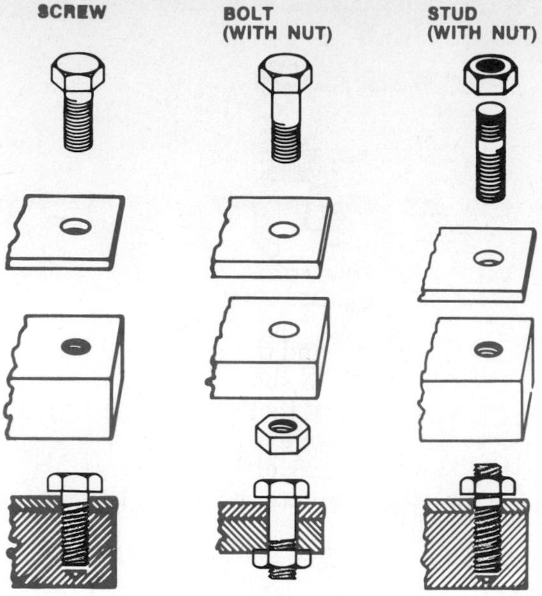
SCREW
BOLT
(WITH NUT)
STUD
(WITH NUT)

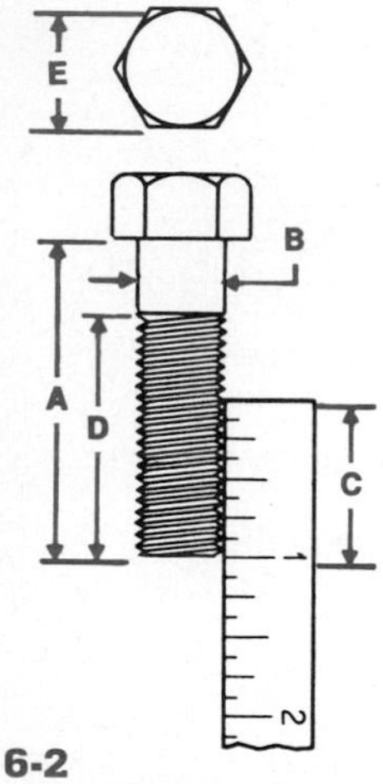
E
B
A
D
C
2

Fig. 6-2
A hex-head bolt with its parts named: (A) length; (B) diameter; (C) pitch, or threads per inch; (D) length of thread; (E) size of wrench required to fit head.

Fig. 6-3
Thread sizes.

Size	Diameter (Decimal)	Threads Per Inch: Coarse (UNC or NC)	Threads Per Inch: Fine (UNF or NF)	Threads Per Inch: Extra-Fine (UNEF or NEF)
0	0.0600	. . .	80	
1	0.0730	64	72	
2	0.0860	56	64	
3	0.0990	48	56	
4	0.1120	40	48	
5	0.1250	40	44	
6	0.1380	32	40	
8	0.1640	32	36	
10	0.1900	24	32	
12	0.2160	24	28	32
$\frac{1}{4}$	0.2500	20	28	32
$\frac{5}{16}$	0.3125	18	24	32
$\frac{3}{8}$	0.3750	16	24	32
$\frac{7}{16}$	0.4375	14	20	28
$\frac{1}{2}$	0.5000	13	20	28
$\frac{9}{16}$	0.5625	12	18	24
$\frac{5}{8}$	0.6250	11	18	24
$\frac{3}{4}$	0.7500	10	16	20
$\frac{7}{8}$	0.8750	9	14	20
1	1.0000	8	12	20
$1\frac{1}{8}$	1.1250	7	12	18
$1\frac{1}{4}$	1.2500	7	12	18
$1\frac{3}{8}$	1.3750	6	12	18
$1\frac{1}{2}$	1.5000	6	12	18

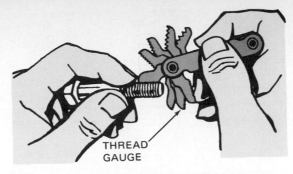

Fig. 6-4
Using a thread gauge.

THREAD
GAUGE

gauge, shown in Fig. 6-4. To use the gauge, find the blade that has the proper number of teeth to fit the threads, as shown in Fig. 6-4. The blade is marked with the pitch, or number of teeth per inch.

Screw threads are puzzling, but you should know about them. A screw that is $\frac{1}{4}$ inch in diameter can have 20, 28, or 32 threads per inch. You must know how to tell the difference. You cannot put a $\frac{1}{4}$-inch, 20-thread nut on a $\frac{1}{4}$-inch, 24-thread bolt.

6-3 THREAD SERIES

There are three thread series: coarse, fine, and extra-fine. By "coarse," "fine," and "extra-fine," we mean the pitch, or number of threads in an inch. A $\frac{1}{2}$-inch bolt, for example, could have coarse threads (13 threads per inch). Or, a $\frac{1}{2}$-inch bolt could have fine threads (20 threads per inch) or extra-fine threads (28 threads per inch). A coarse thread shortens the disassembly and reassembly time. Fewer turns are required to remove or install it. The fine and extra-fine threads are smaller than the coarse threads. Fine and extra-fine threads are used where greater bolt strength and additional accuracy of assembly are required.

6-4 THREAD CLASSES

There are three thread classes. The difference is in the closeness of fit. Class 1 has the loosest fit. It is easiest to remove and install, even when the threads are dirty and somewhat battered. Class 2 has a tighter fit. Class 3 has a very close fit. An external thread, which is used on a bolt, screw, or stud, is called an *A thread*. An internal thread, which is used in a nut or threaded hole, is called a *B thread*.

6-5 COMPLETE THREAD DESIGNATION

Now, let's put together all that you have learned about threads. A thread is designated by size, pitch, series, and class. For example, suppose you have a $\frac{1}{4}$-20 UNC-2A bolt. This means that the bolt is $\frac{1}{4}$ inch in diameter, that it has coarse threads (20 threads per inch), and that the thread is an external, class 2 thread.

You cannot use a $\frac{1}{4}$-28 UNF-2A bolt with a $\frac{1}{4}$-20 UNC-2B nut because the threads don't match. The bolt size and the thread pitch must be the same for a bolt or screw to fit a nut or a threaded hole.

6-6 BOLT AND SCREW STRENGTH

Bolts and hex-head screws are made of materials having different strengths. Figure 6-5 shows how the heads of bolts and hex-head are marked to show their proper use. The *minimum tensile strength* (pounds per square inch) is the pull, in pounds, that a round rod with a cross section of 1 inch can stand before it tears apart or breaks. High-

USAGES IN VEHICLES	SOME USED	MUCH USED	FOR SPECIAL EQUIPMENT	CRITICAL POINTS	COMPETITION MAXIMUM REQUIREMENTS
TYPICAL APPLICATIONS	FENDERS	BELL HOUSINGS	HEAD BOLTS	BEARING CAPS	RACE CARS
MINIMUM TENSILE STRENGTH, P.S.I.	64,000	105,000	133,000	150,000	160,000
MATERIAL	LOW-CARBON STEEL	MEDIUM-CARBON STEEL	MEDIUM-CARBON STEEL	ALLOY STEEL	SPECIAL ALLOY STEEL
QUALITY	INDETERMINATE	MINIMUM COMMERCIAL	MEDIUM COMMERCIAL	BEST COMMERCIAL	BEST QUALITY
HEAD MARKINGS	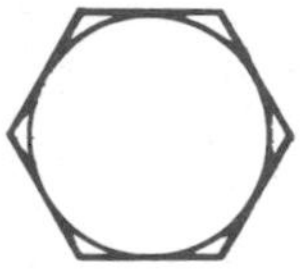	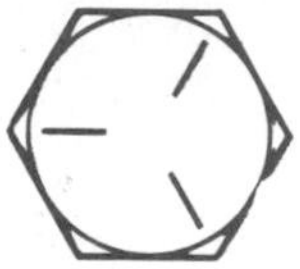	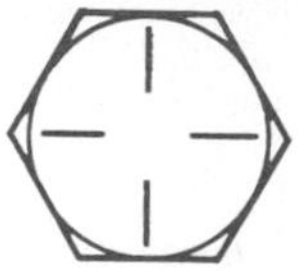	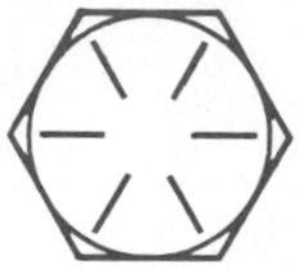	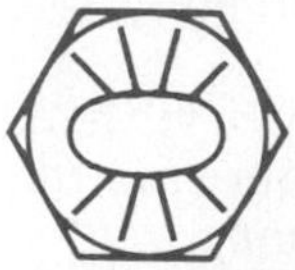

Fig. 6-5
Meaning of USCS bolt-head markings.

quality screws are more expensive and are used only where added strength is necessary.

6-7 METRIC BOLTS, SCREWS, AND THREADS

Metric bolts, screws, and threads are measured in millimeters [mm]. The threads are different from the threads we have been describing. An automotive technician working on both domestic and imported vehicles needs two sets of fasteners and two sets of wrenches.

The different ways that the wrench size for bolts is measured are shown in Fig. 6-6. In both the USC and metric systems, the wrench size is determined by measuring across the flats of the bolt head. In past years, the British Standard system was used in England. In this system, the wrench size is determined by measuring, in inches, across the outside diameter of the threads. Figure 6-7 shows the specifications for metric bolts and nuts used by one manufacturer of imported vehicles. All measurements are in millimeters.

Fig. 6-6
Different ways the wrench sizes for a bolt are determined.

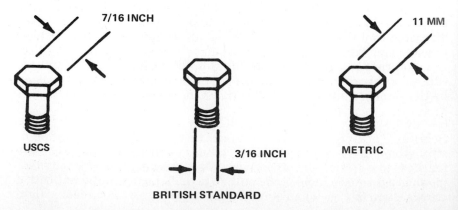

38

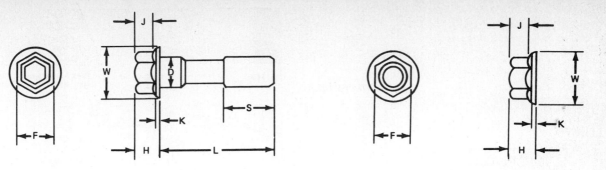

BOLT   NUT

BOLT						
	M6	M8	M10	M12	M14	M16
Pitch	1.0	1.25	1.5	1.75	2.0	2.0
F	10.0	12.0	14.0	17.0	19.0	22.0
H	6.0	8.0	10.5	12.5	14.0	15.0
W	13.0	17.0	20.0	24.0	28.0	32.0
K	1.25	1.45	1.75	2.25	2.55	2.75
J	4.0	5.5	7.0	8.0	9.0	10.0
D	6.0	8.0	10.0	12.0	14.0	16.0
S	18	22	26	30	34	38
L	10-70	12-100	15-200	20-200	25-200	30-200
R	0.14	0.18	0.21	0.25	0.28	0.28

NUT						
	M6	M8	M10	M12	M14	M16
Pitch	1.0	1.25	1.5	1.75	2.0	2.0
F	10.0	12.0	14.0	17.0	19.0	22.0
H	7.0	9.0	11.5	14.0	16.0	18.0
W	13.0	17.0	20.0	24.0	28.0	32.0
K	1.25	1.45	1.75	2.25	2.55	2.75
J	5.0	6.5	8.0	10.0	11.0	13.0

6-8 SCREWS AND BOLTS

Screws enter threaded holes. Bolts are used with nuts. However, screws and bolts look alike. The main difference is in the head and the type of screwdriver or wrench that is used to turn it. A great variety of screws and bolts are used in automobiles. Figure 6-8 shows various screws and bolts and the types of screwdrivers and wrenches needed to turn them. The most common bolts have hexagonal (six-sided), or "hex," heads. The most common screws have slotted heads. But many Phillips-head and Reed-and-Prince-head screws are also used. Find these screws in Fig. 6-8.

6-9 SETSCREWS

The setscrew is a special type of screw (Fig. 6-9). Its purpose is to fasten a collar or gear to a shaft. The setscrew is turned down into a threaded hole in the collar or gear until the point "bites" into the shaft. This holds the collar or gear in position.

Fig. 6-7
Chart showing the specifications for metric nuts and bolts used by Honda. (*Honda Motor Company, Ltd.*)

39

Fig. 6-8

Screwdrivers and wrenches required to drive various types of screws and bolts.

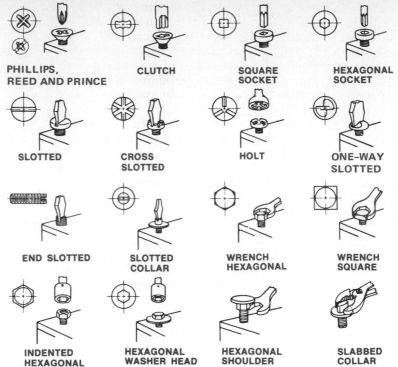

PHILLIPS, REED AND PRINCE   CLUTCH   SQUARE SOCKET   HEXAGONAL SOCKET

SLOTTED   CROSS SLOTTED   HOLT   ONE-WAY SLOTTED

END SLOTTED   SLOTTED COLLAR   WRENCH HEXAGONAL   WRENCH SQUARE

INDENTED HEXAGONAL   HEXAGONAL WASHER HEAD   HEXAGONAL SHOULDER   SLABBED COLLAR

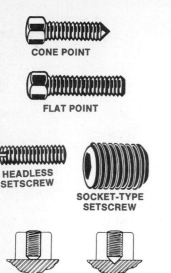

CONE POINT

FLAT POINT

HEADLESS SETSCREW   SOCKET-TYPE SETSCREW

FLAT POINT   CONE POINT

Fig. 6-9

Types of setscrew points.

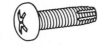

Fig. 6-10

Self-tapping screw.

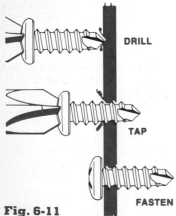

DRILL

TAP

FASTEN

Fig. 6-11

A drill-and-tap screw.

6-10 SELF-TAPPING SCREWS

Self-tapping screws cut their own threads. Figure 6-10 shows one type of self-tapping screw. The end of the screw is smaller and has slots cut in it. These slots form cutting edges. When the self-tapping screw is turned into a hole, threads are cut in the hole. Another type of screw, the drill-and-tap screw, shown in Fig. 6-11, not only cuts its own threads but also drills the hole. The point of the screw is formed into a drill, as you can see. When this screw is used, only one operation is required. The screw drills, taps, and fastens.

6-11 NUTS

Now let's look at various kinds of nuts. You will find several types of nuts in the shop (Fig. 6-12).

The speed nut (Fig. 6-12) is formed from sheet metal and is quickly installed by pressing it down into place on the stud or bolt. It won't take much of a load, so it is useful only for light fastening.

Some nuts have a built-in locking feature. One type of self-locking nut has a slot cut in the side (Fig. 6-13A). When the nut is tightened, the separated sections of the thread pull together and lock the nut on the bolt. The interference nut (Fig. 6-13B) has a collar of fiber or soft metal. The bolt threads cut threads in the soft material. The soft material jams in the threads and prevents the nut from working loose. Another type of self-locking nut (Fig. 6-13C) has vertical slots, and the upper section of the nut is somewhat smaller in diameter than the lower section. Thus the upper threads jam tightly against the bolt threads to lock the nut into place. The Palnut (Fig. 6-13D) is a single-thread nut that provides some locking action when turned down on the nut.

All these self-locking nuts have one common purpose: They prevent the nut from loosening so that parts will not fall off. Another way to keep the nut in place is to use a slotted, or castellated, nut such as the one shown in Fig. 6-12. This type of nut is used with a cotter pin, as shown in Fig. 6-14. The cotter pin is made of soft steel. After the nut is tightened properly, the pin is inserted through a hole in the bolt and two slots in the nut. The two ends of the pin are then bent around the nut, as shown in Fig. 6-14.

To remove the cotter pin, straighten out the two legs and pull it out with pliers. Once a cotter pin has been used, throw it away. Its legs may break off if they are bent again.

Another way to lock a nut on a bolt is to use a second nut tightened against the first. The second nut is called a *jam nut*.

6-12 LOCK WASHERS

A common way to lock a nut or bolt in place is to use a lock washer. Lock washers are placed between the nut or bolt head and a flat washer, as shown in Fig. 6-15. The edges left by the split or by the teeth in the lock washer bite into the metal and keep the bolt or nut from turning. In some assemblies, the flat washer is not used. The lock washer is placed directly against the part.

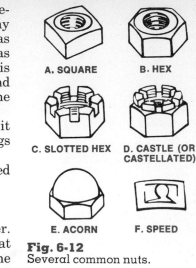

Fig. 6-12
Several common nuts.

A. SELF-LOCKING   B. INTERFERENCE   C. SELF-LOCKING   D. PALNUT

Fig. 6-13
Self-locking nuts.

6-13 SAFETY WIRE

Where a machine is subjected to severe vibration, lock washers and self-locking nuts may not be sufficient to prevent loosening. Cotter pins can be used. Safety wire is also used (Fig. 6-16). The safety wire is threaded through holes in bolt heads or castle nuts, as shown, and twisted tight. It is installed so that all pull exerted by the wire tends to tighten the nut or bolt. Safety wire should never be reused.

6-14 SNAP RINGS

There are two types of snap rings: external and internal (Fig. 6-17). External snap rings are used on shafts to prevent the endwise movement of a gear or collar on the shaft. Internal snap rings are used in housings to keep shafts or other parts in position. Special snap-ring pliers must be used to install and remove snap rings. Figure 6-18 shows

Fig. 6-14
A cotter pin before installation (at top) and after installation (bottom).

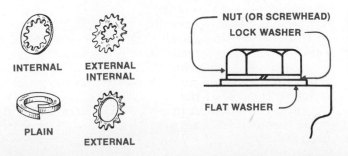

Fig. 6-15
Lock washers (left) and a plain lock washer installed between a flat washer and a nut or bolt (right).

Fig. 6-16
Safety wiring methods, shown for right-hand threads. For left-hand threads, install wire in opposite direction.

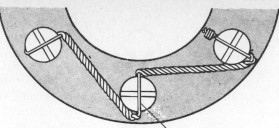

SAFETY WIRE OVER HEAD

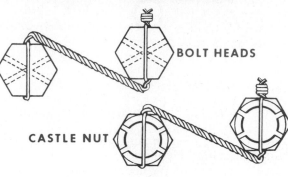

BOLT HEADS

CASTLE NUT

SAFETY WIRE AROUND HEAD
TWIST METHODS

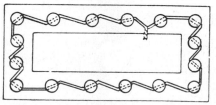

SINGLE-WIRE PLAIN METHOD

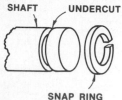

SHAFT   UNDERCUT

SNAP RING

EXTERNAL

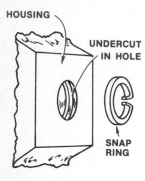

HOUSING

UNDERCUT IN HOLE

SNAP RING

INTERNAL

Fig. 6-17
Internal and external snap rings.

Fig. 6-18
Using snap-ring pliers to remove the snap ring from an automatic-transmission shaft. (*Cadillac Motor Car Division of General Motors Corporation*)

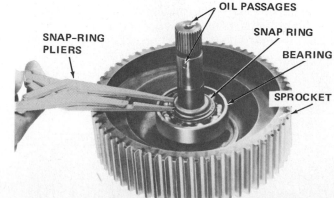

OIL PASSAGES

SNAP RING

BEARING

SPROCKET

SNAP-RING PLIERS

END-PLAY TAKE-UP	INTERNAL — BOWED — FOR HOUSINGS AND BORES	EXTERNAL — BOWED — FOR SHAFTS AND PINS	INTERNAL — BEVELED — FOR HOUSINGS AND BORES	EXTERNAL — BEVELED — FOR SHAFTS AND PINS	EXTERNAL — BOWED E-RING — FOR SHAFTS AND PINS	EXTERNAL — PRONG-LOCK® — FOR SHAFTS AND PINS
AXIAL ASSEMBLY	INTERNAL — BASIC — FOR HOUSINGS AND BORES	EXTERNAL — BASIC — FOR SHAFTS AND PINS	INTERNAL — INVERTED — FOR HOUSINGS AND BORES	EXTERNAL — INVERTED — FOR SHAFTS AND PINS	EXTERNAL — HEAVY-DUTY — FOR SHAFTS AND PINS	EXTERNAL — HIGH-STRENGTH — FOR SHAFTS AND PINS

snap-ring pliers being used to remove the snap rings from an automatic-transmission shaft.

Figure 6-19 shows a special kind of snap ring. This type has two lips with holes into which the pin ends of a special snap-ring pliers fit (Fig. 6-20). With this design, there is less chance that the pliers will slip off the snap ring during removal or installation. Eaton rings (Fig. 6-21) are similar except that they have notches instead of holes.

Fig. 6-19
Truarc retaining, or snap, rings. (*Waldes Kohinoor, Inc.*)

INTERNAL

EXTERNAL

Fig. 6-20
Truarc retaining-ring pliers used to install internal and external rings. (*Waldes Kohinoor, Inc.*)

Fig. 6-21
Installing an Eaton snap ring. (*Eaton Corporation*)

43

6-15 KEYS AND SPLINES

Keys and splines are used to lock gears, pulleys, collars, and other similar parts to shafts so that they will rotate together. Figure 6-22 shows a typical key installation. The key is wedge-shaped and fits into slots, called *keyways,* cut in the shaft and collar (or other part being installed). The key locks the shaft and collar together.

Splines (Fig. 6-23) are internal and external teeth cut in both the shaft and the installed part. When the gear, pulley, or collar is installed on the shaft, it is the same as having a great number of keys between the two parts. In many machines, the splines fit loosely so that the gear or other part is free to move back and forth on the splines. The splines, however, force both parts to rotate together. Splines may be straight or curved, as shown in Fig. 6-23.

6-16 RIVETS

Rivets (Fig. 6-24) are metal pins used to fasten parts together more or less permanently. In the automobile, the rivets are installed cold. In construction work, they may be heated first. One end of the rivet has a head. After a rivet is in place, a driver, or hammer and rivet set, is used to form a head on the other end of the rivet, as shown in Fig. 6-24.

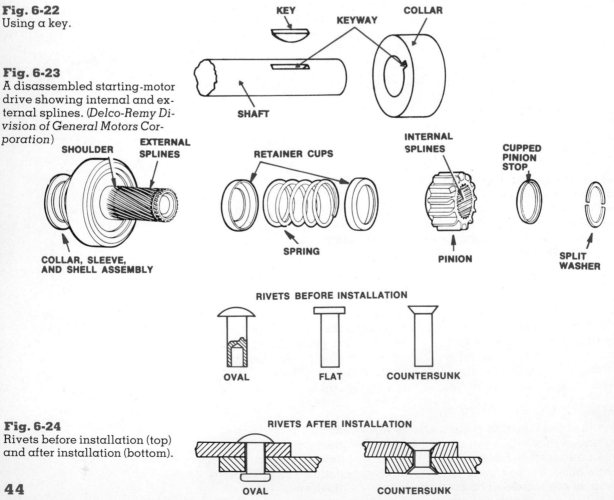

Fig. 6-22
Using a key.

Fig. 6-23
A disassembled starting-motor drive showing internal and external splines. (*Delco-Remy Division of General Motors Corporation*)

Fig. 6-24
Rivets before installation (top) and after installation (bottom).

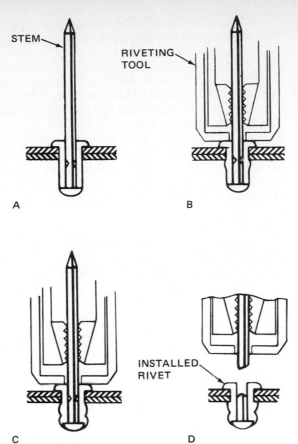

STEM

RIVETING TOOL

A

B

INSTALLED RIVET

C

D

Fig. 6-25
Steps in installing a Pop rivet in a blind hole. (A) Rivet is placed in hole. (B) Riveting tool is placed over stem of rivet. (C) Rivet head compresses. (D) Stem "pops" or snaps off. (*Avdel Corporation*)

6-17 POP RIVETS

Pop rivets (Fig. 6-25) are used to install rivets in blind holes. These are holes where one end of the rivet cannot be reached to flatten it. First the Pop rivet is placed in the hole. Then the riveting tool is put over the stem of the rivet. The stem is pulled up, as shown in Fig. 6-25, so that the base of the rivet is compressed. Then the stem of the rivet is popped off to complete the job.

6-18 THREADED INSERTS

Damaged or worn threads in a cylinder block, cylinder head, or other part can often be replaced with a threaded insert, as shown in Fig. 6-26. First drill out the worn threads; then tap the hole with the special tap that comes with the threaded-insert repair package. This makes new threads in the hole. Then screw the threaded insert into the hole to bring the hole back to its original thread size. One brand of threaded insert is called a *Heli-Coil*. It is shown in Fig. 6-26.

CHECK UP ON YOURSELF

Here is your chance to check up on yourself and find out whether you understand what you are studying. The questions that follow are on automotive fasteners, the chapter you have just read. If you miss a question, just go back and reread the section that covers the question you missed. The answers follow the questions.

45

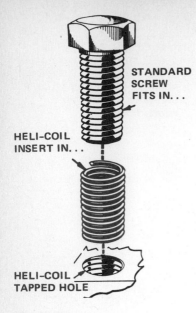

STANDARD SCREW FITS IN...

HELI-COIL INSERT IN...

HELI-COIL TAPPED HOLE

Fig. 6-26
Installing a threaded insert (Heli-Coil) in a tapped hole. (*Chrysler Corporation*)

1. How many threads per inch does a $\frac{1}{2}$-20 UNF-2A bolt have?
2. What is thread pitch in the USC system?
3. What are the three thread series?
4. Of the three classes of threads, which has the closest fit?
5. Metric bolts, screws, and threads are measured in what unit?
6. What is the name of the screw that cuts its own threads?
7. What is the purpose of the self-locking nut?
8. What is the name of the pin that is used with the castellated nut?
9. What are the two types of snap rings?
10. What is the name of the teeth that are cut in both the shaft and the matching collar or gear which is installed on the shaft?
11. What is the name of the pin that is used to fasten parts together more or less permanently?
12. What is the name of the material that is threaded through holes in bolt heads and twisted tight?
13. Where are Pop rivets installed?
14. What is the name of the device used to replace damaged or worn threads?

ANSWERS

1. Twenty (Sec. 6-2). **2.** Number of threads per inch (Sec. 6-2). **3.** Coarse, fine, and extra-fine (Sec. 6-3). **4.** Class 3 (Sec. 6-4). **5.** Millimeters [mm] (Sec. 6-7). **6.** Self-tapping (Sec. 6-10). **7.** To prevent the nut from loosening (Sec. 6-11). **8.** Cotter pin (Sec. 6-11). **9.** Internal and external (Sec. 6-14). **10.** Splines (Sec. 6-15). **11.** Rivet (Sec. 6-16). **12.** Safety wire (Sec. 6-13). **13.** In blind holes (Sec. 6-17). **14.** Threaded insert (Sec. 6-18).

CHAPTER SEVEN
TOOLS IN THE SHOP

After studying this chapter, you should be able to:

1. List and describe the basic hand tools used in the shop and explain how each is used.
2. List and describe the purpose of cutting tools used in the shop and explain how to use them.
3. List and describe power tools used in the shop.

7-1 TOOLS

Two main types of tools are used in the auto shop. One type is called *hand* tools, because your hand supplies the energy needed to operate them. The hammer (Fig. 7-1) and the wrench (Fig. 7-9) are good examples of hand tools. The other type is called *machine,* or *power,* tools. Electricity or compressed air supplies the operating power for these tools. An example of a machine, or power, tool that uses electric power is the valve grinder (Fig. 7-2). The valve grinder has an electric motor that spins a grinding wheel. Tools using compressed air for power are called *pneumatic* tools. "Pneumatic" means of or pertaining to air. The air-powered impact wrench used to remove and install wheel-attaching nuts is an example (Fig. 7-3).

In the next few pages, we are going to look at common hand tools used in the shop. In later chapters, we will look at the power tools that are used for specialized jobs, such as grinding valves, honing engine cylinders, grinding brake disks, and so on.

7-2 HAMMERS

There are several kinds of hammers (Fig. 7-1), but they are all used in about the same way. The ball-peen hammer is the one you will use most often. It is a general, all-purpose hammer. Rawhide-faced, rubber, plastic-tipped, and brass hammers are designed for special jobs. They are used for striking on easily scratched surfaces. The cross-peen hammer is used in metalwork, such as body work on damaged cars.

Figure 7-4 shows you the right and wrong ways to grip a hammer. When using a hammer, grip the end and swing the hammer so that the head strikes the surface squarely, as shown in Fig. 7-4. The swinging action should come from your elbow, not from your wrist or shoulder.

CAUTION

Always make sure that the hammerhead is firmly wedged on the handle. Otherwise, it could fly off and hurt someone. The head is held on the handle by a wedge (Fig. 7-5) or screw in the end of the handle.

Fig. 7-1
Various types of hammers used in the shop.

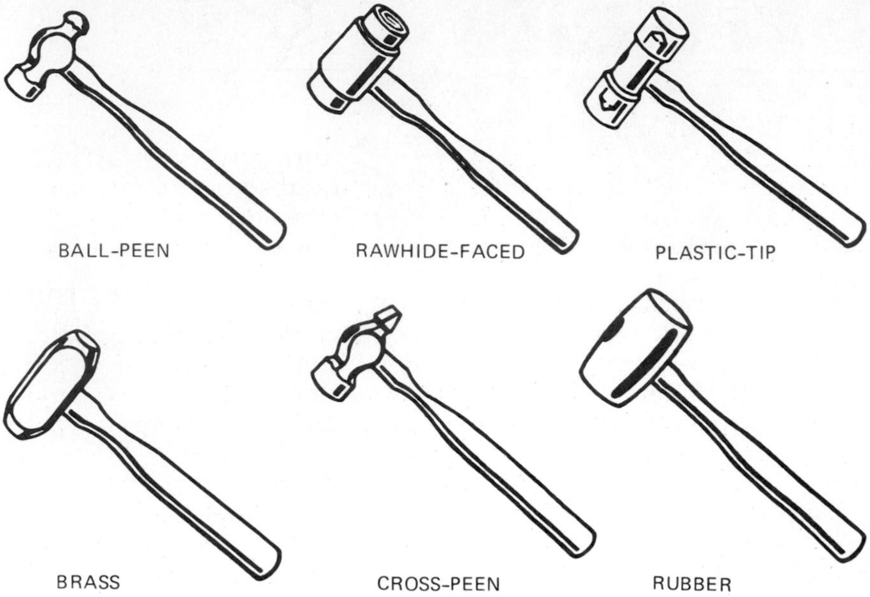

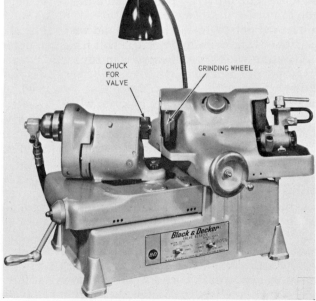

BALL-PEEN
RAWHIDE-FACED
PLASTIC-TIP
BRASS
CROSS-PEEN
RUBBER

Fig. 7-2
A valve grinder. This machine is used to grind, or reface, engine valves. (*Black & Decker Manufacturing Company*)

CHUCK FOR VALVE
GRINDING WHEEL
Black & Decker

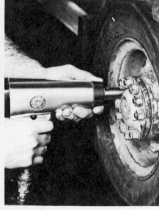

Fig. 7-3
An air-powered impact wrench. This tool is used to remove and install wheel-attaching nuts.

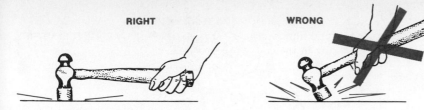

RIGHT WRONG

Fig. 7-4
Right and wrong ways to use a hammer.

7-3 SCREWDRIVERS

The common screwdriver is used to drive, or turn, screws with slotted heads. Figure 7-6A shows a typical slotted-head screwdriver. Figure 7-7 shows how the screwdriver blade fits into the screw slot. When the screw is turned one way, it goes into the workpiece. When it is turned the other way, it is backed out.

The slotted-head screw is only one of several types of screw. See Figs. 6-8 and 7-6B. The differences among the Phillips and the Reed-and-Prince screwdrivers are shown in Fig. 7-8. All have cross slots, but the angles are different. Figure 6-8 shows still other screw heads and the special kinds of screwdrivers needed to turn them. Some of these screws do not have slotted heads at all, but have hexagonal (six-sided) heads. These "hex-head" screws require wrenches to turn them.

Always be sure to pick the right screwdriver for the job. For example, when choosing a common screwdriver, make sure to pick one with a tip that properly fits the screw slot, as shown in Fig. 7-7.

7-4 WRENCHES

Wrenches are used to turn screws or bolts that have hexagonal heads. They are also used to turn nuts that are hexagonal. Bolts with six-sided heads are called "hex-head" bolts. Nuts with six sides are called "hex" nuts. A stud is a headless bolt with threads on both ends. One end of the stud goes into a threaded hole, and a nut is turned down on the other end.

The simplest wrench to use is the open-end wrench (Fig. 7-9). Select the proper size wrench to snugly fit the bolt head or nut, as shown in Fig. 7-10. Then pull or push the wrench to turn the nut or bolt.

7-5 BOX WRENCHES

The box wrench (Fig. 7-11) has an opening into which the bolt head or nut fits, as shown in Fig. 7-12. The advantage of this wrench is that it will not slip off the bolt head or nut. A box wrench can be used in restricted spaces because of the thinness of the wrench head. The typical box wrench has 12 notches or "points" in the head. Using this wrench, you can install a nut or bolt in an area where the wrench can be swung only about 15 degrees. Figure 7-11 shows a combination wrench that has the advantages of both the open-end and the box wrenches.

7-6 SOCKET WRENCHES

The socket wrench is the same as the box wrench except that the head, or socket, is detachable. Figure 7-14 shows sockets. To use a socket wrench, first select a handle. There are several types of handles, as shown in Fig. 7-13. Then select the socket that will fit the bolt head or nut. There are several kinds of sockets (Fig. 7-14). The 12-point is the most common. It needs to be swung only half as far as the 6-point socket before it must be lifted and refitted to the nut for a new grip.

Fig. 7-5
Wedge installation in a ball-peen hammer.

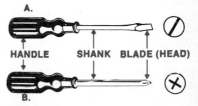

A.

HANDLE   SHANK   BLADE (HEAD)

B.

Fig. 7-6
(A) A typical slotted-head screwdriver. (B) A Phillips or Reed-and-Prince screwdriver.

Fig. 7-7
The screwdriver tip fits into the slot in the screw head.

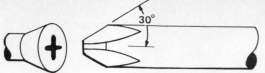

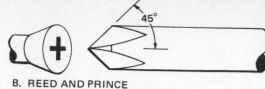

Fig. 7-8   A. PHILLIPS   B. REED AND PRINCE

Difference between the Phillips and the Reed-and-Prince screwdrivers.

Fig. 7-9

An open-end wrench.

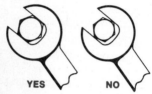

YES   NO

Fig. 7-10

The wrench should fit the nut or bolt head securely.

Fig. 7-11

Box, combination, and open-end wrenches.

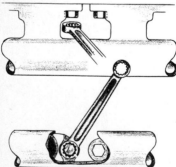

Fig. 7-12

How the box wrench fits around the head of the bolt or nut. (*General Motors Corporation*)

This is convenient when you are working in a tight space. The 8-point socket is useful for turning square pipe plugs. The deep socket is used for spark plugs and hard-to-reach nuts or bolts.

The drive end of the socket, which snaps onto the handle, is square and always sized in fractions of an inch (Fig. 7-15). Figures 7-16 to 7-19 show the ratchet, nut spinner, sliding handle, and speed handle in use. The ratchet handle has a ratcheting device that releases in one direction but catches in the other. When you want to tighten a nut, just flip the lever on the handle head to make the ratchet catch the socket only in the tightening direction.

To work on imported vehicles and domestic cars made to metric measurements, you need metric sockets. USCS sockets will not fit many metric nuts and bolts. Figure 7-20 shows you the difference between metric and USCS sockets. Note that the drive holes in all sockets are the same the world over. They always measure either $\frac{1}{4}$, $\frac{3}{8}$, or $\frac{1}{2}$ inch square.

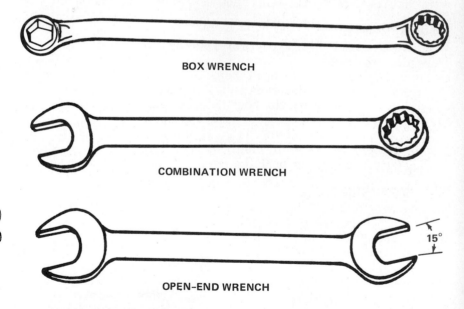

BOX WRENCH

COMBINATION WRENCH

OPEN-END WRENCH

7-7 TORQUE WRENCHES

In automobiles, nuts and bolts must be tightened properly. If they are not tightened enough, they will come loose and something may fall apart. This could cause great trouble, damage to the car, and possibly a serious accident. If nuts or bolts were tightened too much, they would be strained excessively and could break later, again with disastrous results.

To ensure proper tightening of nuts and bolts, you must use torque wrenches. For example, a spec might call for tightening a bolt to "20–

50

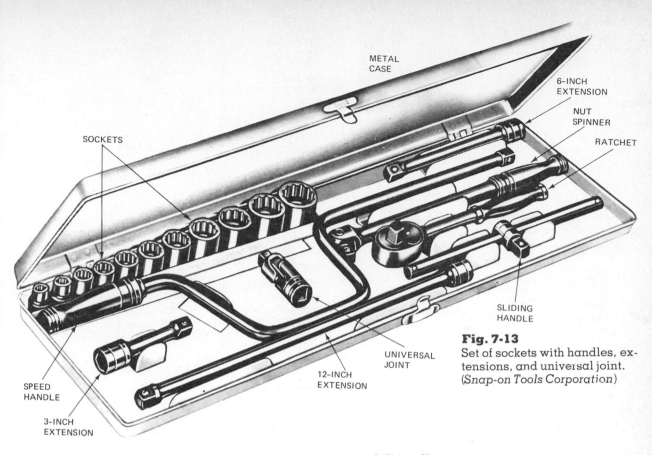

Fig. 7-13
Set of sockets with handles, extensions, and universal joint.
(*Snap-on Tools Corporation*)

24 lb-ft." This means that you have to put a 20- to 24-pound (lb) pull at 1 foot (ft) from the bolt. The torque wrench (Fig. 7-21) lets you do this accurately. You snap the correct socket on the torque wrench, fit the socket on the bolt head, and pull the wrench handle. Watch the indicator needle on the wrench as you gradually increase your pull. When it registers somewhere between 20 and 24, you know you have tightened the bolt correctly. This procedure is called *torquing* the bolt.

NOTE
Threads must be clean and in good shape. Dirty or damaged threads put a drag on the threads as the bolt is turned down. This prevents proper tightening of

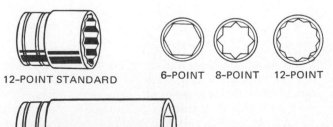

12-POINT STANDARD   6-POINT 8-POINT 12-POINT

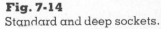

6-POINT DEEP

Fig. 7-14
Standard and deep sockets.

Fig. 7-15
The drive end of a socket is always made for the U.S. Customary System.

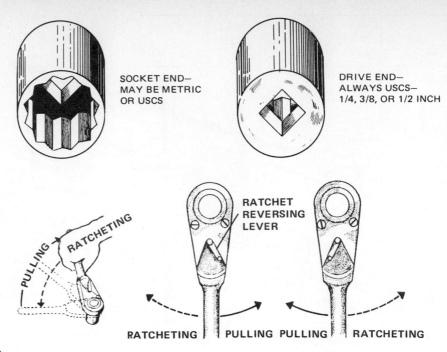

SOCKET END—
MAY BE METRIC
OR USCS

DRIVE END—
ALWAYS USCS—
1/4, 3/8, OR 1/2 INCH

Fig. 7-16
The ratchet handle will ratchet in either direction, according to the position of the control lever.

RATCHET REVERSING LEVER

PULLING RATCHETING

RATCHETING | PULLING PULLING | RATCHETING

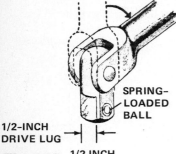

SOCKET END OF HINGED NUT SPINNER SWUNG AT RIGHT ANGLE FOR GREATEST LEVERAGE

SPRING-LOADED BALL

1/2-INCH DRIVE LUG

Fig. 7-17 1/2 INCH
Use of the nut spinner.

the bolt. Therefore, when assembling the various components, make sure that the threads are clean and in good condition.

7-8 PLIERS
Pliers (Fig. 7-22) are a special type of adjustable wrench. The jaws are adjustable because the two legs move on a pivot. Thus pliers can be used to grip or turn an object. *But pliers must not be used on nuts or bolt heads.* They will round off the edges of the hex and roughen the flats so that a wrench will no longer fit properly.

Some pliers have a side cutter, which can be used to cut wires. There are also regular *nippers* which have cutting edges instead of jaws. These are used to cut wire, thin sheet metal, small bolts, and so on.

3/8-INCH DRIVE LUG

Fig. 7-18
Use of the sliding handle.

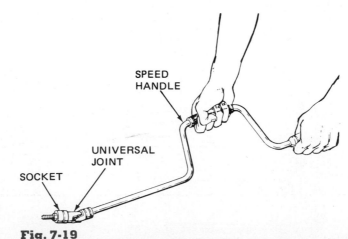

SPEED HANDLE

UNIVERSAL JOINT

SOCKET

Fig. 7-19
Speed handle with universal joint and socket attached. (*Ford Motor Company*)

SOCKET	METRIC SIZE	DECIMAL EQUIVALENT IN INCHES		USCS SIZE	SOCKET	METRIC SIZE	DECIMAL EQUIVALENT IN INCHES		USCS SIZE
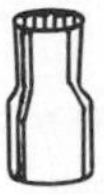	3 mm	0.118	0.125	$\frac{1}{8}$ INCH	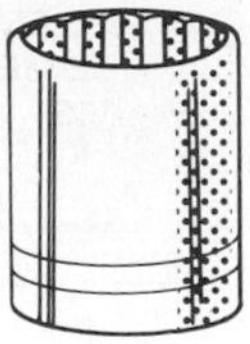	16 mm	0.630	0.625	$\frac{5}{8}$ INCH
	4 mm	0.157	0.187	$\frac{3}{16}$ INCH		18 mm	0.709	0.687	$\frac{11}{16}$ INCH
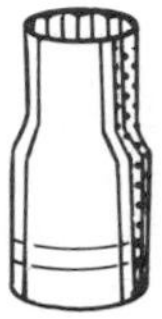	6 mm	0.236	0.250	$\frac{1}{4}$ INCH	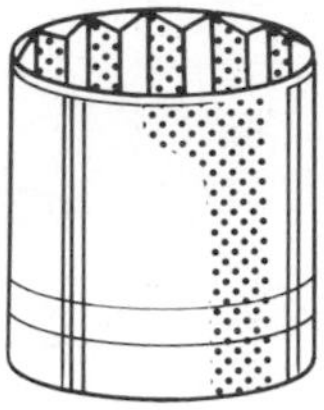	19 mm	0.748	0.750	$\frac{3}{4}$ INCH
	9 mm	0.354	0.312	$\frac{5}{16}$ INCH		20 mm	0.787	0.812	$\frac{13}{16}$ INCH
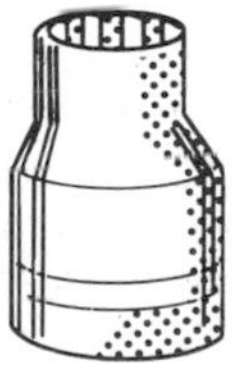	10 mm	0.394	0.375	$\frac{3}{8}$ INCH	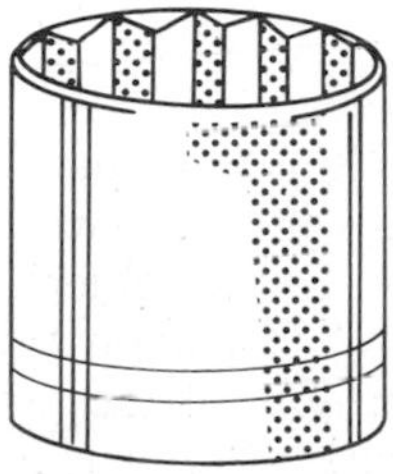	22 mm	0.866	0.875	$\frac{7}{8}$ INCH
	12 mm	0.472	0.437	$\frac{7}{16}$ INCH		24 mm	0.945	0.937	$\frac{15}{16}$ INCH
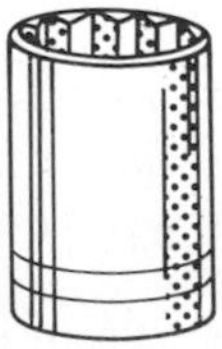	13 mm	0.512	0.500	$\frac{1}{2}$ INCH	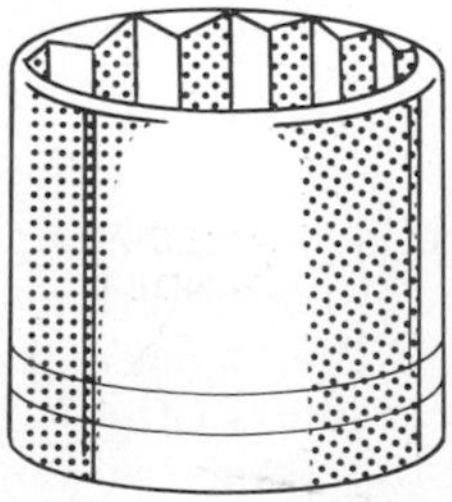	25 mm	0.984	1.00	1 INCH
	15 mm	0.590	0.562	$\frac{9}{16}$ INCH					

Fig. 7-20
Comparison of metric and USCS sizes of sockets. (*Dana Corporation*)

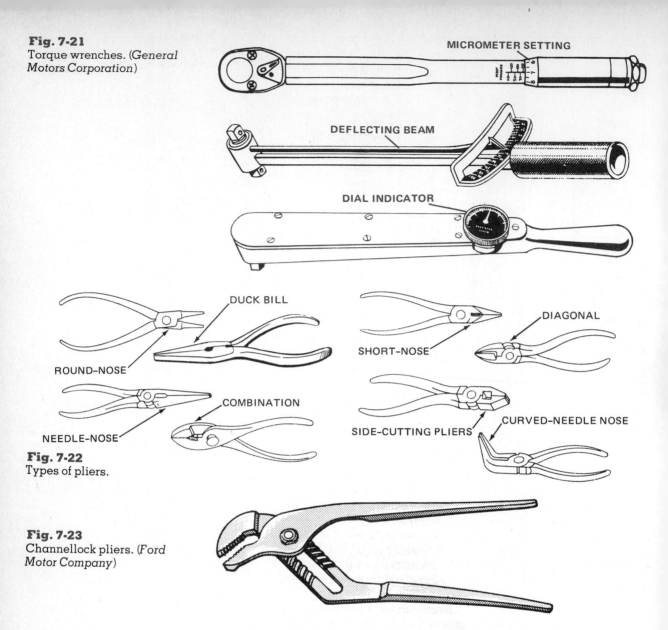

Fig. 7-21
Torque wrenches. (*General Motors Corporation*)

MICROMETER SETTING

DEFLECTING BEAM

DIAL INDICATOR

DUCK BILL

ROUND-NOSE

NEEDLE-NOSE

COMBINATION

SHORT-NOSE

DIAGONAL

SIDE-CUTTING PLIERS

CURVED-NEEDLE NOSE

Fig. 7-22
Types of pliers.

Fig. 7-23
Channellock pliers. (*Ford Motor Company*)

Channellock pliers (Fig. 7-23) are adjustable so that the opening between the jaws can be changed. They have grooves on one jaw and lands on the other, and they can fit in any position. The jaws will then be parallel to the object gripped, regardless of its size.

Vise-grip pliers (Fig. 7-24) can be locked onto an object. This, in effect, gives you an extra hand. The screw allows you to adjust the size of the jaw opening.

7-9 PULLERS

Pullers are used to remove gears and hubs from shafts, bushings from blind holes, cylinder liners from engine blocks, and so on. A puller set has many pieces that can fit together to form different pullers (Fig. 7-25). There are three basic types: the pressure screw (Fig. 7-26), the slide hammer (Fig. 7-27), and the combination (Fig. 7-28). In the

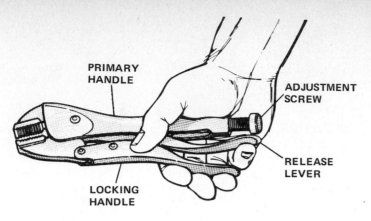

Fig. 7-24
Vise-Grip pliers. (*Ford Motor Company*)

PRIMARY HANDLE

ADJUSTMENT SCREW

RELEASE LEVER

LOCKING HANDLE

pressure-screw type, turning a screw applies the pulling pressure. In the slide-hammer type, the slide hammer hitting the end of the handle provides the pulling pressure.

CHECK UP ON YOURSELF

Here are some questions about hammers, wrenches, and other tools you have studied in this chapter. Don't be discouraged if you miss a question. Just go back and study the material about the item you missed.

1. What are the two main types of tools used in the shop?
2. What kind of hammer is used most often in the shop?
3. What is the most common type of screwdriver?
4. How many sides does a hex nut have?
5. Which wrench is the simplest to use?
6. How many notches are there in the head of a typical box wrench?
7. What are the advantages of a box wrench?
8. What is the advantage of a socket wrench?
9. What are the sizes of the drive holes in sockets?
10. What tool do you use when torquing a bolt?
11. How many legs does a pliers have?
12. What is the device called that is used to remove gears and hubs from shafts?

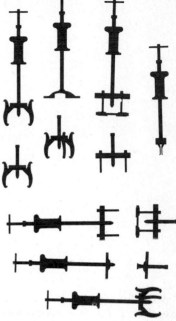

Fig. 7-25
Various assembled pullers. (*Hastings Manufacturing Company*)

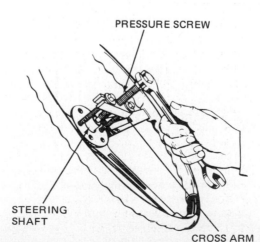

PRESSURE SCREW

STEERING SHAFT

CROSS ARM

Fig. 7-26
Using pressure-screw puller to remove a steering wheel. (*Lisle Corporation*)

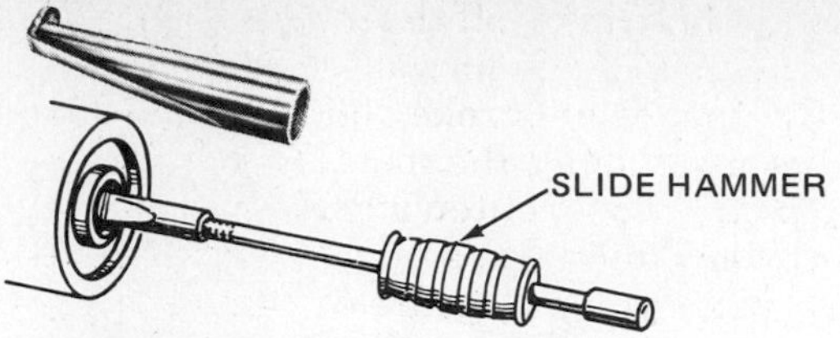

Fig. 7-27
Slide-hammer puller being used to remove a grease retainer. (*Proto Tool Company*)

SLIDE HAMMER

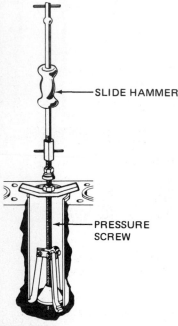

SLIDE HAMMER

PRESSURE SCREW

Fig. 7-28
Combination puller being used to remove a sleeve from an engine cylinder. (*Owatonna Tool Company*)

ANSWERS

1. Hand tools and machine, or power, tools (Sec. 7-1). **2.** Ball-peen hammer (Sec. 7-2). **3.** Type used on slotted-head screws (Sec. 7-3). **4.** Six (Sec. 7-4). **5.** Open-end (Sec. 7-4). **6.** Twelve (Sec. 7-5). **7.** It will not slip off the bolt head or nut, and it can be used in restricted spaces (Sec. 7-7). **8.** The sockets, or heads, are detachable (Sec. 7-6). **9.** $\frac{1}{4}$, $\frac{3}{8}$, or $\frac{1}{2}$ inch square (Sec. 7-6). **10.** A torque wrench (Sec. 7-7). **11.** Two (Sec. 7-8). **12.** Puller (Sec. 7-9).

CUTTING TOOLS

Cutting tools are used to remove metal. Nippers, which were discussed in Sec. 7-8, are a common cutting tool. Other cutting tools include chisels, hacksaws, files, and drills. We will look at these cutting tools now.

7-10 CHISELS

The chisel has a single cutting edge and is driven with a hammer to cut metal. Figure 7-29 shows different kinds of chisels. Figure 7-30 shows how to use a chisel and a hammer. Note that you hold the chisel in your left hand and the hammer in your right. (Of course, if you are left-handed, you hold the chisel in your right hand and the hammer in your left.) Strike the end of the chisel with the hammer. Figure 7-31 shows how a chisel and hammer are used to cut a piece of sheet metal in two. The metal is clamped in a vise. Vises are described later in the book.

Notice that the technician is wearing goggles (Fig. 7-30). They protect the eyes from flying chips that result from the use of the chisel. A flying chip could injure an unprotected eye!

After a chisel has been used for a while, the cutting edge gets dull and the head tends to "mushroom" (Fig. 7-32). The mushroom must be ground off on a grinding wheel, as shown in Fig. 7-33. Grinding off the mushroom from the head of the chisel protects you from getting hurt. The turned-over metal could break off when the head is struck, and a piece of it could fly into your hand and cut you. Figure 7-34 shows how to grind the cutting edge of the chisel.

CAUTION

Always wear goggles or a face shield to protect your eyes when using a chisel. Also, keep the chisel sharp. A dull chisel does a poor job.

7-11 HACKSAWS

The hacksaw (Fig. 7-35) has a steel blade with a series of sharp teeth. The teeth act like tiny chisels. When the blade is pushed over a piece of

Fig. 7-29
Various types of chisels.

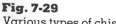

COLD (FLAT)

DIAMOND-POINT

CAPE

ROUNDNOSE

metal, the teeth cut fine shavings, or filings, off the metal. Figure 7-36 shows how to hold and use a hacksaw. Each forward stroke should be full and steady, not jerky. On the back stroke, lift the saw blade slightly so that the teeth do not drag along the metal being cut.

Figure 7-37 shows how to install and tighten a blade in a hacksaw frame. When using a hacksaw, you should use a blade with the proper number of teeth for the metal piece you are going to saw. The teeth must be close enough so that at least two teeth will be working on the metal at the same time. On the other hand, if the teeth are too fine, they will get clogged and stop cutting. Figure 7-38 shows the correct and incorrect number of teeth for different cutting jobs.

7-12 FILES

The file (Fig. 7-39) is a cutting tool with a large number of cutting edges, or teeth. Each is like a tiny chisel. There are many types and shapes of files. The flat file is the most common. Files range in coarseness, or size of individual teeth, from "rough" or "coarse-cut," through "bastard" and "second-cut," to "smooth" or "dead-smooth." See Fig. 7-40. Files also can be single-cut and double-cut. The single-cut file has a series of teeth, like knife blades, that are parallel to one another. The double-cut file has two sets of cuts on the face of the file that are at an angle to each other. The teeth on the double-cut file are pointed.

Figure 7-41 shows how to use a file. Strokes should be steady, and the right amount of pressure should be used. Excessive pressure will clog the file teeth, and it could break the file. Insufficient pressure will not cut the metal, and it can cause the file to chatter, or vibrate.

CAUTION
Always use a file handle (Fig. 7-39). Tighten the file in the handle by tapping the end of the handle on the workbench, as shown in Fig. 7-42. Don't use a file without the handle. You could hurt yourself by ramming the file tang into your hand. Never hammer on the file or try to use it as a pry bar. The file is brittle and will shatter.

7-13 PUNCHES

Punches (Fig. 7-43) are used to knock out rivets and pins from machine parts that are being disassembled, to line up machine parts that are being assembled, and to mark locations of holes to be drilled. Let's take

Fig. 7-30
How to use a chisel and hammer.

Fig. 7-31
How to use a chisel and hammer to cut sheet steel.

Fig. 7-32
At the top, a chisel with a mushroom head and chipped cutting edge. These should be ground off, as shown at the bottom.

Fig. 7-33
Grinding the mushroom from the head of the chisel.

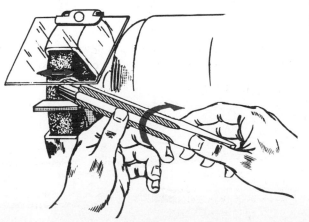

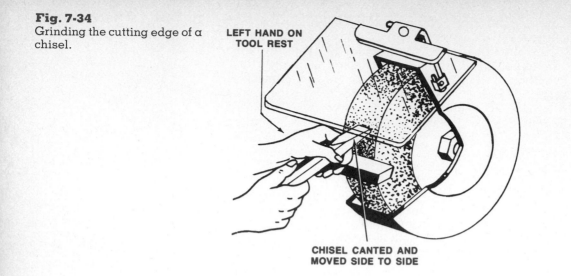

Fig. 7-34
Grinding the cutting edge of a chisel.

LEFT HAND ON TOOL REST

CHISEL CANTED AND MOVED SIDE TO SIDE

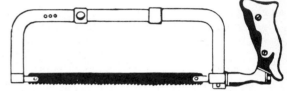

Fig. 7-35
Hacksaws.

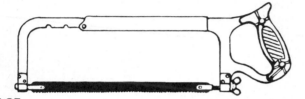

Fig. 7-36
How to hold and use a hacksaw.

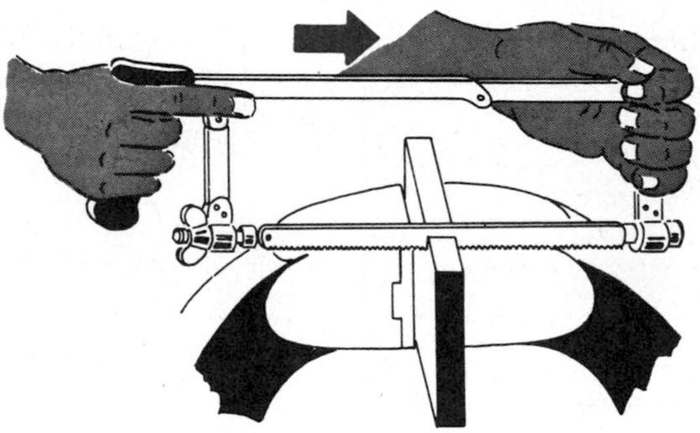

Fig. 7-37
How to install and tighten a blade in a hacksaw frame.

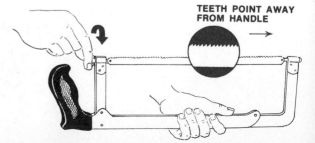

TEETH POINT AWAY FROM HANDLE

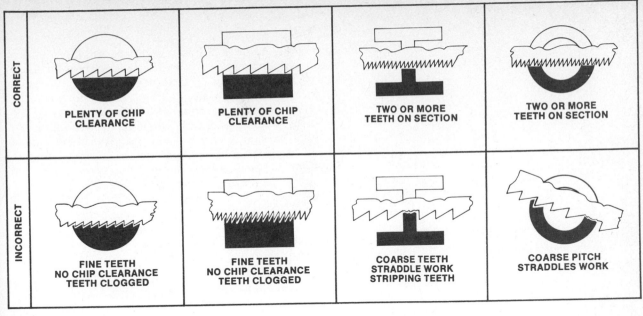

CORRECT	PLENTY OF CHIP CLEARANCE	PLENTY OF CHIP CLEARANCE	TWO OR MORE TEETH ON SECTION	TWO OR MORE TEETH ON SECTION
INCORRECT	FINE TEETH NO CHIP CLEARANCE TEETH CLOGGED	FINE TEETH NO CHIP CLEARANCE TEETH CLOGGED	COARSE TEETH STRADDLE WORK STRIPPING TEETH	COARSE PITCH STRADDLES WORK

Fig. 7-38
Correct and incorrect number of teeth for various jobs.

Fig. 7-39
A typical file with the parts named.

TANG   LENGTH   EDGE
HANDLE   HEEL   FACE   TIP

COARSE   BASTARD   SECOND-CUT   SMOOTH

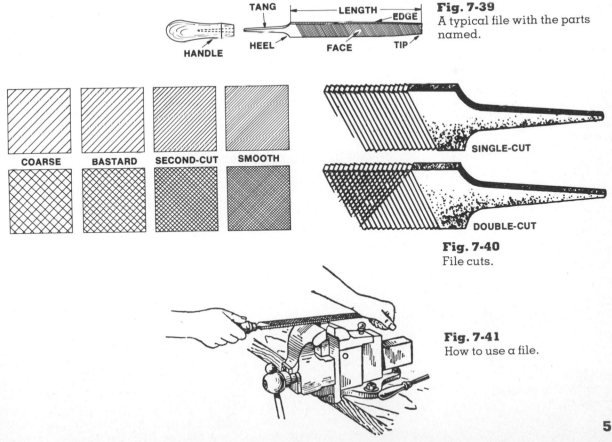

SINGLE-CUT

DOUBLE-CUT

Fig. 7-40
File cuts.

Fig. 7-41
How to use a file.

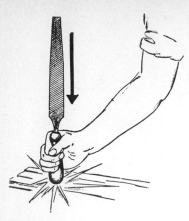

Fig. 7-42
To tighten a file tang in a handle, tap the end of the file handle on the bench.

a look at the different kinds of punches and how they are used for these jobs.

- Knocking out rivets and pins. A starting punch and a pin punch are used to knock out rivets and pins. Some machine parts are held together by rivets and pins. An example is the drive gear on an ignition distributor shaft. The gear is held in place on the shaft by a metal pin that goes through two holes in the gear and a single hole in the shaft. The ends of the pin are rounded off, or *peened over,* by a hammer. To remove the pin, first file off one of the rounded-off ends of the pin. Next, use a starting punch, shown in Fig. 7-44, to break the pin loose. Then use a pin punch to drive the pin out, as shown in Fig. 7-44.
- Aligning machine parts. An aligning punch is used to line up, or align, machine parts. Some machine parts have holes that must align when the parts are assembled. To ensure proper alignment, place the aligning punch through each hole in each part. Then it will be easy to install a bolt or screw through the holes.

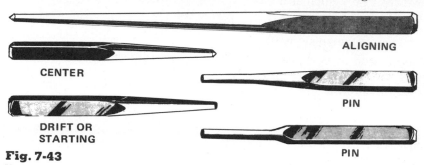

Fig. 7-43
Various types of punches.

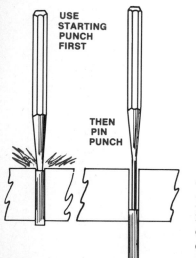

Fig. 7-44
Using starting and pin punches.

- Marking locations of holes to be drilled. A center punch is used to mark locations of holes to be drilled. Marking the location of the hole gives the drill a place to start. This prevents it from wandering on the surface of the workpiece (Fig. 7-45).

  The center punch is also used to mark parts before disassembly so that the parts can be put back together correctly. For example, suppose a cover plate could be put back on a housing in two positions, one right and the other wrong. Before taking the cover plate off, put punch marks next to each other on the housing and the cover plate. Now there can be no question about how the parts are to be reassembled.

7-14 DRILLS

Drills are tools for making holes. The typical drill used in the auto shop is called a *twist drill* (Fig. 7-46). It has a point and two lips, or cutting edges. When the drill is rotated against a piece of metal or wood, the cutting edges shave off material and send it back up the spiral grooves and out of the hole. Twist drills can be used with a hand drill (Fig. 7-47) or an electric drill (Fig. 7-48). Twist drills come in many sizes, and they are numbered according to the size of the hole they make. The smallest twist drills you will use in the shop are $\frac{1}{64}$ inch in diameter. But there are even smaller sizes for special jobs. The largest twist drills you will normally use are less than 1 inch in diameter.

7-15 TAPS AND DIES

Taps and dies are used to cut screw threads. As you can see (Figs. 7-49 and 7-50), both the tap and the die have cutting teeth to perform this job. A tap (Fig. 7-49) is turned down into a hole to cut internal threads. A die (Fig. 7-50) is turned down on a rod to cut external threads.

Occasionally, you will see an auto part with battered threads. For example, you might find a cylinder block with damaged threads. The proper tap, run down into the threaded hole, will often straighten the threads. Damaged threads on bolts or studs can often be cleaned up with a die. Special thread straighteners, called *thread chasers,* can come in very handy. For example, suppose you are working on a cylinder head with damaged studs. A thread chaser may clean up the damage so that the studs will not have to be replaced.

7-16 THREADED INSERT

Sometimes a tapped hole—in a cylinder block, for example—has badly damaged threads that cannot be cleaned up. In this case, you can use a threaded insert, such as a Heli-Coil, as explained in Sec. 6-18 and illustrated in Fig. 6-26.

7-17 STUD EXTRACTORS

When a stud or bolt breaks off, it has to be removed. If the break is above the surface, sometimes you can file two flat surfaces on the stud

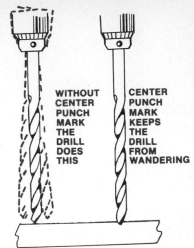

Fig. 7-45
Center-punching a hole location will keep the drill from wandering.

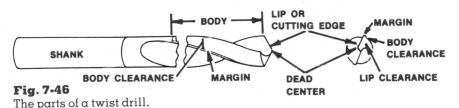

Fig. 7-46
The parts of a twist drill.

Fig. 7-48
An electric drill.

Fig. 7-47
A hand drill.

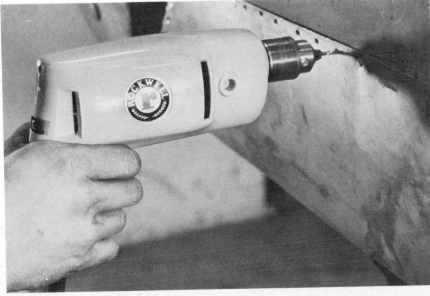

Fig. 7-48
An electric drill.

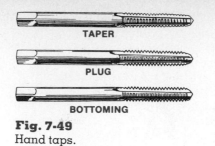

Fig. 7-49
Hand taps.

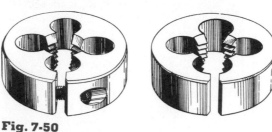

Fig. 7-50
Dies.

Fig. 7-51
Using a stud extractor to remove a broken stud.

or bolt and use a wrench to remove it. If the break is below the surface, you need a stud extractor. First, center-punch the stud and drill a small hole into it. Next, drill a larger hole almost as big as the small diameter of the threads. Leave only a thin shell. Then turn, or drive, the stud extractor into the hole. One type of stud extractor, called *Ezy-Out* (Fig. 7-51), has coarse, spiral threads. As the extractor is turned, the threads bite into the hole in the stud. As the extractor is turned in the reverse direction, the stud backs out.

7-18 VISE
The vise, or bench vise, is used to hold the object being worked on (Fig. 7-52). When the handle is turned, a screw in the base of the vise moves the movable jaw toward or away from the stationary jaw. To protect objects that could be easily damaged, "soft jaws" (Fig. 7-52) are put on the vise jaws. These are caps made of a soft metal such as copper. They are less likely to scratch or dent the object being gripped.

7-19 ARBOR PRESS
The arbor press has a handle that rotates a gear which is meshed with a rack (Fig. 7-53). This causes the rack to move up or down. The lower part of the rack, called the *arbor,* holds the tool. A lot of pressure can be put on the tool with the arbor press. Thus it can be used to press bearings, pins, and other tightly held parts into or out of an assembly.

7-20 GRINDING WHEEL
The grinding wheel is made of an abrasive material containing grains of sharp-edged grit, somewhat like grains of sand. Grinding wheels come in many different sizes and grades. A grinding wheel with large particles is used for coarse work, such as taking the rough edges off metal castings. A fine grinding wheel is used for fine work, such as sharpening tools.

Figure 7-54 shows a pedestal grinder with two grinding wheels. As a rule, in this setup one of the wheels is coarse and the other wheel is

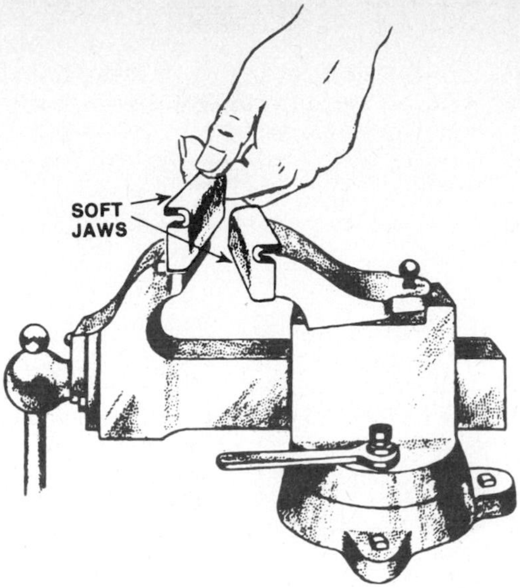

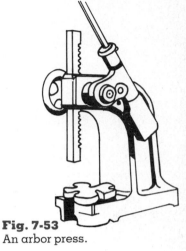

Fig. 7-52
A bench vise showing soft jaws being put into place on the vise jaws.

fine. Figure 7-55 shows a screwdriver tip being ground on a grinding wheel.

Fig. 7-53
An arbor press.

CAUTION

When using a grinder, always wear goggles or a face shield to protect your eyes from flying sparks and metal chips. Be sure the wheel guards are in place and the light is on and aimed at the tool or workpiece you are about to grind. Do not use the grinder until your instructor has explained how to use it and has given you permission to begin. Grinders are safe if used properly. But if you use a grinder improperly, you could hurt yourself!

7-21 USING POWER TOOLS

The shop is equipped with a number of power tools, that is, tools operated by electricity or compressed air. You should carefully follow the instructions for using any of these tools. Keep hands and clothes away from moving machinery, such as the engine fan, the drive belt, and the grinding wheel. Keep hands out of the way when using cutting tools, such as cylinder-boring equipment or a drum lathe. Never attempt to feel the finish while the machine is running. There may be slivers of metal on the surface of the workpiece that could cut your hand. When working on equipment with compressed springs, such as clutches or valves, use care to keep the springs from slipping and jumping loose. They could fly off at high speed and hurt someone. *Never* oil or adjust moving machinery unless the instructions specifically tell you to do so.

CHECK UP ON YOURSELF

Now that you have studied this chapter, let's see how well you understand it. You have to know about chisels, files, and other tools when you work in the shop. Test yourself by answering these questions.

1. Why should you wear goggles when using a chisel?
2. What is the hacksaw blade made of?

Fig. 7-54
A pedestal grinder and two grinding wheels.

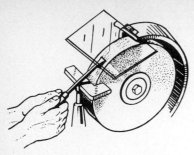

Fig. 7-55
Grinding a screwdriver tip on a grinding wheel.

3. Which file has the biggest teeth?
4. Which punch do you use first to remove a pin from a shaft?
5. What is the purpose of marking hole locations with a center punch?
6. What is the difference between a tap and a die?
7. What is the Ezy-Out?
8. How do you protect objects that could easily be marred when they are in a vise?
9. What safety rule must be followed before you use the grinding wheel?

ANSWERS

1. To prevent chips from flying into your eyes (Sec. 7-10). **2.** Steel (Sec. 7-11). **3.** Rough- or course-cut (Sec. 7-12). **4.** Starting punch (Sec. 7-13). **5.** To keep the drill from wandering (Sec. 7-13). **6.** A tap cuts threads in a hole. A die cuts threads on a rod (Sec. 7-15). **7.** One type of stud extractor (Sec. 7-17). **8.** By using caps, or "soft jaws," made of a soft metal such as copper (Sec. 7-18). **9.** Put on your goggles (Sec. 7-20).

PART TWO
AUTO ENGINE FUNDAMENTALS

Part Two of *The Auto Book* discusses the construction and operation of automobile engines, including the support systems needed for the engine to run. These systems include the lubricating, cooling, and fuel systems. Part Three covers the electrical system. In this part of the book, you will learn about the parts that go together to make the engine and how they all work together to produce power. In addition, you will learn about engine oil and other lubricants as well as about gasoline. There are 12 chapters in Part Two:

CHAPTER EIGHT
AUTOMOTIVE ENGINE OPERATION

After studying this chapter, you should be able to:
1. Explain the various ways in which automotive engines are classified.
2. Describe how the crankshaft and connecting rod convert reciprocating motion to rotary motion.
3. Describe the various valve arrangements used in engines.
4. Explain how the four-cycle engine works.
5. Describe the various types of valve trains.
6. Explain valve timing.

8-1 INTERNAL-COMBUSTION AND EXTERNAL-COMBUSTION ENGINES

There are two kinds of engines: internal-combustion and external-combustion. Internal-combustion engines burn fuel inside the engine. The engines you see in all automobiles are internal-combustion engines.

External-combustion engines burn fuel outside the engine. Steam engines are external-combustion engines. These engines run on steam that is produced by boiling water outside the engine.

8-2 RECIPROCATING AND ROTARY ENGINES

We classify internal-combustion, or IC, engines two ways, according to the *motion* of the internal parts. In the usual automotive engine, the parts reciprocate, or move up and down (Fig. 8-1A). In other engines, such as the Wankel and the turbine, the parts spin, or move in a circular pattern (Fig. 8-1B). The parts that move up and down in automotive engines are called *pistons*. For this reason, reciprocating IC engines are often referred to as *piston engines*.

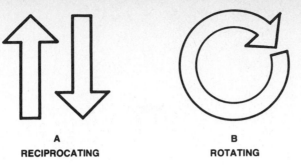

A
RECIPROCATING

B
ROTATING

8-3 ENGINE CYLINDERS

Pistons move up and down in engine cylinders. Most automobile engines have four, six, or eight cylinders. The same action takes place in each cylinder. We will study just one cylinder to find out how the engine works. Figure 8-2 shows a six-cylinder engine partly cut away so that you can see some of the pistons and cylinders.

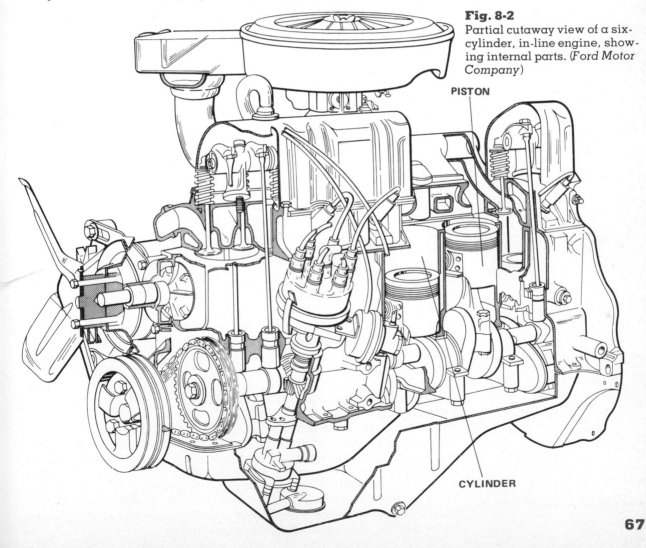

Fig. 8-2
Partial cutaway view of a six-cylinder, in-line engine, showing internal parts. (*Ford Motor Company*)

PISTON

CYLINDER

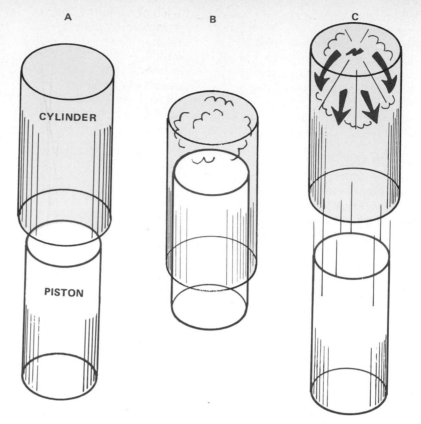

Fig. 8-3

Actions in an engine cylinder. (A) The piston is a metal plug that fits snugly into the cylinder. (B) When the piston is pushed up into the cylinder, trapped air is compressed. (C) If gasoline vapor were mixed with the air and if a spark occurred in the cylinder, the explosion would blow the piston out of the cylinder.

Fig. 8-4

A piston for an engine. (*Ford Motor Company*)

Let us simplify our study by showing only the two parts that interest us now, the cylinder and the piston (Fig. 8-3). What you see in Fig. 8-3 looks like two soft-drink cans, one slightly smaller than the other. The larger can is open at the bottom. The smaller can fits into the larger can, as shown in the middle. If you push the smaller can up into the larger can, you will push or press the air into a smaller volume. That is, you compress the air. Now let's call the cans by their right names. The bigger can is the *engine cylinder*. The smaller one is the *piston*.

When the piston is pushed up into the cylinder, the air in the cylinder is compressed. Suppose there is some gasoline vapor in the compressed air. What would happen if a spark got into the cylinder? There would be an explosion that would blow the piston out of the cylinder, as shown to the right in Fig. 8-3.

8-4 THE CONNECTING ROD AND CRANKSHAFT

Of course, blowing a piston out of a cylinder just once is not enough to make a car move. The piston must move up and down rapidly and remain in the cylinder. Then this up-and-down, or reciprocating, motion must be turned into rotating motion in order for it to rotate the car wheels. The connecting rod and crankshaft do the job of changing the reciprocating motion of the piston into rotary motion.

Figure 8-4 is a picture of a piston. The piston is about 4 inches [100 mm] in diameter and weighs about 1 pound [0.45 kg]. Figure 8-5 shows the piston with the connecting rod attached. Figure 8-6 shows a crankshaft. The part of the crankshaft that does the job of changing the reciprocating motion of the piston into the rotary motion of the wheels is called the *crank*. Figure 8-7 shows how the piston, connecting rod, and crankshaft work together. Only part of the crankshaft is shown in Fig. 8-7. The connecting rod is attached to the piston by a piston pin. The piston pin goes through two holes in the piston and one hole in the connecting rod, as shown in Fig. 8-8. The other end of the connecting rod is attached to a crankpin on the crankshaft (Fig. 8-8). This combination changes reciprocating motion into rotary motion.

8-5 THE CRANKPIN

Note how the crankpin swings around the crankshaft in a circle as the crankshaft rotates (Fig. 8-9). During this circular motion, the piston is moving up and down, or reciprocating, as shown in Fig. 8-10.

When the piston moves up and down in the cylinder, the piston, the connecting rod, and the crankpin go through the eight positions shown in Fig. 8-11. The crankpin moves in a circle. The connecting rod tilts first in one direction and then in the other. The lower end of the connecting rod moves in a circle with the crankpin. Study these eight pictures in Fig. 8-11 to see how the up-and-down motion is changed into rotary motion.

NOTE

The crankpin is also called the *crank throw*, or *connecting rod journal*.

8-6 CRANKS

There are many cranks and connecting rods around you. Look at a bicycle (Fig. 8-12). The pedal and its support form a crank. Your lower leg is the connecting rod. As you pump the pedal, your knee acts as the piston pin and moves up and down. Your foot is the lower end of the connecting rod and moves in a circle as it follows the crank, which is formed by the bicycle pedal and support.

8-7 PISTON STROKE

When the piston moves from top to bottom, or from bottom to top, it completes a *stroke*. The piston completes *two strokes* as it goes through the eight positions shown in Fig. 8-11. In position 1, the piston is at the top. It moves down through positions 2, 3, and 4 to arrive at the bottom position, 5. This is one piston stroke. Then the piston starts back up

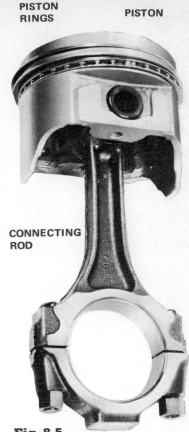

PISTON
RINGS   PISTON

CONNECTING
ROD

Fig. 8-5
A typical piston with connecting rod attached and piston rings installed. (*Ford Motor Company*)

Fig. 8-6
A crankshaft for a four-cylinder engine. (*Chevrolet Motor Division of General Motors Corporation*)

69

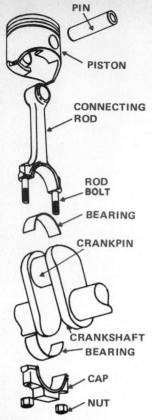

Fig. 8-7
A piston, connecting rod, piston pin, and crank—all in disassembled view.

Fig. 8-8
A piston and connecting-rod assembly attached to the crankpin on the crankshaft.

and moves through 6, 7, and 8 and back to 1. This is the second piston stroke.

When the piston is at the top position, it is said to be at *top dead center* (TDC). When it is at the bottom position, it is said to be at *bottom dead center* (BDC). You will see many mentions of TDC and BDC in this book and in shop manuals because these are the reference points for setting valve and ignition timing.

8-8 FOUR STROKES

You may have heard someone call automobile engines "four-cycle engines." What this means is that the engines are *four-stroke-cycle engines*. In other words, it takes each engine piston four strokes to go through a complete cycle. We will talk more about this later in the chapter.

8-9 MAKING THE ENGINE RUN

Now the piston is moving up and down and the crankshaft is rotating. What is making the piston move? The burning of gasoline in the engine does this job. Let's find out just how it happens.

First, a mixture of gasoline vapor and air goes into the cylinder. Then the piston is pushed up to compress the mixture. Next a spark occurs in the cylinder. This spark ignites the mixture and it explodes, pushing the piston down. It is this push that makes the crankshaft turn and the car wheels rotate. Then the piston must be pushed up to get the burned gases out of the cylinder.

Fig. 8-9
As the crankshaft rotates, the crankpin swings in a circle around the shaft.

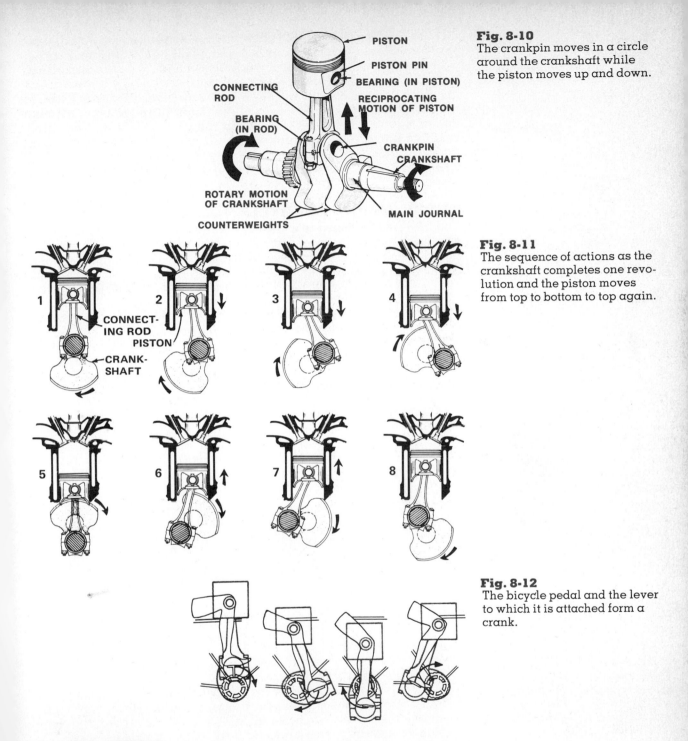

PISTON

PISTON PIN

BEARING (IN PISTON)

CONNECTING ROD

RECIPROCATING MOTION OF PISTON

BEARING (IN ROD)

CRANKPIN

CRANKSHAFT

ROTARY MOTION OF CRANKSHAFT

MAIN JOURNAL

COUNTERWEIGHTS

Fig. 8-10
The crankpin moves in a circle around the crankshaft while the piston moves up and down.

CONNECTING ROD
PISTON
CRANKSHAFT

Fig. 8-11
The sequence of actions as the crankshaft completes one revolution and the piston moves from top to bottom to top again.

Fig. 8-12
The bicycle pedal and the lever to which it is attached form a crank.

8-10 THE VALVES

There must be an opening in the top of the cylinder so that the air-fuel mixture can get into the cylinder. A second opening is needed to get rid of the burned gas. That adds up to two openings. However, these openings cannot remain open all the time. They must be able to open and close at the right time. The valves let the air-fuel mixture into the cyl-

71

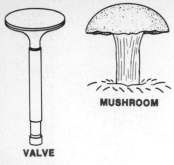

Fig. 8-13

An engine valve, called a mushroom valve because it is shaped somewhat like a mushroom.

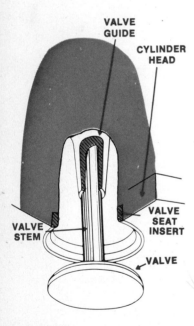

Fig. 8-14

A valve, valve guide, and valve seat. The cylinder head and valve guide have been partly cut away so that the valve stem can be seen.

inder and let the burned gas out. An engine valve is a long metal stem on which there is a flat top. It looks so much like a mushroom (Fig. 8-13) that the valves are called *mushroom valves*. They are also called *poppet valves* because they *pop* up and down.

Each valve moves up and down in a *valve guide* (Fig. 8-14), which is a round hole in the cylinder head. The guide keeps the valve moving up and down in a straight line. When the valve moves up, the valve head fits into a round opening in the cylinder head. This opening is called the *valve port*. When the valve is up, the valve port is closed. The valve head is tight against the edge of the port, and the opening is closed off.

CHECK UP ON YOURSELF

You have really looked into the engine to find out how it runs. The past few pages have given you the fundamentals of engine operation. To see how well you understand what you have studied, answer the following questions.

1. What are the two basic kinds of engines?
2. What are the two basic types of internal-combustion engines?
3. What does IC stand for?
4. What happens to the air-fuel mixture when the piston is pushed up into the cylinder?
5. What is the name of the part of the crankshaft that is offset and swings in a circle as the crankshaft rotates?
6. What is the term that refers to the movement of the piston from top to bottom or from bottom to top?
7. What does TDC mean?
8. What does BDC mean?
9. How many valves are there in a cylinder?
10. There is a round hole in the cylinder head in which the valve moves up and down. What is it called?

ANSWERS

1. Internal-combustion and external-combustion (Sec. 8-1). **2.** Reciprocating, or piston, and rotary (Sec. 8-2). **3.** Internal combustion (Sec. 8-2). **4.** It is compressed (Sec. 8-3). **5.** Crankpin (Sec. 8-5). **6.** A piston stroke (Sec. 8-7). **7.** Top dead center (Sec. 8-7). **8.** Bottom dead center (Sec. 8-7). **9.** Two valves per cylinder (Sec. 8-10). **10.** The valve guide (Sec. 8-10).

HOW THE ENGINE OPERATES

Now we are ready to learn how the engine works. First, one of the valves opens to let the air-fuel mixture into the cylinder. Later, the other valve opens to let the burned gases out. Let's follow the cycle of events all the way through.

A *cycle* is a series of events that repeat themselves. For example, the four seasons—spring, summer, fall, and winter—form a cycle. In an engine, the four-stroke cycle includes the intake stroke, the compression stroke, the power stroke, and the exhaust stroke.

8-11 THE INTAKE STROKE

First, the piston moves down, as shown in Fig. 8-15. As the piston moves down, it produces a vacuum in the cylinder. A *vacuum* is the absence of air or any other substance. Outside air rushes in to fill the vacuum. The same thing happens, for example, when you take in a drink through a straw. You move your jaw down to produce a vacuum in your mouth. Air tries to get in to fill the vacuum. But, instead, the drink gets in the way, and the air pushes the drink up the straw and into your mouth.

During this piston stroke, one of the valves—the intake valve—is open. The valve is down off its seat, and the air-fuel mixture fills the vacuum produced by the downward movement of the piston. This downward movement of the piston is called the *intake stroke* because the cylinder is taking in a mixture of fuel and air. As the air moves toward the cylinder, it first has to pass through the carburetor. The *carburetor* sits on top of the engine and mixes gasoline vapor with the air passing through. Carburetor actions are explained in Chap. 18.

The piston moves all the way down to BDC on the intake stroke. The intake valve is open, and the air-fuel mixture pours into the cylinder. At the end of the intake stroke, the intake valve closes. We will find out later what makes the valve close.

8-12 THE COMPRESSION STROKE

After the piston passes BDC at the end of the intake stroke, it starts to move up. Both valves are closed, so the air-fuel mixture has no place to go. It is pushed, or *compressed,* into a smaller volume (Fig. 8-16). The amount that the mixture of air and gasoline vapor is compressed is called the *compression ratio.*

In a modern engine, the air-fuel mixture is compressed into one-eighth or one-ninth of its original volume. That is like taking 1 quart of air and squeezing it down to less than ½ cup (Fig. 8-17).

If you squeezed the mixture from 1 quart to ½ cup, you would have a compression ratio of 8:1. There are 8 half-cups in 1 quart. When you compress the quart, which is 8 half-cups, into 1 half-cup, you have gone from 8 down to 1. That is, you have compressed the mixture down from 8 to 1. So, the compression ratio is 8 to 1. Usually, the ratio is shown as 8:1. You read this as "8 to 1."

We will discuss compression ratio again in Chap. 9. But first we will go through the rest of the piston actions. The piston moves up from BDC to TDC, compressing the mixture. This stroke is called the *compression stroke.*

8-13 THE POWER STROKE

As the piston nears TDC at the end of the compression stroke, a spark occurs in the top of the cylinder. The spark plug makes the spark (we will find out how this happens later). When a spark occurs in the compressed air-fuel mixture, there is an explosion. The pressure and temperature of the mixture suddenly go up. Every square inch of the piston head gets a push of up to 600 pounds [270 kg] or more. This adds up to as much as 2 tons—4000 pounds [1814 kg]—pushing down on the piston head! That is hundreds of pounds more than the weight of the whole New York Jets football team! See Fig. 8-18. It is easy to understand why the piston moves!

The 2-ton [1814-kg] pressure pushes the piston downward. This downward movement is called the *power stroke* (Fig. 8-19). The powerful push on the piston is carried through the connecting rod to the crank on the crankshaft. The crankshaft turns this downward movement into rotary motion. Then the rotary motion is carried through the gears and shafts to the car wheels so that the car moves.

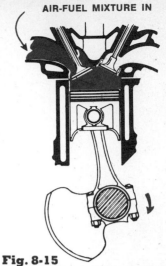

AIR-FUEL MIXTURE IN

Fig. 8-15
The intake stroke. The intake valve, at left, has opened. The piston is moving downward, drawing air and gasoline vapor into the cylinder.

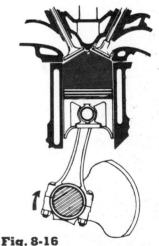

Fig. 8-16
The compression stroke. The intake valve has closed. The piston is moving upward, compressing the mixture.

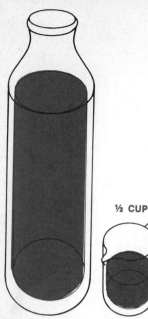

QUART

½ CUP

Fig. 8-17

If you had 1 quart [0.95 L] of air and compressed it to ½ cup [0.12 L], you would compress the air to one-eighth of its original volume.

FOOTBALL TEAM

PISTON

Fig. 8-18

At the start of the power stroke, as much as 4000 pounds [1814 kg] of pressure will be applied to the piston head.

NOTE

The combustion chamber is the space at the top of the cylinder and above the piston in which the burning of the air-fuel mixture takes place (Fig. 8-19). Combustion chambers vary in shape.

8-14 THE EXHAUST STROKE

As the piston reaches BDC on the power stroke, the exhaust valve opens. When the piston moves up again, it pushes out the burned gases through the exhaust port. This upward movement of the piston is called the *exhaust stroke* because the burned gases are pushed out, or exhausted, from the engine cylinder (Fig. 8-20). Finally, as the piston reaches TDC on the exhaust stroke, the exhaust valve closes and the intake valve opens. The piston moves down once more on another intake stroke. The cycle of events in the cylinder is then repeated: intake stroke, compression stroke, power stroke, exhaust stroke. This cycle continues as long as the engine runs.

8-15 PISTON RINGS

Piston rings are essential to the operation of the engine. They are metal rings that fit into grooves in the pistons. You can see these piston grooves in Fig. 8-4. You can see piston rings installed on a piston in Fig. 8-5. The purpose of piston rings is to form a tight seal between the piston and the cylinder wall. As we have seen, there is great pressure above the piston during the compression stroke and the power stroke. The piston itself cannot be made to fit tightly enough in the cylinder to prevent this pressure from leaking past the piston. Leakage could mean serious power loss. The rings press tightly against the cylinder wall and the sides of the piston grooves to provide the needed seal. The rings are covered with oil by the engine lubricating system so that they can slide up and down easily on the cylinder wall. There's more on piston rings in Chap. 13.

8-16 THE FOUR-STROKE CYCLE

Since it takes four piston strokes to complete one cycle, the engine is called a *four-stroke-cycle engine*. The name is usually shortened in print to *four-cycle engine*.

8-17 MULTIPLE-CYLINDER ENGINES

A single cylinder, with a single piston working in it, would not produce enough power to run an automobile. Also, there would be only one power stroke for every two revolutions of the crankshaft. This would make for a very rough ride. So automobiles have engines with four, five, six, or eight cylinders. In these engines, there is one or more power strokes going on all the time. Thus the engine produces a continuous flow of power, and the automobile moves along smoothly.

CHECK UP ON YOURSELF

You are making good progress! You are finding out how the engine runs. Now let's see if you can answer the following questions. If you miss one, just reread the past few pages to get the facts you need.

1. What do we call a series of events that repeats itself?
2. When the piston is moving down and the air-fuel mixture is flowing in, what is the stroke called?

3. What is a vacuum?
4. Can you drink through a straw without first making a vacuum in your mouth?
5. When the piston is moving up and both valves are closed, what is the stroke called?
6. If you could squeeze 1 quart into 1 cup, what would be the compression ratio?
7. When the piston is pushed down by the pressure of the burning air-fuel mixture, what is the stroke called?
8. When the piston is moving up and pushing out the burned gases, what is the piston stroke called?
9. What is the purpose of the piston rings?

ANSWERS
1. A cycle (introductory paragraph). 2. Intake stroke (Sec. 8-11). 3. Absence of air or any other substance (Sec. 8-11). 4. No (Sec. 8-11). 5. Compression stroke (Sec. 8-12). 6. The compression ratio would be 4:1 because there are 4 cups to 1 quart (Sec. 8-12). 7. The power stroke (Sec. 8-13). 8. The exhaust stroke (Sec. 8-14). 9. To provide a good seal between the piston and cylinder wall, preventing leakage of pressure past the piston (Sec. 8-15)

VALVE OPERATION

8-18 THE VALVE TRAIN
So far, we have looked at the four-stroke cycle. We explained the four strokes. We said that the intake valve is open during the intake stroke and that the exhaust valve is open during the exhaust stroke. Typical valves are shown in Fig. 8-21. Note that the intake valve and the exhaust valve are different from each other. The intake valve is larger. Let's find out how these valves are operated.

The assembly of parts that make the valves open and close is called the *valve train*. There are three basic kinds of valve trains, and we will look at them here. The three kinds are the L-head, the I-head or overhead-valve, and the overhead-camshaft.

NOTE
One way of classifying engines is according to the arrangement of the intake and exhaust valves in the cylinder head or cylinder block. The arrangements get their names because of their likenesses to certain letters of the alphabet (Fig. 8-22). In most engines today, the valves are arranged in the shape of an I.

8-19 L-HEAD VALVE TRAIN
The L-head valve train is the simplest valve train. It is found in many of the one-cylinder engines used in lawn mowers, edgers, and so on. Years ago, nearly all automobile engines had L-head valve trains, but not any more. We will explain why after we have discussed the L-head engine.

Figure 8-23 shows the valve train for an L-head engine. The valve moves up and down in a valve guide, which is installed in the cylinder block. The *cylinder block* is the large block of cast iron that encloses the cylinders. All the other engine parts are installed in or on the cylinder block. See Chap. 11 for a detailed look at the cylinder block.

When the valve is down, its head seals off the valve port, so that no air can get into or out of the cylinder. But when it is pushed up, the valve is raised off the valve seat, so that air or gas can pass through.

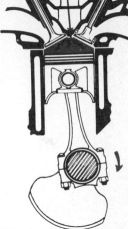

COMBUSTION CHAMBER

Fig. 8-19
The power stroke. The ignition system produces a spark that ignites the mixture. As the mixture burns, high pressure is created, pushing the piston down.

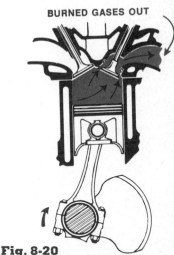

BURNED GASES OUT

Fig. 8-20
The exhaust stroke. The exhaust valve, at right, has opened. The piston is moving upward, pushing the burned gases out of the cylinder.

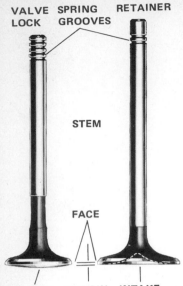

Fig. 8-21
Typical engine valves.
(*Chrysler Corporation*)

About three-quarters of the time, the valve is held down in the closed position by the valve spring.

The stem end of the valve has one or more grooves cut in it. You can see these grooves in Fig. 8-21. When a valve is installed in the engine, the spring is put in place and compressed with a special tool. Then a spring retainer, which is a large washer, is installed, followed by a spring-retainer lock. The lock fits into the grooves in the valve stem. Then, when the spring is released, spring pressure forces the

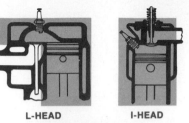

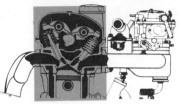

Fig. 8-22
L-head, I-head (overhead-valve), and in-line overhead-cam engines.

Fig. 8-23
A valve train for an L-head engine. The valve is raised off the valve seat with every camshaft rotation.

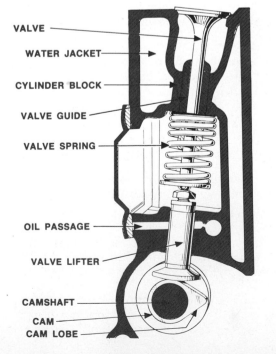

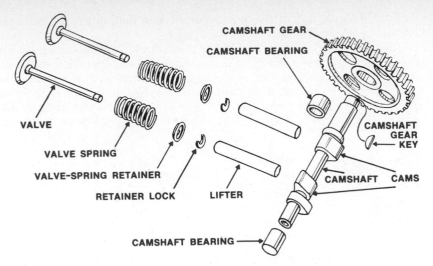

Fig. 8-24
Complete valve train for a one-cylinder engine. (*Cushman Motors*)

CAMSHAFT GEAR

CAMSHAFT BEARING

CAMSHAFT GEAR KEY

VALVE

VALVE SPRING

VALVE-SPRING RETAINER

RETAINER LOCK

LIFTER

CAMSHAFT   CAMS

CAMSHAFT BEARING

spring retainer down on the lock. The lock is held in the grooves in the valve stem.

Figure 8-24 shows the parts of the valve train for a one-cylinder, L-head engine in their proper order of assembly. Notice the cams on the camshaft. These are round collars with a high spot, called the *cam lobe*. The lobe opens the valve, as we will see in a moment.

Spring pressure keeps the valve closed most of the time. The camshaft rotates. It is driven by a gear that is meshed with a gear on the crankshaft. As the camshaft rotates, the cam lobe comes around under the valve lifter. As the lobe moves up under the lifter, it pushes the lifter upward (Fig. 8-25). This, in turn, pushes the valve up so that it opens. Notice that the lifter is between the cam and the end of the valve stem. The lifter takes all the wear caused by the cam rubbing against it. The lifter may also provide a means of adjustment.

As the camshaft continues to rotate, the cam lobe moves out from under the valve lifter. The spring then pulls the valve back down on its seat.

NOTE
The valve lifter is often called the *valve tappet* or the *cam follower*.

8-20 FLAT-HEAD
The L-head engine is also called the *flat-head engine* because the cylinder head is flat on top. Figure 8-26 is a cutaway view of one cylinder of a flat-head engine. Study this picture to find the valves, the piston, and the combustion chamber.

8-21 I-HEAD
Automotive manufacturers stopped making L-head engines and switched to overhead-valve engines. There are several reasons for this change, which are explained later. First, let's look at the I-head engine, also called the *overhead-valve* or the *valve-in-head engine*. As the name implies, the valves are in the cylinder head instead of in the cylinder block.

Figure 8-27 shows the essential parts of the valve train for one cylinder in an overhead-valve engine. Do you see the parts that have been added? They are the pushrods and the rocker arms. The valve springs

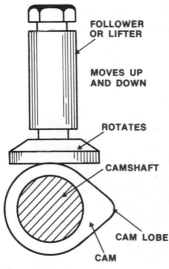

FOLLOWER OR LIFTER

MOVES UP AND DOWN

ROTATES

CAMSHAFT

CAM LOBE

CAM

Fig. 8-25
Every time the cam lobe comes around under the valve lifter, the lifter is raised.

Fig. 8-26
A cutaway view of an L-head engine.

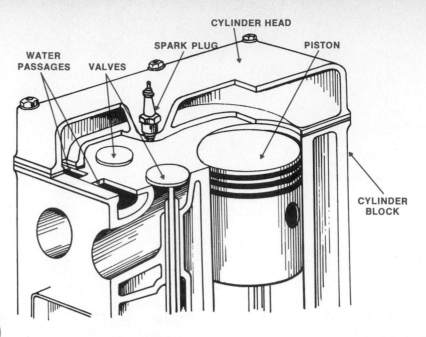

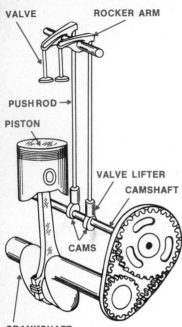

Fig. 8-27
Valve-operating mechanisms for one cylinder of an overhead-valve engine. Only the essential moving parts are shown.

are not shown here, but they are used, just as in the L-head engine. When the cam lobe comes up under the valve lifter, the lobe moves the valve lifter up. This pushes up on the pushrod. The pushrod moves up, pushing up on one end of the rocker arm. The rocker arm is mounted on a shaft so that it can rock back and forth, just like a seesaw. When one end of the rocker arm is pushed up by the pushrod, the other end pushes down on the end of the valve stem. The result is that the valve is pushed down off its seat and it opens.

Fig. 8-28
A sectional view of one bank of a V-8 engine. The rocker arms are mounted on ball pivots. (*Pontiac Motor Division of General Motors Corporation*)

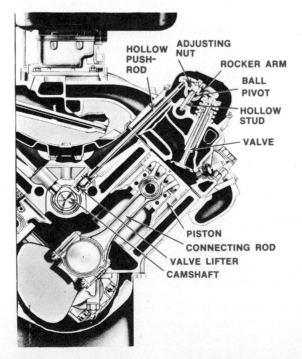

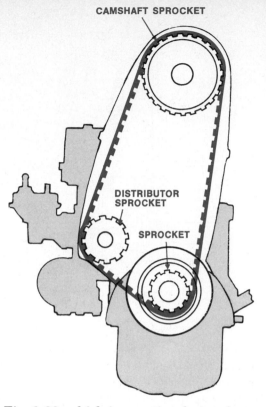

CAMSHAFT SPROCKET

DISTRIBUTOR
SPROCKET

SPROCKET

Fig. 8-29
A simplified drawing of the
drive arrangement for an overhead-camshaft engine. (*Pontiac Motor Division of General
Motors Corporation*)

Take a moment to study Fig. 8-28, which is a sectional view from the end of an engine cylinder. Find the valve, valve spring, rocker arm, pushrod, valve lifter, and cam on the camshaft. Notice that the rocker arm is mounted on a ball pivot instead of a shaft. The action is the same, however. When the valve lifter is pushed up by the lobe on the cam, the pushrod moves up. It then pushes on the rocker arm. The rocker arm rocks, and the valve is pushed down off its seat.

8-22 OVERHEAD-CAMSHAFT ENGINE

In the overhead-camshaft engine, the camshaft is located in the cylinder head. This eliminates the pushrod and puts the cams closer to the valves. With this setup, the valves respond quicker to the cam lobes, and the engine is more responsive. That is, the engine accelerates faster and can have a higher speed (in revolutions per minute, or rpm).

Figure 8-29 shows a simplified drawing of an overhead-camshaft engine and the drive belt. Note that the camshaft sprocket is twice as large as the crankshaft sprocket, just as in other kinds of engines. The drive belt also drives the ignition distributor. As we will explain later, L-head and I-head engines have camshafts with gears that drive the ignition distributor. Many overhead-camshaft engines use the camshaft to drive the distributor. However, on the engine shown in Fig. 8-29, the distributor is driven from the same belt that drives the camshaft. The distributor controls the ignition system and supplies sparks to the spark plugs. Without the sparks, the engine would not run.

In Chap. 14, we look at all kinds of valve trains. We will find out how they work and what the advantages are of the I-head and overhead-camshaft engines.

Fig. 8-30

A simplified drawing of an overhead valve train. The lobe on the cam has moved up under the lifter, raising the lifter and opening the valve. At the same time, the piston is moving up, pushing the burned gases out of the cylinder.

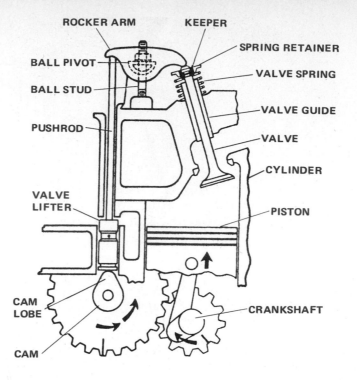

ROCKER ARM   KEEPER
SPRING RETAINER
BALL PIVOT
VALVE SPRING
BALL STUD
VALVE GUIDE
PUSHROD
VALVE
CYLINDER
VALVE LIFTER
PISTON
CAM LOBE
CRANKSHAFT
CAM

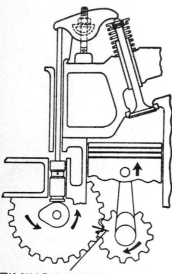

TIMING MARKS

Fig. 8-31

Here the piston has reached the end of the exhaust stroke. The cam lobe has moved out from under the valve lifter, and the valve spring has pulled the valve closed. The other cam on the camshaft—not shown here —is opening the intake valve. The piston is ready to move down on the intake stroke.

8-23 VALVE TIMING

Valve timing refers to the relationship between the valve movement and the piston movement. The valves must move "in time" with the piston. That is, the intake valve must be open during the intake stroke, and the exhaust valve must be open during the exhaust stroke. During the compression and power strokes, both valves must be closed.

How many times does the crankshaft rotate during the four piston strokes? One-half rotation (or 180 degrees) is needed for each piston stroke. And with four piston strokes, the crankshaft must rotate two full turns, or 720 degrees. During these two revolutions of the crankshaft, how many times must the camshaft rotate? Each time the camshaft rotates, both valves open and close. The camshaft rotates only once while the crankshaft rotates twice. In other words, the gear on the crankshaft must turn twice to make the gear on the camshaft turn once.

The camshaft rotates half as fast as the crankshaft because it uses a gear on the camshaft that is twice as big as the gear on the crankshaft (Figs. 8-30 and 8-31). In Fig. 8-30, the lobe on the cam has moved under the valve lifter, causing the valve to open. At the same time, the piston is moving up on the exhaust stroke. This forces the burned gases out through the exhaust port. Further rotation of the crankshaft turns the camshaft so that the lobe moves out from under the valve lifter. This allows the valve spring to close the valve. The actions of the crankshaft and valves during the four piston strokes are shown in the Figs. 8-15, 8-16, 8-19, and 8-20.

Figure 8-32 shows the crankshaft and camshaft gears for a six-cylinder engine. Note the timing marks on the gears. These timing marks must be lined up when the engine is assembled so that the timing between the valves and the piston will be correct.

TIMING MARKS

THRUST-PLATE SCREWS

8-24 TIMING CHAIN

Figure 8-33 shows the timing chain and sprockets used on an overhead-valve engine. Most overhead-valve engines use timing chains and sprockets instead of gears, as shown in Fig. 8-32. The chain is made of metal links that fit the teeth on the two sprockets. The upper sprocket is on the camshaft, and the lower sprocket is on the crankshaft. Note the timing marks on the two sprockets. These must be lined up when the engine is assembled so that the opening and closing of the valves is correctly timed to the piston.

CHECK UP ON YOURSELF

You have now covered most of the fundamentals of engine operation. Answer the questions below to find out how well you understand what you have studied about valves.

1. What is the name of the assembly of parts that operate the valves?
2. What are the three kinds of valve trains?
3. How many cams are there on the camshaft for each cylinder?
4. What are other names for the I-head engine?
5. Name the parts in the I-head valve train.
6. What is meant by valve timing?
7. How many times does the crankshaft rotate during the four piston strokes?
8. What makes the camshaft rotate only half as fast as the crankshaft?
9. What three methods are used to drive the camshaft?

Fig. 8-33
Crankshaft and camshaft sprockets with chain drive on a V-8 engine. (*Chrysler Corporation*)

ANSWERS

1. The valve train (Sec. 8-18). **2.** L-head, I-head or overhead-valve, and overhead-camshaft (Sec. 8-18). **3.** Two (Sec. 8-19). **4.** Overhead-valve, valve-in-head (Sec. 8-21). **5.** Valve, valve spring, valve-spring retainer, retainer lock, rocker arm, pushrod, camshaft, timing chain or gears (Sec. 8-21). **6.** The relationship between valve movement and piston position (Sec. 8-23). **7.** Two (Sec. 8-23). **8.** Camshaft sprocket or gear is twice as large as the crankshaft sprocket or gear (Sec. 8-23). **9.** Two timing gears or two sprockets and chain (Secs. 8-22 to 8-24).

CHAPTER NINE ENGINE MEASUREMENTS

After studying this chapter, you should be able to:

1. Explain what bore and stroke mean.
2. Explain what piston displacement is and how it is calculated.
3. Explain what compression ratio is and how it is calculated.
4. Explain what other engine terms mean, such as horsepower, volumetric efficiency, torque, friction horsepower, brake horsepower, and engine efficiency.

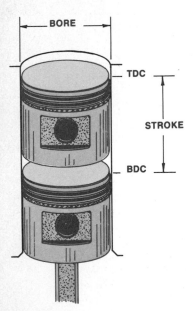

Fig. 9-1
The bore and stroke of an engine cylinder.

To compare one engine with another, you have to take various measurements. It is not very meaningful to say that one engine puts out a lot of power and a different engine "hasn't got it." To compare engines, you have to know what is meant by words like "high compression" and "displacement." In this chapter, you will find out what all this means.

9-1 BORE AND STROKE

We start our study of engine measurement by looking at the engine cylinder. There are two basic cylinder measurements—bore and stroke (Fig. 9-1). The *bore* is the diameter of the cylinder. The *stroke* is the distance the piston moves from BDC to TDC.

When the measurements of an engine cylinder are given, the bore is always mentioned first. For example, a 4- by 3.5-inch cylinder has a bore of 4 inches [102 mm] and a stroke of 3.5 inches [89 mm].

When you listen to professional mechanics, you may hear them talk about an oversquare engine. *Oversquare* means that the bore is greater than the stroke. A 4- by 3.5-inch [102- by 89-mm] engine cylinder is oversquare. A 4- by 4-inch [102- by 102-mm] cylinder is square. Many engines are oversquare. With a shorter stroke, the piston and rings don't have to move as far. There is less wear and less loss of power through friction. The bigger the piston, the more powerful the power strokes. A bigger piston has more area for the high-pressure gases to push down on.

9-2 PISTON DISPLACEMENT

When the piston moves up from BDC to TDC, it pushes away, or *displaces*, a certain volume. You can picture this volume as the diameter

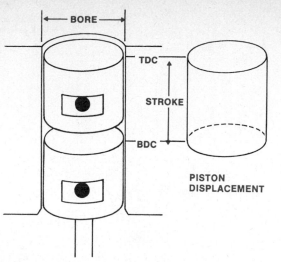

Fig. 9-2
Piston displacement is the volume the piston displaces, or takes the place of, as it moves from BDC to TDC.

of a cylinder, with the top and bottom being the piston head at TDC and at BDC (Fig. 9-2).

For example, an engine cylinder measures 4 inches [102 mm] in diameter. The distance the piston moves from BDC to TCD is 3.5 inches [89 mm]. The displacement of this engine cylinder is the volume of a cylinder 4 inches [102 mm] in diameter and 3.5 inches [89 mm] in length. To calculate the volume, let D stand for diameter and L for length. The symbol π is called *pi*, and it is equal to 3.1416. The calculation is

$$\text{Displacement} = \frac{\pi \times D^2 \times L}{4} = \frac{3.1416 \times 4^2 \times 3.50}{4}$$

$$= \frac{3.1416 \times 16 \times 3.50}{4}$$

$$= \textbf{43.98 cubic inches}$$

The displacement of one cylinder of the engine is 43.98 cubic inches [720.1 cc (cubic centimeters)]. What does 43.98 cubic inches look like? For comparison, 1 quart contains about 60 cubic inches and 1 pint about 30 cubic inches. (Actually, 1 pint is 28.4 cubic inches [473.2 cc].) So 43.98 cubic inches is equal to about 1½ pints (actually 1.52 pints [720.1 cc]). (See Fig. 9-3.) That's for one cylinder. To find the displacement of an eight-cylinder engine, we multiply 43.98 cubic inches [720.1 cc] by 8, to get 351.84 cubic inches [5765.6 cc]. That's about 1½ gallons, or 6 quarts [5.76 L (liters)]. Many technicians don't say "cubic inches." Instead, they say "It's a 350 engine," meaning the engine has a displacement of 350 cubic inches.

When you talk with the technicians who build and race cars, they will tell you that limits are set for engine displacements in most races. In a 500-mile race at Indianapolis (the "Indy 500"), the maximum allowable displacement for nonsupercharged engines was 305.1 cubic inches [5000 cc, or 5 L].

For some engines, especially those made in Europe, the displacement is given in *liters,* a metric measurement. One liter equals 61.02 cubic inches, or 1.057 quarts. The Indy-500 spec of 305.1 cubic inches limited engine displacement to 5 L (305.1 divided by 61.02 is 5 L).

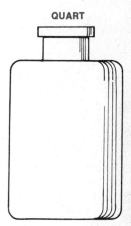

QUART

60 CUBIC INCHES

PINT

½ PINT

PINT AND A HALF

Fig. 9-3   45 CUBIC INCHES.
One quart contains about 60 cubic inches [950 cc]. And 1.5 pints is about 45 cubic inches [760 cc].

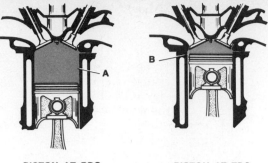

PISTON AT BDC   PISTON AT TDC

9-3 COMPRESSION RATIO

Let's have another look at compression ratio. In Chap. 8 we mentioned that the piston squeezes the air-fuel mixture into a smaller volume, or space. When the volume goes from 1 quart to $\frac{1}{2}$ cup, the compression ratio is 8:1. That is, the volume is reduced to one-eighth of the original volume. In terms of cubic inches, the volume goes from 60 cubic inches (1 quart) to 7.5 cubic inches ($\frac{1}{2}$ cup). This is a ratio of 60:7.5, or 8:1. In metric measurements, the volume goes from 984 to 123 cc. This is a ratio of 984:123, or, again, 8:1.

Figure 9-4 shows an engine cylinder twice—once with the piston at BDC and once with it at TDC. It shows what compression ratio means inside an engine. The cylinder volume is reduced from A to B when the piston moves from BDC to TDC. In other words, the compression ratio is A divided by B.

As an example, suppose A is 45 cubic inches and B is 5 cubic inches. Then the ratio between A and B—which is the compression ratio—is 45 divided by 5, or 9. The compression ratio is 9:1. The volume B above the piston when it is at TDC is called the *clearance volume*. The volume A, with the piston at BDC, is the *air volume*. As you can see, carbon buildup in the combustion chamber increases the effective compression ratio.

9-4 IMPORTANCE OF HIGH COMPRESSION

You should know two important facts about compression ratio. First, when the compression ratio goes up, engine power usually goes up. A car with a higher-compression engine has more acceleration, can pass more quickly on the highway, and has a higher top speed. This is because more push is exerted on the piston during the power stroke because of higher pressure within the combustion chamber. Second, a high-compression engine needs "high-octane" gasoline. If the engine does not get it, the engine will "ping," or detonate. Detonation or spark knock is the sudden explosion of the remaining compressed air-fuel mixture after the spark occurs at the spark plug. The result is a loss of power, engine overheating, and a characteristic rattling sound called *pinging*. You can ruin a high-compression engine with low-octane gas. The engine could detonate so hard that engine parts actually break!

9-5 ENGINE POWER

Now we come to an important engine measurement—horsepower. "How many horsepower?" means "How many horses would it take to equal the maximum power output of the engine?" Let's see what horsepower is. *Horsepower* (hp) is a measure of how hard an engine can work.

9-6 WORK

What is work? You can say that sitting at a desk to figure out an engine repair bill is work. And it is work, because it is part of your job. But it is not what engineers mean when they talk about work.

Engineers have a special meaning for the word "work." To them, it means *changing the position of an object against an opposing force.* Put another way, work means moving an object with a force that overcomes some other force. For example, gravity tends to pull objects down. So when you lift an object against the opposing force of gravity, you are doing work on the object. If you lift a 10-pound [4.5-kg] weight a distance of 5 feet [1.5 m], you are doing 50 ft-lb (foot-pounds) [6.8 m-kg] of work on the weight (Fig. 9-5). The weight will "give back" the work if you drop it.

9-7 ADDING UP THE POWER STROKES

Let's go over work again. During a power stroke in the engine, the high-pressure gas pushes on the piston head with a force of up to 4000 lb [1814 kg]. The automobile is the opposing force. The 4000-pound [1814-kg] force must overcome the opposing force of the automobile to move it along. This is work. The repeated power strokes in all the engine cylinders provide the work necessary to keep the car moving. Therefore, engine power results from the work done on the pistons by the burning gases in the cylinders.

As an example, let's agree that thc 4000 pounds [1814 kg] of pressure pushes the piston down 3 inches, or $\frac{1}{4}$ foot [76.2 mm], as shown in Fig. 9-6. This mcans the push has produced $\frac{1}{4} \times 4000 = 1000$ ft-lb [138 m-kg] of work.

When the power strokcs follow one another very rapidly, the engine is working hard. It is producing a lot of work in a given amount of time. The engine is putting out a lot of *power,* and the car is moving fast. When there are fewer power strokes per minute, the engine is producing less work in the same amount of time. It is putting out less power.

Now you have it. Power is the rate, or the speed, at which work is done. If an engine can do work fast, it is called a *high-powered engine.*

9-8 ENGINE HORSEPOWER

Engine performance is measured in horsepower. One horsepower is the amount of work one horse can do in 1 minute. The average horse can raise a 200-pound [90.8-kg] weight a distance of 165 feet [50.3 m] in 1 minute. Figure 9-7 shows how this measurement can be made. The horse walks 165 feet [50.3 m] in 1 minute. The cable, running over the pulley, raises the 200-pound [90.8-kg] weight 165 feet [50.3 m]. The amount of work done in 1 minute is $165 \times 200 = 33,000$ ft-lb [4560 m-kg]. In other words, 1 hp is 33,000 ft-lb of work per minute.

If the horse took 2 minutes to do the same amount of work (33,000 ft-lb), it would be working only half as hard. It would thus be putting out only 0.5 hp. Three horses would be needed to raise 600 pounds [272.2 kg] a distance of 165 feet [50.3 m] in 1 minute. Why? The work required would be $600 \times 165 = 99,000$ ft-lb [13,680 m-kg], and this work would have to be done in 1 minute.

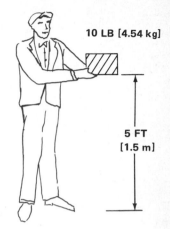

10 LB [4.54 kg]

5 FT [1.5 m]

Fig. 9-5
When you lift an object against the opposing force of gravity, you are doing work on the object.

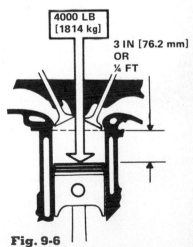

4000 LB [1814 kg]

3 IN [76.2 mm] OR ¼ FT

Fig. 9-6
To move the piston, the pressure on top of the piston must overcome the opposing force of the automobile. This is work.

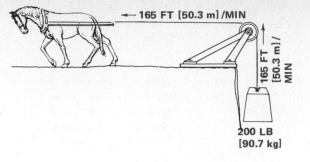

Fig. 9-7
One horse can do 33,000 ft-lb [4560 m-kg] of work in 1 minute.

← 165 FT [50.3 m] /MIN

165 FT [50.3 m] / MIN

200 LB [90.7 kg]

Here is one formula used to figure horsepower:

$$\text{HP} = \frac{\text{ft-lb/min}}{33{,}000} = \frac{L \times W}{33{,}000 \times t}$$

where HP = horsepower
L = distance moved, feet
W = push or pull exerted, pounds
t = time required, minutes

PROBLEM: How many horsepower would it take to raise 3000 pounds a distance of 220 feet in 1 minute?

SOLUTION

$$\text{HP} = \frac{L \times W}{33{,}000 \times t} = \frac{220 \times 3000}{33{,}000 \times 1} = 20 \text{ hp}$$

Another formula uses engine torque as one of the measurements instead of W and L. It is described in Sec. 9-12.

OTHER ENGINE MEASUREMENTS

You can now talk with mechanics and technicians about horsepower, engine displacement, and compression ratio. Some other engine measurements are volumetric efficiency, torque, friction horsepower, and engine efficiency. We look at these engine measurements in the remainder of this chapter.

9-9 VOLUMETRIC EFFICIENCY

The word "volumetric" means having to do with volume. "Efficiency" generally refers to how well a job is done. The two words used together refer to how well the engine cylinder fills up on the intake stroke. Remember, the piston moves down on the intake stroke. The air-fuel mixture pours in to fill the vacuum left by the downward movement of the piston. The mixture doesn't pour in instantly. It needs time to flow through the carburetor and past the intake valve.

There isn't much time for the air-fuel mixture to get into the engine cylinder on the intake stroke. At high engine speed, or high rpm (revolutions per minute), the intake stroke takes less than 0.01 second. The piston moves very fast! So, before the cylinder fills up completely, the intake valve closes and the compression stroke starts. If the cylinder fills up almost completely, then the volumetric efficiency is high. If the cylinder fills up only partly, then the volumetric efficiency is low.

The key idea is this: The less time the mixture has to fill the cylinder, the lower the volumetric efficiency will be. At low engine speed, when the intake stroke takes as long as 0.1 second, the cylinder can almost fill up. The volumetric efficiency is high. This means there is more air-fuel mixture to be compressed and burned. As a result, the power stroke is stronger.

At high engine speed, the intake stroke takes such a short time that the cylinder gets much less air-fuel mixture. The volumetric efficiency is low. There is less air-fuel mixture to be compressed and burned, and the power stroke is weaker.

That is why engine speed cannot be increased indefinitely. As engine speed increases, the intake-stroke time gets shorter and shorter. So the volumetric efficiency gets lower and lower. Less and less air-fuel mixture gets in, and the power output of the engine falls lower and lower. Finally, the power strokes become so weak that they cannot increase the speed any further.

Here is the formula for volumetric efficiency:

$$VE = \frac{\text{actual amount of air-fuel mixture entering cylinder}}{\text{amount entering under ideal conditions}}$$

Suppose that at a certain speed 40 cubic inches [656 cc] of mixture enters the cylinder. However, under ideal conditions, 50 cubic inches [819 cc] could enter. The volumetric efficiency is 40 divided by 50, which is 0.8, or 80 percent.

9-10 IMPROVING VOLUMETRIC EFFICIENCY

The volumetric efficiency (VE) can be improved by increasing the size of the passages through which the air-fuel mixture travels. If the intake valve, the valve port, and the passages through the carburetor are made larger, the air-fuel mixture can get into the cylinder more easily. This is done in modern engines. Engineers call it "improving the engine's breathing." They point out that an engine "breathes" just as you do. It takes in air and then blows it out.

With improved engine breathing, the engine can put out more power at higher speeds. For example, when technicians assemble a racing engine, they enlarge the air-fuel passages as much as possible. This allows the engine to breathe better at high speed. This, in turn, improves the volumetric efficiency of the engine. Suppose an engine has a volumetric efficiency of 80 percent at high speeds. Modifying the engine might raise the actual amount of air-fuel mixture taken in from 40 cubic inches [656 cc] to 45 cubic inches [737 cc]. The VE would then be increased to 90 percent.

You have heard of "two-barrel" and "four-barrel" carburetors. These carburetors are used on high-horsepower engines. The extra barrels are additional air passages that let the engine breathe easier. They give the engine higher volumetric efficiency. The higher volumetric efficiency allows the engine to put out more horsepower, especially at high speeds.

9-11 TORQUE

Torque is twisting, or turning, effort (Fig. 9-8). You apply torque to the steering wheel when you steer a car around a turn. The engine applies torque to the car wheels to make them rotate.

Torque, however, must not be confused with power. Torque is twisting, or turning, effort which may or may not result in motion. In

Fig. 9-8
Torque, or twisting effort, must be applied to loosen and remove the top from a screw-top jar.

other words, torque is the *ability* to do work, or the ability to cause something to rotate.

Torque is measured in pound-feet (lb-ft) or in kilogram-meters (kg-m). Do not confuse this with work, which is measured in foot-pounds (ft-lb) or meter-kilograms (m-kg). For example, suppose you pushed on a crank with a 20-pound [9.1-kg] push. If the crank were 1.5 feet [0.46 m] long, you would be applying $20 \times 1.5 = 30$ lb-ft [4.2 kg-m] of torque to the crank (Fig. 9-9). You would be applying this amount of torque *whether or not* the crank was turning.

9-12 ENGINE TORQUE

Engine torque comes from the pressure of the burning gases in the cylinders. This pressure pushes down on the pistons and causes the crankshaft to turn. The harder the push on the piston, the greater the torque. *Engine torque is not engine power.* Torque is the twisting effort that the pistons apply to the crankshaft. Power is the rate at which the engine is working.

Engine torque varies with the speed of the engine. An engine develops more torque at intermediate speed (with open throttle) than at high speed. Here's the reason: At intermediate speed, there is more time for the air-fuel mixture to enter the cylinder. In other words, the volumetric efficiency is high. This means that more air-fuel mixture enters the cylinder, the combustion pressure goes up, and there is a stronger push on the piston. As a result, more torque is applied to the crankshaft.

At higher speeds, there is less time for the air-fuel mixture to get into the cylinder. Volumetric efficiency drops off. There is less air-fuel mixture to burn, and the combustion pressure is lower. There is less push on the piston, and the engine torque is lower.

The fact that torque drops at high speed is shown in Fig. 9-10. At low speed, about 500 rpm (revolutions per minute), the torque is about 180 lb-ft [24.9 kg-m]. Find this point on the graph by moving up the 500-rpm line until it crosses the curved line. From this point, move

Fig. 9-10

Torque curve of an engine that shows the relationship between torque and speed.

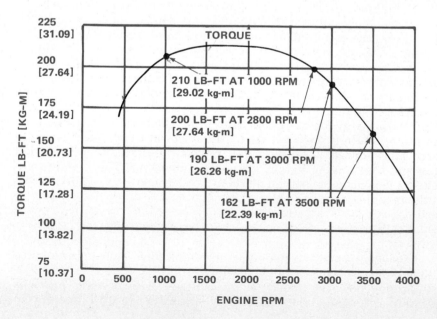

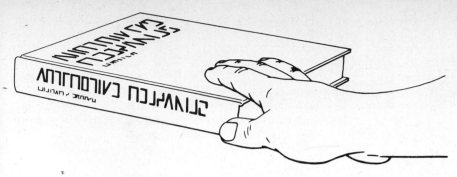

Fig. 9-11
Friction resists the push on the book.

across to the left. You should see that the torque is slightly above 175 lb-ft [24.2 kg-m], or about 180 lb-ft [24.9 kg-m]. As engine speed increases, the torque goes up. Torque reaches a peak in the 1500- to 2000-rpm range. Then it begins to drop. At about 4000 rpm, the torque is less than 125 lb-ft [17.3 kg-m].

This explains why an engine performs better at intermediate speed than at high speed. It is the torque of the engine that gives acceleration and "performance."

Here is another formula for calculating horsepower. It uses the torque developed by the engine.

$$HP = \frac{torque \times rpm}{5252}$$

When you work in the shop and use the shop dynamometer to measure engine output, you will see why this formula is more convenient than the one in Sec. 9-8. You can measure torque or horsepower with the dynamometer.

PROBLEM: How many horsepower are produced by an engine that develops 210 lb-ft of torque at 2400 rpm?

SOLUTION

$$HP = \frac{torque \times rpm}{5252} = \frac{210 \times 2400}{5252} = 96 \text{ hp}$$

9-13 FRICTION HORSEPOWER

Another important engine measurement is friction horsepower. *Friction* is the resistance to motion between two objects in contact with each other. For example, suppose you put a book on a table and push it (Fig. 9-11). Some effort is required to move the book. If you put oil on the table, the book would slide on the oil. You could move the book much more easily, because the oil reduces the friction between the book and the table.

In the engine, all moving parts are covered with oil, or lubricated, so that they will easily slip over one another. Even so, some power is used up just to make them move—to overcome the friction. The power that is used to overcome friction is called *friction horsepower,* abbreviated fhp.

Friction horsepower goes up as engine speed goes up. The graph in Fig. 9-12 shows this. At low speeds, it takes only a few horsepower to overcome the friction in the engine. But as speed increases, the friction loss goes up until, at 4000 rpm, friction is using up 40 hp.

Fig. 9-12
Friction-horsepower curve showing the relationship between friction horsepower and engine speed.

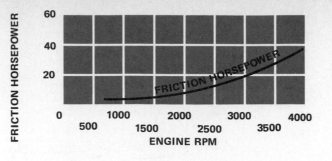

9-14 BRAKE HORSEPOWER

The *brake horsepower* (bhp) of an engine is the usable horsepower that the engine is producing. It is called "brake" horsepower because when engineers first started measuring engine performance, they used a type of brake to measure this power. Today, engine power is measured by a dynamometer. This word comes from "dynamo" and "meter." Originally, the dynamometer was an electric generator with a meter to measure the amount of electricity the generator produced. Today, the term "dynamometer" is applied to several types of power-measuring devices. In use, an engine drives the dynamometer, which measures the amount of power the engine produces. The more power the engine produces, the more power is absorbed by the dynamometer and the higher the meter reads. Engine output is measured as the amount of power the dynamometer is absorbing.

The amount of power that an engine puts out depends on its torque and speed (rpm). As speed goes up, horsepower goes up. And as torque goes up, horsepower goes up. You can see this in the formula in Sec. 9-12. The horsepower calculated by that formula is actually brake horsepower (bhp).

The graph of horsepower output for an engine is shown in Fig. 9-13. Note that the horsepower starts out low at low speed and builds up to about 110 hp at 3500 rpm. After that, as speed increases further, the horsepower output drops off.

The dropoff of horsepower output results from the decrease in torque and the increase in friction horsepower at higher speeds. So the

Fig. 9-13
Curve showing the relationship between brake horsepower and engine speed.

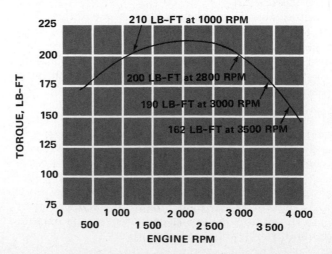

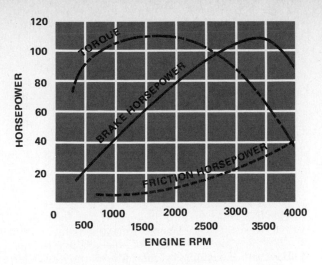

Fig. 9-14
Comparison of the torque, friction-horsepower, and brake-horsepower curves of an engine.

decrease in torque and the increase in friction horsepower keep the engine horsepower from increasing with further increases in rpm.

The graph in Fig. 9-14 combines the three graphs we have been discussing.

NOTE

The four graphs (Figs. 9-10 and 9-12 to 9-14) are for one particular engine only. Different engines have different torque, friction-horsepower, and brake-horsepower curves. The peaks may be at higher or lower speeds. The relationships may not be quite the same as those shown in our graphs.

9-15 ENGINE EFFICIENCY

We noted that the word "efficiency" refers to how well a job is done. In an engine, it is the relationship between the effort exerted and the results obtained. *Engine efficiency* is the ratio of the power actually delivered to the power that could be delivered if the engine operated without any power loss.

Unfortunately, there is considerable power loss in an engine. Power is lost because of friction and because only part of the energy in gasoline is converted to power. A good deal of the potential power in gasoline is lost as heat. The engine cooling system, which is described in Chap. 16, removes about a third of the heat energy of the gasoline. Another third is lost because the exhaust gases are very hot when they leave the engine. More power is lost because of friction. The result is that only about 15 to 20 percent of the energy in the fuel is actually used to move the car.

CHECK UP ON YOURSELF

Once again you have the chance to check up on yourself and find out how well you understand what you studied. The material you covered is different from the material in previous chapters. It describes some of the ways in which engine performance is measured. This is valuable information. Anyone interested in automotive engines should know how engine output is measured, what "compression ratio" means, and so on. Find out how efficiently you have studied this material by answering the following questions.

1. What is bore?
2. What is stroke?
3. What is piston displacement?
4. Compression ratio is a measure of what?
5. Define work.
6. Volumetric efficiency is a measure of what?
7. What is torque?
8. What is friction horsepower?
9. What is brake horsepower?
10. About what percentage of the energy in the gasoline is used to move the car?

ANSWERS

1. Diameter of the cylinder (Sec. 9-1). 2. Distance the piston travels from BDC to TDC (Sec. 9-1). 3. Volume the piston displaces as it moves from BDC to TDC (Sec. 9-2). 4. Amount that the air-fuel mixture is compressed (Sec. 9-3). 5. Changing the position of an object against an opposing force (Sec. 9-6). 6. How well the engine cylinder fills on the intake stroke (Sec. 9-9). 7. Twisting or turning force (Sec. 9-10). 8. Power used up in the engine to overcome friction (Sec. 9-13). 9. Usable horsepower available from the engine (Sec. 9-14). 10. About 15 to 20 percent (Sec. 9-15).

CHAPTER TEN
ENGINE TYPES

After studying this chapter, you should be able to:

1. Explain the various ways in which automotive engines are classified.
2. Explain why the four-cylinder engine has become more popular.
3. Describe the various engine cylinder arrangements.
4. Explain what a turbocharger is and how it works.
5. Describe the various valve arrangements used in engines.
6. Explain the differences between gasoline and diesel engines.
7. Explain what firing order is.
8. Explain how the Wankel engine works.

We have already mentioned some of the different types of automotive engines—L-head, I-head, reciprocating, and rotary. Now we are going to look at other classifications of engines. Automotive piston, or reciprocating, engines can be classified in at least seven different ways:

1. Number of cylinders
2. Arrangement of cylinders
3. Arrangement of valves
4. Types of cooling systems
5. Number of piston strokes per cycle
6. Type of fuel burned
7. Firing order

This is not a complete list, but it will give you an idea of the ways in which engines can be classified.

10-1 NUMBER AND ARRANGEMENT OF CYLINDERS

Almost all automotive piston engines have either four, six, or eight cylinders. Usually, the cylinders in four-cylinder and six-cylinder engines are arranged in a single row, or line. Some V-4 and V-6 engines are made. In these, the cylinders are placed in two rows set at an angle to each other. Flat four- and flat six-cylinder engines have also been made. In these, the cylinders are in two rows across from each other. Eight-cylinder engines are all of the V-8 type. The two rows of cylinders are set at an angle to each other. Figure 10-1 shows the various arrangements. Now let's look at these different engines in detail.

Fig. 10-1
Several cylinder arrange-
ments.

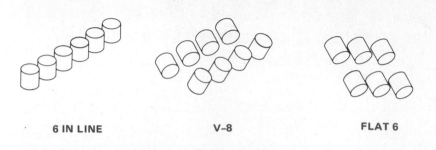

4 IN LINE   V-6   FLAT 4

6 IN LINE   V-8   FLAT 6

10-2 FOUR-CYLINDER, IN-LINE ENGINES

The cylinders in a four-cylinder engine can be arranged in a single line, in pairs set at an angle to form a V or in pairs set opposite one another. A typical four-cylinder, in-line engine is shown in Fig. 10-2. Note that this engine has overhead valves operated by pushrods and rocker arms. Study this picture to locate the pistons, connecting rod (one shown), camshaft, camshaft drive gear, spark plugs, pushrods, rocker arms, and valves. If you look carefully, you will see a spiral gear on the camshaft that is meshed with another spiral gear on a nearly vertical shaft. The purpose of these gears is to drive the oil pump that lubricates the engine. Also, they drive the ignition distributor, not shown in the picture.

The four-cylinder engine has become increasingly popular in recent years. One reason is that there is a definite trend toward small, lightweight cars. This trend has been encouraged by the oil shortage and government regulations regarding car size and increased gasoline mileage requirements. The four-cylinder engine in a small car can give 40 miles per gallon or more on the highway. Large cars with eight-cylinder engines get about 14 or 15 miles per gallon.

The four-cylinder car often does not have the acceleration of cars with larger engines. A partial solution, which we discuss in detail later, is a six-cylinder or eight-cylinder engine that deactivates some of the cylinders when they are not needed. There is one type of six-cylinder engine that cuts out three of the cylinders when the car is cruising. One eight-cylinder engine has electronic controls that can progressively cut out up to four of the cylinders when power demand is low. The controls deactivate the cylinders by not opening the valves. Another solution is to turbocharge the engine. Turbocharging puts more air-fuel mixture into the engine cylinders so that more power is produced. We discuss all this in detail later.

10-3 V-4 ENGINES

Some V-4 engines have been built. Figure 10-3 is a phantom view of a V-4 engine showing the working parts of the engine. You can see the crankshaft, pistons, connecting rods, camshaft, and valve train. The

Fig. 10-2
A partial cutaway view of a four-cylinder, in-line, overhead-valve engine. (*Chevrolet Motor Division of General Motors Corporation*)

extra shaft with a gear (near the bottom of the picture) is a special balance shaft that is needed to balance the engine. A balanced engine runs smoothly and does not vibrate or run unevenly. The difficulty of balancing a V-4 engine is one reason why it has not been more widely used.

10-4 FLAT-FOUR ENGINES

One of the early flat-fours was the Volkswagen engine, shown in sectional view in Fig. 10-4. The four cylinders are arranged in two opposing rows of two cylinders each. The engine is mounted at the rear of the car. It has a rear-wheel drive. Another more recent flat-four is the Subaru, shown in a partial cutaway view in Fig. 10-5. It is used in a front-wheel-drive car. The Volkswagen engine is air-cooled. In this engine, the cylinders are surrounded by flat metal rings, called *fins*. The fins provide large surfaces from which heat can radiate. This prevents engine overheating. The Subaru engine is liquid-cooled. We look more closely at these two kinds of cooling systems later in the chapter.

10-5 FIVE-CYLINDER ENGINES

There are a few five-cylinder automotive engines. Mercedes-Benz produces a five-cylinder diesel engine. Diesel engines are discussed in Sec. 10-15. Audi has a five-cylinder gasoline engine (Fig. 10-6). The five-cylinder engine is somewhat of a compromise between a four- and a six-cylinder. It produces more power than a four- but is not as long or as heavy as a six-cylinder.

10-6 SIX-CYLINDER, IN-LINE ENGINES

Most six-cylinder engines are of the in-line type. In these engines, the six cylinders are arranged in a single row, or line. Figure 10-7 is a partial cutaway view of a six-cylinder, in-line engine. As you can see, it is an overhead-valve engine. The picture is especially good because you can see so many different parts. Find the crankshaft, camshaft, valves,

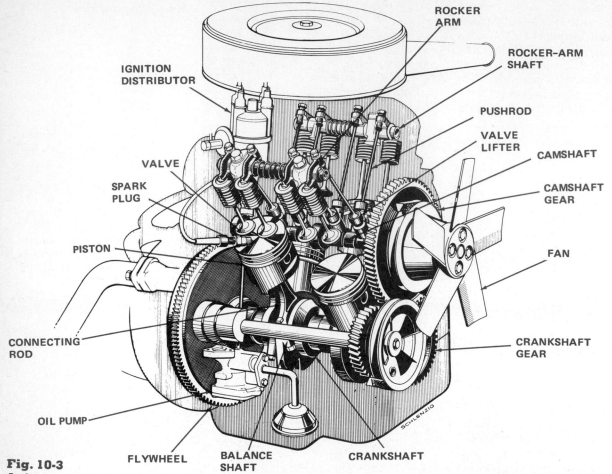

Fig. 10-3
A phantom view of a V-4 engine showing major moving parts in the engine. (*Ford Motor Company of Germany*)

Fig. 10-4
A flat-four-cylinder engine with two banks of two cylinders each, opposing each other. This is an air-cooled engine. (*Volkswagen of America, Inc.*)

rocker arms, pushrods, pistons, connecting rods, and other parts. Notice that you can see the oil pump and the ignition distributor in this picture, as well as the drive gears. The oil pump is located at the bottom in the oil pan. The oil pump supplies oil to the moving parts in the engine, so that they are kept well lubricated. The ignition distributor works with the other parts in the ignition system to supply sparks to the spark plugs.

Another six-cylinder, in-line engine is shown partly cut away in Fig. 10-8. This engine is especially interesting because the cylinders are slanted to one side. It is often called a *slant-six*. The engine has been supplied in two styles: one with a cast-iron cylinder block and the other with a cast-aluminum cylinder block. Cylinder blocks are discussed in Chap. 11.

NOTE

Some engineers are predicting that the six-in-line engine will be phased out over the next several years. The V-6 (Sec. 10-8) will take its place. This is history repeating itself. When the V-8 came along, it superseded the eight-in-line ("straight-eight") engine. Now, the V-6 is predicted to supersede the six-in-line.

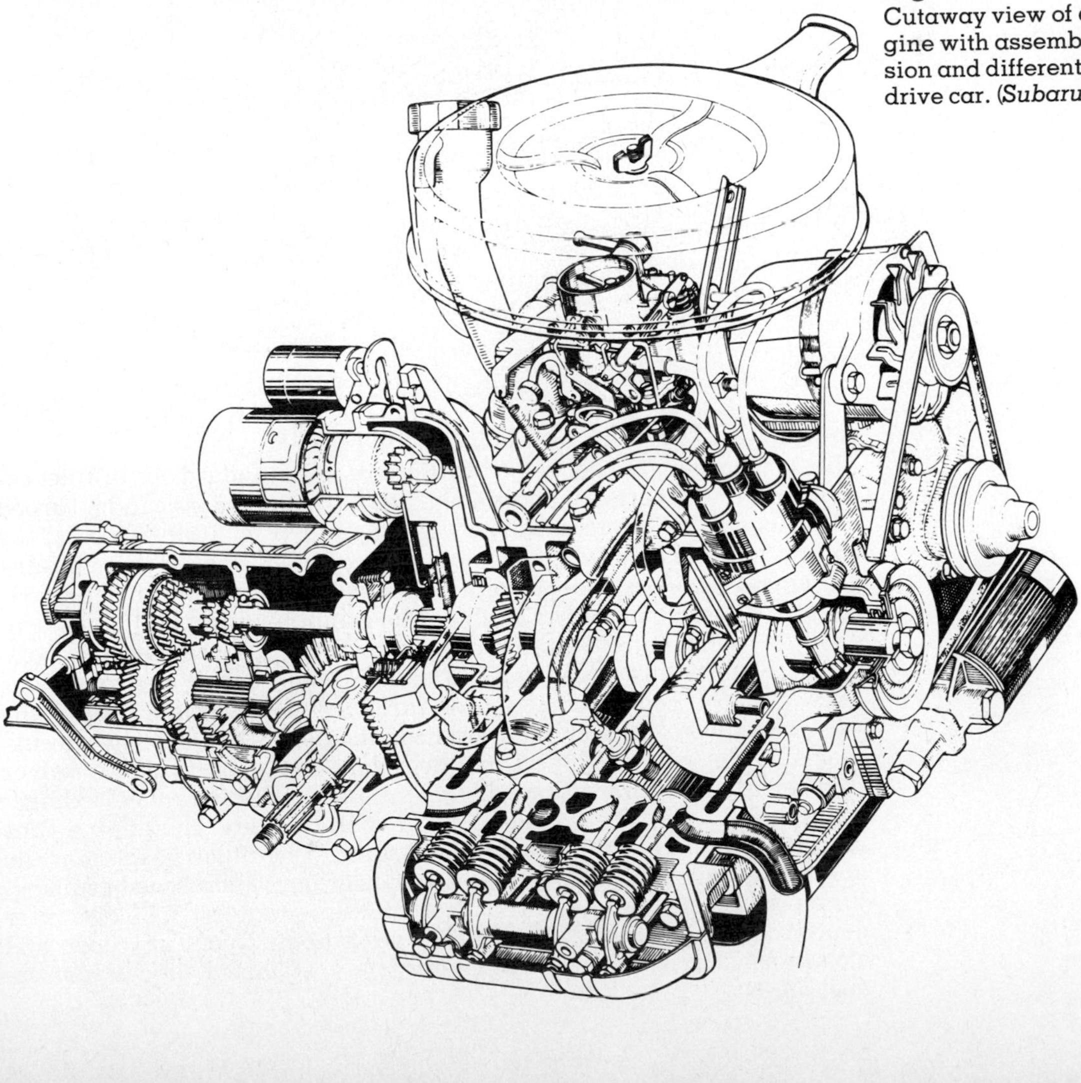

Fig. 10-5
Cutaway view of a flat-four engine with assembled transmission and differential for a front-drive car. (*Subaru*)

Fig. 10-6
Five-cylinder, in-line engine
with related suspension and
steering components for a
front-drive car. (*Audi*)

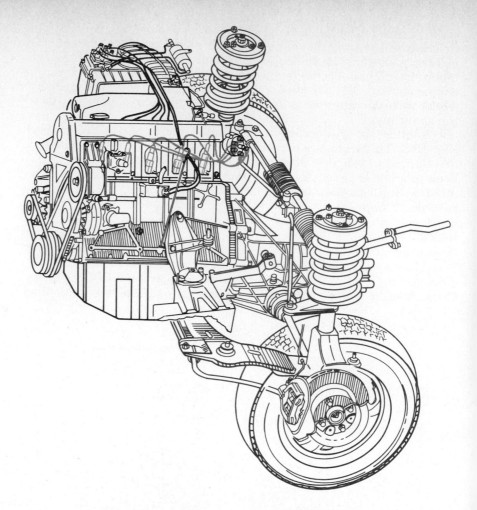

10-7 DUAL-DISPLACEMENT SIX-IN-LINE

This is a new engine developed by Ford. It is a standard six-in-line, except that under certain conditions three of the cylinders can be turned
off. This is done electronically by a computer (Fig. 10-9). That is, the
engine is either a full-displacement (six-cylinder) engine or a half-dis-
placement (three-cylinder) engine. Because of this action, the engine is
called a *dual-displacement* engine. The computer is controlled by sensors that sense intake-manifold vacuum, engine speed, throttle position, coolant temperature, and the transmission gear. When conditions
are right, the computer activates three solenoids located above the
valves in three of the cylinders. These solenoids then actuate mechanisms at the valves of the three cylinders which prevent the valves
from opening. As a result, no air-fuel mixture can enter and no exhaust
gases can escape. The cylinders are inoperative, and the engine runs
on three cylinders. This provides a substantial saving in gasoline while
at the same time supplying adequate power for steady-speed cruising.
When conditions change so that more power is required, the computer
deactivates the solenoids and the valves become free. They open and
close normally, so that the engine reverts to standard six-cylinder operation.

10-8 V-6 ENGINES

Some manufacturers build V-6 engines. These have two rows of three cylinders each, set at an angle to form a V. Figure 10-10 is a cutaway view of a V-6 engine. You can see many details of the parts and interior construction of the engine. Figure 10-11 is a partial cutaway view of a Chevrolet V-6 engine.

10-9 V-6 TURBOCHARGED ENGINE

The turbocharger is a device that sends more than the normal amount of air-fuel mixture into the engine cylinders. Figure 10-12 shows a V-6 turbocharged engine. The exhaust gas spins a rotor which is on the same shaft as a turbine, or a rotary type of air pump. This spins the turbine. When the turbine spins, it sends additional air, under pressure, into the carburetor. This supplies the engine cylinders with additional air-fuel mixture. More power develops. On many turbo-

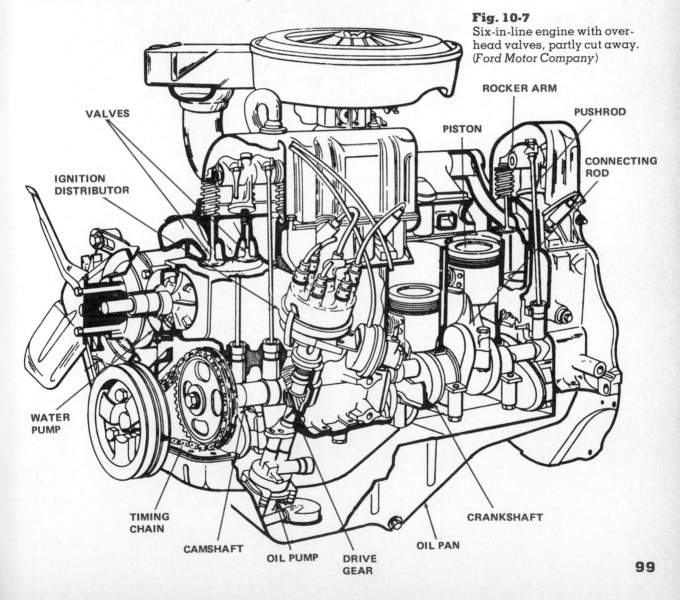

Fig. 10-7
Six-in-line engine with overhead valves, partly cut away. (*Ford Motor Company*)

VALVES

ROCKER ARM

PUSHROD

PISTON

CONNECTING ROD

IGNITION DISTRIBUTOR

WATER PUMP

TIMING CHAIN

CAMSHAFT

OIL PUMP

DRIVE GEAR

OIL PAN

CRANKSHAFT

charged engines, the power output is boosted 30 percent or more. Thus, a 100-hp engine could have its output boosted to 130 hp by a turbocharger. Section 18-33 covers turbochargers in more detail.

10-10 FLAT-SIX ENGINE

The flat-six engine is very similar to the flat-four except that one more cylinder has been added to each bank. A flat-six engine is used in the

Fig. 10-8
A slant-six, in-line, overhead-valve engine, cut away to show internal parts. The cylinders are slanted to permit a lower hood line. (*Chrysler Corporation*)

Fig. 10-9
Schematic drawing of the six-in-line, dual-displacement engine. Under some operating conditions, when full power is not needed, the computer cuts out three of the cylinders. (*Ford Motor Company*)

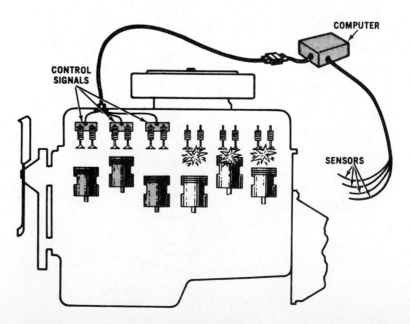

Chevrolet Corvair. This engine is air-cooled and is mounted at the rear of the car.

10-11 V-8 ENGINES

All eight-cylinder automotive engines made today are the V-8 type. They have two rows of cylinders, with four cylinders in each row or bank. The two banks are set at an angle to form a V. Figure 10-13 is a cutaway view of one model of a V-8 engine. Study the picture for a moment and pick out the internal parts of the engine such as the pistons, connecting rods, timing chain, and crankshaft sprocket.

At one time, eight-cylinder, in-line engines were common, but today V-8 engines have taken their place. The V-8 is a shorter, more rigid engine. The cylinders are closer together and have a better chance of getting their share of the air-fuel mixture from the carburetor. The more rigid engine permits higher running speeds and higher compression pressures, with less difficulty from bending of the block and crankshaft. The shorter engine also makes possible more passenger space on the same wheelbase.

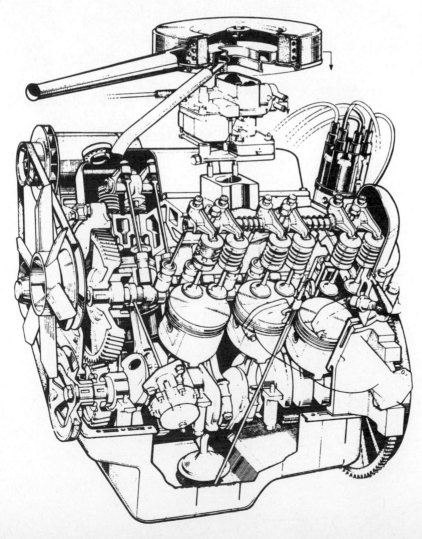

Fig. 10-10
A cutaway view of a V-6 overhead-valve engine. (*Ford Motor Company of Germany*)

10-12 MULTIPLE-DISPLACEMENT V-8 ENGINE

This engine (Fig. 10-14) is an eight-cylinder version of the dual-displacement engine described in Sec. 10-7. However, instead of cutting out half the cylinders, this engine has electronic controls which selec-

Fig. 10-11
Partial cutaway view of a V-6
overhead-valve engine.
(*Chevrolet Motor Division of
General Motors Corporation*)

Fig. 10-12
Turbocharged version of the
Ford V-6 engine. (*Ford Motor
Company*)

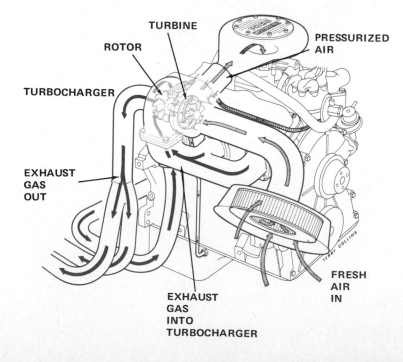

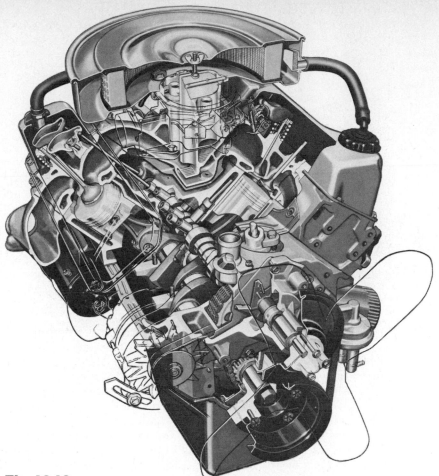

Fig. 10-13
Cutaway view of a V-8 engine. (*Ford Motor Company*)

IDLE (4–CYLINDERS)

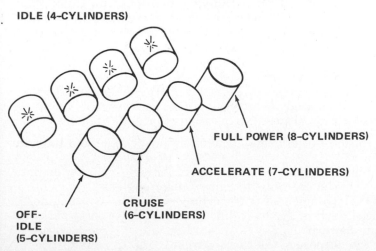

FULL POWER (8–CYLINDERS)

ACCELERATE (7–CYLINDERS)

CRUISE
(6–CYLINDERS)

OFF-
IDLE
(5–CYLINDERS)

Fig. 10-14
Multiple-displacement engine.

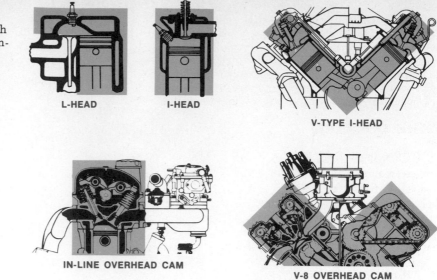

L-HEAD   I-HEAD

V-TYPE I-HEAD

IN-LINE OVERHEAD CAM

V-8 OVERHEAD CAM

tively cut out one, two, three, or four cylinders at a time. The number
of cylinders that the controls cut out depends on the power requirements. When the engine is idling or cruising at a steady speed on a
level highway, the controls cut out four cylinders. Only four cylinders
are needed to provide sufficient power for these operating conditions.
However, when the car encounters a hill, additional power is needed
and the electronic controls put additional cylinders to work. The same
thing happens when the driver "steps on the gas" to increase speed.
Additional cylinders are put to work. The number of cylinders that go
back to work depends on the amount of additional power needed.

10-13 ARRANGEMENT OF VALVES
Another way to classify engines is according to the arrangement of the
valve and valve trains. We have already mentioned, in Chap. 8, the
L-head (or flat-head), the I-head (or overhead-valve), and the overhead-
camshaft arrangements. These arrangements are shown in Fig. 10-15.
We take a good look at valve trains in Chap. 14.

CHECK UP ON YOURSELF
Now is a good time to check up on how well you understand the
facts you have been studying about engines. See how well you know
what you have read. Answer the questions that follow.

1. What is the most usual arrangement for four-cylinder and six-cylinder engines?
2. What is the usual cylinder arrangement for eight-cylinder engines?
3. What has caused the trend to four-cylinder engines?
4. What is the arrangement of the cylinders in a flat-four engine?
5. What is the name of the six-in-line engine in which three of the cylinders can be turned off?
6. What is the purpose of the turbocharger?
7. What is the basic feature of the multiple-displacement engine?
8. What are three valve-train arrangements?

ENGINE COOLING

10-14 COOLING METHODS

There are two methods of engine cooling: liquid cooling and air cooling. Almost all automotive engines are liquid-cooled. The liquid is a mixture of water and an antifreeze solution. The antifreeze solution prevents the water from freezing when the temperature falls below 32°F [0°C]. Another fact not widely known is that the antifreeze also helps to protect the engine from overheating in hot weather.

10-15 AIR-COOLED ENGINES

The Volkswagen and Corvair engines, mentioned previously, are both air-cooled. Also, almost all the small engines used in power mowers and other garden equipment are air-cooled. Figure 10-16 shows a one-cylinder, air-cooled engine. Note the fins that circle the cylinder block and head. These fins have large surface areas that allow heat to be carried away from the cylinders. Many air-cooled engines are equipped with *shrouds*. These are metal shields that direct air from a fan attached to the crankshaft. The air circulates past the fins and helps to keep the engine cool.

10-16 LIQUID-COOLED ENGINES

With few exceptions, all automobile engines are liquid-cooled. The coolant is a mixture of water and antifreeze. In liquid-cooled engines, the cylinder block and cylinder head have water jackets through which the coolant can circulate. You can see the water jackets in many of the

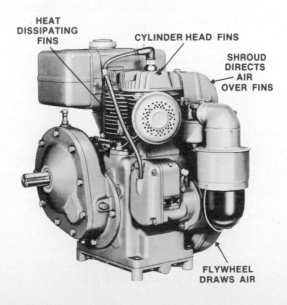

HEAT DISSIPATING FINS

CYLINDER HEAD FINS

SHROUD DIRECTS AIR OVER FINS

FLYWHEEL DRAWS AIR

Fig. 10-16
A one-cylinder, air-cooled engine. (*Teledyne Wisconsin Motor*)

cutaway views of engines on previous pages. Water jackets are spaces which surround the cylinders and the combustion chamber.

Figure 10-17 is a cutaway view of an eight-cylinder engine. The arrows show how the coolant circulates through the water jackets. The coolant is pumped through the engine water jackets by a water pump mounted on the front of the engine. As the coolant flows through the engine water jackets, it picks up heat. It gets very hot, almost to the boiling point. Then it flows into the radiator. The radiator has a series of water passages and also a series of air passages. The pump draws the coolant from the bottom of the radiator, sends it through the engine water jackets, and then sends it back to the top of the radiator. The coolant then moves down through the radiator and loses heat to the air passing through the radiator. The engine fan helps the movement of the air. It draws a strong blast of air through the radiator air passages. Continuous circulation of the coolant between the engine and the radiator removes excess heat from the engine. The engine is thereby protected from overheating. There is more about cooling systems in Chap. 16.

CHECK UP ON YOURSELF

Let's make sure you understand the different engine-cooling methods and how they work. Test yourself by answering the following questions. If you miss a question, study the part that gives you the facts you need.

1. What are the two methods of engine cooling?
2. What do we call the metal shields that direct air around the fins on air-cooled engines?
3. Name the passages through which the coolant circulates in liquid-cooled engines.
4. What causes the coolant to circulate in liquid-cooled engines?
5. What do you call the component in the liquid-cooled engine through which the coolant circulates to lose heat?

ANSWERS

1. Liquid cooling and air cooling (Sec. 10-14). 2. Shrouds (Sec. 10-15).
3. Water jackets (Sec. 10-16). 4. The water pump (Sec. 10-16). 5. The radiator (Sec. 10-16).

10-17 CLASSIFICATION BY PISTON STROKES

Engines can be classified according to the number of piston strokes needed to complete one cycle of operation of the engine. We have already discussed the four-stroke-cycle engine (see Chap. 8), also known as the four-cycle engine. This engine requires four piston strokes to make one complete cycle. There is also the two-stroke-cycle, or two-cycle, engine. In the two-cycle engine, the whole cycle takes place in only two piston strokes. Another book in the McGraw-Hill *Automotive Technology Series, Small Engine Mechanics,* discusses two-cycle engines in detail.

10-18 DIESEL ENGINES

Until now, we have been talking about gasoline engines. All gasoline engines have this in common: The fuel is mixed with air before the air goes into the cylinder. Then the mixture is compressed and ignited by an electric spark at the spark plug.

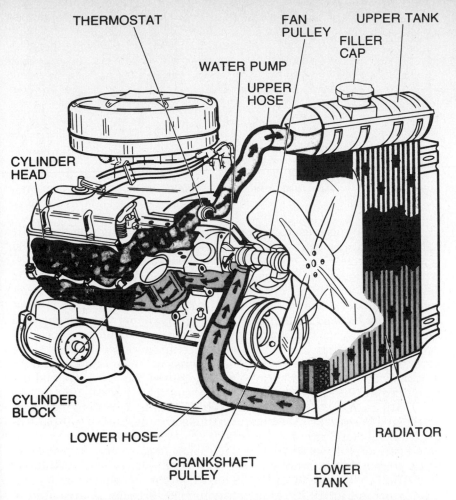

THERMOSTAT

FAN PULLEY

UPPER TANK

FILLER CAP

WATER PUMP

UPPER HOSE

CYLINDER HEAD

CYLINDER BLOCK

LOWER HOSE

CRANKSHAFT PULLEY

LOWER TANK

RADIATOR

Fig. 10-17
A cutaway view of a V-8 engine, showing the cooling system. The arrows show the direction the water flows through the engine water jackets. (*Ford Motor Company*)

In the diesel engine, air alone enters the cylinder. The air is compressed and becomes very hot. This is called *heat of compression*. Then, as the piston nears TDC on the compression stroke, the fuel is injected, or sprayed, into the compressed air. The air is so hot that it ignites the fuel.

When air is compressed, it gets hot. The more it is compressed, the hotter it gets. In the diesel engine, the compression ratio may be as high as 21:1. This means that the air is compressed to only 1/21 of its original volume. This is like compressing 1 quart into less than ¼ cup (less than 2 fluid ounces). See Fig. 10-18. When the air is compressed this much, it gets very hot—up to 1000°F [538°C]. Water boils at 212°F [100°C], so 1000°F [538°C] is really hot! This temperature is high enough to ignite the fuel as it is sprayed into the compressed air.

The fuel used in diesel engines is normally a light oil. It is special in several ways. It ignites easily when sprayed into high-temperature air, and it burns cleanly, leaving little residue such as carbon.

Diesel engines are two-cycle and four-cycle engines, just like gasoline engines. The four-cycle diesel engine requires the usual four piston strokes—intake, compression, power, and exhaust. The essential difference between the gasoline engine and the diesel engine is in the way the fuel is put into the cylinder and the way it is ignited.

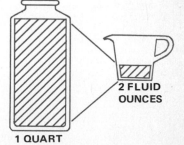

2 FLUID OUNCES

1 QUART

Fig. 10-18
Compressing 1 quart [0.95 L] of air to 2 fluid ounces [60 cc] is a 21:1 compression ratio.

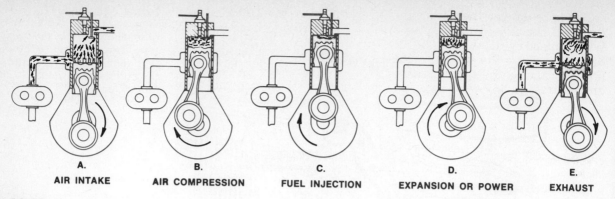

A.	B.	C.	D.	E.
AIR INTAKE	AIR COMPRESSION	FUEL INJECTION	EXPANSION OR POWER	EXHAUST

Fig. 10-19
The sequence of events in the two-stroke-cycle diesel engine.

The two-cycle diesel engine uses a blower, or high-pressure air pump, to ensure fast entry of air and fast exit of the exhaust gases. One type of two-cycle diesel engine has a valve in the cylinder head, which is shown in Fig. 10-19. This is an exhaust valve. Air under pressure is delivered to the cylinder through a series of intake ports in the cylinder wall. This action is shown in Fig. 10-19A. The air is delivered by an air pump, or blower. As the air pours in, the exhaust valve opens, and the fresh air sweeps the burned gases out of the cylinder past the open exhaust valve. Next, as the piston moves up, it closes off the intake ports (Fig. 10-19B). Meanwhile, the exhaust valve has closed. The air is compressed, the fuel is sprayed in and ignited (Fig. 10-19C), and the power stroke (Fig. 10-19D) and the exhaust stroke (Fig. 10-19E) follow.

Until recently, about the only vehicles using diesel engines were trucks and buses. The exception was that some Mercedes-Benz passenger cars had diesel engines (Fig. 10-20). Now, several automotive manufacturers offer diesel engines in their cars. Volkswagen, for example, has a four-cylinder diesel engine in its front-wheel-drive Rabbit car (Fig. 10-21). Oldsmobile has a V-8 diesel engine, shown in partial cutaway view in Fig. 10-22. Many stationary diesel engines are used to drive generators for electricity or to operate machinery.

10-19 DIESEL-ENGINE FUEL SYSTEM

The compressed air in the diesel-engine cylinder, at the end of the compression stroke, is under high pressure. Therefore the fuel must be at a still higher pressure in order for it to be injected into the compressed air. The diesel-engine fuel system includes a high-pressure pump or similar arrangement to inject the fuel into the cylinders. A variety of systems have been used. In one system, a central high-pressure pump feeds all cylinders. In another system, a relatively low-pressure pump delivers fuel to injectors at the cylinders. Each injector has a plunger that is operated by a cam on a camshaft. At the proper time, the cam lobe forces the plunger down, and the plunger sprays fuel into the cylinder.

Diesel engines and diesel-engine fuel systems are different. Before you ever get a chance to work on them, you will be given the special instructions required.

10-20 FIRING ORDER

Another way of classifying piston engines is by their firing order—the order in which the cylinders deliver their power strokes. Engines are designed to deliver the power strokes to the crankshaft in a pattern that will not allow two adjacent cylinders to fire one after the other. When an end cylinder fires, the next cylinder to fire should be near the center or toward the other end of the crankshaft. The purpose of carefully scattering the power strokes along the crankshaft is to avoid undue stress on any one part of the crankshaft. If two or three adjacent

Fig. 10-20

Sectional view of a four-cylinder diesel engine for passenger cars. (*Mercedes-Benz*)

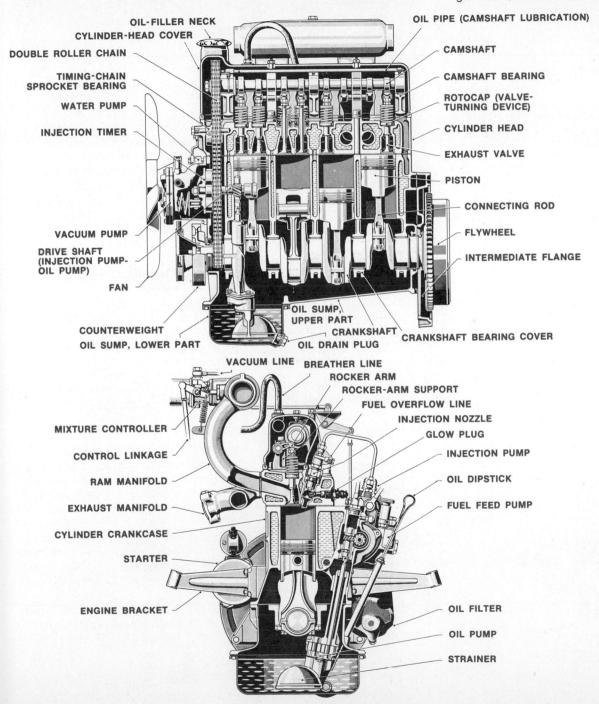

cylinders are fired—bang, bang, bang, like that—this places a strain on the crankshaft, and it may break. A proper firing order prevents this.

Fig. 10-21
Cutaway view of a four-cylinder, overhead-camshaft diesel engine. (*Volkswagen of America, Inc.*)

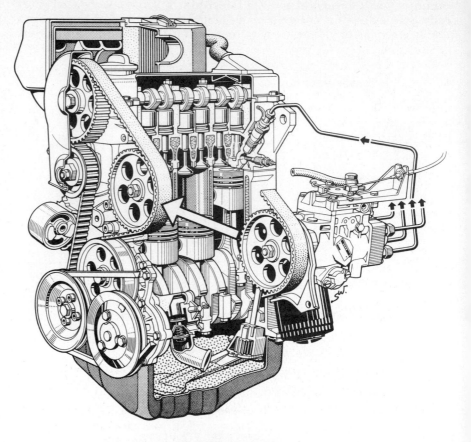

Fig. 10-22
A V-8 diesel engine used in passenger cars and pickup trucks. (*Oldsmobile Division of General Motors Corporation*)

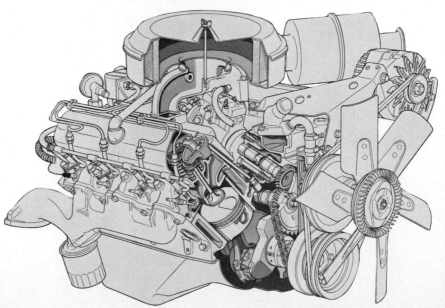

However, in four-cylinder engines, adjacent cylinders do fire one after another. This is because there are only two reasonable firing orders: 1–3–4–2 or 1–2–4–3. In the 1–3–4–2 firing order, number 1 cylinder fires, followed in order by number 3, 4, and 2 cylinders. Cylinders are numbered from front to back.

It is easier to keep the power strokes scattered in a six-cylinder, in-line engine. Two firing orders are possible in these engines: 1–5–3–6–2–4 and 1–4–2–6–3–5. However, all these engines today fire 1–5–3–6–2–4 (Fig. 10-23).

In both four-cylinder and six-cylinder engines, the cylinders are numbered from front to back. The cylinders in V-8 engines are numbered in various ways. One engine manufacturer numbers them from front to rear in this way:

- Right bank: 2–4–6–8
- Left bank: 1–3–5–7

The right bank is the right-hand row as viewed from the driver's seat. The firing order of this engine is 1–8–4–3–6–5–7–2 (Fig. 10-24). See Sec. 12-8 for more information about firing order.

NOTE

The firing order is built in by the car manufacturer, and it cannot be changed without major redesign of the engine. However, in some engines the firing order can be changed by installing a different camshaft and rewiring the ignition.

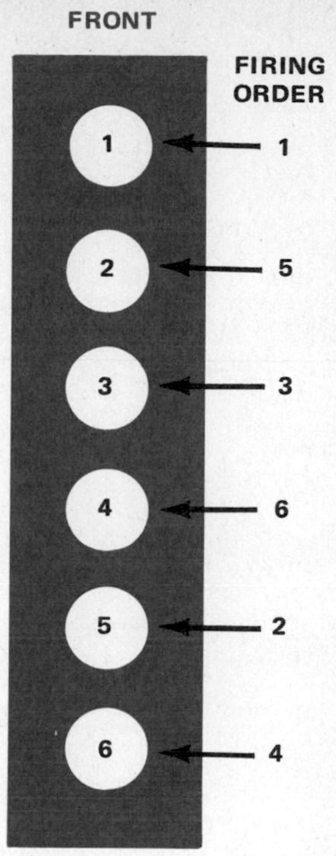

CHECK UP ON YOURSELF

You have just covered two-cycle engines, diesel engines, and firing order. Test your knowledge by answering the following questions.

1. How many piston strokes does it take to complete one cycle in a four-cycle engine?
2. When the air in a diesel-engine cylinder is compressed, how hot does it get?
3. What ignites the fuel in the diesel engine?
4. What do we call the order in which the power strokes occur?
5. What is the purpose of scattering the power strokes along the crankshaft?

ANSWERS

1. Four piston strokes (Sec. 10-17). 2. Up to 1000°F [538°C] (Sec. 10-18).
3. The heat of compression (Sec. 10-18). 4. The firing order (Sec. 10-20).
5. To avoid breaking the crankshaft (Sec. 10-20).

ROTARY ENGINES

10-21 ROTARY ENGINES

Until now, we have been talking about reciprocating engines. These engines have pistons that move up and down, or reciprocate, in cylinders. There is another type of engine that has no pistons. Instead, it has a rotor that is spun by the burning of the fuel in the engine. There are two general types of rotary engines: the *gas turbine* and the *Wankel*. We will take a look at the gas turbine first.

FRONT

FIRING ORDER

1	1
2	5
3	3
4	6
5	2
6	4

Fig. 10-23
Firing order of a six-in-line engine. Cylinders are numbered from front to rear. Firing order is shown by arrows to right.

Fig. 10-24

One V-8 firing order. Cylinders are numbered alternately from front to back. Firing order is shown by arrows from numbers in the center.

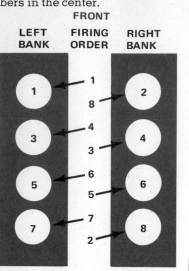

10-22 GAS TURBINES

Gas turbines have been used in a few buses and trucks, but some engineers think we may never see them as a mass-produced engine. Figure 10-25 is a simplified sectional view of a gas turbine. Figure 10-26 is a cutaway view of an actual unit. There are two sections to the gas turbine: the gasifier section, where the fuel is burned, and the power section, where the power from the burned fuel is produced. The turbine can use gasoline, kerosene, or oil for fuel.

The compressor in the gasifier section has an air intake rotor with a series of blades on it. When the air intake rotor spins, it acts as an air pump and supplies the burner with high-pressure air. This is shown by the arrows at the left in Fig. 10-25. In the burner, fuel is sprayed into the compressed air, where the fuel is ignited and burned. The burned gases then flow, at still higher pressures, through the blades of the gasifier section of the turbine. This causes the turbine rotor to spin.

Fig. 10-25
A simplified drawing of a gas turbine. The gasifier section burns fuel and delivers the resulting high-pressure gas to the power section where it spins the power turbine.

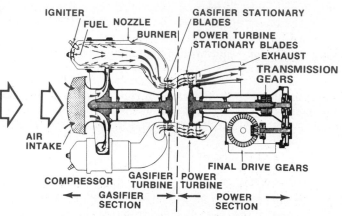

Fig. 10-26
A cutaway view of a gas turbine. (*Caterpillar Tractor Company*)

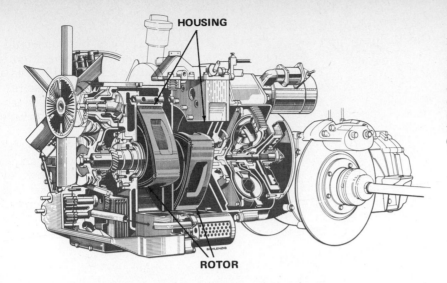

HOUSING

ROTOR

Fig. 10-27
A cutaway view of a two-rotor Wankel engine with attached torque converter and transmission. This engine is the same as the single-rotor engine except that there are two rotors on a single shaft. Each rotor turns in its own chamber. (*NSU of Germany*)

The gasifier turbine rotor is mounted on the same shaft as the air intake rotor. This shaft spins the air intake rotor and supplies the burner with compressed air.

After passing through the gasifier section, the burned gases pass through the power section, causing the power turbine rotor to spin. This rotary motion is carried through shafts and gears to the vehicle drive wheels.

10-23 WANKEL ENGINE

The Wankel engine (Fig. 10-27) is new on the automotive scene. It has a rotor that spins in an oval chamber shaped like a fat figure 8. Several automotive manufacturers have invested a great deal of time and money in doing research and developing the Wankel. The Japanese firm of Toyo Kogyo has produced several hundred thousand automobiles powered by Wankel engines. Other manufacturers have also produced Wankel-powered cars. General Motors spent many millions of dollars on the Wankel engine but then decided not to use it.

The Wankel is also called a *rotary-combustion,* or RC, engine because the combustion chambers rotate, or move in somewhat circular paths. The engine uses a three-lobe rotor (Fig. 10-28) that rotates eccentrically in an oval housing (Fig. 10-29). The three lobes are always in contact with the oval housing, and they form a tight seal. This seal compares with the seal formed by the piston rings against the cylinder wall in the reciprocating engine. The rotor is positioned on the crankshaft by external and internal gears. The four actions—intake, compression, power, and exhaust—are going on at the same time around the rotor when the engine is running. Figure 10-30 shows you how the engine works. The rotor lobes A, B, and C seal tightly against the side of the oval housing. The rotor has recesses in its three faces between the lobes. The dashed lines on the rotors in Fig. 10-30 show the locations of the recesses and how deep they are. It is in these recesses that combustion actually starts. The spaces between the rotor lobes are where intake, compression, power, and exhaust take place.

Let us follow the rotor around as it goes through a complete cycle —intake, compression, power, and exhaust. At I (upper left), lobe A

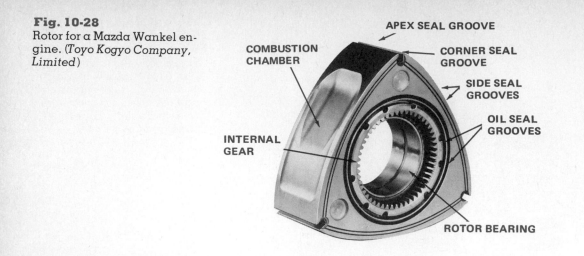

Fig. 10-28
Rotor for a Mazda Wankel engine. (*Toyo Kogyo Company, Limited*)

COMBUSTION CHAMBER

APEX SEAL GROOVE

CORNER SEAL GROOVE

SIDE SEAL GROOVES

OIL SEAL GROOVES

INTERNAL GEAR

ROTOR BEARING

Fig. 10-29
How the rotor fits into the housing. (*Toyo Kogyo Company, Limited*)

has passed the intake port, and the air-fuel mixture is starting to enter. This is shown by the circled 1. As the rotor moves around, at II (upper right), the space between lobes A and C increases, as shown by the circled 2. This motion produces a vacuum, which causes the air-fuel mixture to enter. This action compares with the intake stroke of the piston in the reciprocating engine. At III (lower right), the air-fuel mixture continues to enter as the space between lobes A and C continues to increase, as shown by the circled 3. Then lobe C starts to move past the intake port, as shown in IV (lower left). Further rotor movement carries lobe C past the intake port, so the air-fuel mixture is sealed between lobes A and C, as shown by the circled 4.

To see what happens to the air-fuel mixture, let us go back to I (upper left) again. Here the air-fuel mixture has been trapped between lobes A and B, as shown by the circled 5. Further rotation of the rotor decreases the space between lobes A and B. By the time the rotor reaches the position shown in III, the space (circled 7) is at a minimum. This action is the same as the piston reaching TDC on the compression stroke in the reciprocating engine. Now the spark plug fires and ignites the compressed mixture. Pressure is exerted on the side of the rotor and this forces the rotor to move around. See IV (lower left). This action is the same as the power stroke in the reciprocating engine.

At IV, the high pressure of the burned air-fuel mixture (circled 8) forces the rotor around to position I again. Continued expansion of the burned gases continues to rotate the rotor until the leading lobe passes the exhaust port. Then the burned gases begin to exhaust from between the lobes, as shown by circled 11 and 12 in III and IV. As the rotor continues to rotate, the space between the lobes decreases and the gases are exhausted. This action is the same as the exhaust stroke of the piston in the reciprocating engine.

Following the exhaust stroke, the leading lobe passes the intake port, and the whole cycle is repeated. Note that there are three lobes and three spaces between the lobes. That means that there are three complete cycles of intake, compression, power, and exhaust going on at the same time. The engine is delivering power almost continuously. In a way, a single-rotor Wankel engine is equivalent to a three-cylinder piston engine. A two-rotor Wankel engine might be considered equivalent to a six-cylinder piston engine.

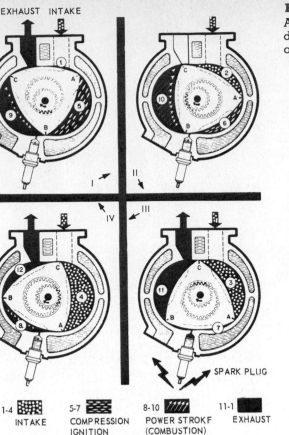

EXHAUST INTAKE

1-4 INTAKE
5-7 COMPRESSION IGNITION
8-10 POWER STROKE (COMBUSTION)
11-1 EXHAUST

SPARK PLUG

Fig. 10-30
Actions in a Wankel engine during one complete revolution of the rotor.

CHECK UP ON YOURSELF

Now you have been introduced to rotary engines. You will rarely see a gas turbine in a car or truck. But you may see an occasional Wankel engine. Now test your understanding of rotary engines.

1. What are the two kinds of rotary engines?
2. What are the two sections in a gas turbine?
3. Where is the air intake rotor located in the turbine?
4. What causes the air intake rotor to spin?
5. What causes the power turbine to spin?
6. How many lobes does the rotor in the Wankel engine have?
7. Why is the Wankel engine also called an RC engine?
8. Where do the four strokes of intake, compression, power, and exhaust take place in a Wankel engine?
9. How many cycles of intake, compression, power, and exhaust are going on in a single-rotor Wankel engine at any one time?

ANSWERS

1. Gas turbine and Wankel (Sec. 10-21).   2. Gasifier and power (Sec. 10-22).
3. In the gasifier section (Sec. 10-22).   4. Movement of high-pressure burned gas through the gasifier turbine blades (Sec. 10-22).   5. Movement of high-pressure burned gas through the power turbine blades (Sec. 10-22).   6. Three (Sec. 10-23).   7. Because the combustion chambers move more or less in circles, or rotate (Sec. 10-23).   8. In the spaces between the rotor lobes (Sec. 10-23).
9. Three (Sec. 10-23).

CHAPTER ELEVEN
ENGINE CONSTRUCTION — CYLINDER BLOCK AND CYLINDER HEAD

After studying this chapter, you should be able to:

1. Explain how cylinder blocks and cylinder heads are made.
2. Explain the purpose of the cylinder block and cylinder head in the engine.
3. Explain the purpose of the engine water jackets.
4. Explain the purpose of the oil pan.
5. Explain the purpose of intake and exhaust manifolds.

In this chapter and in several chapters that follow, we are going to take a close look at the various engine components. We will see how they are made and what they do in the engine.

11-1 CYLINDER BLOCK

The cylinder block is the basic part—the foundation—of the engine. Every other engine part is put inside the block or attached to it. Figure 11-1 shows the main parts that are attached to the block when the engine is assembled. Figure 11-2 shows the parts that are put inside the cylinder block and attached to it. In Fig. 11-2, notice that only one piston and one connecting rod are shown, although the engine uses eight of each. This is done to make the picture easy to study.

The cylinder block is a very complicated piece of cast iron. (Some blocks are built of aluminum. We talk about these later in the chapter.) Figure 11-3 shows one bank of a V-6 engine cylinder block partly cut away. Making a block is a complicated job. First, a sand form—called a *mold*—is made. Then molten iron is poured into this mold.

When the iron has cooled, the sand mold is broken up and removed. This leaves the rough block casting. The casting is then machined to make the cylinder block. The core clean-out holes are needed to clean out the sand cores that were originally in place when the cylinder block was poured.

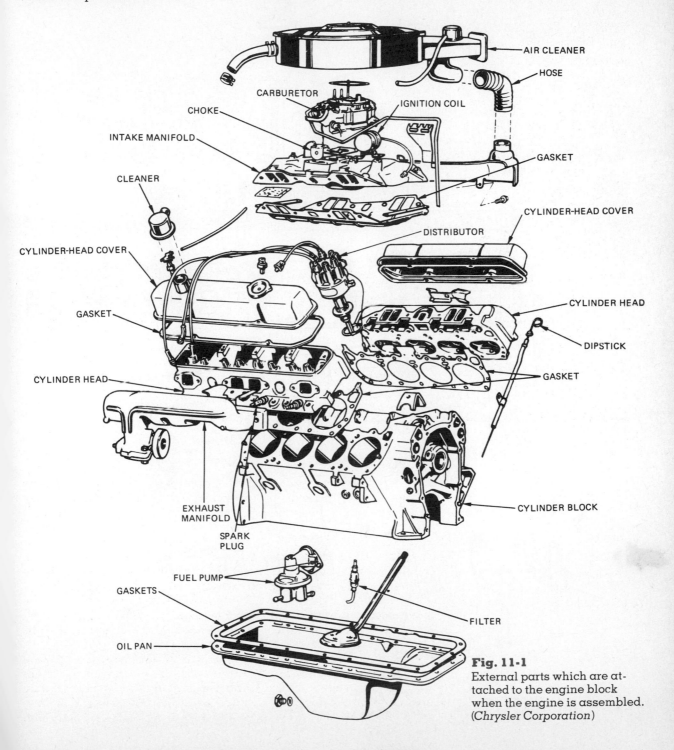

Fig. 11-1
External parts which are attached to the engine block when the engine is assembled. (*Chrysler Corporation*)

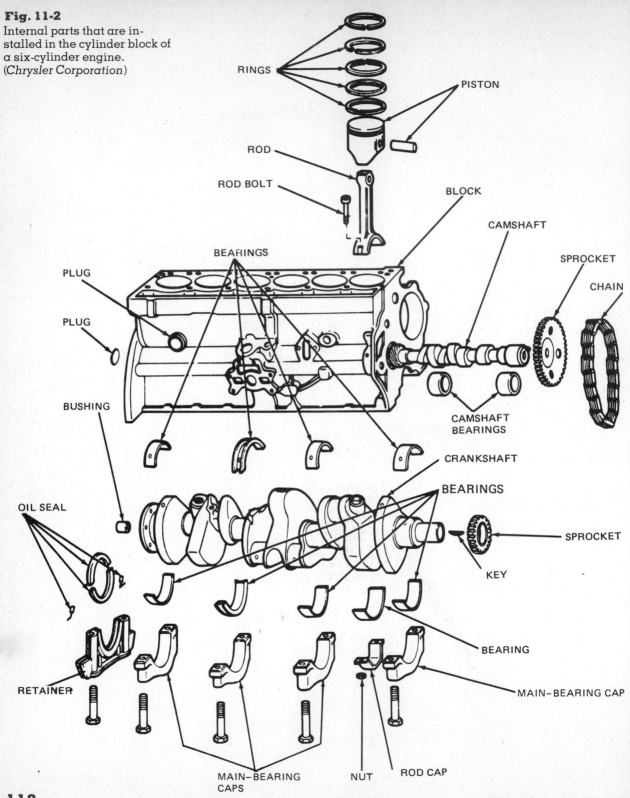

Fig. 11-2
Internal parts that are installed in the cylinder block of a six-cylinder engine. (*Chrysler Corporation*)

RINGS

PISTON

ROD

ROD BOLT

BLOCK

CAMSHAFT

SPROCKET

CHAIN

BEARINGS

PLUG

PLUG

CAMSHAFT BEARINGS

BUSHING

CRANKSHAFT

BEARINGS

OIL SEAL

SPROCKET

KEY

BEARING

RETAINER

MAIN–BEARING CAP

MAIN–BEARING CAPS

NUT

ROD CAP

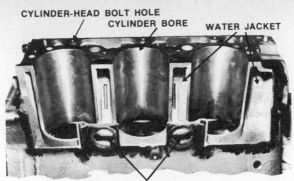

CYLINDER-HEAD BOLT HOLE
CYLINDER BORE
WATER JACKET
CORE CLEAN-OUT HOLES

Fig. 11-3
One bank of a V-6 engine block partly cut away to show the internal construction. (*Truck and Coach Division of General Motors Corporation*)

Cylinder blocks for diesel engines are very similar to those for gasoline engines. The basic difference is that the diesel-engine cylinder block is heavier and stronger. This is because of the higher pressures developed in the diesel-engine cylinders.

The cylinder block contains the cylinders and the water jackets that surround them.

11-2 WATER JACKETS

The water jackets are spaces formed by the inner shells of the cylinders and the outer shell of the cylinder block. You can see the water jackets in Fig. 11-3. This picture shows one bank of a V-6 engine cylinder block, partly cut away so that the water jackets can be seen. The water jackets are spaces surrounding the cylinders through which coolant (water and antifreeze) can flow. The coolant then flows to the radiator. In the radiator, the coolant loses heat. After it is cooled, the coolant returns to the engine. It is this constant circulation of the coolant between the engine and the radiator that keeps the engine from overheating.

11-3 MACHINING THE BLOCK

The job of machining the block includes these operations:

- Drilling holes for attachment of various parts
- Machining the cylinders
- Boring the camshaft-bearing holes
- Smoothing the surfaces to which parts are attached
- Drilling oil passages
- Boring the valve-lifter bores
- Cleaning out the water passages

Figure 11-4 shows a V-8 block. You can see that it takes a lot of work to finish a cylinder block. Also, every machining operation must be done to within 0.001 inch [0.03 mm] or less. The block has water-jacket plugs and oil gallery plugs. The water-jacket plugs are used to plug up the holes to the water jackets after the sand has been cleaned out of the casting. You can see these holes in Fig. 11-3.

The oil gallery plugs are used to plug up the oilholes that are drilled in the casting. These oilholes are called *oil galleries*. They carry the oil flow from the oil pump to various places in the engine where lubricating oil is needed.

There is more information about water jackets and oil galleries in Chaps. 15 and 16.

119

Fig. 11-4
Cylinder block for a V-8 engine.

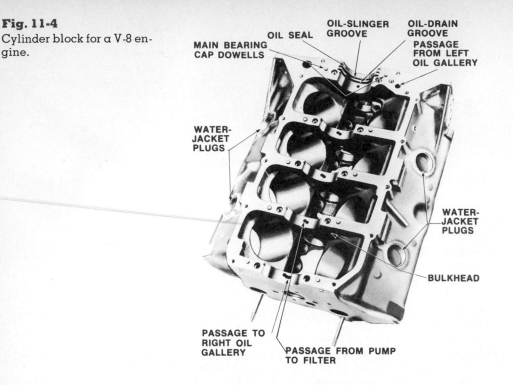

MAIN BEARING CAP DOWELLS — OIL SEAL — OIL-SLINGER GROOVE — OIL-DRAIN GROOVE — PASSAGE FROM LEFT OIL GALLERY — WATER-JACKET PLUGS — WATER-JACKET PLUGS — BULKHEAD — PASSAGE TO RIGHT OIL GALLERY — PASSAGE FROM PUMP TO FILTER

11-4 PARTS ATTACHED TO THE BLOCK

Parts that are attached to the block when the engine is assembled are shown in Fig. 11-1. The cylinder head or heads are mounted on top of the block. The water pump and the timing chain cover are attached at the front. The timing chain is mounted on the camshaft and crankshaft sprockets so that the crankshaft can drive the camshaft. Some engines use a pair of gears to drive the camshaft instead of a timing chain and sprockets. Other engines use sprockets and a toothed belt to drive the camshaft. The clutch housing or automatic transmission is attached at the rear. The crankshaft is hung underneath the block by bearing and bearing caps. You can see the crankshaft and the crankshaft bearings and bearing caps in Fig. 11-2. You can get some idea of how the crankshaft is attached to the block by studying Fig. 10-10. Chapter 12 describes the crankshaft and engine bearings.

11-5 OIL PAN

The oil pan is attached to the bottom of the cylinder block. It is formed from pressed steel, as shown in Fig. 11-5. The oil pan usually holds from 4 to 9 quarts [4 to 8.5 L] of oil, depending on the engine design. Bigger engines require more oil. The oil pan and the lower part of the cylinder block form the *crankcase*. This is a box or case that encloses or encases the crankshaft, and therefore it is called the crankcase.

The oil pump draws oil from the reserve of oil in the oil pan and sends it to all engine parts needing lubrication. The engine-lubricating system is described in detail in Chap. 15.

11-6 ALUMINUM CYLINDER BLOCKS

Several engines have been made with aluminum cylinder blocks. Aluminum is a relatively light metal, weighing much less than cast iron.

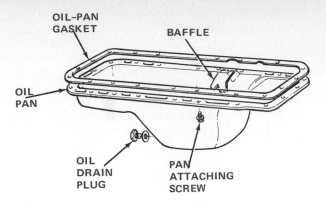

OIL-PAN GASKET

BAFFLE

OIL PAN

OIL DRAIN PLUG

PAN ATTACHING SCREW

Fig. 11-5
An oil pan with gaskets in place, ready for installation on the bottom of the cylinder block. (*Chrysler Corporation*)

Also, aluminum conducts heat more rapidly than cast iron. This means there is less chance for hot spots to develop. However, aluminum is too soft to use as cylinder-wall material. It wears too rapidly. Therefore, aluminum cylinder blocks must have cast-iron cylinder liners. The exception of this is the type of engine used in the Chevrolet Vega, which we will talk about later.

First, let's look at the cast-iron cylinder liners. These are sleeves that are either cast in the block or installed later. In the cast-in type, the cylinder liners are property positioned, and the aluminum is poured around them. By doing this, the liners are cast in the blocks.

There are two types of cast-iron cylinder liners that are installed later: dry and wet. In the dry type, the liners are pressed in place with considerable pressure. They are in contact with the cylinder-bore hole for their full length. In the wet type, the liner is in contact with the engine coolant and is sealed at top and bottom. These liners are removable and can be replaced if they become worn or damaged. Figure 11-6 is a sectional view of an engine with wet cylinder liners.

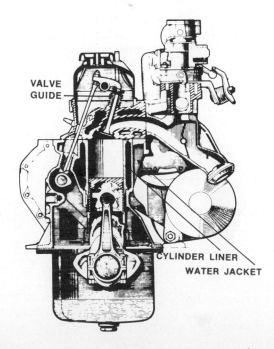

VALVE GUIDE

CYLINDER LINER

WATER JACKET

Fig. 11-6
A sectional view of an engine that uses removable wet cylinder liners. (*Renault*)

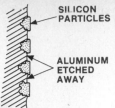

Fig. 11-7
Greatly enlarged view of a
Chevrolet Vega cylinder-wall
surface.

Fig. 11-8
Top and bottom views of a cylinder head for a V-8, overhead-
valve engine. (*Chrysler Corporation*)

Now, let's take a look at the Chevrolet Vega. The engine for this car has a cast-aluminum cylinder block without cylinder liners. The aluminum used is "loaded" with silicon particles. Silicon is an extremely hard substance, and it has very good wearing qualities. In the final preparation of the cylinder block, the cylinders are honed, or smoothed down, and then treated by a special process that etches away the surface aluminum. This leaves only the silicon particles exposed, and the pistons and rings ride on the silicon (Fig. 11-7).

11-7 CYLINDER HEAD
In the liquid-cooled engine, the cylinder head is cast in one piece from iron or aluminum. Aluminum is lighter and runs cooler than iron. However, most engines use the cast-iron head. In a V-type engine, there are two cylinder heads.

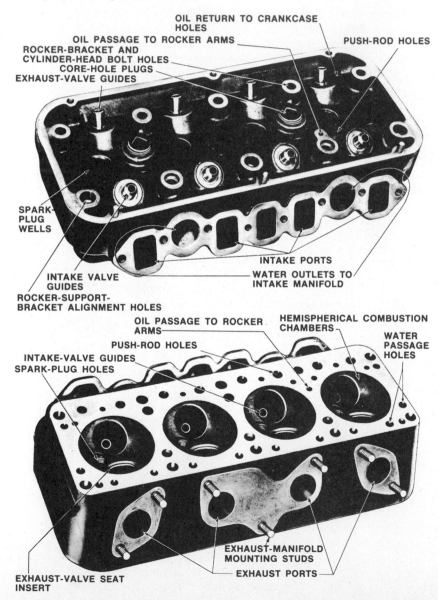

A typical cylinder head for a gasoline V-8 engine is shown in Fig. 11-8. It is a complex casting. There are water jackets in the head, and there are also passages from the valve ports to the openings in the manifolds. The manifolds are described later. As you study Fig. 11-8, locate the parts listed below.

- Tapped holes for the spark plugs
- Coolant-passage holes
- Oil-passage holes
- Pushrod holes
- Tapped holes to attach the rocker-arm brackets
- Tapped holes to attach the manifolds
- Valve-guide holes to carry the valves
- Valve seats

In addition to the above features, some cylinder heads have precombustion chambers. These are small chambers positioned directly above the combustion chambers. Figure 11-9 is a simplified drawing of the arrangement. Initial combustion takes place in the precombustion chamber. We describe the system in Sec. 26-9.

Diesel-engine cylinder heads have a hole for fuel-injection valves instead of spark plugs. As explained in Secs. 10-15 and 10-16, the diesel engine uses a fuel-injection system. The cylinder head includes holes into which the valves for the system are installed.

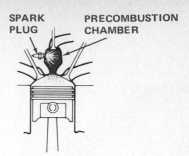

Fig. 11-9
An engine that has a precombustion chamber.

11-8 GASKETS

The joints between the cylinder block and the cylinder head or heads must be tight. They must hold in the high pressure of the burning air-fuel mixture. To ensure a good seal, gaskets are installed between the cylinder block and the cylinder head. Head gaskets are made of thin sheets of soft metal or of asbestos and metal (Fig. 11-10). They are shaped to fit the block, with all openings cut out. When the engine is assembled, the head gasket is placed between the block and the head. Then the head bolts are installed and tightened. This squeezes the gasket between the head and the block, sealing the joint.

Gaskets are also used between the block and the other parts that are attached to the block. Figure 11-11 shows a set of gaskets for a six-cylinder engine.

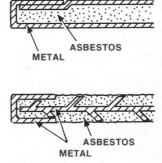

Fig. 11-10
Two types of cylinder-head gaskets.

11-9 INTAKE MANIFOLD

The intake manifold is a casting with a series of passages through which the air-fuel mixture can flow from the carburetor to the engine. The intake manifold for a six-cylinder engine is shown in Fig. 11-12. It is fastened to the side of the cylinder head, as shown in pictures of engines in Chap. 10.

NOTE

Most automotive engines use carburetors which mix gasoline with air to produce the air-fuel mixture. Some automotive engines use fuel-injection systems in which the gasoline is injected, or sprayed, into the air flowing through the intake port. We describe both systems in later chapters.

The intake manifolds for V-6 and V-8 engines sit between the two banks of cylinders (see Figs. 10-10 to 10-12). The carburetor sits on top of the intake manifold. The manifold has the same number of passages

Fig. 11-11
Engine-overhaul gasket set for
a six-cylinder engine, showing
the gaskets and seals used in
the engine. (*McCord Replacement Products Division of
McCord Corporation*)

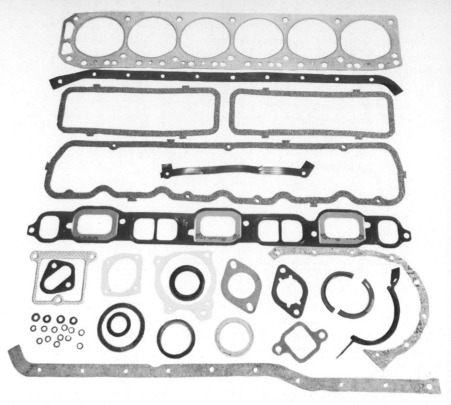

from the carburetor to the cylinders as there are cylinders. Figure 11-13
is a top view of an intake manifold for a V-8 engine. The flat surface
to the left, which has two large holes in it, is the carburetor mounting
pad. The carburetor has two separate barrels. It is, in effect, two separate carburetors, each taking care of half the cylinders. The arrows in
Fig. 11-13 show how the air-fuel mixture flows from the two barrels to
the eight cylinders.

The center passage, marked "exhaust-gas passage," is open when
the engine is cold. The hot exhaust gases, flowing through this passage, heat up the intake manifold. This vaporizes the gasoline better so

Fig. 11-12
The intake manifold for a six-
cylinder, in-line engine.
(*American Motors Corporation*)

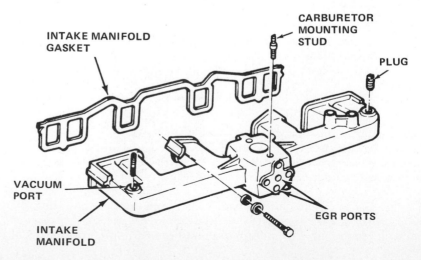

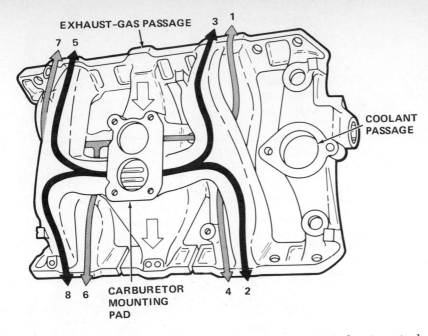

EXHAUST-GAS PASSAGE

COOLANT PASSAGE

CARBURETOR MOUNTING PAD

Fig. 11-13
The intake manifold for a V-8 engine. The arrows show the directions in which the air-fuel mixture flows from the two barrels of the carburetor to the eight cylinders in the engine. The central passage connects the two exhaust manifolds. Exhaust gases flow through this passage during engine warmup. (*Pontiac Motor Division of General Motors Corporation*)

the cold engine runs better. When the engine warms up, a heat-control valve closes to shut off the exhaust-gas passage. We take a more detailed look at the heat-control valve in Chap. 18, when we get to carburetors and the fuel system.

There is one more thing we want to point out in Fig. 11-13. Look at the passage to the right. This is part of the cooling system that connects the cylinder-head water jackets and the hose to the radiator. When the engine is running, coolant circulates through this passage. The flat surface is for mounting the coolant outlet which has the top radiator hose connected to it. We have more to say on this in Chap. 16.

11-10 EXHAUST MANIFOLD

The exhaust manifold is an assembly of tubes carrying exhaust gases from the engine to the car's exhaust system. The exhaust manifold is attached to the side of the cylinder head. Figure 11-14 shows an exhaust manifold for a six-cylinder engine. This is mounted underneath

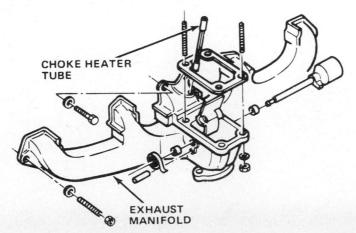

CHOKE HEATER TUBE

EXHAUST MANIFOLD

Fig. 11-14
The exhaust manifold for a six-cylinder, in-line engine. The heat-control valve and parts are shown in a disassembled view. (*American Motors Corporation*)

125

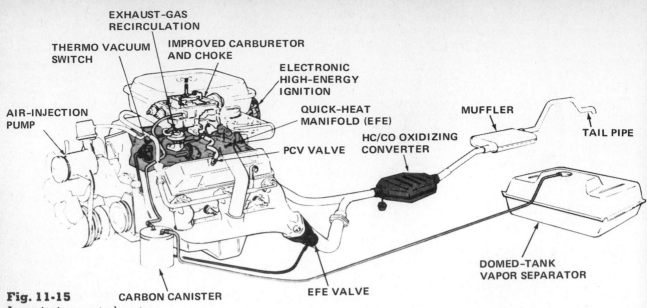

Fig. 11-15
An emission-control system using an under-the-floor catalytic converter. Note that the system uses air injection and other emission-control features. (*General Motors Corporation*)

the intake manifold, shown in Fig. 11-12. The heat-control valve for the six-cylinder engine is mounted in the exhaust manifold. You can see this valve in Fig. 11-14. When the engine is cold, the heat-control valve sends the hot exhaust gases upward. They circulate around the base on which the carburetor is mounted. This puts heat in the air-fuel mixture coming from the carburetor. The heat causes the gasoline to evaporate. This helps the engine to run better when it is cold. As the engine heats up, the heat-control valve automatically closes. When this happens, the hot exhaust gases go directly into the exhaust system without circulating around the mounting base of the carburetor. When the engine is hot, the extra heat is no longer needed to make the gasoline evaporate.

Fig. 11-16
A dual exhaust system for a V-8 engine. Each bank of cylinders has its own exhaust system. (*Ford Motor Company*)

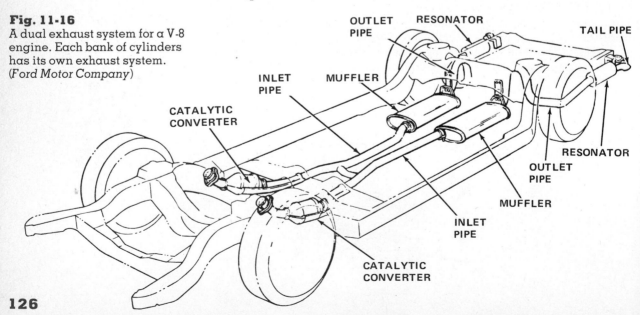

On V-6 and V-8 engines, there are two exhaust manifolds, one for each bank. On some cars, they are connected and exit through a single muffler and tail pipe (Fig. 11-15). Other cars have a dual exhaust system, with separate mufflers and pipes for each (Fig. 11-16).

11-11 EXHAUST SYSTEM

The exhaust system carries the exhaust gases from the exhaust manifold or manifolds to the tail pipe. Figures 11-15 and 11-16 show exhaust systems for V-type engines. The muffler has a series of passages through which the exhaust gases must flow. This softens, or muffles, the sound of the engine.

Since 1975, all cars manufactured in the United States have been equipped with catalytic converters. These devices reduce the amount of pollutants in the exhaust gases. We cover catalytic converters and other emission control devices later.

CHECK UP ON YOURSELF

You are learning about engines. You are on your way to becoming a qualified automotive technician. Now find out how well you understand what you have studied about the cylinder block and the cylinder head by answering the following questions.

1. What do we call the spaces that surround the cylinders and through which the coolant flows?
2. What is attached to the top of the cylinder block?
3. What is attached to the bottom of the cylinder block?
4. What is the name of the part that is installed between the cylinder block and the cylinder head to seal the joint?
5. What is the name of the part that sends heat into the intake manifold when the engine is cold?

ANSWERS

1. Water jackets (Sec. 11-2). 2. The cylinder head (Sec. 11-4). 3. The crankshaft and the oil pan (Secs. 11-4 and 11-5). 4. The head gasket (Sec. 11-4). 5. The heat-control valve (Secs. 11-9 and 11-10).

CHAPTER TWELVE
CRANKSHAFT AND ENGINE BEARINGS

After studying this chapter, you should be able to:

1. Describe a typical crankshaft and explain how it is balanced and lubricated.
2. Explain the purpose of engine bearings and describe their construction.
3. Explain the purpose of the thrust bearing.
4. Describe the vibration damper and how it operates.

The crankshaft is the backbone of the engine. It must take the hard downward thrusts of the pistons and connecting rods when the air-fuel mixture is burned in the cylinders. The crankshaft changes reciprocating motion into rotary motion (Fig. 8-11) and sends it through gears and shafts to the wheels so that the car moves. The crankshaft hangs from the bottom of the cylinder block. It is supported in bearings that allow it to spin without excessive wear or friction. In this chapter we will look at crankshafts and bearings.

12-1 CRANKSHAFT

The crankshaft is made of high-strength steel (Fig. 12-1). It has to be strong enough to take the 4000-pound [1814-kg] thrust of each piston and connecting rod on every power stroke. Also, it must be balanced so that it will run smoothly without a lot of vibration. The crankshaft also does another job. It distributes oil to the connecting-rod bearings.

Let's look at balance first. The crankshaft is composed of a series of cranks. These cranks, together with the connecting rods, change the reciprocating motion of the pistons into rotary motion. Now look at a single crank. As it rotates, centrifugal action keeps pulling the crank away from the centerline of the crankshaft. This off-balance force could cause heavy vibration and very rapid wear of the bearings supporting the crankshaft. To provide balance and to avoid undue wear, the crankshaft has a series of counterweights. These weights balance the rotating forces of the cranks, so there is no force that tends to cause vibration. You can see the counterweights in in Figs. 12-1 and 12-2.

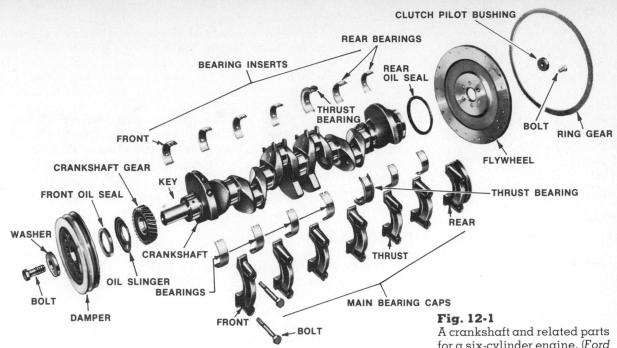

Fig. 12-1
A crankshaft and related parts for a six-cylinder engine. (*Ford Motor Company*)

12-2 LUBRICATING THE CRANKSHAFT BEARINGS

As we explain in Chap. 15, the engine-lubricating system pumps oil to the moving parts in the engine. This oil covers all the moving parts, so that they "float" on layers of oil. The layers of oil arc very thin, but they are thick enough to prevent metal-to-metal contact. When metal-to-metal contact occurs in an engine, serious trouble can result. Metal rubbing on metal will scratch surfaces, waste power, overheat the metal, and can cause complete engine failure.

It is especially important to lubricate with oil the bearings in which the crankshaft turns. The *bearings* are the parts that bear the weight of the crankshaft. The bearings are replaceable. When they wear, they can be removed and new ones can be installed. They are much less expensive to replace than the crankshaft or the cylinder block. Figure 12-1 shows a crankshaft and the bearings that support it. Note that the bearings are thin shells that fit into undercuts in the cylinder block and into the bearing caps.

The bearings supporting the crankshaft are called *main bearings*. Many mechanics just call them the "mains." We will describe bearings later. Note that the round sections of the crankshaft that rest on the bearings are called *journals*. They rotate, or "journey," in the bearings.

The cylinder block has oilholes—called oil galleries—drilled in it which carry the oil from the oil pump to the main bearings. Long holes,

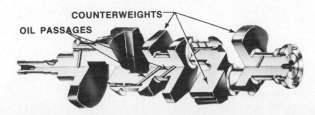

Fig. 12-2
A crankshaft cut away to show the oil passages drilled to the crankshaft journals.

drilled from the front to the back of the block, are connected by short holes drilled in the half-round supports for the crankshaft. These short holes match the holes in the bearings that are installed in the support. The oil flows through the oil galleries to the holes in the bearings. The oil then flows through the bearing holes and onto the crankshaft journals rotating in the bearings. The crankshaft is therefore "floating" on layers of oil. This allows the crankshaft to spin with relatively little effort. Little power is lost, and metal-to-metal contact is prevented.

However, it does take some power to force the crankshaft to rotate on its layers of oil. In Sec. 9-13 we mentioned friction horsepower—the power lost because of friction in the engine. It is the power that is used to overcome the friction between the layers of oil as they slip over one another. There is more about this in Chap. 15, which describes engine-lubricating systems.

12-3 CRANKSHAFT OILHOLES
The crankshaft also has oilholes drilled in it. These oilholes have the job of keeping the connecting-rod bearings lubricated. The connecting rods are attached to the crankpins of the crankshaft by rod caps. Bearing shells are placed between the rods and the rod caps and the crankpins. These bearings must be kept well supplied with oil. The oilholes in the crankshaft do this. You can see the oilholes drilled in the crankshaft in Fig. 12-3. These holes go from the main bearing journals to the crankpins. Some of the oil that is fed to the main bearings flows through these holes to the crankpins. It covers the crankpins and connecting-rod bearings, providing good lubrication.

12-4 ENGINE BEARINGS
Now let's take a closer look at engine bearings. Bearings are needed at every point in the engine where there is rotary motion between engine parts. See Fig. 12-4, which shows the various places bearings are installed in an engine. These engine bearings are called *sleeve bearings*. They are shaped like a sleeve that fits around the rotating journal, or shaft. Some of the bearings are the split type. That is, the bearing is split into two halves. The main and connecting-rod bearings have to be the split type. (Fig. 12-5). Otherwise, they could not be placed on the crankshaft journals or crankpins. Figure 12-6 shows a typical bearing half with the various parts named. Some bearing halves have a groove —the annular groove—which helps distribute the oil around the bearing. The oilhole in the annular groove allows the oil from the holes in the cylinder block and crankshaft to feed through and onto the journal of crankpin.

Fig. 12-3
This drawing shows how the oilholes drilled in the crankshaft feed oil to the main and connecting-rod journals.

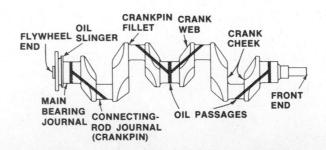

Only one main bearing in an engine is of the thrust type shown in Fig. 12-5. This bearing is called the *thrust bearing*.

The crankshaft is attached to the bottom of the cylinder block by the main bearing caps. The upper bearing halves are installed in the cylinder-block supports. The lower bearing halves are put into the main bearing caps before the caps are bolted in place on the cylinder block.

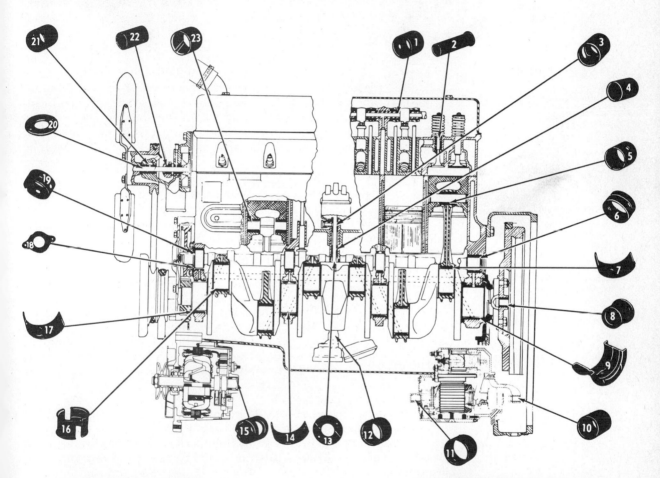

1. ROCKER-ARM BUSHING
2. VALVE-GUIDE BUSHING
3. DISTRIBUTOR BUSHING, UPPER
4. DISTRIBUTOR BUSHING, LOWER
5. PISTON-PIN BUSHING
6. CAMSHAFT BUSHINGS
7. CONNECTING-ROD BEARING
8. CLUTCH PILOT BUSHING
9. CRANKSHAFT THRUST BEARING
10. STARTING-MOTOR BUSHING, DRIVE END
11. STARTING-MOTOR BUSHING, COMMUTATOR END
12. OIL-PUMP BUSHING
13. DISTRIBUTOR THRUST PLATE
14. INTERMEDIATE MAIN BEARING
15. ALTERNATOR BEARING
16. CONNECTING-ROD BEARING, FLOATING TYPE
17. FRONT MAIN BEARING
18. CAMSHAFT THRUST PLATE
19. CAMSHAFT BUSHING
20. FAN THRUST PLATE
21. WATER-PUMP BUSHING, FRONT
22. WATER-PUMP BUSHING, REAR
23. PISTON-PIN BUSHING

Fig. 12-4
Bearings and bushings in a typical engine. (*Johnson Bronze Company*)

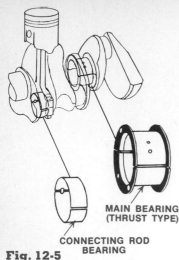

MAIN BEARING (THRUST TYPE)

CONNECTING ROD BEARING

Fig. 12-5
Main bearing of the thrust type and a connecting-rod bearing, in their positions on the crankshaft.

Fig. 12-6
A typical bearing half with the parts named. Many bearings do not have annular and distributing grooves. (*Federal-Mogul Corporation*)

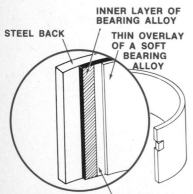

STEEL BACK

INNER LAYER OF BEARING ALLOY

THIN OVERLAY OF A SOFT BEARING ALLOY

Fig. 12-7   **BARRIER PLATING**
The construction of a three-layer bearing. Some bearings have three layers, as shown. Others have two layers. (*Federal-Mogul Corporation*)

132

The connecting rods are attached to the crankpins in a similar way. The upper bearing half is put into the rod. The lower bearing half is installed in the rod cap. Then the cap is bolted to the rod, with the crankpin between the cap and the rod.

12-5 BEARING CONSTRUCTION
Each bearing half is made of a steel or bronze back to which layers of bearing material have been applied. See Fig. 12-7. The bearing material is relatively soft. If wear takes place, it will be the bearing that wears, rather than the much more expensive crankshaft or other moving part.

12-6 BEARING LUBRICATION
Lubrication of the bearings allows the moving part to slide easily on layers of oil. The journal must be slightly smaller than the bearing to provide *oil clearance* (Fig. 12-8), which is about 0.001 inch [0.03 mm]. Oil feeds through the bearing oilhole into this clearance. The oil constantly flows across the bearing and then drops off the edges of the bearing. This movement of the oil cleans the bearings and helps cool them. As the oil moves across the bearing, it picks up heat as well as

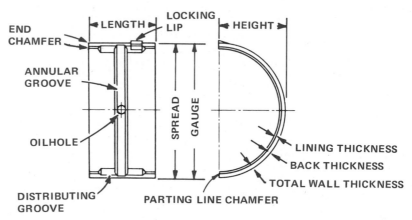

END CHAMFER — **LENGTH** — **LOCKING LIP** — **HEIGHT**

ANNULAR GROOVE

OILHOLE

SPREAD   **GAUGE**

LINING THICKNESS
BACK THICKNESS
TOTAL WALL THICKNESS

DISTRIBUTING GROOVE   **PARTING LINE CHAMFER**

particles of dirt. The oil drops into the oil pan, where it loses heat. The oil pump continuously sends oil through the oil filter to the engine parts. The filter removes dirt from the oil. The oil then goes back up through the engine. This continuous circulation of oil allows the oil to both clean and cool the engine. Chapter 15 describes the engine lubrication system in detail.

12-7 THRUST BEARING
The crankshaft has to be prevented from moving endwise. Normal engine operation tends to push the crankshaft forward and backward. To prevent excessive forward and backward movement, one of the main bearings—called the thrust bearing—has flanges on its two sides, as shown in Fig. 12-5. In the engine assembly, these flanges fit close to the two sides of the crankpin. If the crankshaft tends to shift one way or the other, the crankpin sides come up against the flanges, preventing excessive endwise movement. You can see a thrust bearing in the picture of a crankshaft and its related parts (Fig. 12-1).

12-8 FLYWHEEL

In the engine assembly, a flywheel is attached to the back end of the crankshaft. The flywheel does two jobs (three jobs in some engines): It acts as a stabilizer, and it works with the starting motor to start the engine. A flywheel is shown to the right in Fig. 12-1.

First, the flywheel is a stabilizer. It smooths out the power impulses from the pistons. When a power stroke starts, the push is very strong. The pressure from the burning air-fuel mixture is at the maximum. However, as the piston moves down, the pressure drops. Toward the end of the power stroke, the pressure is only a small fraction of what it was at the beginning. This means that the push on the crankpin starts high but soon tapers off.

The power strokes in an engine follow one another in regular order. The whole sequence for a four-cylinder engine is shown in Fig. 12-9. Although the process is shown in a single circle, we know it takes two revolutions of the crankshaft to produce a complete cycle. First, number 1 cylinder fires, and its piston moves down on its power stroke. This movement is shown by the colored space curving down to the right from the top of the circle numbered 1. Notice that the color thins out near the end of the power stroke (marked to the right as 180 degrees). It thins out because the power stroke weakens toward the end.

Then number 2 cylinder fires, and its piston moves down on the power stroke. The power stroke in number 4 cylinder follows, and then number 3 cylinder fires. The order in which the cylinders fire is called the *firing order*. In Fig. 12-9, the firing order is 1–2–4–3. The firing order in piston engines is described in Sec. 10-20.

As you study Fig. 12-9, you will see that the flow of power is not steady. Each power stroke starts off strong and then fades. If there were no flywheel, you would feel this unsteadiness in the engine. In other words, you would feel a sort of vibration as the separate power strokes hit the crankshaft. The flywheel helps to smooth out these power surges. When a power stroke starts, the engine tends to speed up. Then the engine tends to slow down toward the end of a power stroke. The flywheel resists this speed-up–slow-down action.

Any rotating wheel, including the flywheel, resists any effort to change its speed of rotation. When the engine tends to speed up, the flywheel resists it. When the engine tends to slow down, the flywheel resists it, and this resistance smooths out the power surges.

In the six-cylinder and eight-cylinder engines, the power impulses overlap, as shown in Fig. 12-10. Even in these engines, however, the power impulses do not add up to a perfectly smooth engine. The flywheel helps to smooth out the engine so that the power impulses are less noticeable.

The second job of the flywheel is to work with the starting motor to start the engine. The starting motor is an electric motor that cranks the engine to get it started. This action is described in Chap. 22. There is a ring gear on the flywheel (see Fig. 12-1). When the starting motor works, it meshes a small driving gear with this ring gear. Then the flywheel and the crankshaft are spun, and the engine starts.

A third job of the flywheel on some cars that do not have automatic transmissions is to form part of the clutch. In a car with a manual transmission, you have to shift the gears by hand. The clutch is the mechanism that allows you to shift. We take a more detailed look at the clutch in Chap. 34.

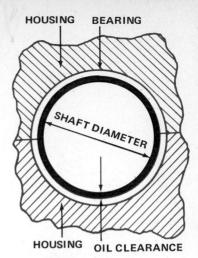

Fig. 12-8
The oil clearance between the bearing and shaft journal.

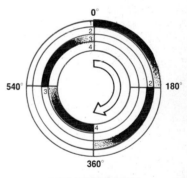

4-CYLINDER ENGINE

Fig. 12-9
Power impulses in a four-cylinder engine. The complete circle represents two full crankshaft revolutions, or 720 degrees. Less power is delivered toward the end of the power stroke because cylinder pressure falls off. This is shown by the lightening of the shaded areas that show the power impulses.

133

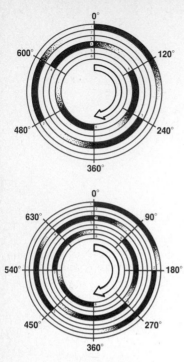

6-CYLINDER ENGINE

8-CYLINDER ENGINE

Fig. 12-10
Power impulses in six- and eight-cylinder engines. The complete circles represent two full crankshaft revolutions, or 720 degrees. Note the power overlap.

12-9 VIBRATION DAMPER

The power impulses from the power strokes hit the crankshaft in one place and then another as the engine runs. Every time a power impulse hits a crankpin, that part of the crankshaft actually twists a little. Then, when the power stroke ends, that part of the crankshaft untwists. This action sets up an oscillating—or back and forth—motion (Fig. 12-11). This motion is called *torsional vibration*. That is, it is a twist-untwist vibration. If it is not controlled, at some speeds torsional vibration can break the crankshaft.

Torsional vibration is controlled by a *vibration damper* (Fig. 12-12), also called a *harmonic balancer*. The vibration damper has a small damper flywheel, which is bonded to the crankshaft pulley by a rubber ring. The damper flywheel is also called the "inertia ring." The vibration damper works in the following way: When the twist-untwist action starts, the inertia ring has a dragging effect. It works through the rubber ring to hold down the twist action. Then, when the untwist motion starts, the inertia ring holds down this action too. The result is that torsional vibration is kept to a minimum.

The pulley part of the vibration damper is connected by belts to drive the water pump and the engine fan. The belts also drive various accessories, such as the alternator, the power-steering pump, and the air-conditioner compressor.

CHECK UP ON YOURSELF

Now that you have studied the crankshaft and the engine bearings, you will want to know how well you understand what you have read. Test yourself by answering the questions that follow.

1. What are the names of the weights on the crankshaft that balance the weights of the crankpins?
2. How does the oil get to the crankshaft journals?
3. What is the name of the parts in which the crankshaft journals rotate?
4. What keeps the crankshaft journals from making metal-to-metal contact with the main bearings?

Fig. 12-11
Showing how the crankpin vibrates torsionally in the crankshaft. Torsional movement is shown greatly exaggerated.

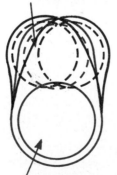

CRANKPIN

MAIN JOURNAL

Torsional vibration. Crankpin moves ahead and back

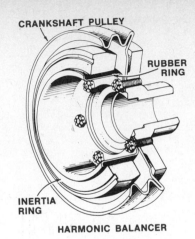

Fig. 12-12
A partial cutaway view of a torsional vibration damper.

CRANKSHAFT PULLEY

RUBBER RING

INERTIA RING

HARMONIC BALANCER

5. What is the purpose of the oilholes in the crankshaft?
6. Why are the main bearings split?
7. What are two other jobs that the engine oil does besides lubricate engine parts?
8. What is the purpose of the thrust bearing?
9. What is the name for the order in which the power strokes take place?
10. What is torsional vibration?

ANSWERS

1. Counterweights (Sec. 12-1). **2.** The oil pump sends it through oil galleries in the cylinder block to holes in the bearings. It flows through these holes onto the crankshaft journals (Sec. 12-2). **3.** Main bearings (Sec. 12-2). **4.** Layers of oil (Sec. 12-2). **5.** To carry oil to the connecting-rod bearings (Sec. 12-2). **6.** To get them around the crankshaft journal (Sec. 12-4). **7.** Cleans and cools (Sec. 12-6). **8.** To prevent excessive endwise movement of the crankshaft (Sec. 12-2). **9.** Firing order (Sec. 12-8). **10.** Twist-untwist action of the crankshaft (Sec. 12-9).

CHAPTER THIRTEEN
PISTONS AND CONNECTING RODS

After studying this chapter, you should be able to:
1. Explain the purpose and construction of connecting rods.
2. Explain how the connecting rod is connected to the piston and to the crankshaft.
3. Explain the purpose of pistons and how they are constructed. Also, explain how expansion is controlled and the purpose of piston-pin offset.
4. Explain the purpose of piston rings and how the two types are constructed and how they work.
5. Describe what happens to oil control as engines wear and explain how replacement rings can help.

The job of the piston and connecting-rod assembly is to carry the high pressure of the burning air-fuel mixture through the connecting rod to the crankshaft. This pressure spins the crankshaft so that the car moves. The piston and the connecting rod are described in Chap. 8. In this chapter we take a closer look at the piston and connecting rod.

13-1 CONNECTING ROD
The connecting rod (Fig. 13-1) is made of high-strength steel. Its purpose is to connect the piston to the crankshaft. It is attached at one end to a crankpin on the crankshaft and at the other end to a piston. The end of the connecting rod that is connected to the crankpin is often called the *rod big end*. The other end, connected to the piston, is called the *rod small end*.

The connecting rod is attached to the crankpin with a rod cap, bolts, and nuts, as shown in Fig. 13-1. Two bearing halves are installed in the rod and cap before the assembly is completed. These bearing halves, and the crankpin they surround, are oiled through oilholes drilled in the crankshaft.

Some connecting rods have oilholes drilled up through them. Oil flows through these holes up to the bearing or bushing at the piston end of the connecting rod. You can see the oilholes in Fig. 13-2.

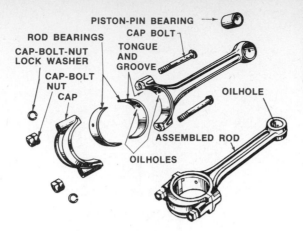

Fig. 13-1
Connecting rod with bearings and bearing cap in disassembled view (at top) and assembled view (bottom). (*Chrysler Corporation*)

The connecting rod is attached to the piston with a piston pin. The piston pin goes through two holes in the piston and one hole in the connecting rod. There are five methods of attaching the piston and rod (Fig. 13-2).

In one method, the piston pin is locked to the connecting rod. The most widely used version of this method is to *press-fit* the pin in the rod (Fig. 13-2D). That is, the fit is so tight that you have to press the pin through the hole in the rod, using high pressure. The press fit holds the pin in place, centered on the connecting rod. The two ends of the pin rest in the holes in the piston. When the connecting rod tilts one way or the other, the piston pin turns with it. A film of oil allows the turning action of the piston pin.

A second method of attaching the piston and rod with the piston pin is shown in Fig. 13-2A. Here the piston pin is not locked to either the piston or the connecting rod. The pin is free to turn in both parts. A pair of lock rings is used, one at each end of the pin. They keep the pin centered. The lock rings fit into undercuts in the piston. An assembly with this arrangement is shown in Fig. 13-3. The other methods shown in Fig. 13-2 are seldom used today in automotive engines.

13-2 PISTON-PIN LUBRICATION
Whether or not the piston pins turns in the piston, or in a bushing in the connecting rod, or in both, it must be lubricated. In some engines,

Fig. 13-2
Five piston-pin arrangements. (*Sunnen Products Company*)

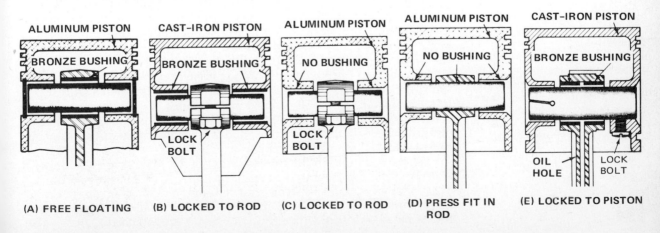

(A) FREE FLOATING   (B) LOCKED TO ROD   (C) LOCKED TO ROD   (D) PRESS FIT IN ROD   (E) LOCKED TO PISTON

Fig. 13-3
A piston and connecting-rod assembly. This type has lock rings to hold the piston pin in position in the piston and connecting rod. (*Chrysler Corporation*)

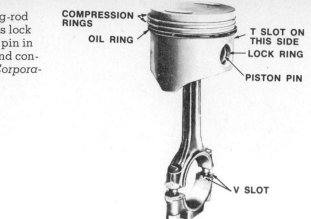

COMPRESSION RINGS

OIL RING

T SLOT ON THIS SIDE

LOCK RING

PISTON PIN

V SLOT

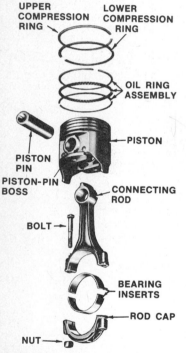

UPPER COMPRESSION RING

LOWER COMPRESSION RING

OIL RING ASSEMBLY

PISTON

PISTON PIN

PISTON-PIN BOSS

CONNECTING ROD

BOLT

BEARING INSERTS

ROD CAP

NUT

Fig. 13-4

A piston and connecting-rod assembly, disassembled so the various parts can be seen. The oil-control ring is of the three-piece type. The piston is the slipper type, which has the skirt partly cut away. (*Ford Motor Company*)

the connecting rod has a hole drilled through it so that oil can flow from the crankpin up to the piston pin (Fig. 13-1).

In most engines, the piston pin is lubricated from oil thrown off the rotating crankpin and rod big end. Some of this oil splashes onto the cylinder walls, where it lubricates the walls and also the piston and piston rings. This oil is scraped off the cylinder walls by the piston rings. Some of the oil that is scraped off gets to the piston pin through holes drilled in the lower piston-ring groove.

13-3 CONNECTING-ROD BALANCE

All connecting rods in an engine must be of equal weight. If one were heavier than the others, an out-of-balance condition would result and produce vibration. This vibration could damage the engine.

When an engine is first assembled in a factory, rods and caps are matched. Therefore, if you disassemble an engine for service, never mix rod caps. For example, never put the rod cap for number 2 cylinder on the rod for number 1 cylinder. If you do, the rod may lock up when it is tightened, or bearing failure may soon result.

13-4 PISTONS

Pistons for automobile engines are made of aluminum; they are about 4 inches [100 mm] in diameter and weigh about 1 pound [454 g]. They are a loose, sliding fit in the engine cylinders. A piston is shown attached to the connecting rod in Fig. 13-3. Figure 13-4 shows all the parts separated. The assembly shown in Fig. 13-4 is the type in which the piston pin is a press fit in the connecting rod.

Notice that the lower edge of the piston is cut away so that the piston skirt is short on the sides. This type of piston is called a *slipper* piston. The piston skirt is shortened on two sides for two reasons. One is that it lightens the weight of the piston. A light piston moves up and down more easily in the cylinder and wastes less power. A lighter piston is also easier on the bearings.

The second reason for the cutaway piston skirt is that it allows a shorter (from top to bottom) engine. Figure 13-5 shows why the cutaway piston skirt allows the shorter engine. The crankshaft has to have counterweights, as explained in Chap. 12. Cutting away the piston skirt allows the connecting rod to be made shorter, but leaves

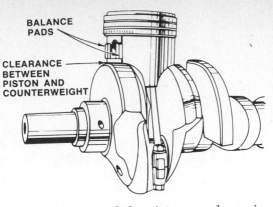

BALANCE PADS

CLEARANCE BETWEEN PISTON AND COUNTERWEIGHT

Fig. 13-5
Slipper piston and connecting rod assembled to the crankshaft. Note the small clearance between the piston and the counterweights on the crankshaft. (*Chevrolet Motor Division of General Motors Corporation*)

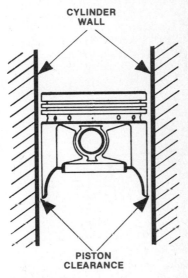

CYLINDER WALL

PISTON CLEARANCE

Fig. 13-6
There must be clearance between the piston and the cylinder wall. Clearance shown here is exaggerated for emphasis.

enough room between the counterweights and the piston, as shown in Fig. 13-5.

13-5 PISTON CLEARANCE

There must be some space between the piston and the cylinder wall (Fig. 13-6). This space, called the *piston clearance*, allows the piston to move up and down easily in the cylinder. The clearance is 0.001 to 0.004 inch [0.03 to 0.10 mm] in most engines.

As cylinder walls wear, the clearance increases. When the clearance gets excessive, the piston fits too loosely. *Piston slap* occurs. In other words, there is so much clearance that the piston shifts from one side of the cylinder wall to the other when the power stroke starts. As the piston hits the other side of the cylinder wall, it makes a hollow, bell-like sound. When you hear this sound, you know the engine is in need of repair.

13-6 EXPANSION CONTROL IN PISTONS

A piston expands when it gets hot. Any metal expands with heat. The cylinder walls expand, too, but not nearly as much as the piston. If the piston were perfectly round, it could expand so much that it would "seize." This means that the piston would expand so much that all clearance would be gone. The piston would jam in the cylinder and stop moving. The connecting rod and crankshaft would continue to move, and the connecting rod or rod bolts might break. If this should happen, the rod probably would go through the cylinder block. The result would be a ruined engine.

To prevent seizure, pistons are built with expansion control. One method of building pistons with expansion control is to make them slightly oval in shape (Fig. 13-7). These slightly oval pistons are called *cam-ground* pistons because they are finished on a machine that uses a cam. The cam moves the piston toward and away from the grinding wheel as the piston revolves. A cam-ground piston is shown in Fig. 13-8. The diameter of the piston at the piston-pin holes (A in Fig. 13-8) is less than the diameter 90 degrees from the holes (B in Fig. 13-8).

In Fig. 13-9, the piston to the left is cold, and only the shaded area has normal clearance. The rest of the piston has excessive clearance with the cylinder wall. As the piston warms up, the metal expands (middle in Fig. 13-9). The excessive clearance around the piston-pin holes provides a place for the metal to go. Expansion increases the area of normal clearance. When the piston is hot, it has normal clearance all around (shaded area to the right in Fig. 13-9).

CIRCLE

OVAL

Fig. 13-7
An oval is a flattened circle.

139

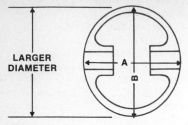

Fig. 13-8
A cam-ground piston viewed from the bottom. When the piston is cold, its diameter at A (at the piston-pin holes) may be from 0.002 to 0.003 inch [0.05 to 0.08 mm] less than at B. (*Chrysler Corporation*)

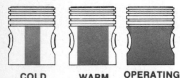

COLD   WARM   OPERATING TEMPERATURE

Fig. 13-9
As the cam-ground piston warms up, as indicated by shading, the expansion of the skirt distorts the piston from an elliptical to a round shape. This increases the area of normal clearance between the piston and the cylinder wall.

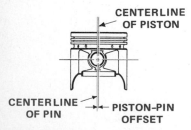

CENTERLINE OF PISTON

CENTERLINE OF PIN — PISTON-PIN OFFSET

Fig. 13-10
The centerline of the piston pin is offset slightly from the centerline of the piston itself to minimize piston slap.

There are other methods of piston expansion control. Some pistons have struts, bands, or belts of special steel cast into the aluminum piston. These steel parts control the expansion so that proper piston clearance is maintained.

13-7 PISTON-PIN OFFSET
In many engines, the piston pin is offset to one side (Fig. 13-10). It is offset to minimize the effect of the sudden, heavy push on the piston at the start of the power stroke. This sudden, heavy push that occurs as the piston starts down tends to slam the piston to one side of the cylinder wall. The action is called piston slap and was discussed earlier in Sec. 13-5. By offsetting the piston pin slightly to one side, the sudden slamming effect is prevented.

CHECK UP ON YOURSELF
It's time to find out how well you understand what you have been reading about pistons and connecting rods. You are learning a great deal about automobiles. Check up on yourself by answering the questions below. If you can't answer a question, study the past few pages to find the answer.

1. What is the name of the part that connects the piston to the crankpin?
2. How is the connecting rod attached to the piston?
3. How is the connecting rod attached to the crankpin?
4. How is the piston pin lubricated?
5. What causes piston slap?

ANSWERS
1. The connecting rod (Sec. 13-1).   2. By the piston pin (Sec. 13-1).   3. By the rod cap, with nuts and bolts (Sec. 13-1).   4. By oil thrown off the connecting-rod bearings (Sec. 13-2).   5. Excessive piston clearance (Sec. 13-5).

PISTON RINGS

13-8 PURPOSE OF PISTON RINGS
Piston rings must provide a good seal between the piston and the cylinder wall. However, there must always be clearance enough for the piston to slide up and down easily in the cylinder without danger of seizure.

If it were not for the piston rings, piston clearance would allow much of the pressure from the burning air-fuel mixture to blow by the piston and escape. "Blowby" is the name given to the unburned air-fuel mixture and burned gases that pass or "blow by" the piston and flow down into the crankcase. When burned gases blow by the piston, power is lost because they cannot add to the push on the top of the piston. Blowby can also cause engine troubles, as you will learn in Chaps. 31 and 32, which discuss engine service.

In addition to providing a seal between the piston and cylinder wall, the piston rings do a second job. They scrape off excessive oil from the cylinder walls and return it to the oil pan. This action keeps oil from working its way up into the combustion chamber, where it would burn. Oil that is burned in the combustion chamber leaves a carbon deposit that can clog valves and piston rings as well as foul spark plugs. Both these conditions cause engine trouble.

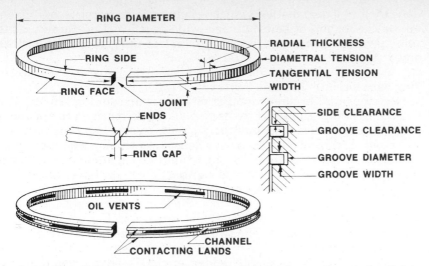

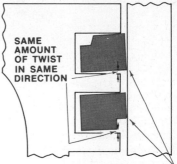

Fig. 13-11
A compression ring (top) and an oil-control ring (bottom). (*Sealed Power Corporation*)

Fig. 13-12
Action of counterbored and scraper compression rings during an intake stroke. Internal forces of the rings tend to twist them so that they put a sharp corner on the cylinder wall. This scrapes the wall clean of any excess oil that has worked up past the oil-control ring. (*Perfect Circle Division of Dana Corporation*)

Actually, there are two types of piston rings. One type fights blowby. The other type scrapes oil off the cylinder walls. The blowby fighters are called *compression rings*. The oil-scraper rings are called *oil-control rings*. We will look at both types of rings in detail.

13-9 RING JOINT GAP
The piston rings are made a little larger than the diameter of the cylinder wall. They are cut at one point, as shown in Fig. 13-11. The cut allows the ring to expand slightly so that it can be slipped over the head of the piston. The ring can then be slid down into the ring groove that has been cut in the piston. Figure 13-3 shows the rings in place in the piston grooves.

13-10 COMPRESSION RINGS
Compression rings are made of cast iron. They are not just plain rings, but have a corner cut out, as shown in Fig. 13-12. The purpose of this is to give the rings a slight twist. This causes the rings to put a sharp corner against the cylinder wall on the intake stroke. The sharp corner is more effective in scraping oil off the cylinder wall. The oil that is scraped off returns to the oil pan rather than working its way up into the combustion chamber to be burned. You can see how the slight twist of the compression rings puts sharp corners against the cylinder wall in Fig. 13-12.

Now, let's see how the compression rings hold in the high pressure of the burning air-fuel mixture and fight blowby. The high pressure works around behind the rings, as shown in Fig. 13-13. The pressure presses the rings down against the lower sides of the ring grooves. The pressure also presses the rings out against the cylinder wall. This provides a good seal at both the cylinder wall and the lower side of the ring groove. Most of the pressure that gets by the upper ring is caught and contained by the lower ring. The two rings, working together, hold in the combustion pressures and, in a good engine, hold blowby to a minimum.

13-11 OIL-CONTROL RINGS
The compression rings help keep oil from getting into the combustion chamber. However, they can do only part of the job. The main job is

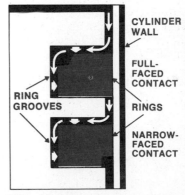

Fig. 13-13
Action of counterbored and scraper compression rings during a power stroke. The combustion pressure presses the rings against the cylinder wall with full-face contact, forming a good seal. (*Perfect Circle Division of Dana Corporation*)

141

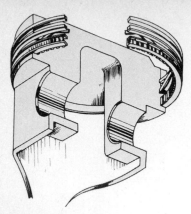

Fig. 13-14
Cutaway views of rings and piston to show construction. The second compression ring has an inner tension ring. The oil-control ring is a three-piece ring consisting of an expander ring and two rails. (*TRW, Inc.*)

EXPANDER–SPACER

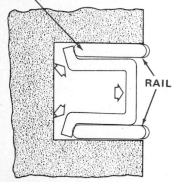
RAIL

Fig. 13-15
The action of the expander spacer, shown by the arrows, forces the rails out against the cylinder wall and up and down against the sides of the ring groove. (*Perfect Circle Division of Dana Corporation*)

done by the oil-control ring, which is below the compression rings (Fig. 13-3). The oil gets on the cylinder walls because oil is thrown off the rod-big-end bearings. An excess amount of oil gets on the cylinder walls. Most of the oil must be scraped off.

Figure 13-11 shows one type of oil-control ring. It is a cast-iron ring with a channel and oil vents cut in it. Oil that the ring scrapes off the cylinder wall passes through these vents and through holes in the back of the ring groove in the piston. The oil then returns to the oil pan. Some of the oil gets onto the piston pins and lubricates them.

Another type of oil-control ring consists of three parts. This ring is made up of two thin rings, or *rails,* and an expander ring between them, as shown in Fig. 13-4. You can see how they fit together in Fig. 13-14. The expander ring pushes the two rails up against the two sides of the ring groove. At the same time, the expander ring pushes the two rails out against the cylinder wall. The arrows in Fig. 13-15 show the direction of these pushes. The two rails do a better job of scraping the oil off the cylinder wall.

Some engines—especially older engines—have two oil-control rings per piston. Because of better design and better rings, most modern engines need only one oil-control ring per piston.

13-12 EFFECT OF ENGINE SPEED ON OIL CONTROL
The higher the engine speed, the poorer job the rings do in controlling the oil. At high speed more oil is pumped through the lubricating system. More oil gets on the cylinder walls. The rings are moving faster and have less time to do their scraping job. The result is that more oil gets past the rings and into the combustion chamber.

13-13 EFFECT OF ENGINE WEAR ON OIL CONTROL
As an engine gets old, its parts wear. The cylinder walls wear unevenly, with more wear at the top where the combustion pressures are greatest. The higher the combustion pressure, the harder the rings are pressed against the cylinder wall (see Fig. 13-13). Uneven wear of the cylinder wall makes it harder for the rings to maintain good contact against the wall. The rings have to change in size, expanding as they move up into the area of maximum wear. The result is that the rings do a poorer job of scraping off oil. More oil works up into the combustion chamber, where it burns.

We have all seen old cars that put out clouds of blue smoke as they go down the highway. They may have worn engines that let more oil get up into the combustion chamber, where it burns. The burning oil turns the exhaust smoke blue. These engines are called "oil pumpers." They "pump" oil up into the combustion chamber. They are also called "smoggers" because the exhaust pollutes the air.

Worn cylinders are not the only cause of burning oil. We will find out about the other causes in later chapters.

13-14 OIL CONSUMPTION
The amount of oil that an engine uses depends on engine speed and engine wear. All engines burn some oil. A new engine operated at moderate speed may not require any additional oil between oil changes. An old engine that is operated at high speed could require oil to be added frequently.

13-15 REPLACEMENT PISTON RINGS

When cylinder walls are worn and old rings are not doing a very good job, good performance can sometimes be restored by installing new piston rings. These rings are sometimes called *rering* sets. They have more tension or more expanders than regular rings. This allows them to follow the changes in the size of the cylinder walls as they move up and down. Therefore they can control the oil better. Their ability to follow the changing size of the cylinder wall also reduces blowby, which results from worn cylinder walls.

Installing new rings is not always the best solution to the problem of worn cylinder walls. A better solution is to hone or bore the cylinders to a larger size and then install oversize pistons and rings. How this is done is explained in Chap. 32. Rings for use in a bored engine sometimes are identified as *rebored* ring sets.

CHECK UP ON YOURSELF

Now, let's see how much you know about piston rings. Answer the questions that follow to find out how well you understand what you have studied.

1. What are the two types of piston rings?
2. Why are the piston rings cut at one place?
3. What is the purpose of the twist in compression rings?
4. What happens to the oil that is not scraped off the cylinder walls by the rings?
5. How does the oil get onto the cylinder walls?
6. What happens to the oil that is scraped off the cylinder walls by the rings?
7. What are the names of the parts that make up the three-piece oil-control ring?
8. What effect does speed have on the piston rings' job of oil control?
9. What are the two main factors that determine how much oil an engine will burn?

ANSWERS

1. Compression rings and oil-control rings (Sec. 13-8). 2. So they can be expanded and slipped over the piston head and into the ring grooves (Sec. 13-9). 3. To enable them to do a better job of scraping the oil from the cylinder walls on the intake stroke (Sec. 13-10). 4. It works up into the combustion chamber where it is burned (Sec. 13-10). 5. From oil thrown off the connecting-rod bearings (Sec. 13-11). 6. It drops back down into the oil pan (Sec. 13-11). 7. Two rails and an expander ring (Sec. 13-11). 8. The higher the speed, the poorer the job the rings do in controlling oil (Sec. 13-12). 9. Speed and engine wear (Sec. 13-14).

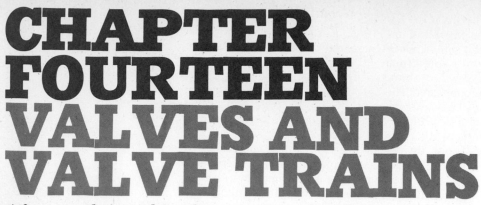

CHAPTER FOURTEEN
VALVES AND VALVE TRAINS

After studying this chapter, you should be able to:
1. Describe the construction and operation of overhead valve trains and their component parts.
2. Describe the construction and operation of overhead-camshaft valve trains.
3. Explain the arrangements for driving the camshaft.
4. Explain what valve timing means and why valves are timed to open early and close late.
5. Explain how hydraulic valve lifters and valve rotators work.

14-1 I-HEAD VALVE TRAIN
The I-head, or overhead-valve, valve train uses pushrods and rocker arms to operate the valves.

NOTE
Chapters 8 and 10 have several cutaway pictures of engines which show I-head valve trains.

The camshaft is driven by a chain or gears from the crankshaft. As the camshaft rotates, the cam lobes on the cams raise the valve lifters. The valve lifters push up on the pushrods. The rocker arms rock, and the valves are pushed down off their seats. In other words, the valves open when the cam lobes move up under the valve lifters.

14-2 DRIVING THE CAMSHAFT
The camshaft is driven by gears or by sprockets and belt or chain. Figures 14-1 and 14-2 show the chain-and-sprocket arrangement for a six-cylinder and an eight-cylinder engine. Many four-cylinder and six-cylinder engines use a pair of gears, as shown in Fig. 14-3. As is explained in Chap. 8, in four-cycle engines the camshaft must turn only once for every two revolutions of the crankshaft. Each intake valve and each exhaust valve open once every complete cycle. One complete cycle takes four piston strokes, or two revolutions of the crankshaft. The

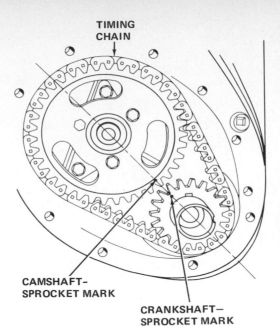

TIMING
CHAIN

CAMSHAFT–
SPROCKET MARK

CRANKSHAFT–
SPROCKET MARK

Fig. 14-1
Crankshaft and camshaft
sprockets with chain drive for a
six-cylinder engine, with timing marks on sprockets.
(*Chrysler Corporation*)

Fig. 14-2
Crankshaft and camshaft
sprockets with chain drive for a
V-8 engine.

camshaft gear or sprocket is twice as big as the crankshaft gear or
sprocket. It takes two crankshaft revolutions to turn the camshaft
once.

The camshaft turns in sleeve bearings or bushings in the cylinder
block. Figure 14-4 shows a camshaft with the bearings and other parts
for a V-8 engine. The bearings are larger than the cams on the camshaft so that the cams can pass through the bearings when the camshaft is installed in the cylinder block.

The chain in Figs. 14-1 and 14-2 is called the *timing* chain. The
timing chain and sprockets determine when the valves open and close;
that is, they "time" the valve action.

Fig. 14-3
Crankshaft and camshaft
gears for a six-cylinder engine.
Note the timing marks on the
gears. (*Buick Motor Division of
General Motors Corporation*)

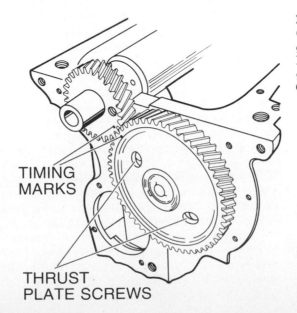

TIMING
MARKS

THRUST
PLATE SCREWS

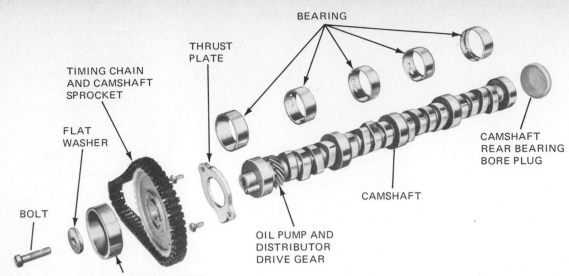

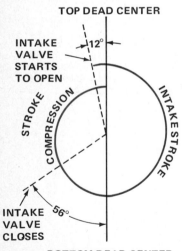

Fig. 14-4
The camshaft and related parts for a V-8 engine. (*Ford Motor Company*)

Fig. 14-5
Intake-valve timing. The complete cycle of events is shown as a 720-degree spiral. This represents two complete crankshaft revolutions. Timing of valves differs for various engines.

14-3 INTAKE-VALVE TIMING

Until now, we have been saying that the intake valve opens when the intake stroke starts and closes when the intake stroke ends. We have also been saying that the exhaust valve opens when the exhaust stroke starts and closes when the exhaust stroke ends.

This is not exactly true. Actually, the intake valve starts to open before the intake stroke starts. And it stays open for some time after the intake stroke ends and the compression stroke starts. The same thing is true for the exhaust valve. It opens before the exhaust stroke starts and remains open for some time after the exhaust stroke ends.

Let's take a closer look at the intake valve. The intake valve doesn't pop open instantly. It takes time for the cam lobe to start pushing the valve lifter up and to get it all the way up. For this reason, the cam is positioned on the camshaft so that it starts opening the intake valve well before the piston reaches TDC at the end of the exhaust stroke. By the time the piston reaches TDC and starts down on the intake stroke, the intake valve is wide open.

Now let's look at the end of the intake stroke. The air-fuel mixture pours into the cylinder as the piston moves down. But the air-fuel mixture takes time to enter the cylinder (see Sec. 9-9). Holding the intake valve open past BDC on the intake stroke gives the air-fuel mixture more time to enter the cylinder. The result is that more air-fuel mixture enters the cylinder, giving a stronger push on the power stroke.

How long is the intake valve open after BDC? The time varies with different engine designs. Typical timing for the intake valve is shown in Fig. 14-5. The intake valve starts to open 12 degrees before TDC at the end of the exhaust stroke. It stays open past BDC after the intake stroke and does not completely close until 56 degrees into the compression stroke. This gives the air-fuel mixture more time to enter so that volumetric efficiency is higher.

Valve timing varies for different engines. It depends on the shape of the lobe on the cam that operates the valve. It also depends on the relationship between the gears or chain and sprockets on the crankshaft and the camshaft.

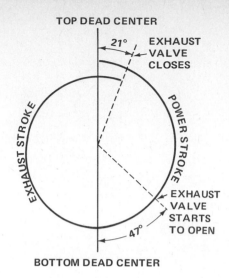

14-4 EXHAUST-VALVE TIMING

The exhaust valve starts to open before the power stroke ends and stays open after the exhaust stroke ends. This gives the exhaust gases more time to get out of the cylinder. Typical exhaust-valve timing for one engine is shown in Fig. 14-6. The exhaust valve starts to open 47 degrees before BDC on the power stroke. It stays open 21 degrees after the end of the intake stroke.

The early opening of the exhaust valve does not waste power, as you might think. By the time the piston has moved down to 47 degrees before BDC, the pressure in the cylinder has already dropped. The purpose of getting the exhaust valve open early is to start the exhaust gases moving out.

In Fig. 14-6 notice that the exhaust valve does not completely close until 21 degrees after TDC on the intake stroke. The upward push of the piston during the exhaust stroke has started the exhaust gases moving out. This upward movement toward the exhaust-valve port continues even after the piston has reached TDC and is starting down on the intake stroke. So, the reason for leaving the exhaust valve open just a little longer is to give most of the remaining exhaust gases a chance to get out too.

14-5 TIMING OF THE TWO VALVES

We have combined the two valve-timing illustrations in Fig. 14-7. You can now see the valve overlap, that is, the time that both valves are open. Both valves are open a total of 33 degrees (12 degrees plus 21 degrees) at the end of the exhaust stroke and at the start of the intake stroke. This provides a valve overlap of 33 degrees.

NOTE

As is explained in Chap. 26 on automotive emission control, the amount of valve overlap can be changed to help reduce certain pollutants in the exhaust gas.

14-6 VALVE GUIDES

The valves slide up and down in valve guides in the cylinder head. In some engines, the valve guides are tubes made of special metal in-

Fig. 14-7
Here, we put together intake-valve timing and exhaust-valve timing.

stalled in the cylinder head (Fig. 14-8). In other engines, the valve guides are integral with the cylinder head, which means that they are holes bored into the cylinder head. The cylinder head for a V-8 engine, shown in Fig. 11-8, has valve guides that have been installed separately. You can see these valve guides in the upper view of the cylinder head. The valve guides must provide a close fit with the valve stems but must also permit the valves to move up and down easily.

CHECK UP ON YOURSELF

Here are some questions that will help you find out how well you understand what you have been studying. If you can't answer all the questions the first time, review the past few pages.

1. What are the mechanisms that drive the camshaft?

Fig. 14-8
Typical engine valves.
(*Chrysler Corporation*)

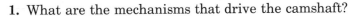

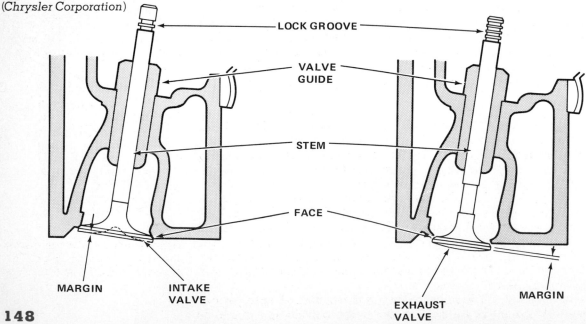

148

2. What is the purpose of holding the intake valve open past BDC after the end of the intake stroke?

3. What is the purpose of opening the exhaust valve before the power stroke is completed?

4. What is the name for the condition during which both intake and exhaust valves are open?

5. What do we call the holes in which the valves slide up and down in the cylinder head?

ANSWERS

1. Gears or sprockets and a chain or belt (Sec. 14-2). **2.** To improve volumetric efficiency. That is, to allow more time for the air-fuel mixture to get into the cylinder (Sec. 14-3). **3.** To give the exhaust gases more time to get out of the cylinder (Sec. 14-4). **4.** Valve overlap (Sec. 14-5). **5.** Valve guides (Sec. 14-6).

14-7 VALVES

Each cylinder has two valves: an intake valve and an exhaust valve (Fig. 14-8). The valve face must closely match the valve seat. In other words, the two must be in full contact all around the seat. This match is necessary for two reasons: First, to keep the combustion pressure from leaking out between the valve face and the valve seat; second, to help conduct heat away from the valve head.

When the engine is running, the exhaust valve gets very hot. It is repeatedly passing the hot exhaust gases, and it can reach a temperature of more than 1000°F [538°C]. Some of the heat is passed down the valve stem to the valve guide. The valve guide is cooled by the coolant circulating in the cylinder head. But much more of the heat is passed from the valve head to the valve seat when the valve is closed. Remember, the exhaust valve is closed nearly three-quarters of the time. With a good match between the valve face and the valve seat, the maximum amount of heat can be passed to the seat. The seat, being in the cylinder head, is cooled by the engine cooling system.

If the contact between the valve face and the valve seat is poor, less heat will be passed to the seat and the valve will run hotter. Also, hot exhaust gases will leak out between the valve and the seat at the points of poor contact. The escaped hot exhaust gases will heat the valve still more and may even burn the valve and the seat. Poor contact, or poor seating, can be caused by dirt or other things. This is explained in greater detail in Chap. 31 on engine service.

14-8 VALVE SEATS

In many engines, the valve seats are integral with the cylinder head. In other words, the valve seats are machined circles bored in the cylinder head. They are carefully ground to match exactly the angle of the valve face. Also, they are carefully centered with the valve guides so that the valves will seat evenly all around.

In some engines, the exhaust-valve seats are metal rings, called *valve-seat inserts,* which are inserted in the cylinder head. Figure 14-9 shows a valve seat in a cylinder head. The seat insert is made of a special metal that can hold up under the heat and pounding it gets in the engine. To install the seat insert, an undercut is made in the cylinder head. Then the insert is pressed into place. This is explained further in the chapters on engine service.

In some engines, the exhaust-valve seats are integral with the cylinder head. A special process called *induction hardening* is used to

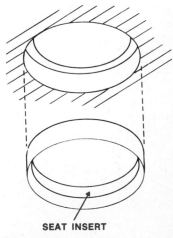

SEAT INSERT

Fig. 14-9

A cutaway view of a valve-seat insert in the cylinder head. The insert is indicated by the arrow.

149

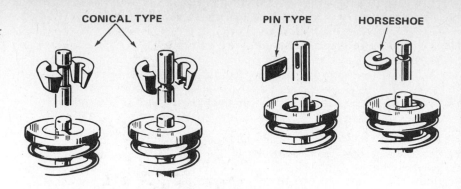

Fig. 14-10
Types of valve-spring-retainer
locks, or keepers.

CONICAL TYPE   **PIN TYPE**   **HORSESHOE**

harden the valve seats in the cylinder head. This improves their wearing ability.

14-9 VALVE-SPRING-RETAINER LOCKS

The valve spring is held onto the end of the valve stem by a spring retainer and a lock. The retainer is a large washer, and the lock is a small piece of steel that fits into or onto the valve stem. Three types of valve-spring-retainer locks are shown in Fig. 14-10. Once the lock is put into place on the valve stem and the spring retainer is released, the retainer holds the lock in place. This maintains valve-spring pressure on the valve stem. The lock prevents the spring retainer from moving farther out toward the end of the valve stem.

14-10 OIL SEALS AND SHIELDS

Oil flows up from the oil pump to lubricate the rocker arms and valve stems. Usually there is so much oil in the cylinder head that the valve stems must be protected from excessive oil. Without protection, oil could work its way down the valve guide, past the valve stem, and into the combustion chamber. Too much oil in the combustion chamber could foul the spark plugs and piston rings. The excessive oil on the valve stems, combined with the high temperature, could cause gum to form on the valve stems. If this happened, the valves would not open

Fig. 14-11
Disassembled and sectional
views of a valve and spring assembly with oil seal and
shield.

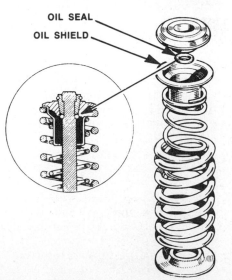

OIL SEAL

OIL SHIELD

and close properly. They could stick in a partly open position. Also, oil could get on the valve seats, and the oil would burn. This would prevent proper valve seating. With either condition, the valves would overheat and burn.

To protect the valve stems from excessive oil, oil shields and seals are used. These are located either at the top of the valve stem, as shown in Fig. 14-11, or at the lower end of the valve stem, as shown in Fig. 14-12. Either way, the seal or shield, made of rubberlike material, prevents oil from getting on the valve stem and seeping down into the combustion chamber.

14-11 VALVE SPRINGS
In many engines, each valve uses only one spring. In other engines, two valve springs are used for each valve. One spring is inside the other (Fig. 14-11).

14-12 ROCKER ARMS
There are several types of rocker arms. One type, shown in Fig. 14-13, is mounted on a shaft that is attached to the cylinder head. Figure 14-

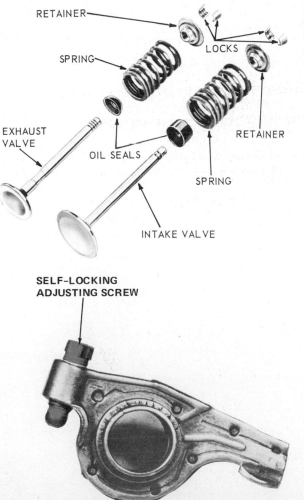

Fig. 14-12
Disassembled view of valves, springs, seals, and related parts for one cylinder. (*Chrysler Corporation*)

Fig. 14-13
One type of rocker arm used in overhead-valve engines. (*Chrysler Corporation*)

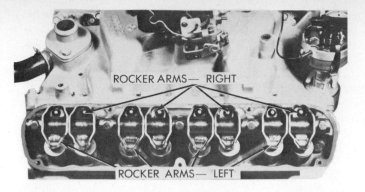

14 shows similar rocker arms mounted on a shaft on the cylinder head. The rocker arm in Fig. 14-13 has a self-locking adjustment screw. The purpose of the screw is to allow for valve-clearance adjustments. The valve must close completely every time. Otherwise, hot combustion gases will flow between the valve seat and the valve face, burning them both. The result will be an expensive service job or a ruined cylinder head.

The adjustment screw in the end of the rocker arm can be turned in or out to adjust the clearance in the valve train. This gives the valve the clearance it needs.

Another kind of rocker arm is shown in Fig. 14-15. This rocker arm is mounted on a stud that is installed in the cylinder head. The rocker arm is held in place by a cup-shaped washer, called a *ball pivot*. It resembles a steel ball that is cut in two and has a hole in its center. The ball pivot is positioned on the stud by a self-locking nut. In operation, the rocker arm rocks back and forth on the ball pivot. The valve train is adjusted by turning the nut up or down on the stud. The ball pivot is lubricated by oil that flows up through the hollow stud from an oil gallery in the cylinder head or through the hollow pushrod (Fig. 14-17).

Fig. 14-15
Rocker arms of the type using ball pivots. (*Chevrolet Motor Division of General Motors Corporation*)

14-13 VALVE ROTATORS

Many engines are equipped with valve rotators, especially on the exhaust valves. These devices turn the valves a little each time they open. Here's the reason why the valves need to be turned. Suppose a valve seats in the same position every time, and suppose one part of the valve seat gets a little carbon on it. The carbon spot will prevent good valve seating at that point. If this happens, the valve overheats at that point because it cannot get rid of its heat. The valve face can overheat enough to actually burn. But if the valve is rotated a little each time it opens, no one point on the valve face gets overheated.

14-14 HYDRAULIC VALVE LIFTERS

Hydraulic valve lifters are used in engines to reduce noise and eliminate valve adjustments. In the past, valve trains without hydraulic valve lifters required adjustment every so often. As normal wear takes place in the engine, the clearances in the valve train increase. There must be some clearance so that the valves will close completely. But this clearance increases with wear. Every time the valve is opened, the valve-train parts must come together to eliminate this clearance. The clearance must be taken up before the lifter and pushrod movement can carry through the rocker arm to the valve stem. Taking up of the clearance produces a noise, called *tappet noise*. Adjustment is required to prevent excessive clearance and noise.

With the hydraulic valve lifter, all clearance in the valve train is taken up by the oil in the lifter every time the valve closes. Then, when the valve train starts to open the engine valve, there is no clearance between metal parts. Because there is no clearance to be taken up, the engine valve opens silently.

Figure 14-16 shows the installation of a hydraulic valve lifter in a V-8 engine. Figure 14-17 shows how the lifter works. The principle of operation is that the lifter is kept filled with oil from the engine lubricating system. This takes up all the clearance. Let's see how it all works.

The picture to the left of Fig. 14-17 shows the situation when the valve is closed. Notice that the lobe of the cam has passed out from under the valve lifter. Oil from the lubricating system is flowing through holes in the valve lifter body and plunger. This oil is under pressure from the engine oil pump. As it flows inside the plunger, most of it flows up through the hollow pushrod to lubricate the rocker arms.

Some of the oil pushes down on the ball-check valve, which opens the valve. This oil then flows under the plunger. The oil raises the plunger enough to take up any clearance—usually only a few thousandths of an inch—in the valve train.

When the cam lobe comes around, as shown at the right in Fig. 14-17, it pushes the valve lifter up. The increase in pressure under the ball-check valve closes the valve. The valve lifter then acts like a solid lifter and moves up to push the pushrod up. The pushrod operates the rocker arm and opens the engine valve. During this interval, some of the oil may leak out from under the plunger. This does not matter, however. As soon as the cam lobe moves out from under the valve lifter and the engine valve closes, any clearance is taken up once again. We described this action in the previous paragraph and showed it at the left in Fig. 14-17.

Fig. 14-16
A sectional view of a V-8 engine, showing the location of the hydraulic valve lifter in the valve train. (*Cadillac Motor Car Division of General Motors Corporation*)

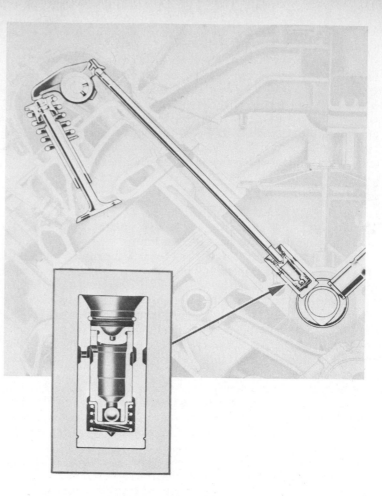

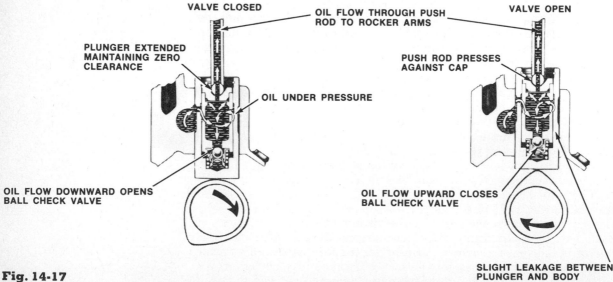

VALVE CLOSED

OIL FLOW THROUGH PUSH ROD TO ROCKER ARMS

VALVE OPEN

PLUNGER EXTENDED MAINTAINING ZERO CLEARANCE

PUSH ROD PRESSES AGAINST CAP

OIL UNDER PRESSURE

OIL FLOW DOWNWARD OPENS BALL CHECK VALVE

OIL FLOW UPWARD CLOSES BALL CHECK VALVE

SLIGHT LEAKAGE BETWEEN PLUNGER AND BODY

Fig. 14-17
The operation of a hydraulic valve lifter. (*Cadillac Motor Car Division of General Motors Corporation*)

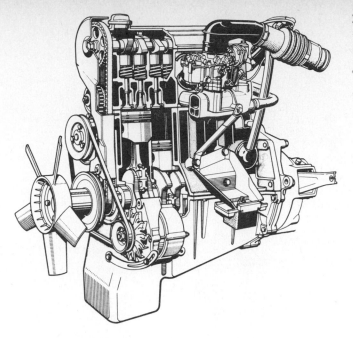

14-15 OVERHEAD CAMSHAFTS

In all the engines we have looked at so far, the camshaft is located in the cylinder block. A pushrod and a rocker arm are required to carry the motion of the valve lifter to the valve. When the camshaft is installed in the cylinder head, as shown in Fig. 14-18, the pushrod is no longer needed. In some engines, the rocker arm is also eliminated. Figure 14-18 shows an overhead-camshaft engine that uses neither pushrods nor rocker arms. The cams work directly on valve tappets that rest on the ends of the valve stems. Figure 14-19 shows an overhead-camshaft engine that uses rocker arms but no pushrods.

What's the advantage of an overhead camshaft? When the camshaft is in the overhead position, the path between the cams and the valves is much shorter. The valves respond quicker. Higher engine speeds are possible because there are fewer valve-train parts to move. Some domestic cars and many imported ones use engines with overhead camshafts.

An engine with a single overhead camshaft is known as a SOHC (single-overhead-camshaft) engine. An engine with two overhead camshafts is called a DOHC (double-overhead-camshaft) engine. The name is often shortened to "overhead-cam engine."

NOTE

Engines using pushrods are often called *pushrod engines* to distinguish them from overhead-cam engines.

CHECK UP ON YOURSELF

The questions that follow will help you review the past few pages, which covered valves, valve lifters, and overhead-camshaft engines. If you can't answer a question, reread the past few pages to find the answer you need.

1. Which of the two valves gets hotter?

155

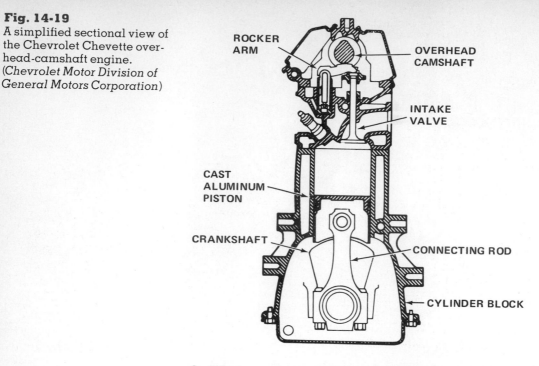

Fig. 14-19
A simplified sectional view of the Chevrolet Chevette overhead-camshaft engine. (*Chevrolet Motor Division of General Motors Corporation*)

ROCKER ARM

OVERHEAD CAMSHAFT

INTAKE VALVE

CAST ALUMINUM PISTON

CRANKSHAFT

CONNECTING ROD

CYLINDER BLOCK

2. What are the two paths the heat takes to get away from the valve head?
3. What do we call the metal rings that are installed in the cylinder head to form the valve seats for the exhaust valve?
4. What do we call the small pieces of steel that are installed on the end of the valve stem to hold the valve-spring retainers and the valve springs in place?
5. Why must excessive amounts of oil be kept off the valve stems?
6. What would happen if an exhaust valve failed to close completely?
7. How is the rocker-arm ball pivot lubricated?
8. What is the job of the valve rotators?
9. When the valve is open, is the check valve in the hydraulic valve lifter open or closed?

ANSWERS

1. The exhaust valve (Sec. 14-7). **2.** Through the valve face to the valve seat, and through the valve stem to the valve guide (Sec. 14-7). **3.** Valve-seat inserts (Sec. 14-8). **4.** Valve-spring-retainer locks (Sec. 14-9). **5.** Excessive oil will work down the valve stem past the valve guide and get into the combustion chamber, where it will burn (Sec. 14-11). **6.** Hot exhaust gas would flow between the valve and the valve seat, burning the valve (Sec. 14-12). **7.** By oil that flows up through the hollow stud from an oil gallery in the cylinder head or through the hollow pushrod (Sec. 14-12). **8.** To rotate the valves slightly so that the valves seat at a different position each time they close (Sec. 14-13). **9.** Closed (Sec. 14-14).

CHAPTER FIFTEEN
ENGINE LUBRICANTS AND LUBRICATING SYSTEMS

After studying this chapter, you should be able to:

1. Explain how oil is produced and the ways in which engine oil is rated as to viscosity and service.
2. Describe the various engine-oil additives and their purpose.
3. Explain how the engine oil circulates in the engine and the various jobs it does.
4. Describe the components in the engine lubricating system and how each works.

The engine has many moving metal parts. If these metal parts rub against one another, they will wear out quickly. The purpose of the lubricating system is to keep metal from rubbing against metal. In this chapter we explain how lubricating systems flood the moving parts with lubricating oil. You will learn how the oil works and how it gets to the moving parts in the engine.

15-1 MOVING PARTS IN THE ENGINE

Look at all the moving parts in the engine (Fig. 15-1). First, there is the crankshaft, which spins in stationary bearings in the cylinder block. The bearings are the parts that bear the weight of the crankshaft. Bearings are replaceable. Therefore, when they wear, they can be removed and new ones can be installed. The bearings supporting the crankshaft are called the *main bearings,* or the *mains.*

Second, there is the connecting rod. The lower end of the connecting rod—the rod big end—is attached to a crankpin on the crankshaft by bearings and a rod cap. The upper end of the rod— the rod small end —is attached to the piston by a piston pin. As is explained in Chap. 13

157

and shown in Fig. 13-2, there are various attachment methods. Regardless of the method, the surfaces or bushings in which the piston pin moves must be lubricated.

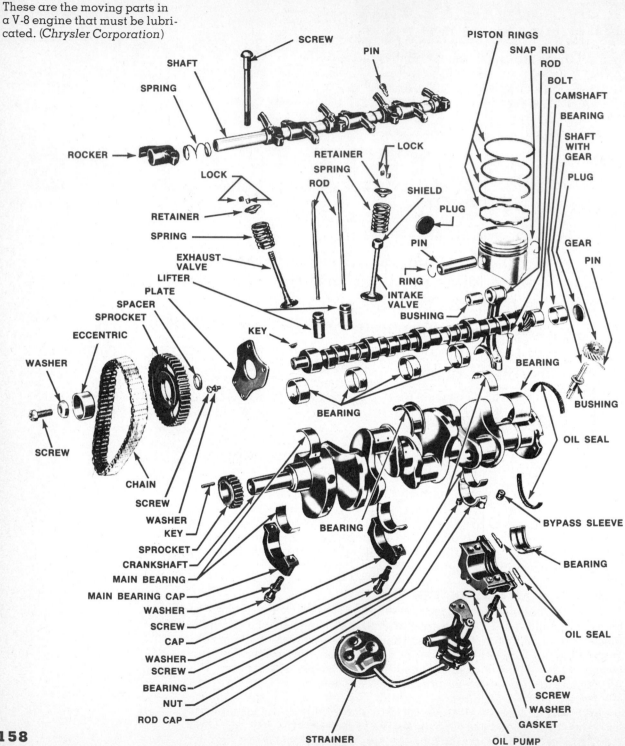

Fig. 15-1
These are the moving parts in a V-8 engine that must be lubricated. (*Chrysler Corporation*)

Third, there is the camshaft, which rotates in bearings. The valve lifters move up and down in bores in the cylinder block. The rocker arms in the cylinder head rock back and forth as the valves move up and down in the valve guides.

Fourth, and most important for engine operation, are the pistons and their rings, which move up and down in the cylinders.

All these parts must be covered with oil so that they can move with relative ease and without metal-to-metal contact. This is the job of the lubricating system. Study Fig. 15-1, which shows the moving parts we have been discussing. Notice that only one piston and rod and only one pair of valves with pushrods and lifters are shown. In the picture, the oil pump can be seen at the bottom of the engine. The oil pump pushes oil up to all the moving parts in the engine.

15-2 ENGINE OIL

Before we explain the lubricating system, let's take a look at oil. Oil is the liquid used in the lubricating system. For many years, the only oil used in engines was made from natural crude oil which came from oil wells drilled deep into the earth. Much of the engine oil used today still comes from crude oil. This crude oil was formed underground millions of years ago in various parts of the world. It must be refined to make it usable. In the refining process, gasoline, kerosene, lubricating oil, and many other products are made.

In recent years, synthetic oils have come out of the chemical laboratory. The manufacturers claim that these have superior lubricating properties. Actually, there are three basic types of synthetic oils. The type most widely used at present is produced from organic acids and alcohols (from plants of various types). A second type is produced from coal and crude oil. A third type is made from crude oil. Although tests have shown these synthetics to have certain superior properties, no automotive manufacturer has given them unqualified approval yet.

Not all oil is the same. There are several grades of oil and several ratings. Oil made for automobiles contains a number of *additives* (chemical compounds that are *added* to the oil) that improve the performance of the oil. Let's take a look at these ratings and additives.

15-3 OIL VISCOSITY AND SERVICE RATINGS

Viscosity refers to the ability of a liquid to flow. An oil with high viscosity is very thick and flows slowly. An oil with low viscosity flows easily. Oil gets thicker as it becomes colder. Therefore, starting a car in cold weather is more difficult than starting it in warm weather. The cold has increased the viscosity of the oil.

Oil viscosity is rated in two ways by the Society of Automotive Engineers (SAE). It is rated for (1) winter driving and (2) summer driving. Winter-grade oils come in three grades: SAE5W, SAE10W, and SAE20W. The "W" stands for winter grade. For other than winter use, the grades are SAE20, SAE30, SAE40, and SAE50. The higher the number, the higher the viscosity (the thicker the oil). All these grades are called *single-viscosity oils*.

Many oils have multiple-viscosity ratings. For example, SAE10W-30 has the same viscosity as SAE10W when it is cold and the same viscosity as SAE30 when it is hot.

Table 15-1
Selecting engine oil based on
outside temperature. (*Chevrolet Motor Division of General
Motors Corporation*)

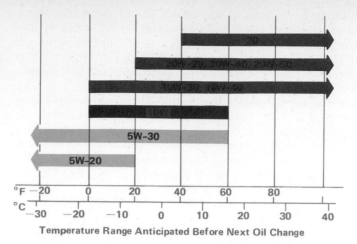

Temperature Range Anticipated Before Next Oil Change

The car manufacturer specifies the viscosity of oil for the engine. Table 15-1 is from a Chevrolet shop manual. The table shows how outside temperature affects the viscosity of oil that an engine needs.

If you study the table, you will see that the higher the outside temperature, the higher the viscosity rating specified. The 5W-30 oil is good for starting and driving in very low outside temperatures. If higher temperatures are expected, a 10W-30 or 10W-40 oil should be used because it will hold its viscosity in the higher temperatures. In other words, 10W-30 or 10W-40 oil will not thin out too much as it heats up.

The service rating indicates the type of service for which the oil is best suited. For gasoline engines, the service ratings are SA, SB, SC, SD, and SE. Here is a brief description of each of these ratings:

- SA—Acceptable for engines operated under the mildest conditions
- SB—Acceptable for minimum-duty engines operated under mild conditions
- SC—Meets requirements of gasoline engines in 1964–1967 model passenger cars and trucks
- SD—Meets requirements of gasoline engines in 1968–1970 model passenger cars and some trucks
- SE—Meets requirements of gasoline engines in 1972 and later cars and certain 1971 model passenger cars and trucks

You will notice that this is an "open-end" series. That is, if the car manufacturers and oil producers see the need for other types of oil, they can bring out "SF" and "SG" service-rated oils.

Diesel engines require different types of oil. They are service-rated CA, CB, CC, and CD. CD is for diesel-engine operations under the most severe conditions.

15-4 OIL ADDITIVES

Certain chemical compounds, called additives, are added to the oil. The purpose of these additives is to give the oil certain properties it does not have in its original refined state. The refining process determines the viscosity and other basic properties of the oil. The additives give the oil other desirable properties. Let's take a look at the additives and what they do.

1. Viscosity Improver

The viscosity improver is a compound that lessens the tendency of the oil to thin out as it gets hot. Without this additive, the oil would not be safe for high-temperature, high-speed operation because it might thin out too much. However, a 10W-40 oil could be used in outside temperatures of 0 to 100°F [−17.8 to 37.8°C].

Multiple-viscosity oils are made by adding a viscosity improver.

2. Pour-Point Depressants

Pour-point depressants are compounds that help prevent the oil from getting too thick at low temperatures. These additives help the oil to flow at low temperatures. In other words, they depress the tendency of the oil to thicken.

3. Inhibitors

Inhibitors are compounds that fight potential oil and lubricating-system troubles. Several inhibitors are used in engine oil. Some fight corrosion and rust. Others fight oxidation of the oil. Oil oxidation takes place because, at fairly high temperatures, the oil is constantly being agitated, or stirred up, in the engine crankcase. The oil is not hot enough to burn. But the oil is hot enough to react with the oxygen in the air. When this happens, oxidation occurs. Oil oxidation results in the formation of new compounds that are harmful to the engine. One compound formed by oil oxidation is a sticky, tarlike material called *sludge* that can clog oil lines. It also causes valves and piston rings to hang up and not work properly. Another compound formed by oil oxidation is similar to varnish. This compound can also cause trouble in the engine.

Another oil additive—an antifoaming compound—helps to prevent the oil from foaming. The oil in the crankcase is constantly being stirred up by the rotation of the crankshaft. This action tends to make the oil foam, just as the action of an egg beater causes egg whites to foam. Foaming prevents normal oil circulation and results in loss of lubrication and engine damage.

4. Detergent-Dispersants

A detergent is similar to soap. When you wash your hands with soap, the soap surrounds and loosens the particles of dirt. You can then rinse off the dirt with water. Similarly, the detergent in the oil loosens the particles of carbon, gum, and dirt on engine parts and carries them away. Some of the particles drop to the bottom of the crankcase, where they are drained away when the oil is changed. Other particles are trapped in the oil filter.

The dispersant action *disperses,* or *scatters,* the particles. This prevents the particles from clotting, or forming clumps, which could clog oil passages and bearings.

5. Extreme-Pressure Compounds

Today's engines are built with heavy valve springs that put high pressure on the valve-train parts. Combustion pressures are also high. The extreme-pressure compounds added to oil help to resist the very high pressure between the engine parts. The extreme-pressure additives fight "squeezing out" by furnishing lubrication even during extreme pressures.

15-5 PURPOSE OF ENGINE OIL

Oil flows in slippery layers onto engine parts, preventing metal-to-metal contact. Figure 15-2 gives you an idea of how the oil works. The picture shows two surfaces that are highly magnified. If you look at a part that is made of very smooth metal (such as a crankpin) under a microscope, you will see tiny rough edges sticking up from the surface of the metal. If two such dry metal surfaces rub against each other, the irregular edges catch each other. Particles of metal are worn off. This action consumes energy and wastes power.

What is worse is that the rubbing and tearing action, or friction, produces heat. Rub your hands together very fast and hard. They get hot. Imagine what would happen in the engine if it ran without oil. Metal parts would be moving against each other at very high pressure. Without oil, these parts would quickly get so hot that the metal would melt and the engine would seize.

The oil prevents this because layers of oil cover the metal surfaces, as shown in Fig. 15-2. They hold the metal surfaces away from each other. Only the oil layers must slip as the two metal parts move. The oil greatly reduces power loss and wear of moving metal parts. But oil does other jobs, as we will discuss below.

15-6 OTHER JOBS FOR THE OIL

The oil reduces friction and wear. It also does other jobs in the engine:

- It removes heat from the engine.
- It absorbs shocks between bearings and other engine parts.
- It forms a seal between the piston rings and the cylinder wall.
- It acts as a cleaning agent.

Let's look at each of these in detail.

15-7 REMOVING HEAT

The engine oil is pumped up from the oil pan at the bottom of the engine through various oil passages to the moving engine parts. As the oil circulates through the engine, the oil gets hot. Then the oil flows back down into the oil pan. The oil pan is much cooler than the engine. It is below the engine and in the path of the air flowing under the moving car. The hot oil therefore loses heat to the air passing under the oil pan. The circulation of the oil between the engine and the oil pan keeps taking heat away from the engine. This helps keep the engine cool.

15-8 OIL COOLERS

In some engines, the oil does not lose enough heat to the oil pan. Because these engines require additional cooling, a separate radiator, or heat exchanger, is used. The heat exchanger is similar to the radiator used in the engine cooling system. It has a series of passages through which the hot oil can flow. It has another series of passages through which coolant from the engine cooling system can flow. The coolant picks up heat from the oil, cooling the oil. The heated coolant then passes through the engine cooling system radiator. There the coolant gives up its heat to the air passing through the radiator.

In air-cooled engines, the hot oil flows through a small oil cooler. Air flowing through the oil cooler carries away heat from the oil.

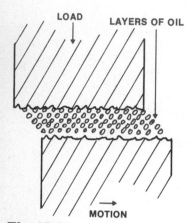

Fig. 15-2

These two highly magnified surfaces show irregularities that you could not see without a microscope. When the surfaces move with relation to each other, the layers of oil prevent metal-to-metal contact.

15-9 ABSORBING SHOCKS

The layers of oil between moving engine parts help to absorb shocks. For example, let's look at the bearing in the big end of the connecting rod. This bearing rests on a crankpin of the crankshaft. When combustion of the compressed air-fuel mixture takes place, a load of up to 4000 pounds [1814 kg] is suddenly put on the rod (Fig. 15-3). This load is carried through the rod bearing to the crank journal. The only thing that prevents metal-to-metal contact is a layer of oil between the bearing and the journal. The layer of oil resists "squeezing out." It acts as a cushion to absorb the sudden shock of the load as combustion takes place.

15-10 FORMING A SEAL BETWEEN RINGS AND WALL

The cylinder walls are covered with oil. We explain later how the oil gets on the cylinder walls. The oil on the cylinder walls lubricates the piston rings as they slide up and down. If you put a drop of oil between your finger and thumb, you can feel how slippery it is. But notice, also, how sticky it is. The oil tends to resist your attempts to separate your finger and thumb. It is the quality of stickiness that allows the oil to form a seal between the piston rings and the cylinder wall. The layer of oil on the cylinder wall fills in most of the irregularities so that there is a good seal.

15-11 ACTING AS A CLEANING AGENT

The oil circulates through the engine and then flows back down into the oil pan. As the oil passes through the engine, it picks up particles of carbon, metal, and dirt. The oil carries all these particles back down to the oil pan. The larger particles fall out. Smaller particles are filtered out by the oil filter.

CHECK UP ON YOURSELF

The past few pages described engine oil, the additives in engine oil, and the purposes of engine oil. Now answer the questions that follow to see how well you understand what you have studied.

1. What prevents metal-to-metal contact of moving parts in the engine?
2. What are the compounds called that are added to the oil?
3. Does SAE10W oil or SAE20W oil have the higher viscosity?
4. What are the five major oil additives?
5. Where does the oil get rid of the heat it picks up from the engine parts?

ANSWERS

1. The engine oil (Sec. 15-1). **2.** Additives (Sec. 15-2). **3.** SAE20W (Sec. 15-3). **4.** Viscosity improvers, pour-point depressants, inhibitors, detergent-dispersants, and extreme-pressure compounds (Sec. 15-4). **5.** In the oil pan (Sec. 15-5).

ENGINE LUBRICATING SYSTEMS

15-12 OIL PUMP

The main purpose of the engine lubricating system is to supply oil to all the moving parts in the engine. The oil pump does this job. It sits in or near the engine oil pan and pumps oil from the pan up to the engine

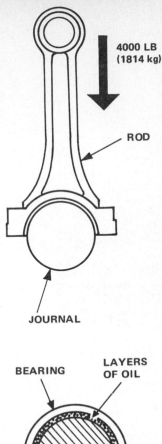

4000 LB
(1814 kg)

ROD

JOURNAL

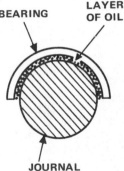

BEARING

LAYERS OF OIL

JOURNAL

Fig. 15-3
The layers of oil between the journal and the rod bearing help to absorb the shock of the sudden load when combustion develops.

parts. In Chap. 10 there are several cutaway pictures of engines, showing the location of the oil pump and the gears that drive it. Figure 15-4 is a simplified drawing of a lubricating system used in a V-8 engine.

The pump sends oil from the oil pan through the oil filter, as shown by the arrows in Fig. 15-4. We explain the oil filter later. The oil then passes through oil lines to the crankshaft bearings, camshaft bearings, valve lifters, pushrods, rocker arms, and valves. These passages are shown by lines in the picture. Then the oil drains back down to the oil pan.

15-13 OIL-PUMP OPERATION

The two common types of oil pumps are the gear-type pump and the rotor-type pump. Let's discuss the gear type first. The oil pump is driven by a pair of spiral gears, as shown in Fig. 15-5. In the arrangement shown, the driving spiral gear is on the end of the engine camshaft. This gear drives a spiral gear on the ignition-distributor shaft. The oil-pump shaft, an extension of the distributor shaft, drives the oil pump.

As the gears are turned in the oil pump, the drive gear drives the driven gear (Fig. 15-5). The spaces between the gear teeth are filled with oil from the oil inlet of the pump. As the gear teeth mesh, the oil is forced out through the oil outlet. Figure 15-6 is a disassembled view of a gear-type oil pump. Larger dirt particles are screened out by a pickup screen, which is submerged in the oil.

The other type of oil pump used in engines is the rotor type. It has a pair of rotors, as shown in Fig. 15-7. The inner rotor has four lobes.

Fig. 15-4

A simplified drawing of the lubricating system for a V-8 engine.

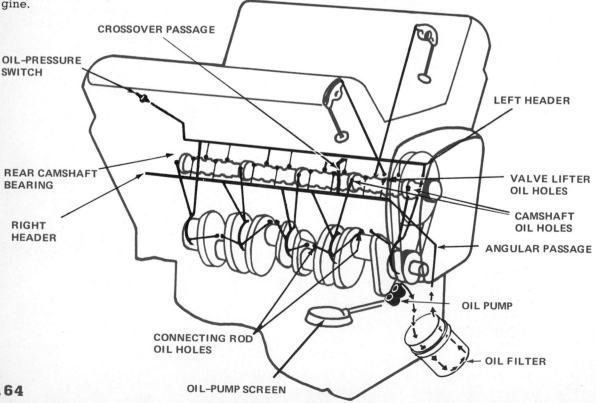

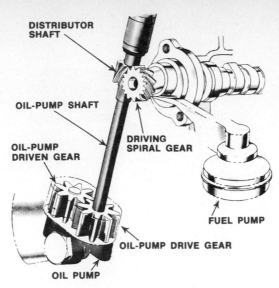

DISTRIBUTOR SHAFT

OIL-PUMP SHAFT

OIL-PUMP DRIVEN GEAR

DRIVING SPIRAL GEAR

FUEL PUMP

OIL-PUMP DRIVE GEAR

OIL PUMP

Fig. 15-5
Oil-pump, distributor, and fuel-pump drives. The oil pump is the gear type. A gear on the end of the camshaft drives the ignition distributor. An extension of the distributor shaft drives the oil pump. The fuel pump is driven by an eccentric on the camshaft.

The outer rotor has four recesses into which the four lobes fit. The outer rotor is offset so that on one side there is space between the lobes of the inner rotor and the recesses of the outer rotor. The inner rotor rotates, driven by the camshaft. The inner rotor forces the outer rotor to rotate along with it. The spaces between the lobes and the recesses fill with oil from the oil inlet. Then, as the lobes move into the recesses, the oil is forced out through the pump outlet.

15-14 RELIEF VALVES
The faster the engine runs, the faster the gears or rotors turn in the oil pump. This means that, without relief, the oil pressure would go very

Fig. 15-6
A disassembled view of a gear-type oil pump. (*Pontiac Motor Division of General Motors Corporation*)

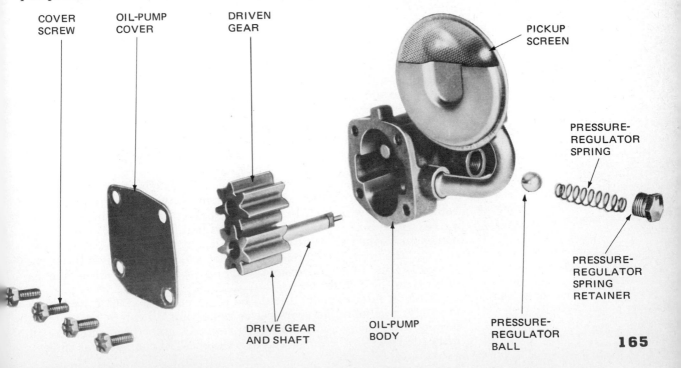

COVER SCREW

OIL-PUMP COVER

DRIVEN GEAR

PICKUP SCREEN

PRESSURE-REGULATOR SPRING

PRESSURE-REGULATOR SPRING RETAINER

DRIVE GEAR AND SHAFT

OIL-PUMP BODY

PRESSURE-REGULATOR BALL

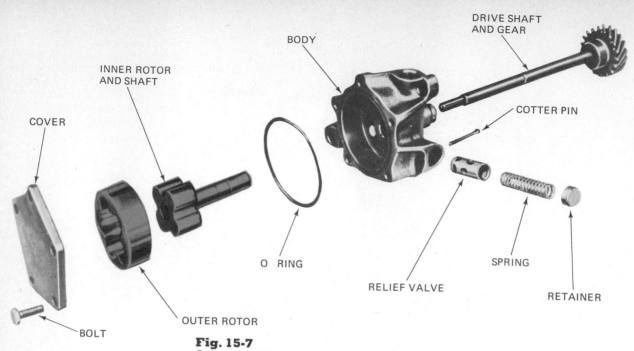

COVER

INNER ROTOR
AND SHAFT

BODY

DRIVE SHAFT
AND GEAR

COTTER PIN

O RING

RELIEF VALVE

SPRING

RETAINER

BOLT

OUTER ROTOR

Fig. 15-7
A disassembled view of a rotor-type oil pump. (*Chrysler Corporation*)

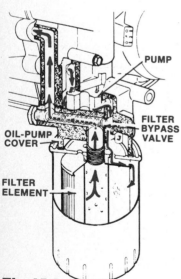

PUMP

FILTER
BYPASS
VALVE

OIL-PUMP
COVER

FILTER
ELEMENT

Fig. 15-8
A cutaway view of a full-flow oil filter with bypass valve. (*Buick Motor Division of General Motors Corporation*)

high. To prevent too much pressure, oil pumps contain a relief valve. This valve contains a ball (Fig. 15-6) or a plunger (Fig. 15-7), which is held in place by a spring. When the pressure starts to go too high, the relief valve pushes the ball or the plunger back against the spring tension. This opens up a relief hole, which allows part of the oil to flow back down into the oil pan. Therefore the pressure is relieved so it does not go too high.

15-15 OIL FILTERS
The oil from the oil pump must first pass through an oil filter before it goes up to the engine. The oil filter is the engine's main protection against dirt. The filter removes particles of carbon and dirt so they do not get into the engine and damage engine bearings and other parts. The filter contains a filtering element made of pleated paper or fibrous material. The oil passes through the filter, and the paper or fibers trap the dirt particles.

Figure 15-8 is a cutaway view of a filter. The filter element is housed in a replaceable can that is thrown away when the element becomes clogged with dirt. In the engine, the filter has a bypass relief valve, which consists of a spring-loaded ball. If the filter element becomes so clogged that all the oil needed by the engine cannot pass through the filter, the increased pressure from the oil causes the valve to open. This allows oil from the pump to bypass the filter and go directly to the engine.

The oil filter element should be replaced before it stops working properly. Car manufacturers recommend that oil filters be replaced periodically. Today many manufacturers recommend replacing the oil filter at the first oil change and every *second* oil change after that.

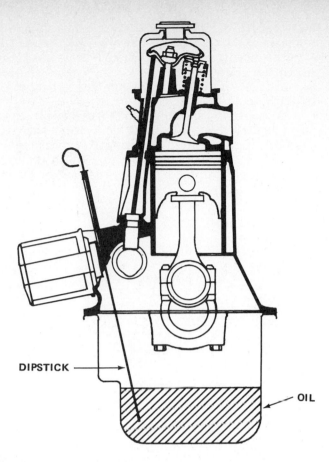

DIPSTICK

OIL

15-16 OIL-PRESSURE INDICATORS

Cars are equipped with some means of showing the driver the oil pressure in the engine. If the pressure drops too low, the engine is not being properly lubricated. Continued operation at low oil pressure will ruin the engine. The driver must be warned of low pressure so that the engine can be stopped.

There are two general types of oil-pressure indicators. In one, a dial on the car instrument panel shows the oil pressure. In the other, a light comes on if the oil pressure drops too low. Both these indicating systems are discussed in Chap. 25, which explains the electrical equipment in the car.

15-17 OIL-LEVEL INDICATORS

A dipstick is used to check the level of the oil in the oil pan (Fig. 15-9). To use the dipstick, pull it out, wipe it off, and put it back in place. Then pull it out again so that you can check the level of the oil shown on the dipstick.

15-18 HOW THE ENGINE LUBRICATING SYSTEM WORKS

Figure 15-10 shows various views of a V-8 engine with the different passages through which oil gets to the engine parts. Let's examine this picture in detail. Start at Fig. 15-10A, which shows a cutaway view of the engine from the side. Oil is picked up from the oil pan by the oil pump and sent through the oil filter (shown in Fig. 15-10D). Then the oil is sent to an oil passage that branches off into two parts. One part sends oil to the crankshaft. The other part sends oil to the valve train.

The oil sent to the crankshaft lubricates (1) the main bearings in which the crankshaft turns, (2) the connecting-rod bearings, (3) the camshaft bearings, and (4) the cylinder walls. Let's see how the oil gets to all these parts.

In the engine shown in Fig. 15-10, the oil enters an oil gallery (or passage) drilled in the cylinder block. From there it flows to the crankshaft bearing supports. These supports are ribs in the bottom of the cylinder block. The oil flows through holes drilled in these bearing-support ribs and through holes in the bearings to reach the crankshaft

Fig. 15-10
The lubrication system of a V-8 engine. The arrows show the flow of oil to the moving parts in the engine. (*Chevrolet Motor Division of General Motors Corporation*)

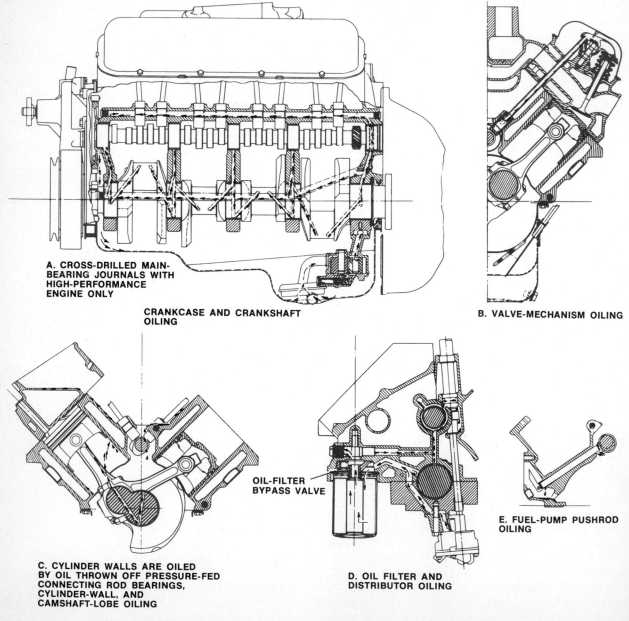

A. CROSS-DRILLED MAIN-BEARING JOURNALS WITH HIGH-PERFORMANCE ENGINE ONLY

CRANKCASE AND CRANKSHAFT OILING

B. VALVE-MECHANISM OILING

C. CYLINDER WALLS ARE OILED BY OIL THROWN OFF PRESSURE-FED CONNECTING ROD BEARINGS, CYLINDER-WALL, AND CAMSHAFT-LOBE OILING

OIL-FILTER BYPASS VALVE

D. OIL FILTER AND DISTRIBUTOR OILING

E. FUEL-PUMP PUSHROD OILING

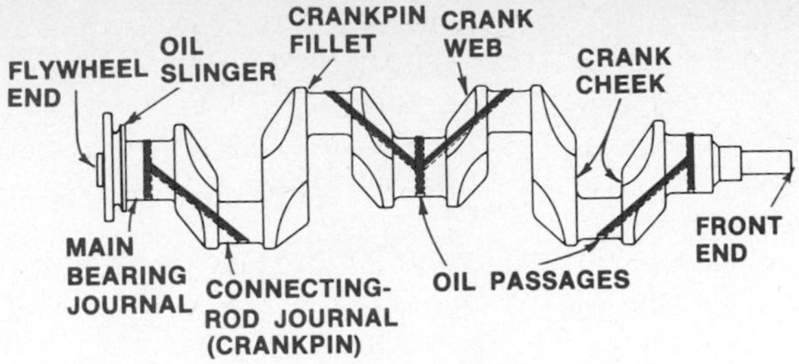

FLYWHEEL END | OIL SLINGER | CRANKPIN FILLET | CRANK WEB | CRANK CHEEK

MAIN BEARING JOURNAL | CONNECTING-ROD JOURNAL (CRANKPIN) | OIL PASSAGES | FRONT END

Fig. 15-11
This drawing shows the oil passages drilled in the crank-shaft.

main journals. Rotation of the journal carries the oil around to the lower bearing half. In this way, the complete bearing is lubricated. Oil flows from the center of the bearing to the edges, where it drops off and returns to the oil pan. This action also cleans the bearings by carrying away any dirt particles trapped between the crankshaft journal and the bearing.

Part of the oil flowing to the bearing takes an additional path. It goes through holes drilled in the crankshaft to reach the connecting-rod bearings. A crankshaft with holes drilled in it is shown in Fig. 15-11. Every time the hole in the crankshaft main journal passes the hole in the main bearing, a spurt of oil flows through the drilled hole to the crankpin. The oil flows over the crankpin to lubricate the connecting-rod bearing. The oil flows out from the center and drops off the edges of the bearing back into the oil pan. Here, too, the oil cleans as it lubricates.

Some of the oil has still not finished its trip through the engine. Oil thrown off the connecting-rod bearings covers the cylinder walls. There it provides lubrication for the pistons, piston rings, and piston pins (Fig. 15-10C).

Some engines further ensure adequate lubrication of the pistons, piston rings, and piston pins by having spit holes in the connecting rod. Some of the oil feeding through the crankshaft holes to the connecting-rod bearings spurts through these spit holes and onto the cylinder walls. You can see this action in Fig. 15-10C. The spurt takes place every time the hole in the connecting rod aligns with the hole in the crankpin. This supplies the pistons, piston rings, and piston pins with the oil they need.

Some of the oil flowing to the main bearing supports flows upward through holes drilled in these supports to the camshaft bearings. You can see this flow in Fig. 15-10A. The camshaft lobes are lubricated by oil thrown off the connecting-rod bearings (see Fig. 15-10C).

15-19 VALVE-TRAIN LUBRICATION

The valve-train oiling arrangement is shown in Fig. 15-10B. Some of the oil from the oil pump flows through an oil gallery to all the valve lifters (Fig. 15-10A). This oil lubricates the valve lifters and fills hydraulic valve lifters. Some of the oil flows from the lifters up through the pushrods, which are hollow. You can see this in Fig. 15-10B. As the oil reaches the top of the pushrods, it spurts out to lubricate the rocker arms, the rocker-arm shaft or ball supports, and the valve stems. Drain holes allow the oil to drop down into the oil pan.

NOTE
Not all engine lubricating systems operate exactly as we have described. One common variation is how the rocker arms get oil. Instead of oiling through hol-

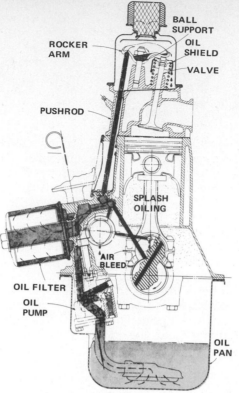

Fig. 15-12
Valve-train lubrication in a six-cylinder, in-line engine. (*Chevrolet Motor Division of General Motors Corporation*)

BALL
SUPPORT

ROCKER
ARM

OIL
SHIELD

VALVE

PUSHROD

SPLASH
OILING

AIR
BLEED

OIL FILTER

OIL
PUMP

OIL
PAN

low pushrods, many rocker arms get oil through the hollow stud on which they pivot.

15-20 SIX-CYLINDER LUBRICATING SYSTEM

Figure 15-12 shows the lubricating system for a six-cylinder engine. The system is the same as just described. Oil flows through oil galleries drilled in the cylinder block to the main and camshaft bearings. Oil flows up the hollow pushrods to the rocker arms and valves. Note in Fig. 15-12 that the valve has an oil shield. This shield keeps excessive oil from covering the valve stem. If there were too much oil, some of it would work down the valve stem through the valve guide and get into the combustion chamber. There it would burn and cause carbon deposits and other trouble.

CHECK UP ON YOURSELF

Find out how much you understand about the lubricating system by answering the following questions.

1. Where does the oil pump get the oil it sends to the engine parts?
2. How does the oil get to the main bearings?
3. How are the cylinder walls and pistons lubricated?
4. How does the oil get up to the rocker arms and valves?

ANSWERS

1. From the oil pan (Sec. 15-12). 2. Through galleries drilled in the cylinder block (Sec. 15-18). 3. From oil thrown off the connecting-rod bearings and from spit holes in the connecting rods (Sec. 15-18). 4. Through hollow pushrods or studs (Sec. 15-19).

CHAPTER SIXTEEN
ENGINE COOLING SYSTEMS

After studying this chapter, you should be able to:
1. Describe the purpose of the engine cooling system and how it works.
2. Explain how the water pump and thermostat work.
3. Describe the construction of the various types of radiators and how they work.
4. Explain the purpose of pressurizing the cooling system and how this is done.
5. Discuss the coolant and its composition.

The burning fuel in the engine produces a lot of heat. Chapter 15 explains that some of this heat is removed by the lubricating oil. Some of the heat leaves the engine in the hot exhaust gases. But most of the heat is carried away by the engine cooling system. It has the job of keeping the engine from getting too hot, or overheating. Let's find out how the engine cooling system does its work.

16-1 PURPOSE OF THE COOLING SYSTEM

The cooling system must cool the engine properly. If the cooling system cools the engine too much, gasoline will be wasted and the engine will not have normal power. If the cooling system does not cool the engine enough, the engine will overheat. Overheating can burn off the film of lubricating oil from the cylinder walls. This would damage the cylinder walls, pistons, and piston rings. The result could be a seized engine!

An overheated engine loses power also. Let's take a look at engine heat. Combustion temperatures in the cylinders can reach 4000°F [2200°C]. That's a high enough temperature to melt the cylinder block. So, this heat must be taken away from the engine before it causes damage. Part of the heat leaves the engine with the hot exhaust gases. The rest of the heat goes into the metal parts around the combustion chamber, the cylinder heads, the cylinder block, and the pistons. Some of this heat is carried away by the engine oil. Most of the heat, however, is removed by the cooling system.

Not all the heat is carried away. Some heat is left so that the engine stays just hot enough to run efficiently.

16-2 TYPES OF COOLING SYSTEMS

There are two kinds of cooling systems: air cooling and liquid, or water, cooling. In the air-cooled engine, air passing the cooling fins on the cylinders and the cylinder heads carries away the excess heat. In the liquid-cooled engine, water mixed with antifreeze, circulating around the combustion chambers, carries away the excess heat. The mixture of water and antifreeze—called *coolant*—cools the engine. An air-cooled engine is shown in Fig. 10-4. Several liquid-cooled engines are shown in Chap. 10. In this chapter we will be discussing liquid-cooled engines.

16-3 LIQUID-COOLED ENGINES

Figure 16-1 is a simplified cutaway view of a cooling system for an engine. The coolant is pumped from the engine to the top of the radiator. It flows down through the radiator, losing heat to the air passing through. Then the coolant is pumped back through the engine by the water pump. Now let's look at each part of the system and find out exactly how it works.

16-4 WATER JACKETS

Water jackets are the spaces that surround the combustion chamber and the cylinder walls. Figure 16-2 shows one bank of a V-6 engine, partly cut away to show the water jackets. In the cylinder block these spaces—the water jackets—are formed by the inner shells of the cylin-

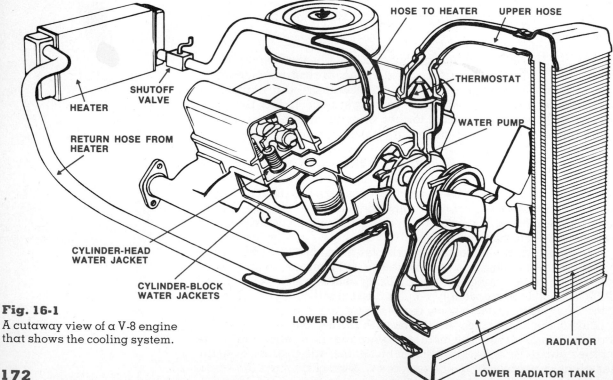

Fig. 16-1
A cutaway view of a V-8 engine that shows the cooling system.

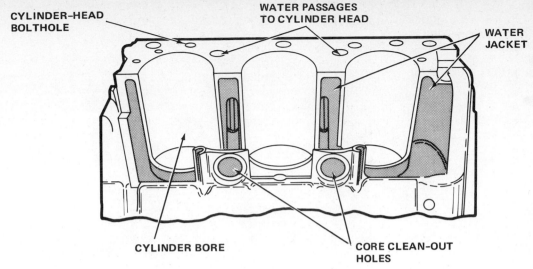

CYLINDER–HEAD BOLTHOLE — WATER PASSAGES TO CYLINDER HEAD — WATER JACKET

CYLINDER BORE — CORE CLEAN-OUT HOLES

Fig. 16-2
One bank of a V-6 engine cut away so that the water jackets can be seen. (*Truck and Coach Division of General Motors Corporation*)

ders and the outer shell of the cylinder block. The water jackets are watertight, and a mixture of water and antifreeze circulates through them. This mixture is called the coolant, and we will use that term from now on.

The coolant passes first through the cylinder-block water jackets and then through the cylinder-head water jackets, picking up heat. Then the hot coolant flows into the radiator. As it flows through the radiator, the coolant loses heat. The cooled coolant then flows back into the bottom of the cylinder-block water jackets to start another trip through the engine.

16-5 WATER PUMP

The water pump forces the coolant to flow through the cooling system. The water pump is mounted at the front end of the engine and is driven by a pulley and a belt from a pulley on the front end of the crankshaft. Figure 16-1 shows the location of the pump in the engine. Figure 16-3 is a cutaway view of a V-8 engine. The pictures give you another view of where the water pump is located. Note that the pulley that drives the pump also carries the engine fan. The fan is described later.

The impeller type of water pump is used in the cooling systems of automobiles. The impeller is a flat plate with a series of curved blades, or vanes. When the impeller spins, the coolant between the blades is thrown outward and is forced through the cooling system. Figure 16-4 shows a disassembled water pump.

A sectional view of a water pump is shown in Fig. 16-5. The shaft on which the pump impeller and the pulley are mounted is supported by a double-row ball bearing. This is a ball bearing with two rows of balls. A seal holds the coolant in the system and prevents it from leaking out past the shaft or the bearing.

Look at Fig. 16-3 again and notice the arrows that show how the coolant circulates. It leaves the bottom of the radiator and goes up to the water pump. It is forced through the engine water jackets by the water pump. The coolant then leaves the water jackets and goes up to the top of the radiator.

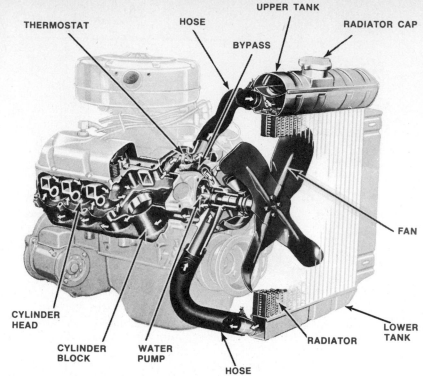

Fig. 16-3
A cutaway view of a V-8 engine showing the cooling system. The arrows show the direction of water flow through the engine water jackets. (*Ford Motor Company*)

THERMOSTAT

HOSE

UPPER TANK

BYPASS

RADIATOR CAP

FAN

CYLINDER HEAD

CYLINDER BLOCK

WATER PUMP

HOSE

RADIATOR

LOWER TANK

16-6 RADIATOR

The radiator has two separate circuits: a coolant circuit and an air circuit. The coolant circuit carries the coolant from a tank at the top of the radiator to a tank at the bottom of the radiator. The air circuit allows air to flow through the radiator from front to back.

Two kinds of radiators are the tube-and-fin radiator (Fig. 16-6) and the ribbon-cellular radiator (Fig. 16-7). Both kinds of radiators are shown cut away so that you can see how they are made.

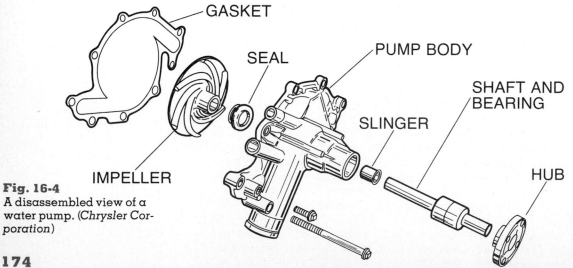

GASKET

SEAL

PUMP BODY

SHAFT AND BEARING

SLINGER

IMPELLER

HUB

Fig. 16-4
A disassembled view of a water pump. (*Chrysler Corporation*)

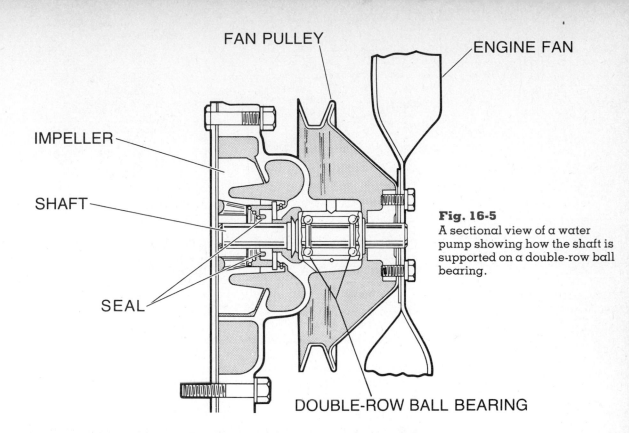

FAN PULLEY

ENGINE FAN

IMPELLER

SHAFT

SEAL

Fig. 16-5
A sectional view of a water pump showing how the shaft is supported on a double-row ball bearing.

DOUBLE-ROW BALL BEARING

The tube-and-fin radiator (Fig. 16-6) is easiest to understand. It has a series of water tubes that go from the top tank to the bottom tank of the radiator. Surrounding these tubes and fastened to them are air fins. Air passes around the outside of the water tubes and between the fins, and it absorbs the heat from the coolant in the tubes.

The ribbon-cellular radiator, shown in Fig. 16-7, is made of a series of metal ribbons soldered together along their edges, forming two sets of passages. One set is formed by the water tubes, which go from the top tank of the radiator to the bottom tank. The other set of passages allows air to pass from the front of the radiator to the back.

Regardless of the type of radiator, the effect is the same. The coolant enters the radiator hot and comes out comparatively cool. The heat is transferred from the coolant to the air passing through the radiator.

16-7 ENGINE FAN

The engine fan helps pull air through the radiator. You can see the location and shape of the engine fan in several of the pictures in this chapter. For example, look at Figs. 16-3 and 16-5. The fan is located at the back of the radiator. It has four or more curved blades. The fan is driven by the belt from the pulley on the engine crankshaft. When the curved blades rotate, they "scoop up" air and push it back toward the engine. This action pulls air through the radiator.

16-8 VARIABLE-SPEED FAN DRIVE

Many engines have a variable-speed fan drive. This drive increases the speed of the fan as the engine gets hot and reduces the speed of the fan as the engine gets cooler. The advantage of the variable speed is the

Fig. 16-6
The construction of a tube-and-fin radiator core.

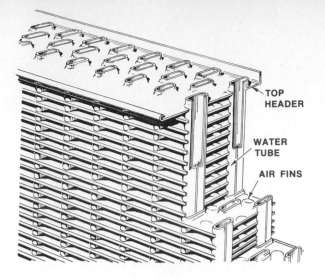

saving of the horsepower it takes to run the fan at high speed. Also the fan is quieter when it runs slower.

One type of variable-speed fan drive has a small fluid coupling. The driving force passes through a fluid in the coupling. When the engine gets hot, more fluid is forced into the coupling, and the fan runs faster. When the engine is cool, less fluid goes into the coupling, and the fan runs slower.

Another type of fan has flexible blades that reduce both the power needed to drive the fan and fan noise at high speed. With this design, the pitch of the blades decreases as fan speed increases, owing to centrifugal force. With the flex fan, power needs and noise are lower at higher speeds.

16-9 DOWN-FLOW AND CROSS-FLOW RADIATORS

The radiators we have been talking about are all down-flow radiators. That is, the coolant flows from a tank at the top of the radiator to a tank at the bottom of the radiator. This system is shown in Fig. 16-8.

In a cross-flow radiator, the coolant flows across the radiator, as is shown by the arrows in Fig. 16-9. The advantage here is that the radia-

Fig. 16-7
The construction of a ribbon-cellular radiator core

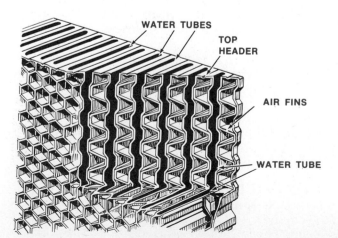

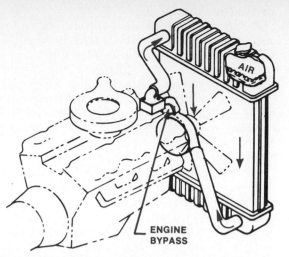

Fig. 16-8
A cooling system using a
down-flow radiator.

tor can be made shorter from top to bottom. Many cars use cross-flow radiators because they take up less height under the hood. This allows car manufacturers to design lower hood lines.

CHECK UP ON YOURSELF

What you have been studying gives you a good start in understanding how cooling systems work. Make sure you understand what you have read before you continue studying this chapter.

1. What are the three main ways that the engine loses heat?
2. What are two kinds of engine cooling systems?
3. In the water pump, what do we call the flat plate with curved blades?
4. What are the two circuits through the radiator?
5. Radiators can be classified according to the direction in which the coolant flows through them. What are the two types?

ANSWERS

1. Through the cooling system, the lubricating system, and in the hot exhaust gases (introductory paragraph). **2.** Air cooling and liquid, or water, cooling (Sec. 16-2). **3.** The pump impeller (Sec. 16-5). **4.** The coolant circuit and the air circuit (Sec. 16-6). **5.** Cross-flow and down-flow (Sec. 16-9).

Fig. 16-9
A cooling system using a cross-flow radiator.

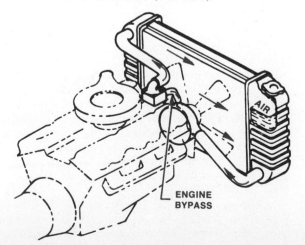

16-10 THERMOSTAT

Sometimes you do not want the cooling system to remove any heat. For example, when the engine is cold, it must be warmed up as fast as possible, because a cold engine wears fast and operates poorly.

Why does a cold engine wear fast? When an engine stops and cools off, most of the oil on the cylinder walls and bearings drips down into the oil pan. When the engine is started again, the oil takes a little while to start circulating. Therefore, for a few seconds the engine is running without enough oil on its moving parts. The result is rapid wear. After the engine is running, the oil begins to circulate to the moving parts.

A cold engine operates poorly because the gasoline does not evaporate very well when it is cold. The air-fuel mixture getting to the cylinders is not always right for good combustion. The result is poor engine operation. As we will study in later chapters, certain devices are used on the engine both to help it run better when cold and to warm it up quickly. Combustion is covered in Chap. 18.

What has all this to do with the thermostat? The thermostat is a device in the cooling system that shuts off circulation of coolant to the radiator when the engine is cold. When the engine is cold, no coolant can flow to the radiator. Instead, it flows through a bypass and back into the engine. This means that the radiator cannot take any heat out of the engine. The heat stays in the engine and makes it warm up faster. The time that the engine operates without proper lubrication and without proper air-fuel mixture is shortened. Then, as the engine gets hot, the thermostat opens the passage to the radiator so that the cooling system can go to work, taking heat out of the engine.

16-11 TYPES OF THERMOSTATS

The thermostat is located at the top of the cylinder head, as shown in Figs. 16-1 and 16-3. There are several types of thermostats, as shown in Fig. 16-10.

All thermostats operate in the same way. When the engine is cold, a valve in the thermostat is closed. This blocks off the coolant passage to the radiator. As the engine warms up, the valve starts to open. This allows coolant to flow to the radiator so that the cooling system can take heat out of the engine.

Most thermostats have a wax pellet that expands with heat. This forces the valve to open so that the circulation of coolant to the radiator can start.

If you look at Figs. 16-3, 16-8, and 16-9, you will see an engine bypass. This bypass allows the pump to circulate coolant through the engine when the engine is cold. When the engine is hot, the coolant circulates between the engine and the radiator.

Two types of thermostats that control the bypass passage and the coolant flow to the radiator are shown in Fig. 16-11. They are called *blocking bypass* thermostats. This type of thermostat has two valves—a primary valve and a secondary valve. The primary valve controls the flow of coolant to the radiator. When the engine is cold, the primary valve is closed. When this valve is closed, no coolant goes to the radiator.

The secondary valve controls the coolant flow through the bypass. When the primary valve is closed, the secondary valve is open. With the secondary valve open, coolant flows through the bypass. When the

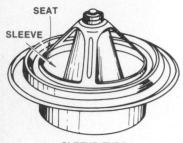

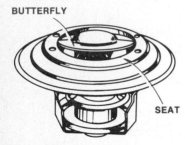

Fig. 16-10
Thermostats for the engine cooling system. (*Chrysler Corporation*)

engine warms up, the primary valve opens and the secondary valve closes. Then coolant begins to pass to the radiator. Both valves work together. As the primary valve opens the passage to the radiator, the secondary valve closes the bypass passage.

16-12 RADIATOR PRESSURE CAP

The cooling systems of most engines are sealed. When the engine gets hot, pressure develops in the cooling system. The increasing pressure increases the boiling temperature of the coolant.

Let's find out how this happens. At normal air pressure, water boils at 212°F [100°C]. If the air pressure is increased, the temperature at which water boils is also increased. For example, if the pressure is raised 15 psi (pounds per square inch) [103 kPa] over normal pressure, the boiling point is raised to about 260°F [127°C].

This is what happens in the sealed cooling system. As pressure goes up, the boiling point goes up. This means the coolant can be safely used at a temperature higher than 212°F [100°C] without its boiling. This is very important. The higher the coolant temperature, the greater the difference between the coolant temperature and the air temperature. The difference in temperatures is what causes the cooling system to work. The hotter the coolant, the faster the heat moves from the radiator to the cooler passing air. A pressurized sealed cooling system can take heat away from the engine faster. That is, the cooling system works more efficiently under higher pressure.

However, the cooling system can be pressurized too much. If the pressure goes too high, it could damage the radiator. To prevent this, the radiator cap has a pressure relief valve (Fig. 16-12). When the pressure goes too high, it raises the valve so that the excess pressure can escape (right, Fig. 16-12).

The radiator cap also has a vacuum valve. This valve lets air or coolant from the expansion tank into the cooling system when the pressure falls too low. This can happen when the engine stops and cools off. The pressure falls in the cooling system. If it falls too much below outside air pressure, it could cause a partial collapse of the radiator. To prevent this, the vacuum valve opens. On cars without an expansion tank, outside air enters to equalize the pressure. On cars with an expansion tank, coolant from the expansion tank flows into the radiator to equalize the pressure (Sec. 16-13).

16-13 COOLING SYSTEM EXPANSION TANK

Many cooling systems now have a separate expansion tank, as shown in Fig. 16-13. The expansion tank is also called a *reservoir*. It is partly

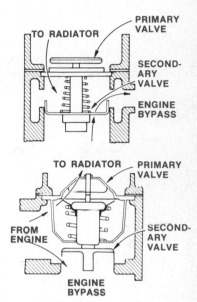

Fig. 16-11
Blocking bypass thermostats.

Fig. 16-12
Radiator pressure cap. (*American Motors Corporation*)

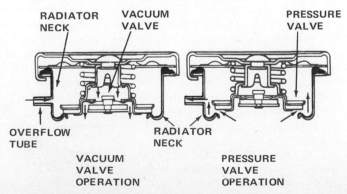

Fig. 16-13
A sealed cooling system.

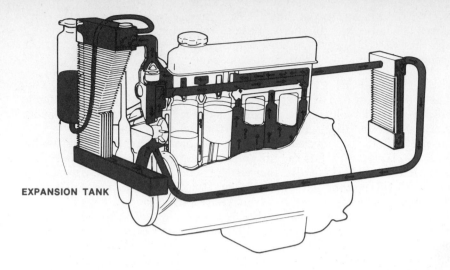

EXPANSION TANK

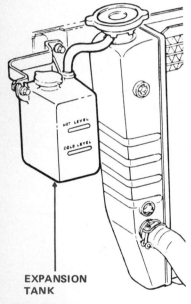

EXPANSION
TANK

Fig. 16-14
An expansion tank, also called
a constant-full reservoir, for a
cooling system.

filled with coolant and connected to the overflow tube in the radiator neck (Fig. 16-12). As the coolant is heated, it expands and the pressure in the cooling system goes up. When the pressure reaches the specified value, it pushes the pressure valve open, as shown to the right in Fig. 16-12. Enough coolant then flows into the expansion tank to prevent further pressure increase. When the engine cools off, the coolant in the cooling system contracts. This produces a partial vacuum in the cooling system. Now, the vacuum valve in the radiator cap opens (left in Fig. 16-12). Coolant from the expansion tank flows back into the radiator. The entire operation works to keep the cooling system filled with coolant at all times. Figure 16-14 shows how the expansion tank is connected to the radiator. Coolant level is checked by looking at the level in the expansion tank. The radiator cap is not removed to check coolant level on cars with a cooling-system expansion tank. You can see the level marks in Fig. 16-14.

16-14 CAR HEATER

Heat from the coolant is used by the car heating system to heat the car interior. The simplest version of the system is shown in Fig. 16-1. It consists of a heater radiator, located in the passenger compartment, that is connected by two hoses to the engine cooling system. Hot coolant flows through the hoses and the heater radiator. A small electric fan forces air through the heater radiator. The air absorbs heat from the heater radiator and warms up the passenger compartment.

A more complex car heater is shown in Fig. 16-15. The principle is the same as for the heater described above. Hot coolant from the engine circulates through a small heater radiator. An electric fan circulates air from the passenger compartment through the heater radiator. The system shown in Fig. 16-15 also includes a defrosting arrangement. The driver can operate controls that will direct the heated air into the passenger compartment. Or the heated air can be directed against the windshield to melt frost or evaporate mist that has formed there.

In some cars the heater is automatically controlled. It usually works with the air-conditioning system to maintain the desired temperature in summer or winter.

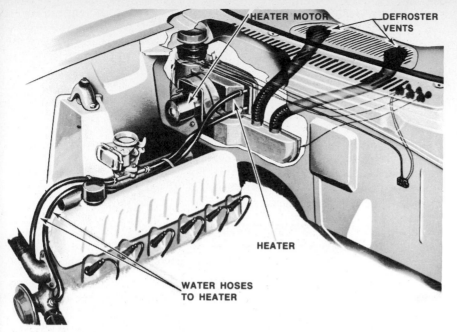

Fig. 16-15
A car heater system. Hot water from the engine cooling system circulates through a small radiator. The fan blows air through the radiator. (*Ford Motor Company*)

HEATER MOTOR

DEFROSTER VENTS

HEATER

WATER HOSES TO HEATER

16-15 ANTIFREEZE SOLUTIONS

Water freezes at 32°F [0°C]. If water freezes in the engine cooling system, it stops coolant circulation. Some parts of the engine will overheat, and this could seriously damage the engine. What is worse, when water freezes, it expands. Water freezing in the cylinder block could expand enough to actually crack the block. Water freezing in the radiator could split the radiator seams. Both conditions cause serious damage. A cracked cylinder block cannot be repaired satisfactorily. A split radiator is also hard to repair.

Freezing of the cooling system can seriously damage the engine. To prevent freezing, antifreeze is added to the water. A mixture that is about one-half water and one-half antifreeze will not freeze even if the temperature reaches −34°F [−38°C]. It seldom gets that cold anywhere in the United States. Higher concentrations of antifreeze in water will prevent freeze-up of the coolant at temperatures as low as −84°F [−64°C].

The most commonly used antifreeze is ethylene glycol. Some antifreeze compounds also plug small leaks in the cooling-system radiator. These antifreeze compounds contain tiny plastic beads or inorganic fibers. They circulate freely with the coolant. If a leak develops, the beads or fibers jam in the leak and plug it. They will not help if the holes are too large.

NOTE

The beads or fibers will not stop leaks in hoses, cylinder-head gaskets, or water-pump seals.

Antifreeze solutions also provide corrosion protection. Compounds are added that fight corrosion inside the engine water jackets and the radiator.

181

Antifreeze solutions should be used year-round in the engine cooling system. One recommendation is that the cooling system be drained, flushed with plain water, and filled with a fresh mixture of antifreeze and water. This should be done every two years.

16-16 TEMPERATURE INDICATORS

There are two kinds of temperature indicators: lights and a gauge. The light system includes a light that comes on when the engine temperature goes too high. This is a warning signal to the driver that something is wrong and that the engine should be stopped before any serious damage occurs. The other system has a gauge on the car instrument panel. A needle or pointer moves across the face of the gauge to show the actual temperature of the coolant in the engine. There's more about temperature indicators in Chap. 25.

CHECK UP ON YOURSELF

Now you have finished the chapter on engine cooling systems. Check up on yourself to find out how well you understand what you have studied by answering the questions that follow.

1. What shuts off the circulation of coolant to the radiator when the engine is cold?
2. How many valves are there in a blocking bypass thermostat? What are their names?
3. How many valves are there in the radiator pressure cap? What are their names?
4. What is the boiling point of water at a pressure of 15 psi [103 kPa] above normal air pressure?
5. What is the purpose of pressurizing the cooling system?

ANSWERS

1. The thermostat (Sec. 16-10). 2. Two: the primary valve and the secondary valve (Sec. 16-11). 3. Two: the pressure relief valve and the vacuum valve (Sec. 16-12). 4. 260°F [127°C] (Sec. 16-12). 5. To increase its efficiency. The higher the pressure, the higher the coolant temperature and the more rapidly the heat can be carried away from the engine (Sec. 16-12).

CHAPTER SEVENTEEN
GASOLINE

After studying this chapter, you should be able to:

1. Describe the composition of gasoline and the additives that go into it.
2. Explain what volatility is and how it affects engine operation.
3. Discuss engine detonation and what is done to prevent it.
4. Explain why lead has been removed from some gasolines.
5. Explain the relationship between compression ratio and detonation.

The most common fuel used in automobile engines is gasoline. However, some automobiles, trucks, and buses have diesel engines that require fuel oil. In this chapter we will talk about gasoline fuel and the systems that use gasoline.

17-1 PROPERTIES OF GASOLINE

Gasoline is a *hydrocarbon* (HC). That is, gasoline is made up of mostly *hydrogen* and *carbon*. These two elements readily unite with oxygen, a common element that makes up about 20 percent of the air. When hydrogen unites with oxygen, water is formed. (The chemical formula for water is H_2O.) When carbon unites with oxygen, carbon monoxide (CO) and carbon dioxide (CO_2) are formed.

If the gasoline in an engine burned completely, only water and carbon dioxide would remain. The trouble is that perfect combustion never happens. Not all the gasoline burns completely. As a result, hydrocarbon and carbon monoxide come out of the tail pipe to pollute the air.

Chapter 26 tells more about air pollution and automotive emission controls. But right now, let's find out more about gasoline.

17-2 SOURCE OF GASOLINE

Gasoline is made from crude oil, from which engine lubricating oil is also made. The crude oil goes through a process called refining. From the refining process come gasoline, lubricating oil, grease, fuel oil, and many other products.

During the refining process, several compounds, called *additives*, are added to gasoline to give it the characteristics of good gasoline. Good gasoline should have

1. Proper volatility, which determines how quickly gasoline vaporizes
2. Resistance to spark knock, or detonation
3. Oxidation inhibitors, which prevent formation of gum in the fuel system
4. Antirust agents, which prevent rusting of metal parts in the fuel system
5. Anti-icers, which fight carburetor icing and fuel-line freezing
6. Detergents, which help keep the carburetor clean
7. Dye for identification

Let's talk about volatility and antiknock first.

17-3 VOLATILITY

After gasoline is mixed with air in the carburetor, the gasoline must vaporize quickly, before it enters the engine cylinders. If the gasoline is slow to vaporize, tiny drops of liquid gasoline will enter the cylinders. Because these drops do not burn, some of the fuel is wasted. It goes out the tail pipe and helps create smog. Also, the gasoline drops tend to wash the lubricating oil off the cylinder walls. This increases the wear on the cylinder walls, piston rings, and pistons.

The ease with which gasoline vaporizes is called its *volatility*. A high-volatility gasoline vaporizes very quickly. A low-volatility gasoline vaporizes slowly. A good gasoline should have just the right amount of volatility for the temperature. If the gasoline is too volatile, it will vaporize in the fuel pump. The result will be a condition called *vapor lock,* which prevents the flow of gasoline to the carburetor. Vapor lock causes the engine to stall from lack of fuel.

17-4 ANTIKNOCK

Spark knock also is called *detonation*. If you have ever been in a car that had detonation, you know the sound. The engine pings, usually under light load. It sounds like someone is tapping on the cylinder walls with a hammer. Look at Fig. 17-1. The horizontal row at the top of the figure shows what happens during normal combustion. The fuel charge—the mixture of air and fuel—starts burning as soon as the spark occurs at the spark plug. The flame sweeps smoothly and evenly across the combustion chamber, much like a balloon being blown up.

Fig. 17-1
Normal combustion without detonation is shown in the horizontal row on top. The fuel charge burns smoothly from beginning to end, providing an even, powerful thrust to the piston. Detonation is shown in the horizontal row on the bottom. The last part of the fuel explodes, or burns, almost instantaneously, to produce spark knock or detonation. (*General Motors Corporation*)

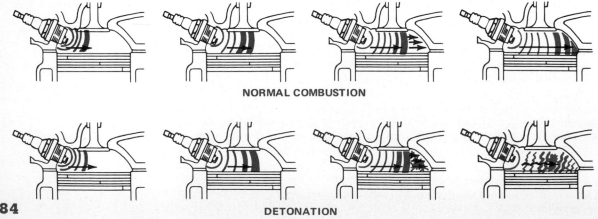

NORMAL COMBUSTION

DETONATION

Now look at the horizontal row at the bottom. The spark starts combustion in the same way. However, before the flame can reach the far side of the combustion chamber, the last part of the charge explodes. The result is a very quick increase in pressure. This is known as detonation, and it gives off a pinging sound.

Detonation can ruin an engine, because the heavy shocks on the piston put a great strain on the engine parts. Continued detonation can cause pistons to chip and parts to break. So detonation must be avoided.

Gasoline refiners have various ways to make gasoline that does not detonate easily. A gasoline that detonates easily is called a *low-octane* gasoline. A gasoline that resists detonation is called a *high-octane* gasoline.

17-5 INCREASING THE OCTANE
One way to increase the octane is to change the refining process. Another way is to add a small amount of tetraethyl lead, also known as "ethyl" or "tel." This additive tends to prevent the last part of the fuel charge from detonating. However, there are two problems with using tetraethyl lead.

One problem is that when gasoline containing tel is burned, some of the lead gets into the air. Lead is a poison, and breathing air containing lead can cause lead poisoning. Lead poisoning can cause illness and death. The other problem is that the lead keeps exhaust emission controls from working as they should. These are two reasons why gasoline without lead is now required for most new cars.

17-6 TWO KINDS OF GASOLINE
One of the emission controls, which we discuss in detail in Chap. 26 is called a *catalytic converter*. The exhaust gases from the engine flow through this device. It reduces the amount of unburned gasoline vapor (HC) and carbon monoxide (CO) in the exhaust gases. However, it will stop doing its job if leaded gasoline is used in the engine. That is the reason most service stations now have pumps labeled "No Lead" or "Unleaded." These pumps sell gasoline without lead for cars requiring it. The other pumps sell leaded gasoline with various octane ratings.

17-7 COMPRESSION RATIOS AND DETONATION
Over the years the compression ratios of automobile engines have gone up. The reason is that higher compression ratios give engines more power. Compression ratio is the amount that the air-fuel mixture is compressed on the compression stroke. The more the air-fuel mixture is compressed, the higher the compression ratio is.

But a high compression ratio can cause a problem because it increases the temperature of the air-fuel mixture. The higher heat of compression may cause the remaining air-fuel mixture to explode before normal combustion is completed. This must not happen because it causes detonation. The compression ratio must be kept low enough to make sure that the fuel charge will not ignite from the heat of compression before the proper time. Also, the higher combustion temperatures cause increased amounts of another exhaust-gas pollutant, nitrogen oxides (NO_x).

17-8 REDUCING COMPRESSION RATIOS

Increasing the combustion temperature increases the formation of NO_x. To have cleaner air, it is desirable to reduce the combustion temperature. One method is to reduce compression ratios. A lower compression ratio means lower combustion temperatures. Then less NO_x is formed during the combustion process. It is for this reason that in recent years engine compression ratios have been reduced compared with those used during the 1960s. This has also reduced engine performance and fuel economy. Other methods of lowering combustion temperature are also used. These are discussed in Chap. 26 and 27 on emission controls.

CHECK UP ON YOURSELF

Let's find out how much you understand about what you have studied in this chapter. Answer the following questions to see if you really know about gasoline and combustion.

1. If gasoline burned completely, what would come out of the tail pipe?
2. What does "volatility" mean?
3. If your car has vapor lock, do you need a gasoline with higher or lower volatility?
4. If the last part of the compressed air-fuel mixture explodes before the flame reaches it, what is the result?
5. What are two ways to raise the octane of gasoline?
6. Why do service stations have gas pumps labeled "No Lead"?

ANSWERS

1. Only water and carbon dioxide (Sec. 17-1). 2. The ease with which a liquid vaporizes (Sec. 17-3). 3. A low-volatility gasoline (Sec. 17-3). 4. Detonation or ping (Sec. 17-4). 5. Change the refining process or add tetraethyl lead to the gasoline (Sec. 17-5). 6. Because cars with catalytic converters must use no-lead gasoline (Sec. 17-6).

CHAPTER EIGHTEEN
AUTOMOTIVE FUEL SYSTEMS USING CARBURETORS

After studying this chapter, you should be able to:
1. Explain the difference between carbureted fuel systems and fuel-injection systems.
2. List the component parts in the carbureted fuel system and the purpose and operation of each, including the fuel pump, fuel filter, air cleaner, and vapor-return line.
3. Describe the purpose, construction, and operation of the carburetor, including the six basic carburetor systems.
4. Explain how the variable-venturi carburetor works.

18-1 TWO FUEL SYSTEMS

For many years, the gasoline-engine fuel system has used a carburetor. The carburetor is a mixing device which mixes air and gasoline vapor in the proper ratios to produce a combustible mixture (Fig. 18-1). This mixture flows from the carburetor through the intake manifold to the engine cylinders, as shown in Fig. 18-1.

Now a second type of fuel system is being installed on some engines. This is the fuel-injection system (Fig. 18-2). In this system, the carburetor is replaced by a throttle body which controls the amount of air moving into the intake manifold. The intake manifold has a series of injectors. The injector sprays a metered amount of gasoline into the intake manifold opposite the intake valve (Fig. 18-3). There the air and fuel mix to form the air-fuel mixture. When the intake valve opens, this air-fuel mixture enters the cylinder.

The basic difference between the two systems is where the gasoline enters the air. In the carburetor, the gasoline enters the air as it passes through the carburetor. In the fuel-injection system, the gasoline is sprayed into the air in the intake manifold. We cover the fuel-injection system in the next chapter.

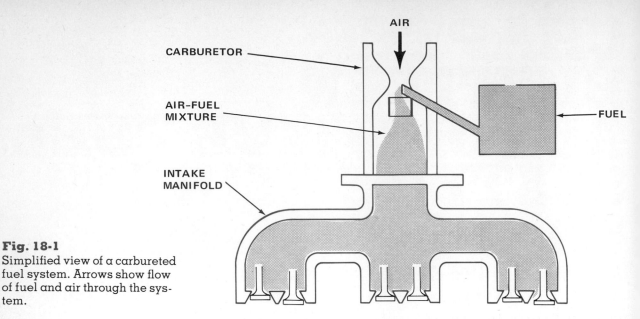

Fig. 18-1
Simplified view of a carbureted
fuel system. Arrows show flow
of fuel and air through the system.

18-2 THE CARBURETED FUEL SYSTEM

The carbureted fuel system is made up of

1. The fuel tank, which stores the liquid gasoline
2. The fuel filter, which filters out dirt particles from the gasoline
3. The fuel pump, which delivers the gasoline from the tank to the carburetor
4. The carburetor, which mixes the gasoline with air and delivers the combustible mixture to the engine
5. The intake manifold, which delivers the air-fuel mixture from the carburetor to the engine cylinders
6. The fuel lines between the tank and the fuel pump and between the fuel pump and the carburetor

A carbureted fuel system for an automobile with a V-8 engine is shown in Fig. 18-4.

18-3 FUEL TANK

The fuel tank is normally located at the rear of the car. It is made of plastic or sheet metal and has two main openings. Gasoline enters the

Fig. 18-2
Simplified view of a fuel-injection system.

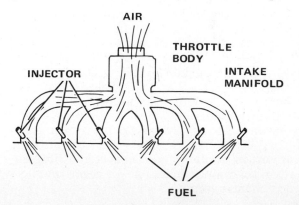

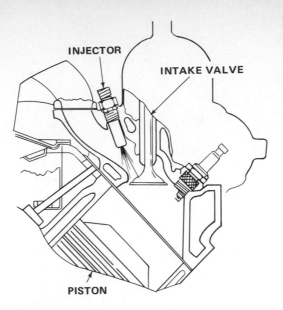

Fig. 18-3
Simplified view showing the method of injecting fuel into the intake manifold just back of the intake valve.

INJECTOR

INTAKE VALVE

PISTON

tank through one opening and leaves the tank through the other opening. Cars manufactured since 1970 have an added system that prevents the escape of gasoline vapors from the fuel tank. It is called the *evaporative control* system. In this system, an extra connection to the gasoline tank sends any fuel vapors to a charcoal canister or to the engine crankcase. The vapors cannot get out of the car and pollute the air. We cover emission control devices in Chap. 26.

18-4 FUEL FILTER
The fuel system has a fuel filter. The filter is made of special paper or other material that lets gasoline through while trapping water and

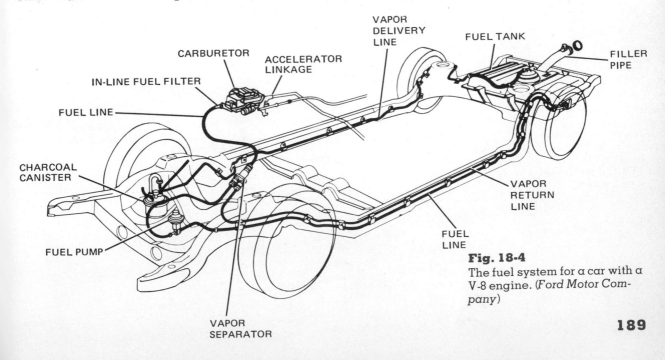

CARBURETOR

IN-LINE FUEL FILTER

FUEL LINE

ACCELERATOR LINKAGE

VAPOR DELIVERY LINE

FUEL TANK

FILLER PIPE

CHARCOAL CANISTER

VAPOR RETURN LINE

FUEL LINE

FUEL PUMP

VAPOR SEPARATOR

Fig. 18-4
The fuel system for a car with a V-8 engine. (*Ford Motor Company*)

Fig. 18-5
Cutaway view of an in-line
fuel filter that shows the magnet which picks up any small
metal particles in the fuel.
(*Ford Motor Company*)

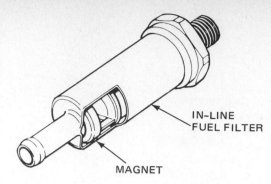

IN-LINE
FUEL FILTER

MAGNET

dirt. Some filters, as shown in Fig. 18-5, are threaded into the carburetor and connected to the fuel line. Other filters are located in the
carburetor, as shown in Fig. 18-6. Some filters contain a small magnet
to trap any metal particles in the fuel, as shown in Fig. 18-5.

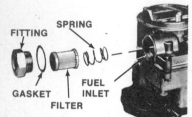

SPRING

FITTING

GASKET

FILTER

FUEL
INLET

Fig. 18-6
The fuel filter located in the
carburetor. (*Buick Motor Division of General Motors Corporation*)

18-5 FUEL PUMP

The fuel pump is mounted on the engine. Its job is to draw gasoline
from the fuel tank and deliver it to the carburetor. The essential parts
of the fuel pump are two one-way valves and a flexible diaphragm (Fig.
18-7). The diaphragm is alternately pulled up and pushed down. This
action alternately produces a vacuum and then pressure in the gasoline chamber of the pump. When the diaphragm is pulled up (Fig.
18-7), the partial vacuum that is created opens the inlet valve. Gasoline flows from the fuel tank, past the inlet valve, and into the gasoline
chamber below the diaphragm. Next, the diaphragm is pushed down
by the spring pressure, producing pressure in the gasoline chamber
(Fig. 18-8). This pressure pushes the inlet valve closed and pushes the
outlet valve open. Then the pressure forces the gasoline out of the gasoline chamber. The gasoline flows through the fuel line to the carburetor.

What pulls the diaphragm up? A rocker arm that rests on an eccentric, or special fuel-pump lobe on the camshaft. As the camshaft ro-

Fig. 18-7
When the eccentric rotates so
that it pushes the rocker arm
down, the arm pulls the diaphragm up. This pulls fuel into
the space under the dia-
phragm. The inlet valve opens
to let in the fuel.

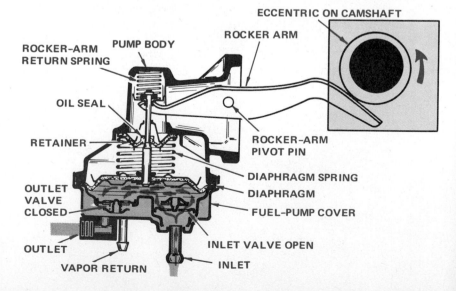

ECCENTRIC ON CAMSHAFT

ROCKER ARM

ROCKER-ARM
RETURN SPRING

PUMP BODY

OIL SEAL

RETAINER

ROCKER-ARM
PIVOT PIN

DIAPHRAGM SPRING

OUTLET
VALVE
CLOSED

DIAPHRAGM

FUEL-PUMP COVER

OUTLET

VAPOR RETURN

INLET VALVE OPEN

INLET

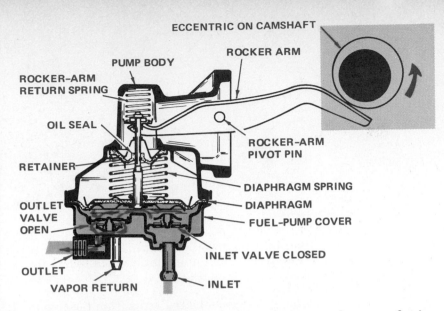

ECCENTRIC ON CAMSHAFT

ROCKER ARM

PUMP BODY

ROCKER-ARM
RETURN SPRING

OIL SEAL

RETAINER

OUTLET
VALVE
OPEN

OUTLET

VAPOR RETURN

ROCKER-ARM
PIVOT PIN

DIAPHRAGM SPRING

DIAPHRAGM

FUEL-PUMP COVER

INLET VALVE CLOSED

INLET

Fig. 18-8
When the eccentric rotates to allow the rocker arm to move up under it, the diaphragm is released. Now the spring pushes down on the diaphragm, creating pressure on the fuel under it. This pressure closes the inlet valve and opens the outlet valve. Now fuel can flow to the carburetor.

tates, the lobe pushes down against the fuel-pump rocker arm, forcing it to pivot. When one end of the rocker arm is pushed down, the other end of the rocker arm pulls up on the diaphragm. Then the lobe moves away from the rocker arm. Now the heavy diaphragm return spring takes over and pushes the diaphragm down.

Study Figs. 18-7 and 18-8 so you can see how the rotation of the camshaft and the movement of the rocker arm cause the pumping action.

18-6 VAPOR-RETURN LINE

Many cars have a vapor-return line. This line allows vapor that has formed in the fuel pump to return to the fuel tank. Figure 18-9 is a view from the top of a car frame, showing the location of the fuel tank, the fuel line, and the vapor-return line. In Figs. 18-7 and 18-8 you can see where the vapor-return line is connected to the fuel pump.

Why is the vapor-return line important? Vapor can form from the combination of vacuum and heat. Gasoline vaporizes more easily in a partial vacuum. The fuel pump, located on the engine, creates a partial vacuum and gets very hot. Therefore vapor can form. If vapor forms, the fuel pump can send the vapor back through the vapor-return line to the fuel tank. If vapor remains in the fuel pump, vapor lock can result. Vapor lock prevents normal pump action and keeps the carburetor

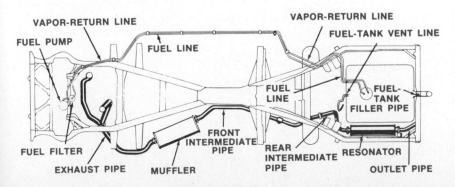

VAPOR-RETURN LINE

FUEL PUMP

FUEL LINE

VAPOR-RETURN LINE

FUEL-TANK VENT LINE

FUEL
LINE

FUEL-
TANK
FILLER PIPE

FUEL FILTER

FRONT
INTERMEDIATE
PIPE

EXHAUST PIPE

MUFFLER

REAR
INTERMEDIATE
PIPE

RESONATOR

OUTLET PIPE

Fig. 18-9
The location of the vapor-return line. Only the frame and part of the fuel system are shown. (*Cadillac Motor Car Division of General Motors Corporation*)

191

Fig. 18-10

A combination fuel filter and vapor separator. It filters the fuel and allows fuel vapor to return to the fuel tank through the vapor-return line. (*Chrysler Corporation*)

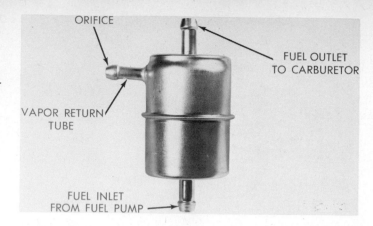

from getting enough gasoline. When this happens, the engine stalls from lack of fuel. The automotive fuel pump is designed to handle liquid fuel only. Pumping stops when a large quantity of vapor gets in the pump.

Actually, the fuel pump keeps fuel circulating from the fuel tank, through the fuel pump, through the vapor-return line, and then back to the fuel tank. Since the fuel is cool, it helps cool the fuel pump so that vapor has less chance to form.

18-7 FILTER SEPARATOR

Some cars have a combination fuel filter and vapor separator located between the fuel pump and the carburetor, as shown in Fig. 18-10. Gasoline from the fuel pump enters the filter separator through the inlet tube and exits through the outlet tube. The fuel is filtered, and if there are vapor bubbles, they enter the return tube. The return tube is connected to the vapor-return line so that the vapor goes back to the fuel tank.

18-8 ELECTRIC FUEL PUMPS

Electric fuel pumps use electricity to draw fuel from the fuel tank and deliver it to the carburetor. There are several kinds of electric fuel pumps. One kind is installed inside the fuel tank. Figure 18-11 shows

Fig. 18-11

The location of the electric fuel pump in the fuel tank. It is mounted on the same support as the fuel-gauge tank unit. (*Chevrolet Motor Division of General Motors Corporation*)

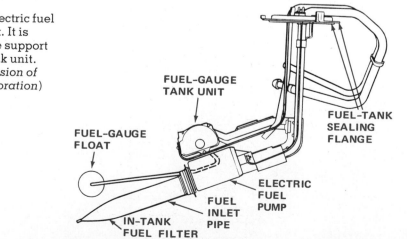

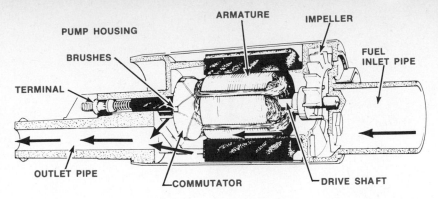

Fig. 18-12
A cutaway view of the tank-mounted electric fuel pump.

PUMP HOUSING
BRUSHES
TERMINAL
ARMATURE
IMPELLER
FUEL INLET PIPE
OUTLET PIPE
COMMUTATOR
DRIVE SHAFT

the mounting arrangement. The fuel pump is mounted on the same support that holds the fuel gauge, which we talk about later. This kind of electric fuel pump has a small electric motor that drives an impeller. The impeller has a series of blades that force the fuel out through the outlet pipe as the impeller spins. Figure 18-12 is a partial cutaway view of the fuel pump.

Another type of electric fuel pump is shown in Fig. 18-13. This unit has an electromagnet. When the ignition switch is turned on, the electromagnet is connected to the car battery. See Chap. 20 for more on electromagnets and Chap. 21 for more on batteries. When the electromagnet is connected to the battery, it pulls on an iron armature. The armature is a flat piece of iron. When the electromagnet pulls on the armature, the armature moves. The armature pulls down on a metal bellows, which produces a partial vacuum in the bellows. In Fig. 18-13 notice that there are two valves above the bellows—an inlet

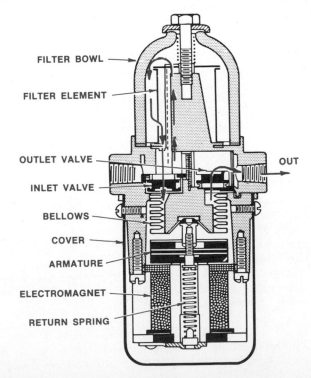

Fig. 18-13
A sectional view of an electric fuel pump of the type that is connected in the fuel line between the fuel tank and the carburetor.

FILTER BOWL
FILTER ELEMENT
OUTLET VALVE
INLET VALVE
BELLOWS
COVER
ARMATURE
ELECTROMAGNET
RETURN SPRING
OUT

Fig. 18-14
A carburetor air cleaner of the
type with a paper element.
(Chrysler Corporation)

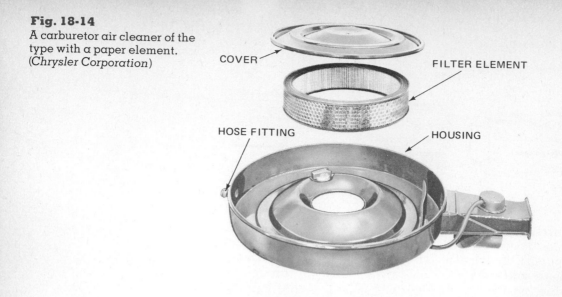

COVER

FILTER ELEMENT

HOSE FITTING

HOUSING

valve and an outlet valve. The partial vacuum opens the inlet valve
and pulls fuel into the bellows.

The downward movement of the armature disconnects the electromagnet from the battery. The electromagnet loses its electricity and
thus its magnetism. It can no longer pull on the armature. So the armature return spring pushes the armature up. This produces a
pressure in the bellows, which closes the inlet valve and opens the outlet valve. Fuel is then pushed into the carburetor.

Compare the pictures of the different fuel pumps. You can see that
the electric fuel pump works the same way as the fuel pump operated
by the camshaft. The only difference is how the vacuum and pressure
in the pump chamber are produced.

18-9 AIR CLEANER

Air mixes with gasoline vapor to make the combustible mixture the
engine needs for power. The engine uses a lot of air when it runs. An
engine can take in up to 100,000 cubic feet of air every 1000 car miles
[2,848,000 L per 1600 km]. That is a lot of air—enough to fill 100
rooms, each measuring 10 feet long by 10 feet wide by 10 feet high [3.1
by 3.1 by 3.1 m]. Air has dirt in it. And 100,000 cubic feet [2,848,000 L]
of air has a lot of dirt! Dirt can ruin an engine and must be kept out.
The air cleaner does this job.

Figure 18-14 shows an air cleaner. It is mounted on top of the carburetor. All air going through the carburetor and into the engine must
first go through the air cleaner. The air cleaner has a filter element
made of fiber, special paper, or spongelike polyurethane. The filter element lets the air through but traps the dirt particles. After long use,
the filter element becomes filled with dirt and must be cleaned or replaced. The air cleaner also reduces the noise made by the air entering
the engine. In addition, the air cleaner helps prevent fires in the carburetor, should the engine backfire.

18-10 THERMOSTATIC AIR CLEANER

The heat-control valve in the exhaust manifold is described in Chap.
12. Its purpose is to put heat into the air going into the carburetor

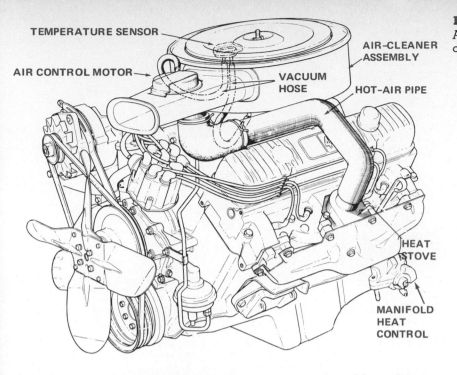

TEMPERATURE SENSOR

AIR CONTROL MOTOR

VACUUM HOSE

AIR-CLEANER ASSEMBLY

HOT-AIR PIPE

HEAT STOVE

MANIFOLD HEAT CONTROL

Fig. 18-15
A heated air system installed on a V-8 engine.

when the engine is cold. The heat helps to vaporize the cold gasoline, so that the cold engine runs better.

The heat-control valve works fine, but it does not work fast enough. Today, the emission laws require faster action. The reason is that when an engine is cold, only part of the fuel burns. The exhaust gases have too much hydrocarbon and carbon monoxide. To get faster action, engines now have heated-air systems which include air cleaners with thermostats. Figure 18-15 shows an engine with this system. Notice that the system includes more than just a thermostat. The system has a hot-air pipe, which is connected to a heat stove above the exhaust manifold. It also has a vacuum hose. Let's see how the system works.

When the engine is cold, the thermostat closes a damper, which shuts off the air passage from the engine compartment. Now all the air to the carburetor must pass through the hot-air pipe connected to the heat stove. In this way, hot air is supplied to the carburetor almost as soon as the engine starts. The fuel vaporizes more completely, and more of it is burned. The exhaust gas is much cleaner because it contains less hydrocarbon and carbon monoxide.

As the engine warms up, the thermostat in the air cleaner begins to open the damper. Air is taken from the engine compartment, not from the heat stove. When the engine is warm, no additional heat is needed to ensure good fuel vaporization. The thermostatic air cleaner is discussed in more detail in Sec. 16-7.

18-11 AUXILIARY AIR INLET

Some air cleaners have another vacuum motor that opens and closes an extra hole in the air-cleaner housing. This type of air cleaner is shown in Fig. 18-16. The vacuum motor operates if a partial vacuum develops in the air cleaner. During cold-engine acceleration, not

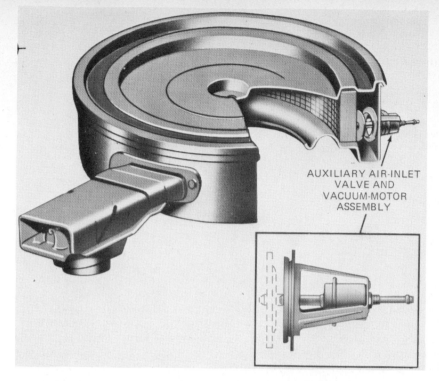

AUXILIARY AIR-INLET
VALVE AND
VACUUM-MOTOR
ASSEMBLY

enough air may get through the heat stove for the thermostatic air cleaner (Sec. 18-10). When this happens, the partial vacuum operates the vacuum motor, and it opens the auxiliary air-inlet passage. Now extra air goes into the air cleaner, and the engine runs properly.

CHECK UP ON YOURSELF

The fuel tank, the fuel pump, and the air cleaner are three important components of the fuel system. Now find out how well you understand the jobs of these components by answering these questions.

1. What are the two basic types of automotive fuel systems?
2. What is the basic difference between the two fuel systems?
3. What is the purpose of the fuel pump?
4. What are the names of the valves in the fuel pump?
5. To what is the inner end of the rocker arm in the fuel pump connected?
6. What is the purpose of the vapor-return line?
7. In the heated-air system, where does the air come from when the engine is cold?
8. What is the name of the device that supplies extra air to the carburetor when the throttle is wide open on a cold engine?

ANSWERS

1. Carburetor (carbureted) and fuel-injection (Sec. 18-1). **2.** Point at which the gasoline enters the air (Sec. 18-1). **3.** To pump fuel from the fuel tank to the carburetor (Sec. 18-5). **4.** Inlet and outlet valves (Sec. 18-5). **5.** To the pump diaphragm (Sec. 18-5). **6.** Return vapor from fuel pump to fuel tank; also, help prevent vapor lock (Sec. 18-6). **7.** From the heat stove on exhaust manifold (Sec. 18-10). **8.** The auxiliary air inlet (Sec. 18-11).

18-12 CARBURETOR TYPES

There are two basic types of carburetor: fixed-venturi and variable-venturi. The *venturi* is the restricted place in the air passage through which the air must flow. As we explain later, this restriction produces a partial vacuum which causes a fuel nozzle to discharge gasoline. The gasoline mixes with the air to produce the combustible mixture that the engine needs to run.

Most carburetors installed on engines made in the United States are of the fixed-venturi type. We will discuss these first. Many imported cars and an increasing number of cars made in the United States are using the variable-venturi (VV) type of carburetor. We discuss these later in the chapter.

18-13 CARBURETOR OPERATION

The carburetor, regardless of type, is a sort of mixing valve. In the carburetor gasoline is mixed with air. The mixture then goes through the intake manifold to the engine cylinders. There, the air-fuel mixture is compressed and burned to make the engine run.

The fixed-venturi carburetor is basically an air horn, a fuel nozzle, and a throttle valve (Fig. 18-17). Let's take a look at these three things. The air horn is a round tube, or barrel. The venturi is a narrow section of the air horn. The fuel nozzle is a small tube through which fuel can flow from the float bowl, or reservoir, in the side of the carburetor. The throttle valve is a round disk mounted on a shaft. Figure 18-18 gives you a better idea of what the throttle valve looks like. When the shaft is turned, the throttle valve is tilted. When it is tilted into the position shown by the dotted lines in Fig. 18-18, the throttle valve is open, and air can flow through the air horn freely.

When the throttle valve is tilted into the position shown by solid lines in Fig. 18-18, the throttle valve is closed. Little or no air can get through the air horn. The throttle valve determines how much air gets through the carburetor. It is the amount of air passing through the carburetor that determines how much fuel flows to the cylinders.

18-14 HOW THE THROTTLE IS CONTROLLED

The throttle is connected to the accelerator pedal in the driver's compartment. A typical arrangement is shown in Fig. 18-19. The accelerator pedal is held in the up position by a spring until the driver presses it. When the driver pushes down the pedal, the pressure on the pedal causes the crank to pivot. Then the crank pulls on the cable. The cable consists of a stiff wire enclosed in a flexible metal cover. The wire can slide back and forth in the cover. When the crank pulls on the cable, the wire inside the cable cover pulls on a lever on the carburetor. The lever is attached to the throttle shaft. The pull on the lever causes the shaft to rotate, and the rotation of the shaft turns the throttle valve in the carburetor. The farther down the driver pushes the accelerator pedal, the farther the throttle valve turns in the carburetor.

18-15 VENTURI EFFECT

The venturi causes fuel to flow out of the fuel nozzle when air flows through the carburetor. The reason is that the air has to flow faster through the venturi than through the rest of the carburetor. This faster flow of air produces a partial vacuum in the venturi. The partial vacuum then causes fuel to flow from the fuel nozzle (Fig. 18-20). The

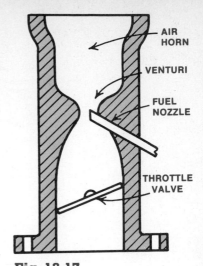

Fig. 18-17
A simple carburetor consisting of an air horn, a fuel nozzle, and a throttle valve.

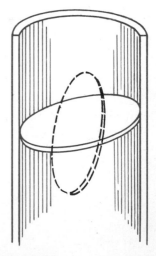

Fig. 18-18
The throttle valve in the air horn of a carburetor. When the throttle is closed, as shown, little air can pass through. But when the throttle is opened, as shown in dashed lines, there is little throttle effect.

197

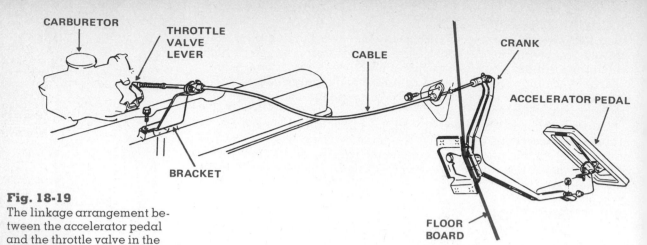

Fig. 18-19
The linkage arrangement between the accelerator pedal and the throttle valve in the carburetor.

more air that flows through the venturi, the greater the vacuum. The greater the vacuum, the more fuel is discharged by the fuel nozzle. There is a relationship between the amount the throttle is open, the amount of air going through the venturi, and the amount of fuel being discharged. This relationship keeps the ratio of air to fuel fairly constant. However, other systems and devices are needed to change the ratio for different operating conditions.

18-15 AIR-FUEL RATIOS
When the engine is started, the air-fuel mixture must be rich. That is, the mixture must have more fuel in it. A mixture of about 9 pounds [4.1 kg] of air to 1 pound [0.45 kg] of fuel, or a ratio of 9:1, is required for starting a cold engine. The reason is that only part of the gasoline vaporizes when the engine is cold. Therefore the engine has to be given more than enough fuel to make sure that enough will vaporize to ensure starting.

When the engine is idling, a less rich mixture is needed—about 12:1. During intermediate-speed, part-throttle operation, a relatively lean mixture of about 15:1 is needed. During high-speed, wide-open-throttle operation, a richer mixture of about 13:1 is needed.

The graph in Fig. 18-21 shows various air-fuel-ratio requirements for different operating conditions. These ratios are only typical. Different engines require different ratios for various operating conditions.

Additional devices and systems are required on the carburetor to produce the changing air-fuel ratios that are needed for different operating conditions.

18-17 CARBURETOR SYSTEMS
The fixed-venturi carburetor has six systems and several devices that provide the correct air-fuel mixture for different operating conditions. These include

1. Float system
2. Idle system
3. Main metering system
4. Power system

198

5. Accelerator-pump system
6. Choke system

Let's look at each system in detail.

18-18 FLOAT SYSTEM

The float system maintains a constant level of gasoline in the float bowl. The fuel nozzle feeds fuel from the float bowl to the air passing through the venturi. If the fuel level in the float bowl were too high, fuel would continue to run out of the fuel nozzle. The air-fuel mixture would be far too rich. Fuel would be wasted, the engine would run poorly or stall, and the exhaust gas would be filled with hydrocarbon and carbon monoxide.

If the fuel level in the float bowl were too low, the vacuum in the venturi would not be able to pull enough fuel out of the float bowl. The mixture would be too lean, and the engine would run poorly or stall.

It is important that the fuel level in the float bowl be held at a constant level (Fig. 18-22). There is a float that is pivoted at one end. The pivot is on the side of the float bowl. At the inlet to the float bowl is a needle valve. When fuel flows to the float bowl, the float rises. This pushes the needle valve into the valve seat in the gasoline inlet. When

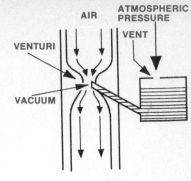

Venturi Effect

Fig. 18-20
Venturi effect. The venturi creates a vacuum when air passes through. Then atmospheric pressure pushes fuel up through the fuel nozzle.

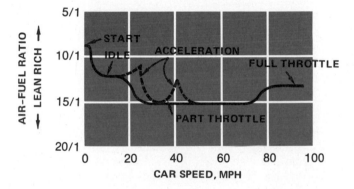

Fig. 18-21
A graph of air-fuel ratios for different car speeds. The graph shows only typical ratios. Car speeds at which the various rates are obtained may vary with different cars. Also, the actual ratios may vary.

the level is high enough, the valve is tightly seated and no additional fuel can enter. When the fuel level drops, the float also drops, allowing the valve to move away from the valve seat. Now more fuel can flow into the float bowl.

In actual operation the float and the needle valve stay in a position that allows just enough fuel to enter the float bowl to maintain a constant level of fuel. In other words, the fuel entering the float bowl just balances the fuel leaving.

Figure 18-23 is a cutaway view of a carburetor, showing an actual float system. Notice that there are two floats connected to a single lever. This lever is pivoted on the side of the float bowl, and its end rests against the end of the needle valve. Many carburetors use only one float.

18-19 IDLE AND LOW-SPEED SYSTEM

When the throttle valve is closed or only slightly open, only a small amount of air can pass through the air horn. With low air speed, there is very little vacuum in the venturi. No fuel will feed from the fuel nozzle. To supply fuel during idle and low speeds, an idle system is built

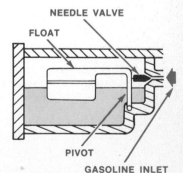

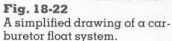

Fig. 18-22
A simplified drawing of a carburetor float system.

Fig. 18-23
A carburetor partly cut away to
show the float system.

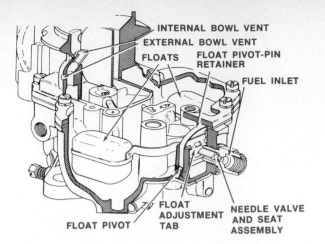

into the carburetor (Fig. 18-24). The system has an opening in the side
of the carburetor below the throttle valve. This hole is called the *idle
port*. In addition to the idle port, there is an idle mixture screw, located
behind the idle port. The port is connected by a passage to the float
bowl.

When the throttle valve is closed and the engine is running, a high
vacuum develops in the intake manifold. The pistons are repeatedly
moving down on their intake strokes, which means they are demand-
ing air-fuel mixture. If the pistons don't get enough air-fuel mixture,
then a vacuum develops. This vacuum is great enough, when the throttle valve is closed, to cause fuel to flow through the fuel passage from
the float bowl to the idle port.

Figure 18-24 shows the idle system in action. If you study this picture, you will see how the air flows down through a passage in the side
of the air horn. The air mixes with the gasoline flowing out of a connecting passage from the float bowl. This mixture moves down to the
idle port and discharges in the lower part of the carburetor. Some air
gets past the throttle valve. This air mixes with the air-fuel mixture

Fig. 18-24
Idle system in a carburetor.
The throttle valve is closed so
that only a small amount of air
can get past it. All fuel is being
fed past the idle adjustment
screw. Arrows show the flow of
air and fuel.

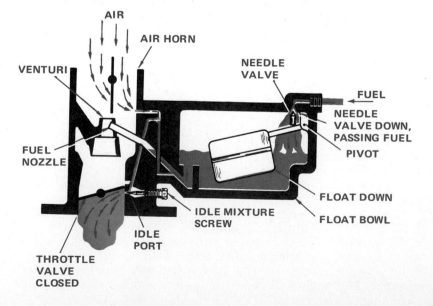

coming from the idle port to form the mixture going to the cylinders.

The idle mixture screw can be turned in or out to change the amount of air-fuel mixture discharging from the idle port. If the screw is turned out, more mixture can discharge. This makes the idle mixture richer. If the screw is turned in, the mixture is made leaner. However, on most carburetors today, the screw has a special cap called an *idle limiter*. It allows only a small adjustment of the screw, which is properly set at the factory. Other carburetors cannot be adjusted after they leave the factory.

18-20 LOW-SPEED OPERATION

If the throttle valve is open just a little for low-speed operation, the edge of the throttle valve moves past the idle port, as shown in Fig. 18-25. More air can flow past the throttle valve now, reducing the vacuum in the intake manifold. So less fuel flows from the idle port. However, the low-speed port now comes into action. The throttle valve has moved past and above the low-speed port. The vacuum in the intake manifold can act on this port as well as on the idle port. Both ports discharge fuel to maintain the required amount of air-fuel mixture.

18-21 MAIN METERING SYSTEM

If the throttle valve is opened farther, more air will flow through. This means that there will be less vacuum in the intake manifold. As a result, the idle and low-speed ports stop discharging fuel. However, with more air flow, there is a vacuum in the venturi. This causes the fuel nozzle to discharge fuel. Therefore, enough fuel enters the carburetor and mixes with the air passing through. Figure 18-26 shows the main metering system in action.

18-22 POWER SYSTEM

When a driver wants full power, the accelerator pedal is pushed to the floor. This causes the throttle valve to open wide. Another system in the carburetor comes into action to deliver additional fuel. This system includes a metering rod and a hole, called the metering-rod jet, in which the rod hangs (Fig. 18-27). Notice that the rod has two diameters. If the rod is raised so that the smaller diameter clears the jet, the result is just the same as though a larger jet had been installed. There is more room for fuel to flow through the jet.

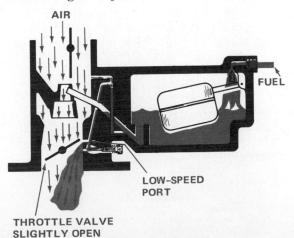

AIR

FUEL

LOW-SPEED PORT

THROTTLE VALVE SLIGHTLY OPEN

Fig. 18-25
Low-speed operation. The throttle valve is slightly open. Fuel is being fed through the low-speed port as well as through the idle port. The dark color is fuel; the light color is air.

201

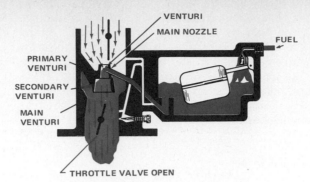

Fig. 18-26
Main metering system in a carburetor. The throttle valve is
open. Fuel is being fed through
the high-speed, or main, nozzle. The dark color is fuel; the
light color is air.

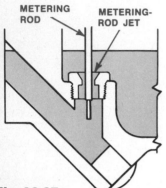

Fig. 18-27
Mechanically operated power
system. When the throttle is
open, as shown, the metering
rod is raised so the smaller diameter of the rod clears the jet.
This allows additional fuel to
flow.

Now let's tie this in with the carburetor (Fig. 18-28). The metering
rod is fastened to the throttle linkage. As the throttle is moved to the
wide-open position, the metering rod is raised. In this position, the metering rod allows more fuel to flow so that full engine power can be
achieved.

The system shown in Fig. 18-28 is a mechanical system. The metering rod is lifted by a mechanical linkage to the throttle. In some carburetors a vacuum piston or diaphragm is used to lift the metering rod.
See Fig. 18-29. In the system shown, a flexible diaphragm is linked to
the metering rod. The space above the diaphragm is connected by a
vacuum passage to the intake manifold. When there is vacuum in the
intake manifold, the vacuum holds the diaphragm up. In this position
the metering rod is up, and the fuel flow is restricted. The up position is
normal for part-throttle operation when the vacuum is fairly high in
the intake manifold.

However, when the throttle is opened wide, the vacuum is lost and
can no longer hold the diaphragm up. A spring pushes the diaphragm
down. At the same time, the metering rod is lowered so that additional
fuel can flow into the carburetor. A richer mixture is delivered to the
engine for full-power operation.

18-23 ACCELERATOR-PUMP SYSTEM

There is another operating condition that needs a richer air-fuel mixture. This condition occurs when the accelerator pedal is pushed down
to increase speed, up to about 30 mph [48 km/h]. To get the power
needed, the engine has to momentarily be fed a richer mixture. The
accelerator pump handles this job. Figure 18-30 shows the system,
which includes a pump that is operated when the throttle is depressed.

Fig. 18-28
A mechanically operated
power system. When the throttle is opened, as shown, the
metering rod is raised. This
allows the smaller diameter of
the rod to clear the jet so that
the additional fuel can flow.

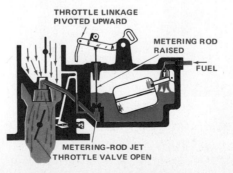

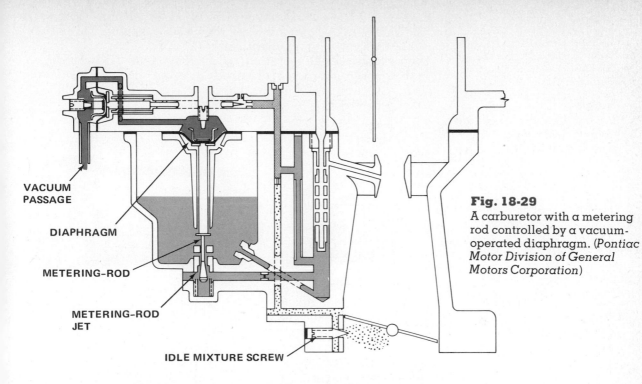

VACUUM
PASSAGE

DIAPHRAGM

METERING-ROD

METERING-ROD
JET

IDLE MIXTURE SCREW

Fig. 18-29
A carburetor with a metering rod controlled by a vacuum-operated diaphragm. (*Pontiac Motor Division of General Motors Corporation*)

The movement causes the pump plunger to be pushed down, as shown in Fig. 18-31. Pushing the pump plunger down forces a shot of fuel out through the pump jet. The fuel discharges into the air-fuel mixture that is moving down the carburetor and enriches the air-fuel mixture.

18-24 CHOKE SYSTEM
When a cold engine is being cranked for starting, extra fuel must be delivered to the engine. The choke does this job. The choke is a round disk located in the air horn, as shown in Fig. 18-32.

When the choke valve is turned to the closed position, as shown in Fig. 18-32, very little air can get past the choke into the air horn. A vacuum develops around the fuel nozzle. During cranking, this vacuum is great enough to cause the fuel nozzle to deliver fuel. This fuel mixes with the air passing through the carburetor to get the engine started.

After the engine starts, the air-fuel mixture must immediately be leaned. In most engines an automatic choke leans the mixture.

18-25 AUTOMATIC CHOKES
An automatic choke is shown in partial cutaway view in Fig. 18-33. It includes a thermostatic spring that winds up or unwinds with changing temperature. When the engine is cold, the spring winds up, closing the choke valve. Then the cold engine gets a rich mixture for starting. As the engine warms up, the thermostatic spring unwinds, opening the choke valve.

During warmup, the choke piston comes into action. When the engine is idling, the piston is pulled down by the intake-manifold vacuum, and the piston opens the choke partly. This prevents too rich an idle mixture. Then, when the throttle is opened for acceleration, the intake-manifold vacuum decreases. This releases the choke piston so that the choke valve moves toward the closed position. This action enriches the mixture for acceleration.

During closed-choke operation, the air-fuel mixture is rich. The result is that more unburned hydrocarbon goes out the tail pipe. To re-

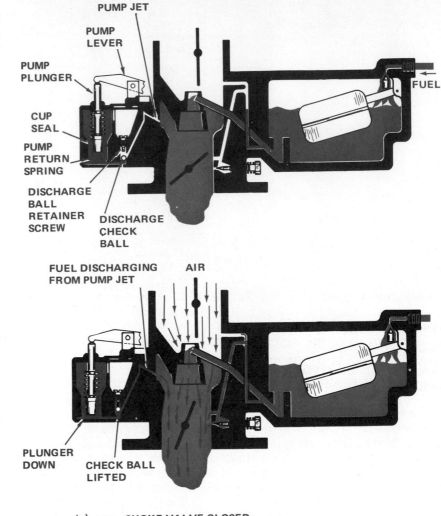

Fig. 18-30
The accelerator-pump system in a carburetor of the type using a pump plunger.

Fig. 18-31
When the throttle is opened, the pump lever pushes the pump plunger down. This forces fuel to flow through the accelerator-pump system and out the jet.

Fig. 18-32
With the choke valve closed, intake-manifold vacuum is introduced into the carburetor air horn, causing the main nozzle to discharge fuel.

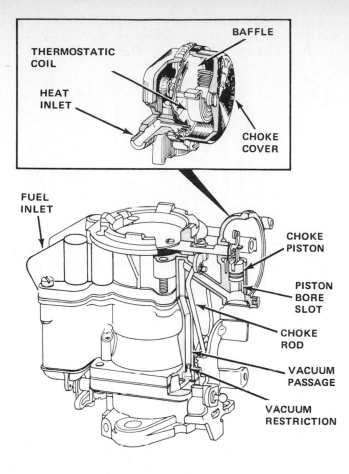

Fig. 18-33
Choke system using a choke piston and thermostatic spring (coil) mounted on the carburetor. (*American Motors Corporation*)

duce the time the choke is closed, some automatic chokes use electric heating elements. The electric heating element speeds up the unchoking action. There is more information on the electric chokes in Chap. 26.

Another type of automatic choke is shown in Fig. 18-34. The thermostat is located in a well on the exhaust manifold. A rod connects the thermostatic coil to the choke valve. This causes faster action because the exhaust-manifold heat does not travel to the coil through a heat tube. Many chokes use a vacuum diaphragm instead of a vacuum piston to pull open the choke valve. A choke of this type is shown in Fig. 18-34.

18-26 FAST IDLE

When the engine is cold, the throttle must be kept partly open so that the engine can idle fast. If the engine slowed down to a normal hot-idle speed, it would stall. To get fast idle with the engine cold, there is a fast-idle cam on the carburetor. This cam is linked to the choke valve. When the engine is cold, the automatic choke holds the choke valve closed. The linkage holds the fast-idle cam in the fast idle position. In this position the linkage has turned the fast-idle cam so that the adjusting screw rests on the high point of the cam. Therefore, the throttle cannot close, and the engine idles fast. Then, as the automatic choke opens the choke valve, the linkage turns the fast-idle cam so that the

Fig. 18-34
Choke system using a vacuum-break diaphragm and a thermostatic spring (coil) mounted in a well in the exhaust manifold. (*Chevrolet Motor Division of General Motors Corporation*)

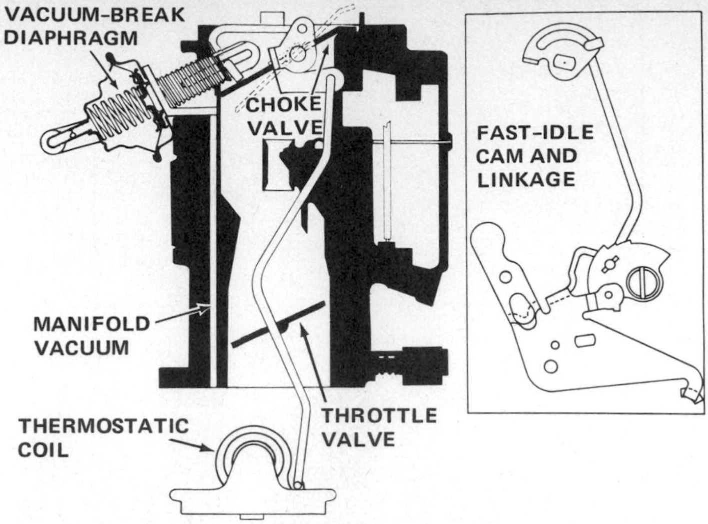

high point moves out from under the adjusting screw. Now the throttle can close to the normal hot-idle position.

18-27 CONTROL DEVICES ON CARBURETORS

Carburetors have other devices to improve driveability, improve fuel economy, and lower air pollution. We describe some of these devices in detail in Chaps. 26 and 27. Here we list them and discuss them briefly.

1. Antidieseling Solenoid

Some engines have a tendency to continue running after the ignition switch is turned off. This is called *run-on,* or *dieseling,* because the engine runs like a diesel, without electric ignition. The carburetors for these engines are equipped with an antidieseling solenoid (Fig. 18-35). When the engine is running normally, the solenoid is connected to the battery. It extends its plunger. The plunger serves as the idle stop and prevents complete closing of the throttle. That is, the throttle cannot close completely. Therefore, normal hot-idle speed results when the driver releases the accelerator pedal. However, when the engine is turned off, the solenoid plunger pulls in. Now the throttle can close completely, shutting off all air flow. The engine stops running.

2. Throttle Return Checks

If the throttle closes too rapidly after the driver releases the accelerator pedal, the air-fuel mixture can be momentarily excessively enriched. This is because the fuel nozzle dribbles fuel for a moment even though the air flow has been shut off. The idle system will also feed a rich air-fuel mixture. This is due to the high vacuum that results when the engine is running fast with the throttle closed. This very rich mixture can cause the engine to stumble or stall. Also, it can damage the catalytic converter. To prevent this, many carburetors are equipped with a throttle-return check (Fig. 18-36). It slows down the throttle closing to prevent the momentary excessive richness.

3. Vacuum Vents

The carburetor and intake manifold have a vacuum in them when the engine is running. This vacuum is used by various other devices on the engine and elsewhere:

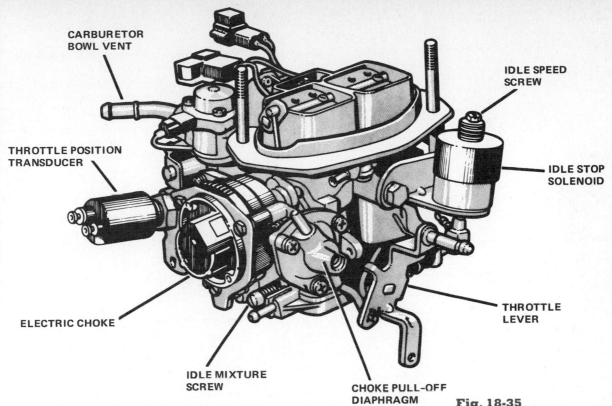

CARBURETOR BOWL VENT

IDLE SPEED SCREW

THROTTLE POSITION TRANSDUCER

IDLE STOP SOLENOID

ELECTRIC CHOKE

THROTTLE LEVER

IDLE MIXTURE SCREW

CHOKE PULL-OFF DIAPHRAGM

Fig. 18-35
Carburetor with an idle-stop (antidieseling) solenoid. (*Chrysler Corporation*)

a. Ignition-distributor vacuum-advance mechanism. This advances the spark during part-throttle operation (Sec. 24-18).

b. Positive crankcase ventilating system. This is a system for ventilating the crankcase without polluting the atmosphere (Sec. 26-4).

c. Evaporative control system. This system traps gasoline vapor from the fuel tank and carburetor float bowl (Sec. 26-5).

d. Thermostatic air cleaner. This system (Sec. 26-7) provides rapid heating of the air entering the carburetor when the engine is cold. This improves cold-engine performance.

e. Exhaust-gas recirculation system. The exhaust-gas recirculation (EGR) system introduces some exhaust gas into the air-fuel mixture going into the engine cylinders. This reduces the formation of one of the air pollutants (NO_x). (See Sec. 26-8.)

CHECK UP ON YOURSELF

You have just completed that part of the chapter which covers fixed-venturi carburetors. Find out how well you understand the details of this type of carburetor by answering these questions.

1. What are the two basic types of carburetor?
2. What are the three basic parts of the fixed-venturi carburetor?
3. What is the venturi effect?
4. Is a 9:1 mixture rich or lean?
5. What happens if the fuel level in the float bowl is too high?
6. What operates the needle valve in the float bowl?

7. When the throttle valve is closed, is the idle port above or below it?
8. What causes the air-fuel mixture to flow from the idle port when the throttle valve is closed?
9. What is the position of the throttle valve when the low-speed port is delivering fuel?
10. What are the two devices in the automatic choke that control the position of the choke valve during cold-engine operation?
11. To what is the linkage from the fast-idle cam connected?
12. What is the device that prevents run-on after the engine is turned off?
13. What is the device that prevents the throttle from closing too fast?

ANSWERS

1. Fixed-venturi and variable-venturi (Sec. 18-12). **2.** Air horn with venturi, fuel nozzle, and throttle valve (Sec. 18-13). **3.** Creates a partial vacuum when air passes through (Sec. 18-15). **4.** Rich (Sec. 18-16). **5.** A very rich mixture results (Sec. 18-18). **6.** Lever on the float in the float bowl (Sec. 18-18).

Fig. 18-36
Carburetor with throttle-return check (dashpot). (*Carter Carburetor Division of ACF Industries*)

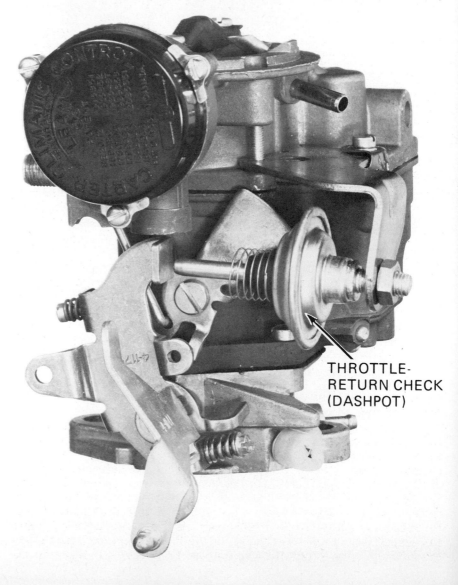

THROTTLE-RETURN CHECK (DASHPOT)

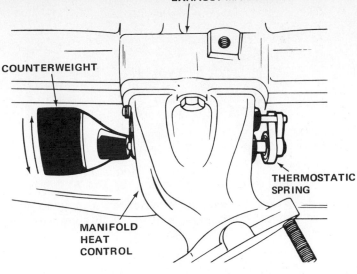

Fig. 18-37
Manifold heat-control valve.
(*Ford Motor Company*)

EXHAUST MANIFOLD

COUNTERWEIGHT

THERMOSTATIC
SPRING

MANIFOLD
HEAT
CONTROL

7. Below the throttle valve (Sec. 18-19). 8. Intake-manifold vacuum (Sec. 18-19). 9. Slightly above the low-speed port (Sec. 18-20). 10. The thermostatic spring and the vacuum piston or diaphragm (Sec. 18-25). 11. To the choke valve (Sec. 18-26). 12. Antidieseling solenoid (Sec. 18-27). 13. Throttle return check (Sec. 18-27).

18-28 MANIFOLD HEAT CONTROL

We have already discussed the importance of vaporizing the fuel during cold-engine operation. If the fuel is not properly vaporized, drops of gasoline will enter the cylinders. They will wash down the cylinder walls and remove the oil, causing the walls, the pistons, and the piston rings to wear fast. In Sec. 18-10 we describe the heated-air system using a thermostatically controlled air cleaner. This air cleaner gets hot air from the heat stove on the exhaust manifold during cold-engine operation.

Now let's take another look at the manifold heat control (Fig. 18-37). It is shown in a cutaway view in Fig. 18-38. The manifold heat-control valve is shown in the closed position to the left in this picture. It is sending the hot exhaust gases up through a passage that surrounds the center of the intake manifold. As the engine warms up, the thermostatic spring unwinds and rotates the heat-control valve into the position shown to the right in Fig. 18-38. In this position, the valve sends the exhaust gases directly into the exhaust pipe, which is connected to the exhaust manifold.

In V-type engines, a different arrangement is necessary, as shown in Fig. 18-39. Here we show a sectional view of the carburetor and intake manifold. The two cylinder heads have been sliced in two at the exhaust valves. Note the exhaust-gas passages through the lower part of the intake manifold and in the two cylinder heads. When the engine is cold, the manifold heat-control valve in one of the exhaust manifolds closes. Now the exhaust gases from that bank of cylinders are forced through the passage in the intake manifold. They quickly heat the intake manifold so that vaporization of the fuel is improved. As the engine warms up, the manifold heat-control valve opens. Now the ex-

209

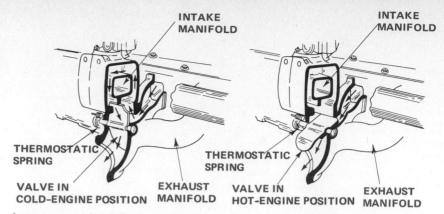

Fig. 18-38
Intake and exhaust manifolds of a six-cylinder, in-line engine cut away so that the location and action of the manifold heat control can be seen. At the left, the heat-control valve is in the cold-engine, or HEAT ON, position, directing hot exhaust gases up and around the intake manifold. (*Ford Motor Company*)

INTAKE MANIFOLD

INTAKE MANIFOLD

THERMOSTATIC SPRING

VALVE IN COLD-ENGINE POSITION

EXHAUST MANIFOLD

THERMOSTATIC SPRING

VALVE IN HOT-ENGINE POSITION

EXHAUST MANIFOLD

haust gases flow in the usual manner to the exhaust pipes connected to the two exhaust manifolds. Figure 12-16 shows a complete exhaust system.

NOTE

Many engines with a thermostatic air cleaner do not have a manifold heat-control valve. It is not needed because the heated-air system adds all the heat necessary to the incoming air-fuel mixture. Heating the air-fuel mixture too much can cause detonation.

18-29 DUAL AND QUAD CARBURETORS
Carburetors with more than a single barrel are used on many engines. More barrels improve driveability. They decrease the tendency of a

Fig. 18-39
The exhaust-gas passage under the intake manifold in a V-8 engine. Note the well in which the carburetor choke thermostat is located. (*Buick Motor Division of General Motors Corporation*)

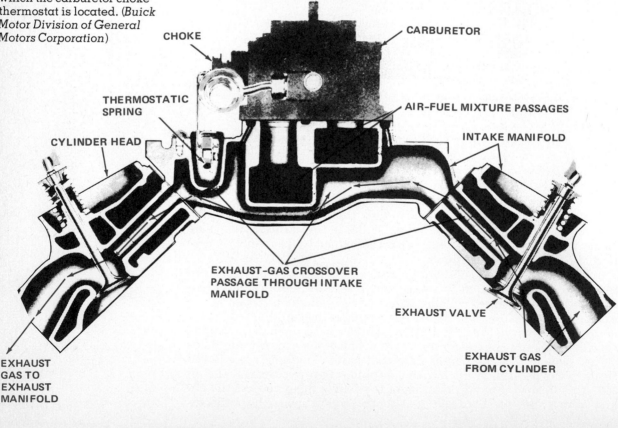

CHOKE

CARBURETOR

THERMOSTATIC SPRING

AIR-FUEL MIXTURE PASSAGES

CYLINDER HEAD

INTAKE MANIFOLD

EXHAUST-GAS CROSSOVER PASSAGE THROUGH INTAKE MANIFOLD

EXHAUST VALVE

EXHAUST GAS FROM CYLINDER

EXHAUST GAS TO EXHAUST MANIFOLD

large single-barrel carburetor to be unresponsive and stumble at low speeds. In addition, more barrels improve air-fuel mixture distribution, thereby reducing exhaust emissions. Adding barrels allows the engine to breathe better. Higher volumetric efficiency and better engine performance result. Volumetric efficiency and engine breathing are explained in Sec. 9-9.

A dual (two-barrel) carburetor is shown from the bottom in Fig. 18-40. Each of the two barrels is, in effect, a complete carburetor. Each barrel feeds half of the cylinders in the engine. Figure 11-13 shows the pattern of air-fuel mixture flow from the two barrels to the eight cylinders of a V-8 engine.

A quad (four-barrel) carburetor is shown from the top in Fig. 18-41. The operation of a quad carburetor is a little different from the operation of a dual carburetor. The quad carburetor can still be considered as two separate carburetors. However, each of these two carburetors has two barrels: a primary barrel and a secondary barrel. During normal low- and intermediate-speed operation, only the primary barrels are operating. One primary barrel feeds half the engine cylinders, and the other primary barrel feeds the other half.

During high-speed driving, when the throttle is open wide, the secondary barrels come into action. Each secondary barrel works with its own primary barrel, adding more air-fuel mixture to the engine.

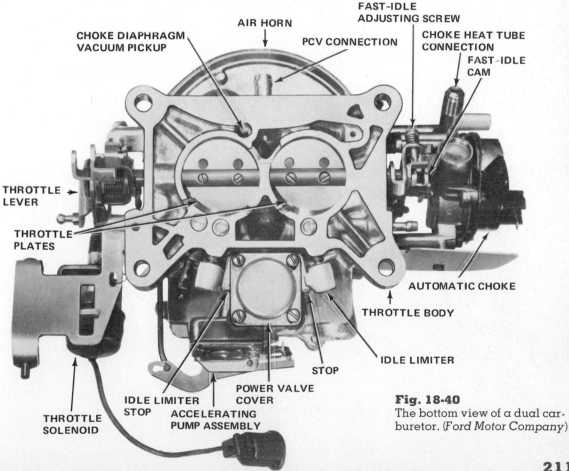

Fig. 18-40
The bottom view of a dual carburetor. (*Ford Motor Company*)

Fig. 18-41
A four-barrel carburetor.
(*Chrysler Corporation*)

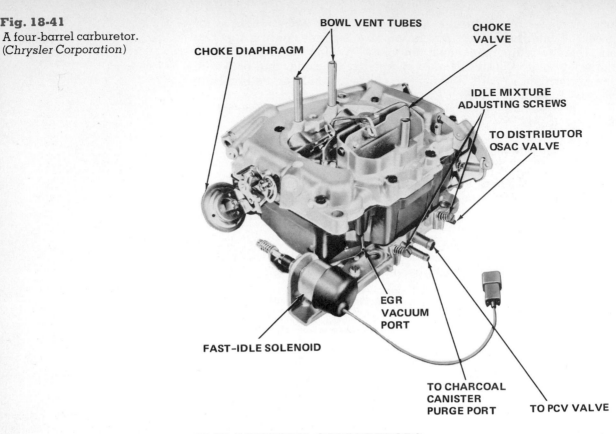

BOWL VENT TUBES

CHOKE
VALVE

CHOKE DIAPHRAGM

IDLE MIXTURE
ADJUSTING SCREWS

TO DISTRIBUTOR
OSAC VALVE

EGR
VACUUM
PORT

FAST-IDLE SOLENOID

TO CHARCOAL
CANISTER
PURGE PORT

TO PCV VALVE

18-30 MULTIPLE CARBURETORS

Some engines use more than one carburetor. The use of more than one carburetor requires a special intake manifold. The additional carburetors supply more air-fuel mixture to improve performance.

18-31 VARIABLE-VENTURI (VV) CARBURETOR

All the carburetors described so far are fixed-venturi types. The size and shape of the venturi do not change. Many imported cars, and an increasing number of cars made in the United States, are using variable-venturi (VV) carburetors. In these, the size of the venturi changes as operating conditions change. We describe two types here: the round-piston type and the somewhat rectangular venturi-valve type. The round-piston type has been used on many imported cars for years. The second VV carburetor we describe is made by Ford. Both types have float systems similar to those in the fixed-venturi units.

18-32 ROUND-PISTON VV CARBURETOR

In this carburetor, the round piston and throttle body form the variable venturi. Figures 18-42 to 18-45 show assembled, sectional, and disassembled views of the carburetor. The piston moves up and down as the vacuum between it and the throttle valve changes. When the throttle is closed so that the engine is idling, there is very little vacuum on the air-cleaner side of the throttle valve. So the piston spring pushes the piston down to its lowest point. The space between it and the lower floor of the throttle body is small. Only a little air can get through. At the same time, the tapered needle is well down in the fuel jet so only a

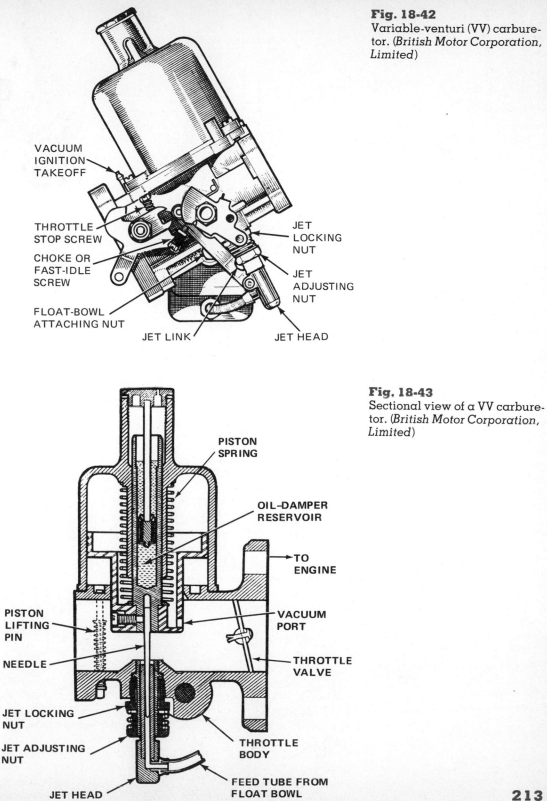

Fig. 18-42
Variable-venturi (VV) carburetor. (*British Motor Corporation, Limited*)

VACUUM
IGNITION
TAKEOFF

THROTTLE
STOP SCREW

CHOKE OR
FAST-IDLE
SCREW

FLOAT-BOWL
ATTACHING NUT

JET LINK

JET
LOCKING
NUT

JET
ADJUSTING
NUT

JET HEAD

Fig. 18-43
Sectional view of a VV carburetor. (*British Motor Corporation, Limited*)

PISTON
SPRING

OIL–DAMPER
RESERVOIR

TO
ENGINE

PISTON
LIFTING
PIN

NEEDLE

VACUUM
PORT

THROTTLE
VALVE

JET LOCKING
NUT

JET ADJUSTING
NUT

THROTTLE
BODY

JET HEAD

FEED TUBE FROM
FLOAT BOWL

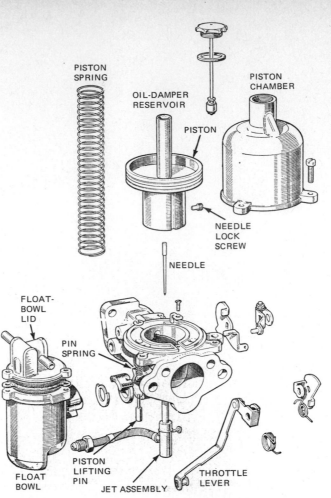

PISTON
SPRING

OIL-DAMPER
RESERVOIR

PISTON CHAMBER

PISTON

NEEDLE
LOCK
SCREW

NEEDLE

FLOAT-
BOWL
LID

PIN
SPRING

FLOAT
BOWL

PISTON
LIFTING
PIN

JET ASSEMBLY

THROTTLE
LEVER

Fig. 18-45
Partial cutaway view of a two-
barrel VV carburetor using
rectangular-shaped venturi
valves. (*Ford Motor Company*)

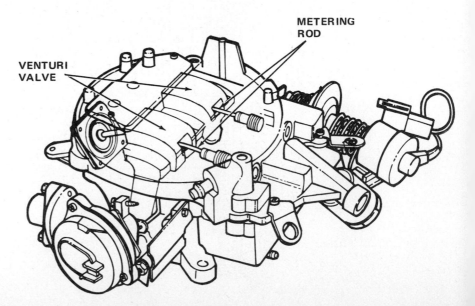

METERING
ROD

VENTURI
VALVE

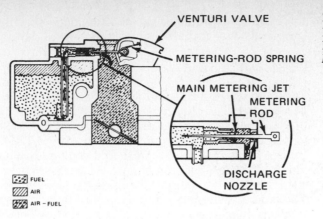

VENTURI VALVE

METERING-ROD SPRING

MAIN METERING JET

METERING
ROD

DISCHARGE
NOZZLE

FUEL

AIR

AIR – FUEL

little gasoline can feed through to the passing air. The resulting air-fuel mixture is right for engine idling.

When the throttle is opened, the intake-manifold vacuum enters the throttle body. This vacuum draws air from the space above the piston, acting through the vacuum port in the lower part of the piston.

The piston is raised by the vacuum, partly lifting the needle out of the fuel jet. Now more air can flow through the carburetor and more fuel can feed into it. The amount of fuel delivered increases to match the additional air flowing through. The wider the throttle opens, the greater the vacuum working on the piston. So it moves up still more. It carries the needle up with it so that the air-fuel ratio stays the same throughout the operating range of the engine.

18-33 FORD RECTANGULAR VV CARBURETOR

This carburetor (Fig. 18-45) is a recent adaptation of the round-piston VV carburetor. It was introduced on some 1978 Ford cars. The piston is rectangular. It is called the *venturi valve*. It slides back and forth across the opening above the throttle valve (Fig. 18-46). Its position is controlled by the amount of vacuum, and this depends on throttle-valve opening. The vacuum control includes a spring-loaded vacuum diaphragm which is connected by a rod to the venturi valve (Fig. 18-47). When the throttle is opened, the intake-manifold vacuum can work on the vacuum diaphragm, causing the venturi valve to move back to increase the venturi opening. Therefore more air can flow through. At the same time, the tapered metering rod (the needle) is pulled out from the fuel jet, allowing more fuel to flow through. This

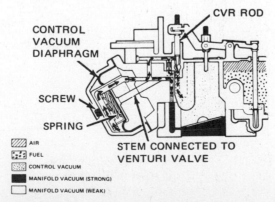

CONTROL
VACUUM
DIAPHRAGM

CVR ROD

SCREW

SPRING

STEM CONNECTED TO
VENTURI VALVE

AIR

FUEL

CONTROL VACUUM

MANIFOLD VACUUM (STRONG)

MANIFOLD VACUUM (WEAK)

additional fuel matches the additional air flowing through so that the proper air-fuel ratio is maintained.

18-34 TURBOCHARGER

The turbocharger, or blower, is a rotary air pump. It forces more air-fuel mixture into the engine cylinders. It includes a rotary compressor located between the carburetor and the intake manifold (Fig. 18-48). Inside the compressor is an impeller that looks like the impeller in the engine cooling-system water pump (Fig. 18-49). When the impeller spins, its blades act like a fan and send additional air-fuel mixture to the intake manifold and engine cylinders. With more air-fuel mixture entering the cylinders, the engine develops more power. Figure 18-49 shows how the impeller is driven. The impeller is mounted on the same shaft as a turbine wheel, which is in the line between the exhaust manifold and the exhaust pipe. Exhaust gases flowing from the engine cylinders through the exhaust manifold spin the turbine wheel. This spins the impeller so that more air-fuel mixture is packed into the engine cylinders.

Figure 18-50 shows a turbocharged V-6 engine. The arrows show the flow of air and exhaust gas through the impeller and the turbine. In this engine, the turbine is in front of the carburetor and sends only air into the carburetor. When the air is under pressure, it picks up a greater quantity of fuel as it goes through the carburetor. The result is the same as when the turbine is located between the carburetor and the intake manifold. The cylinders get additional air-fuel mixture and develop more power.

NOTE

A turbocharged engine is sometimes referred to as a "blown" engine. The turbocharger is "blowing" more charge into the engine. However, this term can be confusing because an engine sometimes "blows." Here the word means that the engine has seized or quit abruptly because of internal damage.

Fig. 18-48
Simplified drawing of a turbocharger which is driven by exhaust gas from the engine.

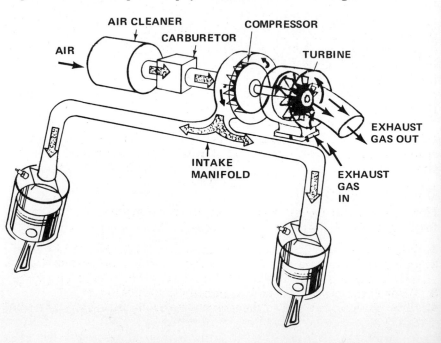

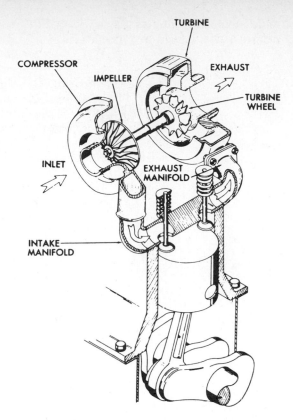

Fig. 18-49
Cutaway view of one cyinder
of a turbocharged engine. (*Joe
Haile Engineering*)

The advantage to using a turbocharger is that a smaller engine which has good fuel economy can produce high power when needed. The Buick turbocharged engine is typical of these installations. Under normal driving conditions, the turbocharger does not develop pressure. But as the throttle is pushed further and further down, the engine manifold vacuum drops to zero. Now the turbocharger engages. Using the exhaust gases coming from the cylinders to spin the turbine, the attached compressor impeller pressurizes the air-fuel mixture flowing into the intake manifold. With a pressure instead of a vacuum in the intake manifold, the cylinders take in an overcharge, or "super-charge," of air-fuel mixture. The engine produces much more power than it would without the turbocharger.

A turbocharged engine operates as a normal engine most of the time. The turbocharger does not add power even at usual highway speeds. During normal driving, it operates only about 5 percent of the time.

CHECK UP ON YOURSELF

Here are some questions about what you have studied in the last few pages of this chapter.

1. What determines the position of the manifold heat-control valve?
2. In a cold V-8 engine, do the exhaust gases from both banks or from only one bank of cylinders add their heat to the intake manifold?
3. What is the purpose of adding barrels to a carburetor?
4. What changes the size of the venturi in the variable-venturi carbu-retor?

217

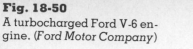

Fig. 18-50
A turbocharged Ford V-6 engine. (*Ford Motor Company*)

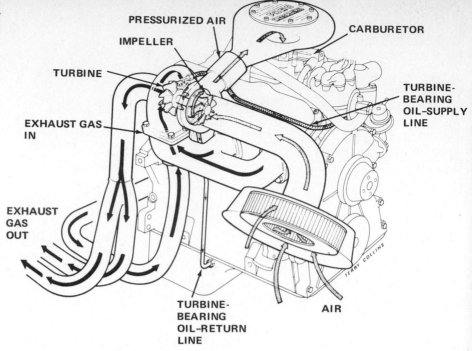

PRESSURIZED AIR

CARBURETOR

IMPELLER

TURBINE

TURBINE-BEARING OIL-SUPPLY LINE

EXHAUST GAS IN

EXHAUST GAS OUT

TURBINE-BEARING OIL-RETURN LINE

AIR

5. What changes the position of the tapered needle in the variable-venturi carburetor?

6. What is the major difference between the two VV carburetors discussed?

7. What controls the position of the venturi piston?

8. What drives the turbocharger?

9. What is the purpose of the turbocharger?

ANSWERS

1. The temperature of the engine, which controls the thermostatic spring (Sec. 18-28). **2.** Exhaust gases from only one bank flow through the exhaust-gas passage in the intake manifold (Sec. 18-28). **3.** To improve performance and driveability (Sec. 18-29). **4.** Movement of the venturi piston (Secs. 18-31 to 18-33). **5.** Movement of the venturi piston in which it is mounted (Secs. 18-32 and 18-33). **6.** The shape of the venturi piston (Secs. 18-32 and 18-33). **7.** Vacuum (Secs. 18-32 and 18-33). **8.** Exhaust gas (Sec. 18-36). **9.** To force more air-fuel mixture into the engine cylinders so they will develop more power (Sec. 18-34).

CHAPTER NINETEEN
FUEL-INJECTION SYSTEMS

After studying this chapter, you should be able to:

1. Describe the construction of, the components in, and the operation of fuel-injection systems.
2. Explain the advantages of the fuel-injection system.

In previous chapters we discussed the carbureted fuel system which is the most widely used fuel system for automobiles. However, the fuel-injection system is becoming more popular for gasoline engines. In this chapter, we describe typical fuel-injection systems used on passenger cars.

19-1 GASOLINE FUEL INJECTION
There are two basic types of fuel-injection systems. In one, the fuel is injected directly into the combustion chamber (Fig. 19-1). This is the system used for diesel engines (Sec. 10-18). The high temperature of the compressed air in the combustion chamber ignites the fuel. The

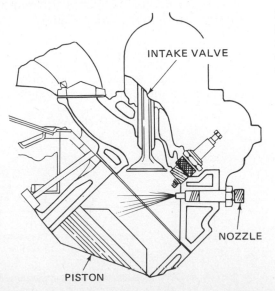

Fig. 19-1
Simplified view showing the method of injecting fuel directly into the combustion chamber of the engine.

INTAKE VALVE

NOZZLE

PISTON

Fig. 19-2
Simplified view showing the
method of injecting fuel into
the intake manifold just in
back of the intake valve.

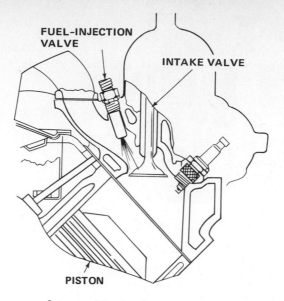

second type of fuel-injection system is used on gasoline engines. It injects the fuel into the intake port opposite the intake valve (Fig. 19-2). This is the type of system we discuss in this chapter.

19-2 ADVANTAGES OF FUEL INJECTION

The fuel-injection system delivers the same amount of air-fuel mixture to each cylinder. At the same time, the fuel-injection system varies the richness to suit the operating conditions. The electronic controls used in electronic fuel-injection systems provide very accurate measuring, or metering, of the fuel. The engine always gets the right amount of fuel for the operating condition, without any lag in fuel delivery. With a carburetor and intake manifold, fuel delivery to the cylinders is not always the same. The air flows around the corners of the intake manifold easily, but the gasoline does not. It is heavier and cannot change directions as easily as air (Fig. 19-3). Some of the drops of gasoline go in a straight line to the end of the manifold. They tend to enrich the mixture going into the end cylinders, or the cylinders farthest from the carburetor.

In contrast, the same amount of fuel reaches each cylinder in a fuel-injected engine (Fig. 19-4). Also, since air alone goes through the throttle body and manifold, the manifold design can be improved for more efficient air flow. The hood height can be reduced. No extra heat

Fig. 19-3
Distribution pattern in an intake manifold. The gasoline particles tend to continue to the end of the manifold, thus enriching the mixture going to the end cylinders. (*Chevrolet Motor Division of General Motors Corporation*)

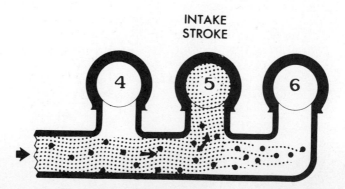

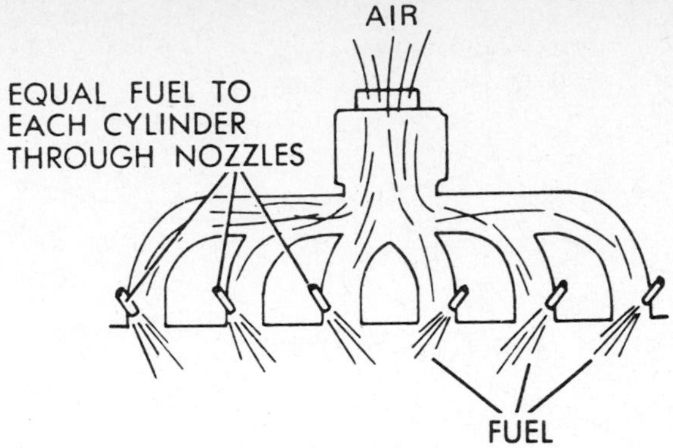

AIR

EQUAL FUEL TO
EACH CYLINDER
THROUGH NOZZLES

FUEL

Fig. 19-4
In a fuel-injected engine, the same amount of fuel reaches each cylinder. (*Cadillac Motor Car Division of General Motors Corporation*)

is required during engine warmup to vaporize the gasoline as with a carburetor. Throttle response is faster because the fuel is under pressure at the injectors.

Because of these advantages, you might ask why all cars do not have fuel-injection systems. Right now, the answer is that the fuel-injection system costs more to make. As it goes into volume production, however, its cost per unit will come down. You can expect to see fuel injection used more in the future.

19-3 EARLY MECHANICAL FUEL-INJECTION SYSTEMS

Early fuel-injection systems for gasoline engines were based on mechanical devices. They were generally considered to be too complicated and hard to keep tuned to be worthwhile. Actually, the modern electronic fuel-injection system is based on recently developed electronic devices. In a following chapter we describe electronic devices such as diodes and transistors and explain how they work. These devices work electrically and produce almost instant response to changing engine conditions. This means that the amount of fuel injected changes as the engine's needs change. The engine always gets the right amount of fuel to suit its operating condition.

19-4 HOW THE ELECTRONIC FUEL-INJECTION SYSTEM WORKS

Figure 19-5 shows the parts of the Cadillac electronic fuel-injection system. This shows the various sensors that feed information to the electronic control unit (ECU). The picture also shows the locations of the other parts of the system. Figure 19-6 shows how the system looks in a sectional view of the engine. Figure 19-7 is a block diagram showing (in the left) the sensors that send information to the ECU. The absolute-manifold-pressure sensor provides an electric signal that changes with the pressure. A second sensor signals electrically the engine speed in revolutions per minute (rpm). A third sensor sends a changing electric signal as the engine coolant temperature changes. A fourth sensor signals intake-manifold air temperature. A fifth sensor signals the throttle position. The ECU takes in all these varying signals, puts them together, and then adjusts the opening time of the injector valves. The valves stay open longer if more fuel is needed. If less fuel is needed, they close earlier.

19-5 FUEL DELIVERY SYSTEM

Figure 19-8 shows schematically the fuel delivery system for the Cadillac electronic fuel-injection system. It includes eight fuel-injection

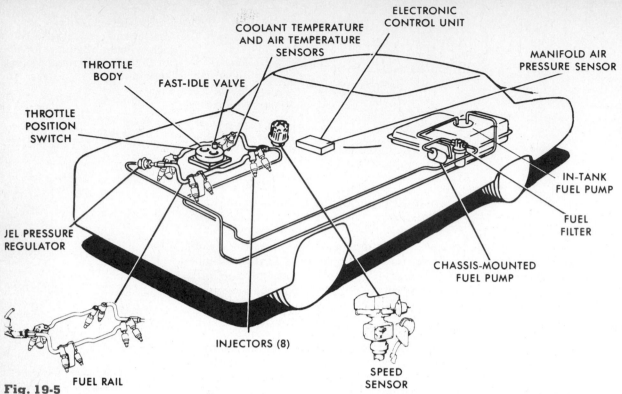

THROTTLE POSITION SWITCH

THROTTLE BODY

FAST-IDLE VALVE

COOLANT TEMPERATURE AND AIR TEMPERATURE SENSORS

ELECTRONIC CONTROL UNIT

MANIFOLD AIR PRESSURE SENSOR

IN-TANK FUEL PUMP

FUEL FILTER

CHASSIS-MOUNTED FUEL PUMP

SPEED SENSOR

INJECTORS (8)

JEL PRESSURE REGULATOR

FUEL RAIL

Fig. 19-5
Components of the Cadillac electronic fuel-injection system. (*Cadillac Motor Car Division of General Motors Corporation*)

valves, one for each engine cylinder. Each valve is placed so that it points at the intake valve for the cylinder. The valves are connected to fuel rails that are connected through a fuel filter to an electric fuel pump. Fuel at constant high pressure is available to the injector valves all the time the engine runs. The fuel pressure regulator prevents excessive pressure.

Each injector valve has a small electric solenoid similar to that shown in Fig. 19-9. When the solenoid is connected to the battery, it pulls back on the nozzle needle, opening the valve. Now fuel can spray out of the valve.

The length of time that the valve stays open is determined by the ECU. The ECU puts together the various signals from the sensors (Fig. 19-7) to determine this. For example, if the manifold-pressure sensor "tells" the ECU that the pressure is high, then the ECU will signal the injector valves to stay open longer. More fuel is needed if there is more air going through the intake manifold.

The timing of the injector valves—that is, when they open—is determined by the engine rpm sensor, located in the ignition distributor (Fig. 19-10). This device includes two reed switches and two magnets. The magnets revolve with the distributor shaft. Every time a magnet passes a reed switch, the switch closes. This signals the ECU and "tells" it to actuate one set of injection valves. When the other switch is operated, the ECU actuates the other set of injection valves.

The speed with which the switches are opened and closed tells the ECU how fast the engine is running. The ECU needs this information so it can adjust the injection-valve actions accordingly.

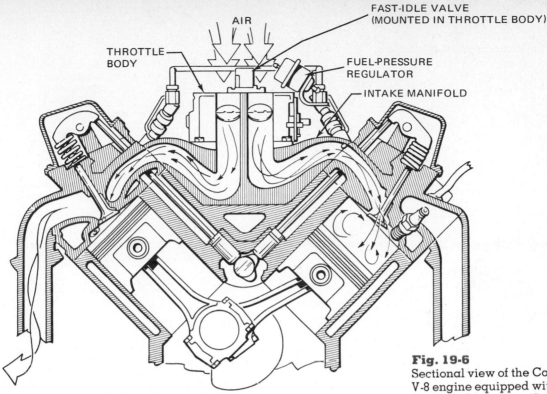

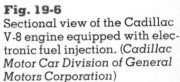

FAST-IDLE VALVE (MOUNTED IN THROTTLE BODY)

AIR

THROTTLE BODY

FUEL-PRESSURE REGULATOR

INTAKE MANIFOLD

Fig. 19-6
Sectional view of the Cadillac V-8 engine equipped with electronic fuel injection. (*Cadillac Motor Car Division of General Motors Corporation*)

19-6 GROUPS OF INJECTION VALVES

Notice that the injection valves do not open individually in time with the cylinder intake-valve opening. Instead, the injection valves are divided into two groups. Half the valves open together. In a four-cylinder engine, this would be two injection valves; in a six-cylinder, three injection valves; in an eight-cylinder (like the Cadillac), four valves. The important point here is that the solenoid injection valves are not actuated individually.

Notice that some of the injection valves are opening many degrees of crankshaft rotation before the intake valves open. Take, for example, the injection valve grouping for a six-cylinder engine (Fig. 19-11).

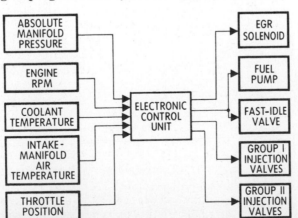

Fig. 19-7
Block diagram showing the sensors (left) that provide information to the electronic control unit. (*Cadillac Motor Car Division of General Motors Corporation*)

223

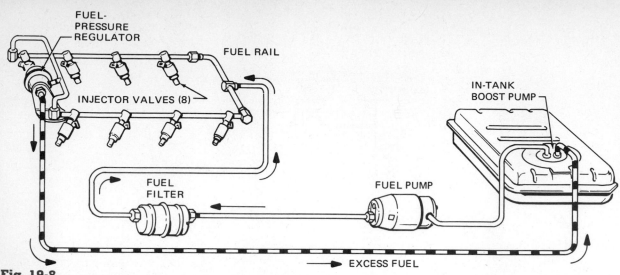

Fuel-pressure regulator, Fuel rail, Injector valves (8), In-tank boost pump, Fuel filter, Fuel pump, Excess fuel

Fig. 19-8
Schematic view of the fuel system used on the Cadillac fuel-injected engine. (*Cadillac Motor Car Division of General Motors Corporation*)

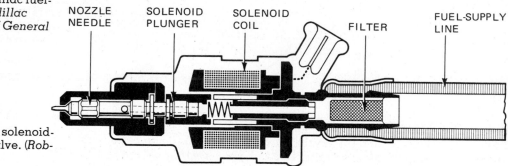

Nozzle needle, Solenoid plunger, Solenoid coil, Filter, Fuel-supply line

Fig. 19-9
Sectional view of the solenoid-operated injection valve. (*Robert Bosch GmbH*)

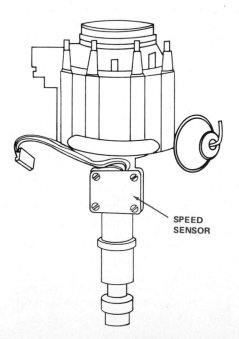

Speed sensor

Fig. 19-10
Ignition distributor used with the Cadillac fuel-injection system. (*Cadillac Motor Car Division of General Motors Corporation*)

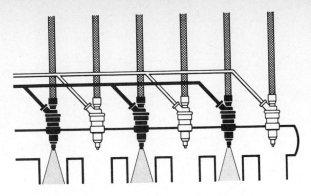

Fig. 19-11
Injection-valve grouping. (Robert Bosch GmbH)

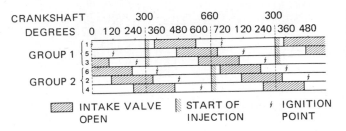

Fig. 19-12
Injection timing chart for a six-cylinder engine. (Robert Bosch GmbH)

Three of the valves open together. Now look at the injecting timing chart for this engine (Fig. 19-12). Note that the individual intake valves open at varying times (crankshaft degrees) after injection. For example, look at the top line, which is for number 1 cylinder. Injection takes place at 300 degrees of crankshaft rotation. Almost 60 degrees later (near 360 degrees), the number 1 intake valve opens and the intake stroke starts. Number 5 cylinder is next in the firing order. Its intake valve opens near 480 degrees, or about 180 degrees after injection. The intake valve for number 3 cylinder opens near 600 degrees, or about 300 degrees of crankshaft rotation after injection. During these varying intervals between fuel injection and intake-valve opening, the fuel is being "stored" in the intake manifold, opposite the intake valves.

Having only two groups of injection valves simplifies the system. Little loss of engine power results from this brief storage of the fuel. The whole action takes place in a small fraction of a second. At highway speed, for example, the time between injection and opening of the intake valve averages only about 0.01 second.

19-7 OTHER ELECTRONIC FUEL-INJECTION SYSTEMS
Figure 19-13 shows another fuel-injection system similar to the one we have described. This shows schematically the various components of the system. The cold-start valve sprays extra fuel into the intake manifold when the coolant temperature switch tells the ECU that the engine is cold. The trigger contacts in the ignition distributor are operated mechanically by a cam on the distributor shaft (Fig. 19-14).

Fig. 19-13
Schematic diagram of an electronic gasoline-injection system. (Robert Bosch GmbH)

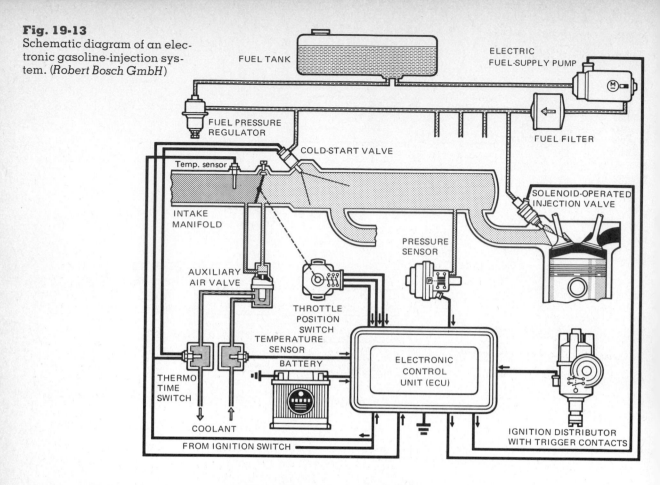

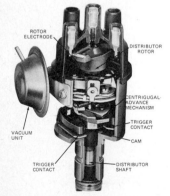

Fig. 19-14
Cutaway view of the distributor, showing the trigger contacts which activate the electronic control. (Robert Bosch GmbH)

CHECK UP ON YOURSELF

Now that you have finished the chapter on fuel-injection systems, find out how well you understand what you read. Answer the questions that follow.

1. What are the two basic fuel-injection systems?
2. Which injection system is used in gasoline engines?
3. What five signals are sent to the electronic control unit in the Cadillac electronic fuel-injection system?
4. How many fuel-injection valves does the Cadillac system have?
5. How many fuel-injection valves operate at any one time?
6. Where is the device that signals the electronic control unit to turn on the fuel-injection valves?
7. How long is it between fuel injection and the opening of an intake valve?
8. Where is the gasoline injected?

ANSWERS

1. Combustion-chamber injection and intake-manifold injection (Sec. 19-1). 2. Intake-manifold injection (Sec. 19-1). 3. Manifold pressure, engine rpm, engine coolant temperature, manifold air temperature, throttle position (Sec. 19-4). 4. Eight (Sec. 19-5). 5. Four (Sec. 19-6). 6. In the ignition distributor (Sec. 19-5). 7. 0.01 second (Sec. 19-6). 8. In front of the intake valve (Sec. 19-1).

PART THREE
AUTO ELECTRICAL SYSTEMS

In Part Three we cover the electrical system used in automobiles. First, we discuss electricity and electronics. We look at some of the functional actions of electricity and then describe diodes and transistors. Next, we cover batteries, starting motors, charging systems, and ignition systems. For each of these, we describe their construction, operation, troubleshooting, and servicing. Part Three ends with a look at other electrical units in the automobile, including wiring circuits, fuses, headlights, horns, indicating devices, and others. There are six chapters in Part Three:

CHAPTER TWENTY
ELECTRICITY AND ELECTRONICS

After studying this chapter, you should be able to:

1. Discuss electricity, electric current, and voltage in terms of electron movement.
2. Explain why insulation is needed.
3. Explain how magnets and electromagnets work and what lines of force are.
4. Explain how diodes and transistors work and how they are put into integrated circuits.
5. List the various electronic devices now used in automobiles.

Electricity does many things for us. It gives us light. It runs much of the machinery around us (refrigerators, factory equipment, television sets, subway trains). It heats our homes. In the car, electricity does several jobs. It starts the engine when we turn the ignition switch on. It makes the sparks that ignite the compressed air-fuel mixture. It operates the radio, the electric gauges, and the lights. Figure 20-1 shows the major parts of the automotive electrical system. In this chapter, we describe all these electrical devices. But, first, let's find out what electricity is all about.

20-1 WHAT IS ELECTRICITY?

Nobody has ever seen what electricity is made of. So we have to rely on the description of scientists. Electricity is composed of tiny particles. The particles are so tiny that it would take billions upon billions of them, all piled together, to make a spot big enough to be seen through a microscope. These particles are called *electrons*. Electrons are all around us in fantastic numbers. In 1 ounce [28 g] of iron, for example, there are about 22 million billion billion electrons. Electrons are normally locked into the elements that form everything in our world.

20-2 ELECTRIC CURRENT

If electrons are forced to move together in the same direction in a wire, we have a flow or current of electrons. We call this flow an *electric cur-*

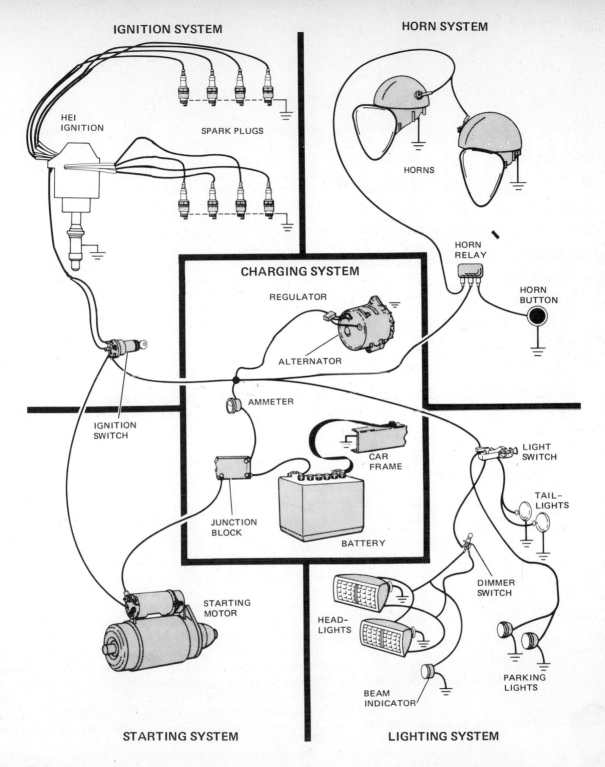

IGNITION SYSTEM

HEI IGNITION

SPARK PLUGS

HORN SYSTEM

HORNS

HORN RELAY

HORN BUTTON

IGNITION SWITCH

CHARGING SYSTEM

REGULATOR

ALTERNATOR

AMMETER

CAR FRAME

JUNCTION BLOCK

BATTERY

LIGHT SWITCH

TAIL-LIGHTS

DIMMER SWITCH

STARTING MOTOR

HEAD-LIGHTS

BEAM INDICATOR

PARKING LIGHTS

STARTING SYSTEM

LIGHTING SYSTEM

Fig. 20-1
A typical car electrical system showing all major parts and the wiring connections. The symbol ⏚ means ground, or the car frame. Because the car frame is used as the return circuit, only half as much wiring is needed. (*Delco-Remy Division of General Motors Corporation*)

rent. The job of the battery and the alternator is to get the electrons to flow in the same direction. When many electrons are moving, we say the current is high. When relatively few electrons are moving, we say the current is low.

20-3 MEASURING ELECTRIC CURRENT

The movement of electrons, or electric current, is measured in *amperes,* or *amps.* One ampere of electric current is a very small amount of current. A battery can put out 200 to 300 amperes as it operates the starting motor. Headlights draw 10 amperes or more. One ampere is the flow of 6.28 billion billion electrons per second.

Nobody can count electrons to find out how many amperes are flowing in a wire. You have to use an ammeter to find this out. The ammeter uses a strange effect of electron flow. This effect is that any flow of electrons, or electricity, produces magnetism.

20-4 MAGNETISM

There are two forms of magnetism: natural and electrical. Natural magnets are made of iron or other metals. Electrically produced magnets are called *electromagnets.* Natural and electromagnets act in the same way. They attract iron objects. Here are two important facts about magnets:

- Magnets can produce electricity.
- Electricity can produce magnets.

We have more to say about magnets and electromagnets and how they act later in this chapter.

20-5 THE AMMETER

Now let's look at how the ammeter measures electric current. The simplest kind of ammeter is shown in Fig. 20-2. This kind of ammeter is found on the instrument panel in many cars. Its purpose is to tell the driver whether the alternator is charging the battery. If the alternator doesn't charge the battery, the battery will run down. If the battery runs down, the car won't start.

Let's see how the ammeter works. The conductor is connected at one end to the battery. The pointer is mounted on a pivot. There is a small piece of oval-shaped iron mounted on the same pivot. This oval-shaped piece of iron is called the *armature.* A permanent magnet, almost circular in shape, is positioned so its two ends are close to the armature. The permanent magnet attracts the armature and tends to hold it in a horizontal position. In this position, the pointer or needle points to zero. Nothing is happening. Now suppose the alternator starts sending current to the battery. This current passes through the conductor. The current produces magnetism. This magnetism attracts the armature and causes it to swing clockwise. This moves the pointer to the "charge" side. The more current that flows, the stronger the magnetism and the farther the pointer moves. The meter face is marked to show the number of amperes flowing.

Now suppose the alternator is not working and you turn on the lights of your car. Current will flow from the battery to the lights. In this situation current will flow in the reverse direction through the conductor in the ammeter. Therefore, the armature is attracted in the opposite direction. It swings in a counterclockwise direction. This

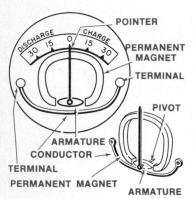

Fig. 20-2
A simplified drawing of a car ammeter, or charge indicator.

moves the pointer to the "discharge" side of the ammeter. The more current that is taken out of the battery, the farther the pointer moves across the discharge side of the ammeter.

20-6 WHAT MAKES THE ELECTRONS MOVE?

Electrons on the move make up electric current. But what makes the electrons move? Too many electrons in one spot. When electrons are concentrated in one place, they try to move. The battery and the alternator are devices that concentrate electrons at one terminal and take them away from the other. Therefore, if the two terminals are connected by a conductor, electrons will flow from the terminal that has too many electrons to the terminal that has too few.

20-7 VOLTAGE

Suppose there are a great many electrons concentrated at one terminal. And suppose there is a great shortage of electrons at the other terminal. When there is a great excess and a great shortage, we say that the electrical pressure is high. We mean that the pressure on the electrons to move from the "too many" terminal to the "too few" terminal is high.

We measure electrical pressure in *volts*. High pressure is high voltage. Low pressure is low voltage. Car batteries are 12-volt units. Twelve volts is considered low pressure. The spark at the spark-plug gap is a flow of electrons at high pressure or voltage. The voltage at the spark-plug gap can be 35,000 volts or more. That's high, but not nearly as high as the voltage on the power lines that carry electricity from power plants to your home and to factories. The voltage on cross-country power lines is several hundred thousand volts.

20-8 INSULATION

If electrons escape from the wire in which they are flowing, electric power is lost. That's the reason that wires are covered with insulation. That's also the reason why power lines are hung from long insulators on the power poles or towers. In addition to power loss, electrons on the loose can be dangerous. For example, if the insulation on the wire to a household appliance or a lamp is damaged, a fire could result. A person who touches the wire or appliance could get an electric shock.

In the car the wires between the battery, the alternator, and other electrical devices are all covered with insulation. The insulation is a nonconductor. This means that electrons, or electric current, cannot flow through it. But if the insulation goes bad, electric current will go where it is not supposed to. It could take a shortcut through the metal of the car frame and the engine. Such a shortcut is called a *short circuit*. It can cause trouble, as you will find out later in the book.

Insulation has the job of keeping the electrons, or the electric current, moving in the proper path, or circuit. Circuits include the wires and the electrical devices in the car.

20-9 MAGNETS—ANOTHER LOOK

Let's take another look at magnets. Magnets act through *lines of force*. These lines of force stretch between the ends of the magnet. The two ends of the magnet are called the *magnetic poles,* or the *poles*. One pole is called the north pole. The other pole is called the south pole. The area surrounding the poles is called a *magnetic field*.

Fig. 20-3
Unlike magnetic poles attract.
As the north pole is moved
near the south pole, the south
pole will pull toward the north
pole.

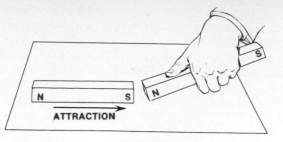

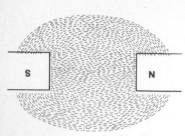

Fig. 20-4
Magnetic lines of force stretching between two unlike magnetic poles try to shorten. This
pulls together the two unlike
poles.

Fig. 20-5
Like magnetic poles repel one
another. When a north pole is
brought near another north
pole, they push away from
each other.

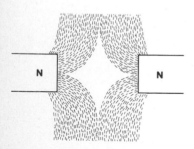

Fig. 20-6
Magnetic lines of force between two like magnetic lines
of force tend to parallel one another. This forces the two like
poles apart.

20-10 LINES OF FORCE

The lines of force have two characteristics. First, the lines of force try
to shorten up. For example, if you hold the north pole of one magnet
close to the south pole of another magnet, the two magnets will pull
together (Fig. 20-3). If we drew the lines of force between the two poles,
the picture would look something like Fig. 20-4. The lines of force,
stretching between the two poles, try to shorten up and thus pull the
two poles together.

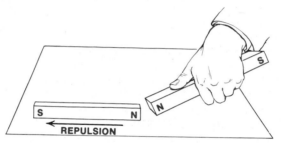

The second characteristic is that the lines of force run more or less
parallel to one another and try to push away from one another. We can
understand this if we bring like poles together—two north poles, for
example (Fig. 20-5). The lines of force run parallel to one another and
try to push away (Fig. 20-6). The magnet that is free to move will move
away as the same pole of the other magnet is brought closer.

We can draw these conclusions:

- Like magnetic poles repel each other. North repels north. South
  repels south.
- Unlike magnetic poles attract each other. North attracts south.
  South attracts north.

20-11 ELECTROMAGNETS

Electromagnets act just like natural magnets. An electromagnet can
be made by wrapping a wire around a rod (Fig. 20-7). We saw what
happened in the ammeter when current flowed one way or another
through the conductor. That is, the current produced magnetism, or
magnetic lines of force.

Current flowing through a single wire, or conductor, will not produce much magnetism. But suppose you wind a conductor, or wire,
around a rod and connect the ends of the wire to a source of electric
current (or electrons). Then the wire winding will produce strong magnetism. In other words, a strong magnetic field will develop around the
coil of wire.

With current flowing through the winding, the winding acts just like a bar magnet. You can point one end of the winding toward a pole of a bar magnet. The winding will either attract or repel the bar-magnet pole. One end of the winding is a north pole, The other end is a south pole. You can change the poles by reversing the leads to the source of current. When the electrons flow through in one direction, one of the poles becomes north. But when the electrons flow through in the opposite direction, the poles reverse. The north pole becomes the south pole, and the south pole becomes the north pole.

An electromagnet such as the one you made by winding wire around a rod is also called a *solenoid*. It is used in several places in the electrical system of the automobile. Solenoids are explained in more detail in a later chapter.

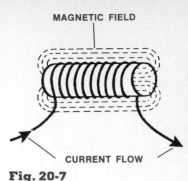

Fig. 20-7
Current flow through a coil of wire (solenoid) produces a magnetic field.

20-12 RESISTANCE

An insulator has a high resistance to the movement of electrons through it. A conductor, such as a copper wire, has a very low resistance. Resistance is found in all electric circuits. In some circuits we want a high resistance in order to keep down the amount of current flow. In other circuits we want as little resistance as possible so that a high current can flow.

Resistance is measured in *ohms*. For example, a 1000-foot [305-m] length of wire that is about 0.1 inch [2.5 mm] in diameter has a resistance of 1 ohm. A 2000-foot [610-m] length of the same wire has a resistance of 2 ohms. In other words, the longer the path, the greater the resistance.

A 1000-foot [305-m] length of wire that is about 0.2 inch [5.1 mm] in diameter has a resistance of only $\frac{1}{4}$ ohm. The heavier the wire, the lower the resistance. The longer the path, or circuit, the farther the electrons have to travel and the higher the resistance to the electric current. With the heavier wire, the path is larger. This means that the resistance is lower.

20-13 OHM'S LAW

There is a definite relationship between amperes (electron flow), voltage (electrical pressure), and resistance. As the electrical pressure goes up, more electrons flow. Increasing the voltage increases the amperes of current. However, increasing the resistance decreases the amperes of current. These relationships are summed up in a formula known as Ohm's law:

Voltage is equal to amperage times ohms.
$$V = I \times R$$

where V is the voltage, I is the current in amperes, and R is the resistance in ohms. The important point about Ohm's law is that increasing the ohms, or resistance, cuts down on the current flowing. We will talk about this again when we discuss the electrical system in the car.

20-14 ONE-WIRE SYSTEMS

For electricity to flow, there must be a complete path, or circuit. The electrons must flow from one terminal of the battery or the alternator, through the circuit, and back to the other terminal. In the automobile, the engine and car frame are used to carry the electrons back to the other terminal. Therefore, no separate wires are required for the re-

Fig. 20-8
The symbol of ground, or the return circuit.

turn circuit from the electrical device to the battery or the alternator. The return circuit is called the *ground*. It is indicated in wiring diagrams by the symbol shown in Fig. 20-8. Look at Fig. 20-1 and you will see many of these symbols. The ground—the engine and car frame—is the other half of the circuit that runs between the source of electricity (battery or alternator) and the electrical device.

20-15 ALTERNATING CURRENT AND DIRECT CURRENT

Most of the electricity generated and used is alternating current (ac). The current flows first in one direction and then in the opposite direction. That is, it alternates. The current you use in your home is ac. It alternates 60 times a second and therefore is called 60-cycle ac. In the metric system, cycles per second are called *hertz*.

The automobile cannot use ac. The battery is a direct-current (dc) unit. When you discharge the battery by connecting electrical devices to it, you take current out in one direction only. The current does not alternate, or change directions. All electrical devices in the car operate on dc only.

20-16 ELECTRONICS

Electronics has opened up a whole new world of electrical devices. These include pocket radios, wrist-watch-size calculators, pocket computers, small television sets, control devices in automobiles and space vehicles, and many more.

Our special interest in this book is what electronics does in the automobile and how it does its job. First, we will look at semiconductors, diodes, and transistors. These are the electronic devices that run electronic equipment. Basically, diodes are one-way electric valves that permit a flow of current through them in only one direction. Transistors are electric switches that can start and stop a flow of current. Both diodes and transistors use materials called semiconductors.

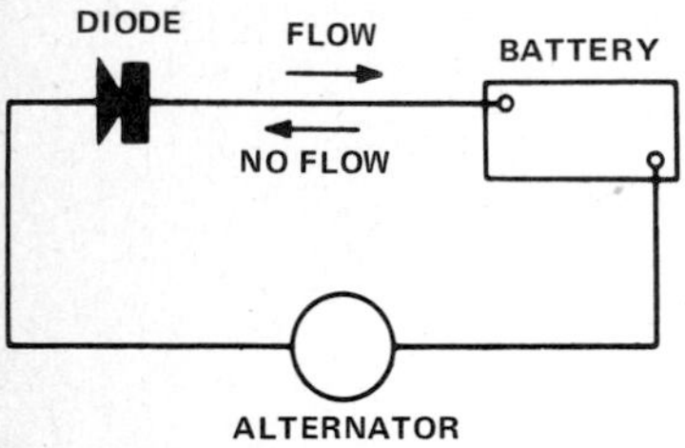

Fig. 20-9
Alternating current from an alternator can be rectified, or changed to direct current, by a diode so that it can charge a battery.

20-17 DIODES

The diode is a device that permits electricity to flow through in one direction but not in the other. Figure 20-9 shows this. The alternator is the device in the automotive electrical system that produces current to charge the battery and operate electrical devices that are turned on. However, the current in the alternator is alternating. Diodes are used to change it to direct current. You cannot use alternating current to charge the battery or operate automotive electrical equipment. Direct current is required. A later chapter describes alternators and the diodes used in them.

20-18 TRANSISTORS

The transistor is a diode with additional semiconductor material added. This added material makes it possible for the transistor to "amplify" the current. That is, a small current applied to the base can turn on or off a large current flow through the transistor. Figures 20-10 and 20-11 show this. In Fig. 20-10 a small current of 0.35 ampere is flowing to the base. When the extra electrons flow into the base after the switch is closed, they form a path through which current can flow from the emitter to the collector in the transistor. This is shown by the arrows in Fig. 20-10.

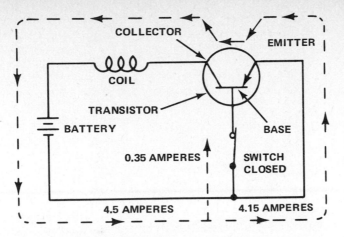

Fig. 20-10
When the switch is closed, current flows.

When the switch is opened, as shown in Fig. 20-11, no current (electrons) flows into the base. There is no path through the transistor for electrons to flow from the emitter to the collector.

A small current to the base allows a large current to flow through the transistor. This small current is called the *signal,* or *trigger current*. When it flows, the large current flows. When the signal current stops, the large current stops.

20-19 INTEGRATED CIRCUITS

Scientists and engineers have found ways to make diodes and transistors extremely small. This makes it possible to group large numbers of these semiconductor devices in a small space. Such groups are called *integrated circuits*. That is, many components are put together, or integrated, into a single package. For example, Fig. 20-12 shows an integrated circuit with 110,000 transistors. Such combinations are used in computers and complex controlling devices. For example, the computer controls that guide space vehicles as they travel out in space and then back to earth have hundreds of thousands of diodes and transistors.

NOTE

Transistors, diodes, and similar devices are called *solid-state* devices because they are solids and have no moving parts (except electrons).

20-20 ELECTRONIC DEVICES IN THE AUTOMOBILE

Much less complex electronic controls are needed for the devices used in automobiles. A partial list of the automotive components using electronic controls follows:

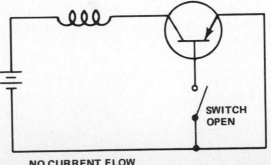

NO CURRENT FLOW

Fig. 20-11
When the switch is open, no current flows.

235

Fig. 20-12
Integrated circuit, showing how many separate devices can be put together into a single component. Note its size in comparison to the rule in front of it. It has 65,000 bits of memory and contains more than 110,000 transistors. (*Digital Equipment Corporation*)

1. Alternator voltage regulator, covered in a following chapter
2. Electronic ignition system, covered in a following chapter
3. Seat-belt interlock system (no longer used, although there may still be some on cars made in 1974)
4. Air bags
5. Anticollision radar
6. Antiskid braking system
7. Electronic fuel injection
8. Electronic engine-control system
9. Accessories such as solid-state clocks, radios, and tape players; headlight dimmer; automatic on-off headlight control; speed controls; automatic temperature controls; and antitheft systems

Some of these devices are covered in this book. For details of other devices, see books in the McGraw-Hill *Automotive Technology Series.*

20-21 ELECTRONICS AND THE MECHANIC

Many mechanics worried about the use of electronics in the automobile. They thought it meant learning a lot of electronic theory. But it did not turn out that way. An electronic circuit is a "go no-go" circuit. Either it works or it doesn't. If it does not work, you replace the electronic device that is bad. There are no adjustments. The testers are simple to use. They plug in and show with lights or meter readings what is working and what is not. You quickly pinpoint a bad part. Installing a new part usually fixes the trouble.

Another advantage is that transistors and diodes never wear out, at least in theory. Connections may go bad. However, the solid-state device continues to do its job until it is overheated or jarred excessively.

CHECK UP ON YOURSELF

It's time to find out what you know about electricity and electronics. Answer the following questions to test yourself.

1. What do we call a flow of electrons moving in the same direction in a wire?
2. The ampere is a measurement of what?

3. What is the purpose of the ammeter?
4. What makes electrons move in a wire?
5. What do we call the material that covers wires and prevents electrons from escaping?
6. Do like magnetic poles attract or repel one another?
7. What do we call a winding that has current flowing through it?
8. Does increasing the resistance in a circuit increase or decrease the amount of current flowing?
9. In the one-wire system used in automobiles, what forms the return circuit?
10. Is the battery a dc or an ac unit?
11. What are the materials called that are used in diodes and transistors?
12. What is the name of the electronic device that will allow current to flow through it in one direction only?
13. What is the name of the electronic device that uses a small electrical signal to allow a large current to flow?
14. What is an integrated circuit?

ANSWERS

1. An electric current (Sec. 20-2). **2.** Current flow (Sec. 20-3). **3.** To tell the driver whether or not the alternator is charging the battery (Sec. 20-5). **4.** Electrical pressure or voltage (Sec. 20-6). **5.** Insulation (Sec. 20-8). **6.** Repel (Sec. 20-10). **7.** An electromagnet (Sec. 20-1). **8.** Decreases the amount of current flowing (Sec. 20-12). **9.** The engine and car frame (Sec. 20-14). **10.** A dc unit (Sec. 20-15). **11.** Semiconductors (Sec. 20-16). **12.** Diode (Sec. 20-17). **13.** Transistor (Sec. 20-18). **14.** A grouping of diodes, transistors, and other electronic components in a small space (Sec. 20-19).

CHAPTER TWENTY-ONE THE BATTERY

After studying this chapter, you should be able to:

1. Explain how batteries are constructed and how they work.
2. Describe the various battery ratings and explain what they mean.
3. Describe battery maintenance and the various ways that batteries can be tested.

The battery is an *electrochemical device*. It produces electricity by converting chemical energy into electrical energy. In this chapter we explain how the battery works, how to keep it working, and what to do when it stops working.

21-1 BATTERY CONSTRUCTION

The 12-volt automobile battery has a series of six cells in the battery case (see Fig. 21-1). Each cell has a number of battery plates with separators between them. When battery liquid, called *electrolyte*, is put into each cell, the cell produces an electrical pressure of 2 volts. The six cells in the battery produce a total of 12 volts. More exactly, each cell has a voltage of 2.1 volts when the electrolyte has a specific gravity of 1.250 and its temperature is 80°F [27°C]. You will learn more about specific gravity later in the chapter.

Many batteries have vent plugs on the cover of each cell. These vent plugs let gas escape from the battery when the battery is being charged. The vent plugs can be removed so that water can be added when the electrolyte level is low.

Some batteries are sealed. Because sealed batteries never need water, they do not need vent plugs (Fig. 21-2).

NOTE
Delco-Remy calls its batteries "Energizers."

21-2 BATTERY ELECTROLYTE

The battery electrolyte is made up of about 60 percent water and 40 percent sulfuric acid (in a fully charged battery). Here is what happens when electric current is taken out of a battery: The sulfuric acid gradually goes into the battery plates, which means the electrolyte gets weaker. As this happens, the battery runs down or goes "dead." It then has to be recharged. The recharging job requires a battery charger. The charger pushes a current of electricity through the battery, restor-

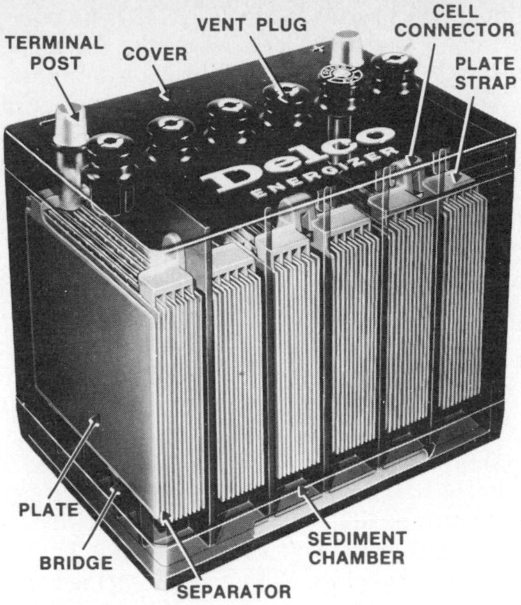

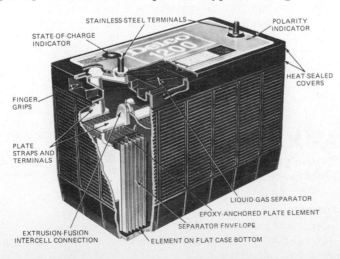

TERMINAL POST COVER VENT PLUG CELL CONNECTOR PLATE STRAP

PLATE BRIDGE SEPARATOR SEDIMENT CHAMBER

Fig. 21-1
A phantom view of a lead-acid storage battery. The case has been drawn as though it were transparent so that you can see the internal construction of the battery. (*Delco-Remy Division of General Motors Corporation*)

ing the battery to a charged condition. The current is pushed into the battery in a direction opposite to the direction in which it was taken out. There's more on this later in the chapter.

21-3 BATTERY RATINGS

The amount of current that a battery can deliver depends on the total area and volume of active plate material. It also depends on the amount and strength of the electrolyte, that is, the percentage of sulfuric acid in the electrolyte. Factors that influence battery capacity include the number of plates per cell, the size of the plates, cell size, and quantity of electrolyte. The ratings most commonly used in referring to battery capacity are discussed below.

1. Reserve Capacity

Reserve capacity is the length of time in minutes that a fully charged battery at 80°F [27°C] can deliver 25 amperes. A typical rating would

STAINLESS-STEEL TERMINALS POLARITY INDICATOR

STATE-OF-CHARGE INDICATOR

HEAT-SEALED COVERS

FINGER GRIPS

PLATE STRAPS AND TERMINALS

LIQUID-GAS SEPARATOR
EPOXY-ANCHORED PLATE ELEMENT
SEPARATOR ENVELOPE
EXTRUSION-FUSION INTERCELL CONNECTION
ELEMENT ON FLAT CASE BOTTOM

Fig. 21-2
Sealed battery of the type that never requires water. Note the state-of-charge indicator in the battery top. (*Delco-Remy Division of General Motors Corporation*)

be 125 minutes. This figure tells how long a battery can carry the electrical operating load when the alternator quits. Some battery manufacturers rate their batteries in ampere-hours. That is, they multiply the number of amperes by the number of hours. For example, the 125-minute rating means the battery is a 52.1 ampere-hour unit.

$$25 \times \frac{125}{60} = 52.1$$

2. Cold Cranking Rate
One of the two cold cranking rates is the number of amperes that a battery can deliver for 30 seconds when it is at 0°F [−18°C] without the cell voltages falling below 1.2 volts. A typical rating for a battery with a reserve capacity of 125 minutes would be 430 amperes. This figure indicates the ability of the battery to crank the engine at low temperatures. The second cold cranking rate is measured at −20°F [−29°C]. In this case, the final voltage is allowed to drop to 1.0 volt per cell. A typical rating for a battery with a reserve capacity of 125 minutes would be 320 amperes.

Other battery ratings include overcharge life units, charge acceptance, and watts. They are described in detail in *Automotive Electrical Equipment,* a book in the McGraw-Hill *Automotive Technology Series.*

21-4 BATTERY MAINTENANCE
Battery failure is one of the more common car troubles. In most cases, battery failure can be avoided if the battery is checked regularly. Here are the maintenance checks you should make:

1. Check the electrolyte level in all cells.
2. Add water if the electrolyte level is low.
3. Clean off corrosion around the battery terminals.
4. Check the battery condition with a tester.

These maintenance steps are described in the following sections.

21-5 CHECKING ELECTROLYTE LEVEL AND ADDING WATER
Follow this simple procedure for checking electrolyte level: Remove the vent caps on the battery and look into the cells. If the electrolyte level is low, add water.

NOTE
You can't check battery cells on sealed batteries. But you can make sure that connections are clean and tight at the terminals. Some sealed batteries have a charge indicator in the cover (Fig. 21-2).

Many batteries have split rings in the cell covers. These rings show whether the battery needs water. The picture in Fig. 21-3 shows you what the electrolyte and split ring look like when the electrolyte level is too low and when it is right.

NOTE
Don't add too much water! Too much water causes the electrolyte to leak out. The electrolyte will corrode the battery carrier and any other metal it touches.

ELECTROLYTE LEVEL LOW

ELECTROLYTE LEVEL NORMAL

Fig. 21-3
The appearance of the electrolyte and split ring when the electrolyte level is too low and when it is correct. (*Delco-Remy Division of General Motors Corporation*)

21-6 CLEANING OFF CORROSION

Battery terminals, especially those located on top of the battery, tend to corrode (Fig. 21-4). Corrosion builds up around the terminals and the cable clamps. To remove corrosion and clean the battery, mix some baking soda in a can of water. Brush on the solution. Wait until the foaming stops, and then flush off with water. If corrosion is bad, use a battery terminal cleaner to clean the terminal posts and cable clamps (Fig. 21-5).

CAUTION

The vent caps must be in place before cleaning the battery. Don't cover the top of the vent cap with either the baking-soda solution or the flushing water. Some of the baking soda might get down into the electrolyte through the vent hole in the cap. If this happens, the battery may be permanently damaged.

Don't be in a hurry for the battery to dry! If you can't wait for the battery to dry by itself, use a throwaway rag or paper towel. Then throw the rag or paper towel into the trash. Never use shop towels for wiping a battery. The shop air hose must never be used to air-dry the battery. The air stream might pull electrolyte out of the cell through the vent cap. Someone nearby could be seriously injured by this spray of battery acid.

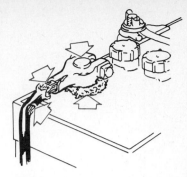

Fig. 21-4
Battery cables with damaged insulation, broken or loose strands, or excessive corrosion should be replaced. Corroded terminals should be cleaned. (*Delco-Remy Division of General Motors Corporation*)

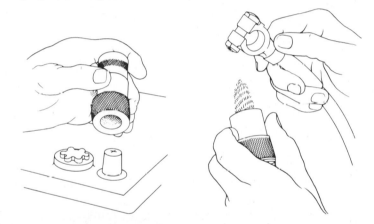

Fig. 21-5
Wire battery brush is used to clean battery-terminal post and cable clamp. (*Buick Motor Division of General Motors Corporation*)

21-7 CHECKING BATTERY CONDITION

There are several methods of testing the battery to find out its condition and state of charge. The hydrometer test and the high-discharge, or battery-capacity, test are the most common. Past testing methods have used a variety of meters. These methods include the 421 test and the cadmium-tip test. When you work in the shop, your instructor will show you how to use the testers available. In the following sections, we cover only the main points of the tests.

21-8 HYDROMETER TEST

The hydrometer tests the *specific gravity,* or *gravity,* of the battery electrolyte. It has a rubber bulb at the top, a glass tube, a float with a stem marked off in figures so that the gravity can be read, and a rubber tube at the bottom (Fig. 21-6). You use the hydrometer by squeezing the bulb, putting the end of the tube into the battery cell, and then releasing the bulb. The electrolyte is drawn up into the glass tube. The float then floats in the electrolyte. The amount the stem of the float sticks out of the electrolyte tells you the state of the charge of the battery (Fig. 21-7).

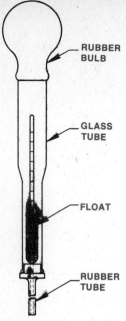

RUBBER BULB

GLASS TUBE

FLOAT

RUBBER TUBE

Fig. 21-6
A battery hydrometer for measuring the specific gravity of battery electrolyte.

If the reading on the stem is between 1.260 and 1.290 gravity, the battery is fully charged. If the reading is between 1.200 and 1.230 gravity, the battery is only half charged. If the reading is around 1.140 gravity, the battery is almost dead and needs a recharge.

NOTE
We do not usually refer to the decimal point in speaking of specific gravity. We say, for example, twelve-sixty (1.260) gravity, or eleven twenty-five (1.125).

CAUTION
The electrolyte contains sulfuric acid! This is a dangerous acid that can give you serious skin burns. If it gets in your eyes, it can cause blindness. Sulfuric acid will eat holes in clothing, make spots on car paint finishes, and corrode any metal it touches. Be very careful when using the hydrometer to avoid spilling the electrolyte.

If you get battery acid on your skin, flush it off *at once* with plenty of water. Then put baking soda (if it is available) on the burned area. Baking soda neutralizes the acid. If you get acid in your eyes, flush your eyes with water over and over again. Then get to a doctor at once! Acid can make you blind.

After you have checked the electrolyte in the battery cell, squeeze the bulb to return the electrolyte to the cell from which you drew it.

If the battery is low, it should be recharged. If the battery is low and old, it may be worn out and a new battery may be needed.

Another type of hydrometer sometimes is used. It is much smaller and simpler to use than the hydrometer discussed above. Basically, the small hydrometer has four small plastic balls in it instead of a float. When electrolyte is drawn into the tube, the condition of the cell is told by the number of balls that float. If all the balls float, the cell is fully charged. If no balls float, the cell is dead.

21-9 METER TESTS
There are different kinds of meter tests. Each one requires a different meter or procedure. We go over some of them briefly in the sections that follow. Your instructor will tell you more about them when you work in the shop.

1. High-Discharge Test
The high-discharge test also is called a high-load test and a battery-capacity test. In this test the tester puts a very heavy discharge on the battery for 15 seconds. Then the battery voltage is measured. Figure

Fig. 21-7
Various specific-gravity readings. (*Delco-Remy Division of General Motors Corporation*)

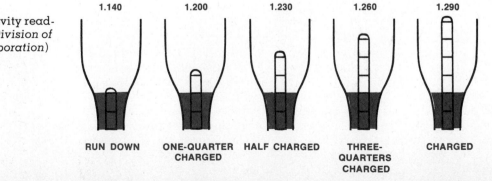

| 1.140 | 1.200 | 1.230 | 1.260 | 1.290 |

RUN DOWN   ONE-QUARTER CHARGED   HALF CHARGED   THREE-QUARTERS CHARGED   CHARGED

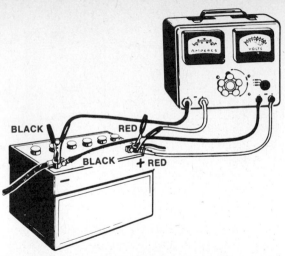

Fig. 21-8
A special testing instrument connected to a battery, ready for a high-discharge test. (*Chrysler Corporation*)

21-8 shows this tester in use. The tester has a knob that can be turned one way or the other to put more or less load on the battery. If it is turned all the way in one direction, the tester will be taking up to 300 amperes from the battery. This is a heavy load. If the battery voltage falls below 9.6 volts during this heavy load, then the battery is either discharged or worn out. If it is worn out, it should be junked. If the battery is only discharged, then it can be recharged and used again.

2. The 421 Test
This test requires a special programmed tester. The 421 tester first applies a discharge load on the battery for a specific number of seconds. Then it gives the battery a short charge for a few seconds. Finally, the battery voltage is measured. The battery tester does all this automatically. You read the results on the voltmeter on the tester. This tells you whether the battery is in good condition, needs charging, or is defective and should be junked.

3. Cadmium-Tip Test
In this test, the vent plugs are removed from the battery, and the tips of the cadmium-tip tester are inserted into the electrolyte of adjacent cells. The meter gives a cell voltage reading that tells you the condition of the cells. Figure 21-9 shows how this battery tester is used. It is called a cadmium-tip tester because the tips are coated with cadmium.

21-10 CHARGING A BATTERY
If a battery is run down but is otherwise in good condition, it can be given a charge with a battery charger and then put back into opera-

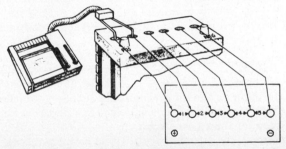

Fig. 21-9
A cadmium-tip tester is used to test each cell in a battery with vent plugs. (*Chrysler Corporation*)

Fig. 21-10
A quick-charger is used to charge a battery. (*Chrysler Corporation*)

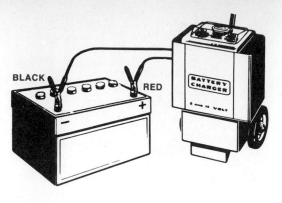

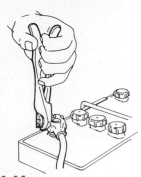

Fig. 21-11
Battery-nut pliers are used to loosen a nut-and-bolt type of battery cable.

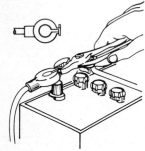

Fig. 21-12
Pliers are used to loosen a spring-ring type of cable clamp from a battery terminal.

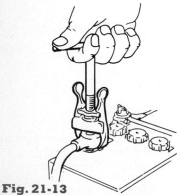

Fig. 21-13
Using a special clamp puller to pull the cable clamp from the battery terminal.

244

tion. The two ways to charge a battery are (1) by the slow-charge method, which usually requires taking the battery out of the car; and (2) by the quick-charge method, which can be done with the battery in the car. Figure 21-10 shows a battery being charged with a quick charger. Certain precautions must be taken, regardless of which charger is used. With the quick charger, it is especially important not to overcharge the battery. If used in the wrong way, this charger can quickly ruin a battery. You will find out all about this when you work in the shop.

21-11 THE IMPORTANCE OF KEEPING A BATTERY CHARGED

There are many reasons why it is important to keep a battery charged. A run-down battery will not start the engine. A discharged, or partly discharged, battery goes bad more quickly. Also, a discharged battery will freeze at about 18°F [−8°C]. But it takes −95°F [−35°C] to freeze a fully charged battery. Because a run-down battery can freeze, it is important to recharge it if it is low in cold weather.

21-12 REMOVING A BATTERY

If you have to remove a battery from a car, you must be careful to avoid damaging it. Battery terminals are of three types. They are lead posts (Figs. 21-11 to 21-13), side screws (Fig. 21-14), and top screws (Fig. 21-2). The battery with the lead posts on top can be ruined if too much pressure is put on the terminals as the clamps are loosened. There are two types of clamps: the nut-and-bolt type (Fig. 21-11) and the spring type (Fig. 21-12). You should use battery pliers, as shown in Fig. 21-11, to loosen the nut-and-bolt type. With either type of clamp, if a clamp sticks, don't pry it off. This can break internal connections. Instead, use the battery-cable puller, as shown in Fig. 21-13.

If you hammer or put pressure on terminals or lift the battery by the terminals, you can break internal connections. This would ruin the battery.

NOTE
When replacing a battery, don't install it backward. Don't connect the negative terminal to the cable clamp that should be connected to the positive terminal. This can cause serious damage. The negative terminal post of the battery is smaller than the positive terminal post (Fig. 21-15). Also, don't carry the battery by the terminal posts. Use a case-type battery carrier (Fig. 21-16).

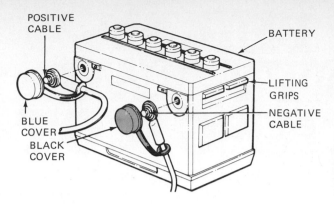

POSITIVE CABLE
BATTERY
LIFTING GRIPS
NEGATIVE CABLE
BLUE COVER
BLACK COVER

Fig. 21-14
Cable connections for a side-terminal battery. (*Cadillac Motor Car Division of General Motors Corporation*)

NEGATIVE POST — SMALL → ← NEG
POSITIVE POST — LARGE → ← +POS

Fig. 21-15
The negative terminal post of the battery is smaller than the positive terminal post.

CAUTION

Always disconnect the ground battery cable first. The ground battery cable is the short cable or uninsulated strap that is fastened to the car frame or engine. When you disconnect this cable first, you can't get into trouble while disconnecting the cable from the insulated terminal. If you don't disconnect the ground cable first, you could accidentally ground the pliers or puller. This would cause a direct short across the battery. The result would be sparks and possible damage to the tool or the cable, or injury to yourself.

CHECK UP ON YOURSELF

Answer the questions that follow to see how well you understand what you have studied about the battery.

1. How many cells does a 12-volt battery have?
2. Why is the battery electrolyte dangerous?
3. What is the name of the tester that checks specific gravity?
4. Which of the two terminal posts of the battery is smaller?
5. If a battery were advertised as a "125-minute" battery, which battery rating does that mean?
6. Why should you disconnect the ground cable first?

ANSWERS

1. Six cells (Sec. 21-1). **2.** Sulfuric acid is very corrosive. It can burn your skin seriously and harm your eyes. It will eat holes in clothing or metal (Sec. 21-8). **3.** Hydrometer (Sec. 21-8). **4.** The negative-terminal post is smaller (Sec. 21-12). **5.** Reserve capacity (Sec. 21-3). **6.** To prevent accidentally shorting the battery (Sec. 21-12).

Fig. 21-16
A case-type battery carrier is used to lift a battery.

CHAPTER TWENTY-TWO
STARTING MOTORS

After studying this chapter, you should be able to:

1. Describe the construction and operation of starting motors.
2. Explain the purpose of the overrunning clutch and how it works.
3. List the possible causes of the trouble if the starting motor does not operate or if it operates slowly but the engine does not start.

Starting motors—also called cranking motors and starters—are small but powerful electric motors that spin the crankshaft to get the engine started. Starting motors are not very complicated, and they seldom need service. Their job is to convert electrical energy from the battery into mechanical energy.

22-1 STARTING-MOTOR OPERATION

The starting motor is operated by electromagnetism. Electricity flowing through wires and through coils of wire, or windings, produces electromagnetism. This leads to two important facts about magnets that you should know when you study starting motors:

- Like magnetic poles repel each other.
- Unlike magnetic poles attract each other.

Now let's put all this together and see how the starting motor works. Look at Fig. 22-1. It will show you how motors work. First, notice the three pieces of copper wire and the shapes they have been bent into: two supports and one swinging loop. Note how the two supports have been fastened to a piece of wood with thumbtacks. Notice also how the swinging loop has been hung from the two supports, between the two poles of the horseshoe magnet.

If the battery is momentarily connected to the two supports, the swinging loop swings out from under the poles of the magnet. Here's the reason. When current flows through the loop, the magnetic field caused by the current opposes the magnetic field from the magnet. The result is that the magnet forces the loop out.

Now, in the electric motor, there are a lot of loops. The magnetic field they move in is very strong. So there is a very strong push on the loops.

22-2 STARTING-MOTOR CONSTRUCTION

The basic parts of the starting motor are the armature and the field-frame assembly (Fig. 22-2). The armature has a series of wire loops, or

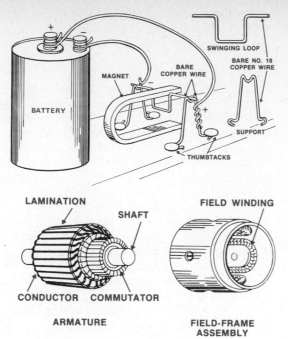

Fig. 22-1
A simple arrangement to demonstrate motor principles. When the circuit is closed by touching the wire to the support, the wire loop swings out from between the magnetic poles.

LAMINATION

SHAFT

FIELD WINDING

CONDUCTOR COMMUTATOR

ARMATURE

FIELD-FRAME ASSEMBLY

Fig. 22-2
The two major parts of a starting motor: the armature and the field-frame assembly.

conductors, mounted in a circle around the supporting shaft. The ends of the conductors are connected to the commutator. The only purpose of the commutator is to connect the loops, during their rotation, to the battery.

The field-frame assembly has field windings. They are called field windings because they produce the magnetic field in which the loops move.

The starting motor has other parts (Fig. 22-3). It has supports for the two ends of the armature shaft. It also has a drive gear to mesh with the flywheel ring gear. When the drive gear meshes with the fly-

Fig. 22-3
A disassembled view of a starting motor using an overrunning clutch and solenoid. (*Delco-Remy Division of General Motors Corporation*)

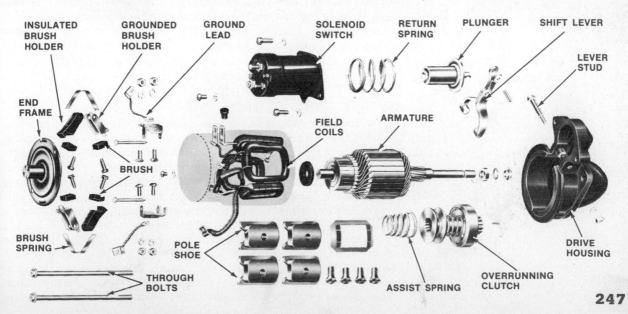

INSULATED BRUSH HOLDER

GROUNDED BRUSH HOLDER

GROUND LEAD

SOLENOID SWITCH

RETURN SPRING

PLUNGER

SHIFT LEVER

LEVER STUD

END FRAME

BRUSH

FIELD COILS

ARMATURE

BRUSH SPRING

POLE SHOE

THROUGH BOLTS

ASSIST SPRING

OVERRUNNING CLUTCH

DRIVE HOUSING

wheel ring gear and the armature spins, the flywheel and the engine crankshaft are rotated. The starting motor also has brushes to connect the armature commutator to the battery.

22-3 STARTING-MOTOR WIRING CIRCUIT

Figure 22-4 shows, in simplified form, the wiring circuit of a starting motor. The current flows into the motor terminal and through the two field windings. From there, it flows through one brush and then through the armature conductors to the other brush. This brush is connected to ground, which is the return circuit to the battery. Ground is explained in Chap. 20. The brushes make sliding contact with the armature commutator. The commutator is made up of separate pieces, or segments, each connected to the end of one of the loops, or conductors. The armature conductors are not shown in Fig. 22-4.

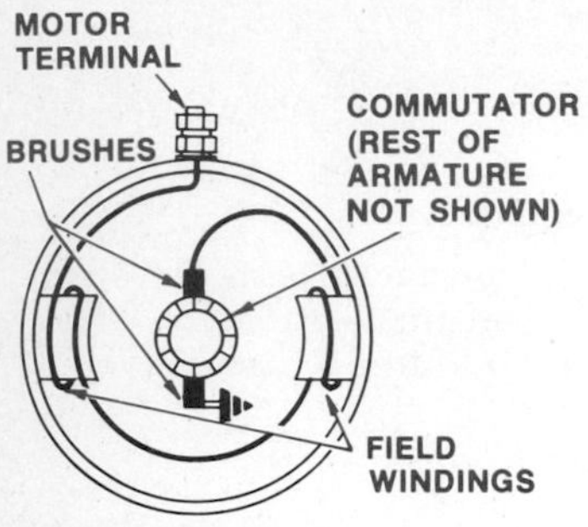

When current flows through the starting motor, a very strong magnetic field is produced by the field windings. Another powerful magnetic field is produced by the armature conductors. The field-winding magnetic field tries to push the armature magnetic field out of the way. The result is a powerful downward push on the loops, which causes the armature to revolve. When the armature is connected to the engine flywheel through the meshing gears, it spins the engine crankshaft so that the engine starts.

22-4 STARTING-MOTOR DRIVES

The drive gear on the end of the armature shaft has only about 12 teeth. It also is called a *drive pinion*. The ring gear on the flywheel has about 15 times as many teeth. Therefore, the armature must turn 15 times in order to turn the flywheel once. In actual operation, the armature will spin about 3000 rpm (revolutions per minute). The spinning turns the flywheel and crankshaft about 200 rpm. This is fast enough to start the engine.

Now let's look at what would happen if the gears remained meshed when the engine started. If the engine were to speed up to 3000 rpm, the armature would be spun up to 45,000 rpm. That speed is fast enough to damage the armature and burn out the armature-shaft bearings. To prevent this from happening, the starting motor has a special drive device. This device meshes the drive gear for starting but de-meshes it once the engine has started. The starting-motor drive used today is the overrunning-clutch drive.

22-5 OVERRUNNING CLUTCH

The overrunning clutch protects the starting-motor armature from damage after the engine starts. A starting motor using an overrunning clutch is shown in end and side sectional views in Fig. 22-5. The starting motor has a solenoid on top to operate the clutch.

Before we describe the solenoid, however, let us see how the clutch works. The clutch is a one-way drive. This means that the clutch will carry rotary motion from the starting-motor armature to the flywheel, but it will not carry the motion the other way.

Two views of an overrunning clutch are shown in Fig. 22-6. The clutch shown has four rollers positioned between the shell and the pinion and collar. The shell is attached to a sleeve. The sleeve has internal spiral splines that mesh with spiral splines on the end of the armature shaft. The sleeve and the shell can move back and forth along the

Fig. 22-4
Simplified wiring circuit of a starting motor.

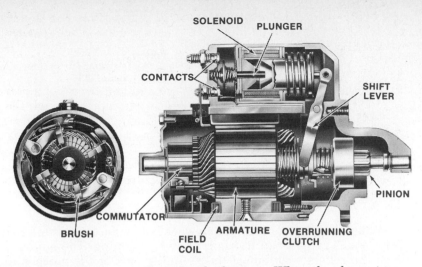

Fig. 22-5
End and side sectional views of a starting motor using an overrunning clutch and solenoid. (*Delco-Remy Division of General Motors Corporation*)

shaft, but they must turn when the shaft turns. When the sleeve turns, the shell turns with it. As the shell turns, it causes the rollers to be pushed along in the notches in the shell. These notches are smaller at one end. As the rollers are pushed along, they jam in the smaller notches. The collar and pinion are locked to the rollers so that the pinion must rotate with the shell and the armature.

Figure 22-7 shows the complete sequence of actions. First, in Fig. 22-7A, we see the pinion disengaged from the flywheel ring gear. Next, in Fig. 22-7B, we see what happens when the solenoid is connected to the battery. The connection is made through the ignition switch and key. When the key is put in the ignition switch and the switch is turned past ON to START, both the ignition system and the solenoid are connected to the battery.

Current flows through the solenoid and produces a magnetic field. The magnetic field pulls the iron plunger into the hollow center of the solenoid. When this happens, the overrunning-clutch assembly is pushed along the armature shaft. The pinion engages with the flywheel ring gear.

Next, as the plunger completes its movement into the solenoid (Fig. 22-7C), the plunger pushes a copper disk against the two heavy contacts in the inner ends of the solenoid terminals. Now current can flow from the battery, through the disk and terminals, and into the starting motor. The starting-motor armature begins to spin. The spinning armature spins the clutch sleeve. The rollers jam between the sleeve shell and the collar on the pinion. The pinion rotates and spins the flywheel, and the engine starts.

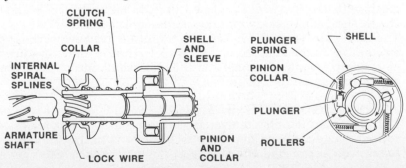

Fig. 22-6
Cutaway and end sectional views of an overrunning clutch. (*Delco-Remy Division of General Motors Corporation*)

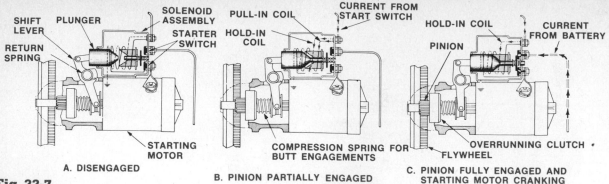

SHIFT LEVER · PLUNGER · SOLENOID ASSEMBLY · PULL-IN COIL · CURRENT FROM START SWITCH · HOLD-IN COIL · CURRENT FROM BATTERY · PINION · STARTER SWITCH · HOLD-IN COIL · RETURN SPRING · STARTING MOTOR · COMPRESSION SPRING FOR BUTT ENGAGEMENTS · OVERRUNNING CLUTCH · FLYWHEEL

A. DISENGAGED
B. PINION PARTIALLY ENGAGED
C. PINION FULLY ENGAGED AND STARTING MOTOR CRANKING

Fig. 22-7
The operation of the solenoid and overrunning clutch as the pinion meshes with the flywheel teeth. (*Delco-Remy Division of General Motors Corporation*)

When the engine starts, the flywheel spins the overrunning-clutch pinion much faster than it originally was spinning. The pinion collar turns the rollers back out of the jamming part of the notches in the sleeve. Now the pinion and collar can spin freely without causing the armature speed to increase.

22-6 SOLENOID WINDINGS

Notice that there are two separate windings in the solenoid; a pull-in winding and a hold-in winding (Fig. 22-7). The pull-in winding has a few turns of a heavy wire. The hold-in winding has many turns of a relatively fine wire. The pull-in winding takes a high current through it and produces a strong magnetic field. A strong field is needed to pull the plunger in and shift the pinion into mesh. After the shift has been completed, a much smaller amount of magnetism is required to hold the plunger in. Notice that the pull-in winding is connected to the two heavy contacts. When the copper disk hits the two contacts to connect the starting motor to the battery, the copper disk shorts out the pull-in winding. The hold-in winding, however, continues to do its job. It is connected from one contact to ground.

The purpose of the pull-in winding is to provide enough magnetism to shift the pinion into mesh. Then the pull-in winding is killed to reduce the load on the battery. The hold-in winding continues to hold the plunger in. This allows the battery to crank the engine without having to waste current where it is no longer needed.

22-7 GEAR REDUCTION

The starting-motor shown in Fig. 22-8 has a gear reduction which increases cranking torque. The shifter fork is enclosed. When it is actuated by the solenoid, it shifts the overrunning-clutch pinion into mesh with the flywheel. It also shifts the large driven gear on the clutch shaft into mesh with the smaller gear on the armature shaft. The gear ratio between the armature and the flywheel, because of the extra gears in the starting motor, is 45:1. That is, the armature turns 45 times to turn the flywheel and the crankshaft once. This provides a high cranking torque for starting.

STARTING-MOTOR SERVICE

In this part of the chapter we explain how to locate troubles in the starting system. If you find that the trouble is in the starting motor, remove the motor and check it further on the bench. Starting-motor

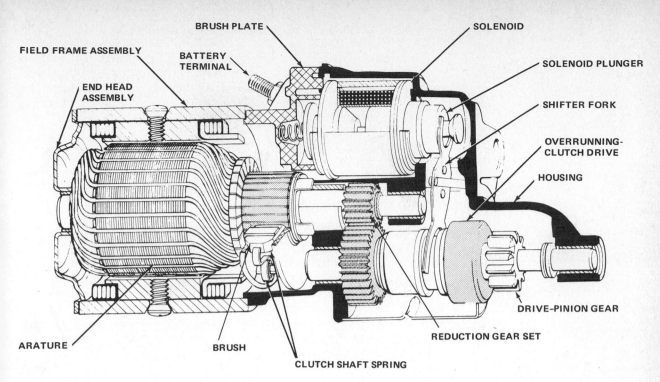

FIELD FRAME ASSEMBLY

BRUSH PLATE

SOLENOID

BATTERY TERMINAL

SOLENOID PLUNGER

END HEAD ASSEMBLY

SHIFTER FORK

OVERRUNNING-CLUTCH DRIVE

HOUSING

ARATURE

BRUSH

CLUTCH SHAFT SPRING

REDUCTION GEAR SET

DRIVE–PINION GEAR

Fig. 22-8
Sectional view of a gear-reduction, overrunning-clutch starting motor. (*Chrysler Corporation*)

service often is done in shops that specialize in automotive electrical work. In many shops, trouble in starting motors is fixed by "R and R." This means that the old starting motor is removed and replaced with a new or rebuilt starting motor.

22-8 TROUBLESHOOTING THE STARTING MOTOR
The basic problems with the starting motor are as follows:

- The starting motor does not crank.
- The starting motor cranks slowly, but the engine does not start.
- The starting motor turns over and cranks the engine at normal speed, but the engine does not start.

The last problem cannot be blamed on the starting motor. If it spins the engine at normal cranking speed, the starting motor has done its job. Now let's look at the other two problems.

22-9 MOTOR DOES NOT CRANK
When you turn the ignition key to START and nothing happens, the first thing you probably think about is a dead battery. You may be right. But before you check the battery, do this. Turn on the headlights and try cranking. Five things could happen when you do this. These are discussed below.

1. No Cranking, No Lights
When you try to start, if the starting motor does not do anything and the lights do not come on, either the battery is dead or a connection is bad. If you think there may be a bad connection, check the connections at the battery, at the starting-motor solenoid, and at the starter switch or relay.

2. No Cranking, Lights Go Out as You Turn the Key

If the lights go out as you turn the key, there may be a bad connection at the battery. The bad connection lets only a little current through—enough for the lights to go on. But when you try to start, all the current goes to the starting motor because the starting motor has much less resistance than the lights. Therefore the lights go out. Try wiggling the battery connections to see if this helps.

3. No Cranking, Lights Dim Only Slightly When You Try to Start

The trouble probably is in the starting motor. Either the pinion is not engaging with the flywheel, or there is an open circuit inside the starting motor. If you hear the starting-motor armature spin, then the overrunning clutch is slipping.

4. No Cranking, Lights Dim Heavily When You Try to Start

This is most likely due to a run-down battery. The battery has enough charge to burn the lights, but not enough charge to deliver 200 to 300 amperes to the starting motor. Low temperatures make it tough on the battery. The starting motor needs more current to start a cold engine because the engine oil is much thicker. The battery should be in good condition and fully charged in the winter to ensure starting. There is one other thing to consider when you get no cranking and the lights dim heavily. The starting motor or the engine may be seized or dragging.

5. No Cranking, Lights Stay Bright When You Try to Start

The trouble probably is either in the starting motor or in the circuit between the ignition switch and the solenoid. You have to check to find the problem. If the trouble is not in the wiring, then it is in the starting motor.

22-10 MOTOR CRANKS SLOWLY BUT ENGINE DOES NOT START

This condition probably is due to a discharged battery. The battery doesn't have enough power to crank the engine fast enough for starting. Low temperature could be a factor here, as it was in number 4 above.

Also, the driver may have run down the battery trying to start the car. For example, there might be a problem in the engine, ignition, or fuel system that is preventing the engine from starting. The driver continued to crank until the battery ran down.

NOTE

Never operate the starting motor for more than 30 seconds at a time. Pause for a few minutes to allow it to cool off. Then try again, if necessary. It takes a very high current to crank the engine. This can overheat the starting motor if it is used for too long a time. Overheating can ruin the starting motor.

The procedure here is to test the battery and replace it or recharge it, if it is low. Or, connect a booster battery and then try to start. If you still can't get the engine started, the trouble is in the engine, not in the battery. As long as the starting motor cranks the engine normally, the starting motor is working properly.

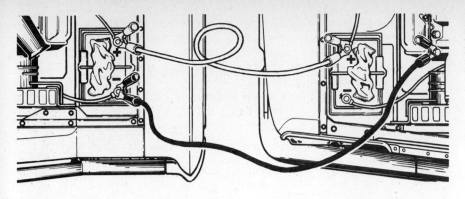

CAUTION

Use care in connecting a booster battery, to avoid hurting yourself or damaging the car electrical equipment. Here is Ford's recommendation for using jumper cables between two cars (for a negative-ground battery). The correct cable connections are shown in Fig. 22-9.

1. Remove the vent caps from both batteries. Cover the holes with cloths to prevent splashing of the electrolyte in case there is an explosion.
2. Shield your eyes.
3. Do not allow the two cars to touch each other.
4. Make sure all electrical equipment except the ignition is turned off on the car you are trying to start.
5. Connect the end of one cable to the positive (+) terminal of the booster battery. Connect the other end of this cable to the positive terminal of the dead battery.
6. Connect one end of the second cable to the negative (−) terminal of the booster battery.
7. Connect the other end of the second cable to the engine block of the car you are trying to start. *Do not connect it to the negative (−) terminal of the car battery!* This could damage electrical equipment.
8. Now start the car that has the booster battery. Then start the car that has the low battery. After the disabled car is started, disconnect the booster cable from the engine block. Then disconnect the other end of this (the negative) cable. Finally, disconnect the positive cable.

22-11 STARTING-MOTOR REPAIR

Repairing a starting motor is a job usually handled by a tuneup technician. Many shops handle starter trouble by replacing the old starting motor with a new or rebuilt one. Figure 22-3 shows a completely disassembled starting motor. The major steps in rebuilding a starting motor are as follows:

- Replace bushings supporting the armature.
- Test the armature and the field coils.
- Turn the commutator if required.
- Replace the field coils if they are damaged.
- Check the solenoid.
- Replace the brushes.

CHECK UP ON YOURSELF

You have now learned about the starting motor. Check up on yourself by answering the questions that follow.

1. What are the two main parts of the starting motor?
2. What type of drive is used in the starting motor?
3. How many windings are there in the solenoid?
4. What is the first check you make when the starting motor will not crank the engine?
5. What is the most likely cause if the engine turns over slowly but does not start?

ANSWERS

1. The armature and the field-frame assembly (Sec. 22-2). **2.** Overruning clutch (Sec. 22-5). **3.** Two windings (Sec. 22-7). **4.** Turn on the lights and try the starting motor (Sec. 22-9). **5.** A discharged battery (Sec. 22-10).

CHAPTER TWENTY-THREE THE CHARGING SYSTEM

After studying this chapter, you should be able to:

1. Describe the difference between a generator and an alternator.
2. Explain why a charging system is needed.
3. Describe the construction and operation of an alternator.
4. Explain the purpose and operation of alternator regulators.
5. Discuss the possible causes of a discharged battery and a low charging rate.

When you take current out of the battery, you have to put it back in, or you will end up with a run-down battery. The alternator does this job by converting mechanical energy taken from the engine into electrical energy. The battery is a storage place for chemical energy, but its capacity is limited. It must always supply current to the starting motor when the engine is cranked. As part of every electric circuit on the car, the battery must be ready to supply current for all these additional electrical loads. But when the engine is running fast enough, the alternator takes over the job as the source of electric current. At this time, the alternator begins to put back into the battery the current taken out for starting. (This is how the battery is kept charged.) In fact, the alternator takes over the job of handling the entire electrical load of everything that is turned on. The alternator, along with the regulator and wiring, is called the *charging system*. Here's what the charging system is all about.

23-1 GENERATOR

For many years, cars used the direct-current generator. You won't see this type of generator today except on old cars and on some small-engine applications and farm tractors. Figure 23-1 shows a generator. It produces electricity when an armature is rotated in a stationary magnetic field.

23-2 ALTERNATOR

The alternator (Fig. 23-2) is short and larger in diameter. It has replaced the generator in automotive vehicles for several reasons. It is

Fig. 23-1
External view of a generator.

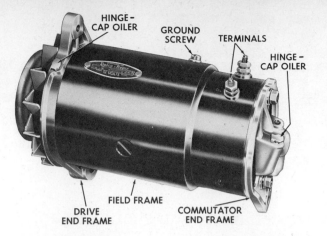

HINGE-
CAP OILER
GROUND
SCREW
TERMINALS
HINGE-
CAP OILER

FIELD FRAME
DRIVE
END FRAME
COMMUTATOR
END FRAME

BATTERY
TERMINAL
GROUND
TERMINAL

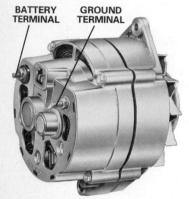

Fig. 23-2
External view of an alternator.

lighter in weight and simpler in construction. It has fewer parts that wear. This makes it easy to service. The charging system requires much less service than the generator and regulator used years ago.

23-3 MAKING ELECTRICITY

Before we describe how the alternator and voltage regulator work, let us review what we know about electricity. Current flowing in a wire held in a magnetic field causes the wire to move. The reverse of this is true. That is, if you move a wire in a magnetic field, you will cause, or *induce,* current to flow in the wire. This process is called *electromagnetic induction* because electricity is induced by magnetism.

You can demonstrate this effect with a strong horseshoe magnet, a wire, and a sensitive ammeter, as shown in Fig. 23-3. Move the wire back and forth through the magnetic field. The meter needle moves first in one direction and then in the other. The same thing would happen if you held the wire stationary and moved the magnet. In either case, current flows through the wire.

Relative motion between the magnetic field and the wire is the key. The wire must cut across the magnetic field. When the wire cuts the magnetic lines of force, current flows in the wire. When the wire moves one way, the current flows in one direction. When the wire is moved in the opposite direction, the current flows in the other direction. This is how we get alternating current in the alternator. We move wires back and forth, or else we move the magnetic field back and forth.

Actually, the "back-and-forth" movement in the alternator is rotary motion. A magnetic field rotates. Here is the basic difference between a generator (dc) and an alternator (ac). In the generator, the magnetic field is stationary and the armature (conductors) rotates. In

Fig. 23-3
Inducing current in a conductor. Moving the conductor back and forth between the magnetic poles induces current in it.

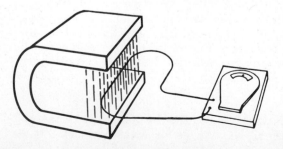

256

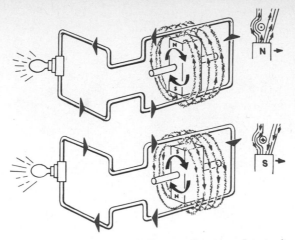

Fig. 23-4

Alternator principles. The magnet rotates inside the stationary wire loop. As it moves through the position shown at the top, current is induced in one direction in the loop. As it moves through the position shown at the bottom, current is induced in the opposite direction. Lines of force and directions of current flow are shown in the top part of the loop in the small drawings to the right. The dot means the current is flowing toward you. The cross means it is flowing away from you.

the alternator, the magnetic field rotates and the conductors (stator) are stationary.

23-4 ALTERNATOR PRINCIPLES

Figure 23-4 shows a simplified alternator. A stationary loop is held around a rotating magnet. As the magnetic field from the magnet cuts through the loop, current is induced in the loop. The current flows first in one direction as the north pole of the magnet passes the upper side of the loop. Then the current reverses direction as the north pole passes the lower side of the loop. In other words, the current that flows in the loop alternates. This makes it alternating current (ac).

The battery and other electrical devices in the automobile cannot use ac. It must be converted into direct current (dc). As we explain later, diodes do this. Diodes are discussed in Sec. 20-17.

23-5 ALTERNATOR CONSTRUCTION

Figure 23-5 shows an end and a side sectional view of an alternator. In the alternator the rotating part is called the *rotor*. Figure 23-6 shows

Fig. 23-5

End and side sectional views of an alternator with built-in diodes. The manufacturer calls this unit a Delcotron. (*Delco-Remy Division of General Motors Corporation*)

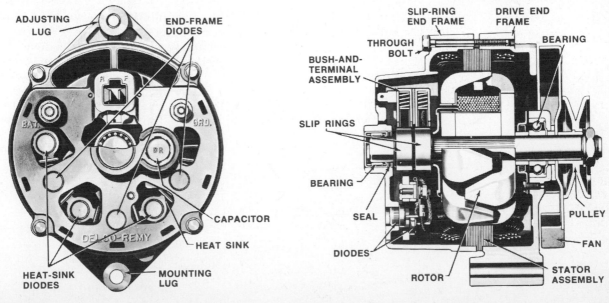

Fig. 23-6
The rotor of an alternator showing the brushes in place on the slip rings. (*Delco-Remy Division of General Motors Corporation*)

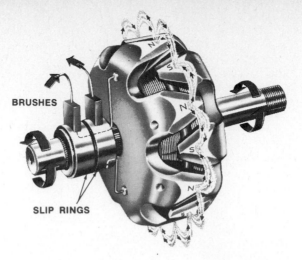

BRUSHES

SLIP RINGS

what the rotor looks like. Notice that the rotor has a winding placed between two pole pieces, as shown in the disassembled view in Fig. 23-7. When current is fed to the winding through the two brushes and slip rings, as shown in Fig. 23-6, magnetism is produced. The magnetism in the winding turns the points on the pole pieces into north and south poles. The magnetic lines of force go between the north and south poles, as shown in Fig. 23-6.

In the assembled alternator, the rotor is inside the stationary conductors, which are grouped together and called the *stator* (Fig. 23-8). When the rotor is rotated, the magnetic field it produces passes through the conductors in the stator. Current is induced in these conductors. The current is ac because north and south poles alternately pass the conductors. But the ac must be converted to dc. At the beginning of this chapter we said that diodes do this job. Now let us find out how the diodes do this.

23-6 DIODES

Diodes are one-way electric valves, as explained in Sec. 20-17. A diode lets current through in one direction but not in the other. For example, if you connect a battery in one direction to a light bulb and a diode, the light will come on. But if you reverse the connections to the battery terminals, the light will not come on because no current will flow.

Now, let's go back to the alternator. Inside it, alternating current is generated. If we connected a simple alternator through a diode to a battery, we get direct current and charge the battery (Fig. 23-9).

Fig. 23-7
The rotor of an alternator, partly disassembled. (*Delco-Remy Division of General Motors Corporation*)

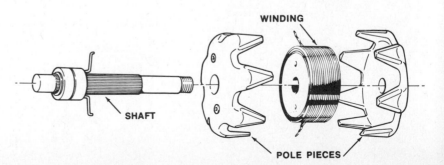

WINDING

SHAFT

POLE PIECES

23-7 DIODES IN OPERATION

The diode is called a *solid-state device*. It has no moving parts. The way the diode works in the alternator is a little more complicated than is shown in Fig. 23-9. There are actually three sets of conductors in the alternator stator. Thus there are three different alternating currents, one in each set of conductors. The alternator is known as a "three-phase unit," which means that there are three sets of conductors in the stator.

The reason for having three phases in an alternator is the same as the reason for adding more cylinders to an automobile engine. More cylinders in an engine provide more power strokes and a smoother flow of power. Three phases in an alternator provide more current and a smoother flow of current.

Let's see how diodes can convert ac into dc. Figure 23-10 shows how the diodes do this job. Notice that there are four diodes, numbered 1, 2, 3, and 4. Now, look at the left picture in Fig. 23-10. Notice that current is coming up through the right lead of the ac source. As the current moves up to the diode assembly, only diode 3 lets the current flow through. So the current moves up and flows to the negative (−) terminal of the battery. The current flows through the battery and back to the diodes. As the current returns to the diodes, only diode 1 lets the current flow through.

A moment later, when the current starts flowing in the opposite direction (it has alternated), the situation is as shown at the right in Fig. 23-10. Now the current is flowing up the left lead from the ac source. The current cannot pass through diode 1, but it can move through diode 2 and from there to the battery. On its return from the battery, the current passes through diode 4 and then down to the ac source.

Four diodes work together as one-way valves. Their operation changes the ac into dc, which can then be used to charge the battery.

23-8 DIODES FOR THREE-PHASE ALTERNATOR

The circuit for the diodes and the stator in a three-phase alternator is shown in Fig. 23-11. There are six diodes. The three sets of conductors in the stator are all connected at the center. The current from each set of conductors makes up the total alternator output. Figure 23-12 shows the location of the diodes in the alternator. They are mounted in the end frame. The six diodes work together to change the ac flowing in the three stator circuits into dc.

Fig. 23-8
The stator of an alternator. (*Delco-Remy Division of General Motors Corporation*)

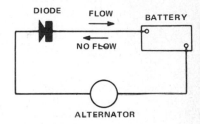

Fig. 23-9
Alternating current from an alternator can be changed to direct current by a diode. The diode allows current to flow in one direction only.

Fig. 23-10
Four diodes connected to an ac source to rectify the alternating current (change it to direct current) to charge the battery. "Rectify" means to change the ac to dc.

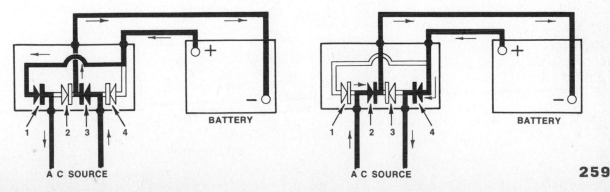

Fig. 23-11
The wiring circuit of an alternator with a six-diode rectifier.

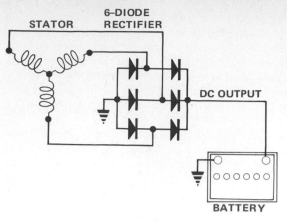

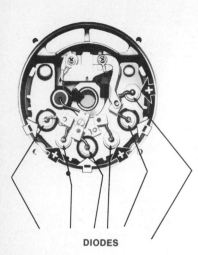

DIODES

Fig. 23-12
The location of the six diodes
in the end frame of an alternator. (*Delco-Remy Division of
General Motors Corporation*)

23-9 ALTERNATOR REGULATORS

Earlier alternators used external regulators which looked like Fig. 23-
13. Modern alternators have solid-state regulators which are mounted
inside the alternator, as shown to the left in Fig. 23-14. These regulators are small and very compact, as you can see in Fig. 23-15. They use
transistors, diodes, resistors, and other electrical components to do
their job. They control alternator voltage by controlling the amount of
current flowing through the rotor, that is, the field windings. When the
regulator fits inside the alternator, this is called an *integral charging
system.*

When the voltage tries to go too high, the voltage regulator cuts
down the amount of current flowing to the field windings. This lowers
the voltage by reducing the strength of the rotating magnetic field. As
a result, there is less current induced in the stator windings. The solid-
state voltage regulator does all this without moving parts. It uses transistors and other solid-state devices.

Fig. 23-13
An ac voltage regulator with
the cover removed. (*Pontiac
Motor Division of General
Motors Corporation*)

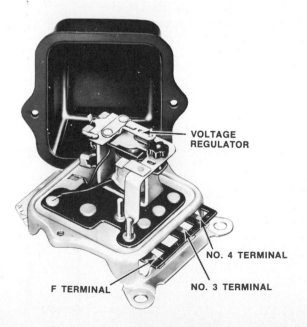

VOLTAGE
REGULATOR

NO. 4 TERMINAL

F TERMINAL

NO. 3 TERMINAL

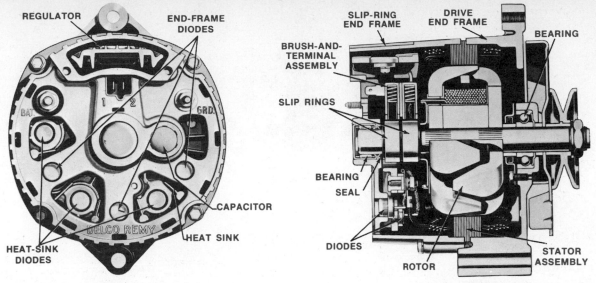

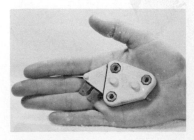

Fig. 23-14
End and sectional views of an alternator with integral diodes and a solid-state voltage regulator. (*Delco-Remy Division of General Motors Corporation*)

23-10 ALTERNATOR SERVICE

Let's look at the possible troubles that an alternator might have and find out what to do when trouble occurs. In some shops, when an alternator shows signs of trouble, the old unit is removed and replaced with a new or rebuilt alternator. When you work in the shop, you will learn how to use testers to check alternator action and how to remove and replace alternators. One important check is to make sure the belt tension is correct. If the belt is worn, you should replace it.

23-11 TROUBLESHOOTING THE ALTERNATOR

Two conditions that occur with the alternator are:

1. Charged battery and a high charging rate
2. Discharged battery and a low charging rate

There could be other problems such as a noisy alternator or faulty ammeter or indicator-light operation. Noise is due to a loose mounting, a bad drive belt, or trouble inside the alternator. If the problem is inside the alterator, the alternator must be removed for bench checking. Bad bearings and some types of diode failure make noise. Faulty indicator-light or ammeter action is caused by a burned-out light, by defective wiring, or by trouble in the separately mounted regulator. If the problem is a bad regulator, it has to be removed and replaced with a new one.

23-12 CHARGED BATTERY AND A HIGH CHARGING RATE

If the alternator continues to push a high charging rate into a charged battery, something is wrong. If it is not corrected, there will be more trouble! The voltage in the car will be high, headlights will burn out, and other electrical devices may be damaged. The battery will be overcharged and will have a very short life.

The most likely cause of a high charging rate with a charged battery is trouble in the regulator. If the regulator is an external unit, it

Fig. 23-15
A solid-state regulator that fits inside an alternator. (*Delco-Remy Division of General Motors Corporation*)

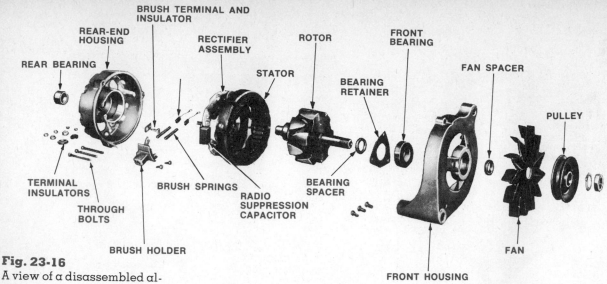

REAR BEARING
REAR-END HOUSING
BRUSH TERMINAL AND INSULATOR
RECTIFIER ASSEMBLY
STATOR
ROTOR
FRONT BEARING
BEARING RETAINER
FAN SPACER
PULLEY
TERMINAL INSULATORS
THROUGH BOLTS
BRUSH SPRINGS
RADIO SUPPRESSION CAPACITOR
BEARING SPACER
BRUSH HOLDER
FAN
FRONT HOUSING

Fig. 23-16
A view of a disassembled alternator. (*Ford Motor Company*)

Fig. 23-17
A rotor that has a pit burned into one of the slip rings.

can be checked and adjusted or replaced. Bad regulators inside the alternator are replaced by disassembling the alternator.

23-13 DISCHARGED BATTERY AND A LOW CHARGING RATE
With a low battery, the charging rate should be high. If the battery is run down and the alternator is producing little or no current, there is trouble. It could be caused by a loose or defective alternator drive belt or by some defect in the alternator or regulator. First, make sure the drive belt is in good condition and tightened to the proper tension. If it is, look at the wiring and connections. A loose connection in the charging circuit can prevent current flow to the battery. The other possibility is trouble in the alternator or regulator. This requires checking and servicing of the alternator or regulator.

NOTE
You need a tester to check alternator output. The meters tell you the voltage and current output from the alternator. Many cars have charge-indicator lights instead of an ammeter in the instrument panel. On these, the only way to tell how much current the alternator is putting out is with a test meter.

23-14 ALTERNATOR REPAIRS
Alternator repairs often are done in a shop that specializes in automotive electrical and tuneup work. Taking an alternator apart is a fairly simple procedure. Remove the pulley nut and the through bolts. Then the alternator can be pulled apart. Figure 23-16 shows a disassembled alternator.

Figure 23-17 shows a rotor that has a pit burned in one of the slip rings. If the pit is not too deep, it can be removed by refacing the slip ring in a lathe. Then the slip ring must be polished with fine polishing cloth. New slip rings can be installed on some rotors.

Many troubles that at first appear to be in the alternator can be traced to the regulator. In Fig. 23-18 the pencil points to a burned-out wire in an externally mounted alternator regulator. This made the red

indicator light on the dash come on. The driver thought that the alternator had gone bad. However, before installing a new regulator, you must find out for sure what caused the regulator wire to burn out.

CHECK UP ON YOURSELF

Now you have the facts about the charging system—alternators and regulators—and know what to do when someone comes into the shop with a run-down battery and no charge going to the battery. See how well you understand what you have studied about alternators by answering the questions that follow.

1. What do we call the part in the alternator that has a winding and two pole pieces?
2. What is the name of the stationary part of the alternator that contains the conductors?
3. In the alternator what are the two slip rings and brushes for?
4. What is the job of the diode?
5. What solid-state devices does the modern voltage regulator use to control alternator output?
6. If the battery is charged and the alternator continues to put out a high charging rate, where would you find the most likely cause?

ANSWERS

1. The rotor (Sec. 23-5). 2. The stator (Sec. 23-5). 3. To feed current to the field winding in the rotor (Sec. 23-6). 4. It acts as a one-way valve for current, thereby changing ac into dc (Sec. 23-6). 5. Transistors, diodes, resistors (Sec. 23-9). 6. In the regulator (Sec. 23-12).

CHAPTER TWENTY-FOUR
THE IGNITION SYSTEM

After studying this chapter, you should be able to:

1. Explain the purpose of the ignition system and describe the components in the system.
2. Describe the two circuits in the ignition system and explain how they work.
3. Explain the difference between the contact-point ignition system and the electronic ignition system, and explain how both systems work.
4. Describe the distributor used in the General Motors high-energy ignition system.
5. Explain the purpose of the centrifugal and vacuum advance mechanisms in the distributor and how they work.
6. Explain the operation of electronic spark timing systems such as the MISAR.

The ignition system produces the sparks that ignite the compressed air-fuel mixture in the engine cylinders. The sparks have to be hot enough to ignite the mixture. Also, they have to arrive at the engine cylinders at exactly the right time. Let's look at the ignition system and find out how it does its job.

24-1 COMPONENTS IN THE IGNITION SYSTEM

Figure 24-1 shows an ignition system in an automobile. Figure 24-2 is a schematic layout of the ignition system, showing the parts. The six major parts in the system are the battery, ignition switch, ignition distributor, ignition coil, wiring, and spark plugs. The ignition coil produces high-voltage surges. The distributor gets these surges to the right spark plugs at the right time. The high-voltage surges produce the sparks at the spark plugs. The heat from these sparks ignites the compressed air-fuel mixture in the engine cylinders so that the pistons move and the engine runs.

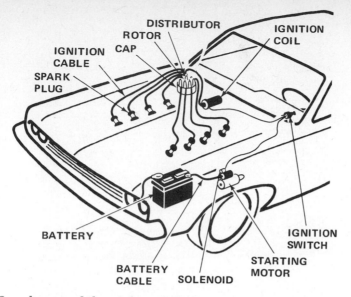

Fig. 24-1
Simplified drawing of an ignition system.

In Fig. 24-2, only one of the eight spark plugs is shown. The distributor cap has been removed from the distributor and placed below it.

24-2 IGNITION DISTRIBUTOR

There are two types of ignition distributors: the type with contact
points (Figs. 24-3 and 24-4), and the electronic type (Figs. 24-17 and
24-19). The contact-point distributor has been around for many years.

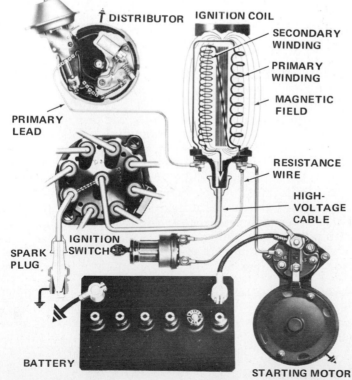

Fig. 24-2
Typical ignition system. It consists of the battery (source of
power), ignition switch, ignition coil (shown schematically), distributor (shown in top
view with its cap removed and
placed below it), spark plugs
(one is shown in sectional
view), and wiring. The coil is
shown schematically with
magnetic lines of force indicated. (*Delco-Remy Division of
General Motors Corporation*)

Fig. 24-3
Top and sectional views of an ignition distributor. In the top view (to left), the cap and rotor have been removed so that the breaker plate can be seen. *(Delco-Remy Division of General Motors Corporation)*

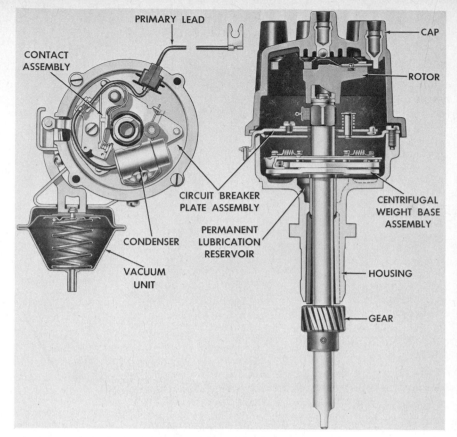

However, in 1973 automotive manufacturers began using electronic ignition systems. In the electronic ignition system, transistors are used as switches instead of contact points. We explain the operation of both systems in following sections.

24-3 OPERATION OF IGNITION SYSTEM
The ignition system has two circuits: the primary circuit and the secondary circuit. Both circuits go through the ignition coil. When the circuit from the battery to the ignition coil is closed (either by contact points or by a transistor), current flows into the coil. Because of the current flow through the coil, a strong magnetic field builds up around it. This loads the coil with electromagnetic energy. Then, when the circuit is opened, the magnetic field collapses. In doing so, it sends a high-voltage surge to the distributor. The distributor sends that surge to the spark plug in the cylinder which is ready to fire.

Now, let's examine the operation of the ignition system in more detail. We will look at the contact-point type first.

24-4 ACTION IN THE IGNITION PRIMARY CIRCUIT
There are two circuits in the ignition system. They are the primary circuit and the secondary circuit. In the contact-point system, the primary circuit (Fig. 24-5) consists of the following:

- Battery
- Ignition switch

- Primary winding in the ignition coil
- Contact points in the distributor

The contact points consist of a stationary point that is connected to ground through the distributor and a movable point that is mounted on a contact arm (Fig. 24-6). The distributor has a shaft on which a cam is mounted. The cam has the same number of lobes as there are cylinders in the engine.

When the engine is running, the distributor shaft turns. The cam repeatedly opens and closes the contact points. Every time a cam lobe comes up under the rubbing block on the contact arm, it pushes the arm out. This separates the movable contact point from the stationary contact point. Then, as the cam continues to move around, the cam lobe moves out from under the rubbing block. Now the spring on the mov-

Fig. 24-4
Partly disassembled distributor. (*Delco-Remy Division of General Motors Corporation*)

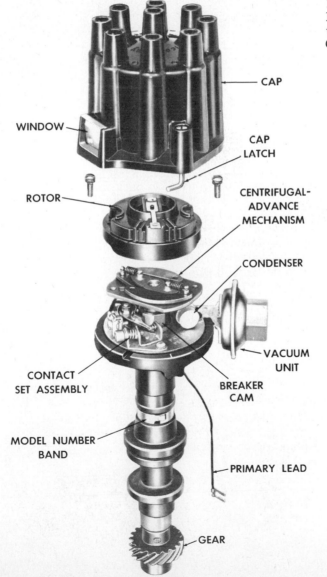

CAP

WINDOW

CAP LATCH

ROTOR

CENTRIFUGAL-ADVANCE MECHANISM

CONDENSER

CONTACT SET ASSEMBLY

VACUUM UNIT

BREAKER CAM

MODEL NUMBER BAND

PRIMARY LEAD

GEAR

267

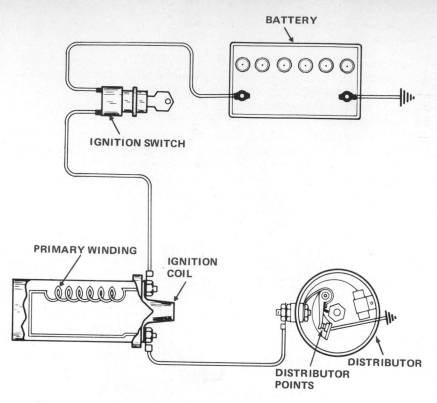

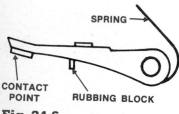

Fig. 24-6
A distributor contact arm.

able contact point pushes it back into contact with the stationary contact point. How long the points stay closed before they open again is called *dwell*. Dwell is the number of degrees of distributor-cam rotation that the points stay closed.

The contact points are often called *breaker points*. This is because they repeatedly break the circuit between the primary winding of the ignition coil and the battery. The cam is often called the *breaker cam*.

Fig. 24-7
Oil-pump, distributor, and fuel-pump drives. The oil pump is the gear type. A gear on the end of the camshaft drives the ignition distributor. An extension of the distributor shaft drives the oil pump. The fuel pump is driven by an eccentric on the camshaft. (*Buick Motor Division of General Motors Corporation*)

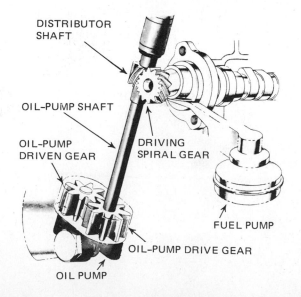

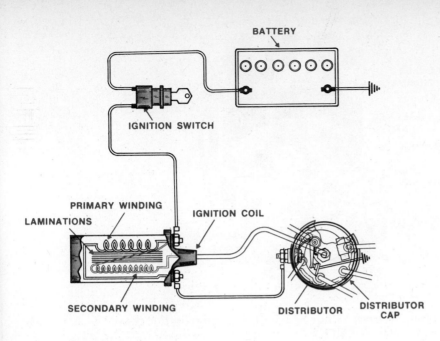

BATTERY

IGNITION SWITCH

PRIMARY WINDING

LAMINATIONS

IGNITION COIL

SECONDARY WINDING

DISTRIBUTOR

DISTRIBUTOR CAP

Every time the contact points close, the primary winding of the ignition coil is connected to the battery (while the ignition switch is turned on). This connection allows current to flow through the primary winding. A magnetic field builds up. (Current flowing in a winding produces a magnetic field around the winding.) Then, when the contact points are separated, the current stops flowing and the magnetic field collapses. It is this buildup and collapse of the magnetic field that produces the high-voltage sparks at the spark plugs.

24-5 DRIVING THE DISTRIBUTOR

The distributor shaft is driven from the engine camshaft by a pair of spiral gears, as shown in Fig. 24-7. The driving gear is on the camshaft. The driven gear is on the distributor shaft. This pair of gears also drives the oil pump, which you can see at the bottom of the picture. The camshaft turns at half the speed of the crankshaft. Because the

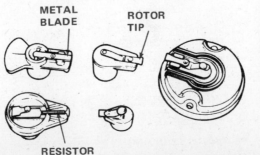

METAL BLADE

ROTOR TIP

RESISTOR

Fig. 24-9
Types of distributor rotors. The one at the lower left has a carbon resistor. The one at the lower right is attached to the advance mechanism by screws. (*Delco-Remy Division of General Motors Corporation*)

269

Fig. 24-10

A cutaway view of a distributor showing how the rotor is mounted on the top of the cam. This picture also shows the construction of the vacuum-advance mechanism. (*Ford Motor Company*)

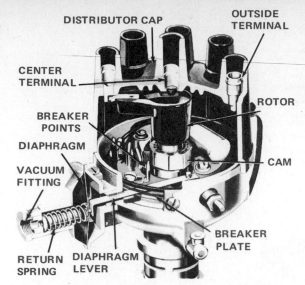

DISTRIBUTOR CAP
OUTSIDE TERMINAL
CENTER TERMINAL
ROTOR
BREAKER POINTS
DIAPHRAGM
CAM
VACUUM FITTING
RETURN SPRING
DIAPHRAGM LEVER
BREAKER PLATE

camshaft gear is meshed with the distributor gear, the distributor shaft turns at half the speed of the crankshaft.

24-6 ACTION IN THE IGNITION SECONDARY CIRCUIT

In Fig. 24-8 we add part of the secondary circuit. Shown here are

- The secondary winding in the ignition coil
- The distributor cap with the wires, or cables, coming from the cap and leading to the spark plugs

This part of the ignition system—the secondary circuit—produces the high-voltage sparks and distributes them to the spark plugs. Every time a piston is nearing TDC on the compression stroke, the secondary

Fig. 24-11

Here we add the rest of the secondary circuit—the high-voltage cable and spark plug.

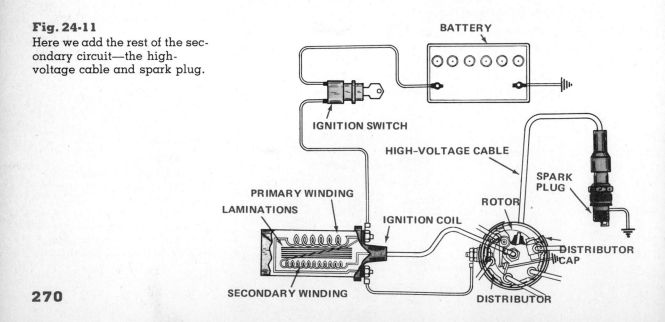

BATTERY
IGNITION SWITCH
HIGH-VOLTAGE CABLE
SPARK PLUG
PRIMARY WINDING
LAMINATIONS
ROTOR
IGNITION COIL
DISTRIBUTOR CAP
SECONDARY WINDING
DISTRIBUTOR

winding sends a high-voltage surge to the spark plug in that cylinder. A spark occurs at the spark plug, the compressed mixture fires, and the power stroke takes place.

24-7 DISTRIBUTOR AND ROTOR ACTION

Let's take a closer look at the distributing action of the distributor. On top of the cam in the distributor is a rotor (Fig. 24-9). The rotor sits on the cam, as shown in Fig. 24-10. As the distributor shaft rotates, the cam and the rotor also rotate. The rotor is a rotary switch. The purpose of the rotor is to connect the center terminal of the distributor cap to the outside terminals of the distributor cap.

The terminals in the cap are insulated from one another and held in place in the cap. You can see three of them cut away in Fig. 24-10. The center terminal of the cap has a carbon button on its lower end. This button rests on one end of the rotor blade. A small spring holds the carbon button and rotor blade in continuous contact. Therefore, the rotor blade is always connected to the secondary winding of the ignition coil. Whenever the coil secondary winding produces a high-voltage surge, the metal blade of the rotor sends the surge to the proper spark plug. That is, the rotor now points to the side terminal which is connected to the spark plug in the cylinder that is ready to fire (Fig. 24-11).

Let's go over this again. First, the cam turns and a lobe opens the contact points. This causes the magnetic field around the coil primary winding to collapse. The collapse produces a high-voltage surge in the secondary winding (we'll explain how later). The rotor is pointing to the side terminal in the distributor cap which is connected to the spark plug that is ready to fire (Fig. 24-12). The surge quickly comes out of the coil secondary winding. It goes through the high-voltage cable to the center terminal of the distributor cap. The surge then jumps a small air gap from the rotor to the side terminal and rushes to the spark plug. Now there is a spark at the gap between the two electrodes in the spark plug. The compressed air-fuel mixture is ignited by the heat from the spark. The engine power stroke results.

24-8 SPARK PLUG

The spark plug (Fig. 24-13) has an insulator to hold the center electrode, the shell to support the insulator, and the ground electrode. When the high-voltage surge enters the spark plug, it flows down the center electrode and jumps from the lower end of the center electrode to the ground electrode just beneath it.

Some spark plugs have a resistor built in, as shown in Fig. 24-14. This resistor limits interference on radio and television receivers. Every high-voltage surge that flows from the coil through the cables to the spark plugs sends out a form of radio wave. The radio wave is actually a magnetic field that can make noise in the radio or blur the television picture. The resistor reduces the current flow through the spark plug. This reduces the interference.

24-9 SECONDARY WIRING

The secondary wiring needs heavy insulation to hold in the high-voltage surges. The secondary cables are usually called *spark-plug wires*. At one time, the high-voltage cables were made of copper wire covered with a heavy rubber or neoprene insulation. Then the conducting core

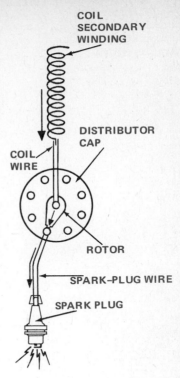

SECONDARY CIRCUIT

Fig. 24-12
Secondary circuit in simplified form. The coil secondary winding is connected to the spark plug through the distributor cap, rotor, and wiring.

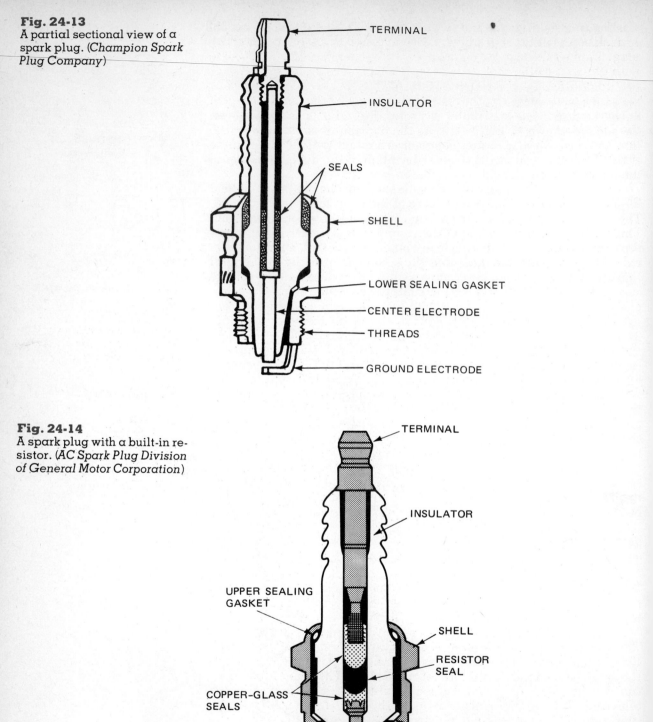

Fig. 24-13
A partial sectional view of a
spark plug. (*Champion Spark
Plug Company*)

TERMINAL

INSULATOR

SEALS

SHELL

LOWER SEALING GASKET

CENTER ELECTRODE

THREADS

GROUND ELECTRODE

Fig. 24-14
A spark plug with a built-in resistor. (*AC Spark Plug Division
of General Motor Corporation*)

TERMINAL

INSULATOR

UPPER SEALING
GASKET

SHELL

RESISTOR
SEAL

COPPER-GLASS
SEALS

LOWER SEALING
GASKET

CENTER
ELECTRODE

SIDE ELECTRODE

was made of linen impregnated with carbon. This core formed a high-resistance path that acted in the same way as the resistor in the spark plug. Later some car manufacturers used fiberglass strands coated with graphite as the conducting core. These cables do the same job as the linen-core cable, but are not damaged as easily. Now spark-plug wires are made of special string that is coated with carbon. A jacket of silicone rubber is placed around the string. Usually, the jacket is called the insulation. These silicone wires are very easily damaged by careless handling. They are easily identified by their size. Normal spark-plug wires are 7 mm in diameter. Silicone spark-plug wires have a diameter of 8 mm.

24-10 IGNITION-COIL ACTIONS

Let's take a closer look at the ignition coil and see how it produces the high-voltage surges. A coil partly cut away is shown in Fig. 24-15. The secondary winding is on the inside. The primary winding is on the outside. The laminations, which consist of strips of iron, help to concen-

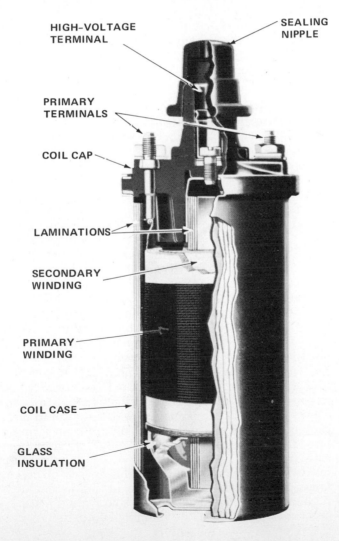

HIGH–VOLTAGE TERMINAL

SEALING NIPPLE

PRIMARY TERMINALS

COIL CAP

LAMINATIONS

SECONDARY WINDING

PRIMARY WINDING

COIL CASE

GLASS INSULATION

Fig. 24-15
A cutaway of an ignition coil. (*Delco-Remy Division of General Motors Corporation*)

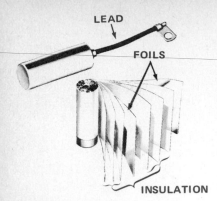

Fig. 24-16
A condenser assembled and with the winding partly unwound.

trate the magnetic lines of force.

When the contact points in the distributor close, they connect the primary winding to the battery. Magnetic lines of force build up almost instantly around the primary winding. Then, when the magnetic field is built up, the contact points open. As soon as current flow stops, the magnetic field collapses rapidly. That is, the lines of force move through the secondary winding at high speed. This produces the high-voltage surge in the secondary winding. The collapse is aided by the condenser, which we will describe later.

Now let's review. In the alternator, which is explained in Chap. 23, magnetic lines of force move through the conductors in the stator to produce electric current. The same thing happens in the ignition coil. The moving lines of force, as they collapse through the secondary winding, induce current in the secondary winding.

Every turn of wire in the secondary winding has a small voltage induced in it by the moving lines of force. Since there are thousands of turns of wire in the secondary winding, thousands of volts build up.

The voltage builds up enough to send a high-voltage surge of current from the center terminal of the coil cap. The current flows through the high-voltage cable to the center terminal of the distributor cap. From there, the current passes down through the rotor and the high-voltage cable to the spark plug that is ready to fire. The high-voltage surge jumps the spark-plug gap to produce the spark that ignites the compressed mixture.

24-11 CONDENSER

The condenser is also called a *capacitor*. It is made of two long strips of metal foil, with insulating strips of wax paper between them, rolled into a winding (Fig. 24-16). The winding is put into a metal can with a bracket so that the assembly can be mounted in the distributor, as shown in Fig. 24-3. The can is connected to one of the two metal strips. The other metal strip is connected to the lead that comes from the center of the can. In the distributor, the can is attached to the plate on which the contact points are mounted. This plate is called the *breaker plate*.

The lead is connected to the movable contact arm. The condenser, therefore, is connected *across* the breaker points. One of the metal strips is connected to the movable contact point. The other metal strip is connected to the stationary (grounded) contact point.

Now, let's see what the condenser does. When the contact points begin to separate, the current stops flowing. However, it tries to continue to flow even after the distributor contacts start to separate. Without the condenser, the current would jump across the separating contact points, making an arc. This arc would waste most of the high-voltage surge. There might not be enough voltage left in the coil to produce the spark at the spark plug. Also, an arc across the points would soon burn the points so that they would no longer make good contact. The condenser prevents an arc from forming. It momentarily provides a place for the current to flow while the contact points separate. In doing this, the condenser brings the current flowing in the primary winding to a quick stop. This speeds up the magnetic-field collapse and increases the voltage in the secondary winding. With a higher voltage, the spark at the spark plug is hotter. A hot spark ensures good ignition of the compressed air-fuel mixture.

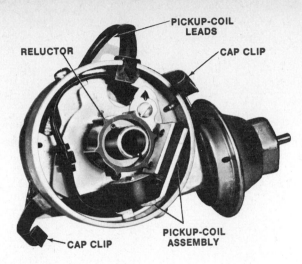

PICKUP-COIL
LEADS

RELUCTOR

CAP CLIP

CAP CLIP

PICKUP-COIL
ASSEMBLY

Fig. 24-17
Top view of the Chrysler electronic ignition distributor. The cap and rotor have been removed to show the reluctor and the pickup coil. (*Chrysler Corporation*)

ELECTRONIC IGNITION SYSTEMS

24-12 ELECTRONIC IGNITION VERSUS POINT-TYPE IGNITION

With the cap on, some electronic-type distributors look the same as distributors using contact points. However, when the caps are removed, the difference between the two is apparent, as you will see in later sections.

The electronic distributor is mounted and driven in the same way as other distributors. Both the contact-point system and the electronic system work almost the same way, especially in the secondary circuit. The big difference is the type of switch used to start and stop current flow to the ignition coil. In the conventional ignition system, contact points do the job. In the electronic ignition system, a transistor is used as the switch. Now, let's take a look at how some of the electronic ignition systems work.

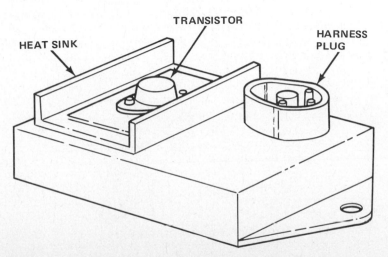

HEAT SINK

TRANSISTOR

HARNESS
PLUG

Fig. 24-18
Electronic control unit for the Chrysler electronic ignition system. (*Chrysler Corporation*)

Fig. 24-19
Schematic wiring diagram for
the Chrysler electronic ignition
system. (*Chrysler Corporation*)

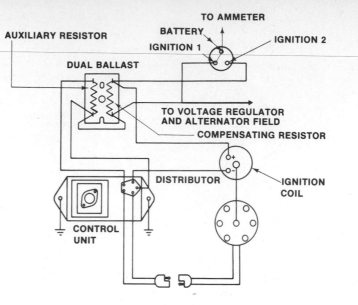

24-12 CHRYSLER ELECTRONIC IGNITION SYSTEM

An electronic ignition system has been used in all Chrysler Corporation cars made in the United States since 1973. In this system, the distributor has a metal rotor with a series of tips on it. This rotor, called the *reluctor,* is shown in Fig. 24-17. The reluctor takes the place of the breaker cam in the contact-point distributor. Notice that the reluctor in Fig. 24-17 has six tips. It is for a six-cylinder engine, so there is one tip for each cylinder. Notice also that the distributor has a permanent magnet and a pickup coil.

The reluctor provides a path for the magnetic lines of force from the magnet. Every time a tip of the reluctor passes the pickup coil, it carries the magnetic field through the coil. This magnetic field produces a voltage signal in the coil. The voltage is very small, but it is enough to trigger the transistor in the electronic control unit into action. Figure 24-18 shows the transistor in the electronic control unit.

The electronic control unit uses a transistor to control the flow of current to the ignition coil. When the voltage signal from the pickup coil arrives at the electronic control unit, the transistor in the control unit cuts off the flow of current to the ignition coil. From the time the current flow to the coil is stopped, the rest of the actions in the secondary

Fig. 24-20
A dual-ballast resistor.
(*Chrysler Corporation*)

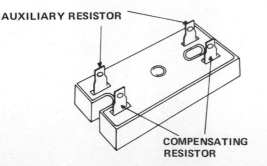

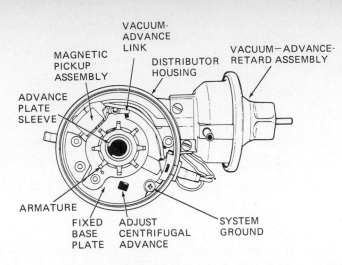

Fig. 24-21
Ignition distributor for an electronic ignition system. Note that Ford calls the rotating part an armature. Chrysler calls it a reluctor. (*Ford Motor Company*)

circuit are the same as in the point-type ignition system. The magnetic field around the coil collapses, creating a high voltage. This high-voltage surge is led from the coil through the distributor cap, rotor, and wiring to the spark plug that is ready to fire.

The tip of the reluctor now rotates past the pickup coil. The voltage

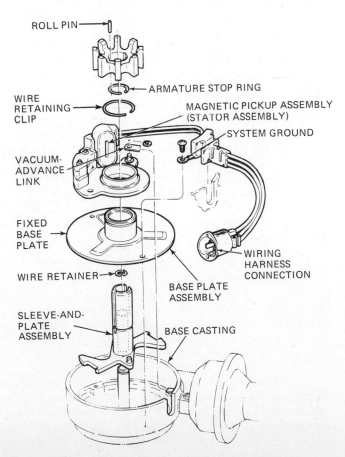

Fig. 24-22
Disassembled view of the distributor for an electronic ignition system. (*Ford Motor Company*)

Fig. 24-23
Proper relationship between
the tooth on the armature and
the core of the stator with the
distributor rotor at the #1 firing
position. (*Ford Motor Company*)

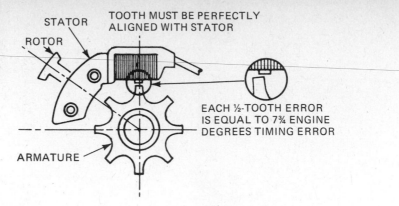

STATOR
ROTOR
TOOTH MUST BE PERFECTLY
ALIGNED WITH STATOR
EACH ½-TOOTH ERROR
IS EQUAL TO 7¾ ENGINE
DEGREES TIMING ERROR
ARMATURE

signal from the pickup coil ends. This allows the electronic control
unit to start current flow to the ignition coil again. As soon as current
flows through the ignition coil, a magnetic field builds up once more
around it. Then the next tip of the reluctor passes the pickup coil, and
the whole series of events is repeated.

In this system, there are no contact points to adjust or wear out.
Everything is automatic. Dwell, or how long current flows through the
ignition coil, cannot be adjusted. The only adjustment required is the
ignition timing, which we shall discuss later.

Figure 24-19 shows the wiring for the Chrysler electronic ignition
system. The dual ballast is a double resistor (Fig. 24-20). It protects the
system from overload but allows maximum current to flow during
cranking. This ensures a hot spark for good starting performance.

24-14 FORD ELECTRONIC IGNITION SYSTEM

The Ford electronic ignition system, which went into 1974 and later
Ford vehicles, is similar to the Chrysler system. Figures 24-21 and
24-22 show top and disassembled views of the distributor used in the
Ford system. Note that the rotor (or armature, as Ford calls it) has
eight tips. So the distributor is for an eight-cylinder engine. In Fig.
24-22, you can see what the pickup coil looks like. Ford calls this the
stator. The core of the stator around which the coil is assembled is
iron. The voltage signal in the pickup coil alternates, or changes direction, at the instant that a tip aligns with the core of the pickup coil.
This is shown in Fig. 24-23.

24-15 GENERAL MOTORS HIGH-ENERGY
IGNITION (HEI) SYSTEM

In 1973, General Motors introduced an ignition distributor that has
the ignition coil and electronic control module mounted in it (Fig.
24-24). This has been used with V-6 and V-8 engines. The wiring is
greatly simplified with this distributor. All connections to the ignition
coil and electronic control module are inside the distributor (Fig.
24-25).

The high-energy ignition system uses special spark plugs with a
wider gap. It may be as much as 0.080 inch [2.03 mm]. A standard
spark plug cannot be used with this system. To get the gap wide
enough on a standard plug, the side electrode must be bent at a severe
angle.

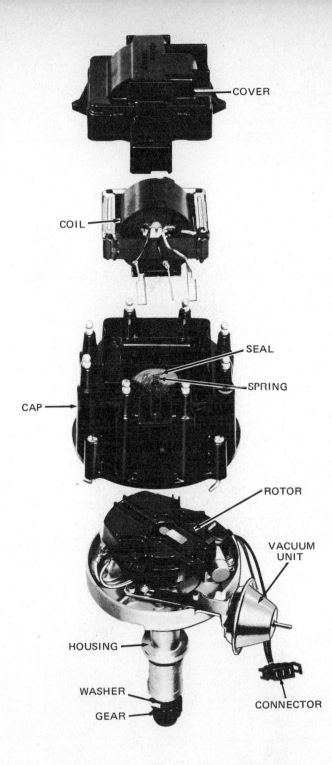

COVER

COIL

SEAL

SPRING

CAP

ROTOR

VACUUM
UNIT

HOUSING

WASHER

GEAR

CONNECTOR

Fig. 24-24
Partly disassembled view of
the High-Energy distributor.
(*Delco-Remy Division of General Motors Corporation*)

Fig. 24-25
Basic wiring diagram of the
General Motors High-Energy
Ignition (HEI) system. *(Delco-
Remy Division of General
Motors Corporation)*

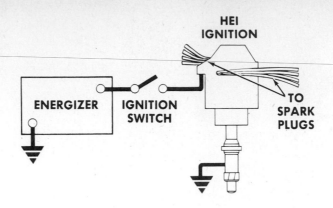

CAUTION

The HEI system produces higher voltage than many other ignition systems—
up to 35,000 volts. This is enough to give you a severe and dangerous shock. Be
careful in working around the high-energy ignition system.

CHECK UP ON YOURSELF

The part of the chapter you have just studied tells you a lot about
the ignition system and how it works to produce the spark that ignites the air-fuel mixture. Now, check your knowledge to find out
how well you understand what you have been reading about the ignition system.

1. What are the six major parts in the ignition system?
2. What are the two types of ignition distributor?
3. What are the two circuits in the ignition system?
4. What is the major difference between the contact-point and the electronic ignition systems?
5. In the contact-point system, does the spark occur at the plug when
   the points close or when they open?
6. How many strips of metal are there in the condenser?
7. How many electrodes does the spark plug have?
8. What is the purpose of the rotor and pickup coil in electronic distributors?
9. What are the special features of the General Motors high-energy ignition system, besides high voltage?

ANSWERS

1. Battery, ignition switch, distributor, ignition coil, spark plugs, and wiring
(Sec. 24-1). **2.** Contact-point and electronic (Sec. 24-2). **3.** Primary and secondary (Sec. 24-3). **4.** The type of switch used to control the flow of current to
the ignition coil primary winding. One uses contact points, and the other operates electronically (Sec. 24-12). **5.** When they open (Secs. 24-7 and 24-10).
6. Two (Sec. 24-11). **7.** Two (Sec. 24-8). **8.** To produce a voltage signal that
switches off the transistor to open the primary circuit (Sec. 24-12). **9.** The
electronic control unit and, in some models, the ignition coil are mounted in the
distributor (Sec. 24-15).

24-16 CENTRIFUGAL-ADVANCE MECHANISM

When the engine is idling or running at low speed, the spark is *timed*
to occur at the spark plug just before the piston reaches TDC on the
compression stroke. As the engine speeds up, there must be some way

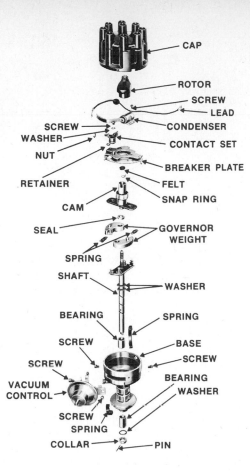

Fig. 24-26
A disassembled distributor.
(*Chrysler Corporation*)

CAP

ROTOR

SCREW

LEAD

SCREW

WASHER

CONDENSER

CONTACT SET

NUT

BREAKER PLATE

RETAINER

FELT

CAM

SNAP RING

SEAL

GOVERNOR
WEIGHT

SPRING

SHAFT

WASHER

BEARING

SPRING

SCREW

BASE

SCREW

SCREW

BEARING

VACUUM
CONTROL

WASHER

SCREW

SPRING

COLLAR

PIN

to advance the spark timing based on the speed of the engine. The centrifugal-advance mechanism in the distributor does this job.

NOTE

Ignition timing refers to the adjustment of the distributor so that the primary current is stopped at the right time. When the primary current is stopped (either by the points opening or by the action of the transistor), a high-voltage surge is produced in the ignition coil secondary winding. This high-voltage surge must reach the right spark plug at the right time. To change the time, the distributor is turned in its mounting. The adjustment shifts the position of the breaker points, or the position of the pickup coil in the electronic system.

When the engine speeds up, things happen much faster in the cylinders. The pistons move up on the compression strokes, go past TDC, and start down in far less time when the engine is running fast. However, the combustion process in the cylinder does not speed up by the same amount.

Therefore, if the spark continued to appear at the spark plug at the same time at high speed as at low speed, this is what would happen. The spark would occur and combustion would start. But the piston would be past TDC and starting down again before the combustion pressure got high. The piston would move down so fast that it would

Fig. 24-27
Position of the advance weights at low speed. There is no centrifugal advance action, so there is only the initial timing advance.

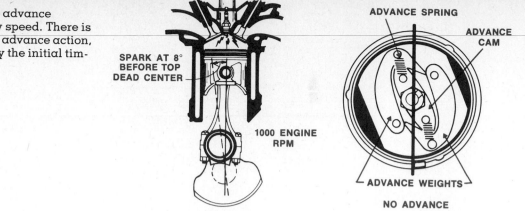

ADVANCE SPRING

ADVANCE CAM

SPARK AT 8° BEFORE TOP DEAD CENTER

1000 ENGINE RPM

ADVANCE WEIGHTS

NO ADVANCE

get ahead of the pressure rise. This would mean a very weak push on the piston and low power. Most of the energy in the burning fuel would be wasted.

To prevent this, distributors have centrifugal-advance mechanisms that advance, or push ahead, the spark as the engine speed increases. You can see the advance mechanism assembled in Fig. 24-4. In the view of the disassembled distributor (Fig. 24-26), you can see the separate parts of the advance mechanism. The parts include a pair of advance weights, also called governor weights. These weights are held by pivots on the base. The base is attached to the distributor shaft. Both weights have advance springs, which hold them in when the engine is idling. Figure 24-27 shows the relationship. At the left, the engine cylinder is shown in sectional view. The engine is running at 1000 rpm (500 distributor rpm). The spark is occurring at 8 degrees before the piston reaches TDC on the compression stroke. This gives the compressed air-fuel mixture enough time to start burning and develop high pressure.

At the right in Fig. 24-27, the positions of the two advance weights are shown with the engine operating at 1000 rpm. There is no advance. This is the basic ignition timing. In other words, with no advance, the

Fig. 24-28
Position of the advance weights at 4000 engine rpm. The weights have moved out against the spring tension to move the advance cam and breaker cam ahead. In the typical engine, the spark now occurs at 28 degrees before TDC, but these figures do not apply to all engines. Different engines have different advances.

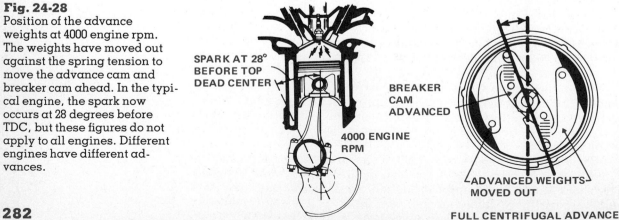

SPARK AT 28° BEFORE TOP DEAD CENTER

4000 ENGINE RPM

BREAKER CAM ADVANCED

ADVANCED WEIGHTS MOVED OUT

FULL CENTRIFUGAL ADVANCE

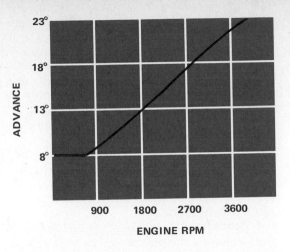

Fig. 24-29
A typical centrifugal-advance curve.

spark occurs at 8 degrees before TDC.

Now look at Fig. 24-28. It shows what happens when the engine is running at 4000 rpm (2000 distributor rpm). The increased speed has caused centrifugal force to push the advance weights out against the tension of the advance springs.

NOTE

The distributor is driven from the camshaft and turns at the same speed as the camshaft. Therefore, the distributor shaft turns at one-half crankshaft speed. This means that 4000 engine rpm is 2000 distributor rpm.

Centrifugal force is the force that acts on any object moving in a curved path. You can swing a pail of water over your head without spilling a drop if you swing it fast enough. The centrifugal force holds the water in the pail, even though the pail is upside down.

As the advance weights push out, their inner ends push against the advance cam, which is free to turn on the upper end of the distributor shaft. As the advance cam turns, it pushes the breaker cam forward in the direction of the rotation. Now the breaker-cam lobes move under the breaker-arm rubbing block earlier. The points are opened earlier. As a result, the timing of the spark is advanced. In Fig. 24-28, the spark has been pushed ahead, or advanced, 20 degrees for a total advance of 28 degrees (8 + 20 = 28) before TDC, when the engine is running at 4000 engine rpm (2000 distributor rpm). This gives the compressed mixture more time to burn and build up pressure on the piston. The energy in the fuel is therefore used more efficiently.

NOTE

The figures shown in Figs. 24-27 and 24-28 are not for any particular engine. They are typical and are given to show how the advance mechanism works.

24-17 CENTRIFUGAL-ADVANCE CURVES

Distributors are designed to provide different advance curves for different engines. The spark is advanced by the centrifugal-advance mechanism for every engine speed. Some engines need more advance than others, and the speeds at which the advances occur differ. For example, the curve in Fig. 24-29 is for one engine. Ignition starts with an advance of 8 degrees for any speed under 900 rpm (450 distributor rpm). As the speed increases, the advance begins. At 2700 engine rpm (1350 distributor rpm), the advance reaches 18 degrees and is at a maximum of 23 degrees at 3600 rpm (1800 distributor rpm).

The shapes of the advance weights and the advance cam, and the tension of the advance springs, are designed so that the engine has the proper advance. No two makes of engine are exactly alike. This is why the advance curves are different for each engine.

24-18 VACUUM-ADVANCE MECHANISMS

There is another condition under which an advance should occur—when the engine is operating at part throttle. At part throttle less air-fuel mixture gets into the cylinders. The mixture takes longer to burn after it is ignited.

So we have the same problem here as we had before. If the mixture burns slower, the piston will be past TDC and moving down before the burning mixture has produced high pressure. As a result, much of the energy in the fuel will be lost. The vacuum-advance mechanism is designed to prevent this loss. Its job is to advance (or retard) the spark timing based on the load on the engine at part throttle. Intake-manifold vacuum indicates these changing conditions.

You can see vacuum-advance mechanisms in Figs. 24-3 and 24-4. Figure 24-10 shows a vacuum-advance mechanism partly cut away. Sectional views of vacuum-advance mechanisms are shown in Figs. 24-3 and 24-30. The mechanism contains a flexible diaphragm that is spring-loaded. The center of the diaphragm is connected by a linkage to the breaker plate, on which the breaker points are mounted. The breaker plate is supported on a bearing so that it can rotate a few degrees one way or the other. Figure 24-31 shows how the vacuum advance works.

The sealed side of the diaphragm is connected by a tube to the carburetor. When the engine is idling, there is no vacuum advance. This is because the throttle is closed, and the throttle valve is below the vacuum port in the carburetor air horn.

When the throttle is partly open, the vacuum in the intake manifold can work on the vacuum port. The vacuum pulls the diaphragm in, as shown at the lower right in Fig. 24-32. Notice how the throttle valve swings past the vacuum passage. This puts the vacuum passage on the intake-manifold side of the throttle valve. The vacuum can then move

Fig. 24-30
The top view of a distributor with cap and rotor removed. The centrifugal-advance mechanism is shown in sectional view. The solid line, arrow, and dashed line show the no-advance and full-advance position of the breaker plate.

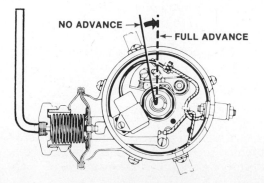

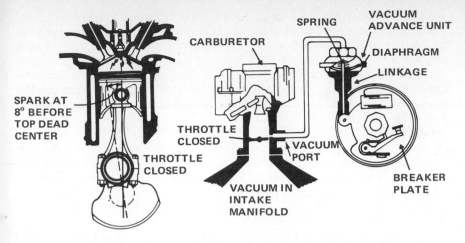

the diaphragm. This rotates the breaker plate a few degrees on its bearing. Therefore, the cam lobes move under the rubbing block of the movable contact lever earlier. This opens the contact points earlier so that the spark is advanced. In Fig. 24-32, the spark has advanced 12 degrees because of the vacuum-advance action. With the original timing of 8 degrees, the total advance becomes 20 degrees before TDC.

With a wide-open throttle, there is very little vacuum in the intake manifold. Therefore, there will be no vacuum advance. Vacuum advance occurs only when there is a vacuum in the intake manifold and during part throttle operation.

24-19 COMBINED ADVANCE
Most distributors have both centrifugal advance and vacuum advance. In a distributor equipped with both, the two advances combine to give the total advance needed for any engine operating condition. Centrifugal advance is based on engine speed. Vacuum advance is based on intake-manifold vacuum. Centrifugal advance always occurs as the engine speed increases. But vacuum advance is determined by the

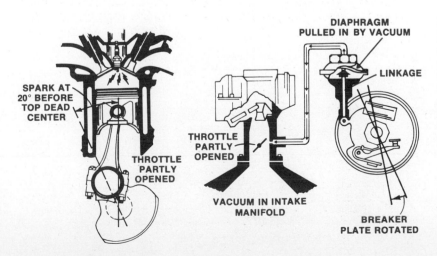

Fig. 24-32
When the throttle is partly opened so that vacuum is applied to the vacuum-advance unit, the breaker plate is rotated, or moved ahead. The cam closes and opens the points earlier to produce a vacuum advance.

position of the throttle and the vacuum in the intake manifold.

A curve showing a typical combined advance is shown in Fig. 24-33. The vacuum advance is shown as being added to the centrifugal advance. In the example shown by a black line, the centrifugal advance is 16 degrees. On top of this is 10 degrees of vacuum advance that is possible if the throttle is only partly open at the engine speed indicated. The result is a total of 26 degrees of spark advance.

24-20 CONTROLLING THE VACUUM ADVANCE
In many engines today there are emission-control devices that turn the vacuum advance on or off to reduce emissions from the engine. We discuss this in Chaps. 26 and 27 on automotive emission-control devices.

24-21 MISAR (MICROPROCESSED SENSING AND AUTOMATIC REGULATION) ELECTRONIC SPARK TIMING (EST)
In 1977, General Motors introduced a new high-energy ignition system which does not have a centrifugal or vacuum advance such as we just described. Instead, it uses an electronic control unit and four engine sensors. The MISAR ignition distributor still distributes the high-voltage surge. But this distributor no longer does the job of starting and stopping current flow to the ignition coil. The job of making and breaking the circuit between the battery and the ignition coil is done by an electronic control unit and four engine monitoring sensors. These are:

1. Crankshaft sensor in 1977 cars. (In 1978 cars, the sensor is inside the distributor)
2. Engine coolant sensor
3. Manifold vacuum sensor
4. Atmospheric pressure sensor

We will now look at these in detail.

24-22 CRANKSHAFT SENSOR
The crankshaft sensor is mounted to the front engine mounting bracket (Fig. 24-34). A disk with square-cut teeth around its outer edge

Fig. 24-33
Centrifugal- and vacuum-advance curves for one engine.

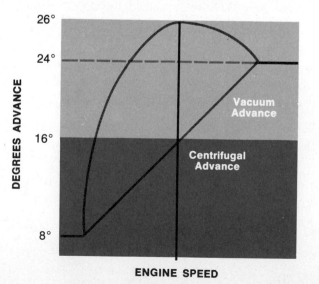

286

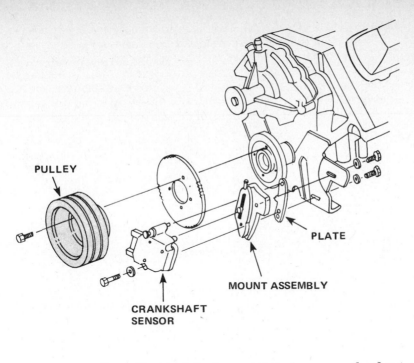

Fig. 24-34
Crankshaft sensor mounting
for the 1977 MISAR ignition system. (*Oldsmobile Division of
General Motors Corporation*)

PULLEY

PLATE

MOUNT ASSEMBLY

CRANKSHAFT
SENSOR

is mounted between the pulley and the harmonic balancer on the front
of the crankshaft (Fig. 24-35). This puts the disk, called a *pulse generator* disk, close to the crankshaft sensor. As the engine runs and the disk
rotates, the square-cut teeth change the magnetic pattern in the
crankshaft sensor. The crankshaft sensor therefore produces a signal
which is fed to the electronic control unit. This signal "tells" the control unit how fast the engine is running and also the position of the
crankshaft. The position of the crankshaft is vital information because
it determines the positions of the pistons on their compression strokes.
Using this information, the control unit adjusts the ignition timing to
suit the engine speed.

The 1978 version of the MISAR system eliminates the crankshaft
disk and sensor, shown in Figs. 24-34 and 24-35. Instead, this sensing
device is assembled inside the distributor. There it can sense the speed
and positions of the distributor shaft, camshaft, and crankshaft. This
provides the information the control unit needs to adjust the timing to
suit the engine speed. At the same time, the sensor in the distributor
"tells" the control unit when to cut off the flow of current to the ignition
coil. This is the same function that the pickup coil has in the other electronic ignition systems described previously.

NOTE
On the 1977 MISAR system, timing is adjusted by moving the crankshaft sensor (Fig. 24-35). The 1978 MISAR system has the speed and position sensor inside the distributor. On the later system, the distributor is shifted in its mounting. Section 29-8 describes ignition timing.

24-23 ENGINE COOLANT SENSOR
Retarding ignition timing tends to raise the engine operating temperature. Advancing the timing will allow the engine to cool down. Checking on this condition is the job of the engine coolant sensor. This sensor

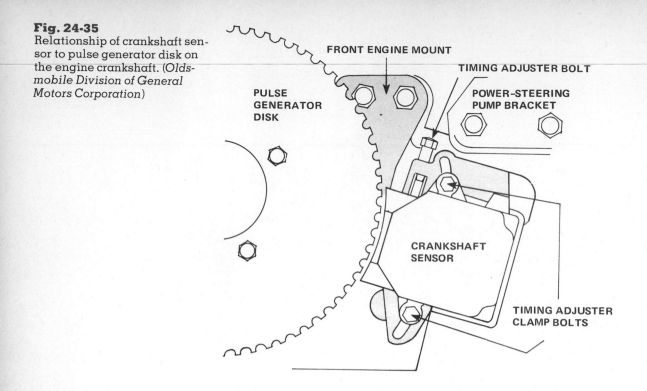

is located in the engine cooling system in the coolant crossover passage at the front of the intake manifold. The sensor changes in resistance as the coolant temperature changes. The resistance falls as temperature goes up. Therefore, current flowing through the sensor increases as the temperature increases. This sends a continuous signal to the electronic control unit which tells it how hot the coolant and the engine are getting. The control unit then adjusts the timing if needed, to prevent engine overheating.

24-24 MANIFOLD VACUUM SENSOR

The manifold vacuum sensor is in the electronic control unit. Figure 24-36 shows the control unit. Note that a manifold vacuum line or tube is connected to it. This line is connected to the intake manifold. Intake-manifold vacuum provides a continuous signal to the control unit. This enables the control unit to adjust the ignition timing to suit variations in intake-manifold vacuum. A high intake-manifold vacuum means less mixture gets into the cylinders, and the mixture burns slower. If the spark is advanced, the mixture is given enough time to burn and deliver its power to the piston. The conventional distributor has a vacuum-advance unit (Figs. 24-3 and 24-4) which provides the advance. But in the MISAR system, the vacuum acts directly on the control unit and causes it to advance or retard the spark as vacuum changes.

24-25 ATMOSPHERIC PRESSURE SENSOR

A second tube running into the control unit (Fig. 24-36) carries atmospheric pressure into the control unit. This corrects the spark timing for different atmospheric pressures. When the car is driven up a mountain so that the air pressure is less, the control unit adjusts the spark timing accordingly. It advances the timing as atmospheric pressure is re-

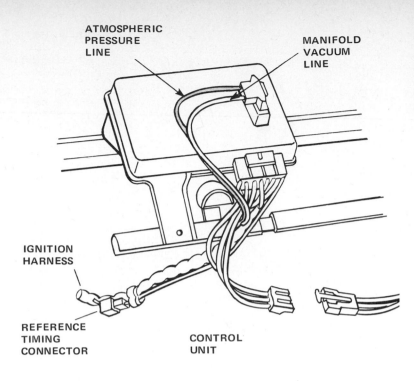

ATMOSPHERIC PRESSURE LINE

MANIFOLD VACUUM LINE

IGNITION HARNESS

REFERENCE TIMING CONNECTOR

CONTROL UNIT

Fig. 24-36
Various connections, including the atmospheric pressure line and the manifold vacuum line, to the control assembly for the MISAR. (*Oldsmobile Division of General Motors Corporation*)

duced. With lower atmospheric pressure, less air-fuel mixture enters the cylinders, and the mixture burns more slowly. Advancing the spark gives the mixture more time to burn and deliver its power to the pistons.

24-26 IGNITION SWITCH

In most cars, the ignition switch is mounted on the steering column, as shown in Fig. 24-37. This locks the steering shaft at the same time the ignition switch is turned off and the ignition key is removed. When this happens, a small gear on the end of the ignition switch rotates and releases a plunger. The plunger enters a notch in a disk on the steering shaft to lock the shaft. If a notch is not lined up with the plunger, the plunger rests on the disk. When the steering wheel, shaft, and disk are turned slightly, the plunger drops into a notch.

When the ignition key is inserted and the ignition switch is turned on, the plunger is withdrawn from the disk to unlock the steering shaft.

The ignition switch has an extra set of contacts that are used when the switch is turned past ON to START. The contacts connect the starting-motor solenoid to the battery so that the starting motor can operate. As soon as the engine is started and the switch is released, it returns to ON and the starting motor is disconnected from the battery.

The alternator field circuit is connected to the battery through the ignition switch when it is turned to ON. When the ignition switch is turned to OFF, the alternator field circuit is disconnected so that the battery cannot run down through the field circuit.

Another job that the ignition switch does is to operate a buzzer if the key is left in the lock when the car door on the driver's side is open.

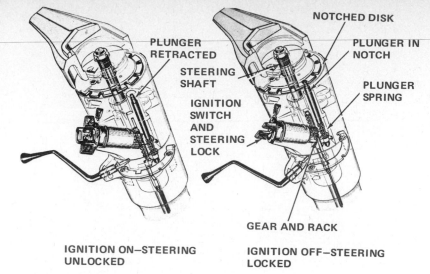

Fig. 24-37
A combination ignition switch and steering-wheel lock in phantom views, showing the two positions of the lock.

NOTCHED DISK

PLUNGER RETRACTED

PLUNGER IN NOTCH

STEERING SHAFT

PLUNGER SPRING

IGNITION SWITCH AND STEERING LOCK

GEAR AND RACK

IGNITION ON—STEERING UNLOCKED

IGNITION OFF—STEERING LOCKED

This is a reminder to the driver to remove the key from the lock when leaving the car. This makes it harder for a thief to steal the car.

Such accessories as the radio and the car heater are also connected to the battery through the ignition switch. This prevents the driver from leaving these units running when leaving the car.

24-27 IGNITION-COIL RESISTOR

In many passenger cars with 12-volt ignition systems, there is a resistance wire in the primary circuit (see Fig. 24-2). This wire is shorted out by the ignition switch when the switch is turned to START. Now, full battery voltage is imposed on the primary winding of the ignition coil for good performance during cranking. With full battery voltage to the coil, the secondary voltage is higher. The sparks are hotter, and the engine starts more easily. After the engine is started, the ignition switch is turned to ON. Now the resistance goes into the ignition primary circuit. This protects the contact points from excess current. Some cars use a separate primary resistor, but it works the same way.

24-28 IGNITION-SYSTEM SERVICE

The ignition system is a basic part of the engine. Whatever happens in the ignition system affects engine operation. If the engine fails to start even though it cranks normally, or if the engine misses, lacks power, overheats, backfires, or pings, the trouble could be caused by a faulty ignition system. In the chapters on engine service, we explain how to troubleshoot an engine to locate problems and how to fix them. The troubles mentioned above could also be caused by something in the fuel system, the cooling system, or the engine itself.

CHECK UP ON YOURSELF

When you work in the shop, you may have to service a faulty ignition system. In this chapter you have been reading about the fundamentals of this important system. Now answer the following questions to see how well you understand what you have studied.

290

1. What is the purpose of turning the distributor in its mounting?
2. What are the two types of advance mechanisms used in distributors?
3. To get a spark advance based on engine speed, is the breaker plate or the breaker cam moved ahead?
4. How is ignition timing adjusted?
5. Does the vacuum-advance mechanism move the breaker plate or the breaker cam ahead?
6. What are the four sensors used in the MISAR system?
7. What is the major difference between the 1977 and 1978 MISAR systems?
8. Where is the ignition switch on most cars?

ANSWERS

1. To change the spark timing (Sec. 24-16). **2.** Centrifugal and vacuum (Secs. 24-16 to 24-18). **3.** Breaker cam (Sec. 24-16). **4.** By turning the distributor in its mounting (Sec. 24-16). **5.** Breaker plate (Sec. 24-18). **6.** Crankshaft, engine coolant, manifold vacuum, atmospheric pressure (Sec. 24-21). **7.** The place at which crankshaft speed and position are sensed (Sec. 24-22). **8.** On the steering column (Sec. 24-26).

CHAPTER TWENTY-FIVE
OTHER ELECTRICAL UNITS

After studying this chapter, you should be able to:
1. Discuss wiring circuits in the automobile, including printed circuits, fuses, circuit breakers, and fusible links.
2. Discuss other components of the electrical system, including headlights, horns, indicating devices, speedometer, odometer, and windshield wipers, and explain how they work.

25-1 WIRING CIRCUITS
The electrical units in the automobile are connected by wires of different sizes. The size of each wire depends on the amount of current the wire must carry. The heavier the current, the larger the wire must be. The wires are gathered together to form wiring harnesses. Each wire is identified by the color of its insulation. For example, wires are light green, dark green, blue, red, black with a white tracer, and so on. The car manufacturers' shop manuals have special illustrations called *wiring diagrams* that show these various wires and their colors. If you have to trace a particular wire, refer to the shop manual to determine its color. Figure 25-1 shows the wiring to the instrument panel for one model car. Figure 25-2 shows the wiring to the fuse block. Note that each wire has its own distinctive color.

25-2 PRINTED CIRCUITS
The instrument panel has a number of indicating devices, switches, and controls (Fig. 25-3). Because the instrument cluster is crowded, there can be problems in making connections between the instruments. The modern solution is printed circuits.

A printed circuit is a flat piece of insulating material or board on which a series of conducting metallic strips are printed. Figure 25-4 shows part of a printed circuit. When a printed circuit is installed on the instrument cluster, the conducting strips carry current between the electrical units. For example, when the indicator bulbs are installed, the contacts on the bulbs rest on the metallic strips to complete the circuit. Figure 25-5 shows how a printed circuit is installed behind the instrument cluster.

25-3 FUSES

Fuses and circuit breakers are installed in various circuits to protect the electrical devices connected in the circuits. Their purpose is to open the circuit in case a short or ground develops and high current starts to flow. If this should happen, the fuse blows or the circuit breaker opens.

A typical older-style cartridge fuse is shown in Fig. 25-6. It contains a soft metal strip, connected at the ends to the fuse caps. When too much current flows through the fuse, the current overheats the metal strip, and it melts, or blows. This opens the circuit and stops the current flow. When this happens, the circuit should be checked to find out what caused the fuse to blow. Then, after the trouble is fixed, a new fuse should be installed. Figure 25-7 shows a fuse panel that takes the round fuse shown in Fig. 25-6.

Instead of the round fuse, many cars today use a U-shaped fuse (Fig. 25-8). This type of fuse can be plugged in and removed easily with your fingers. The fuse block in which these fuses are used is shown in Fig. 25-9.

Fig. 25-1
Instrument-panel wiring for one model of car. (*Buick Motor Car Division of General Motors Corporation*)

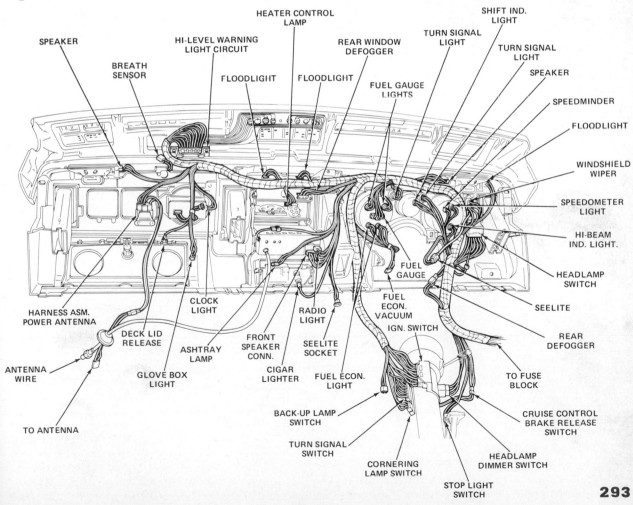

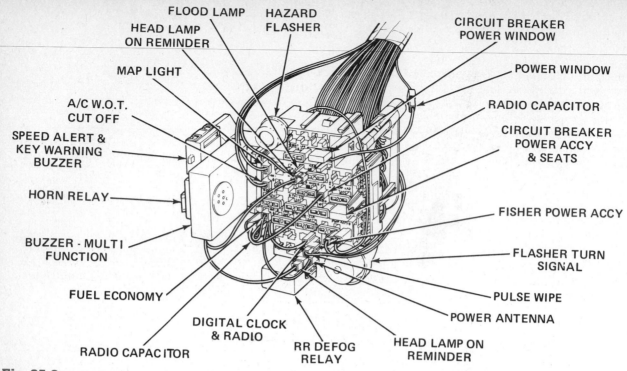

FLOOD LAMP   HAZARD FLASHER

HEAD LAMP ON REMINDER

MAP LIGHT

A/C W.O.T. CUT OFF

SPEED ALERT & KEY WARNING BUZZER

HORN RELAY

BUZZER - MULTI FUNCTION

FUEL ECONOMY

RADIO CAPACITOR

DIGITAL CLOCK & RADIO

RR DEFOG RELAY

HEAD LAMP ON REMINDER

CIRCUIT BREAKER POWER WINDOW

POWER WINDOW

RADIO CAPACITOR

CIRCUIT BREAKER POWER ACCY & SEATS

FISHER POWER ACCY

FLASHER TURN SIGNAL

PULSE WIPE

POWER ANTENNA

Fig. 25-2
Fuse-block wiring. (*Buick Motor Car Division of General Motors Corporation*)

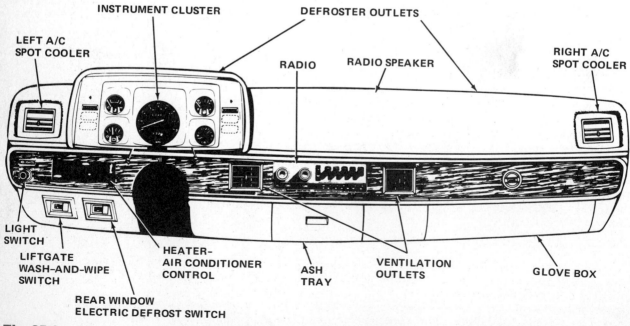

INSTRUMENT CLUSTER   DEFROSTER OUTLETS

LEFT A/C SPOT COOLER

RADIO

RADIO SPEAKER

RIGHT A/C SPOT COOLER

LIGHT SWITCH

LIFTGATE WASH-AND-WIPE SWITCH

REAR WINDOW ELECTRIC DEFROST SWITCH

HEATER- AIR CONDITIONER CONTROL

ASH TRAY

VENTILATION OUTLETS

GLOVE BOX

Fig. 25-3
The instrument panel on a fully equipped late-model automobile. (*Chrysler Corporation*)

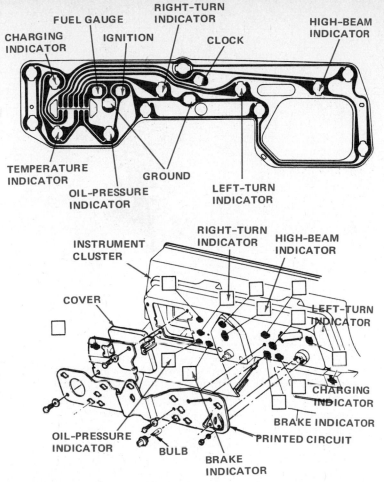

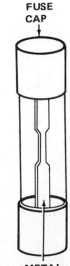

Fig. 25-4
A printed circuit. The black strips are the electrical conductors which form the printed circuit. (*Pontiac Division of General Motors Corporation*)

Fig. 25-5
An instrument-cluster assembly. (*Chevrolet Motor Division of General Motors Corporation*)

25-4 CIRCUIT BREAKERS

Circuit breakers are used in some circuits, such as the headlight circuit. The circuit breaker (Fig. 25-7) has a small winding that carries the current in the circuit. When the current is too high, the winding magnetism opens points to open the circuit. The advantage of the circuit breaker is that it keeps resetting itself. It gives a warning of trouble but does not completely kill the circuit. For example, if excessive current starts to flow in the headlight circuit, the circuit breaker will operate. The lights will flash on and off, warning the driver of trouble. The flashing light gives the driver enough time to pull over to the side of the road and stop.

25-5 FUSIBLE LINK

For added protection, many cars have fusible links in the insulated battery cable and in the larger high-current-carrying wires. Figure 25-10 shows how a fusible link is installed. It is a smaller wire than the wire it is protecting. If a short or ground occurs, the fusible link will burn in two before the larger wire. The other parts of the circuit will not be damaged. Figure 25-11 shows how to repair a burned-out fusible link.

Fig. 25-6
A cartridge fuse.

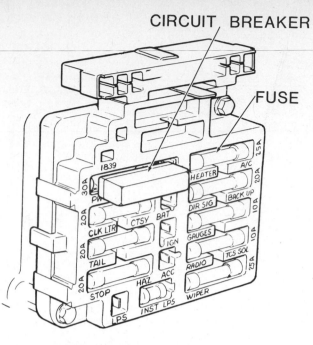

25-6 HEADLIGHTS

A typical lighting system for a car is shown in Fig. 25-12. The complete system includes headlights, parking lights, turn signals, side marker lights, stoplights, backup lights, taillights, hazard warning lights, and interior lights. The interior lights include instrument-panel lights, various warning and indicator lights, and courtesy lights that turn on when a car door is opened.

Figure 25-13 shows a headlight. It has a reflector and a filament at the back and a lens at the front. When the filament is connected to the battery through the light switch, current flows through the filament and it glows white-hot. The light is concentrated by the reflector into a forward beam and is focused by the lens.

Headlights are made in two types and four sizes (two round and two rectangular). The round sizes are $5\frac{3}{4}$ inches [146 mm] in diameter and 7 inches [178 mm] in diameter. The rectangular headlights are $6\frac{1}{2}$ by 4 inches [165 by 100 mm] and 7.9 by 5.6 inches [200 by 142 mm]. Round and rectangular headlights are shown in Fig. 25-14. The type of

Fig. 25-8
A good fuse and a blown miniaturized fuse. Note the terminals to test the fuse. (*Buick Motor Car Division of General Motors Corporation*)

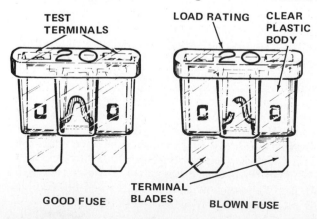

Fig. 25-9
Fuse panel using the miniaturized fuses. (*Chevrolet Motor
Division of General Motors Corporation*)

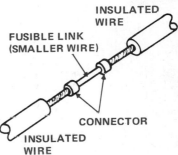

Fig. 25-10
A fusible link connected into a
hot-wire circuit.

headlight is identified by the number 1 or 2 molded into the glass at
the top of the lens. Type 1 has only one filament. Type 2 has two filaments: one for the high beam and the other for the low beam. The high
beam is for driving on the highway when there is no car approaching
from the other direction. The low beam is for city driving and for passing
a car coming in the opposite direction. The use of the low beam for
passing prevents the oncoming driver from being temporarily blinded
by the high beam.

Some cars have only one pair of headlights. These are type 2.
Other cars have two pairs of headlights: one pair of type 1 and one pair
of type 2.

The driver uses the dimmer switch to select the filament that will
glow. For example, on a car having only one pair of headlights (type 2),
the driver operates the dimmer switch to select either the high or low
beam. On a car having two sets of headlights (one set of type 1 and one
set of type 2), the arrangement is different. When the driver operates
the dimmer switch for low-beam driving, one of the filaments in the
type-2 lights comes on. When the driver changes the dimmer switch to
high beam, the other filament of the type-2 lights comes on. At the
same time, the single filament of the type-1 lights comes on.

25-7 AUTOMATIC HEADLIGHT CONTROL
This is an electronic device that automatically selects the proper headlight beam. It holds the lights on the high beam until a car approaches
from the other direction. The headlights of an approaching car trigger
a photoamplifier so that it switches automatically from high to low
beam. When the other car has passed, the photoamplifier automati-

Fig. 25-11
Repairing a burned-out fusible link. (*Buick Motor Car Division of General Motors Corporation*)

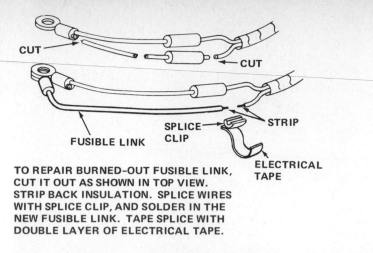

CUT

CUT

FUSIBLE LINK

SPLICE CLIP

STRIP

ELECTRICAL TAPE

TO REPAIR BURNED–OUT FUSIBLE LINK, CUT IT OUT AS SHOWN IN TOP VIEW. STRIP BACK INSULATION. SPLICE WIRES WITH SPLICE CLIP, AND SOLDER IN THE NEW FUSIBLE LINK. TAPE SPLICE WITH DOUBLE LAYER OF ELECTRICAL TAPE.

cally switches back to high beam. The device has several names: Autronic Eye, Guide-Matic, Automatic Headlight Dimmer, and so on.

The photoamplifier is mounted either on the top left side of the instrument panel or behind the radiator grill (Fig. 25-15). In either place the unit is in line with the lights of oncoming cars. The photoamplifier contains a light-sensing photocell that releases electric current when light strikes it. The current is very small, but it is increased by the amplifier section of the photoamplifier. This provides enough current to operate the power relay and shift the headlights from high to low beam. However, the driver can use the manually operated dimmer switch to override the photoamplifier.

25-8 STOPLIGHT SWITCH

The stoplight switch operates lights at the rear of the car to warn the driver behind that you are applying the brakes. Years ago, the switch was connected into the brake hydraulic system. When the brakes were applied, the pressure on the brake fluid operated the switch. Today, with dual-braking systems, this type of switch can no longer be used. Dual-braking systems are really two braking systems in one. One op-

Fig. 25-12
A typical headlight wiring system.

Fig. 25-13
Parts of a headlamp.

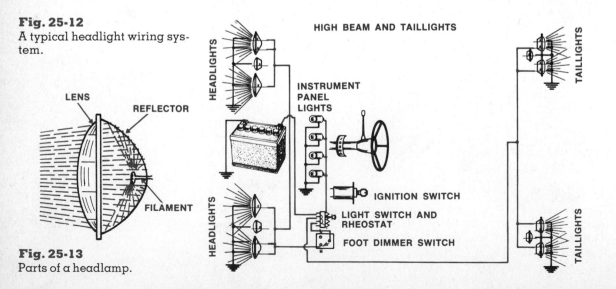

LENS

REFLECTOR

FILAMENT

HEADLIGHTS

HEADLIGHTS

HIGH BEAM AND TAILLIGHTS

INSTRUMENT PANEL LIGHTS

IGNITION SWITCH

LIGHT SWITCH AND RHEOSTAT

FOOT DIMMER SWITCH

TAILLIGHTS

TAILLIGHTS

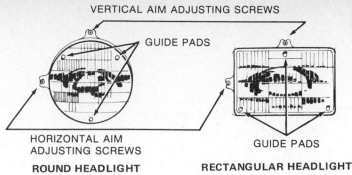

VERTICAL AIM ADJUSTING SCREWS

GUIDE PADS

HORIZONTAL AIM
ADJUSTING SCREWS

GUIDE PADS

ROUND HEADLIGHT

RECTANGULAR HEADLIGHT

Fig. 25-14
Shapes of the round and rectangular headlights.

erates the front brakes; the other operates the rear brakes. If one system fails, the other system can still stop the car.

The stoplight switch used on cars today is shown in Fig. 25-16. It is a mechanical switch that is operated by the brake pedal. When the brakes are applied, the switch contacts close and the stoplights come on.

Fig. 25-15
The locations of the components of the automatic headlight control system. (*Cadillac Motor Car Division of General Motors Corporation*)

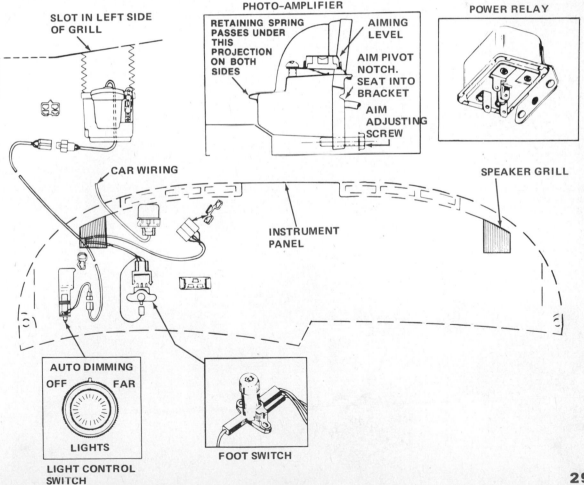

SLOT IN LEFT SIDE
OF GRILL

PHOTO–AMPLIFIER

RETAINING SPRING
PASSES UNDER
THIS
PROJECTION
ON BOTH
SIDES

AIMING
LEVEL

AIM PIVOT
NOTCH.
SEAT INTO
BRACKET

AIM
ADJUSTING
SCREW

POWER RELAY

CAR WIRING

SPEAKER GRILL

INSTRUMENT
PANEL

AUTO DIMMING

OFF   FAR

LIGHTS

LIGHT CONTROL
SWITCH

FOOT SWITCH

Fig. 25-16
A mechanical stoplight switch,
closed, with the brake applied.

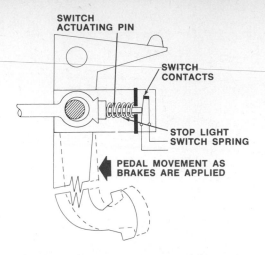

25-9 HORNS AND HORN RELAYS

The automotive horn is the vibrating type. Figure 25-17 is a sectional view of a typical horn. It has a field coil, a set of contact points, and a metal diaphragm. When the horn is operated by closing the horn button, current starts flowing through the field coil. This produces a magnetic field that pulls the diaphragm down. The diaphragm movement produces a click. As the diaphragm moves down, the contacts are separated so no current can flow. The magnetic field in the field coil dies, and the diaphragm is released. It moves up with another click. This action is so rapid that the separate clicks blend to form the horn sound you hear.

The horn relay (Fig. 25-18) has a single winding that is connected through the horn button to the battery when the horn blows. Current

Fig. 25-17
A sectional view of a horn.
(*Delco-Remy Division of General Motors Corporation*)

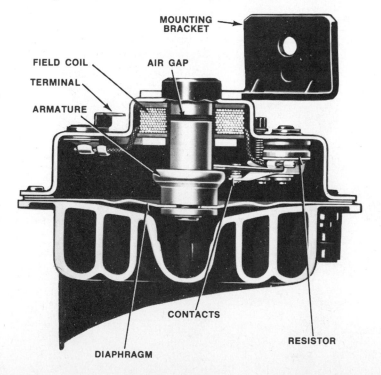

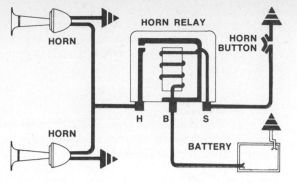

Fig. 25-18
A horn relay and horn circuit.

flowing through the winding produces a magnetic field that pulls the armature down and closes the contact points. This connects the horns directly to the battery, so the horns blow (see Fig. 25-18).

In today's cars, the horn relay has a second job. If the driver leaves the ignition key in the ignition switch and then opens the car door, the horn relay buzzes. The circuit for this arrangement is shown in Fig. 25-19. When the ignition key is left in the ignition switch, the switch closes a warning switch. The warning switch is located in the ignition switch and is connected to the door switch. When the door switch is closed as the door is opened, the circuit is completed to the horn-relay winding. The circuit is completed through a second set of contact points that is above the armature. When the circuit to the winding is completed, the winding magnetism pulls the armature down. This opens the upper points to open the winding circuit. The magnetism dies, and the armature moves back up. The points close and the action is repeated. This produces a buzzing sound that warns the driver to remove the ignition key.

25-10 INDICATING DEVICES

Many cars have an ammeter, or charge indicator; a fuel gauge; an oil-pressure gauge; and an engine-temperature indicator. These instru-

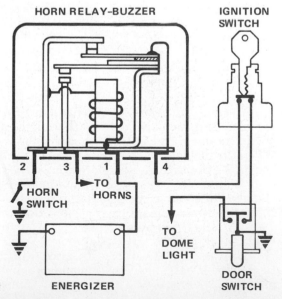

Fig. 25-19
A horn-relay wiring system of the type with the warning system.

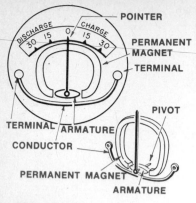

POINTER
PERMANENT MAGNET
TERMINAL
PIVOT

DISCHARGE
30 15 0 15 30
CHARGE

TERMINAL ARMATURE
CONDUCTOR
PERMANENT MAGNET
ARMATURE

Fig. 25-20
A simplified drawing of an ammeter, or charge indicator.

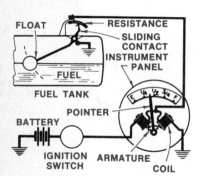

FLOAT
RESISTANCE
SLIDING CONTACT
INSTRUMENT PANEL
FUEL
FUEL TANK
POINTER
BATTERY
IGNITION SWITCH
ARMATURE
COIL

Fig. 25-21
A schematic wiring circuit of a balancing-coil fuel-level indicating system.

ments keep the driver informed of the operating condition of the engine. For example, if the oil pressure drops too low or the temperature goes too high, the indicators tell the driver that something is wrong so that the engine can be stopped before it is damaged. Let's take a look at these gauges.

25-11 AMMETER
In Chap. 20 we describe the ammeter in detail. The ammeter tells the driver which way the current is flowing—to the battery or from the battery. The ammeter also tells how much current is flowing (Fig. 25-20).

25-12 CHARGE INDICATOR LIGHT
Many cars have an indicator light instead of an ammeter. When the alternator is not charging the battery, the light comes on. When the alternator is charging the battery, the light stays out.

25-13 FUEL GAUGES
A typical fuel-gauge circuit is shown in Fig. 25-21. The fuel gauge has two units: a tank unit and a dash unit. The tank unit contains a sliding contact that slides back and forth on a resistance as a float moves up and down in the fuel tank. As the fuel level in the tank drops, the float moves down, and the sliding contact moves to reduce the resistance. This lets more current flow through the left coil in the dash unit. Less current flows through the right coil. As a result, the left coil becomes relatively stronger; that is, it has more magnetism. It pulls the armature around so that the pointer moves to the left, toward E, or empty. When the tank is filled, the float rises. This puts more resistance into the tank-unit circuit. Now, more current flows through the right coil in the dash unit. This coil becomes stronger and pulls the armature and pointer to the right to show that the tank is full.

Another type of fuel gauge is shown in Fig. 25-22. The tank unit works the same way as the one described above. However, the dash unit uses a different system to show the fuel level. This system uses a thermostatic dash unit. It consists of a thermostat with a coil wrapped around it. When the float rises, resistance in the tank unit is reduced. More current flows, and the coil generates more heat. The heat acts on the thermostat, causing it to bend. This pushes the pointer to the right, toward F, or full.

The fuel-gauge system also has a low-fuel-level warning light. The warning light is connected to a thermistor assembly in the fuel tank. When the fuel level is high, the thermistor is covered and kept cool. When the fuel level is low, the thermistor is exposed to the air and gets warm. As the thermistor gets warm, it passes more current. This action is just the reverse of what happens in most electric circuits. Usually, when a circuit gets hot, it passes less current. However, the thermistor passes more current, and the higher current operates the warning relay. The relay closes its points and turns on the warning light.

The instrument voltage regulator (Fig. 25-22) is also a thermostatic device. It cuts down the amount of current flowing to the instruments.

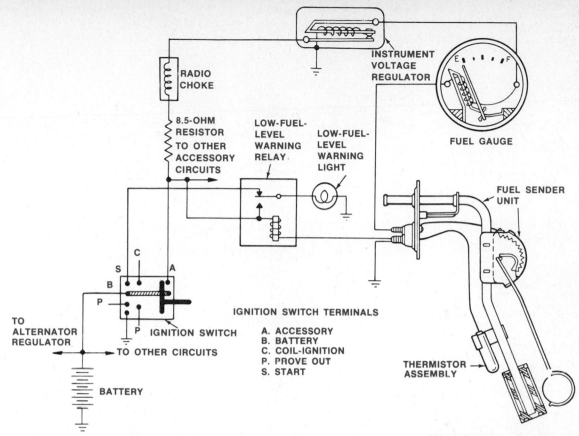

RADIO CHOKE

8.5-OHM RESISTOR TO OTHER ACCESSORY CIRCUITS

INSTRUMENT VOLTAGE REGULATOR

FUEL GAUGE

LOW-FUEL-LEVEL WARNING RELAY

LOW-FUEL-LEVEL WARNING LIGHT

FUEL SENDER UNIT

S C A B P

P IGNITION SWITCH

TO ALTERNATOR REGULATOR

TO OTHER CIRCUITS

BATTERY

IGNITION SWITCH TERMINALS

A. ACCESSORY
B. BATTERY
C. COIL-IGNITION
P. PROVE OUT
S. START

THERMISTOR ASSEMBLY

Fig. 25-22
A schematic wiring circuit of a thermostatic fuel-gauge system which includes a low-fuel-level warning system. (*Ford Motor Company*)

25-14 OIL-PRESSURE INDICATORS

Figure 25-23 shows the wiring circuit of an oil-pressure indicator. The unit is mounted on the engine so that it is subjected to engine oil pressure. The pressure pushes up on the diaphragm. The upward movement causes the sliding contact to move. Increased pressure moves the sliding contact so that the resistance is increased. This means that current flowing through the left coil in the dash unit now flows through the right coil. The right coil gets stronger magnetically and pulls the armature and pointer around to show the higher pressure.

Most cars use an oil-pressure indicator light. The light is off when the oil pressure is normal. But if the pressure drops too low, the light comes on.

25-15 ENGINE-TEMPERATURE INDICATORS

Figure 25-24 shows the wiring circuit of an engine-temperature indicator. The engine unit is immersed in coolant so that the unit senses engine temperature at all times. The unit is a thermistor, and its resistance decreases as it gets hot. This means that the right coil in the dash unit becomes stronger magnetically as the engine heats up. As a result, the armature and pointer are pulled around to show the increased temperature.

Many cars use indicator lights instead of a gauge. Figure 25-25 shows the wiring diagram for an indicator-light system. The system

303

Fig. 25-23
A schematic wiring circuit of a balancing-coil oil-pressure indicator system.

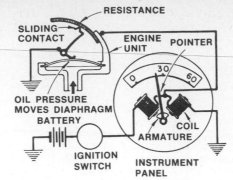

RESISTANCE
SLIDING CONTACT
ENGINE UNIT
POINTER
0 30 60
OIL PRESSURE MOVES DIAPHRAGM
BATTERY
COIL
ARMATURE
IGNITION SWITCH
INSTRUMENT PANEL

Fig. 25-24
A schematic wiring circuit of a balancing-coil engine-temperature indicator system.

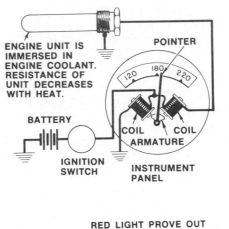

ENGINE UNIT IS IMMERSED IN ENGINE COOLANT. RESISTANCE OF UNIT DECREASES WITH HEAT.
POINTER
120 180 220
BATTERY
COIL ARMATURE
COIL
IGNITION SWITCH
INSTRUMENT PANEL

Fig. 25-25
A temperature indicator system which uses COLD and HOT indicator lights.

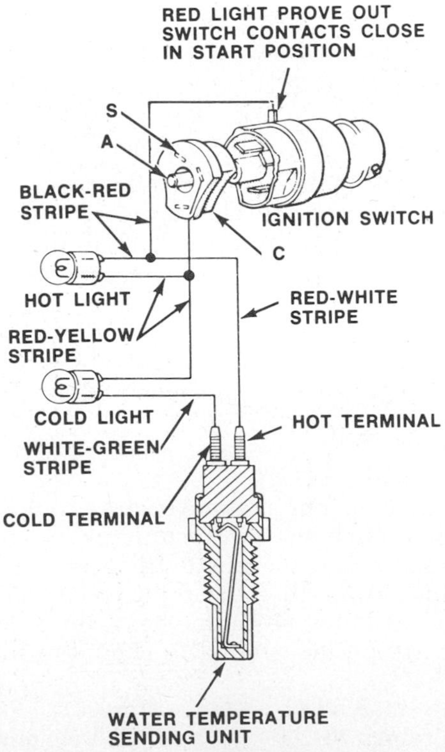

RED LIGHT PROVE OUT SWITCH CONTACTS CLOSE IN START POSITION
S
A
BLACK-RED STRIPE
IGNITION SWITCH
C
HOT LIGHT
RED-YELLOW STRIPE
RED-WHITE STRIPE
COLD LIGHT
WHITE-GREEN STRIPE
HOT TERMINAL
COLD TERMINAL
WATER TEMPERATURE SENDING UNIT

has two lights and a thermostatic engine unit. When the engine is cold, the thermostat blade is straight and contacts the terminal connected to the "cold" light. The cold light comes on to show that the engine is cold. As the engine warms up, the thermostat blade bends and moves away from the cold terminal. The cold light goes out. If the engine gets too hot, the thermostat blade bends so much that it touches the hot terminal. Now the "hot" light, which is red, comes on to warn the driver that the engine is overheating.

25-16 SPEEDOMETER AND ODOMETER

The speedometer and the odometer are not electrical. We discuss them here because they are also mounted in the instrument cluster with the other instruments. The speedometer tells the driver how fast the car is going. The odometer tells the driver the distance the car has been driven. Figure 25-26 is a cutaway view of the assembly.

There is a small magnet mounted on a shaft inside the speedometer. This magnet is driven by a flexible cable from the transmission. The faster the car goes, the faster the magnet spins. This action produces a rotating magnetic field that drags on the aluminum ring surrounding the magnet. The faster the spinning, the more drag on the ring. The spinning action causes the aluminum ring to swing around against the drag of a spring. This, in turn, moves a pointer attached to the ring, which indicates the car speed.

The odometer is operated by a pair of gears from the rotating flexible cable. The motion is carried through the gears to the mileage or kilometer rings on the odometer indicator. These rings turn to show the distance the car has been driven.

25-17 WINDSHIELD WIPERS

Windshield wipers are driven by an electric motor. A typical system is shown in Fig. 25-27. The motor, through gearing, causes the wiper blades to move back and forth on the windshield. Most cars have a windshield washer as part of the windshield-wiper system. When the driver presses a button, a squirt of cleaning liquid covers the windshield. Now the blades can clean the windshield more effectively.

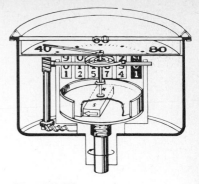

Fig. 25-26
A cutaway view of a typical speedometer-odometer assembly.

Fig. 25-27
Three-speed windshield-wiper assembly and mounting arrangements. (*Chrysler Corporation*)

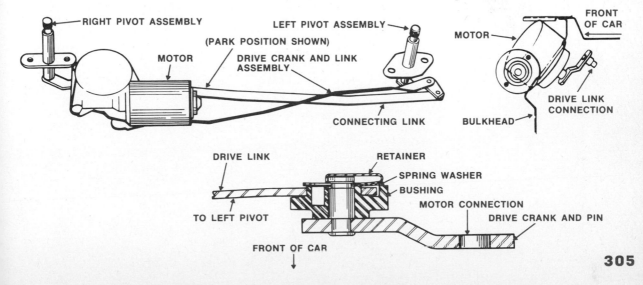

CHECK UP ON YOURSELF

You have learned about the smaller electric circuits in the automobile. Find out how well you understand what you have studied by answering the questions that follow.

1. What is the name of the assembly of wires that connects various electrical components?
2. What is the name of the flat piece of insulating material on which a series of conducting strips are printed?
3. What are two types of protective devices in the automotive electric circuits?
4. What are four indicating devices found on most cars?
5. How is the speedometer driven?

ANSWERS

1. The wiring harness (Sec. 25-1). 2. The printed circuit (Sec. 25-2). 3. Fuses and circuit breakers. The fusible link is a form of fuse (Secs. 25-3 to 25-5). 4. The ammeter, or charge indicator; the fuel gauge; the oil-pressure indicator; and the engine-temperature indicator (Sec. 25-10). 5. By a flexible cable from the transmission (Sec. 25-16).

PART FOUR

AUTOMOTIVE EMISSION CONTROLS

In recent years, there has been a great deal of attention focused on the automobile as an air polluter. In the engine, gasoline is mixed with air to produce a combustible mixture. When this mixture burns in the engine cylinders, the engine runs and the car moves. However, as explained in Chap. 17, complete combustion never occurs. Some polluting gases always come out of the tail pipe. These chemicals contribute to air pollution. They can cause smog which is unhealthy to breathe and to live in. To help control this unhealthy condition, federal and state laws require car manufacturers to install pollution-control or "smog" devices on their cars. These devices cut down the amount of air pollutants given off by cars. There are two chapters in Part Four:

CHAPTER 26 Automotive Emission Controls
         27 Automotive Emission Controls Service

CHAPTER TWENTY-SIX
AUTOMOTIVE EMISSION CONTROLS

After studying this chapter, you should be able to:
1. Explain why automotive emission controls are required.
2. Describe the various emission control devices and explain how they work, including positive crankcase ventilation, evaporative control systems, exhaust gas recirculation, and catalytic converters.

Automobiles are said to be responsible for about half the air pollution in the United States. Smoke from power plant and factory smokestacks, incinerators, and home heating also contributes to air pollution. In this chapter we will concentrate on automotive antipollution devices. They are called automotive emission controls.

26-1 DANGERS FROM SMOG
When the smoke from factories and homes does not blow away and automobiles continue to operate in the same area, smog builds up. Smog makes your eyes sting. When smog is in the air, it is hard to breathe, and your throat and lungs may begin to feel sore. You may cough. People with breathing problems or heart trouble can become very ill, and some may die. Smog damages food and flower crops. Even house paint is affected by smog.

But scientists tell us that all this is only part of the danger. Increasing pollution of the air from smoke and chemicals may cause our weather to change. The earth might heat up so much that the ice caps at the North and South Poles would melt. This would raise the level of the oceans as much as 180 feet [55 m]. Coastal cities such as New York and Los Angeles would be flooded (Fig. 26-1).

26-2 POLLUTION FROM AUTOMOBILES
The automobile gives off pollutants from four places, as shown in Fig. 26-2. Pollutants can come from the fuel tank, the carburetor, the

Fig. 26-1
Melting of the polar ice caps would flood all coastal cities.

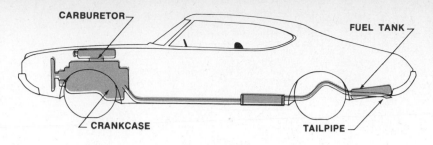

Fig. 26-2
Four possible sources of atmospheric pollution from the
automobile.

crankcase, and the tail pipe. Pollutants, or emissions, from the fuel
tank and carburetor consist of gasoline vapors. Emissions from the
crankcase consist of partly burned air-fuel mixture that has leaked
past the pistons and rings into the crankcase. Emissions from the tail
pipe consist of partly burned air-fuel mixture that did not complete
combustion in the engine cylinders. In addition, there is a pollutant,
called oxides of nitrogen, that forms in any high-temperature combustion process. To understand all these pollutants, let us first review the
combustion process.

26-3 COMBUSTION

Gasoline is a hydrocarbon (HC) made up mostly of hydrogen and carbon. When hydrocarbon burns completely, water (H_2O) and carbon
dioxide (CO_2) are formed. Unfortunately, combustion is never complete. Therefore, some HC remains and some CO (carbon monoxide) is
formed. Carbon monoxide is a poisonous gas.

There is another dangerous gas that the engine gives off: oxides of
nitrogen. Actually, there are several oxides of nitrogen. Nitrogen
makes up about 80 percent of our atmosphere. Oxygen forms almost 20
percent. Usually, nitrogen is an *inert* gas—it will not unite with any
other element. But in the high combustion temperatures in the engine
cylinders, some nitrogen will unite with oxygen to form oxides of nitrogen. The chemical formula for these oxides of nitrogen is NO_x. The "x"
stands for different amounts of oxygen. NO_x unites with atmospheric
moisture in the presence of sunlight to form an acid. This acid contributes to the eye-irritating, cough-producing, effects of smog. Oxides of
nitrogen also are called nitrogen oxides.

To sum up, there are three basic pollutants coming from the engine. These are unburned gasoline (HC), carbon monoxide (CO), and
oxides of nitrogen (NO_x). In addition, there is also loss of HC from the
carburetor and fuel tank. Let's find out how these pollutants are being
controlled.

26-4 CRANKCASE VENTILATION

Air must circulate through the crankcase when the engine is running.
The reason is that water and liquid gasoline appear in the crankcase
when the engine is cold. Also, there is some blowby on the power
strokes. "Blowby" is the name for the leakage of burned gases and unburned gasoline vapor past the pistons and the rings and down into the
crankcase. Water appears as a product of combustion. Water is also
carried into the engine as moisture in the air that enters the engine.
When the engine is cold, this water condenses on the cold engine parts
and runs down into the crankcase. Gasoline vapor also condenses on
cold engine parts and runs down into the crankcase.

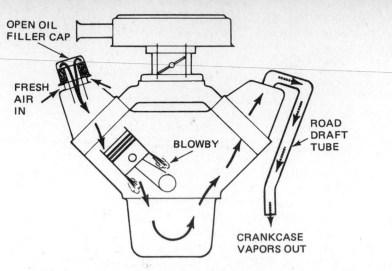

Fig. 26-3
An open crankcase ventilating system. (*Ford Motor Company*)

OPEN OIL
FILLER CAP

FRESH
AIR
IN

BLOWBY

ROAD
DRAFT
TUBE

CRANKCASE
VAPORS OUT

The water, liquid gasoline, burned gases, and gasoline vapor must be cleared from the crankcase. Otherwise, sludge and acids will form. Sludge is a gummy material that can clog oil lines and starve the engine lubricating system. This could ruin the engine. The acids corrode engine parts and also can damage the engine.

In older engines, the crankcase was ventilated by an opening at the front of the engine and a vent tube at the back. The forward movement of the car and the rotation of the crankshaft moved air through the crankcase, as shown in Fig. 26-3. The air passing through removed the water and fuel vapors, discharging them into the atmosphere. This caused air pollution.

To prevent this type of air pollution, engines have a positive crankcase ventilating (PCV) system. A typical system is shown in Fig. 26-4. Filtered air from the carburetor air cleaner is drawn through the crankcase. In the crankcase the air picks up the water and fuel vapors. The air then flows back up to the intake manifold and enters the engine. There, the unburned fuel is burned.

Too much air flowing through the intake manifold during the idle period would upset the air-fuel-mixture ratio and cause poor idling. To

Fig. 26-4
A positive crankcase ventilating system on a V-type engine. (*Ford Motor Company*)

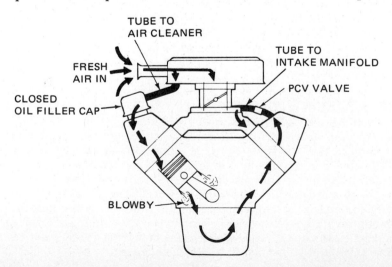

TUBE TO
AIR CLEANER

FRESH
AIR IN

CLOSED
OIL FILLER CAP

TUBE TO
INTAKE MANIFOLD

PCV VALVE

BLOWBY

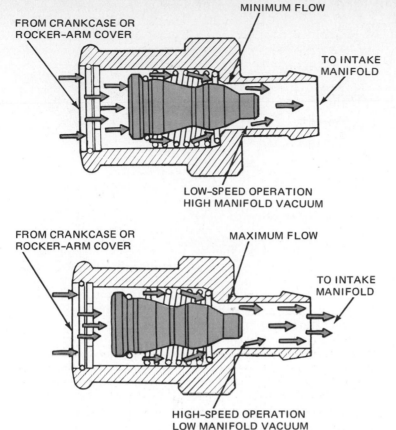

Fig. 26-5
Operation of the PCV valve.
(*Ford Motor Company*)

FROM CRANKCASE OR
ROCKER-ARM COVER

MINIMUM FLOW

TO INTAKE
MANIFOLD

LOW-SPEED OPERATION
HIGH MANIFOLD VACUUM

FROM CRANKCASE OR
ROCKER-ARM COVER

MAXIMUM FLOW

TO INTAKE
MANIFOLD

HIGH-SPEED OPERATION
LOW MANIFOLD VACUUM

prevent this, a regulator valve is used. The valve is called a *positive crankcase ventilation* (*PCV*) valve. The PCV valve allows only a small amount of air to flow during idle. But as engine speed increases, the valve opens to allow more air to flow. Figure 26-5 shows the valve in the two positions.

26-5 EVAPORATIVE CONTROL SYSTEMS

Gasoline vapor can escape from an uncontrolled fuel tank and carburetor. As temperatures change, the fuel tank "breathes." When the fuel tank heats up, the air inside expands. Some of it passes out through the vent in the tank cap (or the tank vent tube). When the tank cools, the air inside contracts and outside air enters. This breathing causes a loss of gasoline vapor, because any air leaving carries gasoline vapor with it. Gasoline vapor also is lost from the float bowl in the carburetor. When the engine is shut off, the float bowl is full. Heat from the engine vaporizes part of or all this gasoline. Then the gasoline vapor passes out through the carburetor vents.

To prevent the loss of gasoline vapor from the fuel tank and the carburetor, evaporative control systems are installed on all late-model cars. The names for this type of system are evaporation control system (ECS), evaporation emission control (EEC), vehicle vapor recovery (VVR), and vapor saver system (VSS).

The system shown in Figs. 26-6 and 26-7 is typical. This system includes a canister filled with activated charcoal. Hose and pipe con-

Fig. 26-6

A fuel evaporation control system. The fuel-return pipe returns excess fuel not needed by the carburetor to the fuel tank. The constant flow of this excess fuel through the fuel pump helps to prevent vapor lock. (*Oldsmobile Division of General Motors Corporation*)

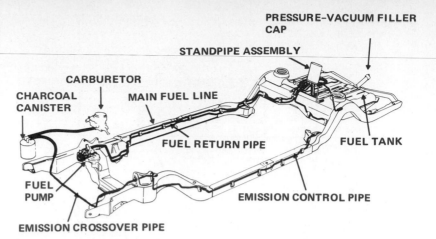

nect the canister to the fuel tank and the carburetor. Any vapor-filled air that leaves the fuel tank passes through the emission-control pipe to the canister. The gasoline vapor is adsorbed by the activated charcoal. That is, the activated charcoal particles in the canister "grab" the molecules of HC in the air coming from the fuel tank. Then, when the engine is started, intake-manifold vacuum draws fresh outside air up through an opening in the canister. This moving air pulls the HC out of the activated charcoal. These vapors are carried back to the carburetor and into the engine. In this way, the canister is purged, or cleaned, of gasoline. Now the canister is ready to do its job again.

While the engine is stopped, any gasoline that evaporates from the carburetor collects as vapor in the carburetor and air cleaner. As soon as the engine starts, this vapor is drawn down through the carburetor and into the engine along with the entering air-fuel mixture.

Figure 26-8 shows a charcoal canister. The fuel tank is sealed. It has a cap like the pressure-vacuum cap used on a radiator in a pressurized cooling system. The cap will open if too much pressure develops in the tank. It will also open to admit air as fuel is withdrawn so that a vacuum does not develop in the tank. Pressure or vacuum in the tank could damage the tank.

Fig. 26-7

A schematic view of the fuel evaporation control system. (*Pontiac Motor Division of General Motors Corporation*)

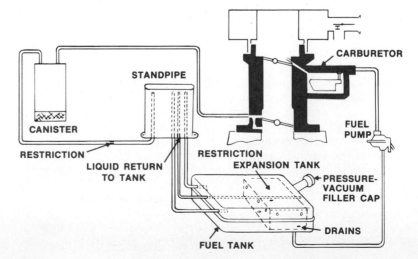

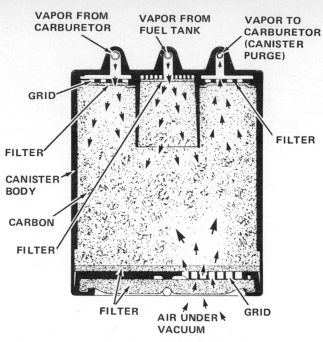

Fig. 26-8
A sectional view of a charcoal
canister for a V-8 engine evaporation control system. (*Pontiac Motor Division of General
Motors Corporation*)

VAPOR FROM CARBURETOR

VAPOR FROM FUEL TANK

VAPOR TO CARBURETOR (CANISTER PURGE)

GRID

FILTER

CANISTER BODY

CARBON

FILTER

FILTER

FILTER

AIR UNDER VACUUM

GRID

The charcoal-canister system shown in Figs. 26-6 and 26-7 uses a standpipe assembly. Because the standpipe assembly is above the fuel tank, no liquid gasoline can flow through the emission-control pipe to the canister. The vent pipe to the canister is open at the top of the assembly and takes vapor-filled air only from the top. The standpipe assembly also is called a vapor-liquid separator.

Other methods of preventing liquid gasoline from getting into the canister are used. One method involves a domed fuel tank (Fig. 26-9). The dome forms the high point of the tank, and the emission-control pipe is connected at this point.

Another arrangement is shown in Fig. 26-10. Here a liquid check valve is used. It mounts in the top of the fuel tank and has a vent hose to the canister. The liquid check valve will pass air but will not pass gasoline.

Some cars have used a different vapor recovery system (Fig. 26-11). This system uses the crankcase instead of a canister as the storage

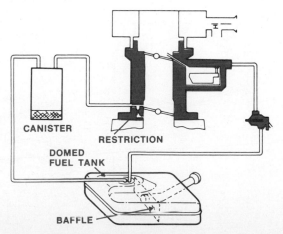

CANISTER

RESTRICTION

DOMED FUEL TANK

BAFFLE

Fig. 26-9
An evaporation control system
of the type using a domed fuel
tank. (*Pontiac Motor Division of
General Motors Corporation*)

313

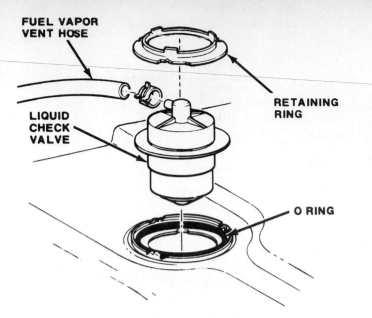

FUEL VAPOR VENT HOSE

RETAINING RING

LIQUID CHECK VALVE

O RING

place for gasoline vapor. When the engine is stopped, the gasoline vapors pass from the vapor separator at the fuel tank, through the fuel-tank vent line, and to the breather cap on the valve cover. From there, the vapors pass down into the crankcase. At the same time, fuel vapors from the carburetor float bowl also flow down into the crankcase. The vapors, being 2 to 4 times heavier than air, sink to the bottom of the crankcase. Then, when the engine is started, the positive crankcase ventilating system clears the crankcase of the vapors. The vapors are carried up to the intake manifold and then into the engine, where they are burned.

26-6 CLEANING UP THE EXHAUST GASES

Complete combustion never occurs in the engine cylinders. So some HC and CO are contained in the exhaust gases. It is possible to increase the combustion temperature and thus burn more of the HC. But

Fig. 26-11
An evaporation control system of the type using the crankcase for fuel-vapor storage. (*Chrysler Corporation*)

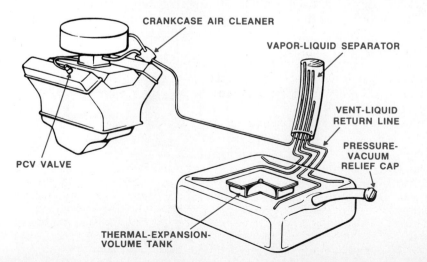

CRANKCASE AIR CLEANER

VAPOR-LIQUID SEPARATOR

VENT-LIQUID RETURN LINE

PRESSURE-VACUUM RELIEF CAP

PCV VALVE

THERMAL-EXPANSION-VOLUME TANK

then, more NO_x is produced. So simply increasing combustion temperatures is not the answer.

Federal regulations require very low amounts of HC, CO, and NO_x in the exhaust gases. For example, the United States standards for cars made in 1980 are as follows:

- HC—0.41 gram (g) per vehicle mile
- CO—7.0 grams per vehicle mile
- NO_x—2.0 grams per vehicle mile

A gram is a very small amount. There are 454 g in 1 pound [0.45 kg], for example. In effect, these standards require almost the complete absence of pollutants in the exhaust gas. Here are the three ways to remove pollutants from the exhaust gas.

1. Controlling the Air-Fuel Mixture

First, gasoline has been changed to reduce lead pollution from the exhaust gas. Also leaner carburetor settings and faster warmup are used, so more of the fuel is burned during startup.

2. Controlling Combustion

Engineers have altered the combustion chambers of engines to improve combustion. They have lowered compression ratios, which also lowers the engine power but helps the emission problem. They have modified ignition timing to prevent excessive emissions during certain operating conditions. And, they have recirculated part of the exhaust gases through the engine to modify the combustion process.

3. Treating the Exhaust Gases

One procedure is to pump fresh air into the exhaust gases as they leave the engine. This supplies additional oxygen so that unburned HC and CO can burn. Another way to treat the exhaust gases is to use *catalysts* in the exhaust line. Catalysts are chemicals that cause a chemical reaction (such as combustion) without actually becoming part of the chemical process.

CHECK UP ON YOURSELF

Check up on yourself by answering these questions.

1. What are the four places in the automobile from which pollutants can be given off?
2. What are the three major pollutants from automobiles?
3. What is the name of the valve in the crankcase ventilation system?
4. What two types of evaporative control systems are used in automobiles to trap fuel vapor?
5. What are the three ways to clean up the exhaust gas?

ANSWERS

1. The carburetor, the fuel tank, the crankcase, and the tail pipe (Sec. 26-2).
2. Gasoline (HC), carbon monoxide (CO), and oxides of nitrogen (NO_x) (Sec. 26-3). 3. The positive crankcase ventilating (PCV) valve (Sec. 26-4). 4. One type uses a canister filled with activated charcoal to adsorb the gasoline vapors. The second type uses the crankcase as the storage place for the gasoline vapors (Sec. 26-5). 5. Control the air-fuel mixture, control the combustion, and treat the exhaust gases (Sec. 26-6).

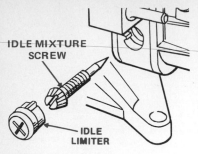

Fig. 26-12
The location of the idle limiter in one model of carburetor. (*Ford Motor Company*)

26-7 CONTROLLING THE AIR-FUEL MIXTURE

Lead is being removed from gasoline. Chapter 17 points out that octane can be increased by adding tetraethyl lead to gasoline. Engines with higher compression ratios can then be built. The reason that lead is now being removed is to let the catalytic converter work better to clean the exhaust gas. We'll get to catalysts in a later section.

NOTE

From the standpoint of pollution, it is desirable to get the lead out of gasoline. Lead is a poisonous substance. In some cities the lead in the exhaust gases increases the lead in the air to almost the danger point. So lead is being removed from gasoline.

Carburetors have been modified to deliver a leaner air-fuel mixture, particularly during idling. Many carburetors have an idle limiter (Fig. 26-12), which is preset at the factory. The idle limiter prevents an excessively rich idle mixture.

Faster warmup and quicker choke action are also important ways of reducing pollutants. During choking, a very rich mixture enters the cylinders. Some of the excess gasoline has no chance to burn. It exits in the exhaust gas as unburned HC. One way to reduce the amount of unburned gasoline in the exhaust is to preheat the mixture during warmup. The thermostatic air cleaner does this job. Figure 26-13 shows the system. It includes a heat stove at the exhaust manifold, a hot-air pipe, and a thermostatic arrangement in the snorkel tube of the air cleaner. The *snorkel tube* is the tube through which air enters the air cleaner.

Figure 26-14 shows the parts of the air cleaner. It has a thermostatic spring, called a temperature-sensing spring, shown in Fig. 26-14. When the entering air is cold, this spring holds the air-bleed valve

Fig. 26-13
The heated-air system installed on a V-8 engine. (*Buick Motor Division of General Motors Corporation*)

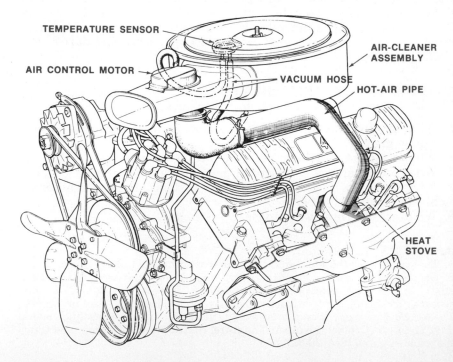

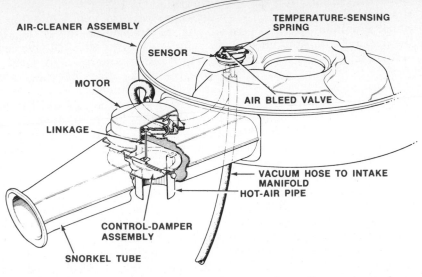

AIR-CLEANER ASSEMBLY

SENSOR

TEMPERATURE-SENSING
SPRING

MOTOR

LINKAGE

AIR BLEED VALVE

VACUUM HOSE TO INTAKE
MANIFOLD
HOT-AIR PIPE

CONTROL-DAMPER
ASSEMBLY

SNORKEL TUBE

Fig. 26-14

An air cleaner with thermostatic control. (*Chevrolet Motor Division of General Motors Corporation*)

closed. Now, intake-manifold vacuum can work on the vacuum chamber in the snorkel tube. The vacuum chamber, called the motor in Fig. 26-14, has a diaphragm, which is raised by the vacuum. This movement of the diaphragm tilts a damper so that the snorkel tube is blocked off. Now all air must come from the heat stove through the hot-air pipe.

Figure 26-15 shows how the air cleaner works. Look at Fig. 26-15B to see what happens when the engine is started cold. The temperature-sensing spring has closed the air bleed valve. Vacuum from the intake manifold can work on the motor. The diaphragm in the vacuum cham-

Fig. 26-15

Four modes of operation of the thermostatic air cleaner. (*Chevrolet Motor Division of General Motors Corporation*)

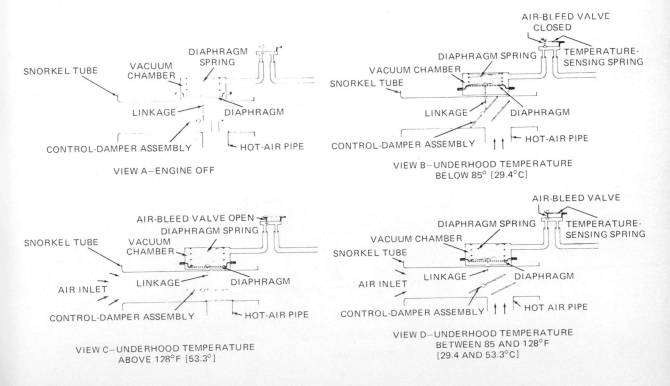

SNORKEL TUBE

VACUUM CHAMBER

DIAPHRAGM SPRING

LINKAGE

DIAPHRAGM

CONTROL-DAMPER ASSEMBLY

HOT-AIR PIPE

VIEW A—ENGINE OFF

AIR-BLEED VALVE CLOSED

DIAPHRAGM SPRING

TEMPERATURE-SENSING SPRING

VACUUM CHAMBER

SNORKEL TUBE

LINKAGE

DIAPHRAGM

CONTROL-DAMPER ASSEMBLY

HOT-AIR PIPE

VIEW B—UNDERHOOD TEMPERATURE BELOW 85° [29.4°C]

AIR-BLEED VALVE OPEN
DIAPHRAGM SPRING

SNORKEL TUBE

VACUUM CHAMBER

LINKAGE

DIAPHRAGM

AIR INLET

CONTROL-DAMPER ASSEMBLY

HOT-AIR PIPE

VIEW C—UNDERHOOD TEMPERATURE ABOVE 128°F [53.3°]

AIR-BLEED VALVE

DIAPHRAGM SPRING

TEMPERATURE-SENSING SPRING

VACUUM CHAMBER

SNORKEL TUBE

LINKAGE

DIAPHRAGM

AIR INLET

CONTROL-DAMPER ASSEMBLY

HOT AIR PIPE

VIEW D—UNDERHOOD TEMPERATURE BETWEEN 85 AND 128°F [29.4 AND 53.3°C]

ber is raised, and linkage to the control damper tilts it. This blocks off the snorkel-tube inlet. All air must come from the heat stove. The exhaust manifold starts to heat up the instant the engine starts. This means that, almost at once, there is hot air flowing through the carburetor. The gasoline vaporizes, more of it burns, and less leaves the engine in the exhaust gas. In addition, the choke opens more quickly.

Now look at Fig. 26-15C. Here you can see what happens shortly after the engine has started. Plenty of hot air comes from the heat stove, and so the temperature-sensing spring begins to open the air-bleed valve. Now the intake-manifold vacuum is only partly successful in pushing up the diaphragm. The control damper only partly blocks off the snorkel tube. Cold air begins to enter from the engine compartment. The cold air mixes with the hot air from the heat stove to give the carburetor warm air at the right temperature.

After the engine has reached operating temperature, the temperature-sensing spring opens the air-bleed valve completely (Fig. 26-15C). Now all air enters through the snorkel-tube inlet. Heated air from the heat stove is no longer needed.

As long as the choke is closed, a rich mixture is being fed to the engine, and the exhaust gas is loaded with unburned HC. To reduce the closed-choke time, some automatic chokes are equipped with an electric heating element (Fig. 26-16). This produces rapid opening of the choke.

26-8 CONTROLLING THE COMBUSTION PROCESS

Late-model engines have been changed somewhat to improve the combustion process. During the 1960s, the compression ratios of engines went up a little each year. About 1969 the average was a little above 9.5:1. Now the average is down around 8:1 or a little higher. NO_x is formed in the high-temperature combustion process. Reducing the compression ratio reduces peak temperatures. This reduces the amount of NO_x that forms. Unfortunately, reducing the compression ratio also reduces engine performance and efficiency.

Fig. 26-16
Arrangement for an electric-assist choke mounted in a well in the exhaust-gas crossover passage of the intake manifold. (*Chrysler Corporation*)

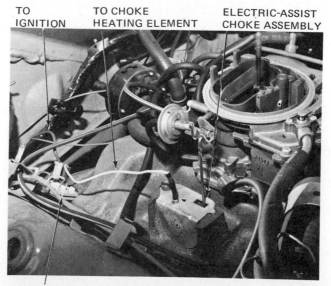

TO IGNITION   TO CHOKE HEATING ELEMENT   ELECTRIC-ASSIST CHOKE ASSEMBLY

CHOKE CONTROL SWITCH

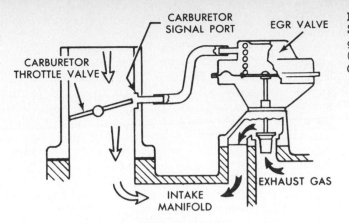

Fig. 26-17
Schematic view of an exhaust
gas recirculation system.
(*Chevrolet Motor Division of
General Motors Corporation*)

Another method of controlling the formation of NO_x in the engine is to recirculate some of the exhaust gas back through the engine. Figure 26-17 shows this system. It is called the *exhaust gas recirculation* (EGR) system. A part of the exhaust gas is picked up from the exhaust manifold and sent through the intake manifold and back through the engine. Usually, less than 10 percent of the exhaust gas is recirculated this way. The exhaust gas mixes with the air-fuel mixture. By absorbing some of the heat of combustion, the cooler exhaust gas lowers the combustion temperature. This reduces the amount of NO_x that forms.

Another way to mix some of the exhaust gases with the incoming air-fuel mixture is to leave part of the exhaust gases in the cylinders. The Chrysler NO_x control system (Fig. 26-18) does this by increasing the exhaust-valve and intake-valve overlap. The camshaft has been ground so that the cams provide this additional valve overlap. We discuss valve overlap in Chap. 14. Valve overlap occurs when the intake valve opens before the exhaust stroke ends, and the exhaust valve stays open after the intake stroke starts. If the amount of overlap is increased, the exhaust gases have more chance to mix with the incoming air-fuel mixture. The presence of the exhaust gases, as the mixture is compressed and ignited, lowers the combustion temperatures so that less NO_x is produced.

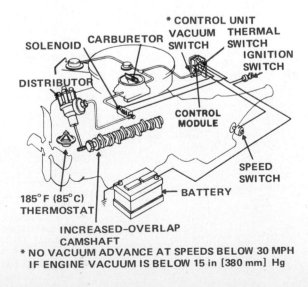

Fig. 26-18
The Chrysler Corporation NO_x
control system for cars with automatic transmissions.
(*Chrysler Corporation*)

The Chrysler NO$_x$ control system, shown in Fig. 26-18, uses other controlling devices. These additions provide control of the distributor vacuum advance during certain operating conditions. The vacuum advance works on intake-manifold vacuum. When the vacuum is high during part throttle, the ignition timing is advanced. The air-fuel mixture is less highly compressed and takes longer to burn. Advancing the spark gives the mixture this additional time. However, the longer burning time also gives NO$_x$ more time to form. More NO$_x$ forms during idle, acceleration in lower gears, and deceleration. To guard against this, the Chrysler control system prevents vacuum advance during these operating conditions.

Figure 26-19 shows one type of General Motors NO$_x$ control system. It is called the *transmission-controlled spark* (TCS) system. It uses a TCS solenoid that is connected electrically to a switch in the transmission. The switch is open only when the transmission is in high gear. When the transmission is in a lower gear, the switch is closed, connecting the TCS solenoid to the battery. The solenoid therefore lifts its plunger. This shuts off the vacuum line from the carburetor to the vacuum-advance unit on the distributor.

The result is no vacuum advance. Then, when the transmission shifts into high gear, the transmission switch opens, and the solenoid is disconnected. Now, the vacuum line from the carburetor to the vacuum unit on the distributor opens so that vacuum advance results.

Fig. 26-19
The General Motors NO$_x$ control system, called the transmission-controlled spark (TCS) system by General Motors. (*General Motors Corporation*)

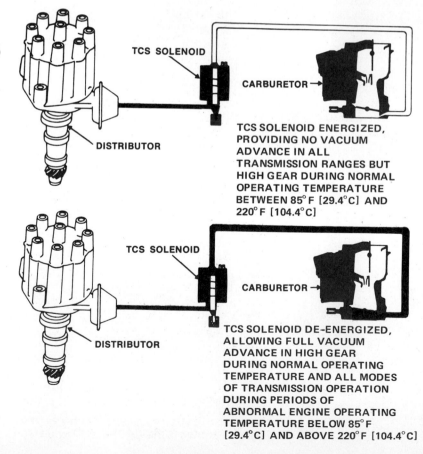

TCS SOLENOID

CARBURETOR

DISTRIBUTOR

TCS SOLENOID ENERGIZED, PROVIDING NO VACUUM ADVANCE IN ALL TRANSMISSION RANGES BUT HIGH GEAR DURING NORMAL OPERATING TEMPERATURE BETWEEN 85°F [29.4°C] AND 220°F [104.4°C]

TCS SOLENOID

CARBURETOR

DISTRIBUTOR

TCS SOLENOID DE-ENERGIZED, ALLOWING FULL VACUUM ADVANCE IN HIGH GEAR DURING NORMAL OPERATING TEMPERATURE AND ALL MODES OF TRANSMISSION OPERATION DURING PERIODS OF ABNORMAL ENGINE OPERATING TEMPERATURE BELOW 85°F [29.4°C] AND ABOVE 220°F [104.4°C]

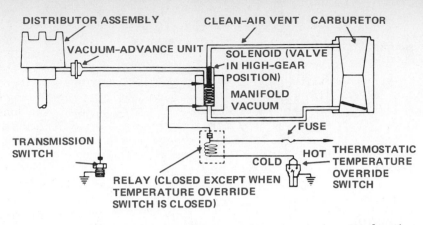

Operating without vacuum advance can cause engine overheating under some conditions. Therefore, the TCS system includes a safety circuit that shuts down the TCS system when the engine overheats. It is shown in Fig. 26-20. The safety circuit includes a thermostatic temperature override switch, which is mounted on the engine, and a relay. If the engine gets too hot, the thermostatic switch closes. This action opens the relay. With the relay open, the solenoid circuit opens. The plunger moves to open the vacuum line to the vacuum-advance unit so that vacuum advance results. The system also restores vacuum advance when the engine is cold.

Vacuum advance is desirable when the engine starts and when the engine overheats. With vacuum advance, cold-engine operation is improved. Also, vacuum advance helps to prevent engine overheating, especially during long idling periods.

There are other vacuum-advance controls to prevent or allow vacuum advance under different operating conditions. When you work in the shop and use the manufacturers' shop manuals, you will find out about these controls and how to service them.

26-9 STRATIFIED CHARGE

Another way to improve combustion and reduce exhaust emissions is to use stratified charge. "Strata" means layers. Stratified charge means that the fuel and air are not mixed uniformly in the cylinder. They are in layers, some rich and some lean. The principle is shown in Fig. 26-21. The spark plug is surrounded by a small amount of rich mixture. A lean mixture fills the combustion chamber and surrounds the small pocket of rich mixture. Combustion starts in the rich mixture. Then, once started, the burning gases can ignite the lean mixture. The result is that the fuel in the combustion chamber is more completely burned. Fewer pollutants appear in the exhaust gas.

A small amount of rich mixture surrounds the spark plug in order to get the combustion started. The lean mixture filling the combustion chamber is so lean that the spark plug cannot ignite it. However, the spark plug can easily ignite the rich mixture. Then, once the rich mixture ignites, its flame is strong enough to burn the lean mixture in the cylinder.

One way to achieve stratified charging is to give the mixture a swirling motion as it enters the cylinder. This can be done by careful placement of the intake port. Another method is the Honda CVCC (Compound Vortex Controlled Combustion) system (Fig. 26-22). Here,

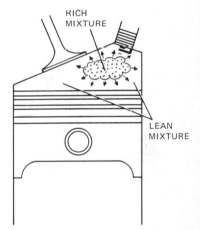

Fig. 26-21
Principle of stratified charging.

321

Fig. 26-22
Combustion chamber and
valve arrangements of a
Honda CVCC engine. (*Honda
Motor Company, Inc.*)

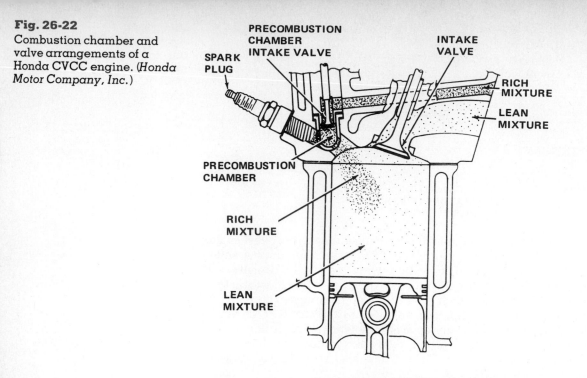

there is a separate small precombustion chamber. The precombustion
chamber has its own intake valve and has the spark plug. Figure 26-23
shows how the system works. The carburetor delivers a rich mixture to
the precombustion chamber and a lean mixture to the main cylinder.
Ignition starts in the precombustion chamber. The rich mixture, as it
burns, streams out into the lean mixture. There it mixes with the lean
mixture, and combustion continues. The result is more complete burning of the fuel and reduced exhaust emissions.

26-10 TREATING THE EXHAUST GASES

After the exhaust gases leave the engine cylinders, the gases can be
treated to reduce the HC, CO, and NO_x content. One method is to blow
fresh air into the exhaust manifolds. This system, called the *air-injection system,* provides additional oxygen to burn HC and CO coming out
of the cylinders. Figure 26-24 shows the details of the system.

The air-injection pump pushes air through the air lines and the air
manifold to a series of air-injection tubes, located opposite the exhaust
valves. The oxygen in the air helps to burn any HC or CO in the exhaust gases. The check valve prevents any backflow of exhaust gases to
the air pump, in case of backfire. The air bypass valve operates during
engine deceleration (when intake-manifold vacuum is high) to momentarily divert air from the air pump to the air cleaner instead of to the
exhaust manifold. This tends to prevent backfiring in the exhaust system.

A variation of this system involves a special chamber, called a
thermal reactor. It is shown in Fig. 26-25. In the V-8 system shown,
there are two reactors, one for each bank of cylinders. These reactors
are basically enlarged exhaust manifolds. Being larger, the reactors
hold the exhaust gases a little longer. This gives the HC and CO additional time to react with the oxygen in the air that is being pumped in.

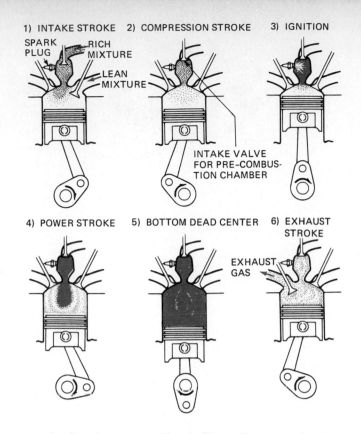

1) INTAKE STROKE 2) COMPRESSION STROKE 3) IGNITION

SPARK PLUG RICH MIXTURE

LEAN MIXTURE

INTAKE VALVE FOR PRE-COMBUS-TION CHAMBER

4) POWER STROKE 5) BOTTOM DEAD CENTER 6) EXHAUST STROKE

EXHAUST GAS

Fig. 26-23
Sequence of actions in the Honda system. (*Honda Motor Company, Inc.*)

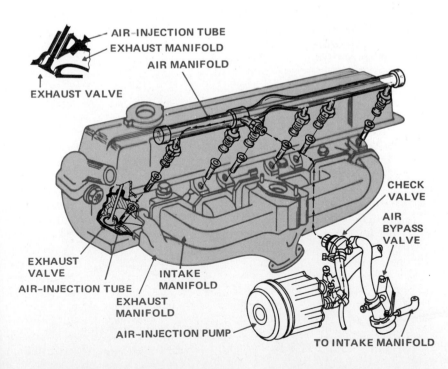

AIR-INJECTION TUBE
EXHAUST MANIFOLD
AIR MANIFOLD

EXHAUST VALVE

CHECK VALVE

AIR BYPASS VALVE

EXHAUST VALVE
AIR-INJECTION TUBE
INTAKE MANIFOLD
EXHAUST MANIFOLD
AIR-INJECTION PUMP

TO INTAKE MANIFOLD

Fig. 26-24
Cylinder head with manifolds and the parts of the Thermactor system detached. The cylinder head has been cut away at the front to show how the air-injection tube fits into the head. (*Ford Motor Company*)

323

Fig. 26-25
A thermal reactor system for
exhaust-emission control.

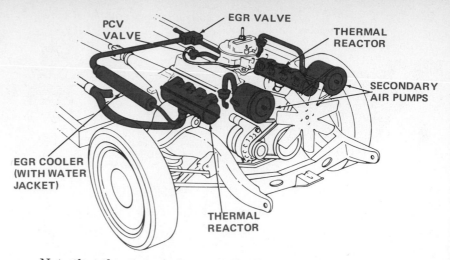

Note that the system shown in Fig. 26-25 also includes an exhaust gas recirculation (EGR) system, which we have already described.

26-11 CATALYTIC CONVERTERS

Catalytic converters provide another way to treat the exhaust gases. A catalyst is a material that causes a chemical reaction without actually becoming a part of the reaction process. The metal platinum can act as one kind of catalyst. When exhaust gas and air are passed through platinum-coated pellets or a coated honeycomb core, the HC and CO react with the oxygen in the air. Harmless water (H_2O) and carbon dioxide (CO_2) are formed. Reducing exhaust emissions with a catalytic converter is a chemical process. It is not a burning process, such as the process in the thermal reactor or in the exhaust manifold in the air-injection system.

Figure 26-26 shows an engine using a catalytic converter, air injection, and other emission-control features. Figure 26-27 is a cutaway view of a catalytic converter. Note the bed of beads. The beads are coated with platinum. As the exhaust gases pass through this bed of

Fig. 26-26
One late-model emission-control system using an under-the-floor catalytic converter. Note that the system uses air injection and other emission-control features described previously. (*General Motors Corporation*)

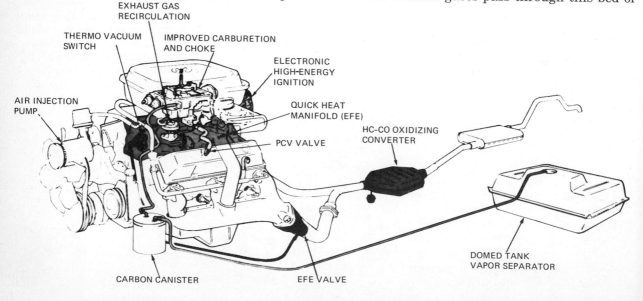

beads, the platinum changes the HC and CO into water (H_2O) and carbon dioxide (CO_2).

Some cars may have a catalytic converter that handles HC and CO, and also nitrogen oxides (NO_x). This type of catalytic converter may be more widely used in the future.

One of the problems with the catalysts is that the lead in leaded gasoline soon coats the catalysts. When this happens, the catalysts are no longer effective. If an engine runs on leaded gasoline, the catalysts stop doing their job in a very short time. This is one reason that lead is being removed from gasoline.

NOTE

Removing the lead from gasoline can have a bad effect on the engine valves. The lead acts as a lubricant for the exhaust-valve faces and seats. A thin coat of lead covers the valve faces and seats. This helps to reduce wear. To prevent valve troubles, manufacturers are hardening the valve seats and coating the valve faces with special metallic compounds. This overcomes the problems brought on by the loss of lead in the gasoline.

26-12 PREVENTING RUN-ON

Some of the emission-control devices have a tendency to allow the engine to keep running after the ignition is turned off. This is sometimes called "dieseling," because the engine acts a little like a diesel engine. It runs without any spark from the ignition system. The high idle-speed setting leaves the throttle partly open. This allows enough air-fuel mixture to enter the cylinders to continue combustion. The combustion is caused by hot spots in the combustion chamber, and the engine continues to run.

Two methods are used to stop the engine once the ignition has been turned off. In one method there is an idle-stop solenoid on the carburetor, as shown in Fig. 26-28. When the ignition is on, the solenoid is connected to the battery. A plunger extends from the solenoid to keep the idle speed up around 650 rpm. This means that the throttle is partly open. However, when the ignition switch is turned off, the solenoid is disconnected and the plunger retracts. This allows the throttle to fully close, stopping the engine.

In some air-conditioned cars, there has to be a higher idle-speed setting when the air conditioner is turned on. The higher idle-speed is necessary to prevent engine stalling because of the extra load of the air conditioner. In some air-conditioned cars, a time-delay switch is used. The switch causes the air-conditioner clutch to engage for about 3 seconds after the ignition is turned off. This action throws an extra load on the engine and causes it to stop.

Fig. 26-28
Idle-stop solenoid mounted on the carburetor to prevent engine dieseling when the ignition is turned off. (*Echlin Manufacturing Company*)

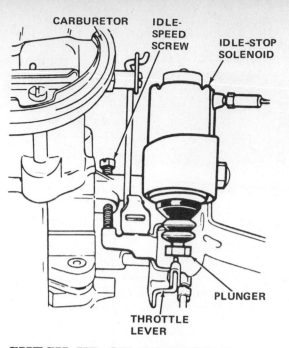

CARBURETOR   IDLE-SPEED SCREW   IDLE-STOP SOLENOID

PLUNGER

THROTTLE LEVER

CHECK UP ON YOURSELF

You have now finished the chapter on automotive emission controls. Find out how well you understand what you just studied by answering the questions that follow.

1. When a cold engine equipped with a thermostatic air cleaner is started, where does the air that goes to the air cleaner come from?
2. Why is it desirable to get quick automatic-choke action?
3. How does the EGR system work?
4. How does the Chrysler NO_x control system mix some of the exhaust gases with the incoming fresh air-fuel mixture?
5. What happens if an engine with a TCS system starts to overheat?
6. In operation, what does the air-injection system do?
7. What is the basic difference between the air-injection system and the thermal reactor?
8. What is the name of one type of catalyst that is used in the catalytic converter?
9. What happens to the catalysts if leaded gasoline is used?
10. What is "dieseling"?

ANSWERS

1. From the heat stove at the exhaust manifold (Sec. 26-7). **2.** A closed choke means a rich mixture to the engine and exhaust gases loaded with unburned HC. Opening the choke fast reduces this (Sec. 26-7). **3.** The exhaust gas recirculation system sends part of the exhaust gases back through the engine to help control the formation of NO_x (Sec. 26-8). **4.** By increasing valve overlap (Sec. 26-8). **5.** Permits vacuum advance in any gear if the engine begins to overheat (Sec. 26-8). **6.** Pumps air into the exhaust manifold to supply additional oxygen so the HC and CO remaining in the exhaust gases can burn (Sec. 26-10). **7.** The thermal reactor is basically an oversized exhaust manifold (Sec. 26-10). **8.** Platinum-coated pellets (Sec. 26-10). **9.** The catalysts become coated with lead and can no longer do their job (Sec. 26-10). **10.** The running of the engine after the ignition has been turned off. Ignition is produced by hot spots in the combustion chamber (Sec. 26-12).

CHAPTER TWENTY-SEVEN
AUTOMOTIVE EMISSION CONTROLS SERVICE

After studying this chapter, you should be able to:
Describe how to service the various emission control devices, including positive crankcase ventilation, evaporative control systems, exhaust gas recirculation, and catalytic converters.

27-1 SERVICING THE PCV SYSTEM

The PCV valve must be replaced at regular intervals and whenever it clogs or sticks. When you install a new PCV valve (Fig. 27-1), inspect and clean the system thoroughly. This includes all hoses, grommets, and connectors. To clean the hoses, soak them in mineral spirits. Then clean the insides with a brush, and wash the outsides. Thoroughly clean all connectors, especially the elbow connection. Wash the oil-filler cap in mineral spirits, and shake it dry. Some types of oil-filler caps must not be dried with compressed air.

After all parts of the PCV system are clean, inspect them carefully. Replace any component that shows signs of damage, wear, or deterioration. Be sure the grommet into which the PCV valve fits is not damaged or torn. Replace any cracked or brittle hose with hose of a similar type. Replace any component, hose, or fitting that does not allow a free flow of air after cleaning.

Fresh ventilation air must be filtered before it enters the crankcase. There are two different methods in use. In one method, the carburetor air-cleaner filter does the cleaning. In this system, the hose for the crankcase ventilation air is connected to the downstream, or clean-air, side of the carburetor air filter. No special service is required. The second method of cleaning the crankcase ventilation air is to use a separate filter, called a PCV filter. This filter, shown in Fig. 27-2, mounts on the inside of the air-cleaner housing. Ventilation air comes into the air cleaner through the inlet or snorkel. It then passes through the PCV filter and into the crankcase.

Fig. 27-1
PCV-valve locations.

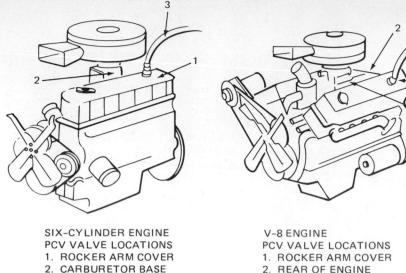

SIX–CYLINDER ENGINE
PCV VALVE LOCATIONS
1. ROCKER ARM COVER
2. CARBURETOR BASE
3. HOSE

V–8 ENGINE
PCV VALVE LOCATIONS
1. ROCKER ARM COVER
2. REAR OF ENGINE
3. CARBURETOR BASE

Whenever the PCV system is serviced, the PCV filter must also be checked. To check the filter shown in Fig. 27-2, remove the retainer clip. Then remove the air-cleaner cover, and take out the PCV filter. Check it for damage, dirt buildup, and clogging. If the filter is clean, reinstall it in the air cleaner. A dirty or damaged PCV filter must be replaced.

27-2 SERVICING EVAPORATIVE CONTROL SYSTEMS

Evaporative control systems require little service. About the only periodic service required is to replace the filter, which is located in the bottom of the canister, at specified intervals. No testers are needed to check evaporative control systems. Almost all problems can be found by visual inspection. Problems are also indicated by a strong odor of fuel. Some technicians use the infrared exhaust analyzer to quickly detect small vapor losses from around the fuel tank, canister, air cleaner, lines, or hose. Any loss will register on the HC meter of the exhaust analyzer.

The crankcase storage system requires an air-tight crankcase to prevent the escape of HC vapor while it is stored there. Crankcase leaks also can be detected with an infrared exhaust analyzer.

Fig. 27-2
A PCV-filter location inside the air cleaner. (*Ford Motor Company*)

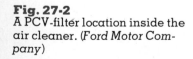

PCV FILTER
FILTER RETAINER
AIR CLEANER HOUSING
RETAINER CLIP
VENT HOSE
ELBOW CONNECTOR

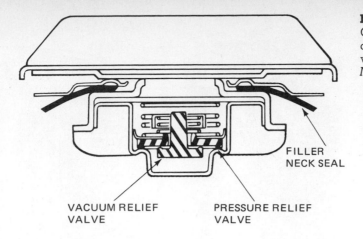

Fig. 27-3
Cutaway view of a fuel-tank cap for the tank used with a vapor-recovery system. (*Ford Motor Company*)

FILLER
NECK SEAL

VACUUM RELIEF
VALVE

PRESSURE RELIEF
VALVE

Most problems with evaporative control systems can be noticed during an inspection. Typical defects are damaged lines, liquid-fuel and vapor leaks, and missing parts. The filler cap can be damaged or corroded so that its valves fail to work properly. A problem with the fuel-tank cap could deform the tank. This could also occur when the wrong cap is installed on the tank. Be sure that the fuel-tank filler cap is of a type specified by the manufacturer for the vehicle. The cap must completely seal the fuel tank.

To service the evaporative control system, inspect the fuel-tank cap (Fig. 27-3). Check the condition of the sealing gasket around the cap. If the gasket is damaged, replace the cap. Check the filler neck and tank for stains resulting from fuel leakage. Usually, you can trace a stain back to its origin. Then fix the cause of the leak. This may require replacing a gasket, clamp, or hose, or replacing the tank.

Inspect all lines and connections in the fuel and evaporative control systems for damage and leakage. Perform any necessary repairs. Check all clamps and connections for tightness.

NOTE
The hoses used in evaporative control systems are specially made to resist deterioration from contact with gasoline and gasoline vapor. When you replace a hose, make sure the new hose is specified by the manufacturer for use in evaporative control systems. Sometimes this type of hose is marked EVAP.

Check the charcoal-canister lines for liquid gasoline. If any is present, replace the liquid-vapor separator or the liquid check valve.

At scheduled intervals, inspect and replace the filter in the canister (Fig. 27-4). Servicing evaporative control systems requires no special tools. To replace the canister filter, remove the canister and turn it upside down (Fig. 27-4). Remove the bottom cover. Pull out the old filter with your fingers, and insert the new filter. If the canister itself is cracked or internally plugged, a new canister should be installed.

27-3 SERVICING THE AIR-INJECTION SYSTEM
In general, no routine service is required on the air-injection system. Hoses should be inspected and replaced, if required, whenever a tuneup is performed. Some systems use a separate filter to clean the air entering the pump. On these systems, the filter should be checked

Fig. 27-4
Replacing the air filter in the
charcoal canister.

FIBER GLASS FILTER

BOTTOM
OF
CANISTER

every year or every 12,000 miles [19,300 km] of operation. It should be cleaned or replaced as necessary. Late-model air pumps use a centrifugal filter. It is replaced only in case of mechanical damage.

The air-pump drive belt should be checked periodically to make sure it is in good condition and at the proper tension (Fig. 27-5). The engine should be hot when the check is made. Inspect the belt for tension, wear, cracks, and brittleness. Install a new belt if necessary. Proper belt tension is important. A loose belt does not turn the air pump. This causes high exhaust-emission levels, and may result in noise. A tight belt overloads the rear bearing in the air pump. If the bearing becomes noisy or fails, replacement of the air pump or bearing is necessary. When tightening the belt, do not pry against the pump housing. It is aluminum and will deform and break easily.

27-4 SERVICING THE TCS SYSTEM

The TCS system (Fig. 27-6) does not require regular service. However, every 12 months or 12,000 miles [19,300 km], or whenever a tuneup is performed, the operation of the system should be checked, and the idle-stop solenoid adjusted (see Fig. 26-28).

27-5 EGR SYSTEM SERVICE

There are differences in manufacturers' recommended service intervals for EGR systems. When the engine is operated with leaded gasoline, the EGR system should be checked for proper operation every 12 months or 12,000 miles [19,300 km]. For engines operated on unleaded gasoline, the EGR system is checked every 24 months or 24,000 miles [38,600 km]. Some cars manufactured by Chrysler have an EGR-maintenance reminder light on the instrument panel. The light comes on automatically at 15,000 miles [24,100 km] to remind the driver to have the EGR system checked. Many late-model cars do not require regular EGR system service. Instead, if a trouble develops in the EGR system, a diagnosis is performed.

A sticking EGR valve should be inspected for deposits. If there is more than a thin film of deposits, clean the EGR valve. Remove any deposits from the mounting surface and from around the valve and seat. The method of cleaning depends on the type of valve (Fig. 27-7).

General Motors recommends cleaning an EGR valve from a V-8 engine by holding the valve assembly in your hand and tapping the protruding stem lightly with a plastic hammer. Then lightly tap the sides of the valve. Shake out the loose particles. If you are not certain of the type of valve or how to clean it, refer to the manufacturer's shop manual.

Fig. 27-5
Use a belt-tension gauge to check the adjustment of the air-pump drive belt. (*Chevrolet Motor Division of General Motors Corporation*)

NOTE
Do not clamp the EGR valve in a vise or wash the EGR valve in solvent. Either may damage the valve and diaphragm.

27-6 SERVICING PRECAUTIONS FOR CATALYTIC CONVERTERS
Manufacturers recommend that the following servicing and operating precautions be observed for vehicles equipped with catalytic converters:

1. Avoid prolonged idling, especially at fast idle after a cold start.
2. Do not attempt to start a car equipped with a catalytic converter by pushing or towing. Use another battery and jumper cables.
3. Avoid excessively prolonged cranking with an intermittently firing or flooded engine.
4. Avoid operating an engine under load if it is missing.

Fig. 27-6
Layout of the transmission-
controlled spark (TCS) system
on the engine and the transmission. (*Chevrolet Motor Division of General Motors Corporation*)

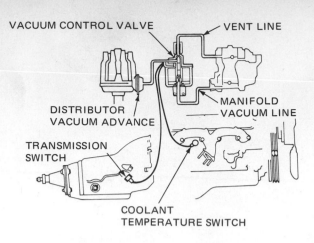

5. The use of liquid engine or carburetor cleaners, which are injected directly into the carburetor, is not recommended.
6. Do not turn off the ignition with the vehicle in motion.
7. Use only unleaded gasoline. Never use low-lead or leaded gasoline.
8. Avoid running out of gasoline while the engine is operating or
while driving on the highway, especially at high speed. This
may damage the converter.
9. Do not use engine or ignition replacement parts which are not
certified, recommended, or approved as being equivalent to
original equipment. The installation of non-original-equip-
ment parts may be a violation of the antitampering provision
of the Clean Air Act.
10. Do not pump the accelerator to start a hot engine that has
stalled.
11. When raising or lowering the car on a hoist, be sure all hoist
arms and other equipment are properly positioned to avoid damaging the converter and other under-car components. If the
hoist makes contact with any part of the car other than the
proper lift points, check all under-body components for physi-
cal damage and clearance before operating the vehicle.
12. A vehicle with a catalytic converter does not require extra
time to cool down, but the converter does. With its heavier
mass and insulation, the converter cools more slowly than the
muffler.
13. When operating an engine equipped with a catalytic converter

Fig. 27-7
Two different types of EGR
valves and how to clean them.
(*Ford Motor Company*)

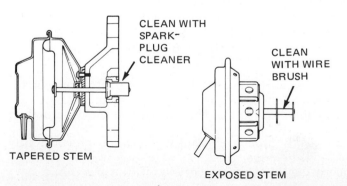

332

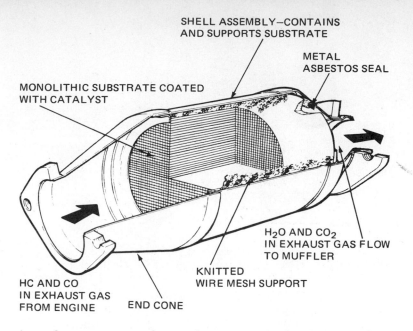

SHELL ASSEMBLY—CONTAINS
AND SUPPORTS SUBSTRATE

METAL
ASBESTOS SEAL

MONOLITHIC SUBSTRATE COATED
WITH CATALYST

H_2O AND CO_2
IN EXHAUST GAS FLOW
TO MUFFLER

KNITTED
WIRE MESH SUPPORT

HC AND CO
IN EXHAUST GAS
FROM ENGINE

END CONE

Fig. 27-8
Construction of the round type of monolithic catalytic converter used by Ford. (*Ford Motor Company*)

in a shop, use normal procedures to vent the engine exhaust gas to the outside with shop exhaust fans.

14. Cylinder balance tests and starting-motor tests can be performed in the same way as on cars without converters.

15. Do not run an engine more than 30 seconds with more than one spark-plug wire removed. The resulting overrich mixture may damage the converter. If possible, use an oscilloscope for ignition-system checks.

27-7 SERVICING THE CATALYTIC CONVERTER

The catalytic converter requires no service or maintenance in normal operation. By law, new-car manufacturers warranty catalytic converters to last for 5 years or 50,000 miles [80,500 km], whichever comes first, in normal usage. The converters used by American Motors Corporation and General Motors have a drain hole in the front bottom of the converter for removing and replacing the pellets. Defective catalytic converters on Chrysler and Ford cars require installation of a new converter. A cutaway view of the round type of monolithic catalytic converter used by Ford is shown in Fig. 27-8. The catalyst in it cannot be replaced. Like the Ford converter, the Chrysler converter must be replaced if it becomes defective or damaged.

No special tools are needed to replace a catalytic converter. Many converters can be removed by raising the vehicle on a hoist and disconnecting the converter at the front and rear. When installing the new converter, use new nuts and bolts. Other converters have the exhaust pipe attached to the converter inlet. To replace the converter, cut the pipe.

If the bottom cover of a catalytic converter on a General Motors car is bulged, distorted, torn, or damaged, the cover can be replaced with the converter on the car. A repair kit is available from General Motors dealers. However, if the inner shell of the converter is damaged, the converter must be replaced. When heat damage to the converter is indicated (bulging and distortion), inspect the remainder of the exhaust

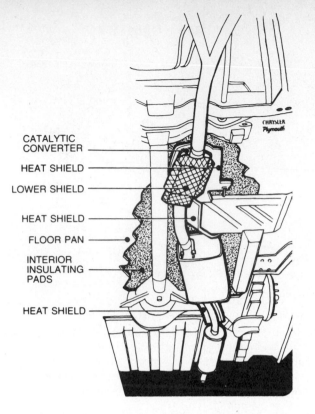

CATALYTIC CONVERTER

HEAT SHIELD

LOWER SHIELD

HEAT SHIELD

FLOOR PAN

INTERIOR INSULATING PADS

HEAT SHIELD

system for damage also. Unless the catalytic converter has a hole in it, or the converter pipe clamps are loose, exhaust-system noise is not the fault of the catalytic converter. Catalytic converters provide virtually no sound deadening. Cars equipped with catalytic converters use conventional mufflers to control exhaust noise.

The use of fuel additives is not recommended on cars equipped with catalytic converters. The additive may harm the catalyst. Before using any fuel additive, in either the fuel tank or the carburetor, check that the additive is approved for use in cars with catalytic converters. Reasonable use of starting fluid will not harm the catalyst, according to General Motors.

During the chemical reaction in the catalytic converter, when the exhaust gas passes over the catalyst, the exhaust-gas temperature may rise to 1600°F [870°C]. Therefore, cars equipped with catalytic converters have heat shields and insulation pads to protect chassis components and the passenger-compartment floor from heat damage (Fig. 27-9).

If a shield is missing, torn, or ripped, it must be replaced. Remove the damaged shield by carefully chiseling the shield loose at its welds. Whenever the vehicle has been operated on gravel roads, in off-road use, or under severe road-load conditions, Ford recommends a shield inspection at 5000-mile [8000-km] intervals.

27-8 SERVICING THE THERMOSTATICALLY CONTROLLED AIR CLEANER

To check the thermostatically controlled air cleaner, first make sure the hoses and heat pipe are tightly connected. See that there are no

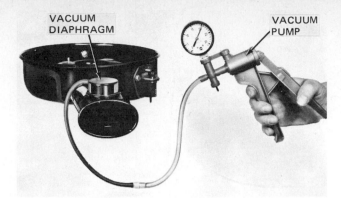

leaks in the system. The system can be checked with a thermometer. Failure of the thermostatic system usually results in the damper door staying open. This means that the driver will probably not notice anything wrong in warm weather. But, in cold weather, the driver will notice hesitation, surge, and stalling. A typical checking procedure follows.

Remove the air-cleaner cover. Install the thermometer as close to the sensor as possible. Allow the engine to cool below 85°F [29°C] if it is hot. Replace the air-cleaner cover without the wing nut.

Start and idle the engine. When the damper begins to open, remove the air-cleaner cover, and note the temperature reading. It should be between 85 and 115°F [29 and 46°C]. If it is difficult to see the damper, use a mirror.

If the damper does not open at the correct temperature, check the vacuum motor and sensor.

With the engine off, the control damper should be in the compartment or cold-air-delivery position (see Fig. 26-15). To determine if the vacuum motor is operating, apply at least 9 in Hg [229 mm Hg] of vacuum to the fitting on the vacuum motor (Fig. 27-10). The vacuum can be from the engine, from a distributor tester, or from a hand vacuum pump (Fig. 27-10). With vacuum applied, the damper should move to the hot-air-delivery position (Fig. 26-15).

If the vacuum motor does not work satisfactorily, it should be replaced (Fig. 27-11). This can be done by drilling out the spot welds and unhooking the linkage. The new motor can be installed with a retain-

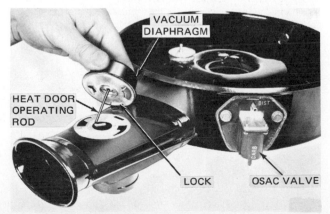

Fig. 27-12

Replacing the temperature
sensor in a thermostatically
controlled air cleaner.
(*Chrysler Corporation*)

ing strap and sheet-metal screws. Other types of vacuum motors have
locking tabs which disengage and engage when the vacuum motor is
rotated (Fig. 27-11).

If the vacuum motor does work well, the sensor should be replaced
(Fig. 27-12). This is done by prying up the tabs on the retaining clip.
The new sensor is then installed, and the tabs are bent down again.

CHECK UP ON YOURSELF

Now you have finished the chapter on servicing automotive emissions controls. Find out how well you understand these procedures
by answering the questions that follow.

1. Where is the PCV filter usually located?
2. What testers are required to check evaporative control systems?
3. What emission-control system requires periodic checking of the
   drive-belt tension?
4. Which emission-control system includes the idle-stop solenoid?
5. What causes an EGR valve to stick?
6. What exhaust emission-control device may be damaged by running
   the engine for a long time with one or more spark-plug wires disconnected?
7. In what type of weather can failure of the thermostatically controlled air cleaner go unnoticed by the driver?

ANSWERS

1. In the carburetor air cleaner (Sec. 27-1). **2.** None (Sec. 27-2). **3.** The air-
injection system (Sec. 27-3). **4.** The TCS system (Sec. 27-4). **5.** Deposits on
the EGR valve (Sec. 27-5). **6.** The catalytic converter (Sec. 27-6). **7.** Warm
weather (Sec. 27-8).

PART FIVE
AUTOMOTIVE ENGINE SERVICE

Engine service includes troubleshooting to find the cause of any trouble and then fixing it. That is, first you analyze the complaint or trouble. Then you do whatever is necessary to eliminate it and restore the engine to normal operating condition. We have divided engine service into valve-train service; connecting-rod, piston, and ring service; and crankshaft and cylinder service. In this part of the book, we have also included separate chapters on engine troubleshooting and engine tuneup. There are six chapters in Part Five:

CHAPTER TWENTY-EIGHT ENGINE TROUBLESHOOTING

After studying this chapter, you should be able to:

1. Explain what troubleshooting is and how analysis of a specific trouble can point to the possible causes and cures.
2. List the 16 engine troubles discussed in the chapter and explain what should be done in each case to pinpoint the cause of trouble.

The person who works as an engine troubleshooter is called an engine *diagnostician,* a word that means diagnostic technician. The purpose of the diagnosis is to answer the question *"What* is wrong?"

The diagnostician begins with the customer's complaints. The diagnostician listens to the engine and uses test instruments to find out exactly what is wrong. Usually, the diagnostician will tell the customer or write on the repair order what must be done to cure the engine trouble. The remedy might be something minor, like a tuneup. Or the remedy could be something major, like grinding valves or replacing piston rings. In this chapter we look at various engine troubles and what causes them. Then we find out how the diagnostician determines which cause produces what trouble.

28-1 ENGINE TROUBLES

First, let's make a list of engine troubles. Then we'll show you how to sort through the possible causes of engine troubles to determine what the problem really is. This process is called *troubleshooting,* or trouble diagnosis. Here are the engine troubles, listed in the order in which we discuss them in later sections of this chapter:

1. Engine does not turn over when startup is attempted.
2. Engine turns over slowly but does not start.
3. Engine turns over at normal speed but does not start.
4. Engine runs but misses.
5. Engine lacks power, lacks acceleration, or lacks high-speed performance.
6. Engine overheats.
7. Engine idles roughly.
8. Engine stalls.

9. Engine backfires.
10. Engine has smoky exhaust—blue, black, or white.
11. Engine uses too much oil.
12. Engine has low oil pressure.
13. Engine uses too much gasoline.
14. Exhaust gas has too much CO or HC.
15. Engine experiences run-on or dieseling.
16. Engine is noisy (knocks, pounds, chatters, thuds, and so on).

Let's discuss each of these troubles in turn. We'll explain what the possible causes might be and how to correct the conditions. In Chap. 29 we describe the modern diagnostic equipment you can use to help you pinpoint the causes of trouble.

NOTE

The first part of this troubleshooting procedure is described in Chap. 22. It is repeated here so you can have the whole procedure in one chapter.

28-2 ENGINE DOES NOT TURN OVER

The first thing you should think about if the engine does not turn over when you try to start it is that the battery is dead. Often, the battery is the trouble. But you have to consider whether the driver ran down the battery while trying to start the car. If the driver did, the real cause of the trouble could be elsewhere. Make sure the gearshift level is in neutral (N) or park (P). What should you do if nothing happens when you try to start? Turn on the headlights and try to start the car again. One of the following will happen:

- Lights stay bright with no cranking action.
- Lights dim a lot with no cranking action.
- Lights go out.
- Lights burn dimly or not at all when you turn them on.

Let's look at each of these in detail.

1. Lights Stay Bright

If the lights stay bright, there is an open circuit between the starting motor and the battery. The open circuit is probably in the wiring circuit, in the starting-motor solenoid, or in the motor itself. Also, the car may not be in neutral, or the neutral safety switch may need adjustment.

2. Lights Dim a Lot

If the lights dim a lot, the battery may be run down. It has enough power to light the lights, but when the load of the starting motor is added, the battery is too weak. Test the battery. If the battery is *not* run down, remove the starting motor for further checks of it and of the engine. The trouble could be a jammed or shorted starting motor or a locked-up engine.

3. Lights Dim a Little

If the lights dim only a little when you try to start, the starting-motor solenoid may have burned or corroded contacts. Because the solenoid draws a little current, the lights dim from the added load on the battery. But the current for cranking cannot get to the starting motor because the corroded contacts are an open circuit in the solenoid. Listen for cranking action. If you hear the buzz of an electric motor running, the overrunning clutch in the starting motor is slipping.

4. Lights Go Out
If the lights go out when you try to start, it is probably due to a bad connection at one of the battery terminals. The connection is good enough to let through the few amperes needed for the lights. But when the starting-motor load of several hundred amperes is added, the connection breaks down. Try wiggling the cable connections at the battery terminals. If that helps, then the terminals should be cleaned. The way to clean terminals is explained in Chap. 21.

5. Lights Burn Dimly or Not At All
If the lights burn dimly or not at all when you first turn them on, the battery is probably run down. Test the battery. If it is run down, you should try to find out what caused it. Maybe the driver ran down the battery trying to start. Then the trouble is in the fuel system, in the ignition system, or in the engine itself. Maybe the alternator output is low, or maybe a short in the electrical system caused a slow drain on the battery. Also, the battery may no longer be able to hold a charge.

28-3 ENGINE TURNS OVER SLOWLY BUT DOES NOT START
If the engine turns over slowly but does not start, the battery may be run down. In cold weather, the engine is much harder to crank. If it is very cold, the engine won't turn over very fast. The driver may have run down the battery trying to start. Other possible causes include a bad battery, a defect in the charging system that prevents the alternator from charging the battery, a defective starting motor, and mechanical trouble in the engine.

28-4 ENGINE TURNS OVER AT NORMAL CRANKING SPEED BUT DOES NOT START
If the engine turns over at normal cranking speed but does not start, the battery and starting motor are in good condition. The cause probably is in the ignition system or the fuel system. One of the following situations probably exists:

- The carburetor is not delivering normal amounts of air-fuel mixture.
- The ignition system is not delivering sparks properly.

Disconnect the lead from one spark plug. Use insulated pliers and hold the clip end about $\frac{3}{16}$ inch [5 mm] from the engine block (Fig. 28-1) Then crank the engine. A good spark should jump to the block. If no spark occurs, the trouble is in the ignition system. If a spark does occur, the trouble probably is in the fuel system.

Failure to start could be due to overchoking. Try cranking with the throttle wide open. If this doesn't work, take off the air cleaner and open and close the throttle several times. If the accelerator pump delivers fuel each time you open the throttle, the carburetor is getting fuel. Two other possible causes remain:

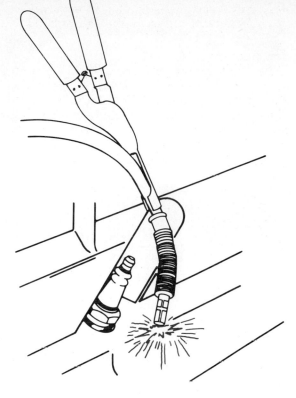

- The ignition timing is off.
- There are problems in the engine, such as fouled spark plugs or defective valves.

Also, a plugged or collapsed exhaust system can build up back pressure. This could prevent normal exhaust and intake so that the engine will not start.

NOTE
The choke should be open when the engine is warm and closed when the engine is completely cold and the ignition is first turned on. If the choke does not work, the engine will be hard to start. If the choke is open, a cold engine will be hard to start. If the choke is closed, a hot engine will be hard to start.

28-5 ENGINE RUNS BUT MISSES
A missing engine is a rough engine. Failure of cylinders to fire normally and in sequence throws the engine out of balance. You can usually feel this condition. The engine lacks power. The quickest way to pinpoint the trouble is to make a visual inspection and then to use diagnostic equipment, such as a vacuum gauge or an oscilloscope. We explain how to use these instruments in Chap. 29. There are also a couple of quick checks that could help you locate the trouble. These quick checks are handy because you don't need testing equipment, and you can make them away from the shop.

First, run the engine at various speeds and under load, such as going uphill, to verify that there is a miss. Next, with the engine idling

Fig. 28-2

To check for a misfiring cylinder, remove each spark-plug wire, one at a time. With the plug wire disconnected, if the cylinder is good, engine speed should drop about 50 rpm. (*Sun Electric Company*)

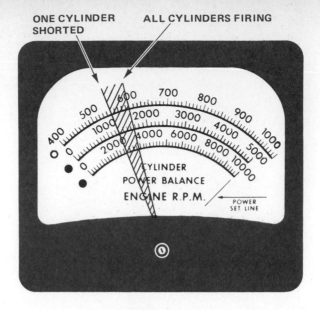

ONE CYLINDER SHORTED

ALL CYLINDERS FIRING

CYLINDER POWER BALANCE
ENGINE R.P.M.

POWER SET LINE

and a tachometer connected, check that each cylinder is firing. To do this, use insulated pliers to remove the spark-plug wire from the spark plug. If the engine speed drops by 50 rpm or more (Fig. 28-2), you know that cylinder is doing its job. If there is no change in engine rpm, the cylinder for that plug is not doing its job. This could be caused by trouble in the distributor or wiring, a fouled plug, or trouble inside the cylinder, such as defective valve action. (There is more on the use of the tachometer in Chap. 29.)

Make another check by holding the spark-plug end of the lead about $\frac{3}{16}$ inch [5 mm] from the engine block (Fig. 28-1). If a spark jumps the gap, the distributor and wiring are probably fine. The trouble is most likely in the cylinder. Stop the engine and take out the plug. If it is badly fouled or burned, the plug is probably the cause of the trouble. Install a new plug and try again. If the old plug is all right, the trouble is probably in the engine itself.

Make the above test with the engine idling. It is a good idea to try the test with the engine under load at higher speeds too. The ideal would be to operate the engine with the car on a dynamometer (covered in Chap. 29). However, if the shop has a dynamometer, then it also will have an oscilloscope, which will enable you to pinpoint many trouble causes.

NOTE

In engine troubleshooting, there are lots of details to think about. These include details about how things should work and which things can go wrong to keep components from working. Here's one way to help you learn: Get some 3-by 5-inch cards. On one side, write down a trouble; on the other side, list the possible causes. Look at the trouble side and try to recall the causes on the other side. Then figure out why each cause can create that trouble.

CHECK UP ON YOURSELF

You have to know many facts to be a good engine diagnostician. So far, you have read about four of the sixteen engine troubles that

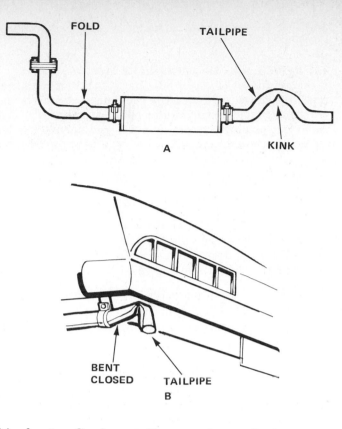

Fig. 28-3
A clogged or restricted exhaust system may cause the engine, cold or hot, to lack power. (*Ford Motor Company*)

are covered in this chapter. See how well you understand what you have studied by answering the following questions.

1. What does it mean if the lights stay bright with no cranking action?
2. What is the most likely cause if the lights dim a lot when you try to start?
3. What is the probable cause if the lights dim only a little when you try to start?
4. If the engine turns over at normal cranking speed but does not start, what two systems should be checked?
5. If shorting out a spark plug does not change the engine speed, what does this mean?

ANSWERS

1. There is probably an open circuit between the starting motor and the battery (Sec. 28-2). **2.** The battery is run down (Sec. 28-2). **3.** There is probably an open circuit in the solenoid (Sec. 28-2). **4.** The ignition system and the fuel system (Sec. 28-4). **5.** The cylinder that was shorted out is faulty and is not delivering power (Sec. 28-5).

28-6 ENGINE LACKS POWER, ACCELERATION, OR HIGH-SPEED PERFORMANCE

A complaint about a lack of power, acceleration, or high-speed performance is hard to analyze. Almost any part of the car, from the engine to the tires, could be the cause. You can get an idea of the cause of the trouble by trying to find out if the engine lacks power when it's either cold or hot, only cold, or only hot. Let's look at each of these conditions. An oscilloscope or dynamometer, along with other test instruments, may be needed to pinpoint the exact cause of this kind of trouble.

1. Engine Lacks Power Cold or Hot

If the engine lacks power whether it is hot or cold, the cause could be a miss, which we covered in the previous section. The cause could also be carburetor trouble (carburetor not delivering normal air-fuel mixture). A clogged exhaust system could restrict normal intake and exhaust action. This could be caused either by a bent or collapsed exhaust or tail pipe or by a clogged muffler (Fig. 28-3). There are many other possible causes outside the engine:

- PCV valve stuck open
- Clogged carburetor air cleaner
- Incorrectly adjusted throttle linkage
- Incorrect gasoline for the engine
- Weak ignition coil
- Incorrect ignition timing

The above are most of the possible "outside" causes. Inside the engine, lack of power could be caused by the following:

- Loss of compression from worn cylinder walls, pistons, or rings
- Bad valves
- Oil too heavy for the engine
- Carbon buildup in the combustion chambers
- Worn camshaft lobes
- Excessive parts wear or mechanical friction

Also, dragging brakes, underinflated tires, or incorrect front-end alignment can rob power from the drive wheels.

2. Engine Lacks Power Only When Cold

If the engine lacks power only when it is cold, the cause is probably an incorrect air-fuel mixture reaching the cylinders or a failure of the warmup systems. For example, if the choke is not working properly, the mixture will be too lean for good cold-engine operation. The manifold heat-control valve or the thermostatic air cleaner may not be operating properly. This means the mixture is not getting the heat it should have. If the thermostat in the cooling system is sticking open, the engine will take a long time to warm up and develop good hot-engine performance. Also, engine valves may stick partly open when cold and cause poor cold-engine performance.

3. Engine Lacks Power Only When Hot

To start normally when hot, the engine must have good compression and no intake-manifold leaks. However, the engine that lacks power only when hot probably is overheating. The causes of engine overheating are discussed in the following section. There are other possible causes of poor hot-engine performance. For example, an automatic choke sticking closed will feed the engine an air-fuel mixture that is too rich. This can reduce engine power. In addition, a rich mixture can foul spark plugs and piston rings with carbon, causing serious engine trouble. You can check the choke by removing the air cleaner and noting choke action as the engine warms up. If the choke does not open, you have pinpointed the trouble.

If the manifold heat-control valve and the thermostatic air cleaner do not work properly, they can feed too much heat to the air-fuel mixture. This prevents adequate amounts of mixture from reaching the cylinders. Engine performance will be poor. If there is vapor lock in the fuel line or fuel pump, not enough fuel or no fuel will reach the carburetor. The engine will perform poorly or stall.

28-7 ENGINE OVERHEATS

Most engine overheating is caused by loss of coolant through leaks in the cooling system. We'll tell you how to check the cooling system later. There are other possible causes of engine overheating. For example, high altitudes and hot climates make engines overheat more easily. Overloading the engine by pulling a big trailer at high speed or up a long hill will overheat the engine. Not enough lubricating oil may cause the engine to overheat and possibly fail! Improperly timed ignition or valves will cause engine overheating. A loose or slipping engine fan belt will result in poor water-pump and fan action and engine overheating. Idling the engine and driving at low speed for long periods can overheat the engine. If the emission-control TCS system is bad, it may prevent vacuum advance even though the engine is getting hot. Therefore, the engine will get even hotter. So the TCS system also needs checking as a cause of engine overheating.

The following conditions in the cooling system are possible causes of engine overheating:

- Thermostat stuck closed
- Clogged cooling-system hoses
- Scale or rust buildup in the engine water jackets or radiator
- Defective water pump
- Not enough coolant in the system

28-8 ENGINE IDLES ROUGHLY

A rough idle can be caused by an improperly adjusted carburetor. It can also be caused by any of the reasons for lack of power described in Sec. 28-6.

28-9 ENGINE STALLS

If the engine starts and then stalls, note when the stalling takes place. Does the engine stall:

- Before the engine warms up?
- As the engine warms up?
- After slow-speed driving or idling?
- After high-speed or full-load driving?

The operating condition will give you a clue to the cause. Let's take a look at these conditions.

1. Engine Stalls before It Warms Up

If the engine stalls before it warms up, the cause is probably fuel-system trouble. Any one of the troubles listed below can cause stalling before the engine warms up:

- Idle mixture or idle speed out of adjustment
- Low float level in the carburetor
- Icing in the carburetor
- Open choke

345

With a low float level, not enough fuel can get to the engine. Icing is caused by cool, moist air entering the cold carburetor. Under some conditions the moisture condenses and turns to ice. This clogs the carburetor throttle and air horn, and the engine stalls.

Ignition-system troubles can cause engine stalling before warmup. If the ignition system is bad enough to cause stalling, it probably would prevent starting. However, there might be an open primary resistance wire. When the engine is cranked, this wire is bypassed. Full battery voltage gets to the ignition coil. Then, when the engine starts, the wire goes back into the circuit. If this wire is open, the engine stalls.

2. Engine Stalls as It Warms Up

If the engine stalls as it warms up, the problem is probably in the fuel system. If the choke does not open, the mixture will become too rich for a warm engine. Then the engine will stall. Also, the manifold heat-control valve or the thermostat in the air cleaner may be sticking. This means the ingoing air-fuel mixture will be overheated. Not enough of the mixture will get to the cylinders for proper combustion. When this happens, the engine stalls.

Another possible cause of stalling is a low hot-idle speed. As the engine warms up, it could stall because the hot-idle speed is too low. Engine overheating (see Sec. 28-7) could cause vapor lock and stalling.

3. Engine Stalls after Low-speed Driving or Idling

The fuel system is a likely cause of this condition. A weak fuel pump might not be able to deliver enough fuel at idle. The fuel pump could be weak at low speed and do a satisfactory job during intermediate- and high-speed driving. The float level in the carburetor may be too high, or the idle mixture may be too rich. These conditions can cause the engine to "load up" with an overrich mixture and stall. Engine overheating also can cause stalling after prolonged low-speed driving or idling. Even an engine in good condition can overheat under these conditions. The reason is that not enough air passes through the radiator to ensure good cooling (see Sec. 28-7).

4. Engine Stalls after High-speed Driving

If the engine stalls after high-speed driving, the problem is usually in the fuel system. High-speed driving builds up heat in the engine. Then, when the car stops—at a stop sign, for example—the heat causes a vapor lock. Stalling can also be caused by engine overheating (see Sec. 28-7).

28-10 ENGINE BACKFIRES

Backfiring is caused by early ignition. Combustion flashes back through the still-open intake valve. After-firing, which is another type of combustion outside the cylinder, occurs in the exhaust line, that is, in the manifold or the muffler. Backfiring or after-firing can result from the following:

- Defective exhaust emission-control air-bypass valve
- Incorrect ignition or valve timing
- Defective high-voltage wiring or distributor cap, which permits cross-firing

- Spark plugs of the wrong heat range that overheat and cause preignition
- Carbon in the engine, which develops hot spots that preignite the mixture
- Hot or sticking valves

Valves will overheat if they do not seat properly or if they have been ground too much. Air-fuel mixtures that are too rich or too lean, caused by carburetor problems, can also cause backfiring.

28-11 ENGINE HAS SMOKY EXHAUST

Smoky exhaust indicates that the engine is burning oil, the air-fuel mixture is too rich, or water has leaked into the combustion chamber. The color of the exhaust can tell you which situation exists. If the exhaust gas has a bluish tinge, the engine is burning oil. See Sec. 28-12, which discusses the problem of the engine using too much oil. If the exhaust gas is more black than blue, the air-fuel mixture probably is too rich. Not all the fuel is burning in the engine. Black exhaust gas can also be caused by misfiring cylinders (see Sec. 28-5). See Sec. 28-14 for causes of too much fuel consumption. Whitish exhaust smoke while the engine is cold may be considered normal. But after warmup, it may indicate water in the combustion chamber. The situation may be caused by a cracked cylinder head or a blown cylinder-head gasket.

28-12 ENGINE USES TOO MUCH OIL

The engine can lose oil in three ways. These are by burning it in the combustion chamber, by leaking it in liquid form, and by passing it out of the crankcase through the PCV system in the form of mist or vapor.

External leaks often can be seen by inspecting the seals around the oil pan, the cylinder-head cover, and the timing-gear housing and at the oil-line and oil-filter connections. Oil and dirt around the leaky spot will show you the leak.

You can check the actual amount of oil the engine uses as follows: Fill the crankcase to the correct level and drive several hundred miles. Then measure the additional amount of oil necessary to bring the oil level back up to the correct level. There is one caution here. If the car is being driven around town in start-and-stop operation, the engine may never get warmed up. This means that the crankcase oil will be diluted with water and unburned gasoline. For a proper check on the oil level, the car should be taken out on the highway and driven long enough for the engine to get hot. Then the water and unburned gasoline will be boiled out of the crankcase.

If oil is being burned in the combustion chambers, the exhaust gas will have a bluish tinge. Oil can enter past the valve guides and valve stems and past the piston rings.

If the valve guides are worn, there will be too much clearance around the valve stems. Oil in the valve compartment will be drawn into the combustion chamber on each intake stroke. If the valve guides are worn, the underside of the valves usually will be covered with carbon. This condition requires replacement of the valve seals or installation of new valve guides and possibly new valves.

Probably the most common cause of too much oil consumption is the failure of the piston rings to keep the oil out of the combustion chambers. Oil gets into the combustion chambers because of worn cylin-

347

der walls and worn or stuck piston rings. Another possible cause is worn engine bearings that throw off excessive amounts of oil onto the cylinder walls. There is more oil than the piston rings can control. So some of the oil gets up into the combustion chambers.

Even with a good engine, oil consumption goes up with engine speed. More oil is pumped at high speed, so more oil gets on the cylinder walls. The piston rings have less time to handle the oil. Also, at high speed, the oil gets hotter and thinner. Therefore it is harder for the piston rings to control. An engine can use two or more times as much oil at high speeds as at low speeds.

28-13 ENGINE HAS LOW OIL PRESSURE

Low oil pressure is often a warning of a worn oil pump or worn engine bearings. Worn bearings can pass so much oil that the oil pump cannot maintain pressure. This can be serious because the center bearings could get most of the oil. The end bearings could be oil-starved and fail from lack of oil. Other causes of low oil pressure include the following:

- Weak oil-pump pressure relief-valve spring
- Worn oil pump
- Oil-line leaks
- Clogged oil line

If the oil is diluted, foaming, or loaded with too much sludge, the oil pump cannot feed enough oil to the engine to keep the pressure up. An overheating engine may cause the oil to thin out because of the high temperature. This could prevent normal oil pressure.

CHECK UP ON YOURSELF

Let's pause for a moment and review the last few pages on engine troubleshooting. Check up on yourself by answering the questions that follow.

1. Could a lack of engine power only when the engine is cold be caused by a defect in the ignition system?
2. Could a sticking choke cause loss of engine power when the engine is hot?
3. Is the ignition system or the fuel system most likely to blame if the engine stalls as it warms up?
4. What is the cause of black exhaust?
5. If the exhaust gas has a bluish tinge, what is the cause?

ANSWERS

1. Probably not. Lack of power when the engine is cold is most likely caused by trouble in the fuel system (Sec. 28-6). 2. Yes. A sticking choke allows an overrich mixture to flow to the engine when the engine warms up. An overrich mixture reduces engine power. In addition, an overrich mixture fouls the plugs and piston rings (Sec. 28-6). 3. The fuel system (Sec. 28-9). 4. Overrich air-fuel mixture (Sec. 28-11). 5. Oil burning in the combustion chamber (Sec. 28-11).

28-14 ENGINE USES TOO MUCH GASOLINE

This means poor fuel economy, or low miles per gallon. The cause of this trouble is hard to pin down. It may be underinflated tires or dragging brakes. Or the trouble may be in the fuel system, the ignition system, or the engine. It could be due to the way the car is driven. A fuel-mileage tester can be used to accurately check fuel consumption (Fig. 28-4). You may need other test instruments to find the cause.

NOTE

Before you make your tests, you should find out the answers to these questions: Is the car operated around town in start-and-stop driving? Does the driver pump the accelerator pedal when idling and insist on being the first to get away when the stoplight changes? If so, the gas mileage is going to be low.

A rough check that does not require testing instruments is to install a set of new or cleaned spark plugs. Then operate the engine for about 20 minutes, and remove the plugs. If they are coated with carbon, the mixture is too rich. The trouble is in the fuel system.

Here are the conditions to check in the fuel system:

- Failure of the choke to open, which means the engine is getting a rich mixture.
- Clogged air cleaner, which can act like a closed choke.
- High float level, which causes too much fuel to be delivered to the carburetor fuel nozzles.
- Idle-mixture screw set too rich.
- Accelerator-pump check valve in the carburetor not closing, which allows fuel to leak past the valve and into the carburetor.
- Metering rod stuck in the high-speed position, which allows the engine to be fed a mixture that is too rich.
- Worn carburetor jets, which allow too much fuel to flow.

Fig. 28-4

Fuel mileage tester. A small container holding exactly 0.1 gallon [0.4 L] is mounted on the driver's door. (*Ford Motor Company*)

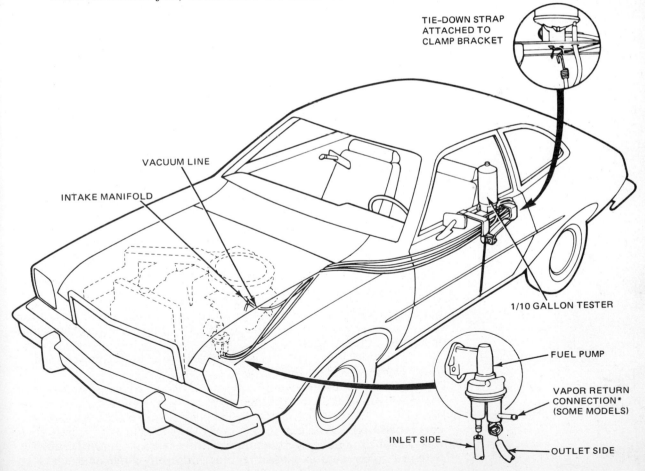

TIE-DOWN STRAP ATTACHED TO CLAMP BRACKET

VACUUM LINE

INTAKE MANIFOLD

1/10 GALLON TESTER

FUEL PUMP

VAPOR RETURN CONNECTION* (SOME MODELS)

INLET SIDE

OUTLET SIDE

Here are the conditions in the ignition system to consider:

- Weak coil or condenser, which could cause missing, particularly at high engine speeds
- Incorrect timing or faulty advance-mechanism action, either of which could prevent full use of the power in the air-fuel mixture
- Dirty or worn plugs or contact points or defective wiring, which could cause missing and high fuel consumption

Here are the conditions in the engine to consider:

- Worn or stuck piston rings
- Worn cylinder walls
- Worn or stuck valves
- Burned cylinder-head gasket

Any of these conditions cause loss of power, which means that more fuel must be burned to get the same engine speed.

28-15 TOO MUCH CO AND HC IN THE EXHAUST GAS

Today automobile-testing procedures include using the exhaust-gas analyzer (Chap. 29). The purpose of exhaust-gas testing is to keep the smoggers off the highway. Many states require exhaust-gas testing of all cars during state inspection. Cars that do not pass the test because they give off too much HC or CO must be repaired before they can be licensed. Later we describe exhaust-gas analyzers and explain how to use them. Here, we want to review why cars emit too much CO and HC and the causes of this problem. Cars emit too much CO and HC because in the combustion process not all the gasoline burns completely. We cover most of the causes of incomplete combustion in Chap. 27, but let's summarize them here:

1. Missing because of ignition problems, such as faulty plugs, high-voltage wiring, distributor cap, ignition coil, condenser, or contact points
2. Improper ignition timing
3. Choke sticking closed, worn jets, high float level, and other conditions listed in Sec. 28-14 which cause excessive fuel consumption
4. Faulty air-injection system, which does not inject enough air into the exhaust manifold to completely burn the HC and CO
5. Defective TCS (transmission-controlled spark) system, which permits vacuum advance in all gear positions instead of in high
6. Defective catalytic converters, which must be replaced or recharged to restore exhaust-gas cleaning

28-16 ENGINE RUN-ON OR DIESELING

Some engines have a tendency to continue running after the ignition switch is turned off (see Sec. 18-26). If an engine does this, the following could be the trouble:

- Incorrect idle-stop solenoid adjustment or defective solenoid
- Engine overheating
- Hot spots in cylinders
- Advanced ignition timing

28-17 ENGINE NOISES

A skilled technician can often pinpoint the causes of engine troubles by listening to the engine operating under different conditions. The technician may use a listening rod or a stethoscope to locate the source of a noise. To do this, the pickup end of the rod or stethoscope is moved around on various places on the engine to find where the noise is loudest (Fig. 28-5). This enables the technician to find out which cylinder has the broken ring or which main bearing is knocking.

CAUTION
Keep away from the moving fan belt and fan when using a listening rod or stethoscope!

Here are descriptions of various noises and what they mean.

1. Valve and Tappet Noise
Valve and tappet noise is a regular clicking that increases with engine speed. The noise is caused by too much clearance in the valve train. If the valve train has mechanical lifters, the valves can be adjusted to minimize the noise. If the valve train has hydraulic valve lifters, the problem may be caused by a sticking plunger in the lifters. This requires servicing or replacement of the lifters.

Other causes of the valve and tappet noise include the following:
- Weak valve springs
- Worn valve-lifter faces
- Lifters loose in the block
- Rough camshaft lobes
- Rough or worn faces on the lifter adjustment screws

Any of these conditions could cause a clicking noise that synchronizes with valve action.

2. Detonation
This is a pinging or chattering sound. It is most noticeable when the car is climbing a hill or accelerating. It can be caused by any of the following:
- Use of a low-octane gasoline
- Carbon deposits in the combustion chamber, which increase the compression ratio and the tendency of the engine to detonate
- Excessively advanced ignition timing

3. Connecting-rod Noise
Connecting-rod noise is usually a light knocking or pounding. The sound is most noticeable when the engine is "floating" (neither accelerating nor decelerating). The sound becomes more noticeable as the driver eases up on the accelerator with the car running at medium speed. To find out which connecting rod is causing the trouble, short out each spark plug in turn. Rod noise will drop off when the cylinder that is responsible is not delivering power. Rod noise can be caused by a worn big-end bearing or crankpin, a bent rod, or insufficient oil.

4. Piston-pin Noise
Piston-pin noise is somewhat like valve and tappet noise, but it has more of a metallic, double-knock sound. It can usually be heard most easily during idle with the spark advanced. It may also be noticeable at car speeds of about 30 mph [48 km/h]. You can check it out by idling the engine and then shorting out spark plugs one at a time. Piston-pin noise will be reduced when the plug in a noisy cylinder is shorted out.

Fig. 28-5
A mechanic's stethoscope being used to locate engine noise.

Causes of piston-pin noise include a worn piston or bushing and lack of oil.

5. Piston-ring Noise
Piston-ring noise is similar to the valve and tappet noise. It is a click, a snap, or a rattle. It is most evident on acceleration. Low ring tension, broken or worn rings, or worn cylinder walls can produce this noise. You can make the following test: Remove all spark plugs and add 1 to 2 fluid ounces [30 to 60 cc] of heavy engine oil to each cylinder. Replace the plugs. Crank the engine for several revolutions to work the oil down past the rings. Then start the engine. If the noise has been reduced, the rings are probably at fault.

6. Piston Slap
Piston slap is a hollow, muffled, bell-like sound. It is caused by the piston rocking back and forth in the cylinder and "slapping" the cylinder wall. Piston slap can be caused by worn cylinder walls or pistons, collapsed piston skirts, or misaligned connecting rods.

7. Crankshaft Knock
Crankshaft knock is a heavy and dull metallic knock. It is most noticeable when the engine is under a heavy load or accelerating, especially if the engine is cold. If the noise is regular, it is probably caused by worn main bearings. If the noise is irregular and sharp, it is probably caused by a worn thrust bearing.

8. Miscellaneous Noises
Other noises coming from the engine compartment can be caused by loose accessories. These include the alternator, starting motor, horn, manifolds, flywheel, crankshaft pulley, and oil pan. Also, noise that seems to come from the engine may be coming from the clutch, transmission, or drive line.

CHECK UP ON YOURSELF
You have just finished the chapter on troubleshooting. Now, check up on yourself by answering the questions that follow.
1. Can trouble in the fuel system and the ignition system cause high fuel consumption?
2. Can trouble in the fuel and ignition systems cause too much HC and CO in the exhaust gases?
3. If you hear a regular clicking that increases with engine speed, what is the probable cause of the noise?
4. If you hear a pinging or chattering sound coming from the engine when the car is going up a hill, what is the most likely cause?
5. If the engine gives off a hollow, bell-like sound, what is the probable cause?

ANSWERS
1. Yes. Troubles in the fuel system can cause an excessively rich mixture. Troubles in the ignition system can cause missing. Both waste fuel (Sec. 28-14). 2. Yes. For the same reasons given in the previous answer (Sec. 28-14). A rich mixture or missing will increase the amount of HC and CO in the exhaust (Sec. 28-15). 3. Excessive valve-tappet clearance (Sec. 28-17). 4. Detonation, resulting from the use of low-octane gasoline or excessive carbon in the combustion chambers (Sec. 28-17). 5. Piston slap, resulting from worn cylinder walls or pistons or misaligned rods (Sec. 28-17).

CHAPTER TWENTY-NINE ENGINE TESTING INSTRUMENTS

After studying this chapter, you should be able to:
List and describe the eight engine testing instruments discussed in the chapter and explain how to use each.

In Chap. 28 we explain how to locate the causes of many engine troubles without using testing instruments. Many of the troubleshooting checks we describe are almost second nature to experienced technicians. They listen to the engine and automatically perform the quick checks they decide are necessary. But to pinpoint the exact cause of other troubles, the experts use test instruments. In this chapter we cover the different instruments that can be used to test the engine.

29-1 ENGINE TESTING INSTRUMENTS
The testers we cover in this chapter are as follows:

1. Tachometer, which measures engine speed in revolutions per minute (rpm)
2. Cylinder-compression tester, which measures the ability of the cylinders to hold compression pressure
3. Cylinder-leakage tester, which finds any points where compression-pressure leakage is occurring
4. Vacuum gauge, which measures intake-manifold vacuum
5. Exhaust-gas analyzer, which measures the amount of pollutants in the exhaust gas
6. Ignition-timing light, which is used to set the ignition timing and check the spark advance
7. Oscilloscope, which shows the overall operating condition of the ignition-system circuits
8. Chassis dynamometer, which checks the engine and vehicle components under actual operating conditions

There are also instruments to test the battery, starting motor, charging system, and cooling system. There are other instruments to test ignition coils, condensers, spark plugs, distributor contact-point dwell, and distributor-advance mechanisms.

29-2 TACHOMETER
The tachometer measures engine speed in revolutions per minute (rpm). It is a necessary instrument because the idle speed must be ad-

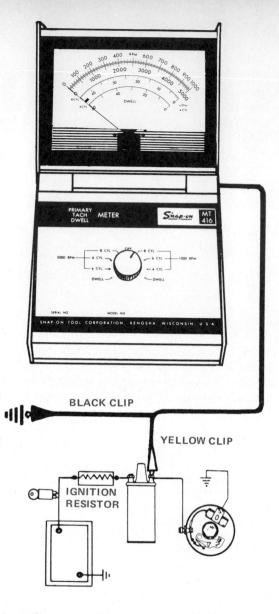

Fig. 29-2
Engine tachometer mounted in a car center console. (*Chrysler Corporation*)

justed to a specific rpm. Also, many tests must be made at specific engine speeds. The tachometer is connected to the ignition system and operates electrically.

The tachometer measures the number of times the primary circuit is interrupted and translates this into engine rpm. The tachometer has a selector knob that can be turned to 4, 6, or 8, according to the number of cylinders in the engine being tested. Figure 29-1 shows a tachometer connected to an engine.

Many high-performance cars have tachometers mounted on the instrument panel (Fig. 29-2). Their purpose is to keep the driver informed about how fast the engine is turning. Knowing this, the driver can keep the rpm within the range at which the engine develops maximum torque. This enables the driver to get the best performance from the engine. Many of these tachometers have a red line at the top rpm on the dial. The red line marks off the danger point for engine speed. This enables the driver to keep the engine below this speed.

Some car tachometers are mechanical instead of electrical. They are driven off a gear on the ignition distributor shaft. They operate somewhat like the speedometer, which we cover in Chap. 26.

29-3 CYLINDER-COMPRESSION TESTER

The cylinder-compression tester measures the ability of the cylinders to hold compression. Pressure, operating on a diaphragm in the tester, causes the needle on the face of the tester to move around to indicate the pressure being applied. Figure 29-3 shows a compression tester being used to measure the pressure in an engine cylinder.

To use the tester, first remove all the spark plugs. A recommended way to do this is to disconnect the wires, loosen the plugs one turn, reconnect the wires, and start the engine. Then, run the engine for a few seconds at 1000 rpm. The combustion gases will blow out of the plug well any dirt that could fall into the cylinder when the spark plugs are removed. The gases also blow out of the combustion chamber any loosened carbon that was caked around the exposed threaded end of the plug. This procedure prevents carbon and dirt particles from lodging under a valve and holding the valve open during the compression test. Now, remove the spark plugs.

Next, screw the compression-tester fitting into the spark-plug hole of number 1 cylinder, as shown in Fig. 29-3. Disconnect the distributor lead from the negative terminal of the coil. This protects the coil, and other electronic units, from damaging high voltage. Hold the throttle wide open and operate the starting motor to crank the engine. The needle on the compression tester will move around to show the maximum compression pressure the cylinder is developing. Write down this figure. Test the other cylinders in the same way.

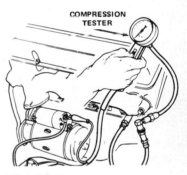

COMPRESSION TESTER

Fig. 29-3
A cylinder-compression tester in use. (*Sun Electric Corporation*)

29-4 RESULTS OF THE COMPRESSION TEST

The manufacturer's specifications tell you what the compression pressure of the cylinders should be. If the results of the test show that the compression is low, there is leakage past the piston rings, valves, or cylinder-head gasket. To correct the trouble, you must remove the cylinder head and inspect the engine parts.

Before you do this, you can make one further test to pinpoint the trouble. Squirt a small quantity of engine oil through the spark-plug hole into the cylinder. Then retest the compression. If the pressure increases to a more normal figure, the low compression is due to leakage past the piston rings. Adding the oil helps seal the rings temporarily so that they can hold the compression pressure better. The trouble is caused by worn piston rings, a worn cylinder wall, or a worn piston. The trouble could also be caused by rings that are broken or stuck in the piston-ring grooves.

If the addition of oil does not increase the compression pressure, the leakage is probably past the valves. This could be caused by

- Broken valve springs
- Incorrect valve adjustment
- Sticking valves
- Worn or burned valves
- Worn or burned valve seats

- Worn camshaft lobes
- Dished or worn valve lifters

There is also the possibility that the cylinder-head gasket is "blown." This means that the gasket has burned away so that compression pressure is leaking between the cylinder head and the cylinder block. Low compression between two adjacent cylinders is probably caused by the head gasket having blown between the cylinders.

Whatever the cause—rings, pistons, cylinder walls, valves, or gasket—the cylinder head has to be removed so that the trouble can be fixed. We discuss engine service later in the book.

29-5 CYLINDER-LEAKAGE TESTER

The cylinder-leakage tester does about the same job as the compression tester, but in a different way. It applies air pressure to the cylinder with the piston at TDC on the compression stroke. In this position, both valves are closed. Very little air should escape from the combustion chamber. Figure 29-4 shows a cylinder-leakage tester. Figure 29-5 shows the tester connected to an engine cylinder and how it pinpoints places where leakage can occur.

To use the tester, first remove all spark plugs. Then remove the air cleaner, the crankcase filler cap or dipstick, and the radiator cap. Set the throttle wide open and fill the radiator to the proper level. You are now ready to begin.

Connect the adapter, with the whistle, to the spark-plug hole of number 1 cylinder. Turn the engine over until the whistle sounds. When the whistle sounds, the piston is moving up on the compression stroke. Continue to rotate the engine until the TDC timing marks on the engine align. When the marks align, the piston is at TDC. Disconnect the whistle from the adapter hose and connect the tester, as shown in Figs. 29-4 and 29-5. Apply air pressure from the shop supply. Note the gauge reading, which shows the percentage of air leakage from the cylinder. Specifications vary, but if the reading is above 20 percent, there is excessive leakage. If the air leakage is excessive, check further by listening at the carburetor, tail pipe, and crankcase filler pipe.

Figure 29-5 shows what it means if you can hear air escaping at any of the three listening points. If air bubbles up through the radiator, the trouble is a blown cylinder-head gasket or a cracked cylinder head. This allows leakage from the cylinder to the cooling system.

Check the other cylinders in the same manner. A special TDC indicator supplied with the tester enables you to quickly find TDC on the other cylinders. When you use the tester, follow the instructions that explain how to use the TDC indicator.

Fig. 29-4
A cylinder-leakage tester. The whistle is used to locate TDC in number 1 cyclinder. (*Sun Electric Corporation*)

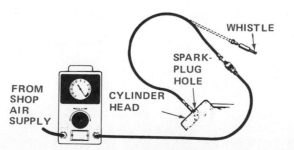

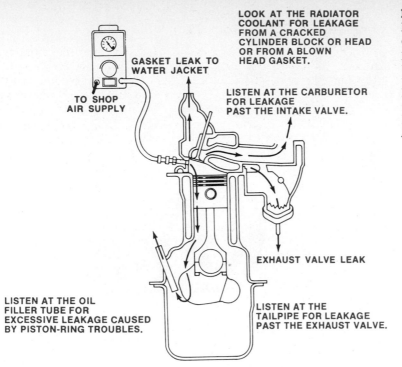

LOOK AT THE RADIATOR
COOLANT FOR LEAKAGE
FROM A CRACKED
CYLINDER BLOCK OR HEAD
OR FROM A BLOWN
HEAD GASKET.

GASKET LEAK TO
WATER JACKET

TO SHOP
AIR SUPPLY

LISTEN AT THE CARBURETOR
FOR LEAKAGE
PAST THE INTAKE VALVE.

EXHAUST VALVE LEAK

LISTEN AT THE OIL
FILLER TUBE FOR
EXCESSIVE LEAKAGE CAUSED
BY PISTON-RING TROUBLES.

LISTEN AT THE
TAILPIPE FOR LEAKAGE
PAST THE EXHAUST VALVE.

Fig. 29-5
Here is how the cylinder-leakage tester works. It applies air pressure to the cylinder through the spark-plug hole with the piston at TDC and both valves closed. Points where air is leaking can then be pinpointed, as shown. (*Sun Electric Corporation*)

29-6 ENGINE-VACUUM GAUGE

The engine-vacuum gauge is an important tester for tracking down troubles in an engine that runs but does not perform as well as it should. This gauge measures intake-manifold vacuum. The intake-manifold vacuum changes with different operating conditions and different engine defects. The way in which the vacuum varies from normal can show you what is wrong inside the engine.

Figure 29-6 shows the vacuum gauge connected to the intake manifold. With the gauge connected, start the engine and operate it as explained below.

The test must be made with the engine at normal operating temperature. The meanings of various readings are explained in the following paragraphs. (See Fig. 29-7.)

- A steady and fairly high reading at idle indicates normal performance. Specifications vary with different engines, but a reading of 17 to 22 inches [432 to 559 mm] of mercury indicates the engine is OK. The reading will be lower at higher altitudes because of the lower atmospheric pressure. For every 1000 feet [305 m] above sea level, the reading will be reduced about 1 inch [25 mm].

NOTE

"Inches of mercury" refers to the way the vacuum gauges are set up. There is no mercury in the gauge. It is just a way of measuring vacuum.

- A steady and low reading indicates late ignition or valve timing or possibly leakage around the pistons. Leakage around pistons (excessive blowby) could be due to worn or stuck piston rings,

Fig. 29-6
A vacuum gauge connected to the intake manifold for a manifold-vacuum test. (*Sun Electric Corporation*)

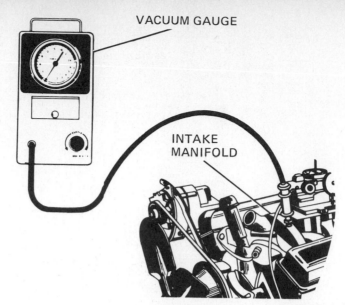

VACUUM GAUGE

INTAKE MANIFOLD

LOW AND STEADY READING INDICATES LOW COMPRESSION, AIR LEAKS, OR LATE IGNITION TIMING

RAPID VIBRATION WHEN ENGINE IS ACCELERATED INDICATES WEAK VALVE SPRINGS

INTERMITTENT DROP OF NEEDLE INDICATES STICKY VALVES

FLOATING MOTION OF NEEDLE INDICATES RICH MIXTURE

Typical Vacuum Gauge Readings

Fig. 29-7
Typical vacuum-gauge readings and their meaning.

worn cylinder walls, or worn pistons. Each of these conditions reduces engine power. With reduced power, the engine does not "pull" as much vacuum.

- A very low reading indicates a leaky intake manifold or carburetor gasket or possible leaks around the carburetor throttle shaft. Air leaks into the manifold reduce the vacuum and engine power.

NOTE
Some engines with high-lift cams and more valve overlap may have a lower and more uneven intake-manifold vacuum.

- Back-and-forth movement of the needle that increases with engine speed indicates weak valve springs.
- Gradual falling back of the needle toward zero with the engine idling indicates a clogged exhaust line.
- Regular dropping back of the needle indicates a valve sticking open or a spark plug not firing.
- Irregular dropping back of the needle indicates that valves are sticking only part of the time.
- Floating motion or slow back-and-forth movement of the needle indicates an air-fuel mixture that is too rich.

A test can be made for loss of compression due to leakage around the pistons as a result of stuck or worn piston rings, worn cylinder walls, or worn pistons. Race the engine for a moment and then quickly release the throttle. The needle should swing around to 23 to 25 inches [584 to 635 mm] as the throttle closes. This indicates good compression. If the needle fails to swing around this far, there is loss of compression. Further checks should be made.

CHECK UP ON YOURSELF
You have now finished the first half of the chapter on engine testing instruments. It is important for you to know how to use the instru-

ments and what the test results mean. Review what you have just studied by answering the following questions.

1. What is the purpose of the tachometer?
2. What is the purpose of the compression tester?
3. What are possible causes of low compression?
4. What is the purpose of the cylinder-leakage tester?
5. What does the engine-vacuum gauge check?

ANSWERS
1. To measure engine speed in rpm (Sec. 29-2). **2.** To measure how well the cylinders can hold compression (Sec. 29-3). **3.** Leakage past the valves, piston rings, or cylinder-head gasket (Sec. 29-4). **4.** To determine if there is leakage of compression and to pinpoint where leakage is occurring (Sec. 29-5). **5.** Intake-manifold vacuum (Sec. 29-6).

29-7 EXHAUST-GAS ANALYZER
At one time the major use of the early type of exhaust-gas analyzer was to adjust the carburetor. It is still used for that purpose. Today the newer type of infrared exhaust-gas analyzer has the added job of checking out the emission controls on the car. We cover the emission controls in Chap. 27. Their main purpose is to cut down on carbon monoxide (CO), hydrocarbon (HC), and oxides of nitrogen (NO_x) in the exhaust gas.

Figure 29-8 shows an infrared exhaust-gas analyzer. It is used by sticking a pickup tube or probe into the tail pipe of the car (Fig. 29-9). The probe draws out some of the exhaust gas and carries it through the analyzer. Two dials on the face of the analyzer, shown in Fig. 29-10, tell you how much HC and CO are in the exhaust gas. The HC meter shows parts per million (ppm). The CO meter reports a percentage. Federal and state laws set the maximum legal limits on the amount of HC and CO permitted in the exhaust gas.

Fig. 29-9
Exhaust-gas analyzer con-
nected for an exhaust-gas test.

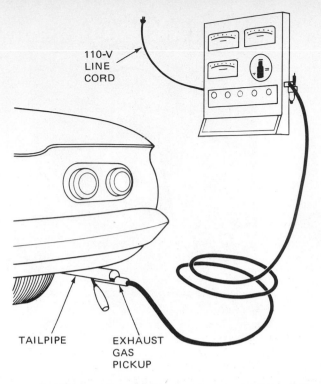

110-V
LINE
CORD

TAILPIPE   EXHAUST
                GAS
                PICKUP

A different kind of tester is required for NO_x, but it works in the same general way. It draws exhaust gas from the tail pipe and runs the gas through the analyzer. The result is reported in terms of the amount of NO_x in the exhaust gas. Generally, NO_x testers are available only in testing laboratories. They are not used today in the automotive service shop.

29-8 IGNITION-TIMING LIGHT
The sparks must reach the spark plugs in the cylinders at exactly the right time. Adjusting the distributor to make the sparks do this is called *ignition timing.* You can adjust the distributor by turning the distributor in its mounting. If you rotate the distributor in the direction opposite to the direction in which the cam rotates, you move the

Fig. 29-10

Hydrocarbon meter and carbon monoxide meter faces. (*Sun Electric Corporation*)

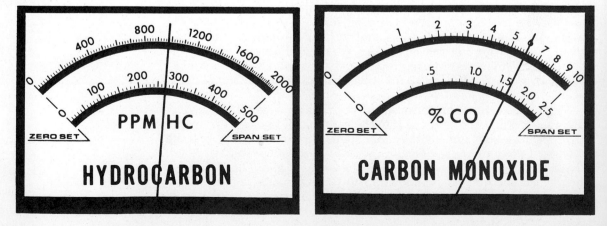

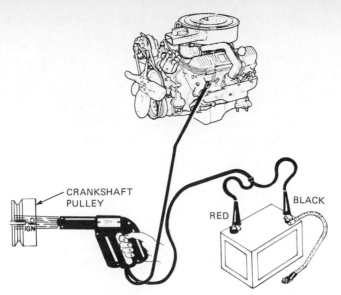

Fig. 29-11
A timing light is used to check
ignition timing.

CRANKSHAFT
PULLEY

RED

BLACK

IGN

contact points (or pickup coil) ahead. Therefore, the points close and open earlier. This advances the spark, so the sparks appear at the plugs earlier. Turning the distributor in the same direction as the direction in which the distributor cam rotates retards the sparks. The sparks appear at the plugs later.

To time the ignition, check the markings on the crankshaft pulley with the engine running. Since the pulley is turning rapidly, you can't see the markings with normal light. But by using a special stroboscopic light called a timing light, you can make the pulley appear to stand still. Use the light this way. Connect the timing-light lead to the number 1 spark plug (Fig. 29-11). Every time the plug fires, the timing light gives off a flash of light (see Fig. 29-12). The light lasts only a fraction of a second. The repeated flashes of light make the pulley seem to stand still.

To adjust the ignition timing, loosen the clamp screw that holds the distributor in its mounting and turn the distributor one way or the

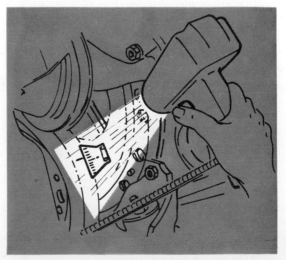

Fig. 29-12
The timing light flashes every
time number 1 spark plug fires.

Fig. 29-13
Ignition-timing marks on the
crankshaft pulley.

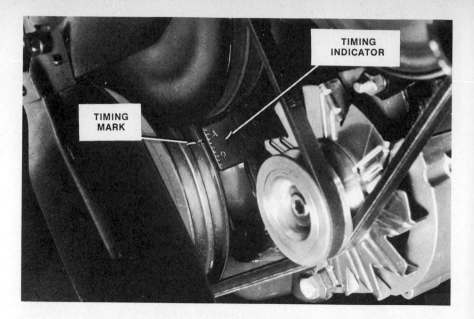

other. As you turn the distributor, the marking on the pulley will move
ahead or back. When the ignition timing is correct, the markings will
align with a timing pointer, or timing mark, as shown in Fig. 29-13.
Tighten the distributor clamp.

NOTE

The 1977 MISAR ignition system, described in Secs. 24-21 to 24-25, is not adjusted by turning the distributor in its mounting. Instead, if the ignition does
require timing, the crankshaft sensor (Fig. 24-35) is shifted. The 1978 MISAR
ignition system is timed by turning the distributor in its mounting. See Sec.
24-22.

29-9 OSCILLOSCOPE

The oscilloscope is a high-speed voltmeter that uses a televisionlike
picture tube to show ignition voltages. Figure 29-14 shows an automotive oscilloscope. The oscilloscope draws a picture of the ignition voltages on the face of the tube. The picture shows what is happening in
the ignition system. To understand the pictures, we have to review the
ignition system.

NOTE

The oscilloscope is usually called a *scope* in the shop. We will use that term
from now on.

When the ignition-coil primary circuit is opened (by either the
points or the transistor), the voltage in the secondary winding jumps
up. It can go up as high as 35,000 volts. This high voltage surges to a
spark plug and produces a spark. That is, the high voltage jumps the
gap between the insulated and grounded electrodes of the spark plug.
It takes a high voltage to start the spark. But after the spark is started,
much less voltage is needed to keep the spark going. The scope draws a
picture of how and when this voltage goes up and then drops back
down.

Fig. 29-14
Engine analyzer. This tester includes an oscilloscope (top center) and devices that check the condenser, distributor contact-point dwell, engine speed, and so on. (*Sun Electric Corporation*)

The picture is drawn on the face of the tube by a stream of electrons. This is exactly the way the picture tube in a television set works. However, in the scope, the stream of electrons draws a picture of just one thing—the ignition-system voltages feeding into the scope. Figure 29-15 shows the face of the picture tube and helps to explain what we mean.

When a voltage, such as the voltage that fires a spark plug, is detected by the scope, a "spike," or vertical line, appears on the face of the tube. This is shown in Fig. 29-15. The higher the voltage, the higher the spike. If the voltage spike goes down, it indicates that the ignition coil or the battery is connected backward.

To understand how the scope picks up the voltages and what the scope pictures mean, first look at what is called the *basic pattern* (Fig. 29-16). The basic pattern is what the scope would show if it were drawing the voltage pattern for one spark plug. To start with, the contact points have opened or the electronic control unit has opened the primary circuit. The high-voltage surge from the coil has arrived at the spark plug. The voltage goes up, from A to B, as shown in Fig. 29-16. This is called the *firing line*. After the spark is established, the voltage drops off considerably and holds fairly steady, from C to D. This is a very short time, measured in hundred-thousandths of a second. But the spark lasts for as long as 20 degrees of crankshaft rotation. This is long enough to ignite the compressed air-fuel mixture in the cylinder.

After most of the magnetic energy in the coil has been converted into electricity to make the spark, the spark across the spark-plug gap

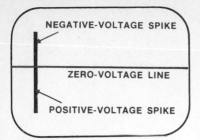

Fig. 29-15
The oscilloscope will draw a horizontal zero-voltage line until a negative or positive voltage pulse enters and causes the trace to kick upward or downward, as shown. The higher the voltage, the farther the trace will move up or down. These sharp upward and downward movements of the trace are called spikes.

Fig. 29-16
A waveform, or trace, showing one complete spark-plug firing cycle. (*American Motors Corporation*)

dies. However, there is still some energy left in the coil. This produces a wavy line, from D to E. This line is called the *coil-condenser oscillation line*. This wavy line means that the remaining energy is pushing electricity back and forth in the ignition secondary circuit. The voltage alternates, but it is no longer high enough to produce a spark. After a very short time, the voltage dies out. Then, at E, the points close or the electronic control unit sends current through the ignition coil once again. Now an alternating voltage is produced in the secondary. This is the result of the buildup of current in the coil primary winding. This is shown by the oscillations following E. The section from E to F is called the *dwell* section. This is the time during which the contact points are closed and current is flowing through the primary winding of the ignition coil. During this time, the magnetic field is building up in the ignition-coil primary. Then, when the points open at F, we are back to A again. The magnetic field collapses, and the whole process is repeated.

29-10 OSCILLOSCOPE PATTERNS

The curves that the scope draws on the tube face are called *patterns*. The patterns can be drawn on the tube face in different ways. For example, the scope can be adjusted to draw a parade pattern, as shown in Fig. 29-17. It is called a parade pattern because the traces for the separate cylinders follow one another across the tube face, like marchers in a parade. Note that they follow from left to right across the screen, in normal firing order, with number 1 cylinder on the left.

By adjusting the scope in a different way, the traces can be stacked one above another, as shown in Fig. 29-18. Stacking the traces this way is called a *raster* pattern. It lets you compare the traces so that you can see if something is wrong in a cylinder. The pattern is read up in the firing order, with number 1 cylinder at the bottom.

A third way to display the traces is to superimpose them (Fig. 29-19), that is, put them one on top of another. This gives a quick comparison and shows whether the voltage pattern from any one cylinder differs from the others. If everything is OK in the cylinders, only one

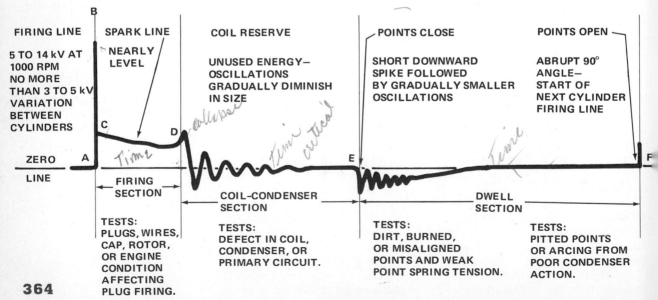

FIRING LINE	SPARK LINE	COIL RESERVE	POINTS CLOSE	POINTS OPEN
5 TO 14 kV AT 1000 RPM NO MORE THAN 3 TO 5 kV VARIATION BETWEEN CYLINDERS	NEARLY LEVEL	UNUSED ENERGY— OSCILLATIONS GRADUALLY DIMINISH IN SIZE	SHORT DOWNWARD SPIKE FOLLOWED BY GRADUALLY SMALLER OSCILLATIONS	ABRUPT 90° ANGLE— START OF NEXT CYLINDER FIRING LINE

ZERO LINE

FIRING SECTION

COIL-CONDENSER SECTION

DWELL SECTION

TESTS: PLUGS, WIRES, CAP, ROTOR, OR ENGINE CONDITION AFFECTING PLUG FIRING.

TESTS: DEFECT IN COIL, CONDENSER, OR PRIMARY CIRCUIT.

TESTS: DIRT, BURNED, OR MISALIGNED POINTS AND WEAK POINT SPRING TENSION.

TESTS: PITTED POINTS OR ARCING FROM POOR CONDENSER ACTION.

364

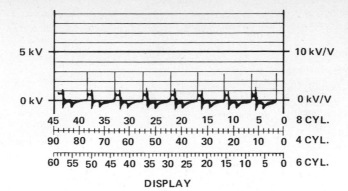

Fig. 29-17
Parade, or display, pattern of the ignition secondary voltages in an eight-cylinder engine. (*Sun Electric Corporation*)

DISPLAY

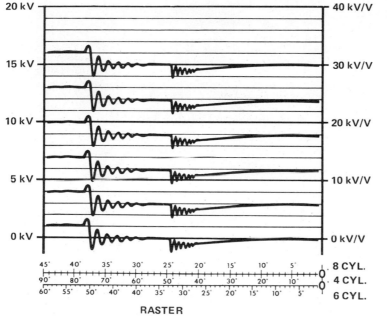

Fig. 29-18
Stacked, or raster, pattern of the ignition secondary voltages in a six-cylinder engine. (*Sun Electric Corporation*)

RASTER

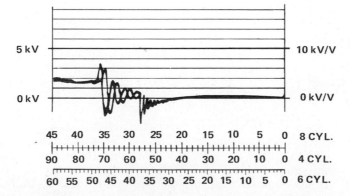

Fig. 29-19
Superimposed pattern of the ignition secondary voltages in a six-cylinder engine. (*Sun Electric Corporation*)

SUPERIMPOSED

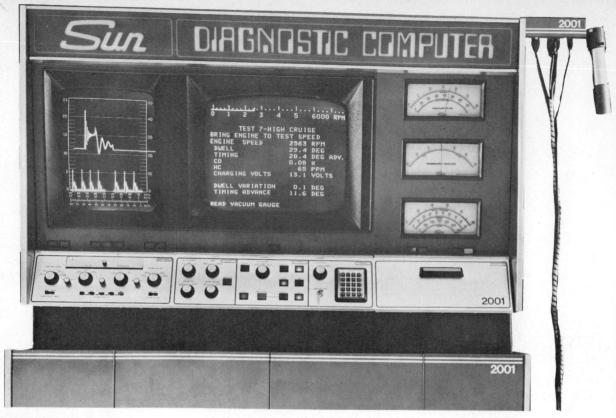

The screen displays:

```
0  1  2  3  4  5  6000 RPM
       TEST 7-HIGH CRUISE
   BRING ENGINE TO TEST SPEED
   ENGINE SPEED         2563 RPM
   DWELL                29.4 DEG
   TIMING               28.4 DEG ADV.
   CO                    0.08 X
   HC                      65 PPM
   CHARGING VOLTS        13.1 VOLTS

   DWELL VARIATION        0.1 DEG
   TIMING ADVANCE        11.6 DEG

   READ VACUUM GAUGE
```

Fig. 29-20

A diagnostic engine analyzer. This tester includes an oscilloscope (top left) and other meters to check engine vacuum, fuel-pump pressure, dwell, and engine rpm. (*Sun Electric Corporation*)

curve would appear on the tube face, because all the curves would fall on top of one another.

29-11 USING THE SCOPE

There are several makes of oscilloscopes. Many are combined in consoles with other test instruments for testing the separate ignition components, engine rpm, intake-manifold vacuum, and so on. Figure 29-20 shows a tester of this type. Figure 29-21 shows the face of a similar tester. Scopes have pickup sensors that can be clamped onto the ignition wires, as shown in Fig. 29-22. It is not necessary to disconnect and reconnect the ignition wiring. The pattern pickup sensor is clamped onto the wire that goes from the coil to the distributor-cap center terminal. The sensor senses the high-voltage surges going to all the spark plugs. The trigger pickup sensor is clamped onto the wire that goes to the plug in number 1 cylinder. The trigger pickup senses when the plug fires. This is the signal to the scope to start another round of traces.

29-12 READING THE PATTERNS

The patterns in Fig. 29-23 show different trouble conditions that occur in the ignition system. The pattern that the scope draws of any cylinder ignition-circuit voltage shows what voltages are occurring in that circuit. The way that the voltage varies from normal shows you where the electrical problem exists. For example, the scope can detect wide or narrow spark-plug gaps, open spark-plug wires, shorted coils or condensers, arcing contact points, improper contact-point dwell, and so on. Many abnormal conditions in an engine change the voltage required to fire the plug. This shows up on the scope. When you work in the shop with the oscilloscope, you will be given more instructions on how to use it.

Fig. 29-21
An oscilloscope with timing light and tachometer, used in tuneup work. (*Sun Electric Corporation*)

Fig. 29-22
To connect an oscilloscope to
the ignition system, test leads
are clipped to terminals and
pickup sensors are clamped on
high-voltage leads. (*Autoscan,
Inc.*)

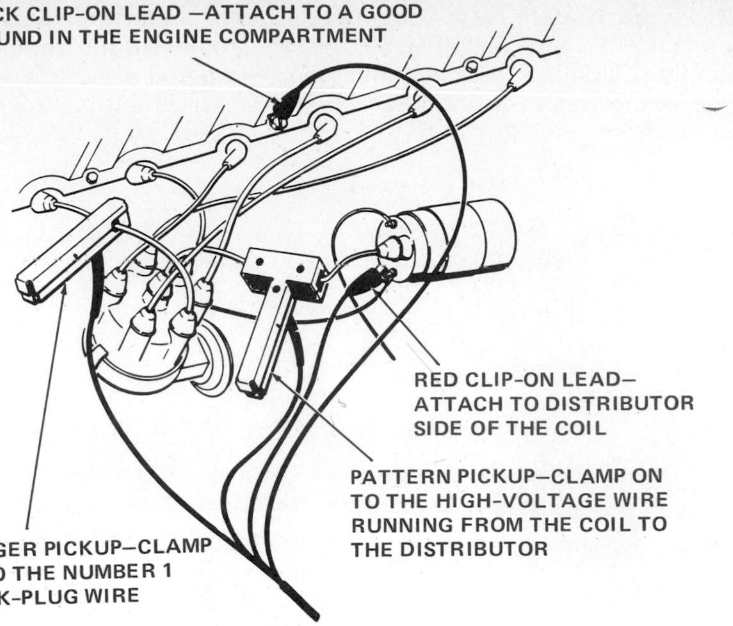

BLACK CLIP-ON LEAD —ATTACH TO A GOOD
GROUND IN THE ENGINE COMPARTMENT

RED CLIP-ON LEAD—
ATTACH TO DISTRIBUTOR
SIDE OF THE COIL

PATTERN PICKUP—CLAMP ON
TO THE HIGH-VOLTAGE WIRE
RUNNING FROM THE COIL TO
THE DISTRIBUTOR

TRIGGER PICKUP—CLAMP
ON TO THE NUMBER 1
SPARK-PLUG WIRE

29-13 DYNAMOMETER

The chassis dynamometer can test engine power output under various
operating conditions. Some dynamometers can duplicate any kind of
road test at any load or speed desired by the dynamometer operator.
The part of the dynamometer that you can see consists of two heavy
rollers mounted at or a little above floor level. The car is driven onto
these rollers, as shown in Fig. 29-24, so that the car wheels can drive
the rollers. Next, the engine is started, and the transmission is put into
gear. The car is then operated as though it were out on an actual road
test.

Under the floor there is a device that can place various loads on
the rollers. This allows the technician to operate the engine under various conditions. The technician can find out how the engine performs
during acceleration, cruising, idling, and deceleration. The test instruments, such as the scope, tachometer, and vacuum gauge, are hooked
into the engine. These instruments then show the actual state of the
engine during various operating conditions.

The dynamometer can also be used to check the transmission and
the differential. For example, the shift points and other operating conditions of an automatic transmission can be checked on the dynamometer. Special diagnostic dynamometers are becoming more popular.
These units have many instruments attached and have motored rollers
that permit testing of wheel alignment, suspension, brakes, and
steering.

29-14 COOLING-SYSTEM TESTERS

There are three basic testers for the cooling system: the hydrometer,
the pressure tester, and the belt-tension tester. The hydrometer checks
the concentration of antifreeze in the coolant (Fig. 29-25). The pressure
tester checks the ability of the cooling system to hold pressure. The
pressure tester is also used to check the radiator pressure cap. The
third tester checks the drive belt tension.

Let's explain these three instruments in more detail. The percentage of antifreeze in the coolant determines how well the car is protected against freezing. The more antifreeze—up to a point—the lower the temperature can go before the coolant freezes. If the coolant freezes in the engine, the engine can be seriously damaged. Water expands as

Fig. 29-23
Various abnormal traces and their causes. (*Ford Motor Company*)

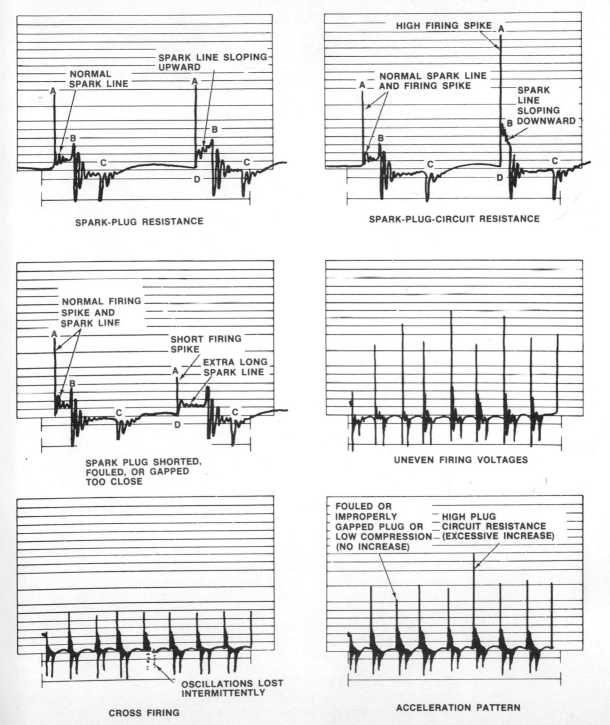

SPARK-PLUG RESISTANCE

SPARK-PLUG-CIRCUIT RESISTANCE

SPARK PLUG SHORTED, FOULED, OR GAPPED TOO CLOSE

UNEVEN FIRING VOLTAGES

CROSS FIRING

ACCELERATION PATTERN

Fig. 29-24
An automobile in place on a chassis dynamometer. The rear wheels drive the dyna-mometer rollers, which are flush with the floor. At the same time, instruments on the test panel measure car speed, engine power output, engine vacuum, and so on. (*Sun Electric Corporation*)

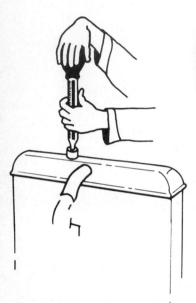

Fig. 29-25
A hydrometer is used to check the strength of the antifreeze in the coolant.

Fig. 29-26
A pressure tester is used to check the cooling system for leaks. (*Texaco, Incorporated*)

it freezes. The expansive force is great enough to crack the cylinder head and the cylinder block. A hydrometer is used to check the coolant (Fig. 29-25).

The pressure tester is a small air pump with a pressure gauge (Fig. 29-26). It is attached to the radiator filler neck. The pump is operated to apply pressure. If the pressure holds steady and there are no signs of leaks, the cooling system is tight.

One type of belt-tension tester is shown in Fig. 29-27. If there is not enough tension, the belt will slip. The fan and water pump will not be driven fast enough, and the engine will overheat. Also, the belt will wear out rapidly. To adjust, move the alternator out slightly.

29-15 PCV-VALVE TESTER

In the positive crankcase ventilating (PCV) system, air passes through the crankcase and then up to the intake manifold. The air passing through picks up the blowby gas that has leaked past the piston rings into the crankcase. The unburned and partly burned gasoline in the blowby then passes through the engine again. There it has another chance to burn.

The PCV valve prevents too much air from flowing into the engine during idle. If the valve sticks open, too much air will flow. The idle mixture will be upset, and the engine will idle roughly and may stall. If the valve sticks closed, not enough air will get through. The blowby products can accumulate in the crankcase. This could seriously damage the engine. These products include corrosive acids and sludge that could plug oil lines and cause the engine to fail from oil starvation. Two types of PCV-valve testers are shown in Figs. 29-28 and 29-29.

29-16 FUEL-SYSTEM TESTERS

Various testers check fuel-system performance. The exhaust-gas analyzer, engine-vacuum gauge, oscilloscope, and other instruments are used to check engine performance. An important part of the engine is the fuel system, and these test instruments also report on the fuel system. There are also fuel-pump pressure and capacity testers that check on how well the fuel pump is doing its job. Figure 29-30 shows a fuel-pump pressure and capacity tester.

29-17 ELECTRICAL-SYSTEM TESTERS
A variety of testers are required to test the electrical equipment on the car. These include the distributor, coil, and condenser testers for the ignition-system components. To check the charging system, ammeters and voltmeters are required. Any of several instruments can be used to

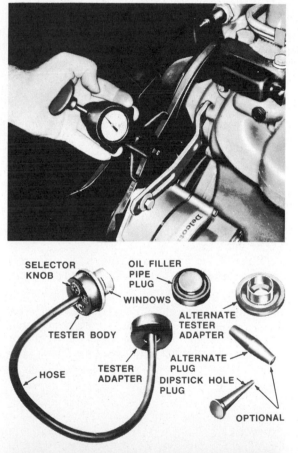

Fig. 29-27
A belt-tension gauge is used to check the tension of the fan belt.

Fig. 29-28
A positive crankcase ventilating system tester. (*Ford Motor Company*)

Fig. 29-29
A PCV tester on a valve cover in readiness for a test. (*Ford Motor Company*)

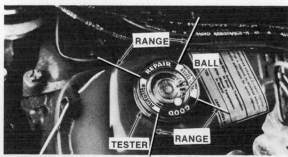

Fig. 29-30

Fuel-pump pressure and capacity tests. (*Ford Motor Company*)

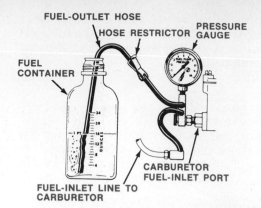

FUEL-OUTLET HOSE

HOSE RESTRICTOR   PRESSURE
GAUGE

FUEL
CONTAINER

CARBURETOR
FUEL-INLET PORT

FUEL-INLET LINE TO
CARBURETOR

check the battery, including a hydrometer, a voltmeter, a 421 tester, and a cadmium-tip tester. We describe these testers in Chap. 22.

Some cars now are equipped with special diagnostic connectors under the hood. By plugging in the special diagnostic tester, the car's electrical system and air conditioning can be quickly checked.

CHECK UP ON YOURSELF

The chapter you have just finished on engine testing instruments gives many facts you need to know to become an automotive technician. Review what you have just studied by answering the questions that follow.

1. What does the exhaust-gas analyzer measure?
2. What does the oscilloscope show on its tube face?
3. What are three types of patterns that the oscilloscope can draw on the tube face?
4. What is the purpose of the chassis dynamometer?
5. What are three basic testers for the cooling system?

ANSWERS

1. The hydrocarbon and carbon monoxide in the exhaust gas (Sec. 29-7). **2.** Ignition voltages (Sec. 29-9). **3.** Parade, raster, and superimposed patterns (Sec. 29-10). **4.** To check the performance of the engine and other automotive components under varying conditions (Sec. 29-13). **5.** Hydrometer, pressure tester, and belt-tension tester (Sec. 29-14).

CHAPTER THIRTY
ENGINE TUNEUP AND CAR-CARE INSPECTION

After studying this chapter, you should be able to:

1. List the 12 steps in the engine tuneup procedure discussed in the chapter.
2. Explain how to perform each step in the tuneup procedure.

Engine service is divided into two parts in this book. In this chapter we discuss the engine checks, adjustments, and replacement of parts that make up a complete engine tuneup.

30-1 ENGINE TUNEUP

Engine tuneup means different things to different people. To some, it means a light, once-over check of the engine, which takes in only the more obvious trouble spots. To others, engine tuneup means using the proper test instruments to carry out a careful, complete analysis of all engine components. In addition, it means adjusting everything to specifications and repairing or replacing defective or worn parts.

NOTE

In this chapter, we combine two procedures. These are engine tuneup and car-care inspection. Engine tuneup includes checking and servicing the engine and its systems. Car-care inspection includes checking other components on the car, such as brakes, steering, suspension, and tires. Together, engine tuneup and car-care inspection cover most things in and on the car that could cause trouble. Most automotive shops find that a customer who comes in for an engine tuneup can also be sold the additional service work found during a car-care inspection.

30-2 ENGINE TUNEUP PROCEDURE

The steps in the complete tuneup procedure are listed below. Each step is discussed further later in the chapter.

1. Service and test battery and starting motor.
2. Check cooling system.
3. Check air cleaner and choke.
4. Check manifold heat control.
5. Check PCV valve.
6. Check filters.
7. Service spark plugs.
8. Check ignition system, including cap, rotor, wiring, coil, condenser, distributor-advance mechanisms, points, and timing.
9. Adjust carburetor idle speed and idle mixture.
10. Check exhaust gas for HC and CO.
11. Check engine performance.
12. Road-test car for overall performance. This means engine, handling, brakes, steering, transmission action, noises, rattles, squeaks, and so on.

NOTE

Although lubricating the chassis and checking and changing the engine oil and the filter are not part of an engine tuneup job, they are part of vehicle maintenance. Many car owners have these done at the same time as a tuneup. So, lubrication and oil changes are covered here along with the tuneup procedure.

30-3 CHECKING AND CHANGING THE OIL AND THE FILTER

You should check the lubrication sticker on the car door jamb to see whether the engine oil should be changed. Often the car owner will want to change the oil during a complete engine tuneup. If the sticker shows the filter needs changing, it should be changed too. A typical factory recommendation is that the oil filter should be changed the first time the oil is changed and then every other oil change after that. When the oil is changed, you should also determine whether a chassis lubrication job is due. There is more on this step in Sec. 30-4.

To change the oil, drive the car over a lift. Make sure the car is placed so the lift arms contact the specified lift points on the car frame. This will properly support the car and will avoid crushing the fuel line, brake line, muffler, or tail pipe. Then raise the lift with the car on it so that you can drain the old oil (Fig. 30-1).

CAUTION

Always make sure the lift lock or safety pin is in place before going under the car. The lock or safety pin keeps the lift from accidentally releasing and allowing the car to settle on the floor.

When the car is up on the lift, position the container under the drain plug, as shown in Fig. 30-1. Then remove the plug and allow the oil to drain. Give the oil enough time to drain completely. Then replace the plug.

CAUTION

If the engine is hot, the oil will be hot enough to burn your hand. Be careful to avoid getting hot oil on your hand.

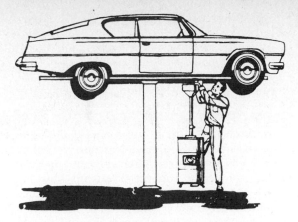

Install a new oil filter if needed (Fig. 30-2). If possible, fill the filter with fresh oil before installation. Lower the car and put in the proper amount and grade of oil. Be sure the oil is the grade called for by the car manufacturer and the viscosity needed for the temperature in which the car will be driven.

When the car is up on the lift, check the muffler, the exhaust pipe, and the tail pipes. A leaky muffler can be deadly. It can leak exhaust gas, which contains carbon monoxide, into the car. Carbon monoxide is a deadly gas. It can make the driver drowsy and lead to an accident.

30-4 LUBRICATING THE CHASSIS

Although lubrication of the chassis is not a part of the engine tuneup procedure, it is often performed with the oil change. Special greases are needed, plus grease guns and dispensers that put the grease where it is needed. To guide the technician, car manufacturers print lubrication, or "lube," charts in their manuals. Figure 30-3 shows such a chart. Oil companies and others produce lube charts for all cars. These are available to service stations and garages. When you work in the shop, you will learn chassis lubrication and servicing procedures.

30-5 SERVICING AND TESTING THE BATTERY AND STARTING MOTOR

We cover battery and starting-motor service in detail in Chaps. 21 and 22. Checking these two parts is the starting point for an engine tuneup. Check the battery state of charge and electrolyte level. If the battery terminals are corroded, they should be cleaned, as explained in Chap. 21. Damaged or corroded battery cables should be replaced. The

Fig. 30-2
An oil filter being removed.
(*Chrysler Corporation*)

battery top should be cleaned if necessary. A low battery should be re-charged. When the battery is worn out, a new one should be installed.

If the starting motor does its job of cranking the engine at normal cranking speed, you can assume that the starting motor is OK. In a complete tuneup procedure, you should check the current draw of the cranking motor. This requires an ammeter.

30-6 CHECKING THE COOLING SYSTEM

Check the radiator hose for wear and tightness. A quick check is simply to squeeze the hose. Note any cracks that appear as well as the hardness of the hose. Then remove the filler cap and note the level and condition of the coolant. Find out how long the car has been driven with the old antifreeze. If the coolant looks dirty and rusty, suggest flushing the cooling system to the customer. This involves flushing out the radiator and replacing the old antifreeze with a new solution. Many manufacturers recommend draining the old coolant and putting in a new solution every two years. Check the coolant with a hydrometer to find out how low the temperature can go without freezing the coolant. If there is not enough antifreeze to protect the engine from freezing, add more antifreeze.

Fig. 30-3
Lubrication recommendations for a late-model car. (*Chevrolet Motor Division of General Motors Corporation*)

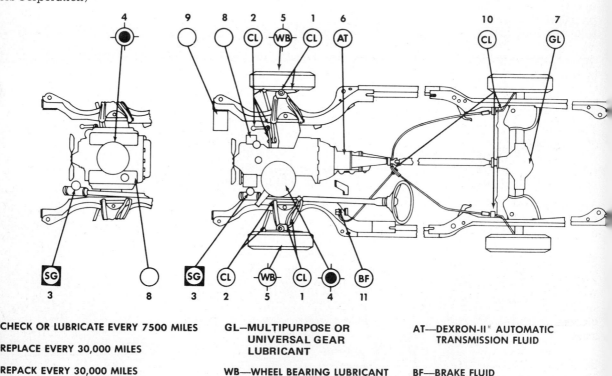

⊘ CHECK OR LUBRICATE EVERY 7500 MILES

⊙ REPLACE EVERY 30,000 MILES

⊖ REPACK EVERY 30,000 MILES

▣ CHECK FOR GREASE LEAKAGE EVERY 30,000 MILES

*REFILL POSITRACTION REAR AXLE WITH SPECIAL LUBRICANT ONLY

GL—MULTIPURPOSE OR UNIVERSAL GEAR LUBRICANT

WB—WHEEL BEARING LUBRICANT

CL—CHASSIS LUBRICANT

AT—DEXRON-II" AUTOMATIC TRANSMISSION FLUID

BF—BRAKE FLUID

SG—STEERING GEAR LUBRICANT

1. Front Suspension
2. Steering Linkage
3. Steering Gear
4. Air Cleaner
5. Front Wheel Bearings
6. Transmission
7. Rear Axle
8. Oil Filter
9. Battery
10. Parking Brake
11. Brake Master Cylinder

Test the cooling system with the pressure tester, as shown in Fig. 29-26. Pressure-test the radiator cap. Inspect the engine, radiator, and hoses for signs of leakage. Use a belt-tension tester to check the tension of the fan belt (Fig. 29-27). Adjust the fan belt if necessary.

CAUTION

There are two things you much watch out for. First, keep your hands away from the engine fan when the engine is running. You can lose fingers if you get your hands caught in the fan or the fan belt! Second, never remove the radiator cap from a hot engine. Always wait until the engine is cool.

CHECK UP ON YOURSELF

You have now gone through the first half of the chapter on engine tuneup. Now find out how well you understand what you have studied. Answer the questions that follow.

1. What two parts do you check first when you start an engine tuneup?
2. How do you determine whether an oil change is due?
3. What is a lube chart?
4. How often should old antifreeze be drained and new antifreeze be added?

ANSWERS

1. The battery and the starting motor (Secs. 30-2 and 30-5). 2. Look at the lubrication sticker on the car door jamb (Sec. 30-3). 3. The lube, or lubrication, chart tells you what kinds of lubricants to use, where to use them, and how often to use them (Sec. 30-4). 4. Antifreeze should be drained and new antifreeze put in every two years (Sec. 30-6).

30-7 CHECKING THE AIR CLEANER AND THE CHOKE

The filter element in the air cleaner requires cleaning or replacement at periodic intervals. In the heated-air system, the air cleaner has a thermostatic control. We discuss the operation of the thermostatic control in Chap. 18. With the engine cold, the damper in the snorkel should be closed. As the engine warms up, the damper should open. You may need a small mirror to check this action. When you take the air cleaner off, note the action of the choke. It should be closed with the engine cold. The choke should open as the engine warms up.

30-8 CHECKING THE MANIFOLD HEAT CONTROL

The manifold heat control should direct heat to the intake manifold when the engine is cold. It should shut off the heat when the engine warms up. If the manifold heat-control valve sticks, it should be cleaned with special solvent. Never oil the valve. This will cause it to stick.

30-9 CHECKING THE PCV VALVE

Figures 30-4 and 30-5 show PCV-valve locations. If the PCV valve sticks open, it can cause poor idle and stalling. Check it with the PCV-valve tester. If a tester is not available, remove the PCV valve from the rocker cover while the engine is running. A hissing noise indicates that the valve is not plugged. Place a finger over the valve inlet. You should feel a strong vacuum. Stop the engine and remove and shake the PCV valve. If the valve is moving freely, you will hear a clicking noise. Most manufacturers recommend that PCV valves be replaced

Fig. 30-4
Locations of the PCV valve in a
V-type engine.

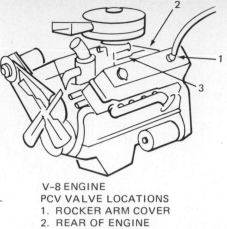

V–8 ENGINE
PCV VALVE LOCATIONS
1. ROCKER ARM COVER
2. REAR OF ENGINE
3. CARBURETOR BASE

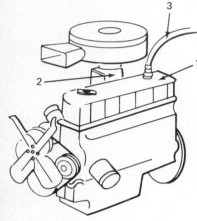

SIX-CYLINDER ENGINE
PCV VALVE LOCATIONS
1. ROCKER ARM COVER
2. CARBURETOR BASE
3. HOSE

Fig. 30-5
Locations of the PCV valve in
an in-line engine.

every two years. Cleaning is not recommended for PCV valves. When checking the PCV valve, always check the PCV system hoses and connections for possible leaks and clogging.

30-10 CHECKING THE FILTERS
There are several filters to be checked. These include the air filter in the air-injection system, the filter at the bottom of the canister in the evaporative systems, the PCV filter in the air-cleaner housing, and the filter in the fuel line. These filters should be checked at the mileages specified by the manufacturer.

30-11 CLEANING OR REPLACING THE SPARK PLUGS
Spark plugs should be removed for examination and cleaned or filed and regapped as necessary.

NOTE
The high cost of labor and the relatively low cost of spark plugs have caused many technicians to recommend installing new plugs instead of cleaning and regapping the old plugs.

The appearance of the plugs tells you a lot about the condition of the engine (Fig. 30-6). If the plug runs too hot or too cold, it should be replaced with a plug of a different heat range. The temperature that a plug will reach depends on the distance the heat must travel from the center electrode to reach the outer shell of the plug and enter the cylinder head. A plug that has a long heat path from the center electrode to the plug shell will run hot. The electrodes will be at a higher temperature (see Fig. 30-7). A plug that has a short heat path from the center electrode to the plug shell will run cold. If the old plug is fouled from carbon deposits, the plug may be running too cold. A plug with a higher heat range should be installed.

A spark-plug cleaner is shown in Fig. 30-8. When the spark plug is placed in the cleaner, the cleaner sends a blast of grit against the electrodes and insulator. The grit cleans the electrodes and insulator. After the cleaning is done, the spark-plug electrodes are filed flat with an ignition file, Then a spark-plug gauge is used to adjust the electrode gap (Fig. 30-9).

30-12 CHECKING THE IGNITION SYSTEM

There are several parts in the ignition system that can be checked with an oscilloscope and timing light while doing a tuneup. These are:

- Cap and rotor
- Wiring

Fig. 30-6

Appearance of spark plugs related to causes. (*Champion Spark Plug Company*)

NORMAL

Brown to grayish tan color and slight electrode wear. Correct heat range for engine and operating conditions.

RECOMMENDATION: Properly service and reinstall. Replace if over 10,000 miles of service.

SPLASHED DEPOSITS

Spotted deposits. Occurs shortly after long-delayed tune-up. After a long period of misfiring, deposits may be loosened when normal combustion temperatures are restored by tune-up. During a high-speed run, these materials shed off the piston and head and are thrown against the hot insulator.

RECOMMENDATION: Clean and service the plugs properly and reinstall.

CARBON DEPOSITS

Dry soot.

RECOMMENDATION: Dry deposits indicate rich mixture or weak ignition. Check for clogged air cleaner, high float level, sticky choke, or worn breaker contacts. Hotter plugs will temporarily provide additional fouling protection.

HIGH-SPEED GLAZING

Insulator has yellowish, varnish-like color. Indicates combustion chamber temperatures have risen suddenly during hard, fast acceleration. Normal deposits do not get a chance to blow off, instead they melt to form a conductive coating.

RECOMMENDATION: If condition recurs, use plug type one step colder.

OIL DEPOSITS

Oily coating.

RECOMMENDATION: Caused by poor oil control. Oil is leaking past worn valve guides or piston rings into the combustion chamber. Hotter spark plug may temporarily relieve problem, but positive cure is to correct the condition with necessary repairs.

MODIFIER DEPOSITS

Powdery white or yellow deposits that build up on shell, insulator, and electrodes. This is a normal appearance with certain branded fuels. These materials are used to modify the chemical nature of the deposits to lessen misfire tendencies.

RECOMMENDATION: Plugs can be cleaned or, if replaced, use same heat range.

TOO HOT

Blistered, white insulator, eroded electrodes and absence of deposits.

RECOMMENDATION: Check for correct plug heat range, overadvanced ignition timing, cooling system level and/or stoppages, lean air-fuel mixtures, leaking intake manifold, sticking valves, and if car is driven at high speeds most of the time.

PREIGNITION

Melted electrodes. Center electrode generally melts first and ground electrode follows. Normally, insulators are white, but may be dirty due to misfiring or flying debris in combustion chamber

RECOMMENDATION: Check for correct plug heat range, overadvanced ignition timing, lean fuel mixtures, clogged cooling system, leaking intake manifold, and lack of lubrication.

- Coil and condenser
- Advance mechanisms
- Points
- Timing

First, remove the cap from the distributor (Figs. 30-10 and 30-11). Then clean and inspect the cap and rotor, as shown in Fig. 30-12. If the cap is defective, install a new cap, as shown at the upper right in Fig. 30-12. Remove the leads, one at a time, and install them in the proper tower in the new cap. In this way, you will not get the leads mixed up.

Fig. 30-7
The heat range of spark plugs. The longer the heat path (indicated by the arrows), the hotter the plug runs. (*AC Spark Plug Division of General Motors Corporation*)

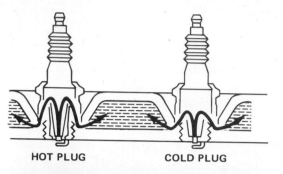

HOT PLUG   COLD PLUG

Fig. 30-8
Spark-plug cleaner and tester. (*Champion Spark Plug Company*)

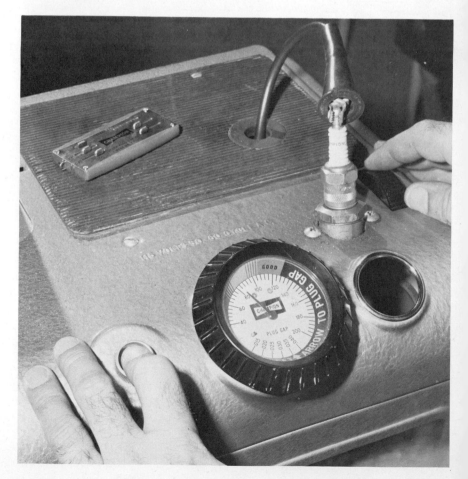

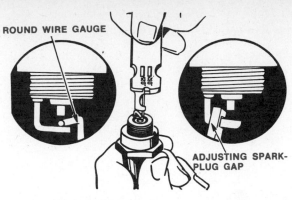

ROUND WIRE GAUGE

ADJUSTING SPARK-PLUG GAP

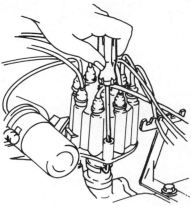

Fig. 30-9
A special gauge and adjusting tool are used to adjust the spark-plug gap.

Check the high-voltage wiring. If it has cracked insulation, replace it. Cracks can allow the high-voltage surges to drain off so that the plug will not fire. The engine will miss.

The coil and condenser should be tested on a coil-condenser tester to find out whether they are in good condition. This test should be made anytime the scope indicates the possibility that they are defective.

The action of the centrifugal and vacuum-advance mechanisms can be checked with a timing light. Section 30-8 explains how to use the timing light. Check the amount of advance at various engine speeds and throttle openings to determine whether the advance mechanisms are working properly. An accurate test can be made if the distributor is removed from the engine and checked on a distributor tester.

Fig. 30-10
Removal of a distributor cap which has spring-loaded clamps. (*Delco-Remy Division of General Motors Corporation*)

If the points are worn or burned, they should be replaced. Points should be adjusted by loosening the locking screw and shifting the stationary point (Figs. 30-13 and 30-14). On General Motors window-type distributors, adjust the points by lifting the window and inserting a $\frac{1}{8}$-inch Allen wrench in the point-adjusting screw. The point opening on new points can be measured with a feeler gauge. A feeler gauge cannot be used on rough points. With rough points, the opening will be greater than the thickness of the gauge (Fig. 30-15).

One way to measure and adjust point opening is with a dwell meter. This meter measures the number of degrees of cam rotation that the points are closed. As the point opening is increased, the dwell angle is reduced. The dwell meter must be used while the engine is running. Also, the distributor tester can be used to measure point opening. The distributor must be removed from the engine and placed in the tester (Fig. 30-16).

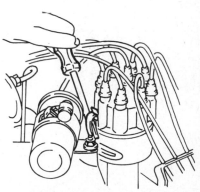

Fig. 30-11
Removal of a distributor cap which has spring clips. (*Delco-Remy Division of General Motors Corporation*)

30-13 INSTALLING AND TIMING THE IGNITION DISTRIBUTOR

Timing the ignition should be done after the various mechanical checks listed above have been completed. Ignition timing is covered in Sec. 29-8. If the distributor has been removed, ignition timing must be made when the distributor is put back in the engine.

Follow the steps listed below to remove the distributor:

1. Disconnect the distributor-to-coil primary wire. Remove the cap and crank the engine so that the rotor is in a position to fire number 1 cylinder. The timing mark on the engine pulley

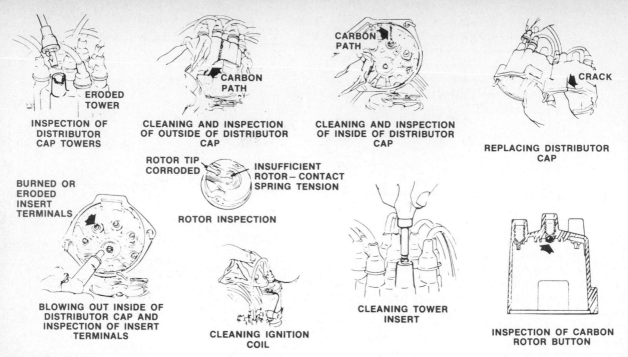

INSPECTION OF
DISTRIBUTOR CAP
TOWERS

ERODED
TOWER

CLEANING AND INSPECTION
OF OUTSIDE OF DISTRIBUTOR
CAP

CARBON
PATH

CLEANING AND INSPECTION
OF INSIDE OF DISTRIBUTOR
CAP

CARBON
PATH

REPLACING DISTRIBUTOR
CAP

CRACK

BURNED OR
ERODED
INSERT
TERMINALS

ROTOR TIP
CORRODED

INSUFFICIENT
ROTOR—CONTACT
SPRING TENSION

ROTOR INSPECTION

BLOWING OUT INSIDE OF
DISTRIBUTOR CAP AND
INSPECTION OF INSERT
TERMINALS

CLEANING IGNITION
COIL

CLEANING TOWER
INSERT

INSPECTION OF CARBON
ROTOR BUTTON

Fig. 30-12
Checking and servicing a distributor cap and rotor. (*Delco-Remy Division of General Motors Corporation*)

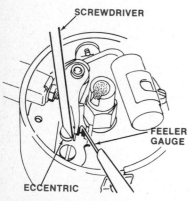

SCREWDRIVER

FEELER
GAUGE

ECCENTRIC

Fig. 30-13
On some distributors, the point opening is adjusted by loosening the lock screw and turning the eccentric with a screwdriver. (*Delco-Remy Division of General Motors Corporation*)

should be aligned with the tab or pointer on the engine front cover or timing-gear cover. Make a slight mark on the distributor housing directly beneath the center of the rotor blade (Fig. 30-17). Now make another slight mark on the block to align with the mark on the distributor housing.

2. Disconnect the vacuum hose from the distributor. Note the position of the distributor in its mounting. Remove the distributor clamping nut and clamp. Remove the distributor. Note the position of the rotor on the distributor housing after removal. The rotor may rotate a little as the distributor is removed. This is due to the movement of the spiral driven gear as it is pulled out of the drive gear on the camshaft.

Follow the steps listed below to install the distributor:

1. Make sure that the timing mark on the pulley aligns with the stationary timing mark and that number 1 piston is at TDC on the compression stroke.
2. Check that the distributor-to-block gasket or seal is in place on the distributor. Turn the distributor rotor to the same position you noted when you removed the distributor.
3. Install the distributor. If you have positioned the rotor correctly, the gear may slide down into the camshaft drive gear or oil pump without trouble. If the distributor housing does not seat flush against the block, hold the distributor housing down lightly. Then bump the starter slightly until the distributor drops into place. Using the marks that you made during distributor removal, check the rotor to make sure it is aligned with the mark on the housing. Then check that the housing is aligned with the mark on the block.

4. Install the distributor clamp. However, leave the nut loose enough to allow the distributor to be rotated for final ignition timing.
5. Attach the distributor-to-coil wire.
6. Install the distributor cap, adjust the ignition timing (see Sec. 29-8), tighten the clamp nut, and reconnect the vacuum hose to the distributor.

NOTE

The 1977 MISAR ignition system, described in Secs. 24-21 to 24-25, is not adjusted by turning the distributor in its mounting. Instead, if the ignition does require timing, the crankshaft sensor (Fig. 24-35) is shifted. The 1978 MISAR ignition system is timed by turning the distributor in its mounting. See Sec. 24-22.

30-14 ADJUSTING THE CARBURETOR

There are certain legal restrictions to carburetor adjustments. The only carburetor adjustments now allowed for late-model engines during tuneup are idle-speed, choke, and throttle adjustments. The idle mixture is preset at the factory. A limiter cap is installed on the idle-mixture screw to prevent improper adjustment. The procedure is listed on the Vehicle Emission Control Information decal in the engine compartment. This decal lists the specific procedure that *must be* followed. If some carburetor trouble has occurred that requires disassembling the carburetor, the locking cap or caps may be removed. Then the idle mixture may be readjusted. Here is the procedure for setting the idle speed and idle mixture.

1. Disconnect the fuel-tank hose from the charcoal canister.
2. Disconnect the vacuum hose to the distributor. Plug the hose leading to the carburetor.
3. Make sure the distributor contact-point dwell and the ignition timing are correct.
4. Adjust the idle speed. On earlier engines there is a screw in the throttle linkage at the carburetor. On later engines equipped with idle-stop solenoids the adjustment screw is in the solenoid. Use a tachometer to measure engine speed. Make the adjustment to get the specified idle speed.
5. Reconnect the distributor vacuum hose and the hose to the charcoal canister.

To set the idle mixture, follow the steps below. This adjustment is allowed only if the carburetor has required disassembly because of some problem in the carburetor.

1. With the limiter caps off, turn the mixture screws in until they lightly touch the seats. Then back them off six full turns.
2. Adjust the idle speed, as already discussed.
3. Connect an exhaust-gas analyzer to the exhaust system. Calibrate the CO (carbon monoxide) meter. Adjust the idle-mixture screws to get the best idle at the specified engine rpm with a CO reading at or below the specified maximum. The engine should be running at normal idle, with automatic transmission in D (drive) or manual transmission in neutral.
4. After setting the idle mixture, recheck the idle speed. If everything is OK, install new limiter caps on the idle-mixture screws.

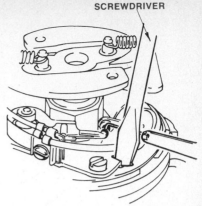

Fig. 30-14
On some distributors, the stationary point base is pried back and forth with a screwdriver to adjust the point opening. (*Delco-Remy Division of General Motors Corporation*)

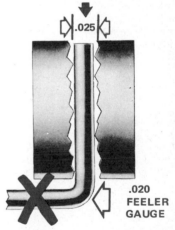

Fig. 30-15
Why a feeler gauge will not accurately measure the point opening of used and rough points. Roughness of the points is exaggerated.

Fig. 30-16
An ignition distributor tester.
(*Sun Electric Corporation*)

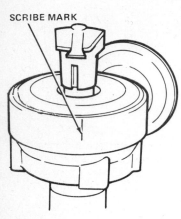

Fig. 30-17
Location of the reference marks made on the distributor housing to indicate rotor position. (*American Motors Corporation*)

Fig. 30-18
Setup for adjusting idle mixture with propane. (*Ford Motor Company*)

30-15 ADJUSTING IDLE MIXTURE WITH PROPANE

Some carburetors have been changed to limit the rich idle-mixture adjustment. Backing out the idle-mixture screws on these carburetors will not greatly enrich the mixture. This means another mixture adjustment procedure is required. The procedure uses propane to artificially enrich the mixture while you make the idle-mixture adjustment. Figure 30-18 shows the setup for doing this.

On these cars, there is a Vehicle Emission Control Information label under the hood (Fig. 30-19). This decal explains how to disconnect and plug hoses to make the adjustment. Factory shop manuals also have detailed explanations of how to use propane to make the adjustments. Making any adjustment that differs from the instructions and specifications on the label may violate state and federal laws.

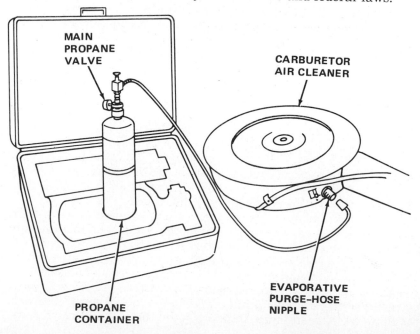

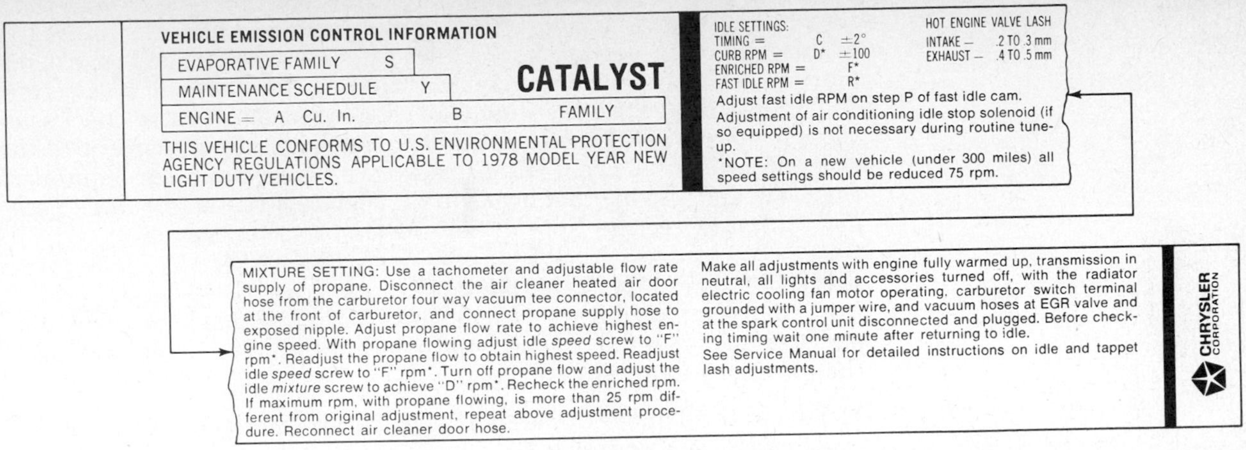

The procedure is that a cartridge of propane is connected to the carburetor or air cleaner. Then propane gas is fed into the air going through the air cleaner and the carburetor. This enriches the air-fuel mixture. Then the idle speed and idle-mixture screws are adjusted to get the proper engine rpm.

Fig. 30-19
Information label or decal that is under the hood or on the engine of new cars. It includes the procedure for adjusting the idle mixture with propane. (*Chrysler Corporation*)

30-16 CHECKING THE EXHAUST GAS FOR HC AND CO

An exhaust-gas analyzer is needed to check the exhaust gas for HC and Co. We describe the tester in Chap. 29 and explain how to use it. If the HC and CO exceed maximum allowable limits, a correction must be made. This can mean checking out the emission-control systems and adjusting the carburetor. Also, failure of the TCS system may allow vacuum advance in all transmission gears. This can increase emissions in lower gears.

Many technicians test the exhaust gas both before and after the tuneup. This tells them how much improvement has been made. That is, they find out how much the HC and CO have been reduced. Also, the results of the test show the customer that the tuneup was needed.

30-17 CHECKING ENGINE PERFORMANCE

Checking engine performance requires a road test or special testing equipment, such as a compression tester, vacuum gauge, oscilloscope, and dynamometer. The use of engine testing instruments is described in Chap. 29.

Compression and vacuum tests can be made during the mechanical checks outlined earlier. For example, when the spark plugs are out for service, the compression can be checked. If the vacuum gauge is connected, the intake manifold vacuum can be checked.

30-18 CHECKING THE CHARGING SYSTEM

The charging system (alternator and regulator) should be checked with a charging system tester. This is to make sure that the alternator can handle the electrical load and keep the battery charged.

30-19 OTHER CHECKS

Tires should be checked for pressure and unusual wear. Unusual wear could mean front-end misalignment. A front-wheel alignment would be required to fix this problem. Brakes should be checked to make sure they have adequate lining and stopping power and no leaks in the hydraulic system. Steering should be checked for freeness and ease of operation. The suspension system, including front-wheel ball joints, should be checked. Lights should be checked also. All these checks, although not part of the actual tuneup procedure, are important to the safe operation of the car. These checks are covered in later chapters of this book and also in other books in the McGraw-Hill *Automotive Technology Series* (see the Note in Sec. 30-1).

CHECK UP ON YOURSELF

You have completed a very important chapter of this book. Now find out how well you understand what you have studied by answering the questions that follow.

1. Should the damper in the snorkel of the air cleaner be open or closed when the engine is cold?
2. If the PCV valve is sticking, should you clean it or replace it?
3. If a spark plug is fouled from carbon deposits, should you install a plug with a lower or a higher heat range?
4. What shop tester is used to test the coil and the condenser while the engine is running?
5. What are the two basic carburetor adjustments?
6. What is the purpose of using propane to adjust some late-model carburetors?

ANSWERS

1. Closed (Sec. 30-7). **2.** Replace it (Sec. 30-9). **3.** Install a plug with a higher heat range to keep the carbon burned off the plug (Sec. 30-11). **4.** The scope (Sec. 30-12). **5.** Idle speed and idle mixture (Sec. 30-10). **6.** To enrich the mixture sufficiently to permit adjusting the idle mixture (Sec. 30-15).

CHAPTER THIRTY-ONE ENGINE SERVICE – VALVES

After studying this chapter, you should be able to:
1. Describe the various valve troubles and explain their causes.
2. List the various valve and valve train services and explain how to perform each.

In this chapter and in Chaps. 32 and 33, we look at the various services that the engine requires. The chapters on engine troubleshooting and engine tuneup tell you how to locate the causes of trouble in the engine. This chapter explains how to fix troubles in valves and valve mechanisms.

31-1 CLEANLINESS
The major enemy of engine service is dirt. A trace of dirt or any other abrasive can ruin an otherwise good service job. You must be very careful to keep everything clean. This means tools, parts, your hands, and the work area.

Before any major engine service job is done, the engine should be cleaned to remove outside dirt and grease. Steam cleaning is one way to clean an engine before disassembly. First, the electrical parts and the air-cleaner opening are covered. Then a spray of soap and steam is directed onto the engine. Parts removed from the engine should be cleaned if they are to be used again. We will talk more about cleaning engine parts in later sections.

31-2 VALVE TROUBLES
Now let's look at valve troubles and their causes. Valve troubles include valve sticking, valve burning, valve and seat breakage, valve-face and seat wear, and valve deposits. We will cover each of these troubles in the following sections.

31-3 VALVE STICKING
Valves will stick open or partly open because of the following conditions:

- Gum or carbon deposits on the valve stems (Fig. 31-1). This is usually due to worn valve guides that allow oil to work past them or to failure of the oil seal or shield on the valve stems.

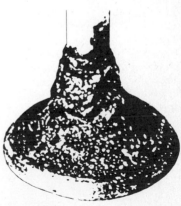

Fig. 31-1
A gummed intake valve. Note the deposits under valve head.

Fig. 31-2
Valve burning resulting from seat distortion. The valve failed to seat in one area. This allowed hot exhaust-gas leakage and burning of the valve. (*TRW Inc.*)

- Warped valve stems. This can result from the valve hitting the piston or a foreign object in the combustion chamber, overheating, an off-center valve seat, or a cocked valve spring.
- Lack of oil.
- Cold engine. However, when the engine warms up, the valves may work free.

If deposits such as gum or carbon are causing valves and piston rings to stick, the engine may have to be disassembled to clean out the deposits. However, special additives can be put in the oil or fuel that help to free valves and rings. One type of liquid additive comes in a pressure can and is sprayed into the running engine through the carburetor.

NOTE

Certain cleaners, which are sprayed directly into the carburetor or added to the fuel, must not be used in cars equipped with a catalytic converter. Such additives may damage the catalytic converter. Always read the label on the container before using it.

31-4 VALVE BURNING

Valve burning is usually an exhaust-valve problem (Figs. 31-2 to 31-4). Valve burning often is due to poor valve seating. This means that the valve does not make good contact with the valve seat over the whole surface of the valve face. In a running engine the exhaust valve can get red-hot. The exhaust valve passes heat to the valve seat to help cool the valve. But when the valve-face-to-seat contact is not good, the valve cannot pass enough heat. It gets too hot and burns. Here are possible causes of poor valve seating:

Fig. 31-3
Valve burning due to failure of the valve to seat fully. Note that the valve is uniformly burned all the way around its face. (*TRW Inc.*)

- Valve sticking
- Tappet clearance too small, so valve cannot close completely
- Cocked or weak valve spring
- Distorted valve seat
- Dirt on valve seat

In addition to poor valve seating, other causes of valve burning include

- Overheated engine due to faulty engine cooling system or engine overload. For example, an engine can be overloaded by pulling a trailer or going up a long hill with wide-open throttle.
- Lean air-fuel mixture.
- Detonation due to engine deposits, low-octane fuel, or wrong ignition timing.

31-5 VALVE BREAKAGE

This can be due to engine overheating or detonation. Valve breakage also is caused by an off-center valve seat. This tends to bend the valve every time it closes. Too much tappet clearance is another cause of valve breakage. Too much tappet clearance increases the impact load on the valve when it closes.

31-6 VALVE-FACE WEAR

This can result from too much tappet clearance, which increases the impact load on the valve when it closes. Dirt on the valve face or valve seat also causes valve-face wear. The causes of valve burning listed in Sec. 31-4 also are possible causes of valve-face wear.

31-7 VALVE DEPOSITS
Too much gum in the fuel will cause gum deposits to form on the intake valves. Carbon deposits may form from an air-fuel mixture that is too rich or from oil passing through a worn intake-valve guide. Incomplete combustion can result in carbon deposits on the exhaust valves. Dirt or the wrong oil can also cause deposits to form on valves.

Fig. 31-4
Valve burning due to guttering. This condition is caused by accumulations of deposits on the valve face and seat. Parts of the deposits break off to form a path through which exhaust gas can pass when the valve is closed. This soon burns channels in the valve face, as shown. (*TRW Inc.*)

31-8 VALVE SERVICES
Nine engine parts in valve trains may require service: valves, valve seats, valve guides, valve springs and retainers, pushrods, rocker arms, valve tappets, camshaft and drive, and camshaft bearings. The service jobs for these parts include

- Adjusting valve-tappet clearance
- Replacing ball studs
- Removing cylinder head
- Removing valves
- Checking valve springs
- Servicing rocker arms and rocker-arm shafts
- Cleaning the cylinder head
- Cleaning, checking, and grinding valves
- Servicing valve guides
- Grinding valve seats
- Installing valves
- Checking pushrods
- Servicing hydraulic valve lifters
- Servicing the camshaft and camshaft bearings
- Installing the cylinder head
- Checking valve-timing gears or sprockets and belt or chain

In this book we discuss each of these services briefly. The *Auto Shop Workbook* describes each of the service jobs in detail, explaining how each job is done step by step.

31-9 ADJUSTING VALVE-TAPPET CLEARANCE
Many engines with hydraulic valve lifters do not normally require adjustment of valve-tappet clearance. However, if valves and valve seats are ground, then some adjustment may be required. The procedure for this type of adjustment is covered later. First, let's take a quick look at a typical procedure for adjustment of valve-tappet clearance on an engine with solid, or mechanical, valve lifters.

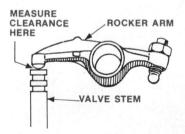

Fig. 31-5
Where to measure clearance in the valve train.

1. Remove the valve cover. Turn the crankshaft until the valves to be adjusted are fully closed. The valve tappets are on the base circle of the cams.
2. On the type of engine that has the rocker arms mounted on a shaft (Fig. 31-5), adjust the valve clearance by turning the self-locking adjustment screw. Get the proper clearance between the end of the valve stem and the rocker arm. Use a box wrench, as shown in Fig. 31-6. An open-end wrench could damage the screw head. Measure the clearance with a feeler gauge. Check the Vehicle Emission Control Information decal under the hood,

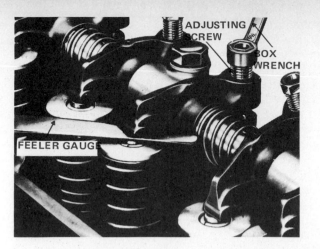

or a shop manual, for the correct specifications. Two settings may be given, one for the intake valve and a different setting for the exhaust valve.

3. Turn the crankshaft to close other valves, and check and adjust them the same way.

4. On the type of engine that has the rocker arms mounted on ball studs (Fig. 31-7), turn the stud nuts up or down. Set the specified clearance between the valve stem and the rocker arm. Turning the stud nut up increases the clearance. Turning it down reduces the clearance.

We mentioned previously that in valve trains with hydraulic valve lifters, no adjustment is usually needed. However, if valves and valve seats with hydraulic lifters are ground, then some adjustment may be required. Here are typical procedures for this type of adjustment.

1. Ford
First, bleed down the hydraulic valve lifter by applying pressure on the lifter to force the oil out and the valve-lifter plunger down. Figure 31-8 shows a valve-lifter bleeding tool being used to do this job. To start with, turn the crankshaft so that the lifter is on the base circle of the

Fig. 31-7
Adjustment of valve-tappet clearance on an engine with the rocker arms independently mounted on ball studs. Backing out the stud nut increases clearance. (*Chevrolet Motor Division of General Motors Corporation*)

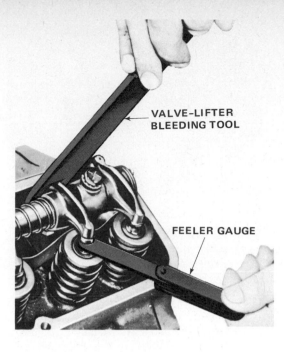

VALVE-LIFTER
BLEEDING TOOL

FEELER GAUGE

cam. This is done by turning the crankshaft so that the piston is at TDC in number 1 cylinder on the compression stroke. Then check the valves that are closed. Turn the crankshaft to close another set of valves and check them. Usually you can check all valves with only two or three positions of the crankshaft. You will find specific instructions on this procedure in the service manual covering the engine you are working on.

To check the valve-lifter adjustment, as shown in Fig. 31-8, apply pressure to the lifter. When the plunger bottoms, measure the clearance between the valve stem and the rocker arm, as shown in Fig. 31-8. If the clearance is too small, then a shorter pushrod must be installed. Because the grinding of valves reduces clearance, a shorter pushrod may be required after the valves and seats are ground. If the clearance is excessive, then a longer pushrod should be installed.

2. Plymouth
The checking procedure for hydraulic valve lifters on Plymouth engines is necessary only when valves have been ground. Use the special tool shown in Fig. 31-9 to measure the increased height of the valve stem above the cylinder head. This is done before the head is assembled and installed on the engine. If the height is too great, the end of the valve stem should be ground off.

3. Chevrolet
This procedure is typical of the General Motors engines using the ball-pivot rocker arm (Fig. 31-10). With the valve lifter on the base circle of the cam, back off the adjustment nut until the pushrod is loose. Then slowly turn the adjustment nut down until all side play, or looseness, is gone. Turn the adjustment nut down one additional turn, or the amount specified in the shop manual.

Fig. 31-9
Measurement of a valve-stem
length with a special tool after
the valve is installed in the
head. (*Chrysler Corporation*)

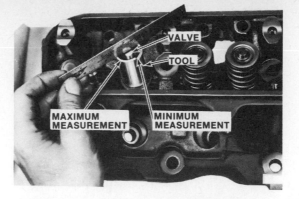

CHECK UP ON YOURSELF

This chapter, plus your shopwork, will give you the information and skill you need to check and adjust valve clearance. Now test your knowledge by answering the questions that follow.

1. What should you keep clean when doing engine service work?
2. What are five basic valve troubles?
3. What could cause gum or carbon to form on valve stems?
4. Which valve is usually the one that burns?
5. What are five causes of poor valve seating?
6. What is the purpose of adjusting the valves on engines with mechanical valve lifters?
7. Generally, when does the valve train using hydraulic valves need adjustment?

ANSWERS

1. Everything—tools, hands, parts, and work area (Sec. 31-1). **2.** Sticking, burning, breakage, face wear, and deposits (Sec. 31-2). **3.** A worn valve guide or failure of the oil seal or shield on the valve stem (Sec. 31-3). **4.** The exhaust valve (Sec. 31-4). **5.** Valve sticking, tappet clearance too small, cocked or

Fig. 31-10
Adjustment of a valve rocker-arm stud nut to properly position the plunger of the hydraulic valve lifter. (*Chevrolet Motor Division of General Motors Corporation*)

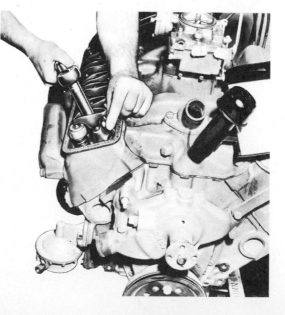

weak spring, distorted seat, and dirt on seat (Sec. 31-4). **6.** To restore correct clearance in the valve train (Sec. 31-9). **7.** Only after valves and valve seats have been ground (Sec. 31-9).

31-10 REPLACING BALL STUDS
Ball studs, if damaged, can be replaced. Some screw into tapped holes in the head. Others are a press fit and must be pulled with a special puller.

31-11 REMOVING THE CYLINDER HEAD
To remove the valves, you must first remove the cylinder head. This means draining the cooling system and removing the carburetor, manifolds, and any other parts that are in the way. Then remove the cylinder-head bolts and take off the head.

31-12 REMOVING VALVES
The cylinder head should be put into a head stand. A valve-spring compressor is used to compress the valve springs (Fig. 31-11). Then the retainer locks, retainers, oil seals, and springs can be removed. Now the valve can be removed. If the stem end is peened over, or mushroomed, do not drive out the valve. This could break the valve guide or cylinder head. Instead, use a small grinding stone to grind off the mushroom.

NOTE

Do not interchange valves and other parts. Each valve, spring, lock, retainer, and pushrod should be reinstalled in the same place in the same cylinder from which it was taken. As you remove each valve, place it in a numbered valve rack. This will prevent mixup on reassembly.

31-13 CHECKING VALVE SPRINGS
The valve springs should be checked for distortion, tension, and color change. If discolored, the spring has been overheated and should be discarded. A bent or weak spring should also be discarded.

Fig. 31-11
A cylinder head mounted in a repair stand with a valve-spring-compressor tool in place. (*Chrysler Corporation*)

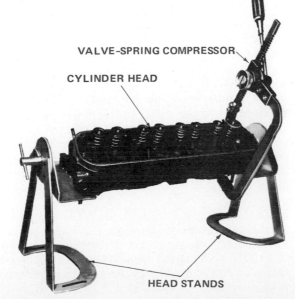

VALVE-SPRING COMPRESSOR

CYLINDER HEAD

HEAD STANDS

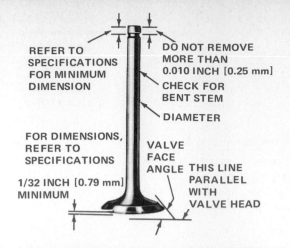

REFER TO SPECIFICATIONS FOR MINIMUM DIMENSION

DO NOT REMOVE MORE THAN 0.010 INCH [0.25 mm]

CHECK FOR BENT STEM

DIAMETER

FOR DIMENSIONS, REFER TO SPECIFICATIONS

1/32 INCH [0.79 mm] MINIMUM

VALVE FACE ANGLE

THIS LINE PARALLEL WITH VALVE HEAD

31-14 SERVICING ROCKER ARMS AND ROCKER-ARM SHAFT

Rocker arms with worn bearing surfaces should be replaced. On some rocker arms, worn or pitted valve ends can be resurfaced in the valve refacer.

31-15 CLEANING THE CYLINDER HEAD

The head should be cleaned of carbon, gasket material, and other deposits with a carbon scraper. A wire brush driven by a drill motor can be used to clean the combustion chambers and ports. Check and clean out water jackets.

CAUTION

Always wear goggles when using a wire brush or compressed air. The goggles protect your eyes from flying particles that could injure your eyes. Be sure you do not blow particles toward anyone working near you when you use compressed air.

31-16 CLEANING, CHECKING, AND GRINDING VALVES

The various parts of each valve should be checked as shown in Fig. 31-12. If the valve faces are rough or pitted, they should be ground in a valve refacer.

31-17 SERVICING VALVE GUIDES

Valve guides must be serviced before valve seats are ground. The valve-seat grinder pilots in the guide. If the guide is not in good condition, the seat will not be ground square and evenly. To service a valve guide, it is first cleaned and then checked for wear. If worn, it must be replaced (if it is the replaceable type) or reamed to a larger size. Then, valves with oversize stems are used. Knurling the valve guides is another method of restoring the guides to good condition.

31-18 GRINDING VALVE SEATS

Whenever valves are ground, the valve seats also must be ground. A valve-seat grinding stone, driven by an air or electric motor, is used to grind valve seats (Fig. 31-13). As the stone rotates on the seat, it removes pits and restores the seat to a smooth, round surface with the proper angle.

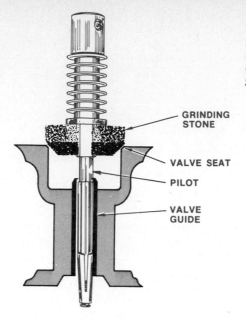

Fig. 31-13
The pilot on which the grinding
stone rotates keeps the valve
seat concentric with the valve
guide. (*Black & Decker Manufacturing Company*)

GRINDING
STONE

VALVE SEAT

PILOT

VALVE
GUIDE

31-19 INSTALLING VALVES
After the cylinder head, valve seats, and valves have been serviced, the
valves are reinstalled in the cylinder head. Valves and related parts
should always go back into the same valve guide and seat from which
they were removed. Coat valves with engine oil. Use a spring compressor (Fig. 31-11) to compress the spring. Then install the oil seal, spring
retainer, and locks.

31-20 CHECKING PUSHRODS
Pushrods should be checked for wear and for being bent. If any defects
are found, install a new pushrod.

31-21 SERVICING HYDRAULIC VALVE LIFTERS
Manufacturers' shop manuals carry detailed servicing procedures for
hydraulic valve lifters. However, many shops replace defective lifters
with new ones instead of servicing used lifters. The reason is that labor
charges to service a lifter can be greater than the cost of a new one.

31-22 SERVICING THE CAMSHAFT AND BEARINGS
Removing a camshaft from an engine is a major job. It is done when the
camshaft needs regrinding or replacement or if the camshaft bearings
need replacement.

31-23 INSTALLING THE CYLINDER HEAD
After the head has been assembled, it is installed on the cylinder block.
Always use a new head gasket. Make sure the mating surfaces between the head and block are clean and smooth. The cylinder-head
bolts should be tightened in the proper sequence and to the proper tension (Fig. 31-14).

All boltholes should be cleaned of dirt or coolant. Threads should
be clean and straight. Dirty or battered threads will not allow normal
bolt tightening, and then the head could come loose. It requires a

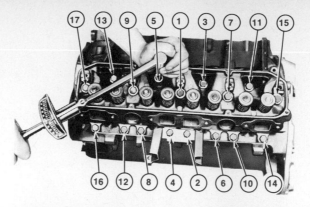

Fig. 31-14
A sequence chart for tightening cylinder-head bolts on a V-8 engine. (*Chrysler Corporation*)

torque above normal to overcome the excessive friction of dirty or battered threads. Dirt or water in a bolthole can result in a broken block. Bolts that do not seat properly leave the cylinder head loose. This will cause a blown gasket.

CHECK UP ON YOURSELF

Now you have finished the chapter on valves. Your related shopwork shows you how to perform the various valve-train jobs discussed in the chapter. Check up on yourself by answering the questions that follow.

1. What is the purpose of putting the valves in a rack as you remove them from the cylinder head?
2. When grinding valves, should you also grind the valve seats?
3. Do dirty or battered threads reduce or increase the torque required to tighten the head bolts?
4. What would cause you to discard a valve spring?
5. Why should you never attempt to force out a valve which is mushroomed on the stem end?

ANSWERS

1. So you can return each valve to the valve seat from which it was taken (Sec. 31-12). 2. Yes (Sec. 31-18). 3. They increase the torque (Sec. 31-23). 4. If the spring is bent, weak, or discolored (Sec. 31-13). 5. This could break the valve guide or cylinder head (Sec. 31-12).

CHAPTER THIRTY-TWO
ENGINE SERVICE—CONNECTING RODS, PISTONS, AND PISTON RINGS

After studying this chapter, you should be able to:

1. Explain how to remove and replace the piston-and-rod assembly.
2. Explain how to service the connecting rod and bearings.
3. Discuss bearing failures and their causes.
4. Explain how to replace rod bearings.
5. Describe piston services.

This chapter covers an important part of engine service—piston-and-rod service. It explains how to remove these parts from the engine and how to service them (see Fig. 32-1). You must keep your tools, parts, hands, and work area clean for good engine service work.

32-1 PREPARING TO REMOVE THE PISTON-AND-ROD ASSEMBLY

Before the piston-and-rod assembly can be removed, the engine oil must be drained and the oil pan removed. Then the cylinder head must be taken off. Next, the cylinders should be examined for wear (Fig. 32-2). If a cylinder is worn, there will be a ridge at the top of it (Fig. 32-3). It is called the *ring ridge*. This ridge marks the upper limit of top-ring travel. You can feel it with your fingernail (Fig. 32-2). If a piston is forced out past this ridge, it could break the rings and piston, as shown in Fig. 32-3.

If you find ring ridges, you must remove them before you take out the pistons. A ring-ridge remover is shown in a cylinder in Fig. 32-4. When the tool is rotated in the cylinder, cutter blades cut off the ridge. Then the pistons can be removed without damage.

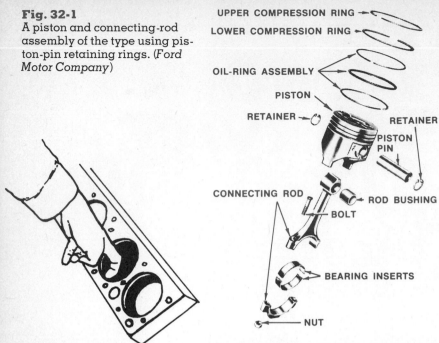

Fig. 32-1
A piston and connecting-rod assembly of the type using piston-pin retaining rings. (*Ford Motor Company*)

UPPER COMPRESSION RING

LOWER COMPRESSION RING

OIL-RING ASSEMBLY

PISTON

RETAINER

RETAINER

PISTON PIN

CONNECTING ROD

ROD BUSHING

BOLT

BEARING INSERTS

NUT

Fig. 32-2
Feeling for ring ridge with fingernail.

Fig. 32-3
How a ring ridge caused by cylinder wear may break the ring if the piston is withdrawn without removing the ridge. (*Sealed Power Corporation*)

32-2 REMOVING THE PISTON-AND-ROD ASSEMBLY

After you have removed the cylinder head and the oil pan, turn the crankshaft so that the number 1 piston is near BDC. Check the connecting rod and the cap for identifying marks. If there are no marks, use a small water-color brush and white metal paint to mark a "1" on the rod cap and the rod. This enables you to return the cap to the rod from which it came, and return rod and cap to the number 1 cylinder.

Next, remove the rod nuts and take off the rod cap. Then use rod guides to cover the rod bolts, as shown in Fig. 32-5. The purpose of the guides is to protect the crankpins from the rod-bolt threads. If exposed, these threads could scratch or nick the crankpins. Short pieces of rubber hose, split and slipped over the bolts, serve the same purpose. With the guides or the hoses in place, slide the piston-and-rod assembly up in the cylinder. Take the assembly out from the top.

As you go from one cylinder to the next to remove the remaining piston-and-rod assemblies, turn the crankshaft to get at the rod nuts. Mark all rods and caps with the number of the cylinder from which they were removed. As you remove the piston-and-rod assemblies, set them in a piston rack in the same order the pistons are numbered.

32-3 SEPARATING THE PISTONS AND THE RODS

To separate the pistons from the rods, remove the piston pins. The procedure varies, depending on the way in which the rod and the piston are attached to the pin. With a free-floating pin, remove the retainers and slip the pin out (see Fig. 32-1). With a press-fit pin, you have to use a special tool to press the pin out of the connecting rod. Do not try to force the pin out with a hammer. If you do, you will probably break the piston.

NOTE

Make sure the pistons have identifying marks so that each piston can be reattached to its matching connecting rod in the correct position. If the piston is installed on a rod backward, piston slap and early piston failure can result. Make sure that each piston-and-rod assembly is returned to the cylinder from which it was taken.

32-4 CHECKING THE CONNECTING RODS

The rods should be cleaned and checked for nicks on the bearing surfaces and sides of the big-end bore. Check especially for cracks around

Fig. 32-4
A ring-ridge-removing tool in place in the top of a cylinder. Cutters remove the ridge as the tool is turned.

Fig. 32-5
A special short guide and long guide used to remove the connecting rod. (*Buick Motor Division of General Motors Corporation*)

SHORT GUIDE

LONG GUIDE

OVERLAY WIPED OUT

LACK OF OIL

CRATERS OR POCKETS

FATIGUE FAILURE

SCRATCHES   DIRT EMBEDDED
INTO BEARING MATERIAL

SCRATCHED BY DIRT

OVERLAY GONE FROM
ENTIRE SURFACE

TAPERED JOURNAL

RADIUS RIDE

RADIUS RIDE

BRIGHT (POLISHED) SECTIONS

IMPROPER SEATING

Fig. 32-6
Types of engine-bearing failure. The appearance of a bearing usually tells what caused its failure. (*Ford Motor Company*)

the piston-pin hole or the cap-bolt holes. Check the rods for alignment. A bent rod can cause trouble with the bearing, piston, and cylinder wall. If any rod has defects, it should be thrown away.

32-5 PISTON-PIN BUSHING IN THE ROD
If the rod is used with a free-floating piston pin, there is a bushing in the small end of the rod. If this bushing is worn, it can be replaced. Then the new bushing is reamed or honed to size.

32-6 INSPECTING THE CONNECTING-ROD BEARINGS
Connecting-rod bearings are the split type. They are precision-insert bearings and are serviced by replacement.

As you take the rod caps off and take the rod-and-piston assembly apart, examine the bearings for wear or other trouble. Figure 32-6 shows various kinds of trouble and their causes. Let's examine each kind of failure.

1. Lack of Oil
If the oil supply fails, bearing material will be wiped off the shell. The friction heat can become so high that the rod will actually weld to the crankpin. When this happens, the engine "throws a rod." The rod freezes to the crankpin and breaks. Part of the rod may go through the cylinder wall. Failure of the oil supply can result from worn bearings, which pass all the oil the pump can send. This oil-starves the bearings farthest from the pump. Oil starvation also can result from low oil level in the oil pan, clogged lines, or a defective oil pump.

2. Fatigue Failure
Fatigue failure of bearings normally is not a problem. However, unusual operating conditions or out-of-round bearing journals can cause this trouble. For example, if an engine is operated under heavy load with wide-open throttle, the upper bearing half may "fatigue out." This type of operation repeatedly overloads the upper bearing half. The hammering effect causes the metal to fatigue and flake out. A similar effect could be caused by an out-of-round journal. The out-of-round section of a journal overloads the bearing each revolution.

3. Scratched by Dirt

If the oil is dirty, particles of dirt will gouge out the soft bearing material and may also scratch the crankpin. The oil can become dirty if the oil and the oil filters are not changed at the proper intervals. If the bearing becomes overloaded with particles, bearing failure will soon occur.

4. Tapered Journal

A tapered journal is larger at one end than at the other. The bigger end puts more load on the bearing. This overload wipes out the bearing material at that end.

5. Radius Ride

If the radius of the journal, where it curves up to the crank cheeks, is not cut away enough, the journal will ride on the edge of the bearing. This action will push the bearing to one side, overheat it, and cause it to fail. Usually, radius ride would occur only after a crankshaft has been reground in an automotive machine shop.

6. Improper Seating

If the bearing is not properly seated in the bearing cap or rod, there will be high spots in the bearing. For example, look at Fig. 32-7. Here you see what happens if particles of dirt are left in the cap or rod when the bearing is installed. The bearing is damaged in two ways. The shell is pushed up at the spot where the dirt particles occur, leaving the bearing with insufficient oil clearance (as at X). This condition causes frictional heating and rapid bearing wear. Also, air space is left between the bearing and rod or cap. This prevents normal heat flow away from the bearing. The condition makes the heating problem worse, so the bearing soon fails.

32-7 CHECKING THE CONNECTING-ROD-BEARING CLEARANCE

There are three ways of checking the clearance between the connecting-rod bearing and the crankpin journal. These are with Plastigage, with shim stock, or with micrometer and telescope gauge.

1. Plastigage

Plastigage is the most popular way to check bearing fit. It is a plastic material that comes in strips. To use Plastigage, first wipe the oil from the bearing and the journal. Then lay a strip of Plastigage on the bearing in the cap, as shown at the left in Fig. 32-8. Next, put the cap into

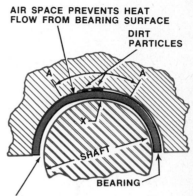

Fig. 32-7
The effect of dirt particles under the bearing shell as a result of poor installation.

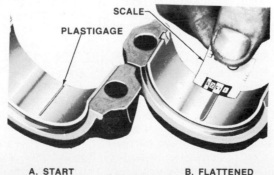

A. START   B. FLATTENED

Fig. 32-8
Bearing clearance is checked with Plastigage. Plastigage in place before installing the cap (left). Measurement of the amount of flattening (or bearing clearance) with a scale (right). (*Buick Motor Division of General Motors Corporation*)

place and tighten the cap nuts to the normal tension. Then remove the cap and measure the amount that the Plastigage has flattened. Check the clearance with the chart on the Plastigage package, as shown in Fig. 32-8. The smaller the clearance, the flatter the Plastigage.

NOTE
Do not move the rod on the crankpin while the cap nuts are tight. Moving the rod will flatten the Plastigage too much and throw off the measurements.

2. Shim Stock
Shim stock is a sheet of thin metal that can be purchased in various thicknesses. To measure clearance with shim stock, first lubricate a strip of stock. Lay it lengthwise in the center of the bearing cap. Then install the cap and lightly tighten the cap nuts. Next, check the ease with which the rod can be moved on the crankpin. If the rod moves easily, there is too much clearance. Remove the cap. Put another strip of shim stock on top of the first strip, and repeat the procedure. Continue adding shim stock, until the rod is hard to move. The thickness of the shims is the clearance.

3. Micrometer and Telescope Gauge
This method requires a micrometer to measure the diameter of the crankpin. It also requires a telescope gauge or an inside micrometer to measure the inside diameter of the rod bearing with the cap in place. Bearing clearance is the difference between the bearing diameter and the crankpin diameter.

CHECK UP ON YOURSELF
These questions will help you review what you have studied about connecting-rod and bearing service. Answer the questions that follow.

1. What is the ring ridge?
2. Why must all rods and caps be numbered?
3. What do engine manufacturers recommend doing with bent connecting rods?
4. What are six types of bearing failure described in the chapter?
5. What are the three methods of checking rod-bearing clearance?

ANSWERS
1. The ring ridge marks the upper limit of cylinder-wall wear produced by ring travel (Sec. 32-1). 2. So that each rod and cap can be returned to the cylinder from which it was removed (Sec. 32-2). 3. Replacing them (Sec. 32-4). 4. Lack of oil, fatigue failure, scratched by dirt, tapered journal, radius ride, and improper seating (Sec. 32-6). 5. Using Plastigage, shim stock, or micrometer and telescope gauge (Sec. 32-7).

32-8 REPLACING CONNECTING-ROD BEARINGS
New connecting-rod bearings are required if the old ones are defective or worn. They are also required if the crankshaft is reground. Grinding the crankshaft is explained in Chap. 33.

NOTE
Engine rebuilders usually install new bearings, even though the old bearings seem to be in good condition. With the engine disassembled, it costs only a little more to install new bearings.

1. Checking the Crankpins

Before installing the bearings, check the crankpins with a micrometer. This check will detect taper or an out-of-round condition. If crankpins are out of round or tapered more than 0.0015 inch [0.038 mm], the crankshaft must be replaced or the crankpins reground. Out-of-round or tapered crankpins are hard on bearings and can cause early bearing failure.

2. Installing New Bearings

When installing new bearings, make sure your hands, the workbench, your tools, and all engine parts are clean. It takes only a little dirt to ruin a bearing. Be sure that the bores in the cap and the rod are clean. Keep the bearings wrapped up until you are ready to install them. Then handle them carefully. Wipe each bearing with a clean, lint-free cloth just before installing it.

Put the bearing shells into place in the cap and the rod. If the shells have locking tangs, make sure the tangs enter the notches provided in the cap and the rod. The tangs in the rod and the tangs in the cap face one another when the cap is properly installed.

3. Bearing Spread

Bearing shells have "spread." The ends are spread out a little beyond the diameter of the rod bore into which the shell fits (see Fig. 32-9). This ensures a snug fit when the shell is pushed into place.

4. Bearing Crush

Bearing shells also have a little additional height over a full half (Fig. 32-10). This additional height is crushed down as the cap bolts are tightened to provide a firm seat in the bearing bore. Firm seating is necessary for adequate heat transfer from the bearing to the cap or the rod.

32-9 SERVICING THE PISTONS

As the pistons are removed from the engine and separated from the connecting rods, they should be examined carefully. If the pistons are in good condition, remove the rings and set aside the pistons for further inspection. The rings are removed with a ring expander, as shown in Fig. 32-11.

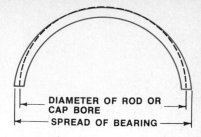

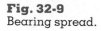

Fig. 32-9
Bearing spread.

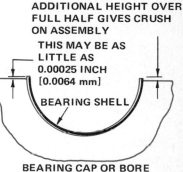

Fig. 32-10
Bearing crush.

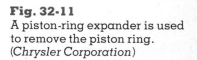

Fig. 32-11
A piston-ring expander is used to remove the piston ring. (*Chrysler Corporation*)

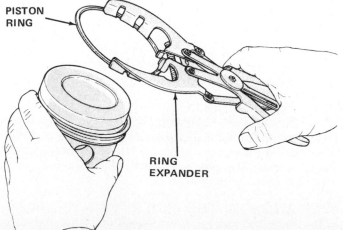

Examine damaged pistons to determine what caused the damage. For example, look at Figs. 32-12 to 32-14. Make sure to correct the condition that caused the damage. Otherwise the new pistons will also be damaged by the condition. Scrape the piston heads clean. Then soak them in a parts-cleaning solution, such as carburetor cleaner, which is safe to use on aluminum. Clean the piston inside and out.

NOTE

Do not clean the piston in caustic, or corrosive, solution or use a wire brush on the piston skirt. These could damage the finish, causing rapid piston failure.

Clean out the ring grooves with a ring-groove cleaner (Fig. 32-15) or with a piece of an old ring. Clean out the oilholes or slots in the back of the ring grooves with a drill or a small, thin screwdriver.

32-10 INSPECTING THE PISTONS

Each piston should be examined for wear, scuffs, cracks, or scratches. Check the fit of the rings in the grooves and the condition of the piston-pin bosses or bushings. We cover these checks in later sections.

Measure the diameter of the piston with a micrometer. Compare this diameter with the diameter of the cylinder in which the piston is to be installed. If there is too much clearance, a new piston will be required. A typical piston clearance is 0.0005 to 0.0015 inch [0.013 to 0.038 mm] on a new or rebored engine. Most American-made engines can be rebuilt without reboring if the cylinder taper does not exceed 0.005 inch [0.13 mm] or if the cylinder out-of-round does not exceed 0.003 inch [0.08 mm].

32-11 NEW PISTONS

New pistons are available in the original size and in various oversizes. When oversize pistons are selected, the cylinders are bored and honed to provide the correct piston clearance. (We describe cylinder service in Chap. 33.)

Engine manufacturers supply oversize pistons of the same weight as the original pistons. There is no engine-balance problem if all pistons are of the same weight, even if some are of different size.

Aluminum pistons usually are supplied with the pin already fitted. This ensures factory specifications for piston-pin clearance.

NOTE

New pistons have a special finish. They must not be buffed with a wire wheel or finished to a smaller size. This would remove the finish and cause rapid piston wear after installation.

32-12 PISTON PINS

If there is excessive clearance between the piston and pin, most manufacturers recommend discarding both. Some pistons have piston-pin bushings. If these are worn, they should be reamed or honed oversize. Then new oversize pins are installed. This work usually is done in an automotive machine shop.

32-13 ALIGNING THE PISTON AND THE ROD

After the piston and rod have been assembled, rod alignment should be checked. This should be done before the piston rings are installed.

Fig. 32-12
The appearance of a piston that has failed from scuffing. Note the scratch or scuff marks that run vertically on the piston. (*TRW Inc.*)

Fig. 32-13
The appearance of a piston that has failed because of detonation. The ring lands, particularly the top one, appear to have been shattered. (*TRW Inc.*)

32-14 SERVICING THE PISTON RINGS

During an engine overhaul, the piston rings should be replaced. Examine the old rings to see if they indicate any engine troubles. For example, scuffed rings may mean that not enough oil is getting to the cylinder walls. If the cylinders are to be rebored, then a new oversize ring set should be selected that has extra tension. Often, there are special springs under these rings to give more tension. The result is that the rings can do a better job, even in tapered cylinders. The rings can expand and contract more as they move up and down in the cylinders.

32-15 FITTING THE PISTON RINGS

The piston rings must be fitted to the cylinder and also to the ring grooves in the piston. First, push the ring down to the bottom of the cylinder with a piston. Then check the piston-ring end gap with a feeler gauge (Fig. 32-16). If the ring gap is too small, make sure you have the right size ring set for the engine. A smaller ring set will have a larger end gap.

NOTE

If you are fitting rings to a tapered cylinder, be sure to fit the ring at the lower limit of ring travel. If you fit the ring to the upper part of the cylinder, the gap will be too small. When the ring moves down into the smaller diameter, the gap will close up and the ring can break. Make sure the ring has a gap at the point of minimum diameter. The point of minimum diameter is at the lower limit of ring travel.

After checking the ring gap, test the fit of the ring in the piston groove. Insert the outside of the ring into the groove, and roll the ring all the way around the piston (Fig. 32-17). If the fit is too tight, the chances are the groove is dirty and needs cleaning out. An additional test should be made after the ring is installed in the groove. Insert a feeler gauge between the ring and the side of the groove to measure

Fig. 32-14
The appearance of a piston that has failed because of preignition. The excessive temperature has melted a hole in the piston head. (*TRW Inc.*)

Fig. 32-15
A groove-cleaning tool is used to clean the piston-ring grooves. (*Ford Motor Company*)

Fig. 32-16
Measurement of the ring gap with the ring in the cylinder. (*Chrysler Corporation*)

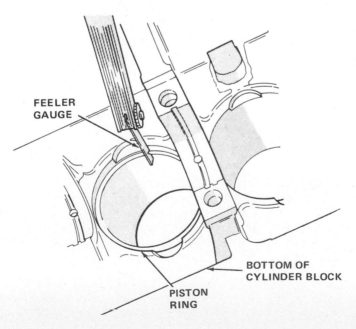

FEELER GAUGE

BOTTOM OF CYLINDER BLOCK

PISTON RING

Fig. 32-17
Checking the fit of the ring in the ring groove. (*Chevrolet Motor Division of General Motors Corporation*)

ring side clearance (Fig. 32-18). Clearance should be at least 0.001 inch [0.025 mm] and not more than 0.004 inch [0.10 mm] for most engines. Check the shop manual for the specifications on the engine you are servicing.

32-16 INSTALLING THE PISTON-AND-ROD ASSEMBLY

After the rings have been installed in the piston grooves, the piston-and-rod assembly is ready for installation. Dip the piston assembly in oil until the pin is covered. Pour out the excess oil. Now the rings must be compressed into the ring grooves so that they will enter the cylinder. Use a ring compressor for this job (Fig. 32-19). Clamp the compressor around the rings, compressing them into the piston grooves. Then push the piston down into the cylinder.

NOTE

Use guide sleeves or rubber tubing to protect the crankpins from the threads on the rod bolts. Also make sure the pistons and the rods are facing in the proper direction.

Remove the rod caps before putting the assembly into the cylinder. Then install the cap to attach the rod to the crankpin. Tighten the nuts to the correct torque. Then turn the crankshaft to make sure it rotates freely.

CHECK UP ON YOURSELF

When you work in the shop, your instructor will check your work. But when you leave school and get a job in a shop, the service manager or shop foreman will inspect your work. Now, see how much you know about bearings, pistons, and piston rings.

1. Why are crankpins checked with a micrometer?
2. What is bearing crush?
3. Why should a piston never be cleaned on a wire wheel?
4. Why should guide sleeves or rubber tubing be used on the rod bolts when installing the connecting rods?

Fig. 32-18
Checking the piston-ring clearance with a gauge. (*Chrysler Corporation*)

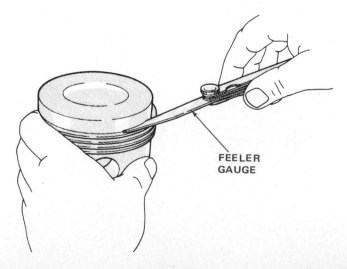

FEELER GAUGE

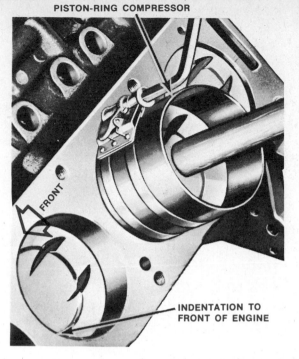

PISTON-RING COMPRESSOR

FRONT

INDENTATION TO
FRONT OF ENGINE

Fig. 32-19
A piston-ring compressor is
used to install a piston with
rings. (*Chevrolet Motor Division of General Motors Corporation*)

ANSWERS

1. To see if they are tapered or out-of-round (Sec. 32-8). **2.** The additional
height of the bearing shell over a full half (Sec. 32-8). **3.** This would remove
the finish and ruin the piston (Sec. 32-11). **4.** To protect the crankpins from
the threads on the rod bolts (Sec. 32-16).

CHAPTER THIRTY-THREE
ENGINE SERVICE— CRANKSHAFT AND CYLINDERS

After studying this chapter, you should be able to:

1. Explain how to check and replace main bearings.
2. Explain how to check and service crankshafts.
3. Explain how to check cylinders for wear and how to service cylinders if needed.

In this chapter we discuss the engine service jobs for the crankshaft and the cylinders. These service jobs include replacing the main bearings and oil seal, checking the crankshaft journals, and honing or boring the cylinders.

33-1 CHECKING THE CRANKSHAFT AND BEARINGS IN PLACE

In some engines the crankshaft main bearings and journals can be checked without removing the crankshaft. The service manual for the engine you are servicing will tell whether the check can be made in this way. We discuss checking crankpins in Chap. 32.

The first step in checking the crankshaft bearings and journals is to drain the engine oil and remove the oil pan. Then, starting at the front of the engine, remove one main-bearing cap at a time to check the bearing and journal. Make sure the caps are numbered and that you know which side of the caps faces the front. Main bearing caps must be replaced on the same journals and in the same position from which they were removed.

Some main-bearing-cap nuts or bolts are locked in place with lock washers or locking tangs. The locking tangs must be bent back before the nuts or bolts can be removed.

If a bearing cap sticks, loosen it carefully to avoid damage. Light taps from a plastic hammer will usually loosen the cap.

NOTE

Heavy hammering or prying can bend or break a cap. A bent or different cap can cause a bad bearing fit. It could require line boring of the block to fit a new cap to the engine.

1. Examining the Main Bearings

Examine the main bearings in the bearing caps for wear or unusual damage (see Fig. 32-6). Both main bearings and connecting-rod bearings can have the same sort of troubles.

NOTE

If one main bearing has to be replaced, then all the main bearings should be replaced. Replacing only one main bearing could throw the crankshaft out of alignment so that the crankshaft would break or the bearings would fail.

If you find that some bearings are more worn than others, check the crankshaft for misalignment.

2. Checking the Crankshaft Journals

There are two ways to measure the main journals with the crankshaft still in the engine. One way is to use a special crankshaft gauge (Fig. 33-1).

The other way to measure the main journal with the crankshaft in the engine is with a special micrometer (Fig. 33-2). Before using the micrometer, remove the upper bearing shell from the cylinder block. We explain how to do this in a later section. The *Auto Shop Workbook* explains in detail these two methods of measurement.

If the journals are worn, tapered, or rough, the crankshaft must be removed for service. This is covered later.

33-2 CHECKING MAIN-BEARING CLEARANCE

Main-bearing clearance can be checked with either Plastigage or shim stock. The procedure is the same as that for checking connecting-rod bearings. This is covered in Sec. 32-7 and in the *Auto Shop Workbook*.

33-3 CHECKING CRANKSHAFT END PLAY

Crankshaft end play becomes excessive if the crankshaft thrust bearing is worn. The thrust bearing (Fig. 33-3) prevents excessive end, or back and forth, movement of the crankshaft. End movement of the crankshaft can cause a knock that will occur every time the clutch is operated (on manual-transmission cars). End play is measured by forcing the crankshaft in one direction as far as it will go. Then the clearance at the thrust bearing is measured with a feeler gauge, as shown in Fig. 33-4.

33-4 REPLACING THE MAIN BEARINGS

If there is too much clearance between the main bearings and the journals, and the journals are in good condition, the bearings should be replaced. Other conditions besides worn bearings also require replacement of bearings (see Fig. 32-6). You will have no problem removing and replacing the bearing half in the cap. But you will have to use the crankshaft to help you remove and replace the upper bearing half.

To remove the upper bearing half, first remove the bearing cap. Loosen the other bearing cap bolts about half a turn so that the crankshaft can rotate easily. Then use the special bearing-removal tool, called a roll-out tool. Insert the round section of the tool into the oilhole in the journal, as shown in Fig. 33-5. Then turn the crankshaft to apply pressure against the end of the bearing. The pressure will force the bearing up and out. Turn the crankshaft so that the roll-out tool

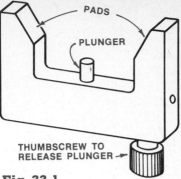

Fig. 33-1
A special gauge for checking the journal diameter. (*Federal-Mogul Corporation*)

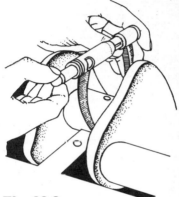

Fig. 33-2
A special micrometer is used to measure the diameter of the crankshaft journal.

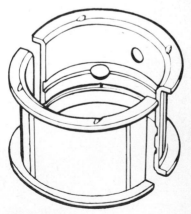

Fig. 33-3
Crankshaft thrust bearing.

409

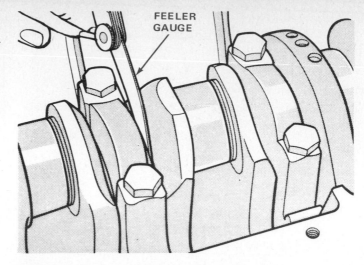

Fig. 33-4
A feeler gauge is used to check crankshaft end play at the end-thrust bearing. (*Chrysler Corporation*)

presses against the plain end of the bearing. Do not press against the end that has the bearing tang.

To install a new bearing upper half, coat the inside of the bearing with engine oil. Leave the outside of the bearing dry. Make sure the crankshaft journal and the bearing bore in the cylinder block are clean. Use the roll-out tool, shown in Fig. 33-5, to push the shell up into place. Then install the bearing cap. Tap the cap with a plastic hammer to make sure the cap is seated. Then tighten the cap bolts. Check the bearing clearance as explained earlier.

NOTE

Some technicians do not install bearings without removing the crankshaft. They say that you may not get the bearing upper half seated properly in the bore. The best way to install bearings is to remove the crankshaft so that you

Fig. 33-5
Removal and installation of the upper main bearing. The crankshaft journal is shown partly cut away so that the tool can be seen inserted into the oilhole in the journal. (*Chrysler Corporation*)

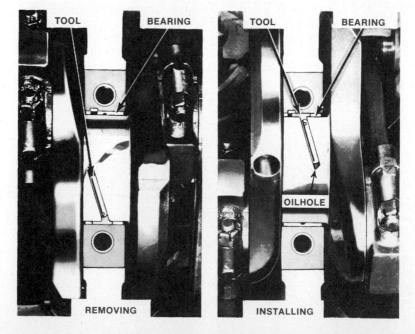

can be sure the bores into which the upper bearings fit are clean. Installing main bearings with the crankshaft in the engine is difficult. It may not be done successfully on all engines.

33-5 REPLACING THE THRUST BEARINGS
Some crankshaft main journals do not have oilholes. For example, the rear main journals of many in-line engines do not have oilholes. The rear main oil seal and, in some engines, the end-thrust bearing are located there. To remove the upper half of this kind of bearing, first start to move the bearing out with a small punch and hammer. Then use pliers with taped jaws to hold the bearing half against the oil slinger, as shown in Fig. 33-6. Turn the crankshaft so that the bearing will rise up out of the bore. Install the new bearing in the same way. Lightly tap the bearing down the final fraction of an inch with a punch and hammer.

33-6 REPLACING THE MAIN-BEARING OIL SEAL
The main-bearing oil seal prevents engine oil from leaking out the rear of the engine, past the rear main bearing. The method of replacing the oil seal varies with different engines. On some engines the crankshaft must be removed in order to install a new seal. On others, the old seal can be pulled out with pliers or a special removing tool. Then the new

Fig. 33-6
Replacement of the rear-main-bearing half with pliers on the engine where the crankshaft has no oilhole in the rear journal. (*Chevrolet Motor Division of General Motors Corporation*)

Fig. 33-7
V blocks and a dial indicator
are used to check a crankshaft
for alignment.

seal can be pushed or pulled into place. Refer to the manufacturer's shop manual for details when you are working on an engine that requires oil-seal replacement.

33-7 REMOVING THE CRANKSHAFT

If the main journals or the crankpin journals are rough or worn, or if misalignment is suspected, the crankshaft must come out of the engine. This operation requires removal of the oil pan and the oil pump. In addition, the connecting rods must be detached. Also, the crankshaft gear or the sprocket and chain or belt must be removed from the front of the engine.

NOTE

For a complete engine overhaul, the cylinder head and piston-and-rod assemblies have to be removed. However, if only the crankshaft is coming out, the piston-and-rod assemblies need not be removed. Instead, they can be detached from the crankpins and pushed up out of the way. Don't push them up too far or the top ring might be pushed up above the top of the cylinder. It would catch on the edge of the cylinder. Then you would have to remove the cylinder head to compress the ring and push it back down into the cylinder.

33-8 CHECKING THE CRANKSHAFT

After the crankshaft has been removed, it should be checked for alignment and for journal wear or damage. Check the alignment by putting the crankshaft in V blocks. As the crankshaft is rotated, the dial indicator will show any out-of-roundness or any misalignment of the main journals (Fig. 33-7).

NOTE

Do not leave the crankshaft with its ends supported on V blocks, as shown in Fig. 33-7, for any length of time. This could cause the crankshaft to sag and go out of alignment from its own weight. To prevent misalignment, set the crankshaft on end or hang it from one end.

If the crankshaft is out of line, a new or reground crankshaft is usually installed. It is difficult to straighten a bent crankshaft.

Next examine the main journals and crankpin journals for wear, scratches, or other damage. Use a micrometer to measure the journals for wear, out-of-round, and taper. Worn journals can be ground in a special crankshaft lathe to return them to a usable condition. (This job is done in an automotive machine shop that specializes in crankshaft regrinding.) Then undersize bearings are used when the engine is reassembled.

33-9 CLEANING THE CRANKSHAFT

After the grinding job, or at any time the crankshaft is out of the engine, the crankshaft should be cleaned in solvent. Use a valve-guide cleaning brush to clean out the oil passages. Then blow out all the passages with compressed air. Any trace of abrasive left in the oil passages will work out and get on the bearings. The abrasive could cause rapid bearing wear and engine damage. Coat all journals with oil after you have cleaned the crankshaft.

CHECK UP ON YOURSELF

Servicing the crankshaft is another important job for the automotive mechanic. See how well you understand what you have learned by answering the questions that follow.

1. If only one main bearing requires replacement, why should they all be replaced?
2. What does it mean when the Plastigage flattens more at one end than at the other?
3. How is the upper bearing half removed without removing the crankshaft?
4. Do the connecting-rod-and-piston assemblies have to be removed if the crankshaft is removed?
5. Why is it important to clean out the oil passages in the crankshaft?

ANSWERS

1. Replacing only one main bearing could throw the crankshaft out of alignment and cause the bearings to fail (Sec. 33-1). 2. That the journal is tapered (Secs. 32-7 and 33-2). 3. A roll-out tool is inserted into the oilhole in the journal; then the crankshaft is rotated (Sec. 33-1). 4. No. The rods can be disconnected by removing the rod caps and then pushing the rods up out of the way (Sec. 33-7). 5. Any trace of abrasive left in the oil passages can work out when the engine is operated. The abrasive could cause rapid bearing failure and a damaged engine (Sec. 33-9).

33-10 CYLINDER WEAR

Engine cylinders do not wear uniformly. They wear more at the top of the ring travel than at the bottom. Here's the reason: When the piston is at TDC at the start of the power stroke, pressures are the greatest. The compression rings apply the greatest pressure against the cylinder walls. Then, as the piston moves down on the power stroke, the pressure decreases. Therefore the cylinder walls wear more at the top of the ring travel than at the bottom, as shown in Fig. 33-8.

Cylinders also tend to wear oval-shaped. This kind of wear is due to the side thrust of the pistons against the cylinder walls on the power stroke. The pistons are pushing down on the connecting rods at an angle, which produces the side thrust.

The washing action of gasoline droplets entering the combustion chamber can also cause cylinder-wall wear. This wear is most likely to occur in an area opposite the intake valve. The ingoing air-fuel mixture, especially when cold, usually contains droplets of liquid gasoline. These droplets hit the cylinder walls and wash off the oil. The result is wear in the area in which the oil has been washed away.

All these kinds of wear must be considered when checking the cylinders to decide how to service them.

33-11 CLEANING AND INSPECTING THE CYLINDER BLOCK

Before deciding whether to rebuild or throw away the cylinder block, you should clean and inspect it. There are several cleaning methods.

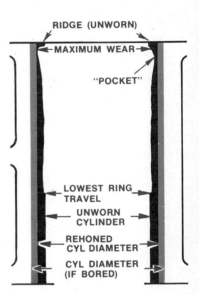

RIDGE (UNWORN)
←MAXIMUM WEAR→
"POCKET"
LOWEST RING TRAVEL
UNWORN CYLINDER
REHONED CYL DIAMETER
CYL DIAMETER (IF BORED)

Fig. 33-8
Taper wear in an engine cylinder (shown exaggerated). Maximum wear is at the top, just under the ring ridge. Honing the cylinder usually removes less material than boring, as indicated. Material removed by honing is shown solid. Material to be removed by boring is shown both solid and shaded.

One method is steam cleaning. A spray of steam and soap washes away the dirt and grease from the outside of the block.

Another cleaning method is to boil the block in a hot, caustic soda solution or similar chemical. Make sure all gasket material is removed from the gasket surfaces. Remove the pipe and expansion plugs so that the oil passages and the water jackets can be boiled out. After removing the block from the boil tank, rinse the block with water. Use compressed air to blow out the oil and water passages. You can also use long rods to clean out any loose deposits in the passages.

Blow out all threaded holes with compressed air. If the threads are not in good condition, use a tap to clean them. Or if they are badly damaged, you may have to use a Heli-Coil, or threaded insert, to repair them, as explained in Sec. 6-18.

Check the block for cracks anywhere, and especially for scratches in the cylinder and main-bearing and cam-bearing bores. Check the head end of the block for warpage by laying a long precision straightedge on it.

33-12 SERVICING THE CYLINDER

New piston rings can be installed in a cylinder with some taper and wear. But the more taper there is, the more blowby, the more oil burning, and the more air pollution there will be. The best way to take care of a cylinder with a large amount of taper is to bore or hone it. As you can see in Fig. 33-8, machine honing may remove most of the taper. But boring may be required to remove it all. We will get to cylinder boring in the next section.

Cylinder wear can be measured with any of the following instruments:

- Inside micrometer
- Telescope gauge and outside micrometer
- Cylinder-bore gauge, which is a special dial indicator

33-13 HONING OR BORING THE CYLINDER

There are two methods of taking metal off the cylinder wall. These are honing and boring. The hone has a series of abrasive stones that are revolved in the cylinder to grind off metal. Boring requires a boring bar, which rotates a cutting tool in the cylinder to shave off metal. Usually, the hone is used to take off small amounts of metal. The boring bar is used if the wear is severe and a lot of metal must come off the cylinder wall. Regardless of which method is used, the cylinder is finished to the proper oversize to fit the oversize piston and rings selected for it.

33-14 CLEANING THE CYLINDER

After honing or boring, the cylinder must be cleaned thoroughly. Even slight traces of grit left on the cylinder walls can cause rapid ring and piston wear. One way to clean the cylinder is to wipe down the cylinder walls with fine crocus cloth. This loosens embedded grit and knocks off any metal fuzz left by the hone or the boring bar. Next, wash down the cylinder walls with soapy water and a stiff brush or mop. Then swab them down with a cloth dampened with engine oil. The job is finished when the cloth comes away from the cylinder walls with no trace of dirt on it.

Clean out the oil and water passages to make sure all dirt and grit are removed.

NOTE

Do not try to clean the cylinder walls with gasoline or kerosene. Neither of these will remove all the grit from the cylinder walls.

33-15 REPLACING CYLINDER SLEEVES

Some engines use replaceable cylinder sleeves. By using special tools, you can usually remove these sleeves and install new ones without trouble. First, the old sleeve must be pulled out. Then a new sleeve is installed.

Cracked blocks, scored cylinders, and cylinders worn so badly that they cannot be serviced in the normal manner—all these can often be serviced by the installation of cylinder sleeves. As a first step, the cylinders are bored oversize to take the sleeves. Then the sleeves are pressed into place.

Figure 33-9 shows a technician using a pneumatic hammer to drive sleeves into place. The cylinder block has been prepared and the sleeves positioned on the cylinder block. Then the pneumatic hammer is used. The hammer uses compressed air, which operates the driving head. It hammers the sleeve down into place in the cylinder block.

The sleeve is then finished to the proper size to take a standard set of rings and a standard piston.

33-16 REPLACING THE EXPANSION CORE PLUG

One of two types of tool should be used to replace an expansion core plug (Fig. 33-10). One type is used for the cup-type plug. Another type is used for the expansion-type plug.

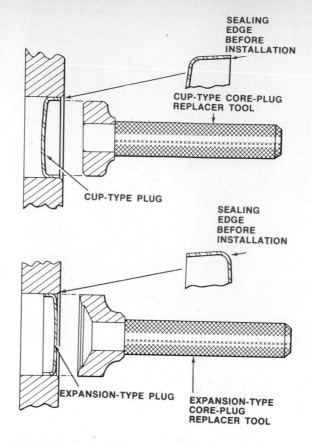

SEALING EDGE BEFORE INSTALLATION

CUP-TYPE CORE-PLUG REPLACER TOOL

CUP-TYPE PLUG

SEALING EDGE BEFORE INSTALLATION

EXPANSION-TYPE PLUG

EXPANSION-TYPE CORE-PLUG REPLACER TOOL

CHECK UP ON YOURSELF

You have completed the part of the chapter on the cylinder and the cylinder block. Answer the questions that follow to see how well you understand what you have studied.

1. Why does the cylinder wear more at the top than at the bottom?
2. What are the three measuring instruments that can be used to check cylinder walls for wear?
3. What are the two methods of servicing cylinder walls?
4. Is the cylinder finished to fit the pistons, or are pistons machined to fit the cylinder?
5. What are the two types of core plugs used in cylinder blocks?

ANSWERS

1. At the start of the power stroke, when the piston is at TDC, the compression rings are forced against the cylinder wall with the greatest pressure (Sec. 33-10). **2.** Inside micrometer, telescope gauge and outside micrometer, and dial indicator (Sec. 33-12). **3.** Honing and boring (Sec. 33-13). **4.** The cylinder is finished to fit the pistons (Sec. 33-13). **5.** Cup and expansion (Sec. 33-16).

PART SIX
AUTO TRANSMISSIONS AND POWER TRAINS

In this part of the book, we cover clutches, manual transmissions, automatic transmissions, drive lines, and differentials. We look at the mechanisms that carry engine power to the driving wheels. Most cars in the United States have the engine at the front, and the rear wheels are driven. However, many imported cars have front-wheel drive, and an increasing number of cars made in the United States are using it. Clutches are used with manual transmissions and provide a means of disconnecting the engine from the transmission when gears are shifted. The automatic transmission does not require a separate clutch. There are five chapters in Part Six:

CHAPTER THIRTY-FOUR AUTOMOTIVE CLUTCHES

After studying this chapter, you should be able to:

1. Explain the purpose, construction, and operation of clutches.
2. Discuss clutch troubles and their possible causes.

The clutch is the assembly that allows power to flow from the engine to the transmission. At one time, almost all cars had clutches. Now most cars are made with automatic transmissions and do not need clutches. However, many cars on the road today are equipped with manually shifted transmissions and clutches.

34-1 PURPOSES OF THE CLUTCH
The clutch is used on cars with transmissions that are shifted by hand. Its purpose is to allow the driver to couple the engine to or uncouple the engine from the transmission. The driver operates the clutch by foot. When the clutch is applied (in the normal running position), the power from the engine can flow through the clutch and enter the transmission. When the clutch is released by foot pressure of the driver, the engine is uncoupled from the transmission. Now, no power can flow through. It is necessary to interrupt the flow of power (to uncouple the engine) to shift gears.

34-2 LOCATION OF THE CLUTCH
The clutch is located just behind the engine, between the engine and the transmission. Figure 34-1 shows the parts of one type of clutch, detached from the engine. When the parts are assembled, the flywheel is bolted to the crankshaft. The friction disk (also called the driven plate) is installed next. It slides onto the end of the transmission shaft, which sticks through the clutch housing. The pressure-plate-and-cover assembly (usually called the pressure plate) is bolted to the flywheel. Then, the other parts are installed, as we will explain in Sec. 34-3.

34-3 CONSTRUCTION OF THE CLUTCH
There are different kinds of clutches. We start our discussion of clutch construction by looking at one of the most common types—the coil-spring clutch. This clutch has a series of coil springs set in a circle. Figures 34-2 and 34-3 show sectional and cutaway views of this clutch. The friction disk (or driven plate) is about 11 inches [275 mm] in diameter.

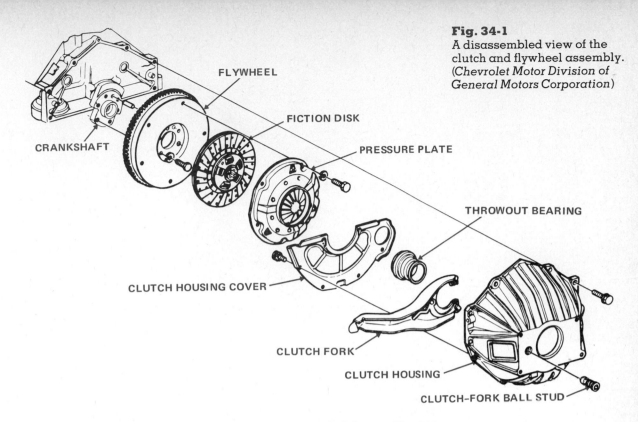

Fig. 34-1
A disassembled view of the
clutch and flywheel assembly.
(*Chevrolet Motor Division of
General Motors Corporation*)

FLYWHEEL

FICTION DISK

PRESSURE PLATE

CRANKSHAFT

THROWOUT BEARING

CLUTCH HOUSING COVER

CLUTCH FORK

CLUTCH HOUSING

CLUTCH-FORK BALL STUD

It is mounted on the transmission input shaft. The disk has splines in
its hub that match splines on the input shaft. These splines consist of
two sets of teeth. The internal teeth in the hub of the friction disk
match the external teeth on the shaft. When the friction disk is driven,
it turns the transmission input shaft.

The clutch also has a pressure plate, which includes a series of coil
springs. The pressure plate is bolted to the engine flywheel (Fig. 34-1).
The springs provide the pressure to hold the friction disk against the

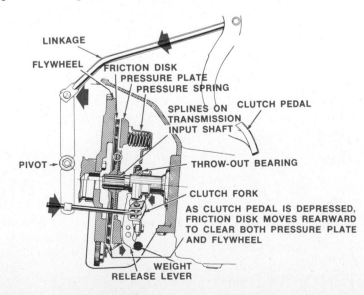

Fig. 34-2
A sectional view of a clutch,
with the linkage to the clutch
pedal. (*Buick Motor Division of
General Motors Corporation*)

LINKAGE

FLYWHEEL

FRICTION DISK
PRESSURE PLATE
PRESSURE SPRING

SPLINES ON
TRANSMISSION
INPUT SHAFT

CLUTCH PEDAL

PIVOT →

THROW-OUT BEARING

CLUTCH FORK

AS CLUTCH PEDAL IS DEPRESSED,
FRICTION DISK MOVES REARWARD
TO CLEAR BOTH PRESSURE PLATE
AND FLYWHEEL

WEIGHT
RELEASE LEVER

419

Fig. 34-3
A partial cutaway view of a
typical clutch. (*Ford Motor
Company*)

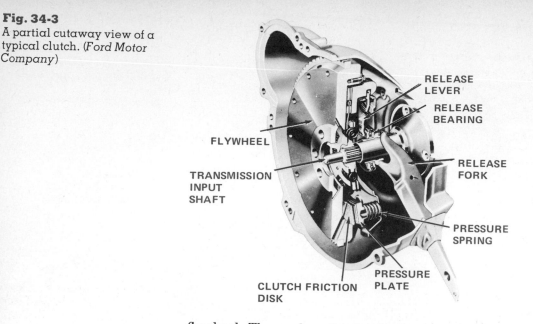

RELEASE
LEVER

RELEASE
BEARING

FLYWHEEL

TRANSMISSION
INPUT
SHAFT

RELEASE
FORK

PRESSURE
SPRING

CLUTCH FRICTION
DISK

PRESSURE
PLATE

flywheel. Then, when the flywheel turns, the pressure plate and the
friction disk also turn. However, when the clutch is released, the
spring pressure is relieved. The friction disk and the flywheel can rotate separately.

34-4 OPERATION OF THE CLUTCH

Let's look at the operation of the coil-spring clutch. Figure 34-4 shows,
at the left, a sectional view of the clutch. The major parts are shown
disassembled at the right. In this clutch, nine springs are used, although only three are shown at the right. Look at the assembled view
at the left. The springs are held between the clutch cover and the
pressure plate. In the condition shown in Fig. 34-4, the springs are
clamping the friction disk tightly between the flywheel and the

Fig. 34-4
A sectional view of the clutch
in the engaged position at the
left. Major clutch parts are
shown to the right.

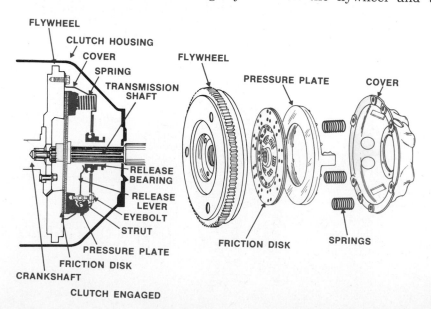

FLYWHEEL

CLUTCH HOUSING
COVER
SPRING
TRANSMISSION
SHAFT

FLYWHEEL

PRESSURE PLATE

COVER

RELEASE
BEARING

RELEASE
LEVER
EYEBOLT
STRUT

PRESSURE PLATE
FRICTION DISK
CRANKSHAFT

FRICTION DISK

SPRINGS

CLUTCH ENGAGED

pressure plate (Fig. 34-5). This forces the friction disk to rotate with the flywheel. In this position the clutch is engaged.

Now look at what happens when the driver operates the clutch pedal to disengage, or release, the clutch (Fig. 34-5). When the clutch is released, the linkage from the pedal forces the release bearing inward (to the left in Fig. 34-6). The release bearing is also called the *throwout bearing*. We will get to the linkage in Sec. 34-6. First, let's see what happens when the release bearing is forced to the left.

As the release bearing moves left, it pushes against the inner ends of three release levers. The release levers are pivoted on eyebolts, as shown in Figs. 34-2, 34-3, and 34-6. When the inner ends of the release levers are pushed in by the release bearing, the outer ends are moved to the right. This motion is carried by struts to the pressure plate (Fig. 34-7). The pressure plate moves to the right (in Fig. 34-6), and the springs are compressed. With the spring pressure off the friction disk, space appears between the disk, the flywheel, and the pressure plate. Now the clutch is released. The flywheel can rotate without sending power through the friction disk.

Releasing the clutch pedal takes the pressure off the release bearing. The springs push the pressure plate to the left (in Fig. 34-4). The friction disk is again clamped tightly between the flywheel and the pressure plate. The friction disk must again rotate with the flywheel. In this position, the clutch is engaged.

34-5 CLUTCH LINKAGE

The purpose of the clutch linkage is to carry the movement of the clutch pedal to the release bearing. A variety of clutch linkages are used. One of the simplest arrangements is shown in Fig. 34-2. Here, pushing down on the clutch pedal pushes the linkage, as shown by the arrows. This action causes the clutch fork to pivot and force the throwout bearing in (at the left in Fig. 34-2). A typical clutch fork with the throwout bearing in place is shown in Fig. 34-8. The clutch fork has a spring-held dust seal to prevent dust from entering the clutch through the fork opening in the clutch housing.

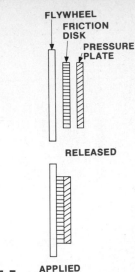

Fig. 34-5
Simplified version of a clutch, showing released and applied positions of the pressure plate and friction disk.

Fig. 34-6
A sectional view of the clutch is the disengaged, or released, position at the left. Major parts are shown to the right.

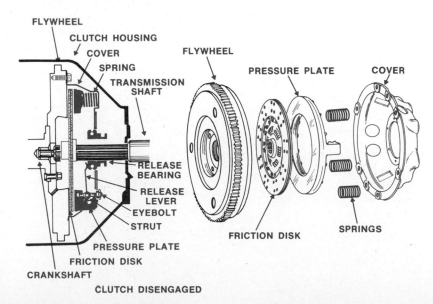

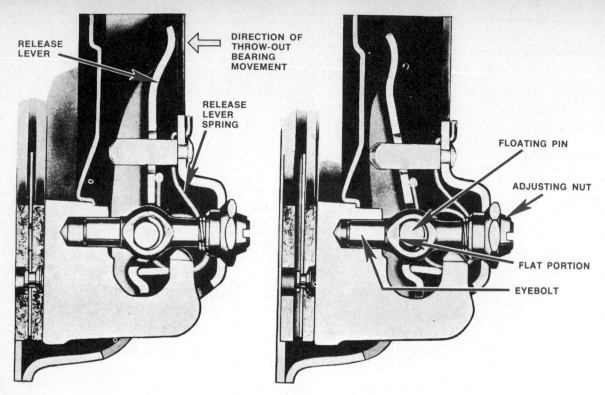

DIRECTION OF THROW-OUT BEARING MOVEMENT

RELEASE LEVER

RELEASE LEVER SPRING

FLOATING PIN

ADJUSTING NUT

FLAT PORTION

EYEBOLT

ENGAGED POSITION

RELEASED POSITION

Fig. 34-7
The two limiting positions of the pressure plate and the release level. (*Oldsmobile Division of General Motors Corporation*)

34-6 FRICTION DISK

The friction disk, or driven plate, is shown partly cut away in Fig. 34-9. It consists of a hub and a plate, with facings attached to the plate. The friction disk has cushion springs and dampening springs. The cushion springs are waved, or curled, slightly. The cushion springs are attached to the plate, and the friction facings are attached to the springs. When the clutch is engaged, the springs compress slightly to take up the shock of engagement. The dampening springs are spiral springs set in a circle around the hub. The hub is driven through these springs. They help to smooth out the power pulses from the engine so that the power flow to the transmission is smooth.

Fig. 34-8
A clutch-fork assembly with release (throwout) bearing. (*Buick Motor Division of General Motors Corporation*)

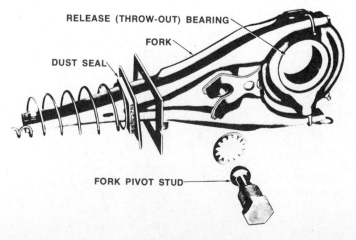

RELEASE (THROW-OUT) BEARING

FORK

DUST SEAL

FORK PIVOT STUD

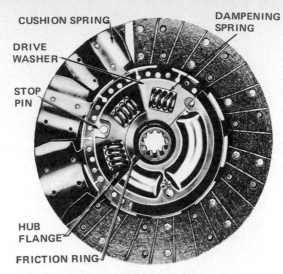

Fig. 34-9
A friction disk, or driven plate. Facings and drive washer have been cut away to show springs. (*Buick Motor Division of General Motors Corporation*)

CUSHION SPRING
DAMPENING SPRING
DRIVE WASHER
STOP PIN
HUB FLANGE
FRICTION RING

34-7 TYPES OF CLUTCHES

We have already described the nine-spring clutch and illustrated it in Figs. 34-2 to 34-7. Now let's look at other types of clutches.

A three-coil-spring clutch is shown in Fig. 34-10. It works the same way as the clutch using nine springs. There are also the diaphragm-spring clutch and the hydraulic clutch. Both are described in the following sections.

34-8 DIAPHRAGM-SPRING CLUTCH

The diaphragm-spring clutch is shown in disassembled view in Fig. 34-1. It is shown in sectional view in Fig. 34-11. The diaphragm spring is a round sheet of steel with a series of fingers pointing toward the center. You can see these fingers in the pressure-plate-and-cover assembly in Fig. 34-1. When the release bearing is forced inward against these fingers, the entire diaphragm caves inward. This action is somewhat like the flexing action of the bottom of an oil can. The movement lifts the pressure plate away from the friction disk. Figures 34-12 and 34-13 show the two positions of the diaphragm spring and the clutch parts.

34-9 HYDRAULIC CLUTCH

The hydraulic clutch is used in vehicles in which the clutch is located far from the foot pedal. Instead of trying to install a complicated link-

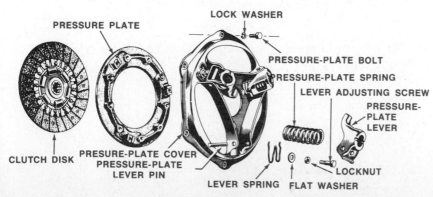

PRESSURE PLATE
LOCK WASHER
PRESSURE-PLATE BOLT
PRESSURE-PLATE SPRING
LEVER ADJUSTING SCREW
PRESSURE-PLATE LEVER
CLUTCH DISK
PRESURE-PLATE COVER
PRESSURE-PLATE LEVER PIN
LEVER SPRING
FLAT WASHER
LOCKNUT

Fig. 34-10
An exploded view of a three-spring clutch.

Fig. 34-11
A flat-finger diaphragm-spring clutch in sectional view, from the top. (*Chevrolet Motor Division of General Motors Corporation*)

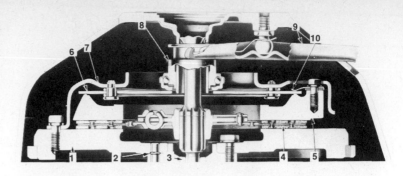

1 FLYWHEEL
2 DOWEL
3 PILOT BUSHING
4 DRIVEN DISK
5 PRESSURE PLATE

6 DIAPHRAGM SPRING
7 COVER
8 THROW-OUT BEARING
9 FORK
10 RETRACTING SPRING

age between the clutch pedal and the clutch, car manufacturers use a hydraulic system. Figure 34-14 shows a disassembled hydraulic clutch. It shows the clutch, the hydraulic cylinders, and the clutch pedal. This arrangement is also used on heavy-duty clutches, with high clutch-spring pressure. High clutch-spring pressure means high clutch-pedal pressure. To reduce this pedal pressure, the hydraulic clutch can be used.

Now let's see how the hydraulic clutch works. When the driver pushes down on the clutch pedal, a pushrod is forced down into a master cylinder. As the pushrod moves down into the master cylinder, the rod forces a piston down into the cylinder. This action puts pressure on the fluid in the cylinder. Some of the fluid is forced out. The fluid flows through a tube and into a servo cylinder at the clutch. A servo converts hydraulic pressure to mechanical movement through a piston. The fluid, flowing into the servo cylinder from the master cylinder, forces the piston in the servo cylinder to move. This movement is carried through a pushrod to the release lever, disengaging the clutch.

CHECK UP ON YOURSELF
See how well you understand what you have studied about clutches and how they work. Answer the questions below.

1. To what is the pressure-plate-and-cover assembly attached?
2. When the release levers are pushed in by the release bearing, what is happening to the outer ends of the release levers?
3. When the clutch is engaged, between which parts is the friction disk clamped?
4. Which is the simpler clutch, the diaphragm-spring type or the coil-spring type?

Fig. 34-12
A diaphragm-spring clutch in the engaged position. (*Chevrolet Motor Division of General Motors Corporation*)

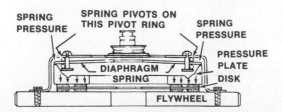

SPRING PRESSURE
SPRING PIVOTS ON THIS PIVOT RING
SPRING PRESSURE
PRESSURE PLATE
DISK
DIAPHRAGM SPRING
FLYWHEEL

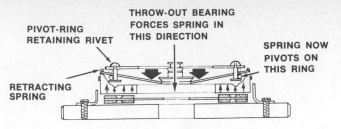

5. In the hydraulic clutch, is there direct mechanical linkage between the clutch pedal and the clutch?

ANSWERS

1. It is attached to the engine flywheel (Sec. 34-3). **2.** The outer ends are pushing struts against the pressure plate to push it away from the friction disk (Sec. 34-4). **3.** The friction disk is clamped between the flywheel and the pressure plate (Sec. 34-4). **4.** The diaphragm-spring clutch (Secs. 34-3 and 34-8). **5.** No. Hydraulic pressure does the job (Sec. 34-9).

CLUTCH TROUBLES

34-10 DIAGNOSING CLUTCH TROUBLE

When you work in the shop, you will see various kinds of clutch trouble and learn how to fix them. Usually, the kind of trouble you find tells you the cause. These troubles are the following:

1. Clutch slips while engaged.
2. Clutch chatters or grabs when engaging.
3. Clutch spins or drags when disengaged.
4. Clutch is noisy when engaged.
5. Clutch is noisy when disengaged.
6. Clutch pedal pulsates.
7. Friction-disk facings wear rapidly.
8. Clutch pedal is stiff.

If the trouble is in the clutch itself, most manufacturers recommend replacing at least the pressure plate and friction disk. In past years, shop manuals carried instructions for disassembly and repair of the clutch. Now let's discuss the different clutch troubles listed above.

34-11 CLUTCH SLIPS WHILE ENGAGED

Slippage while the clutch is engaged could be caused by an incorrect linkage adjustment. That could prevent full spring pressure on the pressure plate and the friction disk. The remedy is readjustment of the linkage. Slippage while the clutch is engaged could also be caused by worn friction-disk facings or weakening of the springs in the pressure plate.

34-12 CLUTCH CHATTERS OR GRABS WHEN ENGAGING

Chattering and grabbing of the clutch are usually due to oil on the facings of the friction disk. Loose facings on the friction disk, heat cracks in the face of the flywheel or pressure plate, broken clutch parts, or binding of the linkage could also cause chattering and grabbing of the clutch.

34-13 CLUTCH SPINS OR DRAGS WHEN DISENGAGED

If the clutch spins or drags when disengaged, the linkage may be out of adjustment. Or, the trouble could be due to internal clutch trouble,

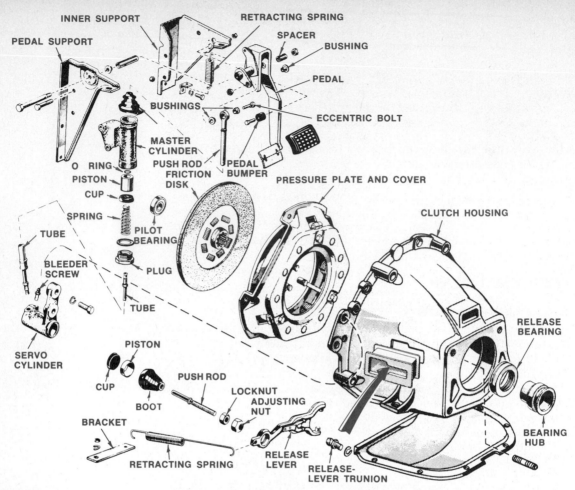

INNER SUPPORT
PEDAL SUPPORT
RETRACTING SPRING
SPACER
BUSHING
PEDAL
BUSHINGS
MASTER CYLINDER
ECCENTRIC BOLT
O RING
PISTON
CUP
PUSH ROD
FRICTION DISK
PEDAL BUMPER
PRESSURE PLATE AND COVER
SPRING
TUBE
BLEEDER SCREW
PILOT BEARING
PLUG
TUBE
CLUTCH HOUSING
SERVO CYLINDER
PISTON
CUP
BOOT
PUSH ROD
LOCKNUT
ADJUSTING NUT
RELEASE BEARING
BRACKET
RETRACTING SPRING
RELEASE LEVER
RELEASE-LEVER TRUNION
BEARING HUB

Fig. 34-14
A disassembled view of a hydraulically operated clutch.

such as lining torn or loose from the friction disk, a warped friction disk or pressure plate, improper clutch adjustment, or binding of the friction-disk hub on the transmission input shaft.

34-14 CLUTCH IS NOISY WHEN ENGAGED
If the clutch is noisy when engaged, the friction disk has broken dampener springs, the disk hub is loose on the transmission input shaft, or there are broken parts in the pressure plate. Also, the transmission might be out of line with the engine.

34-15 CLUTCH IS NOISY WHEN DISENGAGED
If the clutch is noisy when disengaged, the cause probably is a worn or dry clutch release bearing. In this case, the bearing makes a grinding or squealing noise when it goes into action. The pilot bushing in the end of the crankshaft could be worn or in need of lubricant. Also, the release levers could be out of adjustment. In the diaphragm-spring clutch, worn retracting springs can produce noise.

34-16 CLUTCH PEDAL PULSATES
Clutch-pedal pulsations can be felt when light pressure is applied to the clutch pedal. There are several possible causes. The engine and

transmission might not be aligned, the pressure plate or friction disk might be warped or misaligned, or the release levers might be out of adjustment.

34-17 FRICTION-DISK FACINGS WEAR RAPIDLY
Rapid wear of the friction-disk facings will result if the driver "rides" the clutch pedal, by resting a foot on the pedal. This partly releases the clutch, causing clutch slippage and rapid friction-disk wear. Incorrect linkage adjustment or misalignment of internal parts also produces excessive wear of the friction-disk facings.

34-18 CLUTCH PEDAL IS STIFF
A stiff clutch pedal, or a pedal that is hard to press down, probably is due to a misaligned or binding clutch linkage. A stiff clutch pedal can also be caused by a lack of lubricant in the clutch linkage.

34-19 SERVICING THE CLUTCH
Internal clutch troubles call for complete clutch replacement. However, if the trouble is in the linkage—if it is binding or out of adjustment, or if the pedal free play is wrong—the linkage can be lubricated and readjusted. "Free play" is the amount of free clutch-pedal travel before the clutch begins to disengage. On the hydraulic clutch, the level of the fluid in the master-cylinder reservoir should be checked periodically and fluid added if necessary. Refer to the manufacturer's shop manual for details.

CHECK UP ON YOURSELF
See what you understand about the troubles that clutches can have. Try to answer the questions below.

1. What are the eight possible troubles a clutch can have?
2. What are some causes of noise when the clutch is engaged?
3. What are some causes of noise when the clutch is disengaged?
4. What kind of trouble can be caused by riding the clutch pedal?
5. What should be done if the linkage is binding or out of adjustment?

ANSWERS
1. See Sec. 34-10, which lists the eight possible troubles. 2. Broken damper springs on the friction disk, loose disk hub on the transmission input shaft, and misaligned transmission (Sec. 34-14). 3. Worn or dry release bearing, worn pilot bushing at the end of the crankshaft, or pilot bushing in need of lubricant (Sec. 34-15). 4. Clutch slippage and rapid friction-disk wear (Sec. 34-17). 5. It should be lubricated and readjusted (Sec. 34-19).

CHAPTER THIRTY-FIVE
MANUAL TRANSMISSIONS

After studying this chapter, you should be able to:

1. Explain the purpose, construction, and operation of manual transmissions, including how shifts are made and how synchronizers work.
2. Explain what overdrive is and how it is achieved in the transmission.
3. Discuss transmission troubles and possible causes of each.

Manual transmissions are transmissions that are shifted by hand. A car needs some sort of transmission. The engine should be turning fairly fast and producing considerable power to start the car moving. The engine must be turning fast while the car wheels are turning slowly. Later, when the car is out on the highway, the engine is turning fast and the wheels also are turning fast. The transmission takes care of this changing gear or speed ratio, as we will explain. In a manual transmission, the driver selects the gear ratio by hand. Most cars now are equipped with automatic transmissions. These transmissions shift gears automatically. We describe automatic transmissions in Chap. 36.

35-1 GEARS

Before we get into transmissions, let's look at gears. There are many types of gears used on the automobile. All are basically similar. They all have teeth of one sort or another that mesh to carry motion from one gear to another. The simplest gear is the spur gear (Fig. 35-1). It is like a wheel with teeth. Two spur gears are shown meshed in Fig. 35-2. By "meshed" we mean that the teeth of one gear are fitted into the teeth of the other gear. When one gear rotates, the other gear also rotates. The smaller gear often is called the *pinion* gear.

The sizes of the two gears determine the relative speed with which they turn. The big gear turns more slowly than the small gear. But the smaller gear has greater turning force. This turning force is called *torque*. When speed is lost through gears, torque is gained.

For example, suppose the car is in first gear and the engine crankshaft is turning ten times to make the car wheels turn once. This gear

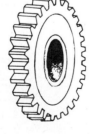

Fig. 35-1
A spur gear.

428

reduction is achieved both in the transmission and at the rear axle, in the differential (the driving mechanism at the rear wheels). We explain the differential in Chap. 38. With the 10:1 gear reduction, there is a great increase in torque. The driven gear turns at one-tenth the speed of the driving gear, but the driven gear delivers 10 times more torque. This increase in torque gives the car the ability to accelerate rapidly.

Figure 35-3 shows two meshing spur gears, one with 12 teeth and the other with 24. The larger gear turns only half as fast as the smaller gear. In other words, while the large gear is making one complete revolution, the smaller gear is making two revolutions. If the larger gear is driving the smaller gear, there is a speed increase. There is also a torque reduction. The smaller gear turns faster, but it has less torque. If the smaller gear is driving the larger gear, there is a speed reduction but a torque increase. Let's see how these characteristics of gears are used in transmissions.

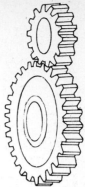

Fig. 35-2
Two spur gears with their teeth meshed.

NOTE

Gears used in transmissions are not plain spur gears with straight teeth. Transmission gears have teeth that are twisted, as shown in Fig. 35-4. These are called *helical* gears. They run more quietly than spur gears and distribute the torque load over a larger area of each tooth.

35-2 FUNCTION OF THE TRANSMISSION

The simplest manual transmission used on passenger cars has three forward-gear ratios between the engine and the car wheels. The crankshaft must revolve about 12, 8, or 4 times to turn the car wheels once.

In first gear, the crankshaft turns about 12 times for each car-wheel rotation. This ratio increases the engine torque enough to get the car moving. Then, in second gear, the crankshaft turns about 8 times to turn the car wheels once. After the car is moving, less torque is needed for acceleration. In second gear the engine turns fast enough to produce a car speed of up to about 30 mph [48 km/h].

In third or high gear, the engine crankshaft turns about 4 times to turn the car wheels once. While the car is in motion and in third gear, normally it is not necessary to shift to lower gears. However, if additional torque is required, as when climbing a steep hill, the transmission can be shifted to a lower gear to get the higher torque.

35-3 TYPES OF MANUAL TRANSMISSIONS

Today, many cars with manual transmissions are equipped with four-speed transmissions instead of three-speed. For example, during one year about 7 percent of Ford Motor Company cars were equipped with four-speed transmissions. About 1 percent were equipped with three-speed transmissions. The other 92 percent had automatic transmissions.

Some cars have five-speed transmissions. These transmissions have a fifth forward speed, which actually is an overdrive. We describe all these transmissions in following sections.

35-4 A SIMPLIFIED TRANSMISSION

We now describe how the transmission works, using a simplified version of a three-speed transmission shown in Fig. 35-4. The simplified transmission is shown in Fig. 35-5. It has three shafts and eight spur

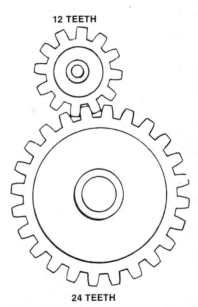

12 TEETH

24 TEETH

Fig. 35-3
Two meshing spur gears of different sizes.

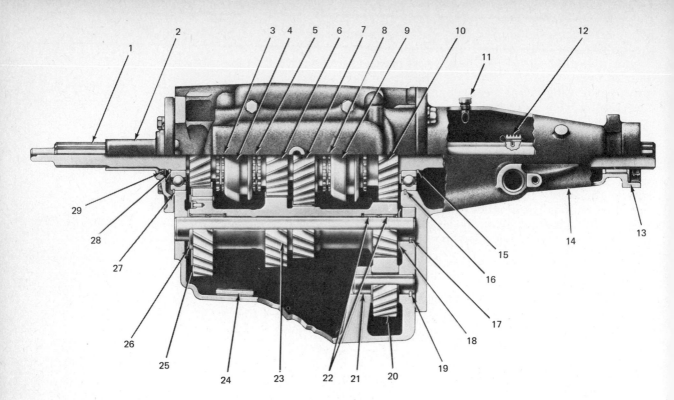

Fig. 35-4
Sectional view of a three-speed transmission. (*Chevrolet Motor Division of General Motors Corporation*)

1. CLUTCH GEAR
2. CLUTCH GEAR BEARING RETAINER
3. 3RD SPEED SYNCHRONIZER RING
4. 2ND-3RD SPEED CLUTCH ASSY.
5. 2ND SPEED SYNCHRONIZER RING
6. 2ND SPEED GEAR
7. 1ST SPEED GEAR
8. 1ST SPEED SYNCHRONIZER RING
9. 1ST—REVERSE CLUTCH ASSY.
10. REVERSE GEAR

11. VENT
12. SPEEDOMETER GEAR AND CLIP
13. REAR EXTENSION SEAL
14. REAR EXTENSION
15. REAR BEARING-TO-SHAFT SNAP RING
16. REAR BEARING-TO-EXTENSION SNAP RING
17. COUNTERGEAR WOODRUFF KEY
18. THRUST WASHER
19. REVERSE IDLER SHAFT WOODRUFF KEY
20. REVERSE IDLER GEAR

21. REVERSE IDLER SHAFT
22. COUNTERGEAR BEARINGS
23. COUNTERGEAR
24. CASE MAGNET
25. ANTI-LASH PLATE ASSY.
26. THRUST WASHER
27. CLUTCH GEAR BEARING
28. SNAP RING
29. CLUTCH GEAR RETAINER LIP SEAL

gears of varying sizes. The transmission housing and bearings are not shown. Four of the gears are rigidly connected to the countershaft. These are the driven gear, second-speed gear, first-speed gear, and reverse gear. When the clutch is engaged and the engine is running, the clutch-shaft gear drives the countershaft driven gear. This turns the countershaft and the other gears on the countershaft. The countershaft rotates in a direction opposite, or counter, to the rotation of the clutch-shaft gear. With the gears in neutral, as shown in Fig. 35-5, and the car stationary, the transmission main shaft is not turning.

The transmission main shaft is mechanically connected by shafts and gears in the rear axle to the car wheels. The two gears on the transmission main shaft may be shifted back and forth along the splines on the shaft. This is done by operating the gearshift lever in the driving compartment. The splines are matching internal and external teeth that permit endwise (axial) movement of the gears but cause the gears and shaft to rotate together. Note that a floor-type shift lever is shown in the illustrations. This type of lever illustrates more clearly the lever action in shifting gears. The transmission action is the same, regardless of whether a floor-type shift lever or a steering-column shift lever is used.

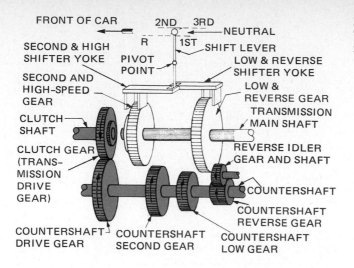

FRONT OF CAR

SECOND & HIGH SHIFTER YOKE

SECOND AND HIGH-SPEED GEAR

CLUTCH SHAFT

CLUTCH GEAR (TRANSMISSION DRIVE GEAR)

COUNTERSHAFT DRIVE GEAR

2ND   3RD

R   1ST

NEUTRAL

SHIFT LEVER

PIVOT POINT

LOW & REVERSE SHIFTER YOKE

LOW & REVERSE GEAR

TRANSMISSION MAIN SHAFT

REVERSE IDLER GEAR AND SHAFT

COUNTERSHAFT

COUNTERSHAFT REVERSE GEAR

COUNTERSHAFT SECOND GEAR

COUNTERSHAFT LOW GEAR

Fig. 35-5
Transmission with gears in neutral.

35-5 SHIFTING INTO FIRST

Suppose the gearshift lever is operated to place the gears in *first* (Fig. 35-6). The large gear on the transmission main shaft is moved along the shaft until it meshes with the small gear on the countershaft. The clutch is disengaged for this operation, so that the clutch shaft and the countershaft stop rotating. When the clutch is again engaged, the transmission main shaft rotates, as the driving gear on the clutch shaft drives it through the countershaft. The countershaft is turning more slowly than the clutch shaft, and the small countershaft gear is engaged with the large transmission mainshaft gear. A gear reduction of approximately 3:1 is achieved. That is, the clutch shaft turns three times for each revolution of the transmission main shaft. There is further gear reduction in the differential at the rear wheels. This produces a still higher gear ratio (approximately 12:1) between the engine crankshaft and the wheels.

NOTE

The actual gear ratio varies in different transmissions. A typical gear ratio for a transmission used in some General Motors cars is 2.58:1. The clutch gear (and engine crankshaft) turns 2.58 times to turn the main shaft of the transmission once.

35-6 SHIFTING INTO SECOND

Now suppose the clutch is operated and the gearshift lever is moved to *second* (Fig. 35-7). The large gear on the transmission main shaft demeshes from the small first-speed countershaft gear. The smaller transmission main-shaft gear is slid into mesh with the large second-speed countershaft gear. This provides a somewhat reduced gear ratio, so that the engine crankshaft turns only about twice when the transmission main shaft turns once. The differential gear reduction increases this gear ratio to approximately 8:1.

35-7 SHIFTING INTO THIRD

When the gears are shifted into *third* (Fig. 35-8), the two gears on the transmission main shaft are demeshed from the countershaft gears. Also, the second-and-third-speed gear is forced axially against the

431

Fig. 35-6
Transmission with gears in
first.

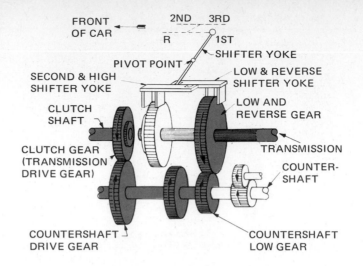

FRONT OF CAR

2ND 3RD

R 1ST

SHIFTER YOKE

PIVOT POINT

SECOND & HIGH SHIFTER YOKE

LOW & REVERSE SHIFTER YOKE

CLUTCH SHAFT

LOW AND REVERSE GEAR

CLUTCH GEAR (TRANSMISSION DRIVE GEAR)

TRANSMISSION

COUNTER-SHAFT

COUNTERSHAFT DRIVE GEAR

COUNTERSHAFT LOW GEAR

clutch-shaft gear. External teeth on the clutch-shaft gear mesh with
internal teeth in the second-and-third-speed gear. Then the transmission main shaft turns with the clutch shaft. A ratio of 1:1 is obtained.
The differential reduction produces a gear ratio of about 4:1 between
the engine crankshaft and the wheels.

35-8 SHIFTING INTO REVERSE

When the gears are placed in *reverse* (Fig. 35-9), the larger of the transmission main-shaft gears is meshed with the reverse idler gear. This
reverse idler gear is always in mesh with the small reverse gear on the
end of the countershaft. Putting the idler gear between the countershaft reverse gear and the transmission main-shaft gear causes the
transmission shaft to rotate in the opposite direction. That is, it rotates
in the same direction as the countershaft. This reverses the rotation of
the wheels, so that the car backs.

The description above outlines the basic operation of all transmissions. However, more complex transmissions are used on modern cars.
These include helical gears and synchromesh devices that synchronize

Fig. 35-7
Transmission with gears in
second.

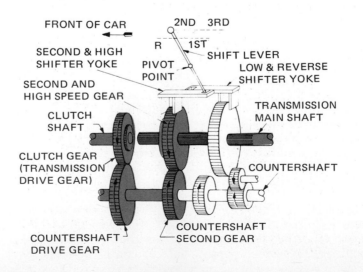

FRONT OF CAR

2ND 3RD

R 1ST

SECOND & HIGH SHIFTER YOKE

PIVOT POINT

SHIFT LEVER

LOW & REVERSE SHIFTER YOKE

SECOND AND HIGH SPEED GEAR

CLUTCH SHAFT

TRANSMISSION MAIN SHAFT

CLUTCH GEAR (TRANSMISSION DRIVE GEAR)

COUNTERSHAFT

COUNTERSHAFT DRIVE GEAR

COUNTERSHAFT SECOND GEAR

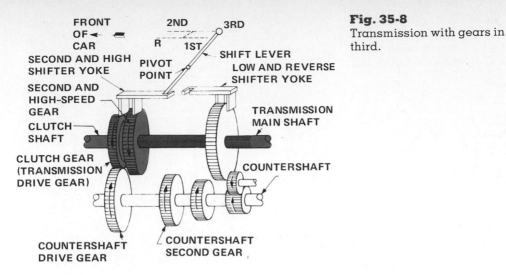

Fig. 35-8
Transmission with gears in third.

the rotation of gears that are about to be meshed. This eliminates clashing of the gears and makes gear-shifting easier.

NOTE
Shifts are made with the clutch disengaged so that no power is flowing into the transmission. This makes shifting and meshing of the gears much easier.

CHECK UP ON YOURSELF

You need to know about manual transmissions to be a general automotive mechanic. Answer the following questions to review what you have studied.

1. One gear with 10 teeth is meshed with a gear with 30 teeth. Which gear will rotate faster, and how much faster will it turn?
2. If a small gear drives a big gear, is torque increased or decreased?
3. What are the two things that the gearshift lever does when it is moved?
4. In the simplified gear system, shown in Fig. 35-6, with which gear is the main drive gear, or clutch gear, meshed?

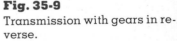

Fig. 35-9
Transmission with gears in reverse.

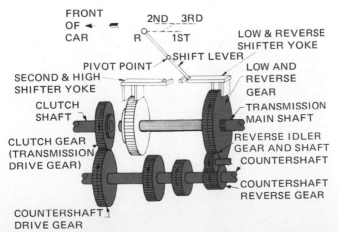

SYNCHRONIZER
RING

SYNCHRONIZER
SLEEVE

EXTERNAL
TEETH

KEYS

SYNCHRONIZER
RING SPRING

INTERNAL
TEETH

EXTERNAL
SPLINES

5. What is the clutch sleeve mounted on?

ANSWERS
1. The gear with 10 teeth will turn three times as fast as the gear with 30 teeth (Sec. 35-1). **2.** Torque is increased but speed is reduced (Sec. 35-1). **3.** It selects the gear to be moved; then it moves the gear into the desired gear position (Sec. 35-4). **4.** The countershaft driven gear (Sec. 35-5). **5.** The main shaft (Sec. 35-5).

35-9 SYNCHRONIZERS
Whenever the car is moving and in gear, the clutch gear is spinning and the main shaft is turning. When the clutch is disengaged, the clutch gear continues to spin until friction slows it down and stops it. When shifting into second or third, the driver tries to mesh gears that may be moving at different speeds. To avoid broken or damaged teeth and to make shifting easy, synchronizing devices (Fig. 35-10) are used in transmissions. Synchronizers make the gears rotate at the same speed when they are about to mesh.

One type of synchronizer, shown in sectional view in Fig. 35-11, has a pair of synchronizing cones. One is an outside cone on the gear, and the other is an inside cone on the sliding sleeve. The sliding sleeve has splines that engage the splines on the gear to produce meshing. The picture at the left, labeled "neutral position," shows the general construction of the synchronizing device. The picture at the upper right shows what happens at the moment the drum, or sliding clutch sleeve, touches the gear. That is the moment when the two cones come into contact.

When contact is made, the gear and the drum are brought into synchronization. This means that they revolve at the same speed. Now, further movement of the shift lever moves the sliding sleeve into mesh with the gear. The splines on the sliding sleeve and the splines on the gear engage, as shown at the lower right. Lockup is completed. When the clutch is engaged, power can flow through the sliding sleeve and the gear.

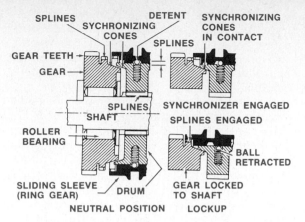

Fig. 35-11
The operation of a transmission synchronizer using cones.

There are other kinds of synchronizing devices (see Fig. 35-10). But they all work in the same general manner. Whenever two gears are about to be meshed, the synchronizer brings them into synchronization. The teeth, or splines, that are about to engage are moving at the same speed, so no clash can occur.

35-10 THREE-SPEED FULLY SYNCHRONIZED TRANSMISSION

The three-speed, fully synchronized transmission is similar to the transmission shown in Fig. 35-4. The difference is that there is full synchronization in reverse as well as in the forward gears. Figure 35-12 shows the gears in the fully synchronized transmission in neutral and in the various gear positions. The fully synchronized transmission has another sliding clutch sleeve for the first-and-reverse gear positions. Study Fig. 35-12 to trace the power flow through the transmission in the four gear positions. The sliding clutch sleeve is called a *synchronizer assembly* in this picture.

35-11 FOUR-SPEED TRANSMISSION

The additional forward speed in the four-speed transmission gives the car more flexibility. A popular arrangement is a four-speed transmission with a floor-mounted shift lever. The combination is called "four on the floor." Figures 35-13 and 35-14 show the gears in a four-speed transmission in neutral. Study these pictures to understand how each forward gear is selected by moving a synchronizer.

35-12 FOUR-SPEED TRANSMISSION WITH OVERDRIVE

This transmission is shown in cutaway view in Fig. 35-15. In third gear, the ratio through the transmission is 1:1. This means the input and output shafts turn at the same speed. However, in fourth, the output shaft turns faster than the input shaft. That is, the output shaft "overdrives" the input shaft. By shifting into overdrive, the engine speed is reduced while the car speed is maintained. This means less engine wear and lower fuel consumption.

35-13 FIVE-SPEED TRANSMISSION WITH OVERDRIVE

The five-speed transmission provides five forward speeds. The fifth speed is overdrive.

35-14 GEARSHIFT LEVERS AND LINKAGES

Gearshift levers for transmissions are located either on the steering column or on the floor. Figure 35-16 shows the shifting patterns for the two locations. Figure 35-17 shows the shift pattern for a floor-mounted shift lever for a four-speed transmission. Let's take a closer look at the column shift.

To shift into first, the driver pushes down on the clutch pedal to disconnect the transmission momentarily from the engine. Then the driver lifts the shift lever and moves it back for first gear. When the lever is lifted, it pivots on its mounting pin and pushes down on the linkage rod in the steering column. This downward movement pushes the crossover blade at the bottom of the steering column. You can see this crossover blade in Fig. 35-18. When the crossover blade is pushed down, a slot in the blade engages a pin in the first-and-reverse shift lever (see Fig. 35-18). Now, when the shift lever is moved into first, the first-and-reverse lever is rotated.

To see what happens next, look at Fig. 35-19. The movement of the first-and-reverse lever on the steering column is carried to the transmission by a linkage rod. The first-and-reverse lever on the transmission is rotated. This moves the first-and-reverse shift fork inside the

Fig. 35-12
Positions of synchronizer assemblies and power flow through a three-speed, fully synchronized transmission.

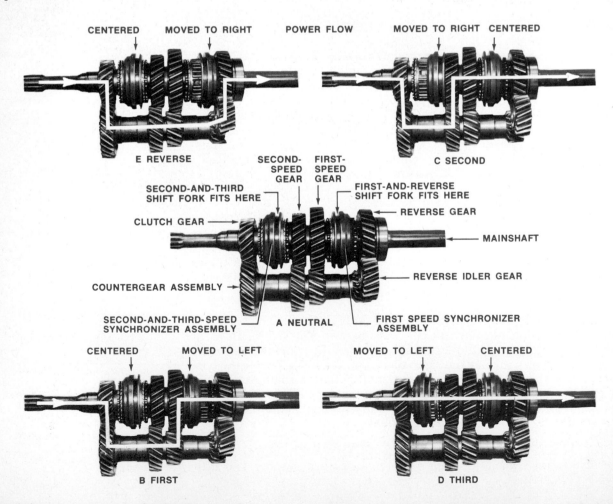

transmission so that the first-and-reverse gear, or synchronizing drum, is moved. Figure 35-20 shows the first-and-reverse shift fork and the second-and-third shift fork.

If the shift is being made into second or third, the second-and-third shift lever at the bottom of the steering column is moved. This motion moves the second-and-third lever on the transmission. The second-and-third shift fork then moves the sliding clutch sleeve, or synchronizing drum, to shift into second or high.

Study Figs. 35-16, 35-18, and 35-19 to see how the linkage works. There are various kinds and arrangements of linkages in different cars. A typical floor-mounted gearshift linkage is shown in Fig. 35-21.

Fig. 35-13
Sectional view of a four-speed transmission. (*Chevrolet Motor Division of General Motors Corporation*)

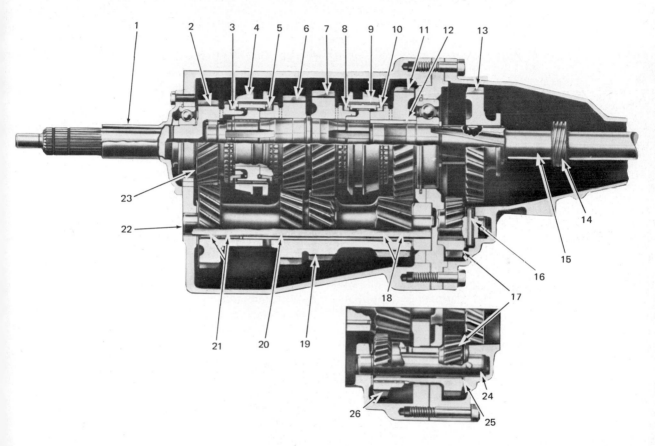

1. BEARING RETAINER	9. FIRST-AND-SECOND-SPEED CLUTCH ASSEMBLY	17. REVERSE IDLER GEAR (REAR)
2. MAIN DRIVE GEAR	10. FIRST-SPEED SYNCHRONIZING RING	18. COUNTERGEAR BEARING ROLLER
3. FOURTH-SPEED SYNCHRONIZING RING	11. FIRST-SPEED GEAR	19. COUNTERGEAR
4. THIRD-AND-FOURTH-SPEED CLUTCH ASSEMBLY	12. FIRST-SPEED GEAR SLEEVE	20. COUNTERSHAFT BEARING ROLLER SPACER
5. THIRD-SPEED SYNCHRONIZING RING	13. REVERSE GEAR	21. COUNTERSHAFT BEARING ROLLER
6. THIRD-SPEED GEAR	14. SPEEDOMETER DRIVE GEAR	22. COUNTERGEAR SHAFT
7. SECOND-SPEED GEAR	15. MAINSHAFT	23. OIL SLINGER
8. SECOND-SPEED SYNCHRONIZING RING	16. REVERSE IDLER SHAFT ROLL PIN	24. REVERSE IDLER SHAFT
		25. THRUST WASHER
		26. REVERSE IDLER GEAR (FRONT)

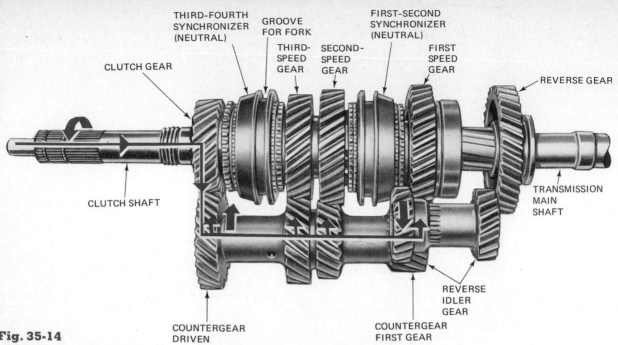

THIRD-FOURTH
SYNCHRONIZER
(NEUTRAL)

GROOVE
FOR FORK

THIRD-
SPEED
GEAR

SECOND-
SPEED
GEAR

FIRST-SECOND
SYNCHRONIZER
(NEUTRAL)

FIRST
SPEED
GEAR

CLUTCH GEAR

REVERSE GEAR

CLUTCH SHAFT

TRANSMISSION
MAIN
SHAFT

COUNTERGEAR
DRIVEN

REVERSE
IDLER
GEAR

COUNTERGEAR
FIRST GEAR

Fig. 35-14
Gear train and shafts of a four-
speed transmission. (*Chevrolet
Motor Division of General
Motors Corporation*)

MANUAL-TRANSMISSION TROUBLES

35-15 DIAGNOSING TRANSMISSION TROUBLE

The type of trouble a transmission has is often a clue to the cause of the
trouble. The first step in any transmission service job is to find the
cause of trouble. We list the various troubles below. Then, in following
sections, we list possible causes of the various troubles. Internal transmission troubles are fixed by disassembling the transmission. Or the
old transmission can be replaced by a new or rebuilt unit. Many shops
prefer to handle transmission service by replacing the complete unit. A
list of the possible transmission troubles follows.

1. Hard shifting into gear.
2. Transmission sticks in gear.

Fig. 35-15
First-speed gear. (*Chevrolet
Motor Division of General
Motors Corporation*)

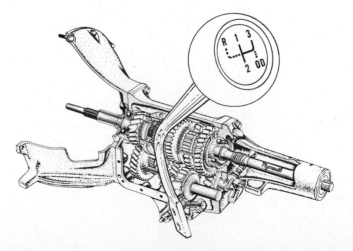

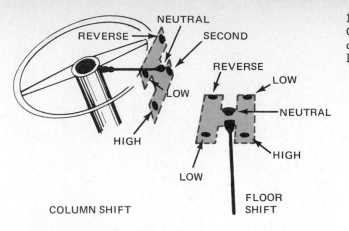

Fig. 35-16
Gearshift patterns for steering-column and floorboard shift levers.

NEUTRAL

REVERSE

SECOND

REVERSE

LOW

LOW

NEUTRAL

LOW

HIGH

HIGH

LOW

COLUMN SHIFT

FLOOR SHIFT

3. Transmission slips out of first or reverse.
4. Transmission slips out of second.
5. Transmission slips out of third.
6. No power through the transmission.
7. Transmission is noisy in neutral.
8. Transmission is noisy in gear.
9. Gears clash in shifting.
10. Oil leaks.

If the trouble is in the linkage, then the linkage should be lubricated and adjusted, as explained in the manufacturer's service manual. If the trouble is internal, then either disassemble the transmission for service or replace it with a new or rebuilt unit.

35-16 HARD SHIFTING INTO GEAR

If shifting into gear is hard, the reason may be that the clutch is not releasing. The clutch may need adjustment. Another possible cause of this trouble is a gearshift linkage that is out of adjustment or in need of oiling. The shifter fork inside the transmission might be bent. If so, it should be replaced. Also, the sliding gear or drum might be tight on the shaft splines, or the synchronizing unit might be damaged.

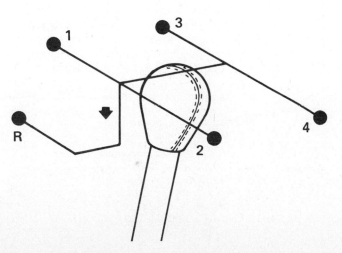

Fig. 35-17
Gearshift pattern on transmission with four forward speeds and reverse. The gearshift lever must be pressed down before it is moved into reverse. (*American Motors Corporation*)

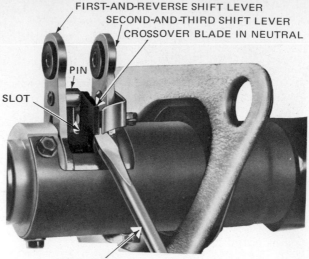

FIRST-AND-REVERSE SHIFT LEVER
SECOND-AND-THIRD SHIFT LEVER
CROSSOVER BLADE IN NEUTRAL
PIN
SLOT
SCREWDRIVER

35-17 TRANSMISSION STICKS IN GEAR

If the transmission sticks in gear, the clutch may not be releasing and may need adjustment. The gearshift linkage may need adjustment or oiling. Internal trouble, such as the gear or drum frozen on the shaft, may also be the cause.

35-18 TRANSMISSION SLIPS OUT OF FIRST OR REVERSE

If the transmission slips out of first or reverse, the gearshift linkage may be out of adjustment. Other possible causes of this trouble are gear or drum loose on the shaft, worn gear teeth, too much end play of the gears, and worn bearings.

35-19 TRANSMISSION SLIPS OUT OF SECOND

The transmission may slip out of second if the gearshift linkage is out of adjustment. This trouble may also be caused by a loose gear or drum on the main shaft or by too much shaft end play. The gear teeth may be worn.

35-20 TRANSMISSION SLIPS OUT OF THIRD

The transmission may slip out of third if the gearshift linkage is out of adjustment. The engine and transmission may be misaligned. Other causes of this trouble are too much main shaft end play, worn gear teeth, and worn bearings or synchronizing unit.

Fig. 35-19

The gearshift linkage between the shift levers at the bottom of the steering column and the transmission lever on the side of the transmission. (*Chrysler Corporation*)

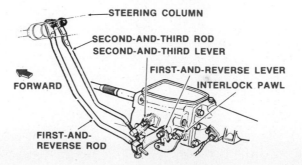

STEERING COLUMN
SECOND-AND-THIRD ROD
SECOND-AND-THIRD LEVER
FIRST-AND-REVERSE LEVER
INTERLOCK PAWL
FORWARD
FIRST-AND-REVERSE ROD

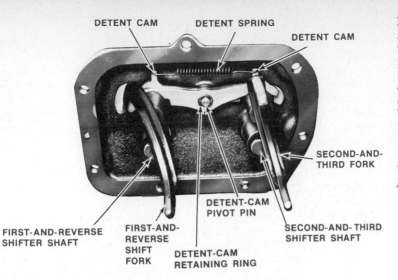

DETENT CAM   DETENT SPRING
DETENT CAM

SECOND-AND-
THIRD FORK

DETENT-CAM
PIVOT PIN

FIRST-AND-REVERSE
SHIFTER SHAFT

FIRST-AND-
REVERSE
SHIFT
FORK

DETENT-CAM
RETAINING RING

SECOND-AND-THIRD
SHIFTER SHAFT

Fig. 35-20
A transmission side cover, viewed from inside the transmission. The shift forks are mounted on the ends of levers attached to shafts. The shafts can rotate in the side cover. The detent cams and springs prevent more than one of the shift forks from moving at any one time. (*Chevrolet Motor Division of General Motors Corporation*)

35-21 NO POWER THROUGH THE TRANSMISSION

There may be no power through the transmission if the clutch is slipping. The clutch may require adjustment. If it has internal defects, it may need replacement. If there is damage such as broken gear teeth, shifter fork, gear, or shaft, there may be no power through the transmission.

35-22 TRANSMISSION IS NOISY IN NEUTRAL

Noise from a transmission in neutral is probably caused by a worn or dry clutch-shaft bearing, worn or dry countershaft bearings, worn gears, or too much shaft end play.

35-23 TRANSMISSION IS NOISY IN GEAR

Clutch defects, which require clutch replacement, may cause noise that seems to come from the transmission. Causes of noise in the transmission when it is in gear are worn, chipped, or broken gears and synchronizers; worn bearings; and lack of lubricant. The trouble also may be caused by some of the same conditions that make the transmission noisy in neutral.

35-24 GEARS CLASH IN SHIFTING

If the gears clash in shifting, the probable cause is a synchronizer defect. The trouble could also be due to gears sticking on the shaft or failure of the clutch to release.

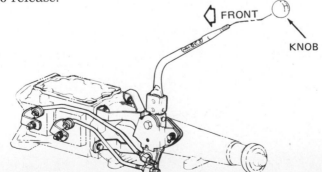

FRONT

KNOB

Fig. 35-21
The gearshift linkage arrangement of a transmission with a floor-mounted shift lever. (*Pontiac Motor Division of General Motors Corporation*)

441

35-25 OIL LEAKS

Oil will leak from the transmission when the drain plug is loose, the side-cover gasket is damaged or loose, the side-cover bolts are loose, or the shift-lever seals in the side cover are damaged. Leakage at the rear of the transmission is caused by wear of the transmission rear seal or the drive line yoke. Oil will leak from the transmission because of foaming resulting from the use of improper lubricant or overfilling. Loose transmission-bearing retainer bolts and a cracked transmission case are other causes.

35-26 SERVICING THE MANUAL TRANSMISSION

Transmission troubles can be repaired in two ways. These are disassembling the transmission and replacing defective parts or replacing the old transmission with a new or rebuilt unit. If the problem is in the linkages between the shift lever and the transmission, it can usually be fixed with a linkage adjustment. You should have the manufacturer's service manual for the specific model of car you are working on. Different linkage arrangements and different adjustment procedures are required for different cars.

CHECK UP ON YOURSELF

Review the last few pages you have been studying by answering the following questions.

1. What is the name of the device that allows gears to be shifted without gear clash?
2. In the synchronizer described in the chapter, what are the two parts that come together first when a shift is made?
3. At what two places are gearshift levers located?
4. What does "four on the floor" mean?
5. What does "overdrive" mean?
6. What are the eight possible transmission troubles listed in the chapter?
7. What are the two ways of handling trouble inside a transmission?

ANSWERS

1. The synchronizer (sec. 35-9). **2.** The synchronizing cones (Sec. 35-9). **3.** On the steering column or on the floor (Sec. 35-14). **4.** A four-speed transmission with a floor-mounted shift lever (Sec. 35-11). **5.** The transmission output shaft turns faster than the input shaft (Sec. 35-12). **6.** Refer to Sec. 35-15 for the list. **7.** Either disassemble the transmission to fix the trouble or replace the old transmission with a new or rebuilt unit (Secs. 35-15 and 35-26).

CHAPTER THIRTY-SIX
AUTOMATIC TRANSMISSIONS

After studying this chapter, you should be able to:

1. Describe the purpose, construction, and operation of a torque converter.
2. Discuss planetary-gear construction and operation.
3. Discuss the hydraulic control system in an automatic transmission and how it controls the bands and clutches.

Automatic transmissions do the job of shifting gears without any help from the driver. They start out in low as the car pulls away from a stop. Then, the automatic transmission shifts from first gear into second and then into third gear as the car picks up speed. The gear-shifting is done hydraulically with oil pressure.

There are two basic parts to the automatic transmission. These are the torque converter and the planetary-gear train. The torque converter passes the power from the engine to the gear box. And that's where the shifting action takes place. In this chapter we will look at torque converters, planetary gears, and the methods used to produce the shifting.

36-1 FLUID COUPLING

The fluid coupling is a special sort of clutch. It uses oil to carry power from the engine crankshaft to the gears. A basic fluid coupling is shown in Fig. 36-1. The assembly is like a hollow doughnut, sliced in two. Each hollow half has a series of semicircular plates, called vanes. The two halves are enclosed in an outer cover that is attached to the flywheel. Figure 36-2 shows the arrangement. The driving half of the fluid coupling, called the pump or impeller, is attached to the crankshaft. The driven half, called the *turbine,* is attached to the transmission shaft.

There is no direct mechanical connection between the pump (driving member) and the turbine (driven member). If no oil were used in the assembly, the two members could rotate independently of each other. However, filling the fluid coupling with oil makes the difference. When the pump rotates, it throws oil into the turbine. The oil between the vanes of the pump is thrown out by centrifugal force.

443

Fig. 36-1
A simplified version of the two members of a fluid coupling, viewed from inside. (*Chevrolet Motor Division of General Motors Corporation*)

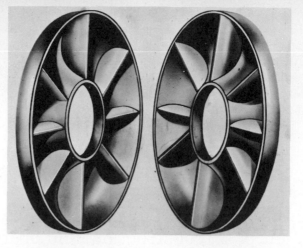

Centrifugal force is the force that pushes things outward from the center around which they revolve. The oil caught between the vanes of the pump has no place to go except into the turbine. The oil is thrown into the turbine with great force and hits the vanes at an angle. In this way, the moving oil applies pressure to one side of the vanes. The push against the vanes forces the turbine to turn. This action is shown in Fig. 36-3.

Fig. 36-2
A sectional view of a fluid coupling.

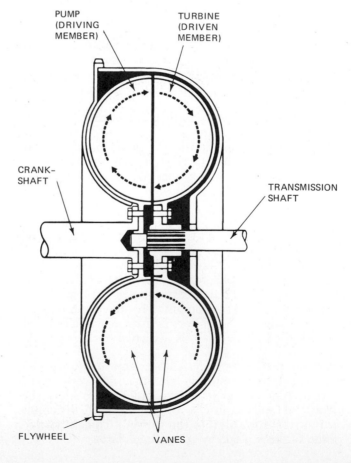

PUMP
(DRIVING
MEMBER)

TURBINE
(DRIVEN
MEMBER)

CRANK-
SHAFT

TRANSMISSION
SHAFT

FLYWHEEL

VANES

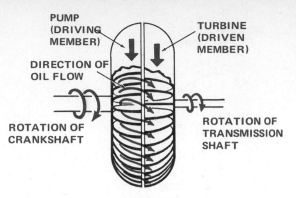

36-2 CURVED VANES

In the fluid coupling, the vanes are straight. Because of this, the fluid coupling can only transmit torque. It cannot increase or multiply torque.

To direct the oil better, the vanes of the pump and turbine are curved, as shown in Fig. 36-4. Also, a smaller doughnut, called a split guide ring, is centered in the vanes of the pump and the turbine. The purpose of the split guide ring is to help guide the oil in its path from the pump to the turbine. This makes the oil produce higher pressure against the vanes of the turbine. A fluid coupling that has curved vanes and a split guide ring is called a *torque converter*.

36-3 THE THIRD MEMBER

To make the torque converter more effective, a third member is required. This member is called the reaction member, or *stator*. Its purpose is to change the direction of the oil coming off the turbine (driven member) vanes. It changes the direction of the oil into a helping direction. To see how this is done, look at Fig. 36-5.

At the left in Fig. 36-5, a jet of oil is hitting a round bucket attached to a wheel. The oil pushes on the bucket and tries to turn the wheel. But the push is not great. This is because the oil does not give up much of its energy of motion during the one pass through the bucket.

However, when a curved vane is added, as shown at the right in Fig. 36-5, things are different. Now when the oil leaves the bucket, it hits the curved vane and is directed back into the bucket. In this way, the oil gives the bucket another push. Actually, the oil could make several circuits between the bucket and the vane. Each time the oil enters the bucket, it gives the bucket another push. This effect is called *torque multiplication*.

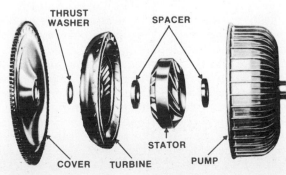

Fig. 36-4
The turbine, stator, and pump (impeller) used in a torque converter. (*Ford Motor Company*)

445

Fig. 36-5
The effect of a jet of oil on a bucket attached to a wheel. If the oil enters and leaves as at the left, the push on the bucket and wheel is small. But if the oil jet is redirected into the bucket by a curved vane, as at the right, the push is increased. (*Chrysler Corporation*)

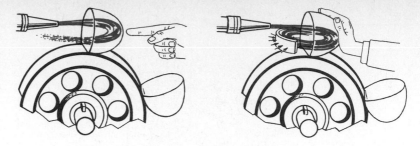

Do you see how torque multiplication occurs in the torque converter? As the oil leaves the turbine, the oil hits the stator vanes and is redirected into the pump in a helping direction. The pump then throws the oil back into the turbine. This is a continuous action. The repeated pushes of the oil on the curved turbine vanes increase the torque on the turbine. In many torque converters, the torque is more than doubled. For each 1 lb-ft [0.14 kg-m] of torque entering the pump, the turbine delivers more than 2 lb-ft [0.28 kg-m] of torque to the transmission shaft. This is torque multiplication.

However, torque multiplication takes place only when the pump is turning considerably faster than the turbine. This happens during acceleration from a stop sign, for example.

36-4 STATOR ACTION

Now let's take a look at the complete stator action, from the time the car starts moving until it is moving at highway speed. To begin with, there is torque multiplication. The pump is turning fast while the turbine is turning slowly. This means the engine is turning fast while the car wheels are turning slowly. What happens here is the same as what happens when the manual transmission is in low gear. Speed is reduced and torque is increased.

However, as the car comes up to speed, the turbine begins to "catch up" with the pump. The effect is the same as if the driver had upshifted a manual transmission. Now, the oil leaving the turbine is no longer moving so forcefully in a hindering direction. The reason is that the turbine is taking up most of the energy caused by the motion of the oil. Therefore, the oil could pass directly into the pump in a helping direction. The stator is no longer needed. Actually, the stator vanes are now in the way. To get the vanes out of the way, the stator is mounted on an overrunning clutch.

The overrunning clutch is a one-way clutch that uses sprags or rollers to provide lockup. It allows the stator to revolve freely, or "freewheel," in one direction. The clutch locks up the stator if it tries to turn in the other direction. Figure 36-6 shows how the stator is mounted on the overrunning clutch.

Figure 36-7 shows the details of one type of overrunning clutch. It consists of a hub, an outer ring that is part of the stator, and a series of rollers. The rollers are located in the notches in the other ring. The outer ring is called the overrunning-clutch cam. The notches are smaller at one end than at the other. The rollers have springs behind them. When there is a push on the stator vanes from the oil leaving the turbine, the stator attempts to rotate backward. This causes the rollers to roll into the smaller ends of the notches. There, they jam and lock

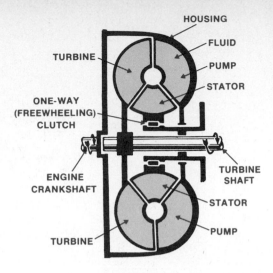

Fig. 36-6
A simplified sectional view of a torque converter showing locations of turbine, stator, pump, and one-way clutch. (*Ford Motor Company*)

the stator to the hub. Therefore the stator cannot turn backward. However, as the turbine speed approaches the pump speed, the direction of the oil no longer has to be changed as it leaves the turbine. It now begins to hit the other side of the stator vanes. The stator starts to revolve in a forward direction. The rollers roll out of the smaller ends of the notches into the larger ends. There, they cannot jam, and the stator spins freely.

36-5 PLANETARY GEARS

Automatic transmissions have two or more *planetary-gear* sets. The planetary-gear set shown in Fig. 36-8 can do many things. In the car automatic transmission, the job of the planetary-gear set is to reduce speed and increase torque, to reverse direction, and to act as a solid shaft. The planetary-gear set consists of an internal gear (also called a ring gear), a sun gear, and a pair of planet pinions on a carrier and shaft. Before we describe how the planetary gears do their job, let's review gears.

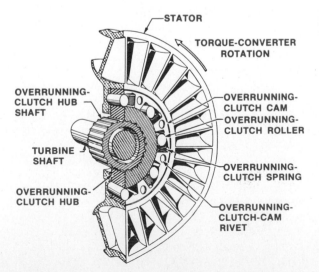

Fig. 36-7
Details of an overrunning, or one-way, clutch used to support the stator in a torque converter. (*Chrysler Corporation*)

Fig. 36-8

A planetary-gear system. The planet pinions rotate on shafts that are mounted on a planet-pinion carrier. The planet-pinion carrier is attached to a shaft that is exactly aligned with the sun-gear shaft. These shafts are exactly centered in the internal gear.

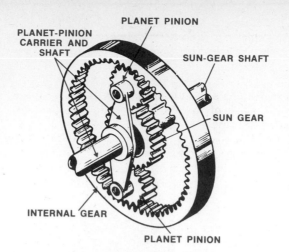

Fig. 36-9
Two meshing spur gears with the same number of teeth.

Fig. 36-10
The idler gear causes the driven gear to turn in the same direction as the driving gear.

36-6 GEAR COMBINATIONS

When two gears are in mesh, as shown in Fig. 36-9, they turn in opposite directions. But if another gear is put into the gear train, as shown in Fig. 36-10, the two outside gears turn in the same direction. The middle gear is called an *idler* gear. It doesn't do any work—it is idle.

To get a combination of two gears to rotate in the same direction, you can use one internal gear. The internal gear, also called an annulus gear or ring gear, has teeth on the inside. When the pinion gear and the internal gear rotate, they both rotate in the same direction (Fig. 36-11).

Now, if another spur gear is added in the center, meshed with the pinion gear, the combination is a simple planetary-gear system (Fig. 36-12). The center gear is called the sun gear because the other gears revolve around it. This is similar to the way the planets in our solar system revolve around the sun. The spur gear between the sun gear and the internal gear is called the planet pinion. This is because it revolves around the sun gear, just as planets revolve around the sun. Now let's study the planetary-gear system.

36-7 PLANETARY-GEAR OPERATION

Let's complete the planetary-gear set by adding another planet pinion, as shown in Fig. 36-13. This gives us the combination shown in Fig. 36-8.

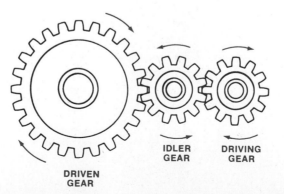

NOTE

The planetary-gear sets used in automatic transmissions usually have three or four planet pinions. But there are various other combinations, as we will see when we explain the complete assemblies.

The two planet pinions rotate on shafts that are a part of a planet-pinion carrier (see Fig. 36-8). Each of the two gears and the planet-pinion carrier are called members. The internal gear, the sun gear, and the planet-pinion-and-carrier assembly are all members. When one member is held stationary and another turns, there will be a speed increase, a speed reduction, or a direction reversal. The result depends on which member is stationary and which turns. Let's see how this works.

1. Speed Increase #1

Suppose the sun gear is held stationary and the planet-pinion carrier turns. Then the internal gear will increase in speed. Why? Follow this closely! When the carrier revolves, it carries the planet pinions around with it. This movement makes the planet pinions rotate on their shafts. As the pinions rotate, they cause the internal gear to rotate also (see Fig. 36-14). Note the conditions. The sun gear is stationary. The planet-pinion carrier is moving, carrying the pinions around with it. The planet pinions "walk around" the sun gear, which means they rotate on their shafts. As the planet pinions turn, they drive the internal gear ahead of them. This provides a speed increase through the planetary-gear set, when the internal gear is connected to the output shaft. Automatic transmissions do not use this condition.

2. Speed Increase #2

Another combination is to hold the internal gear stationary and turn the planet-pinion carrier. In this case, the sun gear is forced to rotate faster than the planet-pinion carrier. There is a greater speed increase than in case #1. This condition normally is not used in automatic transmissions.

3. Speed Reduction #1

If the internal gear turns while the sun gear is held stationary, the planet-pinion carrier turns slower than the internal gear. With the internal gear turning the planet-pinion carrier, the planetary-gear set provides speed reduction and a torque increase. This is the way second gear is obtained in many automatic transmissions.

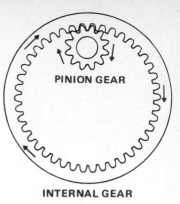

Fig. 36-11

If one internal gear is used with one external gear, both the driven and the driving gears will turn in the same direction.

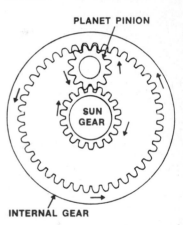

Fig. 36-12

If a sun gear is added to the arrangement shown in Fig. 36-11, the result is a simple planetary-gear system.

Fig. 36-13

To complete the planetary-gear system, a second planet pinion is added. This pinion balances the forces so that the system will run smoothly. Planetary-gear systems in automatic transmissions have three or four planet pinions.

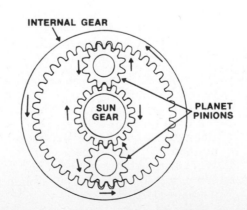

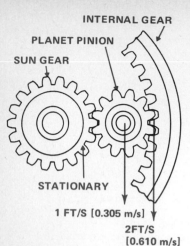

INTERNAL GEAR

PLANET PINION

SUN GEAR

STATIONARY

1 FT/S [0.305 m/s]

2 FT/S
[0.610 m/s]

Fig. 36-14
If the sun gear is stationary and the planet-pinion carrier turns, the ring gear will turn faster than the carrier. The planet pinion pivots about the stationary teeth. If the center of the pinion shaft moves at 1 foot per second [0.3 m/s], the tooth opposite the stationary tooth will move at 2 feet per second [0.6 m/s] since it is twice as far away from the stationary tooth as the center of the shaft.

Fig. 36-15
This chart shows the various conditions that are possible in the planetary-gear system if one member is held and another turned.

4. Speed Reduction #2

If the internal gear is held stationary and the sun gear turns, there is speed reduction. The planet pinions must rotate on their shafts. They also must walk around the internal gear, since they are in mesh with it. As the pinions rotate, the planet carrier rotates. But it rotates at a slower speed than the sun gear. This condition provides the greatest increase in torque. It is used for first gear in automatic transmissions.

5. Reverse #1

To get reverse, the planet-pinion carrier can be held stationary and the internal gear can be turned. In this case, the planet pinions act as idlers and cause the sun gear to be driven in the reverse direction. Here, the planetary-gear set acts as a direction-reversing system, with the sun gear turning faster than the internal gear. However, there is no need for a "high-speed" reverse gear in an automatic transmission. Therefore, this condition is not used in passenger cars.

6. Reverse #2

A second way to get reverse is to hold the planet-pinion carrier stationary and turn the sun gear. The internal gear turns in a reverse direction, but slower than the sun gear. This is the condition used to provide reverse gear in an automatic transmission.

7. Direct Drive

When any two members of a planetary-gear set are locked together by the action of a clutch piston, the planetary-gear set acts as a solid shaft. Locking any two members together causes the input and output shafts to turn at the same speed.

All the conditions discussed above are listed in the chart in Fig. 36-15. The three conditions used in automatic transmissions are listed in columns 2, 3, and 6 of Fig. 36-15. The planetary-gear sets used in automatic transmissions are controlled by bands and clutches to give direct drive, speed reduction, and reverse.

Conditions	1	2	3	4	5	6	
Internal Gear	D	H	T	H	T	D	D —Driven
Carrier		T	T	D	D	H	H	H —Held
Sun Gear	H	D	H	T	D	T	I —Increase in Speed
Speed	I	I	L	L	IR	LR	L —Reduction in Speed

R —Reverse

T —Turn

CHECK UP ON YOURSELF

Automatic transmissions sometimes are a challenge to understand. You should know how they work. Review what you have studied by answering the questions that follow.

1. What is used in the torque converter to carry power from the pump to the turbine?
2. What is the stator doing when the pump is turning much faster than the turbine?
3. Does the stator work when the pump and the turbine are turning at about the same speed?
4. What is the stator mounted on?
5. What are the purposes of a planetary-gear set in an automatic transmission?

6. When a pinion gear meshes with an internal gear, do both revolve in the same, or in opposite, directions?
7. What is the name of the center gear in the planetary-gear set?
8. What is the name of the gears between the sun gear and the internal gear in the planetary-gear set?
9. If the sun gear is held stationary and the internal gear turns, is the planet-pinion carrier driven faster or slower than the internal gear?
10. If the planet-pinion carrier is held stationary, which of the other two members should be turned to get a speed reduction in reverse?

ANSWERS

1. Oil (Sec. 36-1). 2. The stator is redirecting oil from the turbine back into the pump in a helping direction (Sec. 36-3). 3. No. The stator rotates so that its vanes can be out of the way of the oil (Sec. 36-4). 4. An overrunning clutch. (Sec. 36-4). 5. Increase torque, reduce speed, and reverse direction (Sec. 36-5). 6. Both revolve in the same direction (Sec. 36-6). 7. The sun gear (Sec. 36-6). 8. Planet pinions (Sec. 36-6). 9. The planet-pinion carrier turns slower (Sec. 36-7). 10. The sun gear (Sec. 36-7).

HYDRAULIC CONTROLS

36-8 HYDRAULIC SHIFT CONTROLS

We have seen how the power flows into the transmission through the torque converter and how planetary gears operate. Now let's find out how the planetary gears are controlled.

There are two hydraulically operated controls: a band and a clutch. The band is a brake band that wraps around the clutch drum. When the band is applied, or tightened on the drum, the drum is held stationary. Inside the drum, the clutch consists of a series of clutch plates. Half of the plates are splined to one member of the planetary-gear set. The other half are splined to one of the other members. When the clutch is applied by oil pressure, the two sets of clutch plates are forced together. When the oil pressure is released, the clutch releases. This allows the two sets of clutch plates to rotate independently of each other.

One set of clutch plates is called the *drive plates*. The other set is called the *driven plates*. The drive plates are lined on both sides with a thin layer of friction material. It is similar to the facing on a friction disk in a standard clutch. Driven plates are plain metal, without any lining or facing on either side.

36-9 BAND AND CLUTCH

Let's put the two controls—the clutch and the band—onto the planetary-gear set. Figure 36-16 is a sectional view of a planetary-gear set with a band and clutch. We explain later how the band and clutch are applied. First, we want to see what happens when they are applied.

The band is shown in Fig. 36-17. It is positioned around the sun-gear drum. When the band is applied, the sun gear is held stationary. This means that the planetary-gear set acts as a speed reducer. The internal gear is turning because it is mounted on the input shaft. This arrangement forces the planet pinions to rotate. They walk around the stationary sun gear and carry the pinion carrier around with them. The carrier, which is attached to the output shaft, rotates at a slower speed than the internal gear.

Fig. 36-16

A sectional view showing the two controlling mechanisms used in the front planetary set in an automatic transmission. One controlling mechanism consists of a brake drum and brake band; the other is a multiple-disk clutch.

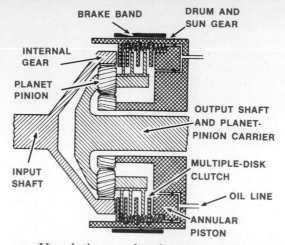

Now let's see what happens if the clutch is applied instead of the band. Oil pressure that enters the clutch through the oil line causes the clutch to apply. The oil pressure forces the piston in the sun-gear drum to the left (in Fig. 36-16). The clutch plates are pushed together so that the clutch is engaged. With this situation, the planet-pinion carrier and the sun gear are locked together. The planetary-gear set is now in direct drive. The planetary-gear set is locked. Figure 36-18 shows the clutch plates. Note that they are alternately splined to the drum and the clutch hub.

NOTE

The arrangement shown in Fig. 36-16 is only one of several arrangements used in automatic transmissions. In some transmissions, when the band is applied, it holds the internal gear or the planet-pinion carrier stationary. Many transmissions lock different members together when the clutch is applied. The principle is the same in all transmissions, however. In the planetary-gear set, there is a gear reduction when the band is applied. There is direct drive when the clutch is applied.

Fig. 36-17

A transmission brake band. (*Chrysler Corporation*)

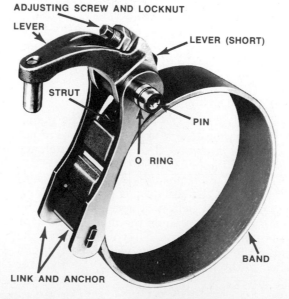

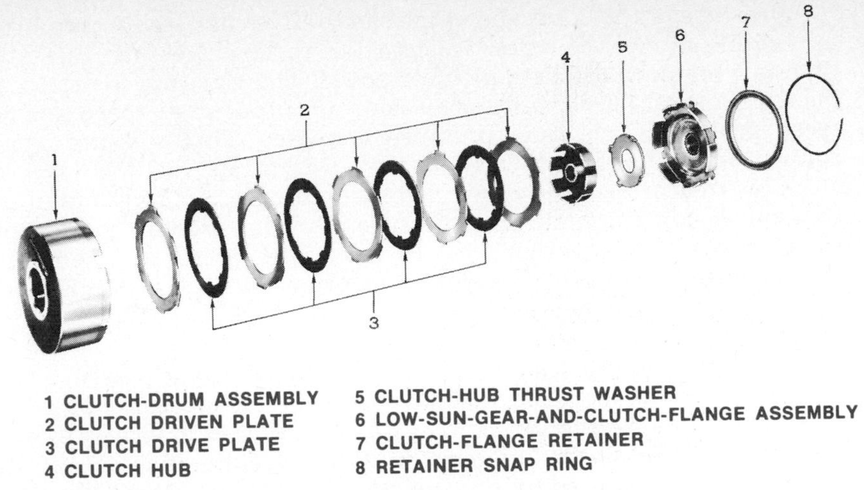

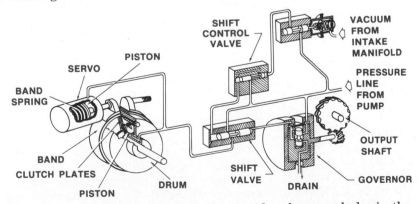

Fig. 36-18
Parts of a clutch. (*Chevrolet Motor Division of General Motors Corporation*)

1 CLUTCH-DRUM ASSEMBLY
2 CLUTCH DRIVEN PLATE
3 CLUTCH DRIVE PLATE
4 CLUTCH HUB
5 CLUTCH-HUB THRUST WASHER
6 LOW-SUN-GEAR-AND-CLUTCH-FLANGE ASSEMBLY
7 CLUTCH-FLANGE RETAINER
8 RETAINER SNAP RING

36-10 HYDRAULIC CIRCUITS

Figure 36-19 is a simplified diagram of a hydraulic control circuit for a single planetary-gear set in an automatic transmission. Notice how the action of the band is controlled by a servo. In hydraulic systems, a servo is a device that converts hydraulic pressure to mechanical movement, as the oil acts on a small piston inside the servo. Later we will look at the circuits for automatic transmissions that use two or more planetary-gear sets. Automatic transmissions use more than one planetary-gear set.

The major purpose of the hydraulic circuit is to apply and release a band and a clutch. By this action, the hydraulic circuit controls the shift from gear reduction (low gear) to direct drive (high gear). The shift must take place at the right time. This depends on car speed and throttle opening. These two factors produce two varying oil pressures that work against the two ends of the shift valve.

Fig. 36-19
A schematic diagram showing the hydraulic control system for the brake-band servo and the clutch. In the system shown, the band is normally on and the clutch off. This arrangement produces gear reduction. But when the shift valve is moved, pressure from the oil pump is admitted to the front of the brake-band piston and to the clutch piston. This movement causes the brake to release and the clutch to apply. Now, with the clutch locking together two planetary members, the planetary system goes into direct drive.

The *shift valve* is a spool-type valve inside a bore, or hole, in the valve body. Figure 36-20 shows what the spool valve looks like. Pressure at one end of the spool valve comes from the governor.

NOTE
The automatic transmission governor is a device that controls, or governs, gear-shifting in relation to car speed. In the hydraulic circuit, the governor controls pressure on one end of the shift valve.

Fig. 36-20
A spool valve for a shift valve.

Pressure at the other end of the spool valve changes as vacuum in the intake manifold changes. This is called throttle pressure. First, the governor pressure changes with car speed. The governor is driven by the output shaft from the transmission. As output-shaft speed and car speed go up, the governor pressure increases. This pressure works against one end of the shift valve, as shown in Fig. 36-19.

Governor pressure is a modified line pressure. An oil pump in the transmission produces the line pressure. This line pressure passes into the governor. The governor lets out part of this pressure. The higher the car speed, the more pressure the governor releases. It is this modified pressure—the governor pressure—that works on one end of the shift valve.

Working on the other end of the shift valve is a pressure that changes as intake-manifold vacuum changes. Line pressure enters the modulator valve at the top. The *modulator valve* is a spool valve attached to a spring-loaded diaphragm. When vacuum increases in the intake manifold, caused by the throttle being partly closed, this vacuum pulls the diaphragm in and moves the spool valve. The motion cuts off the line pressure going to the shift control valve. When this happens, the shift control valve moves to the right, cutting off pressure from the left end of the shift valve. This means that the shift valve is pushed to the left. As a result, line pressure can pass through the shift valve. Therefore, line pressure is applied to the clutch and the servo at the planetary-gear set. With this condition, the band is released and the clutch is applied. This action shifts gears by locking the planetary-gear set in direct drive.

Now let's put it all together and see how the hydraulic control circuit works. To start with, there is no pressure going to the planetary-gear controls. The clutch is released, and the band is applied. The band is applied by the pressure of the heavy spring in the servo.

NOTE

Figure 36-19 is a *simplified* version of the actual systems found in automatic transmissions. In automatic transmissions oil pressure is used to help the spring hold the band tight. However, the basic principles are as shown in Fig. 36-19.

With the clutch released and the band applied, the planetary-gear set is in gear reduction, or low. As car speed increases, the governor releases more and more pressure. This pressure is applied to one end of the shift valve. The pressure on the other end of the shift valve depends on intake-manifold vacuum, or engine speed and throttle opening. As long as the throttle is held open, there is little manifold vacuum. The pressure on the left end of the shift valve is high. This holds the planetary-gear set in low for good acceleration. However, as car speed continues to increase, the governor pressure becomes great enough to push the shift valve to the left. This lets line pressure through to the planetary-gear set. Now the band is released and the clutch is applied. This shifts the planetary-gear set into direct drive.

If the throttle is partly closed after the car reaches intermediate speed, intake-manifold vacuum increases. The vacuum cuts off line pressure to the modulator valve. This cuts off line pressure to the shift control valve. When this happens, the shift control valve moves to the right, cutting off pressure to the left end of the shift valve. The shift valve then moves to the left, pushed by governor pressure. This applies line pressure to the planetary-gear set. The clutch applies and the band releases. Now the planetary-gear set goes into direct drive.

The reason for this roundabout way of getting pressure to the left end of the shift valve is to vary the upshift according to driving conditions. When the car is accelerating, high torque is needed. The gears should stay in low. Then, when cruising speed is reached, less torque is needed. The driver eases up on the throttle. This increases intake-manifold vacuum so that the upshift occurs. If the driver again wants fast acceleration, the throttle is pushed to the floor. This reduces intake-manifold vacuum, and the planetary-gear set downshifts into low (gear reduction). This increases torque to the drive wheels.

36-11 FORD C6 AUTOMATIC TRANSMISSION

You cannot become an automatic-transmission expert by reading a few pages of a book. But you should know what the transmission looks like inside and how it does its job. Most automatic transmissions have three forward speeds and one reverse. All have torque converters. To learn more about automatic transmissions, we will study the Ford C6 transmission. This transmission is shown in cutaway view in Fig. 36-21, and its complete hydraulic circuit is shown in Fig. 36-22.

1. The Manual Shift Valve

The action starts at the manual shift valve, shown at the bottom in Fig. 36-22. After starting the engine, the driver moves the selector

Fig. 36-21
A cutaway view of the Ford C6 automatic transmission. (*Ford Motor Company*)

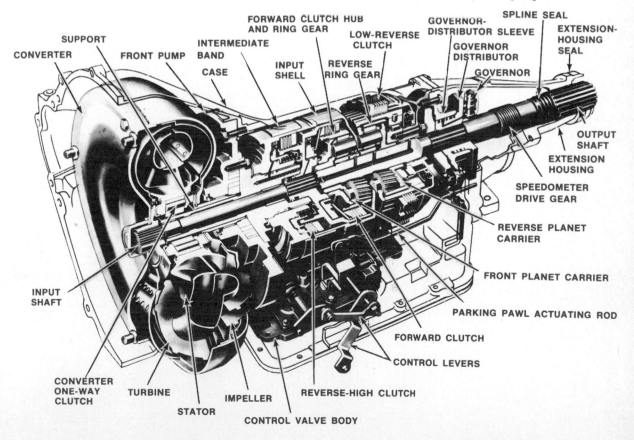

Fig. 36-22
The complete hydraulic system of the Ford C6 automatic transmission. (*Ford Motor Company*)

lever on the steering column or console to the driving range desired. The driver can put the selector lever in R, or reverse, to back up the car. Or the driver can put it in D, or drive, for normal operation. In D the transmission will automatically upshift from first to second to third. If

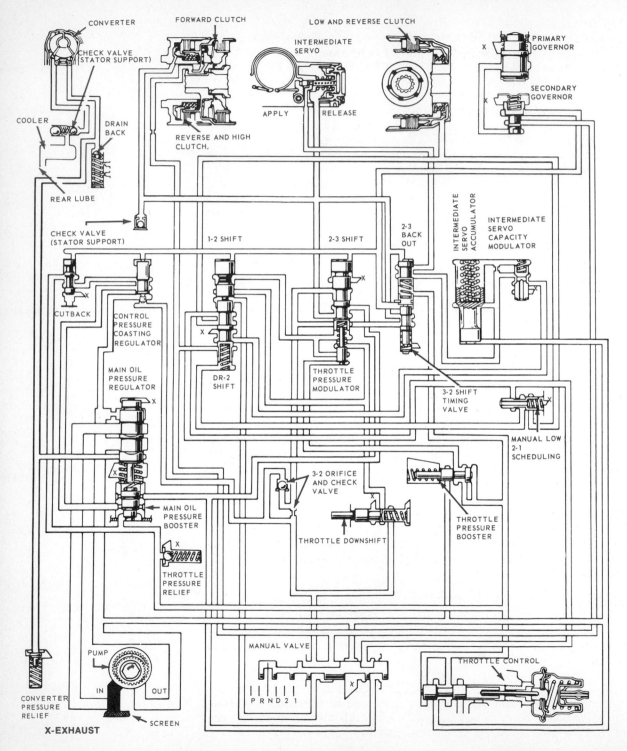

the driver does not want the transmission to shift up to third, the driver can move the selector lever to 2 or 1. In 2 the transmission will remain in second. In 1 the transmission will remain in first. The driver may need 1 or 2 for slowing down on a long hill.

2. Upshifting
Let's assume the driver selects D. Starting out, the transmission is in low. Then, as car speed increases, the shifts are made from low to second and from second to third. Shift points are determined by car speed and throttle opening.

3. The Planetary-gear Sets
The Ford C6 transmission has two interconnected planetary-gear sets, as shown in Fig. 36-21. They share the sun gear, which is common to both. By controlling the two planetary-gear sets, the transmission provides three forward speeds and one reverse.

NOTE
In the Ford C6 transmission, a clutch takes the place of one of the bands. This is described later.

4. First Gear
In first gear, the forward clutch is applied. This locks the front planetary ring gear to the input shaft, and it turns with the input shaft. As the ring gear rotates, it drives the planet pinions. They, in turn, drive the sun gear. This produces a gear reduction through the front planetary-gear set. As the sun gear turns, it drives the rear planet pinions. The rear planet pinions drive the ring gear of the rear planetary-gear set. The ring gear is splined to the output shaft, so the shaft turns. There also is gear reduction in the rear planetary-gear set. With gear reduction in both sets, the transmission is in low, or first, gear.

5. Second Gear
When the upshift to second gear takes place, the hydraulic system applies the intermediate band. This band holds the sun gear and the reverse-and-third clutch drum stationary. Now, there is gear reduction in the front gear set only. The transmission is in second.

6. Third, or Direct Gear
When the hydraulic system produces the shift into third, both the forward clutch and the reverse-and-third clutch are applied. This locks the planetary-gear sets so that there is direct drive through both. The transmission is in third gear.

7. Reverse
In reverse, the reverse-and-third clutch and the low-and-reverse clutch are both applied. This condition causes gear reduction through both planetary-gear sets. Also, the direction of rotation is reversed in the rear set.

36-12 OTHER AUTOMATIC TRANSMISSIONS
A variety of automatic transmissions are used in automobiles. However, they all work in about the same way. All have planetary-gear sets that are controlled by bands and clutches.

36-13 SERVICING THE AUTOMATIC TRANSMISSION

Special training and special tools are needed to diagnose and correct all automatic-transmission troubles successfully. Essential tools you need are a tachometer, a vacuum gauge, and an oil-pressure gauge.

However, there are many services that the mechanic can perform on automatic transmissions. These services include

- Adjusting linkages
- Checking fluid level in the transmission
- Adding fluid if necessary
- Draining old fluid
- Cleaning screens and filters
- Adjusting bands

Procedures vary from one transmission make to another. Some manufacturers recommend draining the fluid and putting in fresh fluid at periodic intervals. Other manufacturers do not recommend this service. Before attempting any of the above services on an automatic transmission, look up the proper way to do the job. Refer to the manufacturer's service manual that covers the transmission you are about to service.

CHECK UP ON YOURSELF

Now you should have a good idea of how automatic transmissions work. Test yourself on what you know by answering the questions that follow.

1. What are the two controls used in automatic transmissions to control the planetary-gear sets?
2. In the simplified version of the planetary-gear set and its controls, which control device puts the gear set into reduction?
3. Which control device puts the planetary-gear set into direct drive?
4. What is the purpose of the governor in the automatic transmission?
5. What are the two pressures that work on the two ends of the shift valve?

ANSWERS

1. A band and a clutch (Secs. 36-8 and 36-9). **2.** The band (Sec. 36-9). **3.** The clutch (Sec. 36-9). **4.** To vary the shift points according to car speed (Sec. 36-10). **5.** Governor pressure and throttle pressure (Sec. 36-10).

CHAPTER THIRTY-SEVEN DRIVE LINES

After studying this chapter, you should be able to:
Discuss the purpose, construction, and operation of the drive line and its component parts, including the universal and slip joints.

Drive lines, also called drive shafts and propeller shafts, carry the power from the transmission to the car wheels. In most automobiles the engine is at the front, and the rear wheels are driven. A long drive shaft is required. However, when the engine is at the front and the front wheels are driven (front-drive cars), two short drive shafts are used. Cars that have engines at the rear with rear drive (rear-drive cars) also use two short drive shafts.

In this chapter, we will look at the two common arrangements. These are front-mounted engine with rear wheels driven and front-mounted engine with front wheels driven.

FRONT-MOUNTED ENGINE WITH REAR WHEELS DRIVEN

37-1 CONSTRUCTION OF THE DRIVE SHAFT (REAR WHEELS DRIVEN)

The drive shaft connects the transmission output shaft to the differential at the wheel axles. The transmission and the engine are more or less rigidly attached to the car frame. But the rear wheels are attached to the car frame by springs. They allow the rear wheels to move up and down. As a result, the following conditions occur:

- The drive line must change length as the wheels move up and down.
- The angle of drive must change as the wheels move up and down.

Figure 37-1 shows how the length of the drive line and the angle of drive change as the wheels move up and down. In the top part of the picture, the wheels and differential are in the up position. The drive angle is small. Also, the drive line is at its maximum length. In the bottom part of the picture, the differential and wheels are in the down position. This is their position when the wheels drop into a hole in the road. In this position, the drive angle is increased. Also, the drive-line length is reduced, because as the rear wheels and differential swing

Fig. 37-1

As the rear-axle housing, with differential and wheels, moves up and down, the angle between the transmission output shaft changes and the length of the shaft also changes. The reason the drive shaft shortens as the angle increases is that the rear axle and differential move in a shorter arc than the drive shaft.

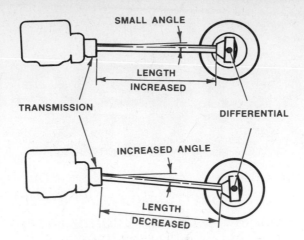

down, they also move forward. The rear wheels and differential must move this way because they are attached to the springs.

Most drive shafts are hollow tubes, with two or more universal joints and a slip joint. (We describe these joints in the following sections.) Figure 37-2 shows one common type of drive shaft. Some drive shafts are the two-piece type and have a support bearing at the center. Figure 37-3 shows one type of rear suspension and drive shaft.

37-2 UNIVERSAL JOINT

The universal joint allows driving power to be carried through two shafts that are at an angle to each other. Figure 37-4 shows a simple universal joint. It is a double-hinged joint, consisting of two Y-shaped yokes and a cross-shaped member. The cross-shaped member is called the spider. The four arms of the spider are assembled into bearings in the ends of the two yokes.

In operation, the driving shaft causes one of the yokes to rotate. This causes the spider to rotate. The spider then causes the driven yoke and shaft to rotate. When the driving and driven shafts are at an angle, the yokes swing around in the bearings on the ends of the spider arms.

A cross-and-two-yoke universal joint is shown in Fig. 37-5. It is almost the same as the simple universal joint shown in Fig. 37-4. However, the four bearings on the ends of the spider arms are needle bearings.

With the cross-and-two-yoke universal joint, there is a change in speed when the drive shaft and the driven shaft are at an angle to each

Fig. 37-2
The drive shaft connects the transmission with the differential. This is a one-piece shaft with two universal joints and one slip joint.

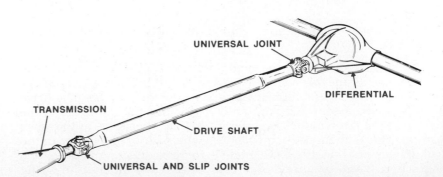

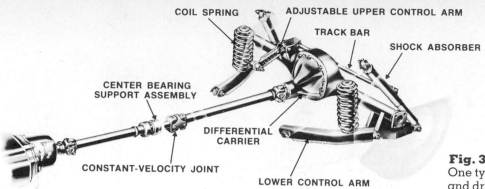

COIL SPRING

ADJUSTABLE UPPER CONTROL ARM

TRACK BAR

SHOCK ABSORBER

CENTER BEARING
SUPPORT ASSEMBLY

DIFFERENTIAL
CARRIER

CONSTANT-VELOCITY JOINT

LOWER CONTROL ARM

Fig. 37-3
One type of rear suspension and drive shaft. (*Buick Motor Division of General Motors Corporation*)

other. The change in speed occurs because the driven yoke and driven shaft speed up and then slow down twice with every revolution of the drive line. The greater the angle between the drive and driven shafts, the greater the speed-up-and-slow-down action. This type of action causes increased wear of the universal joint. To eliminate the speed-up-and-slow-down action, constant-velocity universal joints are used on many cars.

A constant-velocity universal joint is shown in Fig. 37-3 and in exploded view in Fig. 37-6. The constant-velocity universal joint consists of two universal joints linked by a ball and socket. The ball and socket splits the angle of the drive and driven shafts between the two universal joints of the constant-velocity unit. Because the two universal joints operate at the same angle, the speed-up-and-slow-down action is canceled out. The speedup resulting at any instant from the action of one universal joint is canceled out by the slowdown of the other. Therefore no speed change occurs between the two shafts connected to a constant-velocity universal joint.

37-3 SLIP JOINT

Any change in drive-line length is taken care of by a slip joint. A slip joint is shown in Fig. 37-7. It consists of external splines on the end of one shaft and matching internal splines on the mating hollow shaft. The splines cause the two shafts to rotate together but permit the two to slip back and forth inside the hollow shaft. This movement allows the effective length of the drive shaft to change as the wheels move up and down.

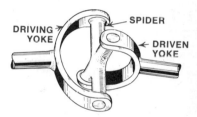

DRIVING YOKE

SPIDER

DRIVEN YOKE

Fig. 37-4
A simple universal joint.

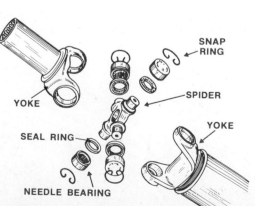

SNAP RING

SPIDER

YOKE

YOKE

SEAL RING

NEEDLE BEARING

Fig. 37-5
A cross-and-two-yoke universal joint in disassembled view.

461

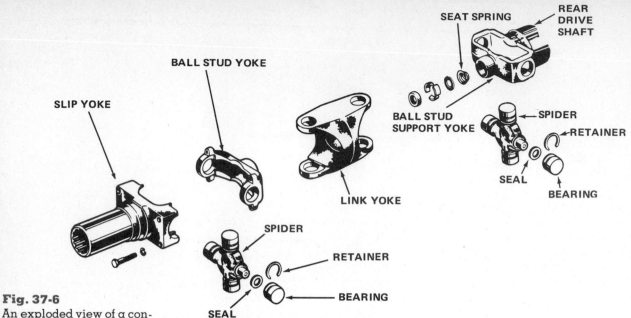

Fig. 37-6
An exploded view of a constant-velocity universal joint.

37-4 FRONT-WHEEL DRIVE

Front-wheel drive, or front drive, is becoming more popular. With front-wheel drive, the long drive shaft to the rear axle is eliminated. This also eliminates the tunnel in the floor pan of the car required for the drive shaft. Front-wheel drive is especially popular on smaller cars. Figure 37-8 shows the engine and power train layout used in most small front-drive cars today. Some large cars such as the Oldsmobile Toronado and the Cadillac El Dorado also have front drive.

Driving the front wheels makes the front suspension more complicated. The front wheels must swing from side to side so that the car can be steered. Also, they must be supported in such a way that they can be driven. This requires universal joints in both front-wheel drive shafts. These constant-velocity universal joints are designed to drive the wheels even though they are turned many degrees from straight ahead.

Figure 37-8 shows the drive shafts and universal joints in a front-drive car. The inner ends of the two drive shafts are connected to a transaxle, which is combined transmission and differential. (We cover the differential in Chap. 38.) Figure 37-9 shows a similar front-drive

Fig. 37-7
The slip joint uses matching external and internal splines.

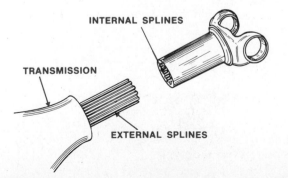

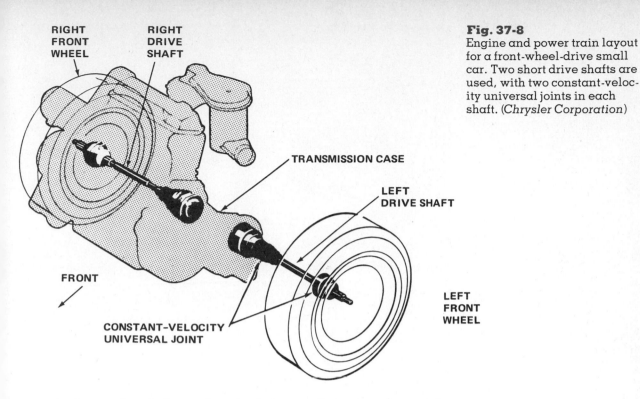

Fig. 37-8
Engine and power train layout for a front-wheel-drive small car. Two short drive shafts are used, with two constant-velocity universal joints in each shaft. (*Chrysler Corporation*)

RIGHT FRONT WHEEL

RIGHT DRIVE SHAFT

TRANSMISSION CASE

LEFT DRIVE SHAFT

FRONT

LEFT FRONT WHEEL

CONSTANT-VELOCITY UNIVERSAL JOINT

car raised on a shop hoist so that the layout and construction can be seen. Each drive shaft has universal joints and slip joints covered by rubber boots. See also Fig. 10-5, which shows a flat-four front-mounted engine for a front-drive car.

37-5 REAR DRIVE WITH REAR-MOUNTED ENGINE
Some cars have the engine mounted at the rear. In these cars, short drive shafts carry the engine power to the rear wheels. Each drive shaft has universal joints and slip joints. Some models of Volkswagen use this type of rear drive (Fig. 37-10).

37-6 FOUR-WHEEL DRIVE
Some vehicles, especially those that are used off the road, can drive all four wheels (Fig. 37-11). The driver has a way to select two-wheel or four-wheel drive. In some four-wheel-drive vehicles, engagement and disengagement of the front axle are automatic. This is called "full-time" four-wheel drive. Each drive shaft to the front and rear axles has universal joints and slip joints.

37-7 SERVICING THE UNIVERSAL
JOINT AND DRIVE SHAFT
Universal joints and drive shafts usually require no service. Most universal joints are prelubricated and do not need additional lubrication. However, in case of wear or damage, the universal joints may be replaced. Refer to the manufacturer's shop manual to determine the proper servicing and replacement procedures.

Fig. 37-9
Front-wheel-drive car raised
on a hoist so that the layout
and parts can be seen.
(*Chrysler Corporation*)

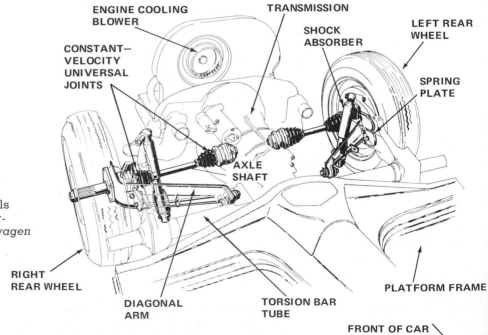

Fig. 37-10
Some Volkswagen models
have rear drive with rear-
mounted engine. (*Volkswagen
of America, Inc.*)

ENGINE COOLING
BLOWER

CONSTANT—
VELOCITY
UNIVERSAL
JOINTS

TRANSMISSION

SHOCK
ABSORBER

LEFT REAR
WHEEL

SPRING
PLATE

AXLE
SHAFT

RIGHT
REAR WHEEL

DIAGONAL
ARM

TORSION BAR
TUBE

PLATFORM FRAME

FRONT OF CAR

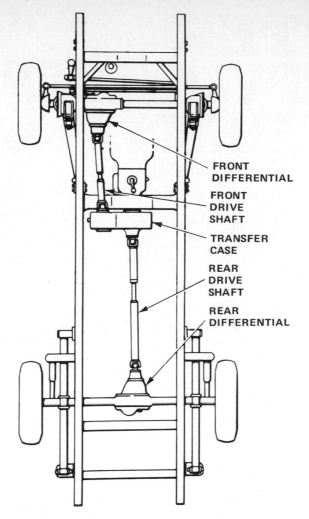

Fig. 37-11
The suspension and drive-train parts of a Ford Bronco. This is a four-wheel-drive vehicle. The transfer case allows the driver to use rear-wheel or four-wheel drive. (*Ford Motor Company*)

FRONT DIFFERENTIAL

FRONT DRIVE SHAFT

TRANSFER CASE

REAR DRIVE SHAFT

REAR DIFFERENTIAL

CHECK UP ON YOURSELF

Drive shafts seldom require service. However, you should know how to service them. Now see how well you understand what you have studied by answering the questions that follow.

1. Between what two parts is the drive shaft connected?
2. Besides carrying the engine power to the wheels, what are the other two things the drive shaft does?
3. How many bearings does a single universal joint have?
4. How many single universal joints does the constant-velocity universal joint have?
5. What two joints does the drive shaft have?

ANSWERS

1. Between the transmission at the front and the differential at the rear (Sec. 37-1). **2.** Changes in length and changes the angle of drive (Sec. 37-1). **3.** Four bearings (Sec. 37-2). **4.** Two joints (Sec. 37-2). **5.** The universal joint and the slip joint (Sec. 37-2 and 37-3).

CHAPTER THIRTY-EIGHT DIFFERENTIALS

After studying this chapter, you should be able to:

1. Discuss the purpose, construction, and operation of differentials.
2. Explain how the nonslip differential is constructed and how it works.
3. Discuss differential troubles and their possible causes.

Power from the engine flows through the drive shaft to the differential. When the power arrives at the differential, the power is split and sent to the two driving wheels. If the car is moving in a straight line, both driving wheels travel at the same speed. But if the car is making a turn, the outer wheel must travel farther and faster than the inner wheel. The differential makes this possible.

38-1 PURPOSE OF THE DIFFERENTIAL

When the car rounds a turn, the outer wheel must travel farther than the inner wheel. For example, suppose a rear-drive car makes a left turn, as shown in Fig. 38-1. The inner rear wheel, turning on a 20-foot [6.1-m] radius, travels 31 feet [9.4 m] during the 90-degree turn. The outer rear wheel, being nearly 5 feet [1.5 m] from the inner wheel, turns on a 24⅔-foot [7.5-m] radius (in the car shown), and it travels 39 feet [11.9 m].

Fig. 38-1
The difference of wheel travel as the car makes a 90-degree turn with the inner wheel turning on a 20-foot [6.1-m] radius.

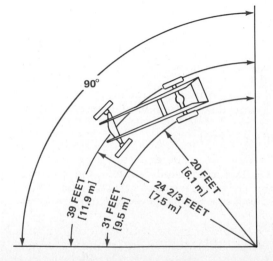

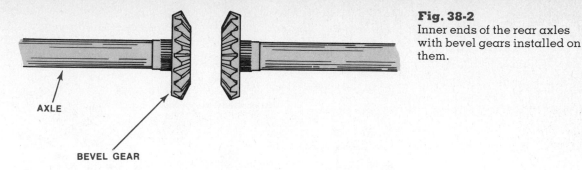

If the drive shaft were geared rigidly to both rear wheels, each wheel would have to skid an average of 4 feet [1.2 m] to make the turn. Doing this, the tires would not last very long. Also, what is worse is that the car would be difficult to control during turns. The job of the differential is to avoid these troubles. The differential allows one drive wheel to turn faster than the other when the car goes around a curve.

38-2 CONSTRUCTION OF THE DIFFERENTIAL

To study differential construction and operation, we will build up, gear by gear, a simple differential. The two drive wheels are mounted on axles. On the inner ends of the axles are bevel gears, which are called differential side gears, or axle gears (Fig. 38-2). A bevel gear is shaped like part of a cone (Fig. 38-3). All the teeth are at an angle. When two bevel gears are put together so that their teeth mesh, one shaft can be driven by the shaft that is at a 90-degree angle (Fig. 38-4).

Figure 38-5 shows the main parts of a differential. The parts are separated so that they can be seen clearly. Refer to this picture as you assemble the differential.

First, in Fig. 38-6, we add the differential case to the two wheel axles and differential side gears. The differential case has bearings that permit it to rotate on the two axles. Next, we add the two pinion gears and the supporting pinion shaft (Fig. 38-7). The shaft fits into the differential case. The two pinion gears are meshed with the differential side gears.

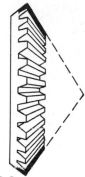

Fig. 38-3
The bevel gear would come to a point, but the pointed end has been cut off.

NOTE

Pinion gear is the name given to the smallest gear in a gear set.

Now we add the ring gear (Fig. 38-8). The ring gear is bolted to the flange on the differential case. Finally, we add the drive pinion (Fig. 38-9). The drive pinion is at the end of the drive shaft. When the drive shaft rotates, the drive pinion rotates, which rotates the ring gear.

38-3 OPERATION OF THE DIFFERENTIAL

The drive pinion on the end of the drive shaft drives the ring gear. The rotation of the ring gear causes the differential case to rotate. When the differential case rotates, the two pinion gears and their shaft move around in a circle with the differential case. Because the two side gears, or axle gears, are meshed with the pinion gears, the side gears must rotate. This causes the axles to rotate. The wheels turn and the car moves.

Suppose one drive wheel is held stationary. If the differential case rotates, the pinion gears would have to rotate on their shaft. The pin-

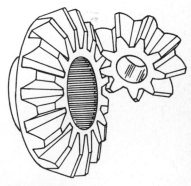

Fig. 38-4
Two meshing bevel gears.

467

ion gears would have to rotate on their shaft. The pinion gears would walk around the stationary side gear. As the pinion gears rotate on their shaft, they carry the rotary motion to the other side gear, causing it to rotate. The wheel that is not held will then rotate at twice its normal speed.

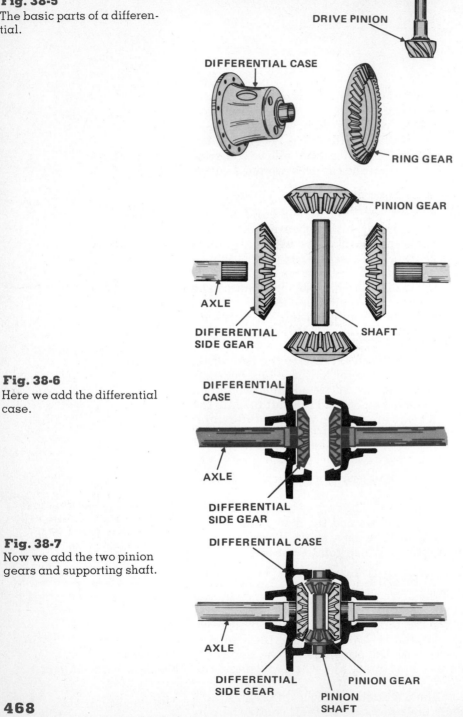

Fig. 38-5
The basic parts of a differential.

DRIVE PINION

DIFFERENTIAL CASE

RING GEAR

PINION GEAR

AXLE

DIFFERENTIAL SIDE GEAR

SHAFT

Fig. 38-6
Here we add the differential case.

DIFFERENTIAL CASE

AXLE

DIFFERENTIAL SIDE GEAR

Fig. 38-7
Now we add the two pinion gears and supporting shaft.

DIFFERENTIAL CASE

AXLE

DIFFERENTIAL SIDE GEAR

PINION SHAFT

PINION GEAR

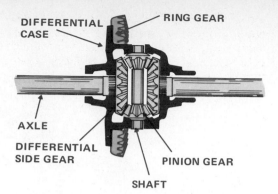

Fig. 38-8
Here we add the ring gear.

DIFFERENTIAL CASE

RING GEAR

AXLE

DIFFERENTIAL SIDE GEAR

PINION GEAR

SHAFT

You can now see how the differential can allow one drive wheel to turn faster than the other. Whenever the car goes around a turn, the outer drive wheel travels a greater distance than the inner drive wheel. The two pinion gears rotate on their shaft and send more rotary motion to the outer wheel.

When the car is moving down a straight road, the pinion gears do not rotate on their shaft. They apply equal torque to the side gears. Therefore both drive wheels rotate at the same speed.

38-4 DIFFERENTIAL CONSTRUCTION
Figure 38-10 is a partial cutaway view of a differential and rear-axle assembly. The pinions and gears are all of heavy construction to carry the power from the drive line. Figure 38-11 is a disassembled view of another differential and rear-axle assembly. Notice that in Fig. 38-11 different names are used for the different gears. For example, the drive pinion and the ring gear are called "gear and pinion." The pinion gears are called simply "pinion." Different manufacturers often use different names for the same parts in their cars. You must watch out for this in automotive work.

38-5 NONSLIP DIFFERENTIAL
The differential we have just studied delivers the same amount of torque to each drive wheel when both wheels have equal traction. When one wheel has less traction than the other, for example, when

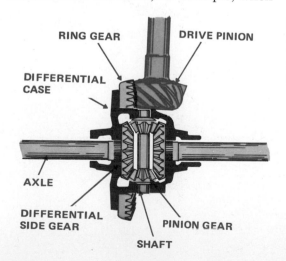

RING GEAR

DRIVE PINION

DIFFERENTIAL CASE

AXLE

DIFFERENTIAL SIDE GEAR

PINION GEAR

SHAFT

Fig. 38-9
To complete the basic differential, we now add the drive pinion. The drive pinion is meshed with the ring gear.

469

Fig. 38-10

A cutaway view of a differential and rear axle. (*Ford Motor Company*)

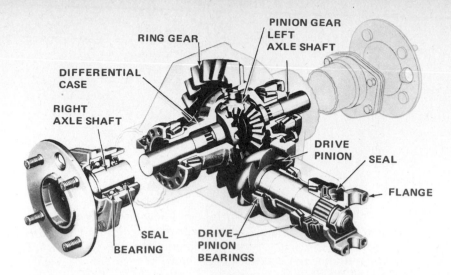

RING GEAR

PINION GEAR
LEFT
AXLE SHAFT

DIFFERENTIAL
CASE

RIGHT
AXLE SHAFT

DRIVE
PINION

SEAL

FLANGE

SEAL

BEARING

DRIVE-
PINION
BEARINGS

one wheel is slipping on ice, the other wheel cannot deliver torque. All the turning effort goes to the slipping wheel. To provide good traction even though one wheel is slipping, a nonslip differential is used in many cars. It is very similar to the standard differential. However, a nonslip differential can prevent wheel spin and loss of traction.

Fig. 38-11

A disassembled view of a differential. (*Chrysler Corporation*)

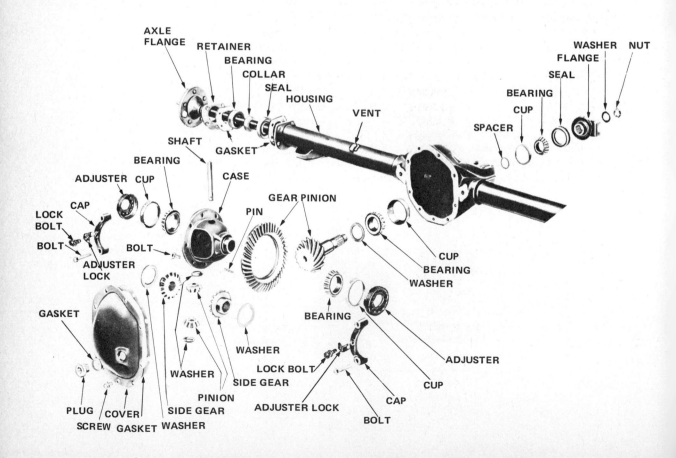

AXLE
FLANGE

RETAINER

BEARING

COLLAR

SEAL

HOUSING

VENT

WASHER   NUT

FLANGE

SEAL

BEARING

CUP

SPACER

SHAFT

GASKET

BEARING

CASE

ADJUSTER   CUP

CAP

LOCK
BOLT

BOLT

BOLT

ADJUSTER
LOCK

PIN

GEAR PINION

CUP
BEARING
WASHER

GASKET

BEARING

WASHER

ADJUSTER

CUP

CAP

BOLT

PLUG   COVER

SCREW   GASKET   WASHER

WASHER

PINION
SIDE GEAR

LOCK BOLT

SIDE GEAR

ADJUSTER LOCK

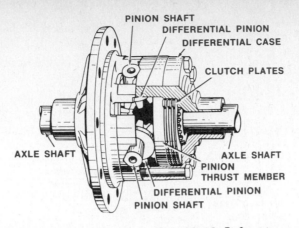

One type of nonslip differential is shown in Fig. 38-12. It has two sets of clutch plates. Also, the ends of the pinion-gear shafts lie rather loosely in notches in the two halves of the differential case. Figure 38-13 is a sectional view of the nonslip differential. During normal straight-road driving, the power flow is as shown in Fig. 38-14.

The rotating differential case carries the pinion-gear shafts around with it. Since there is considerable side thrust, the pinion shafts tend to slide up the sides of the notches in the two halves of the differential case. As the pinion shafts slide up, they are forced outward. This force is carried through the pinion thrust members to the two sets of clutch plates. The clutch plates lock the axle shafts to the differential case. Therefore both wheels turn.

If one wheel spins on ice or tends to slip, the pressure is released on the clutch plates feeding power to that wheel. The torque is sent to the other wheel. This prevents the wheel on the ice from slipping.

During normal driving, if the car rounds a curve, pressure is released on the clutch for the inner wheel just enough to permit some slipping. Figure 38-15 shows the action. This release of pressure permits the outer wheel to turn faster than the inner wheel.

38-6 DIAGNOSING DIFFERENTIAL TROUBLES

The first sign of differential trouble usually is noise. The kind of noise you hear can help you determine what is causing the trouble. However, you have to be sure that the noise actually is coming from the differential. It is sometimes possible to be fooled by universal-joint, wheel-

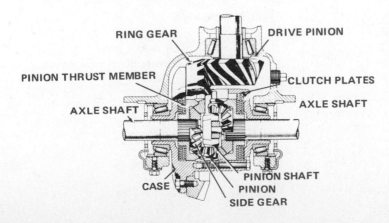

Fig. 38-13
A sectional view of a nonslip differential. (*Chrysler Corporation*)

Fig. 38-14
The power flow through a
nonslip differential on a
straightaway. (*Chrysler Corporation*)

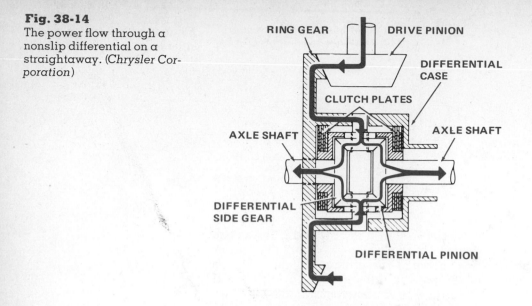

bearing, or tire noise. Note whether the noise is a hum, a growl, or a
knock. Note whether the noise is produced when the car is operating on
a straight road or only on turns. Note whether the noise is more noticeable when the engine is driving the car or when the car is coasting.
Usually a meaningful test for differential noise cannot be made by running the car with the drive wheels jacked up.

1. Humming

A humming noise is often caused by incorrect internal adjustment of
the drive pinion or the ring gear (Fig. 38-16). Incorrect adjustment prevents normal tooth contact and can cause rapid tooth wear and early
failure of the differential. The humming noise will take on a growling
sound as the wear progresses. Check the shop manual covering the car
you are servicing when you make differential adjustments.

Fig. 38-15
The power flow through a
nonslip differential when
rounding a turn. (*Chrysler Corporation*)

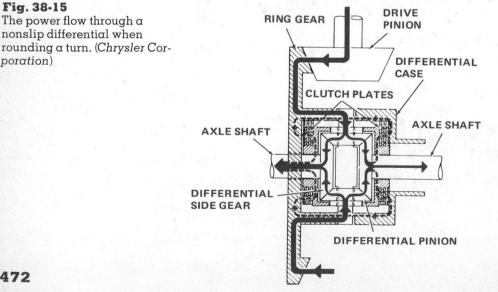

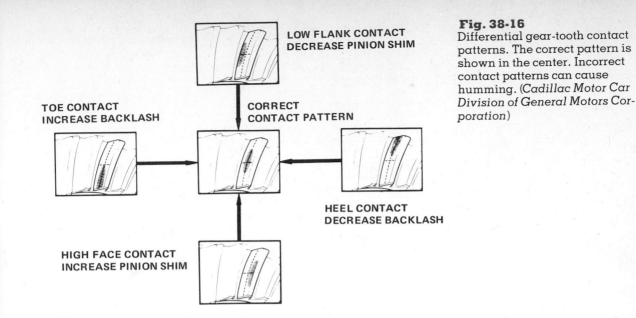

LOW FLANK CONTACT
DECREASE PINION SHIM

TOE CONTACT
INCREASE BACKLASH

CORRECT
CONTACT PATTERN

HEEL CONTACT
DECREASE BACKLASH

HIGH FACE CONTACT
INCREASE PINION SHIM

Fig. 38-16
Differential gear-tooth contact patterns. The correct pattern is shown in the center. Incorrect contact patterns can cause humming. (*Cadillac Motor Car Division of General Motors Corporation*)

2. Noise on Acceleration

If the noise is louder when the car is accelerating, there probably is heavy contact on the heel ends of the gear teeth. If the noise is more evident when the car is coasting, there probably is heavy toe contact. Both these conditions must be corrected. Refer to the manufacturer's shop manual for servicing procedures.

3. Noise on Curves

If the noise is present only when the car is going around a curve, the trouble is inside the differential case. Pinion gears tight on the pinion shaft, damaged gears or pinions, too much backlash between gears, or worn differential-case bearings can cause this trouble. When the car rounds a curve, these parts inside the differential case are moving relative to one another.

38-7 SERVICING THE DIFFERENTIAL

Repair and overhaul procedures on drive axles and differentials vary from one car model to another. Always refer to the manufacturer's shop manual that covers the car you are working on when you begin to repair a differential.

CHECK UP ON YOURSELF

Test yourself on the chapter you have just finished on drive axles and differentials by answering the questions that follow.

1. What is the purpose of the differential?
2. How many gears are there in the simple differential described in the chapter?
3. In the differential, with what gear is the drive pinion meshed?
4. When the car is rounding a curve, do the pinion gears turn on the shaft?
5. Does the nonslip differential have one set or two sets of clutch plates?

ANSWERS

1. To allow one drive wheel to turn faster than the other when the car goes around a curve (Sec. 38-1). **2.** Six: two axle gears, two pinion gears, ring gear, drive pinion (Sec. 38-2). **3.** With the ring gear (Sec. 38-2). **4.** Yes (Sec. 38-3). **5.** Two sets of clutch plates (Sec. 38-5).

PART SEVEN
AUTOMOTIVE SUSPENSION, STEERING, BRAKES, AND TIRES

In Part Seven we discuss the other essential parts of the automobile. In earlier chapters we learned how the engine operates to produce power and how this power is carried through the transmission and drive line to the car wheels. Now we learn how the car body is suspended on springs for a smooth ride and how the car is steered and braked. We also learn about the tires on which the car wheels ride. There are six chapters in Part Seven:

CHAPTER THIRTY-NINE AUTOMOTIVE SPRINGS AND SUSPENSION

After studying this chapter, you should be able to:

1. Explain the purpose of springs, describe the three types used on automobiles, and explain how each is attached and how it works.
2. Describe the different types of front-suspension systems.
3. Discuss the purpose and operation of shock absorbers.
4. Explain how the automatic level control works.

Springs are part of the suspension system of the automobile. Their purpose is to absorb any road shocks that result from the wheels hitting holes or bumps. Let's look at the various kinds of springs and suspension systems and see how they work.

39-1 FUNCTION OF SPRINGS

The car frame supports the weight of the engine, the power train, the car body, and the passengers. The frame, in turn, is supported by the springs. There is a spring at each wheel. The weight of the car frame, body, and so on applies an initial compression to the springs. The springs will further compress or expand as the car wheels hit bumps or holes in the road. Springs alone cannot do the complete job of absorbing road shocks. The tires absorb the impact of many bumps and holes in the road. The springs in the car seats also help to absorb shock. As a result, very little shock from road bumps and holes gets to the passenger.

39-2 TYPES OF SPRINGS

There are three basic types of automotive springs. They are leaf, coil, and torsion bar. In addition, air suspension is used in some trucks and buses. Air suspension was offered for passenger cars some years ago, but it was not popular.

Most cars use either coil springs or torsion-bar springs at the front wheels (Figs. 39-1 and 39-2). Some cars use coil springs at the rear

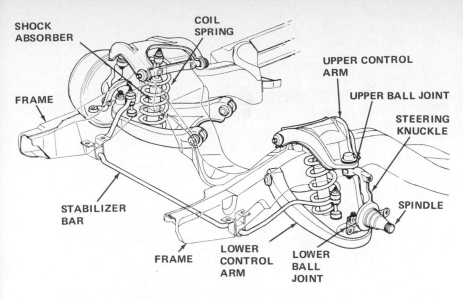

Fig. 39-1
Front-wheel suspension. The wheels mount on bearings on the tapered spindles of the steering knuckles. (*Chevrolet Motor Division of General Motors Corporation*)

SHOCK ABSORBER

COIL SPRING

UPPER CONTROL ARM

UPPER BALL JOINT

STEERING KNUCKLE

FRAME

SPINDLE

STABILIZER BAR

FRAME

LOWER CONTROL ARM

LOWER BALL JOINT

wheels. Others use leaf springs. We describe these types of springs in detail in the following sections.

39-3 LEAF SPRINGS

The leaf spring most commonly used in automobiles is made up of several long plates, or leaves. Figure 39-3 shows a typical leaf-spring installation at a rear wheel. Figure 39-4 shows how the spring at each rear wheel is mounted on the frame. Before we discuss how the leaf spring is attached, let's see how leaf springs work.

The leaf spring acts like a flexible beam. An ordinary solid beam strong enough to support the car weight would not be very flexible. For

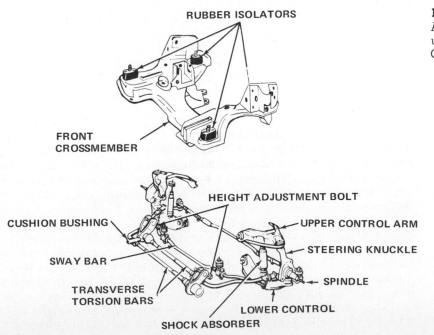

Fig. 39-2
A front-suspension system using torsion bars. (*Chrysler Corporation*)

RUBBER ISOLATORS

FRONT CROSSMEMBER

HEIGHT ADJUSTMENT BOLT

CUSHION BUSHING

UPPER CONTROL ARM

SWAY BAR

STEERING KNUCKLE

SPINDLE

TRANSVERSE TORSION BARS

LOWER CONTROL

SHOCK ABSORBER

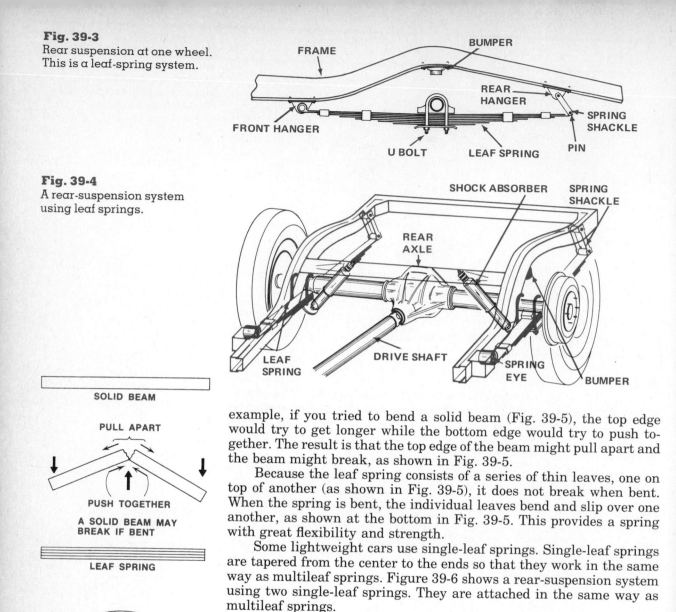

Fig. 39-3
Rear suspension at one wheel. This is a leaf-spring system.

Fig. 39-4
A rear-suspension system using leaf springs.

Fig. 39-5
Compare the effects of bending a solid beam and a leaf beam, or spring.

example, if you tried to bend a solid beam (Fig. 39-5), the top edge would try to get longer while the bottom edge would try to push together. The result is that the top edge of the beam might pull apart and the beam might break, as shown in Fig. 39-5.

Because the leaf spring consists of a series of thin leaves, one on top of another (as shown in Fig. 39-5), it does not break when bent. When the spring is bent, the individual leaves bend and slip over one another, as shown at the bottom in Fig. 39-5. This provides a spring with great flexibility and strength.

Some lightweight cars use single-leaf springs. Single-leaf springs are tapered from the center to the ends so that they work in the same way as multileaf springs. Figure 39-6 shows a rear-suspension system using two single-leaf springs. They are attached in the same way as multileaf springs.

39-4 LEAF-SPRING INSTALLATION
Now let's look again at Figs. 39-3 and 39-4. The spring leaves are of graduated length. The front end of the longest leaf is bent into a circle to form a spring eye. The spring eye is attached to the spring hanger by a bolt. Rubber bushings insulate the bolt from the spring hanger (Fig. 39-7). The rubber bushings serve two purposes. They absorb vibration and prevent it from getting up to the car frame. The bushings also allow the spring eye to twist back and forth as the leaf spring bends.

The rear end of the spring also is bent to form a spring eye. This spring eye is attached to the car frame through a spring shackle. The shackle is needed to take care of the changes in the length of the leaf spring as it bends. As the spring is pushed upward or downward by bumps or holes in the road, the length between the two spring eyes is changed. The shackle forms a swinging support that permits this

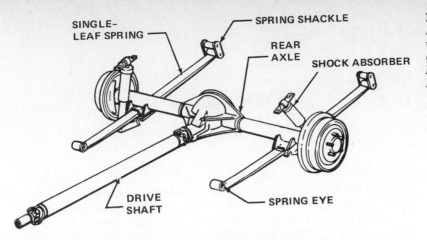

SINGLE-
LEAF SPRING

SPRING SHACKLE

REAR
AXLE

SHOCK ABSORBER

DRIVE
SHAFT

SPRING EYE

Fig. 39-6
A rear-suspension system using a tapered-plate, or single-leaf, spring. (*Chevrolet Motor Division of General Motors Corporation*)

change in length. Figure 39-8 shows a disassembled spring shackle. The shackle includes rubber bushings to absorb vibration and prevent it from getting up to the car frame.

The center of the spring is hung from the rear-axle housing by a pair of U-bolts. The rear of the car is, in effect, hung from the axle housing by two pairs of U-bolts. There are rubber bumpers on the car frame above the axles. The purpose of these bumpers is to absorb the shock that would result if the axle housing actually moved up far enough to hit the frame. The axle housing would move up this far only if the wheels hit a very large bump or if the rear of the car were carrying a very heavy load.

Two shock absorbers, one for each spring, are shown in Fig. 39-4. We describe shock absorbers in Sec. 39-14.

39-5 COIL-SPRING REAR SUSPENSION

In the rear-suspension systems of many cars, coil springs are used instead of leaf springs. The coil spring is made from a length of steel rod wound into a coil (see Fig. 39-1). The coil spring is very elastic and will compress when a weight is put on it. The heavier the weight, the more the spring will compress. Figure 39-9 shows a car using a coil spring at each wheel.

A rear-suspension system using coil springs is shown in Fig. 39-10. Each spring is assembled between spring seats in the car frame and lower control arms, or pads on the axle housing. When the rear wheels hit a hole or a bump in the road, the springs expand or compress to absorb the shock.

The coil-spring rear-suspension system shown in Fig. 39-10 has four control arms. Two of the arms are upper control arms, and two are lower control arms. The purpose of the arms is to keep the rear-axle

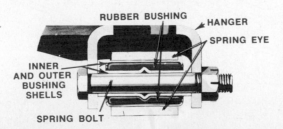

RUBBER BUSHING

HANGER

SPRING EYE

INNER
AND OUTER
BUSHING
SHELLS

SPRING BOLT

Fig. 39-7
Details of the bushing in a spring eye through which the spring eye is attached to the hanger on the car frame.

Fig. 39-8
A disassembled view of a
spring shackle for a leaf
spring.

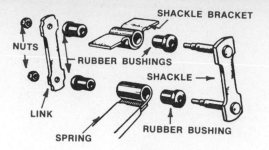

housing in alignment with the frame. The two upper control arms are pivoted on the rear cross member and the differential carrier. The upper control arms prevent sideward movement of the axle housing. The two lower control arms are pivoted on the frame and the axle housing. The lower control arms prevent forward-and-backward movement of the housing. These arms permit the rear-axle housing to move up and down. But they prevent sideward or forward-and-backward movement. As in other suspension systems, a shock absorber is used at each wheel. Figure 39-1 shows a coil-spring rear-suspension system on a front-wheel-drive car. Notice how the rear springs are mounted. Additional control arms are not needed on this car.

39-6 COIL-SPRING FRONT SUSPENSION
The front-suspension system is more complicated than the rear-suspension system. The front-suspension system must allow the wheels to move up and down. It must also allow the wheels to pivot from side to side so that the car can be steered. Figure 39-11 shows two

Fig. 39-9
A phantom view showing the
locations of the coil springs at
the front and rear of the car.
(*Chrysler Corporation*)

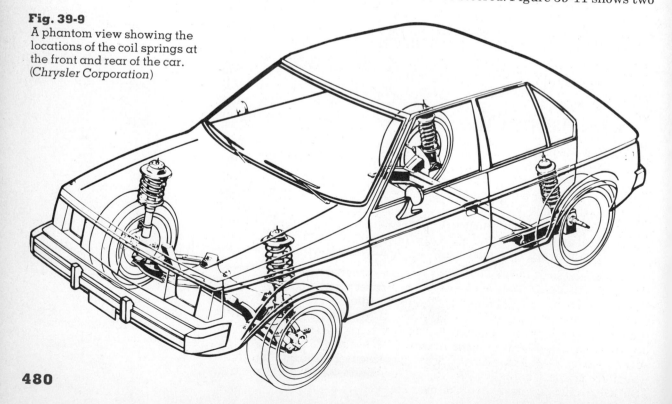

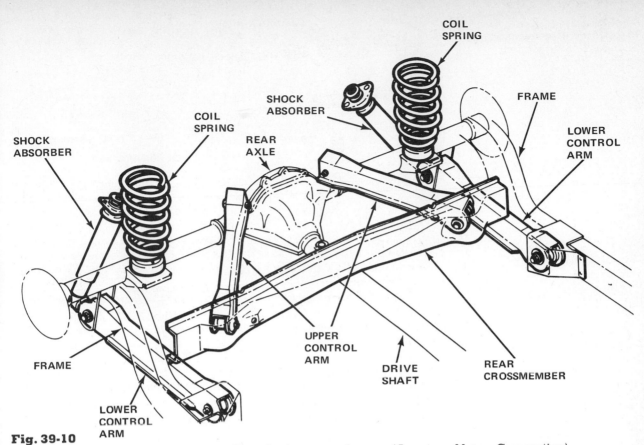

Fig. 39-10

A rear-suspension using coil springs. Note the four control arms. (*American Motors Corporation*)

views of a front-suspension system using coil springs. At the left, you see the essential parts of the system. At the upper right, you see the coil-spring suspension at one wheel in partial cutaway view. Figure 39-1 shows a similar system.

In the system shown in Fig. 39-11, the coil spring is held between a spring seat in the car frame and a lower control arm. The inner ends of both the lower and upper control arms are pivoted on the car frame. The outer ends of the control arms are connected to the steering knuckle. The steering knuckle is attached to the control arms through ball joints. These ball joints allow the steering knuckles to swing to the left or right for steering. In the assembled car, the wheels are mounted on the spindles of the steering knuckles. Swinging the knuckles from left to right pivots the front wheels so that the car can be steered. We cover steering systems in detail in Chap. 40.

Now let's see how the coil-spring front-suspension system works. Figure 39-12 shows what happens when a front wheel hits a bump in the road. Figure 39-13 shows what happens when a front wheel drops into a hole in the road. When a front wheel hits a bump (Fig. 39-12), the wheel moves up, as shown by the dashed lines. As the wheel moves up, the two control arms pivot upward. This action compresses the spring between the lower control arm and the car frame. When a front wheel drops into a hole (Fig. 39-13), the control arms pivot downward. This allows the spring to expand.

481

Fig. 39-11
A coil-spring front-suspension
system.

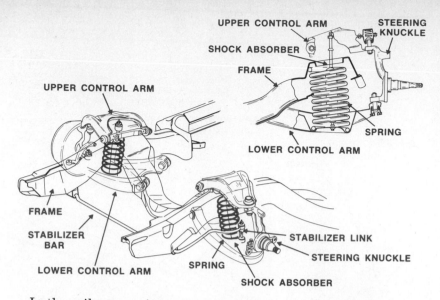

In the coil-suspension system shown in Figs. 39-11, 39-12, and 39-13 the shock absorbers are centered in the springs. We cover shock absorbers in Sec. 39-13.

CHECK UP ON YOURSELF

See how well you understand what you have studied so far about springs and suspension systems by answering the questions below.

1. What are the three types of car springs?
2. To what is the spring eye on the front end of the leaf spring attached?
3. Why does the leaf spring require a spring shackle?

Fig. 39-12
Front suspension at one wheel, showing the action as the wheel meets a bump in the road. Note how the upward movement of the wheel, shown in dashed lines, raises the lower control arm, causing the spring to compress.

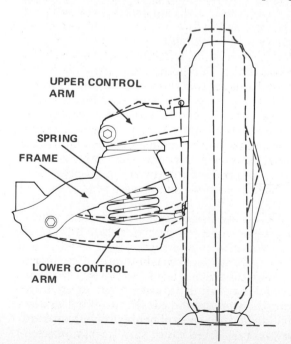

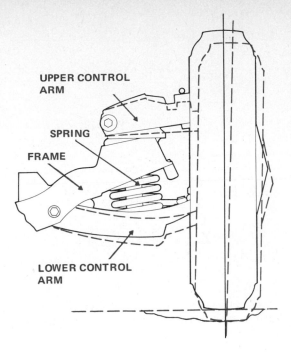

UPPER CONTROL
ARM

SPRING

FRAME

LOWER CONTROL
ARM

Fig. 39-13
Front suspension at one wheel, showing the action as the wheel meets a hole in the road. Note how the downward movement of the wheel, shown in dashed lines, lowers the lower control arm, permitting the spring to expand.

4. In the coil-spring front-suspension system, to what are the outer ends of the control arms connected?

5. In the coil-spring front-suspension system, to what are the inner ends of the control arms connected?

ANSWERS
1. Leaf, coil, and torsion bar (Sec. 39-2). **2.** A spring hanger (Sec. 39-4). **3.** Because the distance between the two spring eyes of the leaf spring changes as the spring flexes (Sec. 39-4). **4.** To the steering knuckle through ball joints (Sec. 39-6). **5.** To the car frame (Sec. 39-6).

39-7 SECOND TYPE OF COIL-SPRING FRONT SUSPENSION

Another type of front-suspension system has the coil springs mounted between the upper control arm and a spring tower that is part of the front-end sheet metal (Fig. 39-14). The action of this type of coil-spring front-suspension system is the same as the action of the system explained in Sec. 39-6. When the wheel meets a bump or a hole, the control arms pivot and compress or expand the spring. The system shown in Fig. 39-14 has a lower control arm with only one point of attachment to the frame. This system uses a strut rod to prevent the outer end of the lower control arm from swinging forward or backward.

39-8 MacPHERSON FRONT SUSPENSION

The MacPherson front suspension (see Fig. 39-9) is similar to the coil-spring suspension shown in Fig. 39-14. However, the top of the coil spring fits into a tower that is part of the body sheet metal. No upper control arm is needed. The shock absorber is built into a strut that connects the lower control arm to the mounting assembly in the tower. Figures 39-9 and 39-15 show the system in a car. Figure 39-16 shows the MacPherson strut partly disassembled. The MacPherson front-suspension system includes a strut, coil spring, stabilizer, and shock

Fig. 39-14
A coil-spring front-suspension
system of the type having the
spring above the upper control
arm.

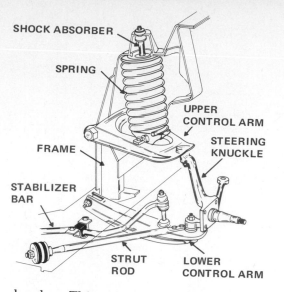

SHOCK ABSORBER

SPRING

UPPER
CONTROL ARM

STEERING
KNUCKLE

FRAME

STABILIZER
BAR

STRUT
ROD

LOWER
CONTROL ARM

absorber. This system is widely used on small cars. A variation of it
also is used for the rear suspension in some cars.

39-9 STRUT

In many front-suspension systems, the lower control arm has only one
point of attachment to the frame. Figure 39-14 shows this type of system. With this system an extra part is required. It is called a strut or a
brake-reaction rod. The strut is fastened between the outer end of the
lower control arm and the car frame. The purpose of the strut is to prevent the outer end of the lower control arm from swinging forward or
backward during braking or when the wheel hits holes or bumps in the
road. In the type of front-suspension system shown in Fig. 39-11, no
strut is needed because the lower control arm has two points of attach-

Fig. 39-15
MacPherson front suspension.
(*Volkswagen of America, Inc.*)

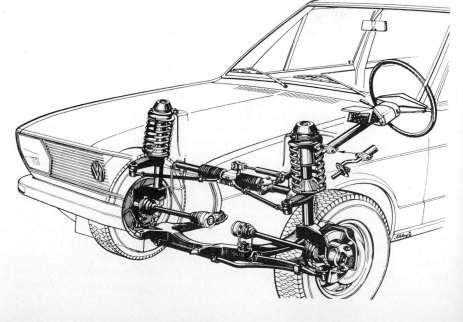

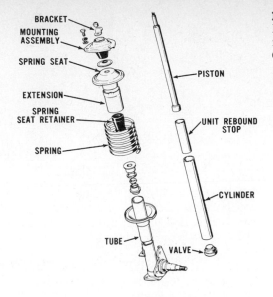

Fig. 39-16
Disassembled MacPherson front suspension. (*Ford Motor Company*)

BRACKET

MOUNTING ASSEMBLY

SPRING SEAT

EXTENSION

SPRING SEAT RETAINER

SPRING

TUBE

PISTON

UNIT REBOUND STOP

CYLINDER

VALVE

ment to the frame. These two points of attachment provide enough forward-and-backward rigidity for the lower control arm.

39-10 STABILIZER BAR

In Figs. 39-1 and 39-11, you can see a part labeled "stabilizer bar." This bar is a long steel rod, fastened at each end to the two lower control arms. The stabilizer bar is sometimes called a sway bar.

When the car goes around a curve, centrifugal force tends to keep the car moving in a straight line. The car therefore "leans out" on the turn. This "lean out" is also called "body roll." With lean-out, or body roll, additional weight is thrown on the outer spring. This weight puts additional compression on the outer spring, and the lower control arm pivots upward. As the lower control arm for the outer wheel pivots upward, it carries the end of the stabilizer bar up with it. At the inner wheel on the turn, there is less weight on the spring. Weight has shifted to the outer spring because of the centrifugal force. Therefore, the inner spring tends to expand. The expansion of the inner spring tends to pivot the lower control arm downward. As this happens, the lower control arm for the inner wheel carries the end of the stabilizer bar downward.

Now, the outer end of the stabilizer bar is carried upward by the outer lower control arm. The inner end is carried downward by the inner lower control arm. This combined action twists the stabilizer bar. The resistance of the bar to twisting opposes the tendency of the car to lean out on turns. There is less body roll than there would be without the stabilizer bar.

39-11 TORSION-BAR FRONT SUSPENSION

In the torsion-bar front-suspension system, two steel bars serve as the springs (see Figs. 39-2 and 39-17). One end of the bars is locked to a cross member of the frame. The other end of the bars is attached to the lower control arms. In operation, the lower control arms pivot up and down, twisting the torsion bars. The effect is very similar to the actions of the coil and leaf springs. Torsion bars that run across the car, as

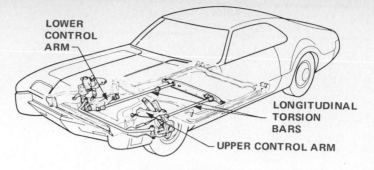

Fig. 39-17
Front suspension of a front-wheel-drive car using torsion bars. The bars are locked at the rear to the frame. They are attached at the front to the inner ends of the lower control arms. They twist varying amounts as varying loads are applied. The front wheels can move up and down, as with other suspension systems. (*Oldsmobile Division of General Motors Corporation*)

shown in Fig. 39-2, are called transverse torsion bars. When the torsion bars are installed so that they run from front to rear on the car, they are called longitudinal torsion bars. This type is shown in Fig. 39-17.

39-12 LIGHT TRUCK FRONT SUSPENSION

Two other types of front suspensions are used on light trucks. The twin I beam front-suspension system (Fig. 39-18) uses two I beams. Each front wheel is supported at the outer end by an I beam. The opposite ends of the I beams are attached to the car frame by pivots. Coil springs are used at each wheel.

Another front-suspension system for trucks is shown in Fig. 39-19. This system uses a single I beam front axle. A leaf spring and a shock absorber are used at each wheel.

39-13 SHOCK ABSORBERS

Shock absorbers are needed because springs do not "settle down" fast enough. After a spring has been compressed and released, it continues to shorten and lengthen, or oscillate, for a time. You can demonstrate to yourself the action of a spring by hanging a small weight on a spring, as shown in Fig. 39-20. Lift the weight and then let it drop. As the weight drops, it expands the spring. Then the spring pulls the weight up. The weight then drops again. The spring, as it lengthens and shortens, keeps the weight moving up and down for some time. These oscillations are shown by the wavy line at the right in Fig. 39-20.

Let's see what would happen if the car springs were not controlled and acted the same way. A wheel hits a bump. The spring compresses. Then the spring expands after the wheel passes the bump. The expan-

Fig. 39-18
A twin I beam front-suspension system using coil springs. (*Ford Motor Company*)

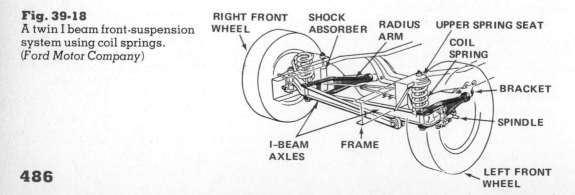

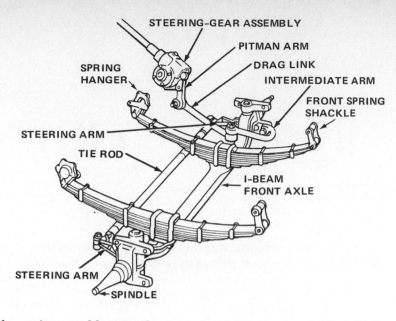

STEERING-GEAR ASSEMBLY

PITMAN ARM

SPRING HANGER

DRAG LINK

INTERMEDIATE ARM

FRONT SPRING SHACKLE

STEERING ARM

TIE ROD

I-BEAM FRONT AXLE

STEERING ARM

SPINDLE

sion of the spring would cause the car to be thrown upward. Now, having overexpanded, the spring would shorten again. This action could cause the wheel to momentarily leave the road, and the car would drop down. The action would be repeated until the oscillations gradually died out.

Such spring action on a car would produce a very bumpy and uncomfortable ride. Also, this action could be dangerous, because a bouncing wheel makes the car difficult to control. So a device is needed to control the oscillating action of the spring. This device is the shock absorber.

39-14 OPERATION OF THE SHOCK ABSORBER

The shock of the wheel meeting a bump or a hole is absorbed by the shock absorber. Because of the shock absorber, as soon as the wheel passes the hole or the bump, it returns to contact with the road and does not bounce. The most commonly used shock absorber is the direct-acting or telescope type (Fig. 39-21). Several illustrations in this chapter show the locations of the shock absorbers at the front and the back of the car. In operation, the shock absorbers lengthen and shorten as

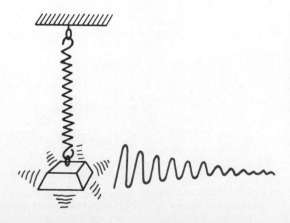

Fig. 39-20
If a weight hanging from a coil spring is set into up-and-down motion, it will oscillate for some time. The distance it moves up and down will gradually shorten, as indicated by the curve. Finally, the motion will die out.

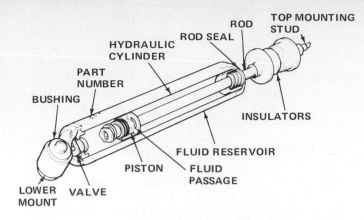

Fig. 39-21
A cutaway view of a direct-acting shock absorber (*Ford Motor Company*)

Labels: TOP MOUNTING STUD, ROD, ROD SEAL, HYDRAULIC CYLINDER, PART NUMBER, BUSHING, INSULATORS, FLUID RESERVOIR, PISTON, FLUID PASSAGE, VALVE, LOWER MOUNT

the wheels meet irregularities in the road. As they do this, a piston inside the shock absorber moves up and down in a chamber filled with fluid. Movement of the piston puts the fluid under high pressure and forces it to flow through the small openings. Since the fluid can pass through these openings only slowly, the fluid slows the motion of the piston. This, in turn, restrains the movement of the spring.

Figure 39-21 shows a shock absorber in cutaway view. During compression and rebound, the piston moves up and down. The fluid in the shock absorber is forced through small openings in the piston. You can see one of the fluid passages through the piston in Fig. 39-21. This action controls spring movement.

When the wheel receives a sudden severe shock, pressure in the shock absorber could go so high that it would rip open. To prevent this, a valve in the shock absorber opens when the internal pressure gets excessive. When the valve opens, it allows a slightly faster spring movement. However, some restraint is still imposed on the spring.

39-15 AUTOMATIC LEVEL CONTROL

The automatic-level-control system takes care of changes in the amount of load in the rear of the car. In a car without automatic level control, additional weight makes the rear end of the car squat. This changes the handling characteristics of the car. It also causes the headlights to point upward. The automatic level control prevents this by automatically raising the rear end of the car to level when a load is

Fig. 39-22
An automatic-level-control system. The dotted lines show the lower ride height of the car before the automatic level control restores the correct height.

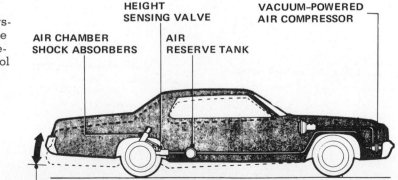

Labels: HEIGHT SENSING VALVE, VACUUM-POWERED AIR COMPRESSOR, AIR CHAMBER SHOCK ABSORBERS, AIR RESERVE TANK, AUTOMATIC ADJUSTMENT TO 3-PASSENGER HEIGHT

488

added. The system also automatically lowers the rear end of the car to level when the load is removed.

The automatic-level-control system includes a compressor, an air-reserve tank, a height-control valve, and two special shock absorbers with built-in air chambers (Fig. 39-22). The compressor is operated by engine intake-manifold vacuum. The vacuum operates a pump that builds up air pressure in the reserve tank. When a load is added to the rear of the car, additional air is passed through the height-control valve to the two rear shock absorbers. These shock absorbers have air chambers, as shown in Fig. 39-23. The air entering this chamber raises the upper shell of the shock absorber. As the upper shell of the shock absorber is raised, the rear of the car is returned to its normal level.

Figure 39-24 shows an electronic type of automatic-level-control system. The air is supplied by an electric air compressor, instead of a vacuum-powered air compressor. No separate height-control valve is needed. A photo-optic sensor (electric eye) is built into the left rear shock absorber. The sensor tells the electronic control module when any change in height has occurred. If a load has been added to the car and additional height is needed, the electronic control module turns on the air compressor.

In both types of automatic level control, a time-delay device is used. It allows air to enter or leave the shock absorber only after a change in level has lasted about 15 seconds. This prevents fast valve action, which could raise or lower the car after each bump or hole in the road. The automatic-level-control system works only when loads are added to or removed from the rear of the car.

39-16 SERVICING THE SUSPENSION SYSTEM

Suspension-system service is closely tied in with wheel alignment and steering service. In Chap. 40 we discuss steering systems. In Chap. 41 we cover servicing procedures for steering and suspension systems.

CHECK UP ON YOURSELF

Answer the questions that follow to test your understanding of the last half of the chapter on springs and suspension.

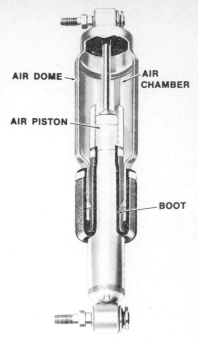

Fig. 39-23
A cutaway view of the special shock absorber (called a Superlift by the manufacturer) used in the automatic level control.

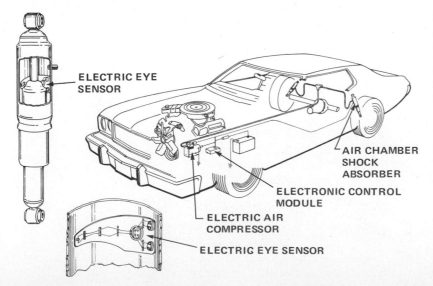

Fig. 39-24
An electronic automatic-level-control system. It uses an electric eye to switch the electric air compressor on and off. (*Monroe Auto Equipment Company*)

1. What are the two types of lower control arms used on front-suspension systems? Which type uses a strut rod?
2. What is the purpose of the stabilizer bar?
3. What is the purpose of the strut rod?
4. What is the purpose of the shock absorber?
5. What is the purpose of automatic level control?

ANSWERS

1. The type with a single point of attachment to the frame and the type with two points of attachment to the frame. The type with a single point of attachment uses a strut (Sec. 39-9). 2. To reduce body roll (Sec. 39-10). 3. To keep the lower control arm from swinging forward or backward (Sec. 39-9). 4. To control spring movement and prevent spring oscillations after the wheel has passed a bump or a hole (Sec. 39-13). 5. To maintain normal height of the rear end of the car regardless of load in the car (Sec. 39-15).

CHAPTER FORTY
STEERING SYSTEMS

After studying this chapter, you should be able to:

1. Explain the construction, purpose, and operation of steering systems.
2. Discuss front-end geometry and the various angles involved.
3. Describe the construction and operation of manual- and power-steering gears.

The steering system allows the driver to guide the car down the road and turn right or left, as desired. The system includes the steering wheel, which the driver turns, linkages, and the front-wheel supports. Most steering systems were manual until a few years ago. Then power steering became popular. Now it is installed on about 95 percent of the cars manufactured in the United States.

40-1 OPERATION OF THE STEERING SYSTEM

Figure 40-1 is a simplified view, from above, of a steering system. We describe the method of supporting the front wheels on steering knuckles in Chap. 39. The steering knuckles are attached to the upper and lower control arms by ball joints. These ball joints permit the steering knuckles to swing from right to left. This movement turns the front wheels one way or the other so that the car can be steered.

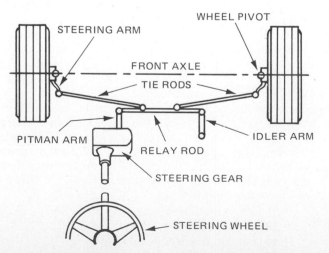

Fig. 40-1
A simplified drawing of a steering system.

In the simplified steering system, you see the steering wheel, steering gear, tie rods, steering arms, and wheels. When the steering wheel is turned, gears inside the steering gear cause the pitman arm to swing to the left or right. As the pitman arm swings, it pulls or pushes on the tie rods. This action pulls or pushes on the steering arms. The steering knuckles and wheels turn the amount desired by the driver in order to steer the car.

Before we describe the steering gears and linkages in detail, let's discuss the various angles in the front-suspension system.

40-2 FRONT-END GEOMETRY

The term "front-end geometry" or "steering geometry" refers to the various angles between the front wheels, the frame, and the attachment parts. The angles that we will discuss in this chapter are listed below:

1. Camber
2. Steering-axis inclination
3. Caster
4. Toe
5. Turning radius

We will look at each of these angles in the following sections. The technician checks these angles when doing a wheel alignment. Each angle is important. If the angles are off, the car will be harder to control and the tires will wear rapidly.

40-3 CAMBER

Camber is the tilting of the front wheels from the vertical (straight up and down). When the wheel tilts outward at the top, the camber is positive (Fig. 40-2). When the tilt is inward, the camber is negative. The amount of tilt is measured as the number of degrees from the vertical. This measurement is called the camber angle. On a moving car, an average running camber of zero provides the longest tire life.

The purpose of camber is to give the wheels a slight outward tilt to start with (on most cars). Then, when the car is loaded and moving, the load will bring the wheels to vertical again. When the wheels are set to zero camber, then loading the car could give the front wheels a negative camber. The tops of the wheels would tilt inward. When the car is rolling forward, the car will pull toward the wheel with the most positive camber.

Any amount of camber—positive or negative—will cause uneven tire wear. The tilt puts more of the load on one side of the tread rather than centering the load over the entire tread.

40-4 STEERING-AXIS INCLINATION

Steering-axis inclination is the amount the ball joints are tilted inward from the vertical. You can see this angle in the simplified view in Fig. 40-2. An actual cutaway front suspension at one wheel is shown in Fig. 40-3. Steering-axis inclination is measured by drawing a line through the centers of the two ball joints. Then you measure how many degrees this line is off from the vertical. There are three reasons for having steering-axis inclination:

- It helps provide steering stability.
- It reduces steering effort.
- It reduces tire wear.

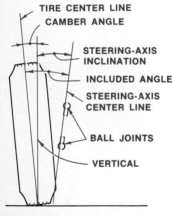

Fig. 40-2
Camber angle and steering-axis inclination. The angles are shown exaggerated.

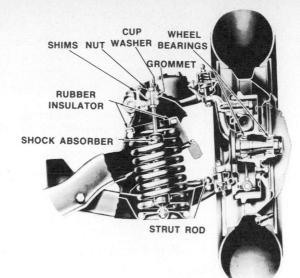

SHIMS NUT CUP WASHER WHEEL BEARINGS

GROMMET

RUBBER INSULATOR

SHOCK ABSORBER

STRUT ROD

Fig. 40-3
A passenger-car front suspension using coil springs. The frame, wheel, and other parts are partly cut away to show suspension parts. (*Pontiac Motor Division of General Motors Corporation*)

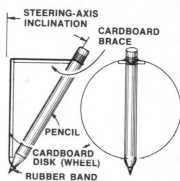

STEERING-AXIS INCLINATION

CARDBOARD BRACE

PENCIL

CARDBOARD DISK (WHEEL)

RUBBER BAND

Fig. 40-4
A cardboard disk to serve as the wheel, a rubber band, and a cardboard brace demonstrate the effects of steering-axis inclination.

The inward tilt, or inclination, of the steering axis tends to keep the wheels pointed straight ahead. It also helps recovery, or the return of the wheels to the straight-ahead position, after a turn. To demonstrate this for yourself, cut out a cardboard disk and a cardboard brace, as shown in Fig. 40-4. Tape them together and attach them to a pencil with a rubber band, as shown in Fig. 40-4. The cardboard disk represents the wheel. The pencil represents the ball-joint center line. The brace at the top holds the disk and the pencil apart so as to get steering-axis inclination. In Fig. 40-4, the angle is greatly exaggerated.

Now, hold the pencil at an angle to the table top so that the wheel is vertical, as shown in Fig. 40-5. Then rotate the pencil, but do not change its angle. As you do this, the wheel is carried around and down toward the table top. If the wheel could not move down, the pencil would be moved up.

This actually is what happens in the car. The wheel is in contact with the ground. It cannot move down. Therefore, when the wheel is swung away from straight ahead, the end of the spindle moves down. This forces the ball joints to move up. The result is that the car body is actually lifted. The lift is not very much, only about 1 inch [25 mm] or

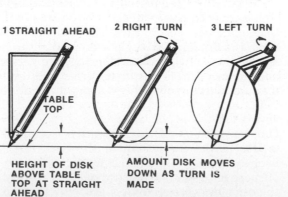

1 STRAIGHT AHEAD   2 RIGHT TURN   3 LEFT TURN

TABLE TOP

HEIGHT OF DISK ABOVE TABLE TOP AT STRAIGHT AHEAD

AMOUNT DISK MOVES DOWN AS TURN IS MADE

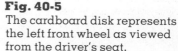

Fig. 40-5
The cardboard disk represents the left front wheel as viewed from the driver's seat.

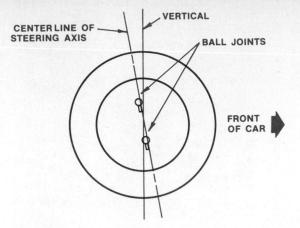

less. But it is enough to help bring the wheels back to the straight-ahead position when the car completes a turn. Now you know one purpose of steering-axis inclination: When the front wheels are turned away from straight ahead, the front end of the car is raised slightly. Then the weight of the car helps to bring the wheels back to the straight-ahead position when the turn is completed. Steering-axis inclination provides steering stability and reduces the effort required to return the steering wheel to straight ahead. Steering-axis inclination cannot be adjusted, but it can be measured. Incorrect steering-axis inclination means that the steering knuckle is bent.

40-5 CASTER

In addition to being tilted inward toward the center of the car, the steering axis is also tilted forward or backward. Backward tilt from the vertical is called *positive caster*. This tilt is shown in Fig. 40-6. Caster provides steering stability. It does this because the wheel trails behind the point at which the forward push is applied (see Fig. 40-7). If you push on a table leg that has a caster, the caster wheel will trail behind the leg. You can see that the wheel trails behind the push. In the car, the push is at the center line of the steering axis, as shown in Fig. 40-6. This puts the push ahead of the wheel. Therefore, the wheel tends to point straight ahead. This helps steering stability. Positive caster helps to keep the wheels pointed straight ahead. It helps overcome any tendency for the car to wander or steer away from straight ahead.

Positive caster increases steering-wheel returnability. Because of this, cars with power steering often have slightly more positive caster than manual-steering cars. The additional positive caster helps overcome the tendency of the power steering to hold the wheels in a turn. But because of the power steering, the driver does not notice that the additional positive caster requires greater turning effort. Cars with manual steering often have a small negative caster.

40-6 TOE

On a car with *toe-in,* the distance between the tires on the front wheels is less at the front than at the back (Fig. 40-8). The actual toe-in usually is less than 0.5 inch [13 mm]. But toe-in is very important. The purpose of toe-in is to ensure parallel rolling of the front wheels when the car moves forward. To start with, there is toe-in. But when the car

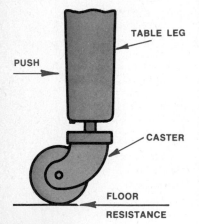

Fig. 40-7
The wheel of the caster trails behind and follows in the direction of the push when the table leg is moved.

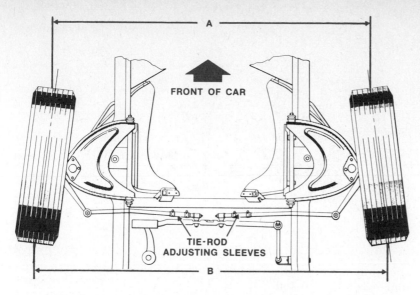

Fig. 40-8
Front-wheel toe-in. The wheels are shown from above and the front of the car is at the top. To find toe-in, subtract B from B. Toe-in is greatly exaggerated in this illustration. (*Bear Manufacturing Company*)

TIE-ROD
ADJUSTING SLEEVES

begins to move forward, the backward push of the road on the tires takes up the play in the steering linkage. This brings the tires into parallel, so they both roll straight ahead.

40-7 TURNING RADIUS

Turning radius, or *toe-out on turns,* is the difference in angles between the two front wheels when they are making a turn. Look at Fig. 40-9. The inner wheel follows a smaller arc. Therefore it must be turned more than the outer wheel. In the example shown, the inner wheel turns 23 degrees away from straight ahead, but the outer wheel turns in only 20 degrees. The way the linkage is attached to the steering knuckles produces this difference (Fig. 40-10). In the example shown, the tie rod is pushing against the left steering-knuckle arm almost at a right angle. The right end of the tie rod not only moves to the left but also swings down. This swing-down effect turns the right wheel more than the left.

40-8 STEERING LINKAGES

There are several types of steering linkages. All have the same job. They carry the movement of the pitman arm to the steering-knuckle arms. Figure 40-11 shows the parts of one type of steering linkage. It includes an intermediate rod, which is supported at one end by the pitman arm and at the other end by the idler arm. The outer ends of the intermediate rod are attached to the steering-knuckle arms by short tie rods. Notice that the tie rods have adjuster sleeves. The purpose of these sleeves is to adjust toe-in. When an adjuster sleeve is turned, it shortens or lengthens the effective length of the tie rod. This swings

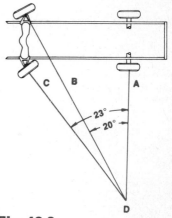

Fig. 40-9
Toe-out on turns, also called *turning radius.*

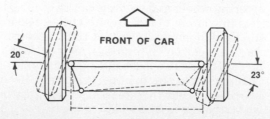

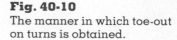

FRONT OF CAR

20°

23°

Fig. 40-10
The manner in which toe-out on turns is obtained.

Fig. 40-11
Basic parts of a steering
linkage.

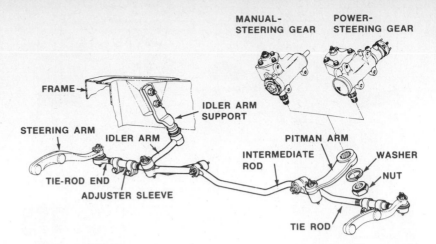

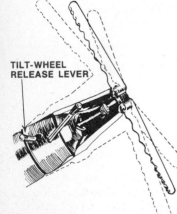

Fig. 40-12
A tilt steering wheel. Lifting
the release lever permits the
steering wheel to be tilted to
various positions, as shown.
(*Buick Motor Division of General Motors Corporation*)

the front wheel slightly one way or the other. Later, we will explain
how toe-in is adjusted.

CHECK UP ON YOURSELF

Here is your chance to check up on yourself. If you can answer all
the questions that follow, you have done a good job studying the
first half of the chapter. If you miss one or more, study the section to
find the answer.

1. What is camber?
2. What is steering-axis inclination?
3. What is caster?
4. What is toe?
5. What is turning radius?

ANSWERS

1. The tilting of the front wheels from the vertical (Sec. 40-3). **2.** The amount
the ball joints are tilted inward from the vertical (Sec. 40-4). **3.** The tilt of the
ball joints forward or backward from the vertical (Sec. 40-5). **4.** The pointing
in of the front wheels so that the wheels are closer together at the front than at
the back (Sec. 40-6). **5.** The difference in angles between the two front wheels
during turns. The inner wheel on a turn turns out more than the outer wheel
(Sec. 40-7).

40-9 TILT STEERING WHEEL

Many cars have steering wheels that can be tilted at various angles.
The purpose of the tilt steering wheel is to allow the driver to change
the angle as desired. The driver can also change the position of the
steering wheel during a long drive. Figure 40-12 shows a tilt wheel.

Some cars also have a telescoping steering wheel. This wheel (Fig.
40-13) can be extended or shortened to suit the driver. Another type of
steering wheel and column can be swung to the right when the driver
gets into or out of the car. All these steering column devices have locking mechanisms, which lock the wheel into the position selected. Also,
the tilt steering column has an interlock to the transmission selector
lever. This device locks out the transmission until the steering column
is returned to the driving position. The interlock is a safety feature
which prevents the steering column from being accidentally moved
while the car is in operation.

40-10 COLLAPSIBLE STEERING COLUMN

The collapsible steering column is a safety device. It will collapse on impact. For example, in a front-end collision, the driver will be thrown forward and into the steering wheel. This will cause the steering column to collapse and thereby cushion the driver's impact.

NOTE

A driver wearing a shoulder belt will not be thrown into the steering wheel.

There are several types of collapsible steering columns. These include the "Japanese-lantern" type, the tube-and-ball type, and the shear-capsule type. Figure 40-14 shows the Japanese-lantern type. It gets its name from the fact that on impact the column collapses like a Japanese lantern. The tube-and-ball type, shown in Fig. 40-15, has two tubes with balls between them. On impact, the balls must make

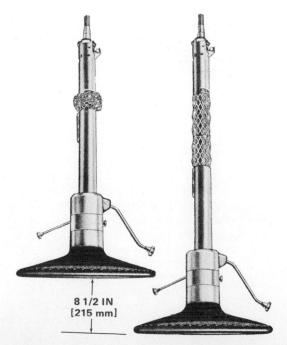

Fig. 40-14
An energy-absorbing, or collapsible, steering column of the "Japanese-lantern" design. The column collapses on impact, as shown to the left.

497

Fig. 40-15
An energy-absorbing, or collapsible, steering column of
the tube-and-ball design.
(*General Motors Corporation*)

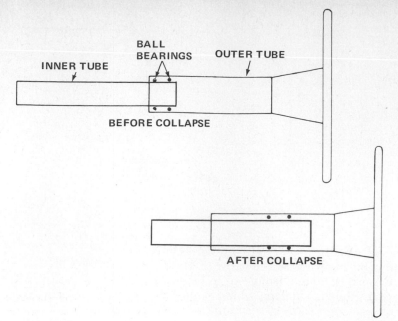

INNER TUBE

BALL
BEARINGS   OUTER TUBE

BEFORE COLLAPSE

AFTER COLLAPSE

grooves in the tubes to permit movement. This action absorbs the
shock. On the shear-capsule type (Fig. 40-16), the impact cuts the capsule to permit the steering column to collapse. The shearing action absorbs the shock.

40-11 STEERING LOCK

The combination ignition switch and steering-wheel lock (Fig. 40-17)
does several jobs. It locks the steering wheel when the ignition switch
is turned off. When the ignition key is inserted and the ignition switch
is turned to ON, the gear rotates. This pulls the rack and plunger out of
the locking position. Then, when the switch is turned to OFF, the rotation of the gear moves the rack and plunger toward the locked position.
If the plunger is lined up with a notch in the disk, the plunger moves in
to lock the steering wheel. If it is not lined up, the plunger is spring-

Fig. 40-16
Shear-capsule type of collapsible steering column.

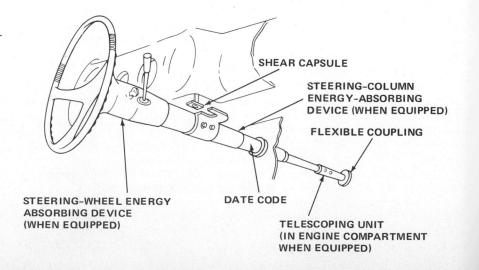

SHEAR CAPSULE

STEERING-COLUMN
ENERGY-ABSORBING
DEVICE (WHEN EQUIPPED)

FLEXIBLE COUPLING

STEERING-WHEEL ENERGY
ABSORBING DEVICE
(WHEN EQUIPPED)

DATE CODE

TELESCOPING UNIT
(IN ENGINE COMPARTMENT
WHEN EQUIPPED)

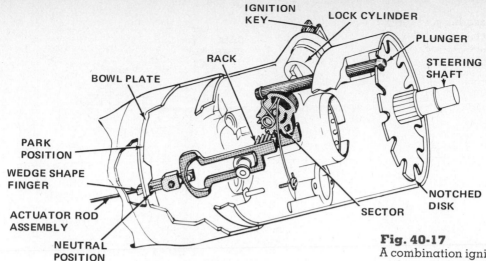

IGNITION KEY — LOCK CYLINDER

PLUNGER

STEERING SHAFT

RACK

BOWL PLATE

PARK POSITION

WEDGE SHAPE FINGER

ACTUATOR ROD ASSEMBLY

NEUTRAL POSITION

SECTOR

NOTCHED DISK

Fig. 40-17
A combination ignition switch and steering lock, showing the ignition switch off and the steering locked. (*Buick Motor Division of General Motors Corporation*)

loaded against the disk. Then a slight turn of the steering wheel will bring a notch into line. The plunger will drop into the notch to lock the steering wheel.

NOTE

The ignition switch also serves as a starting switch. When it is turned past ON to START, it connects the starting motor to the battery. This cranks the engine for starting.

40-12 STEERING GEARS

There are two types of steering gears. These are manual and power. We will discuss manual steering first. The steering gear converts the rotary motion of the steering wheel into straight-line motion, which moves the linkage to the steering arms on the steering knuckles. This swings the front wheels left or right for steering.

The steering gear has two essential parts. They are a worm gear on the end of the steering shaft and a matching sector gear or toothed roller attached to the sector shaft.

Figure 40-18 shows one type of steering gear. As the steering shaft and worm gear rotate, the sector gear must follow the worm gear. The sector gear is moved toward one end of the worm or the other, as the ball nut moves up and down on it. The sector-gear movement causes the pitman arm to swing one way or the other.

Friction is kept low by using balls between the major moving parts. The balls roll between the worm teeth and the grooves cut in the hole in the ball nut. As the worm turns, the balls roll in the worm teeth. The balls must also roll in the grooves inside the ball nut. As the worm rotates, the balls cause the nut to move up or down along the worm. This motion is carried by the teeth on the outside of the ball nut to the teeth on the sector gear. The sector gear must move. This movement rotates the sector shaft which swings the pitman arm.

The steering gear in Fig. 40-18 is called a *recirculating ball steering gear*. The balls move from one end of the worm gear to the other. When the balls reach the end, they enter ball-return guides. which take them back into the ball nut.

499

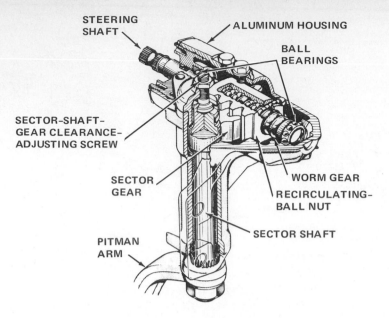

Fig. 40-18
A phantom view of a recirculating-ball steering gear.
(Chrysler Corporation)

STEERING SHAFT

ALUMINUM HOUSING

BALL BEARINGS

SECTOR-SHAFT-GEAR CLEARANCE-ADJUSTING SCREW

SECTOR GEAR

WORM GEAR

RECIRCULATING-BALL NUT

SECTOR SHAFT

PITMAN ARM

40-13 RACK-AND-PINION STEERING

The rack-and-pinion steering gear, used on some small cars, is shown in Fig. 40-19. This system has a pinion gear on the end of the lower steering shaft (Fig. 40-20). The pinion is meshed with a rack of gear teeth cut on the underside of the major cross member of the steering linkage. When the steering wheel is turned, the pinion turns. This moves the rack to the left or right. The movement is carried through tie rods to the steering arms at the front wheels.

Fig. 40-19
A rack-and-pinion steering system. *(Ford Motor Company)*

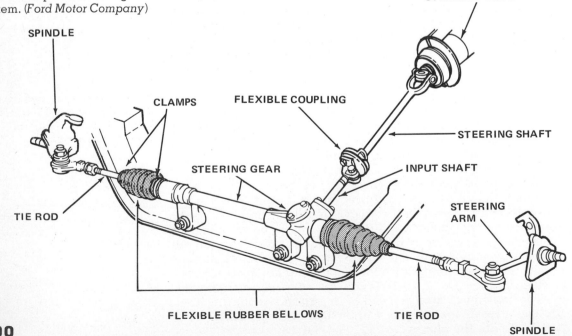

STEERING COLUMN

SPINDLE

CLAMPS

FLEXIBLE COUPLING

STEERING SHAFT

STEERING GEAR

INPUT SHAFT

STEERING ARM

TIE ROD

FLEXIBLE RUBBER BELLOWS

TIE ROD

SPINDLE

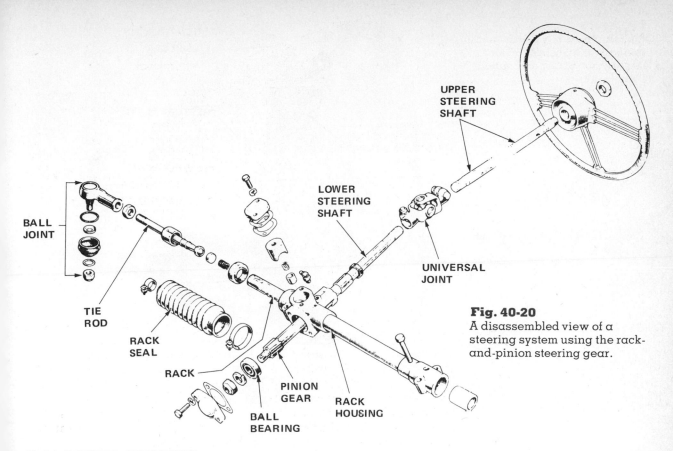

BALL
JOINT

TIE
ROD

RACK
SEAL

RACK

BALL
BEARING

PINION
GEAR

RACK
HOUSING

LOWER
STEERING
SHAFT

UPPER
STEERING
SHAFT

UNIVERSAL
JOINT

Fig. 40-20
A disassembled view of a
steering system using the rack-
and-pinion steering gear.

40-14 POWER STEERING

In the power-steering system, a pump sends fluid under pressure into
the steering gear. This high-pressure fluid does about 80 percent of the
work of steering. Figure 40-21 shows the power-steering system for a
car with a six-cylinder engine. The steering-gear assembly looks almost like the manual-steering gear, except that the power-steering

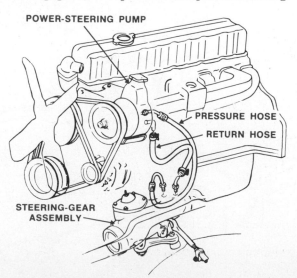

POWER-STEERING PUMP

PRESSURE HOSE

RETURN HOSE

STEERING-GEAR
ASSEMBLY

Fig. 40-21
The power-steering system for
a six-cylinder car. (*Chevrolet
Motor Division of General
Motors Corporation*)

501

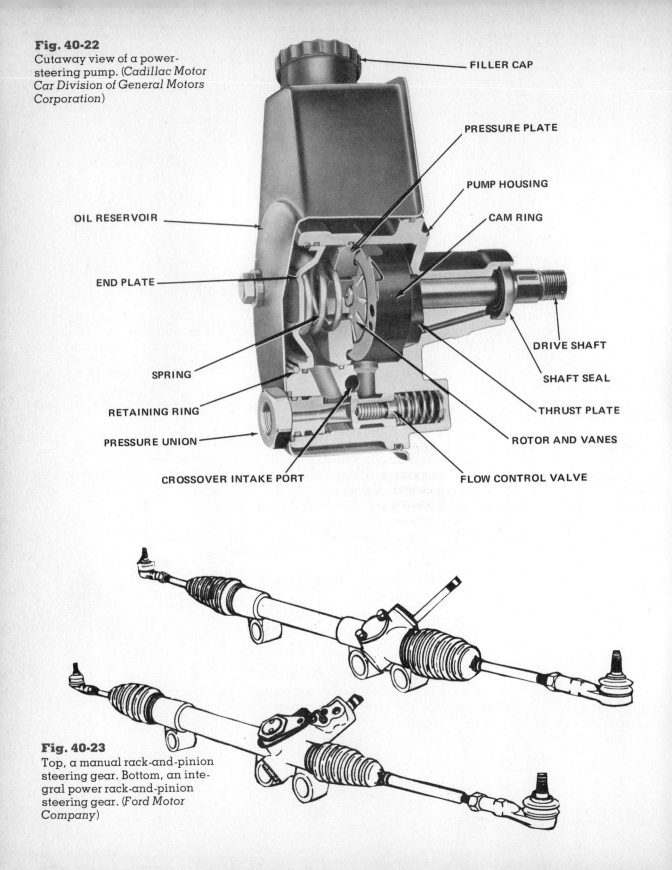

Fig. 40-22 Cutaway view of a power-steering pump. (*Cadillac Motor Car Division of General Motors Corporation*)

FILLER CAP

PRESSURE PLATE

PUMP HOUSING

CAM RING

OIL RESERVOIR

END PLATE

DRIVE SHAFT

SHAFT SEAL

THRUST PLATE

SPRING

RETAINING RING

ROTOR AND VANES

PRESSURE UNION

CROSSOVER INTAKE PORT

FLOW CONTROL VALVE

Fig. 40-23 Top, a manual rack-and-pinion steering gear. Bottom, an integral power rack-and-pinion steering gear. (*Ford Motor Company*)

gear is larger. Figure 40-21 shows the mounting arrangement for the steering gear and pump in one model of Chevrolet. The pump is driven by a belt from the crankshaft pulley. In operation, the pump produces a high pressure on the power-steering fluid. This fluid is a special oil.

Figure 40-22 shows the working parts of a typical power-steering pump. The rotor rotates, and the vanes move in and out of the slots in the pump rotor. As the vanes move out of the slots, the space between the vanes increases. Fluid is drawn into the space. Then, with further rotation, the vanes are pushed back into the slots. This decreases the space between the vanes. The fluid is forced out under pressure. It goes through hoses to the steering-gear assembly. The pump has a flow-control or pressure-relief valve, which opens if the pressure goes too high.

40-15 AN INTEGRAL POWER-STEERING GEAR

This basically is a manual-steering gear that has a hydraulic control system built into it. Figure 40-11 shows a manual-steering gear and an integral power-steering gear. The integral power-steering gear looks similar to the manual-steering gear on the outside. However, the power-steering gear is slightly larger, and it has two hoses connected to it. Figure 40-23 shows a manual rack-and-pinion steering gear (at the top) and a power-steering gear of the same type for the same car (at the bottom). Figure 40-24 shows what a typical power-steering gear looks like in sectional view. It is a recirculating-ball steering gear, with a piston and a spool valve added. The piston ball nut has a rack on it, as shown in Fig. 40-24. This rack is meshed with the sector gear on the sector shaft. When the sector shaft moves, the attached pitman arm turns with it.

Power-steering gears made by different manufacturers sometimes vary in appearance and construction. But they all work in the same general way. When the car is driven straight ahead, fluid pressure from the pump is equal to both sides of the piston. This is the condition shown in Fig. 40-24. However, when a turn is made, the twisting force on the input shaft causes a valve to operate. This valve moves to open passages that send fluid at high pressure to one side of the piston-and-

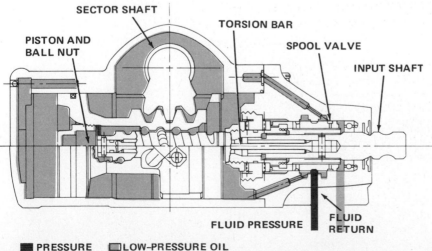

Fig. 40-24
A cutaway view of a rotary-valve power-steering gear. (*Ford Motor Company*)

SECTOR SHAFT

TORSION BAR

PISTON AND BALL NUT

SPOOL VALVE

INPUT SHAFT

FLUID PRESSURE

FLUID RETURN

■ PRESSURE ▢ LOW–PRESSURE OIL

503

Fig. 40-25
Linkage-type power-steering system. (*Ford Motor Company*)

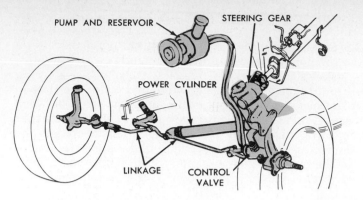

ball nut. Most of the steering effort required to make the turn is supplied by the high-pressure fluid.

40-16 LINKAGE-TYPE POWER STEERING

A linkage type of power steering can be added to certain models of cars built with only manual steering. The linkage type of power steering has a separate power cylinder and control valve. They are connected into the steering linkage as shown in Fig. 40-25. When a turn is made, the control valve operates to send high-pressure fluid to one or the other end of the piston in the power cylinder. One end of the power cylinder is fastened to the car frame. The other end connects to the steering linkage, as shown in Fig. 40-25. Figure 40-26 shows the action in the hydraulic system and power cylinder during a right turn.

CHECK UP ON YOURSELF

See how well you understand what you have studied about steering systems. Check up on yourself by answering these questions.

1. What are three arrangements for changing the steering wheel position?

Fig. 40-26
Action in the linkage-type power-steering system during a right turn. (*Ford Motor Company*)

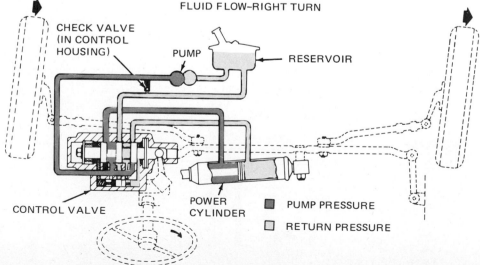

2. What are the three basic jobs that the combination ignition switch does?

3. In the rack-and-pinion steering gear, where is the pinion? Where is the rack?

4. Where does the pressure that operates the power-steering gear come from?

5. In the power-steering gear described, what actuates the control valve?

ANSWERS

1. Tilt steering wheel, telescoping steering wheel, and tilt steering wheel and column (Sec. 40-9). **2.** Lock ignition, lock steering wheel, and serve as a starting switch (Sec. 40-11). **3.** The pinion is on the end of the steering shaft. The rack is part of the steering linkage (Sec. 40-13). **4.** From a pump driven by a belt from the crankshaft pulley (Sec. 40-14). **5.** The twisting of a torsion bar (Sec. 40-15).

CHAPTER FORTY-ONE
STEERING AND SUSPENSION SERVICE

After studying this chapter, you should be able to:

1. Discuss the diagnosis of steering and suspension troubles and their possible causes and corrections.
2. Explain the procedures for checking wheel alignment and making necessary adjustments.

In this chapter we cover the highlights of steering and suspension service. Checking wheel alignment means measuring camber, caster, toe, steering-axis inclination, and turning radius. When you work in the shop, you will be given instructions on how to service specific models of cars and how to use the alignment equipment in the shop.

41-1 DIAGNOSING STEERING AND SUSPENSION TROUBLES

Here we list the various troubles that can occur because of conditions in the steering or suspension system:

1. Excessive play in the steering system.
2. Hard steering.
3. Car wander.
4. Car pulls to one side during normal driving.
5. Car pulls to one side during braking.
6. Front-wheel shimmy at low speed.
7. Front-wheel tramp (high-speed shimmy).
8. Steering kickback.
9. Tire squeal on turns.
10. Incorrect tire wear.
11. Hard or rough ride.
12. Sway on turns.
13. Spring breakage.
14. Sagging springs.
15. Noises.

Let's take a closer look at each of these troubles.

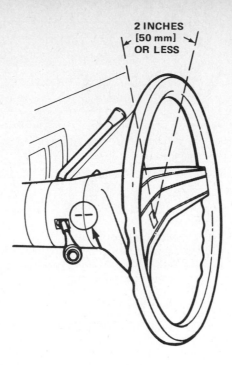

2 INCHES
[50 mm]
OR LESS

41-2 EXCESSIVE PLAY IN THE STEERING SYSTEM

Excessive play in the steering system shows up as free movement of the steering wheel without corresponding movement of the front wheels (Fig. 41-1). A small amount of free play is desirable because it makes steering easier. But when the play is excessive, it can make steering harder. The steering-wheel rim should move less than 2 inches [50 mm] before the front wheels begin to move. Excessive play can be due to the following causes:

- Looseness in the steering gear or linkage
- Worn steering-knuckle parts
- Loose wheel bearings

The tie rods and linkage may be checked for looseness by raising the car. Grasp the front wheels and push out on both wheels at the same time (Fig. 41-2). Then pull in on both wheels at the same time. Excessive movement means worn linkage parts.

Worn steering-knuckle parts such as ball joints can be checked by raising the car. Then grasp the wheel at the top and bottom (Fig. 41-3). If you can wobble the wheel, there is looseness in the wheel bearings or ball joints. Have someone apply the brakes as you again try to rock the wheel. If applying the brakes eliminates the free play, the wheel bearing is loose.

Figures 41-4 and 41-5 show how to check for ball-joint wear. Axial play is checked by moving the wheel up and down. Radial play is checked by rocking the wheel back and forth. Some cars have wear-indicating ball joints. On these, a visual check may be all that is necessary (Fig. 41-6). When the grease-fitting nipple has receded into the ball-joint socket, replace the ball joint.

A quick check for steering-gear wear or looseness can be made by watching the pitman arm while an assistant turns the steering wheel.

Fig. 41-2
Checking tie rods and linkage for looseness.

The steering wheel should be turned one way and then the other with the front wheels on the floor. If steering-wheel rim movement of 2 inches [50 mm] or more is required to make the pitman arm move after reversing wheel direction, there is looseness in the steering gear.

41-3 HARD STEERING

If hard steering occurs just after the steering system has been worked on, the trouble probably is due to excessively tight adjustments in the steering gear or linkages. If hard steering occurs at other times, it could be due to any one of the following problems:

- Inoperative power steering
- Low or uneven tire pressure
- Excessive friction in the steering gear or linkage or at the ball joints
- Improper front-wheel alignment—incorrect camber, caster, or steering-axis inclination
- Frame misalignment
- Sagging springs

Fig. 41-3
Checking for wear in the steering knuckle and wheel bearings. (*Bear Manufacturing Company*)

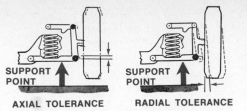

Fig. 41-4
To check ball joints for wear on
a suspension system with the
spring on the lower arm, support the wheel under the arm,
as shown.

On a car with power steering, failure of the power steering will cause the steering system to change to mechanical steering. It will require greater steering effort to turn the steering wheel. When this happens, the power-steering system and the pump should be checked. First, check the fluid level in the pump fluid reservoir. If the problem is not low fluid level, install a pressure gauge in the system and check the pressures.

The steering linkage can be checked for binding by raising the front end of the car. Turn the steering wheel from left to right. If you feel any binding, disconnect the linkage from the pitman arm. If this relieves the hard steering, the trouble is in the linkage. If hard steering is still a problem, the trouble is in the steering gear itself.

41-4 CAR WANDER

Car wander shows up as trouble in keeping the car moving straight ahead. The steering wheel has to be kept moving to prevent the car from wandering from one side of the road to the other. Possible causes of car wander are the following:

- Low or uneven tire pressure
- Linkage or steering-gear binding
- Improper front-wheel alignment—incorrect camber, caster, or steering-axis inclination
- Loose rear springs
- Unevenly distributed load in the car
- Looseness in the steering-gear linkage or at the ball joints

Both binding and looseness in the steering gear or linkage can cause car wander. With binding, the wheels cannot resume their normal straight-ahead position. With looseness, the wheels are not under direct control of the driver.

41-5 CAR PULLS TO ONE SIDE DURING NORMAL DRIVING

This condition is very tiring to the driver. Continual pressure has to be kept on the steering wheel to keep the car moving straight ahead. The trouble could be due to any of the following:

- Uneven tire pressure
- Uneven camber or caster

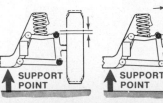

Fig. 41-5
To check ball joints for wear on
a suspension system with the
spring on the upper arm, support the front end on the frame,
as shown.

- Tight wheel bearing on one side
- Uneven springs—sagging, loose, or broken
- Wheels not tracking because of a bent frame or other bent parts

Anything that tends to unbalance the forces acting on the wheels will make the car pull to one side.

41-6 CAR PULLS TO ONE SIDE DURING BRAKING
If the car pulls to one side during braking, there may be uneven braking at the two front wheels. Conditions that could cause the car to pull to one side during braking include

- Loose strut rod
- Uneven braking action at the front wheels
- Uneven tire inflation
- Incorrect or uneven caster
- Causes listed in Sec. 41-5

41-7 FRONT-WHEEL SHIMMY AT LOW SPEED
With front-wheel shimmy at low speed, the front wheels oscillate on the ball joints. The wheels try to turn in and then turn out. This action

Fig. 41-6
How wear-indicating ball joints show that ball-joint replacement is necessary. In a worn ball joint, the grease-fitting nipple recedes into the socket, as shown to the right.

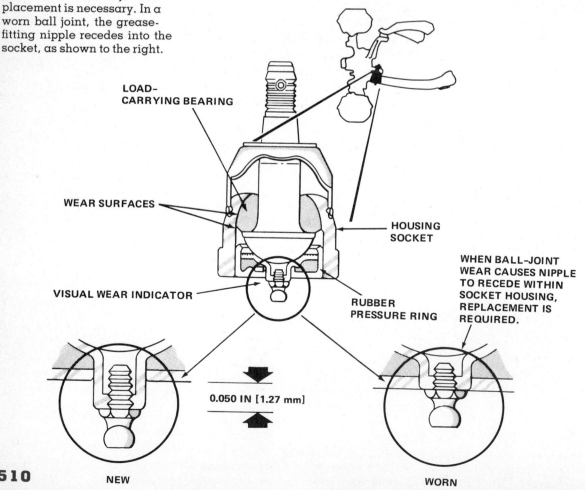

LOAD-CARRYING BEARING

WEAR SURFACES

HOUSING SOCKET

VISUAL WEAR INDICATOR

RUBBER PRESSURE RING

WHEN BALL-JOINT WEAR CAUSES NIPPLE TO RECEDE WITHIN SOCKET HOUSING, REPLACEMENT IS REQUIRED.

0.050 IN [1.27 mm]

NEW

WORN

causes the front end of the car to shake from side to side, or shimmy. Low-speed shimmy can result from any of the following:

- Uneven or low tire pressure
- Looseness in the steering gear or linkages or at the ball joints
- Front springs too flexible or too weak
- Incorrect or unequal camber
- Irregular or unmatching tire treads

If tire treads are worn unevenly, the worn spots can cause a change in the road resistance to the tire. With each tire revolution, there is a tendency for the tire to toe-out more and then less.

41-8 FRONT-WHEEL TRAMP (HIGH-SPEED SHIMMY)

Front-wheel tramp, or high-speed shimmy, is often confused with low-speed shimmy. In front-wheel tramp, the tires tend to move up and down, or bounce, rather than turn in and out as they do with low-speed shimmy. Sometimes the tires bounce so high that they leave the road. The basic conditions that can cause this trouble are as follows:

- Wheels are out of balance.
- Wheels have too much runout.
- Shock absorbers are defective.
- Causes listed in Sec. 41-7.

Wheels that are out of balance have more weight on one side than on the other. As the wheel rotates, the heavy part causes the wheel to run off center. As the heavy part swings around the top, it tends to pull the tire up off the road. Wheels that have too much runout do not run true. They wobble as they rotate. This condition also tends to pull the tire off the road as the tire rotates.

If the shock absorbers are not working, they cannot stop the spring oscillations after bumps. The tires will tend to keep bouncing up and down.

41-9 STEERING KICKBACK

Steering kickback, or steering shock, is felt as sharp and rapid movements of the steering wheel when the front wheels meet obstructions on the road. It is normal to have some kickback. When the kickback becomes excessive, checks should be made. Excessive kickback could be caused by any of the following:

- Low tire pressure
- Sagging springs
- Defective shock absorbers
- Looseness in the steering gear or linkages

41-10 TIRE SQUEAL ON TURNS

If turns are taken too fast, some tire squeal can be expected. If tire squeal on turns is not due to excessive speed, then it is probably due to low or uneven tire pressure or to incorrect front-end alignment.

41-11 INCORRECT TIRE WEAR

If the tires wear abnormally, the kind of wear is often a good indication of the cause. Figure 41-7 shows different types of tire wear and their causes and corrections. Here are the causes:

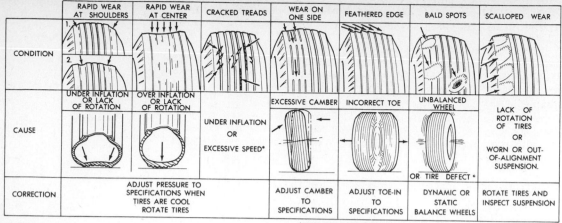

	RAPID WEAR AT SHOULDERS	RAPID WEAR AT CENTER	CRACKED TREADS	WEAR ON ONE SIDE	FEATHERED EDGE	BALD SPOTS	SCALLOPED WEAR
CONDITION	1. 2.						
CAUSE	UNDER INFLATION OR LACK OF ROTATION	OVER INFLATION OR LACK OF ROTATION	UNDER INFLATION OR EXCESSIVE SPEED*	EXCESSIVE CAMBER	INCORRECT TOE	UNBALANCED WHEEL OR TIRE DEFECT*	LACK OF ROTATION OF TIRES OR WORN OR OUT-OF-ALIGNMENT SUSPENSION.
CORRECTION	ADJUST PRESSURE TO SPECIFICATIONS WHEN TIRES ARE COOL ROTATE TIRES			ADJUST CAMBER TO SPECIFICATIONS	ADJUST TOE-IN TO SPECIFICATIONS	DYNAMIC OR STATIC BALANCE WHEELS	ROTATE TIRES AND INSPECT SUSPENSION

*HAVE TIRE INSPECTED FOR FURTHER USE.

Fig. 41-7
Types of tire wear and their causes and corrections. (*Chrysler Corporation*)

- Wear at tread sides from underinflation.
- Wear at tread center from overinflation.
- Wear at one tread side from excessive camber.
- Featheredge wear from excessive toe-in or toe-out on turns. Either of these drags the tire sideways to produce the featheredge wear.
- Cornering wear from excessive speed on turns.
- Uneven or spotty wear from mechanical problems such as unbalanced wheels, grabbing brakes, and so on.
- Rapid wear from high speed.

41-12 HARD OR ROUGH RIDE
A hard or rough ride may be due to excessive tire pressure. The trouble also may be caused by defective shock absorbers or excessive friction in the spring suspension.

41-13 SWAY ON TURNS
If the car sways out excessively on turns, this could be due to a faulty stabilizer bar. Weak or sagging springs and incorrect caster are other possible causes.

41-14 SPRING BREAKAGE
Spring breakage seldom occurs. The most common cause is overloading of the car. Another cause is defective shock absorbers that allow the springs to overwork. Leaf springs can break if the center or U-bolts are loose or if the spring shackle binds.

41-15 SAGGING SPRINGS
Sagging springs could be due to a broken leaf in a leaf spring or to a weak spring. Two other possible causes of sagging springs are a defective shock absorber and installation of the wrong coil spring.

41-16 NOISES
Noises in the steering or suspension system could come from looseness in the system. Also, noises could be caused by a lack of lubrication at points needing it.

41-17 SERVICING STEERING LINKAGES AND SUSPENSIONS

Steering and suspension service includes

- Removal, replacement, and adjustment of tie rods
- Removal and replacement of other linkage parts, including idler arm, center link, stabilizer bar, and struts
- Removal and replacement of upper and lower control arms and springs
- Removal and replacement of shock absorbers
- Removal and replacement of wheels
- Checking front-end alignment and adjusting camber, caster, and toe

For specific details on any of these jobs, refer to the manufacturer's service manual covering the car you are working on.

41-18 WHEEL ALIGNMENT

There are many different types of wheel aligners. Some are mechanical types that attach to the wheel spindles (Fig. 41-8). Others also have

CASTER-CAMBER GAUGE

TURNING-RADIUS GAUGE

Fig. 41-8
Front wheel on a turning-radius gauge with the caster-camber tester attached to the wheel hub. (*Bear Manufacturing Company*)

513

lights that display the measurements on a screen in front of the car (Fig. 41-9). In adjusting front alignment, you measure camber, caster, and toe-in. These are the three things you adjust. You also check steering-axis inclination and toe-out on turns. These are not adjustable. If they are out of specifications, parts are bent or damaged and must be replaced. However, before you make the alignment checks, here are the preliminary things you must do:

- Check and correct tire pressure.
- Check and adjust wheel bearings.
- Check and adjust wheel runout.
- Check ball joints. If they are too loose, replace them.
- Check steering linkages. Make any corrections necessary.
- Check rear leaf springs for cracks, broken leaves, and loose U-bolts. Make any corrections necessary.
- Check front-suspension height (on Chrysler-built cars).

41-19 WHEEL BALANCE

The wheel may be checked for balance on or off the car. This job is done by two methods: static and dynamic balancing. To static-balance (or "bubble-balance") a wheel, it is taken off the car. The wheel is placed on a static balancer that detects any imbalance (Fig. 41-10). A wheel that is statically out of balance is heavier in one section. This will cause the bubble in the center of the balancer to move off center.

Fig. 41-9
Adjusting the wheel gauge to make a wheel-alignment check. Note the horizontal and vertical lines of light shining on the screen. (*Hunter Engineering Company*)

Fig. 41-10
A static or bubble balancer. (*John Bean Division of FMC Corporation*)

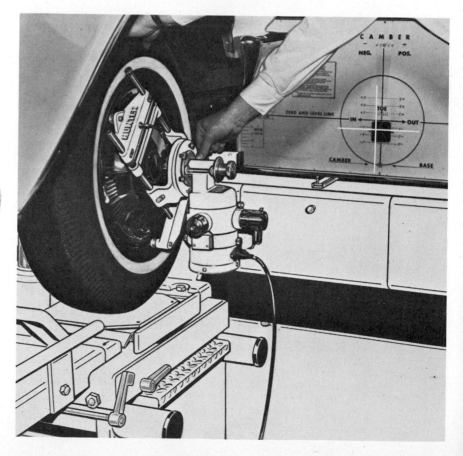

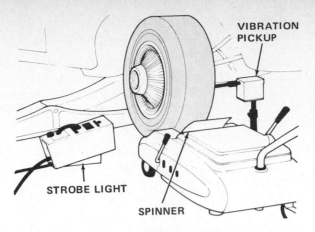

Fig. 41-11
An electronic wheel balancer.
A magnet is attached to the
brake backing plate. Through
a short arm, any movement of
the magnet is sensed by a vibration pickup. This causes the
strobe light to flash, indicating
where to attach a wheel
weight. (*Ford Motor Company*)

To balance the wheel, weights are added until the bubble returns to center.

To dynamic-balance (or "spin-balance") a wheel, the wheel is run at high speeds either on or off the car. Figure 41-11 shows an electronic wheel balancer being used to balance a wheel on the car. Lack of balance shows up as a tendency of the wheel to move off center or out of line. In the shop you will learn more about wheel balancing.

If a wheel is out of balance, one or more weights are installed on the wheel rim, as shown in Fig. 41-12.

CAUTION

To prevent injury from stones thrown out of the spinning tire, off-the-car wheel balancers should have a safety hood (Fig. 41-13). The hood fits around or over the tire while it is spinning to catch any stones that fly from the tire tread.

41-20 ADJUSTING CAMBER AND CASTER

Several different ways to adjust camber and caster have been used. Some of the methods include adjustment by removing or installing shims, by turning a cam, by shifting the inner shaft, and by shortening

Fig. 41-12
Balancing a wheel by placing a weight on the wheel rim. (*Bear Manufacturing Company*)

or lengthening the strut rod. Now, we will review several of these methods.

1. Adjustment by Installing or Removing Shims

The shims are located at the upper control-arm shafts. They are placed either inside or outside the frame bracket. Figure 41-14 shows the location of the shims in many General Motors cars. The shims are inside the frame bracket. Figure 41-15 shows the location of the shims in many Ford cars. The shims are outside the frame bracket. When the shims are inside the frame bracket (Fig. 41-14), adding shims moves the upper control arm inward. This reduces positive camber. When the shims and shaft are outside the frame bracket (Fig. 41-15), adding shims moves the upper control arm outward. This increases positive

Fig. 41-13
A wheel balancer with a safety hood installed over the tire. (*Hennessy Industries, Inc.*)

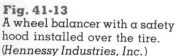

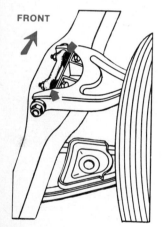

Fig. 41-14
The location of caster and camber adjusting shims (indicated by heavy arrows). Note that the shims and upper control-arm shaft are inside the frame bracket. (*Bear Manufacturing Company*)

camber. If shims are added at one of the attachment bolts and removed from the other, the outer end of the upper control arm shifts one way or the other. This increases or decreases caster. Figure 41-16 shows these adjustments.

2. Adjustment by Turning a Cam
There have been several variations of this method. Figure 41-17 shows an arrangement used on some Chrysler-built cars. The two bushings at the inner end of the upper control arm are attached to the frame brackets by two attachment bolts and cam assemblies. When the cam bolts are turned, the camber and caster are changed. If both are turned the same amount and in the same direction, the camber is changed. If only one cam bolt is turned, or if the two are turned in opposite directions, the caster is changed.

3. Adjustment by Shifting Inner Shaft
This system uses slots in the frame at the two points where the inner shaft is attached (Fig. 41-18). When the attaching bolts are loosened, the inner shaft can be shifted in or out to change camber. Only one end is shifted to change caster.

4. Adjustment by Changing Length of Strut Rod
This arrangement allows changing the caster by changing the length of the strut rod (Fig. 41-19). Camber is changed by turning the cam on which the inner end of the lower control arm is mounted.

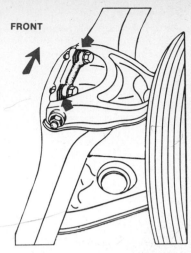

FRONT

Fig. 41-15
The location of caster and camber adjusting shims (indicated by heavy arrows). Note that the shims and upper control-arm shaft are outside the frame bracket. (*Bear Manufacturing Company*)

Fig. 41-16
Caster and camber adjustments on some cars using shims. (*Chevrolet Motor Division of General Motors Corporation*)

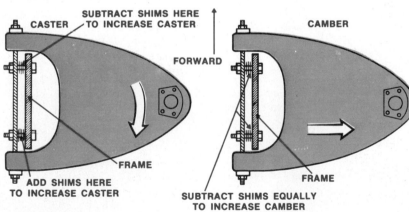

PIVOT SHAFT INBOARD OF FRAME

CASTER — SUBTRACT SHIMS HERE TO INCREASE CASTER

CAMBER

FORWARD

ADD SHIMS HERE TO INCREASE CASTER — FRAME

FRAME

SUBTRACT SHIMS EQUALLY TO INCREASE CAMBER

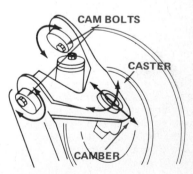

CAM BOLTS

CASTER

CAMBER

Fig. 41-17
Turning the cam bolts moves the upper control arm toward or away from the frame to adjust caster and camber. (*Ammco Tools, Inc.*)

41-21 ADJUSTING TOE
After adjusting caster and camber, toe is adjusted (Fig. 41-20). Place the front wheels in the straight-ahead position. Then check the position of the spokes in the steering wheel. If they are not aligned, they can be properly positioned while setting toe. Toe is adjusted by turning the adjuster sleeves in the linkage (Fig. 41-20).

41-22 SERVICING THE STEERING GEAR
Manual steering gears have two basic adjustments. One of these takes up the worm-gear and steering-shaft end play. The other adjusts the backlash or free play between the worm and sector.

517

Other adjustments are required on power-steering gears. Refer to the manufacturer's shop manual covering the unit being serviced before attempting to adjust or repair a power-steering gear.

NOTE

Studying about trouble diagnosis is challenging. There are so many things you have to keep in mind. One way you can learn how to diagnose troubles is to get some 3- by 5-inch plain cards. Write a trouble on one side of a card. Then, on the other side, write the possible causes. For example, you would write "Excessive Play in the Steering System" on one side of the card. On the other side, you would write down the possible causes, like this:

1. Looseness in the steering gear or linkage
2. Worn steering-knuckle parts
3. Loose wheel bearings

Review the cards often. Look at the trouble and try to remember the causes you wrote on the other side of the card. After you review the cards enough times, you will know the troubles and their causes.

Fig. 41-19
Adjusting caster by changing the length of the strut rod. (*Ford Motor Company*)

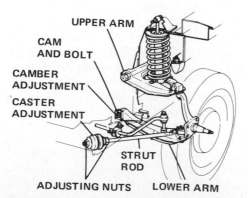

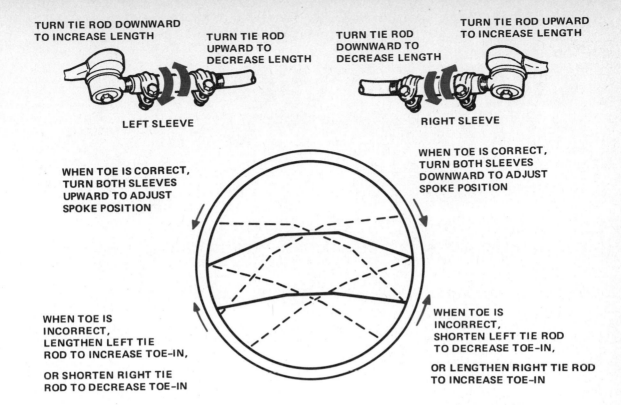

TURN TIE ROD DOWNWARD TO INCREASE LENGTH

TURN TIE ROD UPWARD TO DECREASE LENGTH

LEFT SLEEVE

TURN TIE ROD DOWNWARD TO DECREASE LENGTH

TURN TIE ROD UPWARD TO INCREASE LENGTH

RIGHT SLEEVE

WHEN TOE IS CORRECT, TURN BOTH SLEEVES UPWARD TO ADJUST SPOKE POSITION

WHEN TOE IS CORRECT, TURN BOTH SLEEVES DOWNWARD TO ADJUST SPOKE POSITION

WHEN TOE IS INCORRECT, LENGTHEN LEFT TIE ROD TO INCREASE TOE-IN,

OR SHORTEN RIGHT TIE ROD TO DECREASE TOE-IN

WHEN TOE IS INCORRECT, SHORTEN LEFT TIE ROD TO DECREASE TOE-IN,

OR LENGTHEN RIGHT TIE ROD TO INCREASE TOE-IN

Fig. 41-20
Adjusting toe-in and aligning the spokes in the steering wheel. If the steering wheel is in its proper position, adjust both tie rods equally to maintain the position of the spokes. (*Ford Motor Company*)

CHECK UP ON YOURSELF

When you think you understand this chapter, answer the questions below.

1. How can you check the tie rods and linkages for looseness?
2. How can you check for loose steering-knuckle parts?
3. What is low-speed shimmy?
4. What is front-wheel tramp?
5. What three adjustments are made during a front-end alignment?

ANSWERS

1. Raise the front end. Push out on both front wheels at the same time. Then pull in on both wheels at the same time (Sec. 41-2). 2. Raise the front end. Grasp the top and bottom of the front wheel and see if you can wobble it (Sec. 41-2). 3. Tendency of the front wheels to oscillate on the ball joints (Sec. 41-7). 4. Tendency of the front wheels to bounce up and down (Sec. 41-8). 5. Camber, caster, and toe (Sec. 41-18).

CHAPTER FORTY-TWO
AUTOMOTIVE BRAKES

After studying this chapter, you should be able to:

1. Explain the purpose, construction, and operation of automotive brakes.
2. Describe the difference between drum and disk brakes.
3. Explain how power brakes work.
4. Discuss the purpose of antilock devices and how they work.

We know the purpose of brakes. When you press the brake pedal, the car slows and stops. The brake that we operate with our foot during normal driving is called the foot brake, or service brake. Cars also have a parking brake. In this chapter we find out how the brakes work.

42-1 BRAKE OPERATION
Braking action starts at the brake pedal. When the pedal is pushed down, brake fluid is sent from the master cylinder to the wheels. At the wheels, the fluid pushes brake shoes, or pads, against revolving drums or disks. The friction between the stationary shoes, or pads, and the revolving drums or disks slows and stops them. This slows or stops the revolving wheels, which, in turn, slow or stop the car.

Figure 42-1 shows the brake lines, or tubes, through which the fluid flows. There are two chambers and two pistons in the master cylinder. One chamber is connected to the front-wheel brakes. The other chamber is connected to the rear-wheel brakes. This is called a *dual braking system*. There is a reason for splitting the system into two sections. If one section should fail, the other can still work. It will provide braking until the failed section can be fixed.

In earlier braking systems, there was only one chamber in the master cylinder, which was connected to all four wheel brakes. If that one section failed, the whole system failed. The dual braking system provides added safety because the rear and front sections seldom fail at the same time.

42-2 DUAL-BRAKING SYSTEM
A schematic layout of a dual-braking system is shown in Fig. 42-2. Some brake lines connect the master cylinder to the rear wheels. Other brake lines go from the pressure-differential valve to each of the front

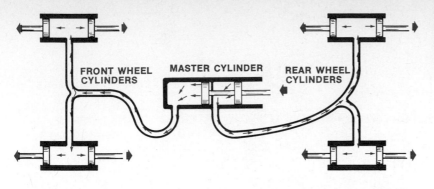

wheels. The brake fluid must first pass through the pressure-differential valve. This valve turns on a red brake warning light on the instrument panel if either of the brake systems fails. (We cover the pressure-differential valve in Sec. 42-15.) In many brake systems, one section of the master cylinder is connected to the front wheels. The other section is connected to the two rear wheels.

There are two different types of brakes used at the wheels. They are drum brakes and disk brakes. Figure 42-2 shows a system using front disk brakes and rear drum brakes. Both the drum brake and the disk brake do the same job; they are constructed differently.

42-3 MASTER CYLINDER

Figure 42-3 shows a master cylinder in cutaway view. This master cylinder has two main parts. The top part is a plastic fluid reservoir. The lower part is an aluminum body with a highly polished bore. It contains the pistons, springs, and seals.

In the car, a pushrod connects the brake pedal to the primary piston in the master cylinder. When the brake pedal is pushed down, the pushrod pushes the primary piston in the master cylinder. The fluid trapped ahead of the piston is pushed out of the master cylinder and into the brake line connected to two wheels. The fluid flows through the brake line to the wheel cylinders or calipers.

When the pushrod moves the primary piston, the secondary piston also is pushed to the left (in Fig. 42-3). Movement of the secondary piston sends brake fluid to the brakes at the other wheels.

Not all master cylinders are constructed like the one shown in Fig. 42-3. Figure 42-4 shows a typical master cylinder with a one-piece

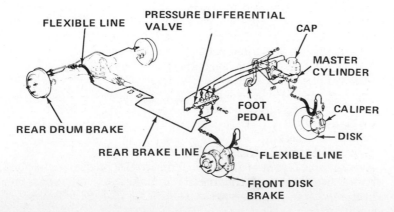

Fig. 42-2
Layout of a dual-braking system. (*Ford Motor Company*)

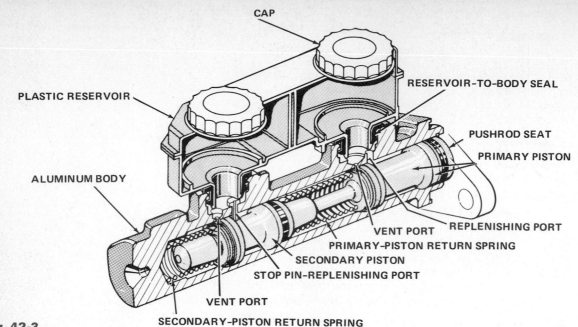

Fig. 42-3
Cutaway view of a master cylinder. (*Chrysler Corporation*)

body in exploded view. However, all master cylinders have the same basic parts and work in the same general way.

42-4 BRAKE LINES

The brake fluid is carried by steel pipes called brake lines from the master cylinder to the various valves and then to the brakes at the wheels. You can see the brake lines and how they are connected in Fig. 42-2. Brake lines usually pass under the floor pan, where they are exposed to stones and other road damage. Because of this, brake lines

Fig. 42-4
Exploded view of a typical master cylinder with a one-piece body. (*Chevrolet Motor Division of General Motors Corporation*)

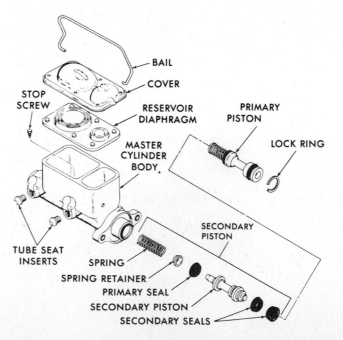

often are wrapped with a wire "armor' to protect them against damage.

A short, flexible brake hose (or "flex hose") is used to connect the stationary brake lines to the brake assemblies that move up and down and swing with each front wheel for steering (Fig. 42-5). Steel tubing will crack if it vibrates or is flexed too much. Only a single flexible hose is needed at the rear axle to take care of the up-and-down movement of the housing. This line is shown in Fig. 42-2.

42-5 BRAKE FLUID
Brake fluid is a very special fluid that is little affected by high or low temperatures. It is *not* a type of engine oil. Brake fluid does not damage the metal or rubber parts in the brake system. Engine oil will damage

Fig. 42-5
Brake lines for a front wheel on a front-wheel-drive car. (*Chrysler Corporation*)

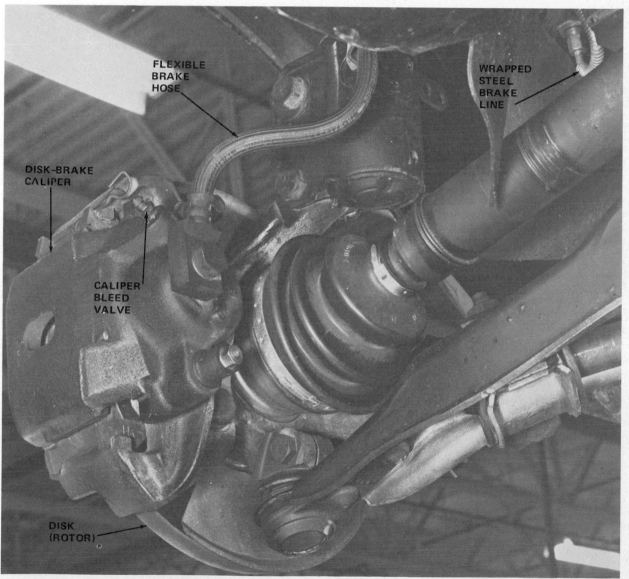

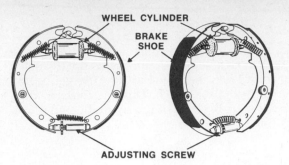

Fig. 42-6
These are the operating components of drum brakes for the rear (left) and front (right) wheels.

WHEEL CYLINDER

BRAKE SHOE

ADJUSTING SCREW

the brake system. For this reason, only the brake fluid recommended by the manufacturer should be put into the brake system.

CAUTION

Never put engine oil in a brake system. Engine oil will cause rubber parts in the system, such as the piston cups, to swell and break apart. This could cause complete brake failure. Use only the brake fluid recommended by the car manufacturer!

42-6 DRUM BRAKES

The drum brake has an iron, steel, or aluminum drum to which the wheel is bolted. The drum and wheel rotate together. Inside the drum and attached to the steering knuckle or axle housing is the brake assembly (Fig. 42-6). At the front wheels, the brake is attached to the steering knuckle. In Fig. 42-7 (center) you can see the boltholes by which the front-wheel brake is attached. At the rear wheels, the brake is attached to the axle housing. You can see the boltholes in the axle housing in Fig. 42-7 (left).

Figure 42-6 shows the moving parts of the drum brake. There are two brake shoes at each wheel. The bottoms of the shoes are held apart by an adjusting screw—also known as a *star wheel*. The tops of the shoes are held apart by a wheel cylinder. The shoes are made of metal. Glued (called *bonded*) or riveted to each shoe is a facing of friction material. The facing is called the *brake lining*. These brake linings are made of a tough material such as asbestos. It can hold up under the rubbing pressure and heat produced during braking.

Figure 42-7 shows the addition of the brake backing plate and the wheel spindle. The brake backing plate is bolted to the steering axle at

Fig. 42-7
Complete drum-brake assembly. Left, the rear brake, with holes through the backing plate for attachment to the axle housing. Center, the front brake, with the spindle in place. Right, the brake drum is partly cut away to show the shoe inside.

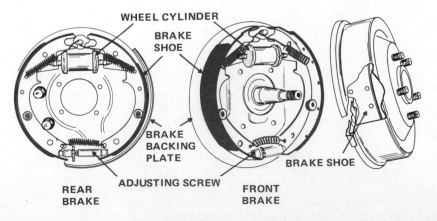

WHEEL CYLINDER

BRAKE SHOE

BRAKE BACKING PLATE

ADJUSTING SCREW

BRAKE SHOE

REAR BRAKE

FRONT BRAKE

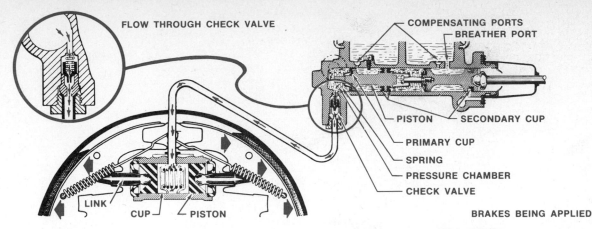

FLOW THROUGH CHECK VALVE

COMPENSATING PORTS
BREATHER PORT

PISTON — SECONDARY CUP
PRIMARY CUP
SPRING
PRESSURE CHAMBER
CHECK VALVE

LINK — CUP — PISTON

BRAKES BEING APPLIED

Fig. 42-8
Conditions in a drum-brake system when the brakes are applied. Brake fluid flows from the master cylinder to the wheel cylinder. This causes the wheel-cylinder pistons to move out and apply the brakes.

the back wheels, or to the steering knuckle at the front wheels. At the right in Fig. 42-7, you can see the brake drum in place over the brake shoes. The drum has been partly cut away so that you can see one of the shoes.

The shoes are attached at one point to the brake backing plate. The attachment is loose so that the shoes can move around slightly. We have now described all the internal brake parts. Now let's discuss how the parts work.

42-7 OPERATION OF THE DRUM BRAKE

When brake fluid is forced from the master cylinder, it flows through the brake lines into the wheel cylinder (Fig. 42-8). A wheel cylinder is shown disassembled at the top and in sectional view at the bottom of Fig. 42-9. There are two pistons, with piston cups, inside the wheel cylinder. When the brake fluid is forced into the wheel cylinder, the brake fluid pushes the pistons apart. This action pushes the brake-shoe actuating pins out. Therefore the brake shoes are forced tightly against the rotating brake drum. The friction between the brake linings and the drum slows or stops the rotation of the drum and the wheel.

Fig. 42-9
The wheel cylinder for a drum brake, disassembled at the top and in sectional view at the bottom.

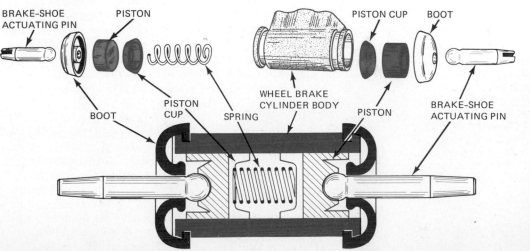

BRAKE-SHOE ACTUATING PIN   PISTON   PISTON CUP   BOOT

BOOT   PISTON CUP   SPRING   WHEEL BRAKE CYLINDER BODY   PISTON   BRAKE-SHOE ACTUATING PIN

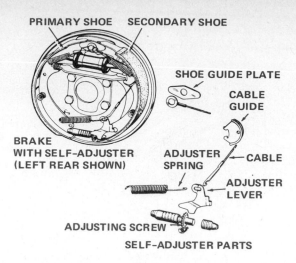

PRIMARY SHOE SECONDARY SHOE

SHOE GUIDE PLATE

CABLE GUIDE

BRAKE
WITH SELF-ADJUSTER
(LEFT REAR SHOWN)

ADJUSTER
SPRING

CABLE

ADJUSTER
LEVER

ADJUSTING SCREW

SELF-ADJUSTER PARTS

42-8 SELF-ADJUSTING BRAKES

Drum brakes have self-adjusters that automatically adjust the brakes as the brake lining wears. Repeated use of the brakes gradually wears the brake lining off the shoes. As the lining wears, the distance between the lining and the drum increases. Then the brake pedal has to be pushed down farther to move the shoes the additional distance to contact the drum.

Brakes on older cars without self-adjusters have to be adjusted periodically. To adjust the brakes, turn the adjusting screw, or star wheel. When the adjusting screw is turned, the lower ends of the shoes are moved out. This eliminates the excessive distance between the shoes and the drum.

Figure 42-10 shows one type of self-adjusting brake. It includes an adjuster lever and spring. Every time the brakes are applied, the brake shoes move outward. The cable guide of the automatic adjuster moves outward with the secondary shoe. This outward movement causes the adjuster lever to pivot on the secondary shoe. If the brake linings have worn enough, the lever will pivot and move back of one of the teeth on the adjusting screw. Then, when the brakes are released, the adjusting screw will be turned a full tooth. This is enough to spread the lower ends of the shoes slightly. The excess clearance between the brake lining and the drum is eliminated to compensate for the lining wear.

In the brake shown, the actual adjustment takes place, if needed, when the car is backed up. When the car is backed up and then braked, the secondary shoe is shifted enough to produce the adjustment.

42-9 RETURN STROKE

When the brakes are released, the spring tension on the brake shoes pulls the shoes away from the brake drum. Also, the return springs in the master cylinder push the pistons back toward the released position. All these actions draw brake fluid out of the wheel cylinders and back into the master cylinder. The brake-fluid flow is shown by the white arrows in Fig. 42-11. However, some pressure is trapped in the brake line and wheel cylinder by the check valve in the master cylinder. As the pressure drops in the brake line, the check valve closes. It traps a slight pressure in the line and in the wheel cylinder. This pressure

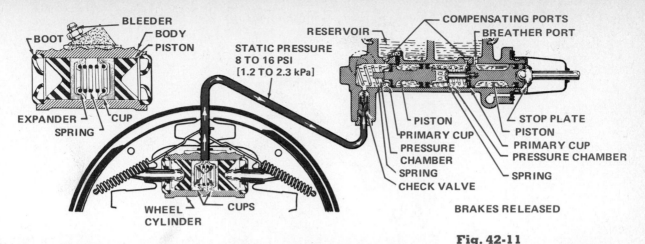

BLEEDER
BODY
PISTON
BOOT

STATIC PRESSURE
8 TO 16 PSI
[1.2 TO 2.3 kPa]

RESERVOIR

COMPENSATING PORTS
BREATHER PORT

EXPANDER
SPRING
CUP

PISTON
PRIMARY CUP
PRESSURE
CHAMBER
SPRING
CHECK VALVE

STOP PLATE
PISTON
PRIMARY CUP
PRESSURE CHAMBER
SPRING

WHEEL
CYLINDER
CUPS

BRAKES RELEASED

causes the piston cups in the wheel cylinder to be held tight against the wheel-cylinder wall, as shown by the colored arrows in Fig. 42-11. Therefore, no air can leak into the line, and no brake fluid can leak out of the wheel cylinders.

Fig. 42-11
Conditions in a drum-brake system when the brakes are released. Brake fluid flows back to the master cylinder, as shown. (*Buick Motor Division of General Motors Corporation*)

CHECK UP ON YOURSELF

Now check up on yourself. Answer the questions that follow to find out if you understand how drum brakes work.

1. How many pistons are there in the dual master cylinder?
2. What carries the brake fluid from the master cylinder to the wheel cylinders or calipers?
3. Why should oil never be put into the brake system?
4. Against what do the brake shoes push the lining when the brakes are applied?
5. What happens when the adjusting screw in the brake is turned?

ANSWERS

1. Two (Secs. 42-6 and 42-3). **2.** Steel brake lines and flexible hose (Sec. 42-4). **3.** Oil swells the rubber parts in the brake system, and complete brake failure could result (Sec. 42-5). **4.** The inner surface of the brake drum (Sec. 42-7). **5.** The brake shoes are moved closer to, or farther away from, the drum (Sec. 42-8).

42-10 DISK BRAKES

The disk brake has a metal disk (also called a rotor) instead of a drum. Figure 42-12 shows a wheel partly cut away so that the positions of the caliper and disk can be seen. A flat shoe, or disk brake pad, is located on each side of the disk. In operation these two flat shoes are forced tightly against the rotating disk. The shoes squeeze the rotating disk to stop the car. Figure 42-13 shows how the disk brake works. Fluid from the master cylinder forces the pistons to move in, toward the disk. This action pushes the friction pads tightly against the disk. The friction between the shoes and the disk slows and stops it. This provides the braking action. Pistons are made of either plastic or steel.

There are three general types of disk brakes. They are the floating-caliper type, the fixed-caliper type, and the sliding-caliper type. Floating-caliper and sliding-caliper disk brakes use a single piston. Fixed-caliper disk brakes have either two or four pistons. Each type of disk brake is described in a following section.

527

Fig. 42-12
A disk-brake assembly, showing the location of the caliper
assembly on the disk. (*Ford
Motor Company*)

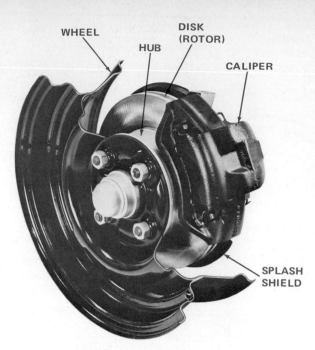

WHEEL

HUB

DISK
(ROTOR)

CALIPER

SPLASH
SHIELD

Fig. 42-13
Sectional views, showing how
hydraulic pressure forces friction pads (linings) inward
against the brake disk to produce the braking action.

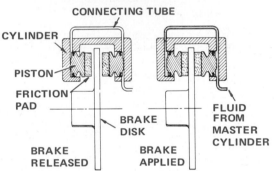

CONNECTING TUBE

CYLINDER

PISTON

FRICTION
PAD

BRAKE
DISK

FLUID
FROM
MASTER
CYLINDER

BRAKE
RELEASED

BRAKE
APPLIED

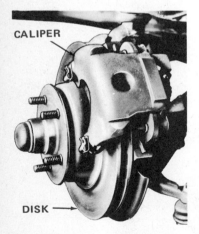

CALIPER

DISK

Fig. 42-14
A floating-caliper disk brake.
(*Ford Motor Company*)

42-11 FLOATING-CALIPER DISK BRAKE

Figure 42-14 shows a floating-caliper (also called a pin-caliper) disk
brake at a front wheel. The wheel has been removed so that you can see
the brake assembly. The caliper is the part that holds the two brake
shoes on each side of the disk. In the floating-caliper brake, two steel
guide pins thread into the steering-knuckle adapter. The caliper floats
on four rubber bushings which fit on the inner and outer ends of the
guide pins. The rubber bushings allow the caliper to move in or out
slightly when the brakes are applied. Figure 42-15 is a sectional view
from above of a floating-caliper disk brake. Figure 42-16 is a disassembled view of a floating caliper. In this type of brake, the guide pins locate and restrain the shoes.

When the brakes are applied, the brake fluid flows to the cylinder
in the caliper and pushes the piston out. The piston forces the inner
shoe against the disk. At the same time, the hydraulic pressure in the
cylinder causes the whole caliper to move inward. This pulls the outer
shoe against the disk. As a result, the two shoes squeeze the disk
tightly. This action causes the caliper to move forward slightly in the
direction that the disk is turning. The slight movement of the caliper

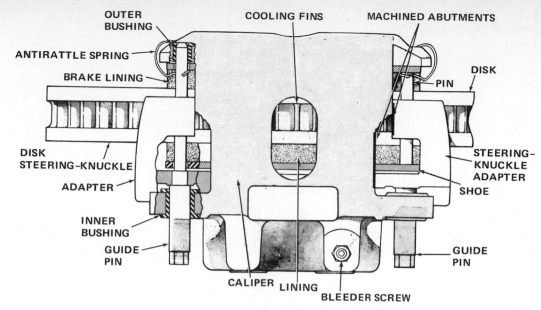

Labels for Fig. 42-15:
OUTER BUSHING
COOLING FINS
MACHINED ABUTMENTS
ANTIRATTLE SPRING
BRAKE LINING
PIN
DISK
DISK STEERING-KNUCKLE
STEERING-KNUCKLE ADAPTER
ADAPTER
SHOE
INNER BUSHING
GUIDE PIN
GUIDE PIN
CALIPER LINING
BLEEDER SCREW

brings together the machined abutments on the caliper and on the adapter (Fig. 42-15).

42-12 FIXED-CALIPER DISK BRAKE

This brake has four pistons, two on each side of the disk. The reason for the name "fixed caliper" is that the caliper is bolted solidly to the steering knuckle. When the brakes are applied, the caliper cannot move. Figure 42-17 is a sectional view of the fixed-caliper disk brake. Figure 42-18 is a disassembled view. You can see how the caliper attaches solidly to the steering knuckle and cannot move. When the brakes are applied, the four pistons push the inner and outer brake shoes in against the disk. Some brakes of this type have used only two pistons, one on each side of the disk.

Fig. 42-15
A sectional view from the top of a floating-caliper disk brake. (*Chrysler Corporation*)

Fig. 42-16
Disassembled view of a floating caliper. (*Chrysler Corporation*)

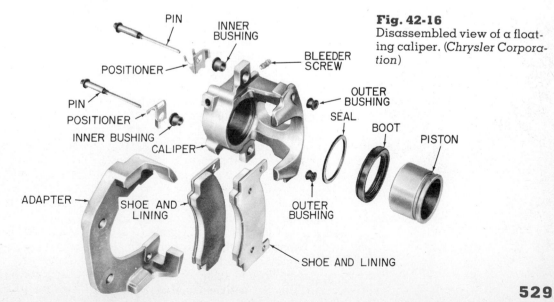

Labels for Fig. 42-16:
PIN
INNER BUSHING
POSITIONER
BLEEDER SCREW
PIN
POSITIONER
OUTER BUSHING
INNER BUSHING
SEAL
BOOT
PISTON
CALIPER
ADAPTER
SHOE AND LINING
OUTER BUSHING
SHOE AND LINING

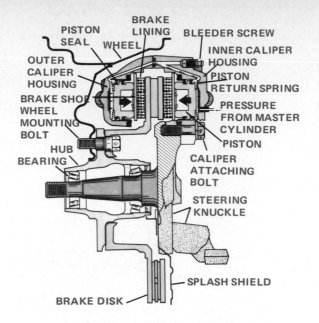

Fig. 42-17
A sectional view of a fixed-caliper disk brake.

PISTON SEAL
BRAKE LINING
WHEEL
BLEEDER SCREW
INNER CALIPER HOUSING
OUTER CALIPER HOUSING
PISTON RETURN SPRING
BRAKE SHOE
WHEEL MOUNTING BOLT
PRESSURE FROM MASTER CYLINDER
PISTON
HUB BEARING
CALIPER ATTACHING BOLT
STEERING KNUCKLE
SPLASH SHIELD
BRAKE DISK

42-13 SLIDING-CALIPER DISK BRAKE

The sliding-caliper is similar to the floating-caliper disk brake. Both types use a single piston. Machined abutments on the adapter position and align the caliper. Figure 42-19 shows a disassembled sliding caliper. A support key (or retainer clip) on each end of the caliper keeps it in position on the adapter. However, the support key allows the caliper to slide in and out slightly. The outer brake shoe is flanged to fit machined fingers on the caliper. The inner shoe is held in position by the adapter.

42-14 SELF-ADJUSTMENT OF DISK BRAKES

Disk brakes are self-adjusting. Each piston has a seal on it to prevent fluid leakage (Fig. 42-19). When the brakes are applied, the piston moves toward the disk. This distorts the piston seal, as shown to the right in Fig. 42-20. When the brakes are released, the seal relaxes and

Fig. 42-18
A disassembled view of a fixed-caliper disk brake.

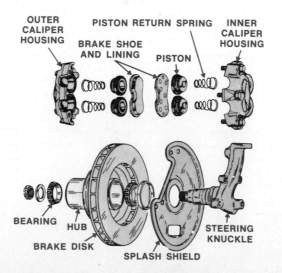

OUTER CALIPER HOUSING
PISTON RETURN SPRING
INNER CALIPER HOUSING
BRAKE SHOE AND LINING
PISTON
BEARING
HUB
BRAKE DISK
SPLASH SHIELD
STEERING KNUCKLE

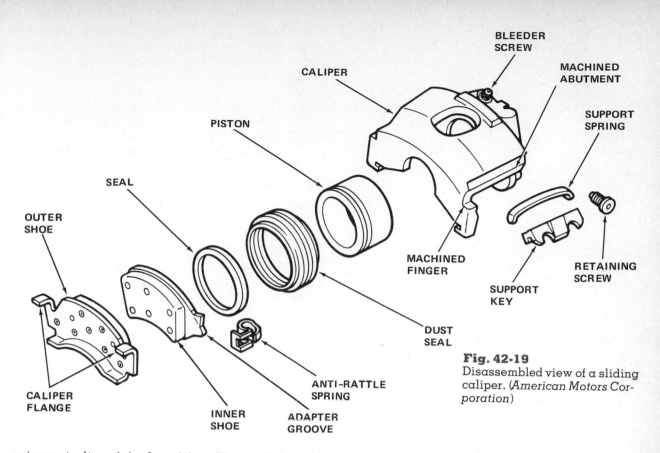

CALIPER

PISTON

SEAL

OUTER
SHOE

CALIPER
FLANGE

INNER
SHOE

ADAPTER
GROOVE

ANTI-RATTLE
SPRING

BLEEDER
SCREW

MACHINED
ABUTMENT

SUPPORT
SPRING

MACHINED
FINGER

SUPPORT
KEY

RETAINING
SCREW

DUST
SEAL

Fig. 42-19
Disassembled view of a sliding
caliper. (*American Motors Corporation*)

returns to its original position. This pulls the piston away from the
disk. As the brake linings wear, the piston "overtravels" and takes a
new position in relation to the seal. This action provides self-adjust-
ment of disk brakes.

Many brake shoes have a wear indicator or "tell-tale tabs," as
shown in Fig. 42-21. The purpose of the wear indicator is to make a

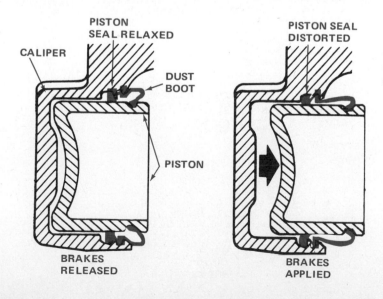

CALIPER

PISTON
SEAL RELAXED

DUST
BOOT

PISTON

BRAKES
RELEASED

PISTON SEAL
DISTORTED

BRAKES
APPLIED

Fig. 42-20
The action of the piston seal
when the brakes are applied
and when they are released.
(*American Motors Corporation*)

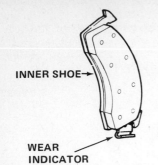

Fig. 42-21

An inner shoe with a wear indicator on it for a sliding-caliper disk brake. (*Cadillac Motor Car Division of General Motors Corporation*)

noise. This warns the driver that the brake linings are thin and new linings are required. When the brake linings are worn, the tab touches the disk when the brakes are applied. This gives off a scraping noise.

42-15 METERING VALVE
Figure 42-22 shows the valves which may be used in brake systems that include disk brakes. Some disk brake systems have a metering valve. This valve keeps the front disk brakes from applying until after the rear drum brakes apply. If the front brakes are applied first, the rear brakes might skid. Also, by delaying the front brake action at low speeds, disk-brake lining life is increased.

42-16 WARNING LIGHT
The dual brake system uses a pressure-differential valve (Fig. 42-22) to operate a warning light. The purpose of this light is to warn the driver if one or the other half of the braking system has failed. The valve has a piston that is centered when both front and rear brakes are operating normally, as shown in Fig. 42-22. However, if one section should fail, there is low pressure on one side of the piston. The high pressure from the normally operating side will push the piston to the low-pressure side. This pushes up the plunger of the brake-warning light switch. It is mounted in the top center of the pressure-differential valve. Contacts inside the switch are closed. This connects a warning light on the instrument panel to the battery. The light then flashes on every time the brakes are applied to warn the driver that there is brake trouble.

42-17 PROPORTIONING VALVE
The proportioning valve (Fig. 42-22) provides balanced braking on cars with front disk brakes and rear drum brakes. During hard braking, more of the car weight is transferred to the front wheels, as shown in Fig. 42-23. As a result, more braking is needed at the front wheels and less at the rear wheels. If equal brake pressure were applied, the rear wheels could skid. The proportioning valve reduces maximum pressure to the rear brakes.

Fig. 42-22

Valves used in a brake system that includes disk brakes. (*Ford Motor Company*)

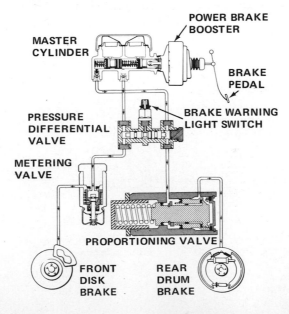

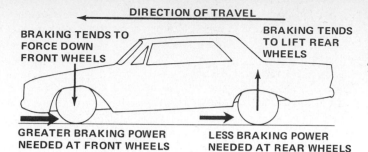

42-18 COMBINATION VALVE

In many cars the pressure-differential valve, the metering valve, and the proportioning valve are combined in a single unit. Figure 42-24 is a sectional view of this combination valve.

42-19 ANTILOCK BRAKE SYSTEMS

About 40 percent of all car accidents involve skidding. The most efficient braking takes place when the wheels are still revolving. Once the brakes lock the wheels and the tires begin to skid, braking is much less effective. Antilock brake systems use devices that relieve the hydraulic pressure at the wheels which are about to skid. This action reduces braking effort that would cause a skid. Here is how one system works.

Figure 42-25 shows the antilock system at a front wheel. A magnetic wheel is attached to the brake disk. As the wheel and disk revolve, the magnetic wheel produces an alternating current in the sensor. The sensor is a coil of wire, or a winding, that bolts to the brake splash shield and does not move. Chapter 23, which covers the alternator in the electrical system, explains that the rotor carries a magnetic field through the stator windings. This produces an alternating current (ac) in the stator windings. In the same way, the magnetic wheel produces an alternating current in the sensor. A similar action takes place at the other wheels. The signals from the car wheels are fed into a logic control unit.

When the brakes are applied, the logic control unit compares the ac signals from the wheels. The frequency of the ac increases with the speed of the wheel. If the frequency of the ac from all wheels is about

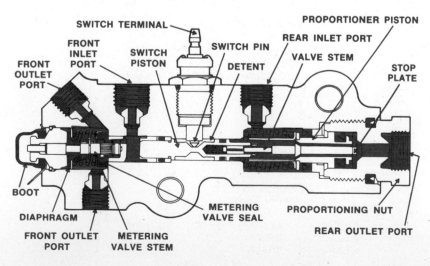

Fig. 42-24
A combination valve with warning-light, metering, and proportioning valves all in the same assembly. (*Chevrolet Motor Division of General Motors Corporation*)

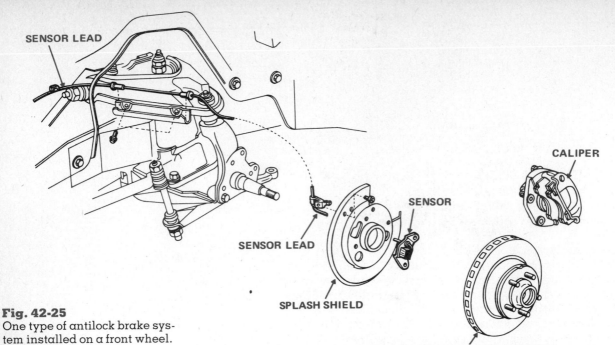

Fig. 42-25
One type of antilock brake system installed on a front wheel. (*Chrysler Corporation*)

SENSOR LEAD

CALIPER

SENSOR

SENSOR LEAD

SPLASH SHIELD

BRAKE DISK WITH MAGNETIC WHEEL

the same, normal braking is indicated. However, if the signal from any wheel shows a rapid decrease in frequency, it means that the wheel is slowing down too fast. It is beginning to skid.

When the logic control unit senses a rapid drop in the frequency of the signal, it immediately "tells" the modulator for that wheel to "ease up." The logic control unit signals the modulator to reduce the hydraulic pressure to the brake for that wheel. When the pressure is reduced, the braking effect at that wheel is reduced and it continues to turn. This prevents the skid.

42-20 STOPLIGHT SWITCH

Figure 42-26 shows a mechanical stoplight switch. When the brake pedal is pushed down for braking, it causes the contacts in the stoplight switch to close. This connects the stoplights to the battery so that

Fig. 42-26
A mechanical stoplight switch shown closed, with the brakes applied. (*Ford Motor Company*)

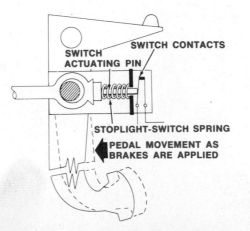

SWITCH
ACTUATING PIN

SWITCH CONTACTS

STOPLIGHT-SWITCH SPRING

PEDAL MOVEMENT AS
BRAKES ARE APPLIED

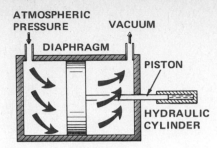

ATMOSPHERIC PRESSURE VACUUM

DIAPHRAGM

PISTON

HYDRAULIC CYLINDER

Fig. 42-27
When there is a vacuum on one side of the diaphragm and atmospheric pressure on the other side, the diaphragm will move toward the vacuum side.

the stoplights come on. Figure 42-26 shows the action during braking with the contacts closed.

42-21 POWER BRAKES

About 90 percent of all American-built cars have power brakes. With power brakes, only a light pressure is required to slow or stop the car. When the brake pedal is pushed down, a vacuum booster takes over and does most of the work of pushing the pistons into the master cylinder. The vacuum comes from the engine intake manifold. Figure 42-27 is a simplified drawing that shows how the power-brake system works. The system includes a hydraulic cylinder in which a tight-fitting piston can move. When vacuum is applied to one side of the diaphragm, atmospheric pressure causes the diaphragm to move to the right. This movement pushes the piston into the hydraulic cylinder (called the master cylinder in the actual power-brake system).

In the power-brake system, the brake pedal does not directly work on the master cylinder. Instead, the brake pedal works a vacuum valve, which then admits vacuum to the power cylinder. Figure 42-28 shows the layout of a power-brake system. Figure 42-29 is a sectional view of a power-brake assembly.

Figure 42-30 shows another complete power-brake assembly when the brakes are released. The floating control valve is preventing any atmospheric pressure from entering the power brake. Figure 42-31 shows what happens when the brake pedal is pushed down to apply the brakes. When the brake pedal is pushed down, the pushrod moves the air valve away from the floating control valve. Now, atmospheric pressure can flow past the valves and into the space to the right of the diaphragm. The atmospheric pressure forces the diaphragm to the left. The pushrod pushes the master-cylinder pistons into the master cylinder. This action causes braking to take place.

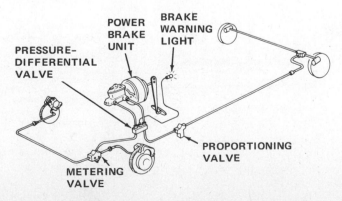

PRESSURE-DIFFERENTIAL VALVE

POWER BRAKE UNIT

BRAKE WARNING LIGHT

METERING VALVE

PROPORTIONING VALVE

Fig. 42-28
A typical power-brake system. (*Wagner Lockheed*)

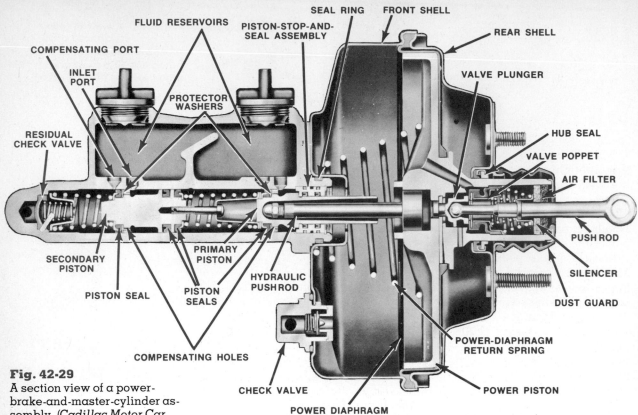

Fig. 42-29
A section view of a power-brake-and-master-cylinder assembly. (*Cadillac Motor Car Division of General Motors Corporation*)

The reaction disk, next to the air valve, gives the driver some braking "feel." A small proportion of the braking effort being applied by the power-brake unit feeds back through the reaction disk. This feedback is felt by the driver through the pushrod and linkage to the brake pedal.

When the brake pedal is released, the air valve moves back to contact the floating control valve. This contact reseals the power-brake

Fig. 42-30
A power-brake unit shown with the brakes released.

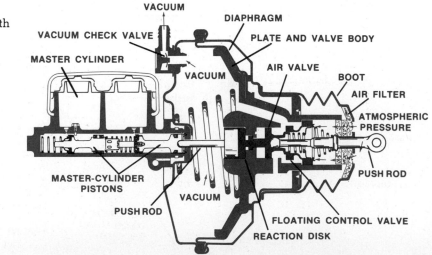

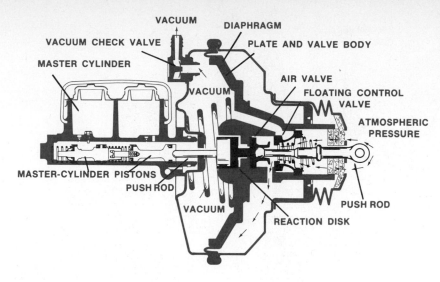

VACUUM

VACUUM CHECK VALVE

MASTER CYLINDER

DIAPHRAGM

PLATE AND VALVE BODY

VACUUM

AIR VALVE

FLOATING CONTROL VALVE

ATMOSPHERIC PRESSURE

MASTER-CYLINDER PISTONS

PUSH ROD

VACUUM

REACTION DISK

PUSH ROD

unit from atmospheric pressure so that the conditions shown in Fig. 42-30 are restored.

Some cars are equipped with a hydraulic brake booster (Fig. 42-32). It uses hydraulic pressure supplied by the power-steering pump to assist in applying the brakes. The ports shown in Fig. 42-32 are connected to the power-steering system. The hydraulic booster is smaller than the vacuum booster. Also, the hydraulic booster can supply about twice the assist power of a vacuum booster.

42-22 PARKING BRAKES

The parking brake is operated by a separate foot pedal or handbrake lever. Operation of the parking brake causes the rear brakes to be applied mechanically for parking. The pedal or lever is connected to the

Fig. 42-32
A hydraulic-type power-brake booster. (*Ford Motor Company*)

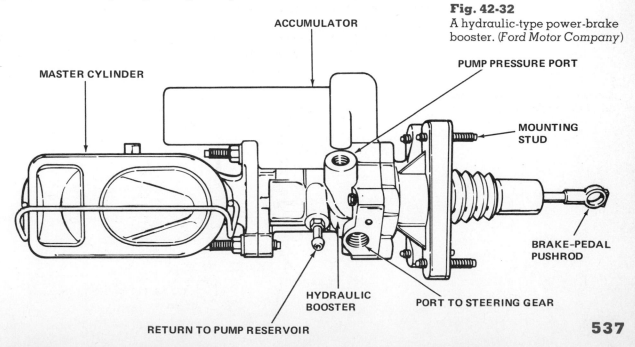

ACCUMULATOR

PUMP PRESSURE PORT

MASTER CYLINDER

MOUNTING STUD

BRAKE–PEDAL PUSHROD

HYDRAULIC BOOSTER

PORT TO STEERING GEAR

RETURN TO PUMP RESERVOIR

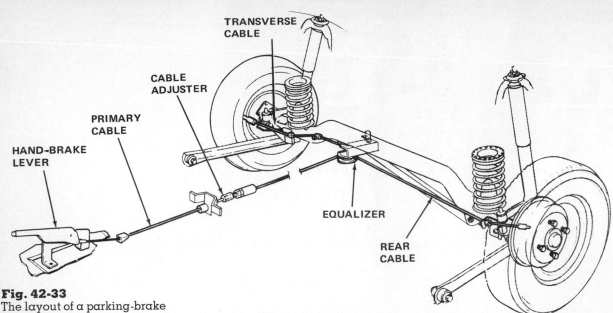

Fig. 42-33
The layout of a parking-brake system. Operation of the hand-brake lever pulls on the brake cables so that the rear brakes are mechanically applied. (*Ford Motor Company*)

rear-wheel brake shoes by cables or linkage. One system is shown in Fig. 42-33. When the lever is operated, the cable forces the brake shoes to move into contact with the brake drums.

In some cars the parking brake is released by a vacuum cylinder. This happens when the engine is started and the transmission selector lever is moved out of park.

CHECK UP ON YOURSELF
Now check up on yourself to find out how well you understand what you have been studying on disk brakes.

1. What are the three general types of disk brakes?
2. How many pistons does the fixed-caliper disk brake have?
3. What is the purpose of the wear indicator on some disk brake shoes?
4. What is the purpose of the brake warning light?

ANSWERS
1. The floating-caliper, the fixed-caliper, and the sliding-caliper (Sec. 42-11). **2.** Two or four (Sec. 42-12). **3.** To warn the driver that the brake linings are worn by making a noise (Sec. 42-14). **4.** To notify the driver if one or the other part of the dual-braking system has failed (Sec. 42-16).

CHAPTER FORTY-THREE
BRAKE SERVICE

After studying this chapter, you should be able to:

1. Discuss possible drum-brake troubles, their possible causes and corrections.
2. Discuss possible disk-brake troubles, their possible causes and corrections.

In this chapter we discuss brake troubles and their possible causes. We will also look at the various services required to fix different brake troubles. Manually operated drum and disk brakes are discussed first. Then we will cover power brakes. When you work in the shop, you will learn the procedures and how to use the special brake tools.

CAUTION
Brake lining usually is made of asbestos. Breathing asbestos dust could cause lung cancer. For this reason, do not use the air hose to blow away dust from the brakes. Instead, wipe away dust with a damp cloth. Avoid breathing any brake dust. Wash your hands after handling dusty brake parts and brake lining.

43-1 DRUM BRAKE TROUBLES
First let's list and discuss drum brake problems. In following sections we'll discuss disk brake problems. The kinds of trouble that you might find in drum brakes are as follows:

1. Brake pedal goes to floorboard.
2. One brake drags.
3. All brakes drag.
4. Car pulls to one side during braking.
5. Soft, or spongy, pedal.
6. Poor braking requiring excessive pedal pressure.
7. Brakes too sensitive or brakes grab.
8. Noisy brakes (brake squeal).
9. Air in system.
10. Loss of brake fluid.
11. Brakes do not self-adjust.
12. Brake warning light comes on.

Now, let's look at each of these troubles in detail.

43-2 BRAKE PEDAL GOES TO FLOORBOARD
This condition seldom occurs with a dual brake system. One section might fail, but it would be rare for both to fail at the same time. When

the brake pedal goes to the floorboard, braking action does not take place. This trouble means that either there is not enough brake fluid in the master cylinder or the brake shoes are worn or out of adjustment. Loss of brake fluid could be due to leaks. Also, air trapped in the hydraulic system could cause the trouble.

43-3 ONE BRAKE DRAGS
When one brake drags, the brake shoes are not moving away from the drum when the brakes are released. This problem could be caused by any of the following:

- Incorrect parking-brake adjustment
- Weak or broken shoe return springs
- Shoes out of adjustment
- Sticking piston in wheel cylinder
- Restricted brake line that will not release pressure
- Loose wheel bearing that allows the wheel to wobble so that the drum hits the brake shoes

43-4 ALL BRAKES DRAG
If all the brakes drag, the probable cause is that the master-cylinder pistons are not returning completely. The pushrod linkage needs adjustment or the master cylinder should be rebuilt or replaced. If the linkage is out of adjustment, the piston cups in the master cylinder are prevented from clearing the compensating ports. Therefore, pressure is not relieved as it should be. Instead, pressure continues to be applied to the brake fluid so that the brake shoes do not retract properly. A similar condition could result from the use of engine oil in the hydraulic system. Engine oil causes the rubber parts, such as the piston cups, to swell. *Engine oil must never be put into the brake system!*

43-5 CAR PULLS TO ONE SIDE DURING BRAKING
This trouble means that more braking friction is being applied to one drum or disk than the other. This problem could be caused by any of the following:

- Grease or brake fluid on lining
- Broken self-adjuster
- Restricted brake line or hose
- Sticking wheel-cylinder piston
- Brake backing plate loose
- Mismatched brake linings
- Incorrect tire pressures
- Unmatched tires on same axle
- Front wheels out of line

Brake linings with grease or brake fluid on them must be replaced. A leaky wheel cylinder could cause brake fluid to get onto the brake linings. At the rear, a defective axle seal or high lubricant level in the differential could allow oil to leak past the seal onto the brake linings (Fig. 43-1).

43-6 SOFT OR SPONGY PEDAL
This trouble probably is caused by air in the brake system. Sometimes it can be caused by incorrect brake-shoe adjustments. See Sec. 43-10 for causes of air leaking into the system.

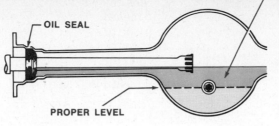

Fig. 43-1
A high lubricant level in the differential and rear-axle housing may cause leakage past the oil seal, resulting in soaked brake linings. (*Pontiac Motor Division of General Motors Corporation*)

43-7 POOR BRAKING REQUIRING EXCESSIVE PEDAL PRESSURE

Poor braking requiring excessive pedal pressure could be caused by any of the following:

- Power booster failure
- Piston stuck in wheel cylinder
- Brake linings soaked with water
- Brake linings hot
- Brake drums glazed
- Shoes out of adjustment
- Failure of one section of the dual brake system

When brake linings become soaked with water, they may lose braking ability. Usually, good braking will be restored as soon as the linings dry out.

If brakes are used continuously for a period of time, such as when coming down a long hill, they may overheat and "fade." The linings become so hot that they are ineffective. To prevent excessive braking when coming down a long hill, the driver should shift to a lower gear so that the engine is allowed to do part of the braking. The excessive heating may also glaze the brake drum so that it becomes too smooth for effective braking. The remedy here is to refinish the drums to remove the glaze. Also, if the brake linings are charred or burned, they should be replaced.

If the system is a power-brake system, failure of the power booster will require a high pedal pressure. See Sec. 43-25 for causes of power-brake failures.

43-8 BRAKES TOO SENSITIVE OR BRAKES GRAB

When the brakes are too sensitive, slight pressure on the brake pedal may cause the brakes to grab. The causes of these problems could be any of the causes listed in Sec. 43-5 and any of the following conditions:

- Binding linkage.
- Defective power brake.
- Defective combustion valve.
- Backing plates loose.
- Brake shoes out of adjustment.
- Brake drums scored.
- Wrong type of brake lining for car.
- Brake linings have grease on them.

43-9 NOISY BRAKES (BRAKE SQUEAL)

If the linings wear down so much that the rivets touch the brake drum, the brakes may squeal when applied. Noise also could result from warped brake shoes or a rough or worn brake drum. Figure 43-2 shows various types of brake drum defects. Loose parts can cause rattles. Some cars have brake squeal caused by vibration between the shoes and the drums.

43-10 AIR IN SYSTEM

If air gets into the hydraulic system, the brakes will be spongy. The result will be poor braking action. This trouble could be due to a plugged filler vent in the master cylinder. If the vent becomes plugged, air could be drawn into the system on the return stroke of the piston, as

Fig. 43-2
Various types of brake-drum defects that require drum service. (*Bear Manufacturing Company*)

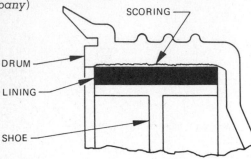

SCORED DRUM

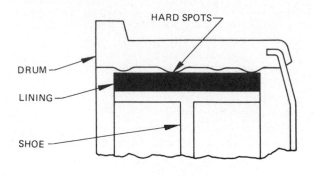

HARD SPOTS

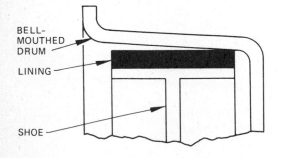

BELL-MOUTHED DRUM

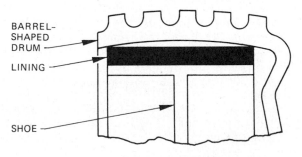

BARREL-SHAPED DRUM

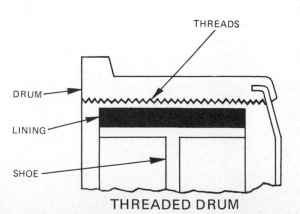

THREADED DRUM

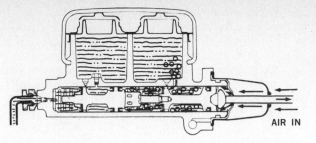

Fig. 43-3
If the cover vent becomes plugged, air may be drawn into the system on the return stroke of the pushrod, past the primary piston seal. Air entering this way is shown by the arrows and bubbles. (*Pontiac Motor Division of General Motors Corporation*)

shown in Fig. 43-3. This is not likely to happen on a dual master cylinder with a rubber reservoir diaphragm (Fig. 42-4). Loose connections or damaged brake lines could also allow air to get in the system. However, the most common cause of air in the system is low brake fluid in the master cylinder. This condition results from loss of brake fluid, which is discussed in Sec. 43-11.

43-11 LOSS OF BRAKE FLUID
Loss of brake fluid is due to a leak. The leak could be in the master cylinder, a wheel cylinder, a connection, or a brake line. Usually, the point of leakage is easy to find because it will be covered with dirt that has stuck to the fluid as it leaked out. If the leak occurs after a brake job, the brake-shoe actuating pin in a wheel cylinder may not be properly installed. If the pin is installed in a cocked position, as shown in Fig. 43-4, the piston will not set straight and a leak may result.

43-12 BRAKES DO NOT SELF-ADJUST
Failure of the brakes to self-adjust could be caused by defects in the adjuster mechanism. For example, the self-adjuster cable may be broken, the lever might not engage the star wheel, or the self-adjuster might be put together incorrectly.

43-13 BRAKE WARNING LIGHT COMES ON
The warning light on the instrument panel comes on if one section of the dual braking system fails. Both sections of the dual braking system should be checked so that the trouble can be found and fixed. It is dangerous to drive a car with only one brake section working. Only half of the wheels are being braked.

CHECK UP ON YOURSELF
Brakes are necessary for safe operation of the car. A knowledge of brakes—how they work and how to service them—is essential to the auto mechanic. Check up on yourself to find out how well you understand drum brake troubles and their possible causes.

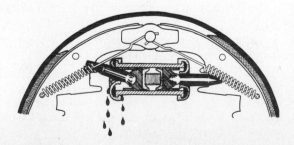

Fig. 43-4
Incorrect installation of the actuating pin will cause a side thrust on the piston, which will permit leakage of brake fluid from the wheel cylinder. The pin must always align in the notch in the brake shoe.

1. What could cause the brake pedal to go to the floorboard?
2. What are the possible causes of the car pulling to one side during braking? (There are nine causes listed in Sec. 43-5.)
3. What is the probable cause of a soft or spongy pedal?
4. With drum brakes, what are the possible causes of excessive pedal pressure being required to produce braking? (There are seven causes listed in Sec. 43-7.)
5. What is the most common cause of air in the brake system?

ANSWERS
1. Either there is not enough brake fluid or the brake shoes are worn or out of adjustment (Sec. 43-2). **2.** See Sec. 43-5. **3.** Air in the brake system (Sec. 43-6). **4.** See Sec. 43-7. **5.** Low brake fluid in the master cylinder (Sec. 43-10).

43-14 DISK BRAKE TROUBLES
Many of the troubles with drum brakes can also occur with disk brakes. However, there are a number of problems that occur only with disk brakes. The following possible troubles may occur:

1. Excessive pedal travel.
2. Brake roughness or chatter (pedal pulsations).
3. Excessive pedal effort.
4. Pull.
5. Noises.
6. Brakes heat up during driving and fail to release.
7. Leaky caliper cylinder.
8. Grabbing or uneven brake action.
9. Brake pedal can be depressed without braking action.
10. Brake warning light comes on (See Sec. 43-13).

43-15 EXCESSIVE PEDAL TRAVEL
Excessive pedal travel could be caused by any of the following:

- Excessive disk runout. This means that the disk wobbles as it rotates. When this happens, the pistons are pushed farther into the caliper. Therefore, additional pedal movement is required to push the pistons out. The runout of the disk is checked with a dial indicator (Fig. 43-5). If runout is excessive, the disk is refinished or a new disk is required.
- Air in the system or insufficient brake fluid in the master cylinder
- Warped or tapered shoes
- Loose wheel bearing
- Damaged piston seal
- Trouble in the power-brake booster
- Failure of one section of the dual braking system

43-16 BRAKE ROUGHNESS OR CHATTER (PEDAL PULSATIONS)
Brake roughness or chatter could be caused by a disk with too much runout (see Sec. 43-15). Brake roughness or chatter could also be caused by a disk whose two sides are not parallel (the disk is thicker in one part than in another). A loose wheel bearing could also cause the trouble.

544

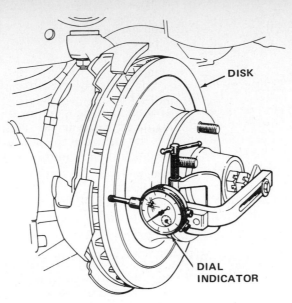

Fig. 43-5
Checking a disk for runout
with a dial indicator. (*Chevrolet Motor Division of General
Motors Corporation*)

DISK

**DIAL
INDICATOR**

43-17 EXCESSIVE PEDAL EFFORT

The most common cause of excessive pedal effort is trouble in the
power-brake unit. If this is not the cause, then other possible causes
are the following:

- Failure of one section of the dual-braking system
- Brake fluid or grease on the brake linings
- Worn linings
- Incorrect linings
- Sticking piston in caliper

43-18 PULL

If the car pulls to one side when the brakes are applied, it means there
is more braking action on that side. Possible causes could be any of the
following:

- Brake fluid or grease on brake linings
- Sticking piston in caliper
- Damaged or bent brake shoe
- Uneven tire pressure
- Unmatched tires on same axle
- Caliper loose on steering-knuckle adapter
- Front end out of alignment
- Unmatched brake linings
- Broken spring or loose suspension parts
- Restriction in brake hose or brake line

43-19 NOISES

Some noises occur with disk brakes. For example, a groan will sometimes result when the brakes are slowly released. Rattles could be
caused by loose parts or excessive clearance between the shoe and the
caliper. Scraping noises could be caused by the following:

- Long mounting bolts
- Disk rubbing the caliper, which could be caused by loose mounting bolts

- Loose wheel bearings
- Worn brake linings, which allow the wear indicator to scrape the disk

43-20 BRAKES HEAT UP DURING DRIVING AND FAIL TO RELEASE

This trouble occurs when the shoes maintain contact with the disk. The trouble could be caused by the driver "riding" the brake pedal. Another possible cause is the failure of the power-brake booster to release properly. Also, the pedal linkage could be stuck, or a piston could be stuck in the caliper.

43-21 LEAKY CALIPER CYLINDER

A leaky caliper cylinder probably is caused by a damaged or worn piston seal or by scores or corrosion on the piston or in the cylinder.

43-22 GRABBING OR UNEVEN BRAKE ACTION

This trouble could be due to trouble in the power-brake booster or to any of the conditions listed in Sec. 43-18.

43-23 BRAKE PEDAL CAN BE DEPRESSED WITHOUT BRAKING ACTION

When this trouble occurs, it means that the pistons are not pushing the brake shoes out into contact with the disk. This trouble will happen if the brakes have been serviced. In such a case, pumping the brake pedal several times may work the pistons out enough to produce normal braking. If this action does not produce normal braking, then the trouble may be due to the following:

- Leaks in the system
- Damaged piston seals
- Air in the system
- Leaks past the primary cups in the master cylinder

43-24 SERVICING THE BRAKES

When you work in the shop, you will learn the various brake jobs. They are listed below.

1. Adjustments

On earlier drum brakes without self-adjusters, adjustments were required periodically to compensate for lining wear. With the self-adjusting drum brakes and with disk brakes, no adjustments are required.

2. Replacing Brake Linings

When linings wear, the shoes must be replaced. On drum brakes, replacement of the shoes requires removal of the wheel and brake drum to get at the shoes (Fig. 43-6). On most disk brakes, the shoes are replaced after removing the wheel and the caliper (Fig. 43-7).

3. Drum and Disk Service

Some manufacturers recommend installing new disks if the old ones are worn or scored. Other manufacturers recommend refinishing the disks. Drums can be ground or turned to remove irregularities or

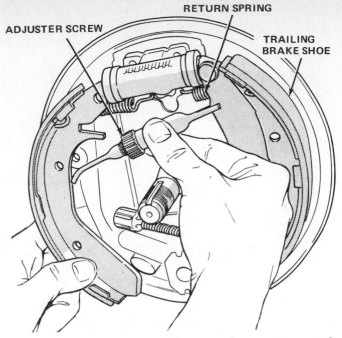

Fig. 43-6
Replacing the brake shoes on a
rear drum brake of a front-
wheel-drive car. (*Chrysler Corporation*)

scores. However, care must be taken to make sure that not too much
metal is removed. The removal of too much metal from a brake drum
leaves the drum too thin for effective braking action. Also, it may be
too thin for safe use.

4. Master Cylinders
Master cylinders may require disassembly for replacement of internal
parts. Honing of the cylinder may also be required. Some technicians
prefer to install a new or rebuilt master cylinder.

5. Wheel Cylinders
Wheel cylinders may require disassembly for replacement of the pistons or cups. Honing of the cylinder may also be required. If the bore

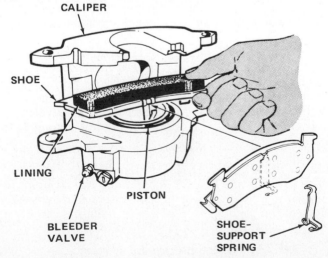

Fig. 43-7
Installing the inner shoe. Note
the location of the support
spring. (*Chevrolet Motor Division of General Motors Corporation*)

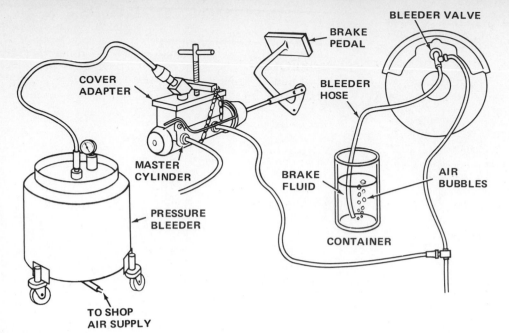

does not clean properly, a new or rebuilt wheel cylinder should be installed.

6. Calipers
New seals are required if the old seals are worn. Cylinders should be cleaned if they are corroded or rough.

7. Installing Brake Lines
Brake lines are made of special steel and rubber tubing. Only tubing recommended by the manufacturer must be used.

8. Flushing the Hydraulic System
If dirt, engine oil, or other damaging material has gotten into the system, the system must be flushed. Clean brake fluid or flushing compound must be forced through the system to wash it out.

9. Filling and Bleeding the Hydraulic System
After flushing, or at any time that brake fluid must be added, the hydraulic system must be bled (Fig. 43-8). All air must be removed from the system. Air is removed by applying pressure at the master cylinder and then opening each bleeder valve in turn at each wheel. This bleeds off any air in any of the lines going to the wheel cylinders or calipers.

43-25 POWER-BRAKE TROUBLES
The power-brake booster is an assist unit. It helps to apply the brakes. Operation of the power-brake system is discussed in Chap. 42. Let's look at the troubles that power-brake units can have and find out what might cause them. The possible causes are the following:

    1. Excessive pedal pressure required.
    2. Brakes grab.

3. Pedal goes to floorboard.

4. Brakes fail to release.

43-26 EXCESSIVE PEDAL PRESSURE REQUIRED
When excessive pedal pressure is required, it usually means that there is trouble inside the power booster. The trouble can be caused by any of the following:

- Defective vacuum check valve
- Collapsed hose
- Plugged vacuum fitting
- Clogged air inlet
- Faulty diaphragm
- Any of the causes listed in Secs. 43-7 and 43-17

43-27 BRAKES GRAB
In the power-brake booster, when the brakes grab, the trouble could be caused by a damaged reaction, or "brake-feel," mechanism or by a sticking air or vacuum valve. Conditions listed in Secs. 43-8 and 43-22 can also cause brakes to grab.

43-28 PEDAL GOES TO FLOORBOARD
This condition could be due to any of the troubles listed in Secs. 43-2 and 43-23. In some models of power brakes, the trouble could also result from failure of the compensating valve to close or from a leaking hydraulic-plunger seal.

43-29 BRAKES FAIL TO RELEASE
If the brakes fail to release, the trouble could be due to a broken diaphragm return spring, faulty check-valve action, or a sticking hydraulic-plunger seal. The causes listed in Secs. 43-4 and 43-20 could also prevent the brakes from releasing.

CHECK UP ON YOURSELF
You have now covered the story on brakes—how they work and how to find out what the trouble is when they do not work as they should. Now check up on yourself and find out how well you understand what you have studied about disk and power-brake troubleshooting.

1. With disk brakes, what are four possible causes of excessive brake-pedal effort?
2. With disk brakes, if the brake pedal can be depressed without causing braking action, what four conditions should you consider?
3. What is the purpose of flushing the brake system?
4. What is the purpose of bleeding the brake system?
5. What are five conditions in the power-brake booster that could make excessive pedal pressure necessary to obtain braking action?

ANSWERS
1. See Sec. 43-17. **2.** See Sec. 43-23. **3.** To remove dirt, oil, or other foreign material from the system (Sec. 43-24). **4.** To remove air from the system (Sec. 43-24). **5.** See Sec. 43-26.

CHAPTER FORTY-FOUR
TIRES AND WHEELS

After studying this chapter, you should be able to:
1. Discuss the purpose and construction of various types of tires, including bias and radials.
2. Discuss space-saving spare tires such as the collapsible and compact types.
3. Discuss tire wear and possible causes of abnormal wear.
4. Discuss the various kinds of tire service and how they are done.

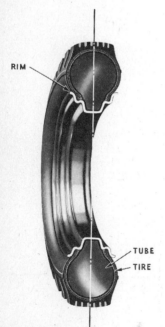

Fig. 44-1
The tire rim and tire are cut away so that the tube can be seen.

Improved tire design and improved highways make tire trouble much less common today than it was years ago. Yet there is still need for tire service occasionally. The automative technician should know how tires are made and how they do their job. Also, you should know what various patterns of abnormal wear mean. Abnormal tire wear usually is a sign of trouble in the steering, suspension, or brake system.

44-1 PURPOSE OF TIRES
The tire does two jobs. First, the tire is an air-filled cushion that absorbs most of the shock caused by road irregularities. The tire flexes, or gives, as it meets bumps and holes in the road. This absorbs the shock before it reaches the passengers. Second, the tire grips the road to provide good traction. Good traction enables the car to accelerate, brake, and take turns without skidding.

44-2 TIRE CONSTRUCTION
There are two general types of tires: those with inner tubes and those without tubes, called tubeless tires. On the tube type, both the tube and the tire are mounted on the wheel rim, as shown in Fig. 44-1. The tube is a hollow rubber doughnut that is inflated with air after it is installed inside the tire and the tire is put on the wheel rim. This inflation causes the tire to resist any change of shape.

Tubes are used in some truck tires and in motorcycle tires. Today tubes seldom are used in passenger car tires. Cars use tubeless tires. The tubeless tire does not use an inner tube. The tubeless tire is mounted on the rim so that the air is retained between the rim and the tire, as shown in Fig. 44-2.

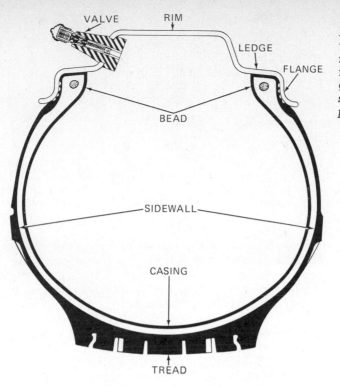

VALVE   RIM

LEDGE

FLANGE

BEAD

SIDEWALL

CASING

TREAD

Fig. 44-2
A sectional view of a tubeless
tire, showing how the tire bead
rests between the ledges and
flanges of the rim to produce a
good seal. (*Pontiac Motor Division of General Motors Corporation*)

The amount of air pressure used in the tire depends on the size and load it is to carry. Passenger car tires are inflated from about 22 to 30 psi [155 to 205 kPa]. Tires on heavy-duty trucks or buses may be inflated up to 100 psi [690 kPa].

Tubeless tires and tube tires are made in about the same way. Layers of cord, called plies, are shaped on a form and impregnated with rubber. The rubber sidewalls and treads are then applied and vulcanized into place to form the completed tire (Fig. 44-3). "Vulcanizing" is a

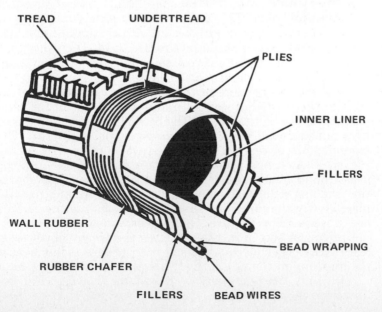

TREAD   UNDERTREAD

PLIES

INNER LINER

FILLERS

WALL RUBBER

BEAD WRAPPING

RUBBER CHAFER

FILLERS   BEAD WIRES

Fig. 44-3
A cutaway view of a tubeless
tire, showing tire construction.
(*Chevrolet Motor Division of
General Motors Corporation*)

Fig. 44-4

The three types of tire construction, as determined by the way the plies are laid. (*Chevrolet Motor Division of General Motors Corporation*)

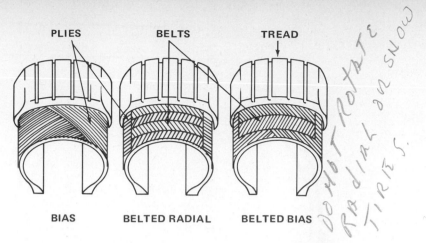

PLIES   BELTS   TREAD

BIAS   BELTED RADIAL   BELTED BIAS

Do not rotate radial or snow tires.

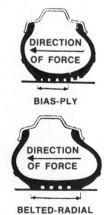

BIAS-PLY   BELTED-RADIAL

Fig. 44-5
Footprints of a nonbelted bias-ply tire and a belted-radial tire on a flat surface. Notice that the radial tire puts more rubber on the road.

DIRECTION OF FORCE

BIAS-PLY

DIRECTION OF FORCE

BELTED-RADIAL

Fig. 44-6
The difference in the amount of tread a bias-ply tire and a radial tire applies to the pavement during a turn.

process of heating the rubber under pressure. This molds the rubber into the desired form and gives it the proper wear characteristics and flexibility. The number of layers of cord, or plies, varies according to the intended use of the tire. Passenger-car tires have 2, 4, or 6 plies. Heavy-duty truck and bus tires may have up to 14 plies. Tires for extremely heavy-duty service, such as earthmoving equipment, may have up to 32 plies.

44-3 BIAS VERSUS RADIAL PLIES

There are two ways to apply the plies: on the bias (diagonally) and radially (Fig. 44-4). For many years most tires were of the bias type, as shown in Fig. 44-4. These tires had the plies crisscrossed. As you can see in Fig. 44-4 (left), one layer runs diagonally one way and the other layer runs diagonally the other way. This makes a carcass that is strong in all directions because of the overlapping plies. However, the plies tend to move against one another in bias tires. This generates heat, especially at high speed. Also, the tread tends to "squirm" or close up as it meets the road (Fig. 44-7). This increases tire wear.

Tires with radial plies (Fig. 44-4, center) were introduced to remedy these problems. In a radial tire, all plies run parallel to one another and vertical to the tire bead. Belts are applied on top of the plies to provide strength parallel to the tire bead. Then the tread is vulcanized on top of the belts. The belts are made of rayon, nylon, fiber glass, and steel mesh.

Radial tires now are installed on about 80 percent of all new cars built in the United States. All radial tires work in the same way, regardless of the belt material. The belt provides added strength. Radial tires put more rubber on the road than a bias-ply tire. The radial is more flexible, so more of the tread stays on the pavement, as shown in Fig. 44-5. Also, the tread has less tendency to heel up when the car goes around a curve, as shown in Fig. 44-6. This keeps more rubber on the road and reduces the tendency of the tire to skid. Radial tires wear more slowly than bias-ply tires. This is because the radial-tire tread does not squirm as the tire meets the pavement. The bias-ply tire tends to squirm, as shown in Fig. 44-7. As the treads pinch together, they slide sideways. This causes tread wear. There is less heat buildup on the highway in the radial tire. This also slows radial tire wear.

Bias-ply tires may also be belted, as shown in Fig. 44-4 (right). These are called *belted-bias tires*. They cost less than radial tires. However, even some tire manufacturers who make belted-bias tires recommend the radial tire as the best.

CAUTION
Never mix radial and bias-ply tires, either belted or unbelted, on a car. Mixing the two types can cause poor car handling and increase the possibility of skidding. This precaution is very important for snow tires. Regular bias-ply snow tires on the rear and radials on the front can result in oversteer. This can cause spin-out on wet or icy roads.

44-4 TIRE TREAD
The tread is the part of the tire that rests on the road. There are many different tread designs, as shown in Fig. 44-8. Snow tires have large rubber cleats molded into the tread for cutting through snow to improve traction.

Some tires have steel studs that stick out through the tread. Studs help the tire get better traction in ice and snow. However, some people claim studded tires shorten the life of the road surface. Because of this possibility, studded tires are banned in certain areas.

44-5 TIRE VALVE
Air is put into the tire, or into the inner tube, through a valve that opens when an air hose is applied to it (Fig. 44-2). Sometimes the valve is called a Schrader valve. On a tubed tire, the valve is mounted in the inner tube and sticks out through a hole in the wheel. On the tubeless tire, the valve is mounted in the hole in the wheel rim (Fig. 44-2). When the valve is closed, spring pressure and air pressure inside the tire or tube hold the valve on its seat. Most valves carry a valve cap, which is screwed down over the valve end. The cap protects the valve from dirt and acts as an added safeguard against air leaks.

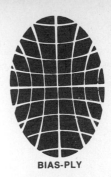

BIAS-PLY

BELTED-RADIAL

Fig. 44-7
Bias-ply treads tend to "squirm" as they meet the road. The radial tire treads tend to remain apart.

Fig. 44-8
Several types of tire tread.

553

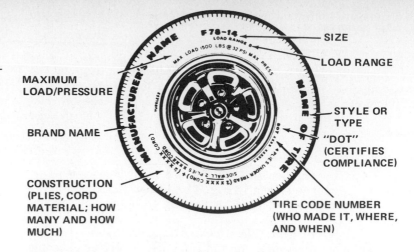

44-6 TIRE SIZE

Tire size is marked on the sidewall of the tire. An older tire might be marked 7.75-14. This means that the tire fits on a wheel that is 14 inches [356 mm] in diameter at the rim where the tire bead rests. The 7.75 means that the tire itself is about 7.75 inches [197 mm] wide when it is properly inflated.

Figure 44-9 shows a tire with an explanation of each mark on it. Tires have several markings on the sidewall. The markings include a letter code to designate the type of car the tire is designed for. D means a lightweight car, F means intermediate, G means a standard car. H, J, and L are for large luxury cars and high-performance vehicles. For example, some cars use a G78-14 tire. The 14 means a rim 14 inches [356 mm] in diameter. The 78 indicates the ratio between the tire height and width, as shown in Fig. 44-10. This tire is 78 percent as high as it is wide. The ratio of the height to the width is called the *aspect ratio* or

Fig. 44-10
Four aspect ratios of car tires. (*American Motors Corporation*)

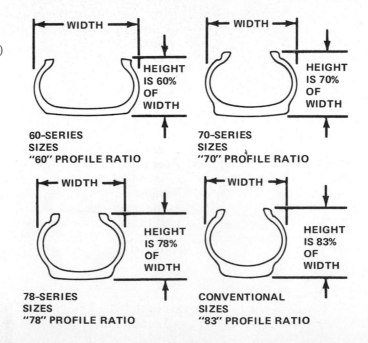

WIDTH — HEIGHT IS 60% OF WIDTH

60-SERIES SIZES "60" PROFILE RATIO

WIDTH — HEIGHT IS 70% OF WIDTH

70-SERIES SIZES "70" PROFILE RATIO

WIDTH — HEIGHT IS 78% OF WIDTH

78-SERIES SIZES "78" PROFILE RATIO

WIDTH — HEIGHT IS 83% OF WIDTH

CONVENTIONAL SIZES "83" PROFILE RATIO

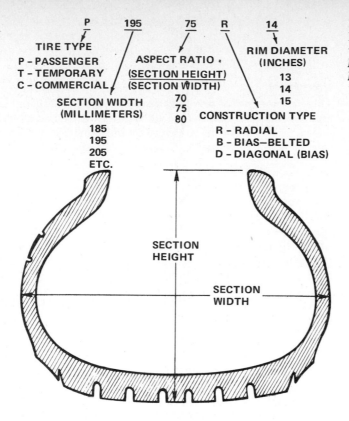

TIRE TYPE
P - PASSENGER
T - TEMPORARY
C - COMMERCIAL

SECTION WIDTH
(MILLIMETERS)
185
195
205
ETC.

ASPECT RATIO
(SECTION HEIGHT)
(SECTION WIDTH)
70
75
80

RIM DIAMETER
(INCHES)
13
14
15

CONSTRUCTION TYPE
R - RADIAL
B - BIAS—BELTED
D - DIAGONAL (BIAS)

SECTION HEIGHT

SECTION WIDTH

Fig. 44-11
Meaning of the size designation for a metric tire. (*Chevrolet Motor Division of General Motors Corporation*)

profile ratio. There are four aspect ratios: 83, 78, 70, and 60. The lower the number, the wider the tire looks. For example, a 60 tire is only 60 percent as high as it is wide.

The addition of an R to the sidewall marking, such as in GR78-14, indicates that the tire is a radial. Also, if a tire is a radial, the word "radial" must be molded into the sidewall. Some radial tires are marked in the metric system. For example, a tire marked 175R13 is a radial tire which measures 175 mm [6.9 inches] wide. It mounts on a wheel with a diameter of 13 inches [330 mm].

Some cars use metric size tires. The meaning of each letter and number of a metric tire size is shown in Fig. 44-11. This is the latest size designation for tires. Comparing the two tire-size labels, a tire formerly marked as an ER78-14 now is marked P195/75R14.

To identify the load that a tire can safely carry, each tire is classified into a load range. The load range indicates the allowable load for the tire as inflation pressure is increased. In Fig. 44-9, you can see that the tire is marked "Load Range B." Most passenger car tires are in load range B. There are three load ranges for passenger car tires: B, C, and D. Under the old system, "ply rating" was used to indicate load range. The load range B tire has the same load-carrying capacity as the tire with a 4-ply rating. Load range C equals a 6-ply rating tire. Load range D equals an 8-ply rating tire.

Fig. 44-12
A collapsible spare tire with inflator. (*Pontiac Motor Division of General Motors Corporation*).

44-7 COLLAPSIBLE SPARE TIRE
This tire (Fig. 44-12) is designed to save space in the luggage compartment. It is installed on the wheel in a deflated condition. It barely pro-

Fig. 44-13
A compact spare tire. (Olds-
mobile Division of General
Motors Corporation)

trudes beyond the rim. There is a pressure can of inflation propellent, called the inflator, in the luggage compartment. Instructions on how to install and safely inflate the collapsible spare tire are printed on the inflator can. We describe the procedure in Sec. 44-27.

CAUTION

This tire must not be driven more than 150 miles [240 km] and at a speed of 50 mph [80 km/h] or less. To exceed these limits is to risk a blowout of the collapsible spare tire. Also, the tire must not be inflated from the usual air hose in the shop or in a service station. This can cause the tire to explode.

44-8 COMPACT SPARE TIRE

Another tire that saves space in the luggage compartment is the compact spare tire (Fig. 44-13). This spare is lighter and considerably smaller than the standard tire being used on the car. The compact spare tire can be driven for the 1000- to 3000-mile [1600- to 4800-km] life of the tread. It is mounted on a narrow 15 × 4 wheel. The tire must not be mounted on any other wheel. No other tire, wheel cover, or trim ring should be installed on the special wheel. Also, the compact spare tire should not be used on the rear of a car equipped with a nonslip differential. The collapsible spare tire is smaller in diameter than the tire on the other side of the rear axle. Differential action must take place continuously. This may cause damage and failure of the nonslip differential.

NOTE

The compact spare tire is for emergency use only. As soon as the standard tire has been repaired, reinstall it on the car. The compact spare carries an inflation pressure of 69 psi [415 kPa]. It provides a rough and noisy ride.

44-9 WHEELS

Most cars use a pressed steel or disk wheel. This type of wheel also is called a *safety-rim* wheel. Figure 44-14 shows how a disk wheel is made. The outer part, called the rim, is of one-piece construction and is welded to the disk. This forms the seamless and airtight wheel that is needed to mount a tubeless tire. The center of the rim is smaller in diameter than the rest. This gives the rim the name "drop center." The center well is necessary to permit removal and installation of the tire. The bead of the tire must be pushed off the bead seat and into the smaller diameter. Only then can the tire beads be worked up over the rim flange. We discuss tire service later in the chapter.

The 14-inch [356-mm] wheel is used on most cars today. However, some smaller cars have 12-inch [305-mm] and 13-inch [330-mm] wheels. For 14-inch [356-mm] wheels, three different rim widths often are used, depending on the tire specified for the car. The rim widths are 4.5 inches [114 mm], 5 inches [127 mm], and 6 inches [152 mm]. Optional larger tires usually require larger rim widths.

Most manufacturers recommend that a wheel be replaced if it is bent or leaks air. The new wheel must be exactly the same as the old wheel. Installation of the wrong wheel could cause the wheel bearing to fail, the brakes to overheat, the speedometer to read inaccurately, and the tire to rub the body and frame.

44-10 SPECIAL WHEELS

Plain steel wheels, decorated with hub caps or wheel covers, are used on cars today. A large variety of special wheels are available for almost any vehicle. These wheels can be classified as styled steel wheels or styled aluminum wheels. A very popular wheel is the "mag" wheel, similar in appearance to the magnesium wheels used on some race cars (Fig. 44-15). However, for passenger cars, mag wheels are made of aluminum. The term "mag wheel" is used to mean almost any chromed, aluminum-offset, or wide-rim wheel of spoke design.

Some aluminum wheels are lighter than the steel wheels they replace. Lighter wheels reduce unsprung weight. This improves handling and performance. Also, some aluminum wheels can improve brake and tire performance by allowing them to run cooler.

CHECK UP ON YOURSELF

Find out how well you understand what you have studied about tires and wheels. Answer the questions below.

1. What are the layers of cord called?
2. What does "vulcanizing" mean?
3. What are the two ways of applying the plies?
4. What are the belts made of?
5. What types of tires increase the usable space in the luggage compartment?
6. What are two types of wheels?

ANSWERS

1. Plies (Sec. 44-2). 2. Heating rubber under pressure so that it will take the desired shape and other characteristics (Sec. 44-2). 3. Diagonally and radially

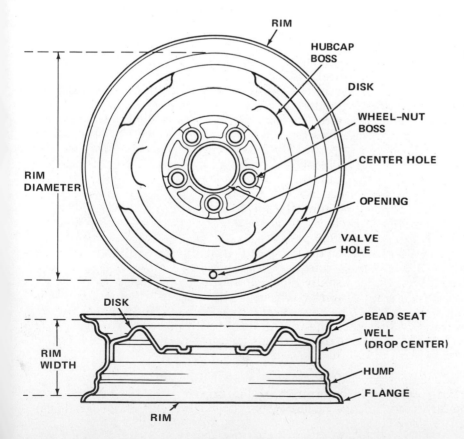

RIM

HUBCAP BOSS

DISK

WHEEL-NUT BOSS

CENTER HOLE

OPENING

VALVE HOLE

RIM DIAMETER

DISK

BEAD SEAT

WELL (DROP CENTER)

HUMP

FLANGE

RIM WIDTH

RIM

Fig. 44-14
Construction of a car wheel.
(*American Motors Corporation*)

(Sec. 44-3). **4.** Rayon, nylon, fiber glass, or steel mesh (Sec. 44-3). **5.** Collapsible spare tire and compact spare tire (Secs. 44-7 and 44-8). **6.** Disk wheel and mag wheel (Secs. 44-9 and 44-10).

TIRE AND WHEEL SERVICE

44-11 TIRE SERVICE
Tire service includes periodic checking of the air pressure and addition of air as needed. Failure to maintain correct air pressure can cause rapid tire wear, early tire failure and poor fuel economy. Incorrect air pressure can also cause handling problems, as we will explain in Sec. 44-12. Tire service includes periodic inspection of the tire for abnormal wear, cuts, bruises, or other damage. In addition, tire service includes the repair and replacement of tires.

44-12 TIRE INFLATION AND TIRE WEAR
The driver has more effect on tire life than any other factor. Good drivers usually get longer tire life than careless drivers. Rapid tire wear can be caused by rapid starting and stopping, severe braking, high-speed driving, and striking or rubbing curbs. Too little air in the tire can cause hard steering, front-wheel shimmy, steering kickback, and tire squeal on turns. Also, the tire with too little air will wear on the shoulders and not in the center of the tread, as shown at the upper

Fig. 44-15
A mag wheel. (*Shelby International, Inc.*)

left in Fig. 44-16. The additional flexing that results from insufficient air pressure also can damage the sidewalls, even causing separation of plies.

The underinflated tire is subject to rim bruises. That is, if the tire should strike a rut or stone, or bump a curb too hard, the tire will flex so much that it will be pinched against the rim. Any of these different kinds of damage can lead to early tire failure.

With overinflation, the tire rides on the center of the tread so that only the center wears, as shown at the upper center in Fig. 44-16. The overinflated tire will not flex normally, with the result that the tire cords can be weakened or even broken.

44-13 TOE-IN OR TOE-OUT TIRE WEAR

Excessive toe-in or toe-out causes the tire to be dragged sideways as it is moving forward. For example, a tire on a front wheel that toes-in 1 inch [25 mm] from straight ahead will be dragged sideways about 150 feet [46 m] every mile [1.6 km]. This sideward drag scrapes off rubber, as shown at the upper right in Fig. 44-16. Note the feather-edges of rubber that appear on one side of the tread. If both sides show

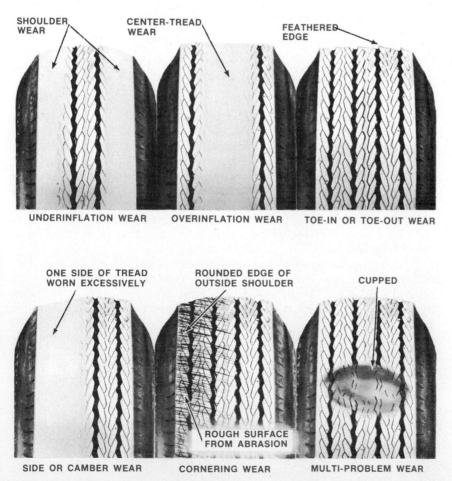

Fig. 44-16
Patterns of abnormal tire-tread wear. (*Buick Motor Division of General Motors Corporation*)

this type of wear, the front end is misaligned. If only one tire shows this type of wear, the steering arm probably is bent. This condition causes one wheel to toe-in more than the other.

44-14 CAMBER WEAR
If a wheel has excessive camber, the tire will run more on one shoulder than on the other. The tread will wear excessively on that side, as shown at the lower left in Fig. 44-16.

44-15 CORNERING WEAR
Cornering wear, shown at the lower center in Fig. 44-16, is caused by taking curves at excessive speeds. The tire not only skids, but also tends to roll, producing the diagonal type of wear shown. The remedy is to have the driver slow down around curves.

44-16 UNEVEN TIRE WEAR
Uneven tire wear, with the tread unevenly or spottily worn, as shown at the lower right in Fig. 44-16, can result from several mechanical problems. These problems include misaligned wheels, unbalanced wheels, uneven or grabbing brakes, overinflated tires, or out-of-round brake drums.

44-17 HIGH-SPEED WEAR
Tires wear more rapidly at high speed than at low speed. Tires driven consistently at 70 to 80 mph [112 to 129 km/h] will give less than half the mileage of tires driven at 30 mph [48 km/h].

44-18 CHECKING TIRE PRESSURE AND INFLATING TIRES
To check tire pressure and inflate the tires, first determine the correct inflation pressure for the tire. You can find this specification printed on a tire placard on one of the door jambs (or at some similar place) on the car. Specifications are for cold tires. Tires that are hot from being driven or from sitting in the sun will have an increased air pressure. Air expands when hot. Tires that have just come off the interstate highway may show as much as a 5- to 7-psi [35- to 48-kPa] increase.

As a hot tire cools, it loses pressure. Never bleed a hot tire to reduce its pressure. If you do this, then when the tire cools, its pressure could drop below the specified minimum.

There are times when the tire pressure should be on the high side. For example, one tire manufacturer recommends increasing the pressure by 4 psi [28 kPa] for high speed, trailer pulling, or extra-heavy loads. However, never exceed the maximum pressure specified on the tire sidewall.

If the tire valve has a cap, always install the cap after checking pressure or adding air.

44-19 TIRE ROTATION
The amount of wear a tire gets depends on its location on the car. For example, the right rear tire wears about twice as fast as the left front tire. This is because roads are slightly crowned (higher in the center) and also because the right rear tire is driving. The crown causes the car to lean out a little, so the right tires carry more weight. The combination of this and carrying power through the right rear tire causes it to wear faster. To equalize wear as much as possible, tires should be

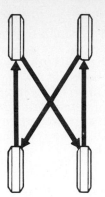
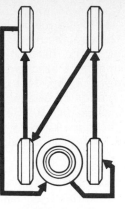

BIAS–PLY TIRE
FOUR–WHEEL
ROTATION

BIAS–PLY TIRE
FIVE–WHEEL
ROTATION

FIVE–WHEEL ROTATION

FOUR–WHEEL ROTATION

BIAS AND
BIAS–BELTED TIRES

RADIAL TIRES

Fig. 44-17
Tire-rotation patterns for cars with and without a rotatable spare tire. (*Chevrolet Motor Division of General Motors Corporation*)

rotated any time wear is noticeable and at the mileage specified by the car manufacturer. One manufacturer recommends rotating radial tires after the first 7500 miles [12,000 km] and then every 15,000 miles [24,000 km]. Bias tires should be rotated every 7500 miles [12,000 km]. Figure 44-17 shows the recommended rotation pattern for bias, bias-belted, and radial tires. Bias and bias-belted tires can be switched from one side of the car to the other. However, radial tires are not switched from one side to the other. To do this reverses their direction of rotation. This could cause handling and wear problems.

On cars with a collapsible spare tire or a compact spare tire, use the four-wheel rotation pattern shown in Fig. 44-17. Always mark the location (LR or RR) on the side of a studded tire before removing it from the wheel. Studded tires should never be rotated. A studded tire should be put back on the same wheel from which it was removed. Also mount the tire so that it rolls in the same direction.

44-20 TIRE INSPECTION

The purpose of inspecting the tires is to determine whether they are safe for further use. When an improper wear pattern is found, the technician must know the causes of abnormal tread wear (Fig. 44-16). The technician must correct the cause or notify the driver of what is wrong. When the tires are found to be serviceable, they can be rotated (Fig. 44-17). After the tires are cool, check and adjust the inflation pressures.

When inspecting a tire, check for bulges in the sidewalls. A bulge is a danger signal. It can mean that the plies are separated or broken and that the tire is likely to go flat. A tire with a bulge should be removed from the rim so that the tire can be checked inside and out. If the plies are broken or separated, the tire should be thrown away. To make a complete tire inspection, remove all stones from the tread. This is to make sure that no tire damage is hidden by the stones. Also, any time the tire is to be spin-balanced, remove all stones from the tread. This will ensure that no person is struck and injured by stones thrown from the tread as the tire rotates.

561

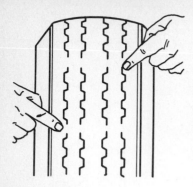

Fig. 44-18
A tire tread worn down so much that the tread-wear indicator shows.

Fig. 44-19
Using a penny to check tread wear.

Many tires have tread-wear indicators, which are filled-in sections of the tread grooves. When the tread has worn down enough to show the indicators (Fig. 44-18), the tire should be replaced. There also are special tire-tread gauges that can be inserted into the tread grooves to measure how much tread remains. A quick way to check tread wear is with a Lincoln penny, as shown in Fig. 44-19. If at any point you can see all Lincoln's head, the tread is excessively worn. Some state laws require a tread depth of at least $\frac{1}{32}$ inch [0.79 mm] in any two adjacent grooves at any location on the tire. A tire with little or no tread has poor traction on the road and will produce poor braking.

NOTE

A tire can look OK from the outside and still have internal damage. To completely inspect a tire, remove it from the rim. Then examine it closely, inside and out.

44-21 TUBE INSPECTION

Tubes usually give little trouble if correctly installed. However, careless installation can cause trouble. For example, if the wheel rim is rough or rusty or if the tire bead is rough, the tube may wear through. Dirt in the casing can cause the same trouble. Another condition that can cause trouble is installing a tube that is too large in the tire. Sometimes an old tube (which may have stretched) is put in a new tire. When a tube that is too large is put into a casing, the tube can overlap at some point. The overlap will rub and wear and possibly cause early tube failure.

A radial tire that is used with a tube must have a special radial-tire inner tube in it. If regular tubes are used in radial tires, the tube splice may come apart.

Always check carefully around the valve stem when inspecting a tube. If the tube has been run flat or at low pressure, the valve stem may be broken or tearing away from the tube. Valve-stem trouble requires installation of a new tube.

44-22 REMOVING A WHEEL FROM THE CAR

Radial tires must be removed from the car to be repaired. Also, if the tire has been run flat, remove the tire for inspection. To repair a tire, first take off the hub cap or wheel cover. Then remove the wheel from the car. If you are using a lug wrench, loosen the lug nuts before raising the car. It is easier to loosen the lug nuts first, because the wheel will not turn if the car weight is on it. On some cars the lug nuts on the right side of the car have right-hand threads. The lug nuts on the left side have left-hand threads. The reason is that the forward rotation of the wheels tend to tighten the nuts, not loosen them. Figure 44-20 shows the technician using an air-powered impact wrench to remove the lug nuts.

NOTE

When using an impact wrench, use an impact socket with it. A regular socket may crack when used on an impact wrench.

44-23 DEMOUNTING A TIRE FROM A DROP-CENTER RIM

With the wheel off the car, make a chalk mark across the tire and rim so you can reinstall the tire in the same position. This preserves the

Fig. 44-20
Using an impact wrench to re-
move the lug nuts. (*Mobil Oil
Corporation*)

balance of the wheel and tire. Next, release the air from the tire. This
can be done by holding the tire valve open or removing the valve core.
The tire should then be removed from the rim, using a shop tire
changer.

44-24 USING SHOP TIRE CHANGERS

Today many shops have an air-powered tire changer, such as shown in
Fig. 44-21. After the bead is pushed off the rim (this is called "breaking
the bead"), a tool is used with the tire changer to lift the bead up over
the rim (Fig. 44-22). The powered tire changer also has a tool to re-
mount the tire on the rim.

44-25 REMOUNTING THE TIRE ON THE RIM

To mount the tire on the rim, use the tire changer. Coat the rim and
beads with rubber lubricant or a soap-and-water mixture. This will
make the mounting procedure easier. Do not use a nondrying lubricant, such as antifreeze, silicone, grease, or oil. They will allow the tire
to "walk around" the rim so that the tire balance is lost. Oil or grease
will damage the rubber. When you are remounting the same tire that
was removed from the rim, make sure the chalk marks on the tire and
rim align. After the tire is on the rim, reposition the beads against the
bead seat. Slowly inflate the tire (Fig. 44-23). If the beads do not hold
air, use a tire-mounting band to spread the beads. You usually will
hear a "pop" as the beads seat on the rim. Then install the valve core
and inflate the tire to the recommended pressure.

CAUTION
Do not stand over the tire while inflating it. If the tire should explode, you could
be injured.

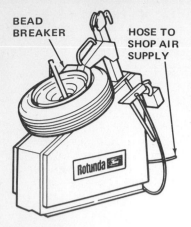

Fig. 44-21
Using an air-powered tire changer to "break the bead" so the tire can be removed from the wheel.

Fig. 44-22
Using the powered tire changer to lift the upper bead above the rim. The center post rotates, carrying the bead-lifting tool around with it.

44-26 CHECKING THE WHEEL

When the tire is off the wheel, check the rim for dents and roughness. Steel wool can be used to clean rust spots from standard steel wheels. Aluminum wheels can be cleaned only with mild soap and water. File off nicks or burrs. Then clean the rim to remove all filings and dirt. A wheel that has been bent should be discarded. A bent wheel may be weakened by heating, welding, or straightening so that it could fail on the highway.

Some wheels now have decorative plastic inserts. The plastic can be cleaned by using a sponge and soap and water.

44-27 TIRE VALVE

If the valve in the wheel requires replacement, remove the old valve and install a new one. There are two types: the snap-in type (see Fig. 44-2) and the type that is secured with a nut. To remove the snap-in type, cut off the base of the old valve. Lubricate the new valve with rubber lubricant. Then attach a tire-valve installing tool to the valve and pull the new valve into place.

On the clamp-in type that is secured with a nut, remove the nut to take the old valve out. Be sure to tighten the nut sufficiently when installing the new valve.

44-28 SERVICING THE COLLAPSIBLE SPARE TIRE

We describe the space-saving collapsible tire in Sec. 44-7. It is installed on the wheel deflated (Fig. 44-12). The wheel must be installed on the car before the tire is inflated.

CAUTION

Do not inflate the tire before the wheel is mounted on the car. Follow the safety cautions listed on the inflator can.

The inflator can has detailed instructions on how to install and inflate the tire. Briefly, here is the inflation procedure:

1. If the temperature is 10°F [−12°C] or below, the inflator must be heated. Put the inflator over the defroster outlet of the car. Set the heater at "Defrost" at the highest temperature. Then run the blower at the fastest speed for 10 minutes.

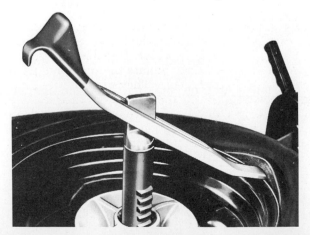

2. Do not inflate the tire off the car. First bolt the wheel to the car with the air valve at the bottom. Remove the plastic cap from the inflator and the cap from the tire valve.
3. Push the inflator onto the valve stem until you hear the sound of gas entering the tire.

CAUTION
Keep your hands off the metal parts of the inflator. They become extremely cold during discharge. You could freeze your fingers!

4. When the sound stops, wait 1 minute. Then remove the inflator and install the valve cap. The gas in the inflator, when completely used up, will properly fill the tire.

NOTE
After you have inflated the tire and have removed the jack so that the tire rests on the pavement, the tire may look underinflated. This can happen especially in cold weather. Drive slowly for the first mile [1.6 km]. This will warm up the tire and increase the pressure.

5. If the inflator is the nonrefillable type, dispose of it in a safe waste receptacle. Do not burn or puncture the inflator. If it is the refillable type, it can be recharged with the proper equipment.
6. The collapsible spare tire must not be driven farther than necessary. The maximum distance is 150 miles [240 km]. As soon as the regular tire has been repaired and installed in place of the collapsible spare tire, remove the valve core from it. This will allow the gas to escape so that the tire collapses. It can then be stored, as before, in the luggage compartment.

CAUTION
This tire must not be used for more than 150 miles [240 km] and at speeds not to exceed 50 mph [80 km/h]. To exceed these limits is to risk a blowout of the collapsible spare tire. Also, do not inflate this tire from the usual air hoses in service stations or from the shop air hose. This can cause the tire to overinflate and explode.

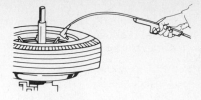

Fig. 44-23
Inflation of the tire while seating the beads. Never exceed a pressure of 40 psi (276 kPa) in a passenger car tire. (*Tire Industry Safety Council*)

TUBE AND TIRE REPAIR

44-29 TUBE REPAIR
If a tire tube has been punctured but has no other damage, it can be repaired with a patch. Remove the tube from the tire to find the leak. Inflate the tube and then submerge it in water. Bubbles will appear where there is a leak. Mark the spot. Then deflate the tube and dry it.

There are two ways to patch a tube leak. They are the cold-patch method and the hot-patch method. With the cold-patch method (also known as "chemical vulcanizing"), first make sure the rubber is clean, dry, and free of oil or grease. Buff, or roughen, the area around the leak. Then cover the area with vulcanizing cement. Let the cement dry until it is tacky. Press the patch into place. Roll it from the center out with a "stitching tool" or with the edge of a patch-kit can.

With the hot-patch method, prepare the tube in the same way as for the cold patch. Put the hot patch into place and clamp it. Then, with a match, light the fuel on the back of the patch. As the fuel burns, the

Fig. 44-24
Installing a head-type plug in
a radial tubeless tire. (*Rubber
Manufacturers Association*)

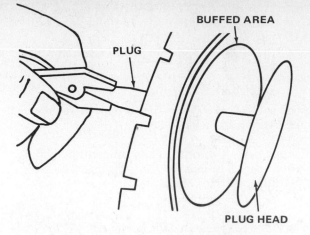

heat vulcanizes the patch to the tube. After the patch has cooled, recheck the tube for leaks by submerging the tube in water.

Another kind of hot patch uses a vulcanizing hot plate. The hot
plate supplies the heat required to bond the patch to the tube.

NOTE
The hot-patch method is preferred to the cold-patch method by many technicians.

44-30 TIRE REPAIR
No attempt should be made to repair a tire that has been badly damaged. If the plies are torn or have holes in them, the tire should be
thrown away. A puncture bigger than $\frac{1}{4}$ inch [6.36 mm] should not be
patched. Instead, the tire should be replaced. Even though you might
be able to patch the tire so it will hold air, it would be dangerous to use.
The tire might blow out on the highway.

To repair small holes in a tubeless tire, first make sure that the
object that caused the hole has been removed. Check the tire for other
puncturing objects. Sometimes a tubeless tire can carry a nail for a
long distance without losing air.

A radial tire should be removed from the wheel for repair. The
plug should be of the head type and applied from inside the tire (Fig.
44-24). Figure 44-25 shows the area of a tire in which a puncture can
be repaired. Punctures outside this area require replacement of the
tire.

NOTE
Leaks from a tubeless tire are located in the same way as leaks from a tube.
With the tire on the wheel and inflated, submerge the tire and wheel in water.
Bubbles will show the location of any leaks. If a water tank is not available,
coat the tire with soapy water. Bubbles will show the location of leaks.

If air leaks from around the spoke welds of the wheel, you can repair the leaks. Clean the area and apply two coats of cold-patch vulcanizing cement on the inside of the rim. Allow the first coat to dry before
applying the second coat. Then cement a strip of rubber patching material over the area.

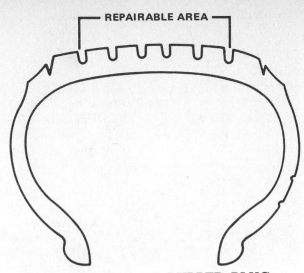

REPAIRABLE AREA

Fig. 44-25
The area of a tire in which a puncture can safely be patched. (*Chrysler Corporation*)

44-31 REPAIRING A PUNCTURE WITH A RUBBER PLUG—TIRE ON RIM

A temporary repair of a small puncture with the tire still mounted on the rim can be made (Fig. 44-26). However, this repair is only a temporary fix. As soon as possible, the tire must be removed from the rim and repaired from the inside, as explained in Sec. 44-32.

Remove the puncturing object and clean the hole. Apply vulcanizing cement to the outside and inside of the hole. There are different kinds of rubber plugs. The kind shown in Fig. 44-26 is installed with a plug needle. To use this plug, cover the hole with vulcanizing cement. Then select a plug of the right size for the hole. The plug should be at least twice the diameter of the hole. Roll the small end of the plug into the eye of the needle. Dip the plug into vulcanizing cement. Push the needle and plug through the hole. Then pull the needle out. Trim off the plug $\frac{1}{8}$ inch [3.2 mm] above the tire surface. Check for leakage. If there is no leakage, the tire is ready to use after it is inflated. However, the tire should not be driven faster than 40 mph [64 km/h] or farther than 75 miles [120 km]. For continued use, the tire must be removed from the wheel and a permanent repair made.

44-32 REPAIRING A TIRE REMOVED FROM THE RIM

There are three methods of repairing holes in tires. These are the rubber-plug, the cold-patch, and the hot-patch method. Permanent repairs are made from inside the tire, with the tire off the rim.

- Rubber-plug method. Rubber plugs can be used in the same way as explained in Sec. 44-31. The basic difference is that the repair is made from inside the tire. The area inside the tire around the puncture is buffed and cleaned. Then the plug is installed from inside the tire.

- Cold-patch method. In the cold-patch method, first clean and buff the inside area around the puncture. Then coat the area around the puncture with vulcanizing cement. Allow it to dry for 5 minutes. Next, remove the backing from the patch. Place the patch over the puncture, stitching it down with the stitching tool. Start stitching at the center and work out, making sure to stitch down the edges of the patch.

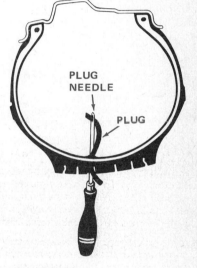

PLUG NEEDLE

PLUG

Fig. 44-26
A tire cut away to show a needle being used to insert a rubber plug into a hole in the tire.

Fig. 44-27
Repairing a tubeless tire by the
hot-patch method.

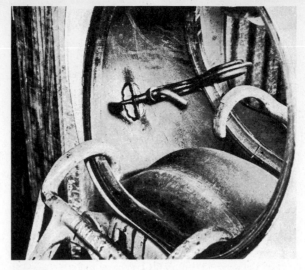

NOTE

Make sure no dirt gets on the cement or patch during the repair. Dirt could allow leakage.

■ Hot-patch method. The hot-patch method is very similar to the cold-patch method. The difference is that after the patch has been put into place over the area, heat is applied. This is done by lighting the patch with a match or with an electric hot plate, according to the type of patch being used (Fig. 44-27).

After the repair is done, mount the tire on the rim. Inflate and test it for leakage, as explained in Sec. 44-30.

44-33 REPAIRING A TIRE THAT USES A TUBE

If a tire that uses a tube has a small hole, clean out the hole. Then repair the tube. No repair to the tire is necessary. The tube will hold the air. However, if the hole is large, up to ¼ inch [6.3 mm] in diameter, the tire should be repaired with a patch on the inside. This prevents dirt or water from working in between the tire and tube and causing tube failure.

CHECK UP ON YOURSELF

You have now completed the chapter on tires and wheels. Now answer the questions that follow to help you review them.

1. If the tire wears on the shoulders and not in the center of the tread, what is the probable cause?
2. If the tire wears in the center of the tread and not on the shoulders, what is the probable cause?
3. If the tire wears more on one side of the tread than on the other, what is the probable cause?
4. Should you inflate the tire to specification when it is hot or cold?
5. What is a tire-wear indicator?

ANSWERS

1. Underinflation of the tire (Sec. 44-12). **2.** Overinflation of the tire (Sec. 44-12). **3.** Excessive wheel camber (Sec. 44-14). **4.** Cold (Sec. 44-18). **5.** Filled-in sections of the tread grooves that show up when the tread has worn down to them (Sec. 44-10).

PART EIGHT
AUTO AIR-CONDITIONING SYSTEMS

In this part, we cover heating and air-conditioning systems used in automotive vehicles. Many of these systems are manually controlled by knobs which the driver can turn to get the desired temperature. Others are automatic. The driver sets the temperature desired, and the system automatically heats or cools as necessary to maintain that temperature in the car. There are two chapters in Part Eight:

CHAPTER 45 Heating and Air Conditioning
        46 Heater and Air-Conditioner Service

CHAPTER FORTY-FIVE
HEATING AND AIR CONDITIONING

After studying this chapter, you should be able to:

1. Discuss the construction and operation of car heaters and air conditioners.
2. Explain how a refrigeration system works.
3. Describe how the various valves and other components in the air-conditioning system work.

Today all cars have heaters, and about 80 percent of all new cars have air conditioners. In this chapter we will cover the various heating and air-conditioning systems. You adjust some systems manually. In other systems, you set the controls, and the system automatically maintains the temperature you selected. For example, if heat is needed inside the car, the heating system goes to work. Or, if the interior of the car needs cooling, the air-conditioning system goes to work.

45-1 CAR HEATER

Older car heaters consisted of a small radiator, or heater core, mounted under the car dash. The radiator, or heater core, was connected by two hoses to the engine cooling system. When heat was needed, a small electric motor behind the heater radiator was turned on. The motor turned a fan that blew air through the heater radiator. The air was heated, and the interior of the car was warmed by it. The heat came from the engine cooling system. Modern car heaters work the same way, but they have additional controls to provide better regulation of the heat.

Figure 45-1 shows the hose connections between the engine cooling system and the car heater. In operation the water pump in the engine cooling system keeps hot coolant flowing through the heater radiator core. Therefore the heater core is hot. The amount of heat that gets into the car interior is determined by the amount of air that is allowed to flow through the heater core. In a modern car-heating system, three doors are provided to adjust the air flow.

Figure 45-2 shows a schematic diagram of the system. The amount of air that enters is determined by the blower speed. The blower motor

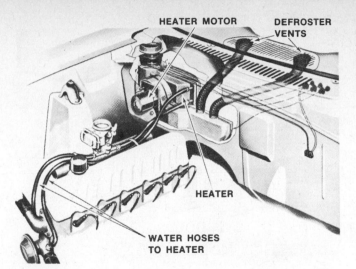

Fig. 45-1
Car heater system. Hot coolant from the engine cooling system circulates through a small radiator. The fan blows air through the radiator.

HEATER MOTOR

DEFROSTER VENTS

HEATER

WATER HOSES TO HEATER

is connected to the battery through a switch. It can be turned to operate the blower slow or fast (and at an intermediate speed in many systems).

After the air enters the system, its direction of flow is determined by the position of the temperature door. In Fig. 45-2 three positions of this door are indicated, labeled A, B, and C. If the temperature door is open wide (position C), then most of the air entering has to pass through the heater core. Maximum heating is obtained. If the door is closed (position A), then no air can pass through the heater core. The air temperature is unchanged.

The air door determines the amount of air, either hot or cold, flowing through the system. It can be adjusted for full air flow (position 1) or for no air flow at all (position 2), or any place in between.

The defroster door can be adjusted so that the heated air is directed up through the defroster outlets to the inside of the windshield. Or the defroster door can be adjusted so that most of, or all, the heated air is directed into the car.

The doors to the system, shown in Fig. 45-2, are operated by cables attached to heater controls on the instrument panel.

45-2 VACUUM-OPERATED HEATER CONTROLS

Figure 45-3 shows a heater-control system that uses vacuum motors to control the system. The unit is mounted under the instrument panel.

Fig. 45-2
The air flow through an automotive heater. (*Chevrolet Motor Division of General Motors Corporation*)

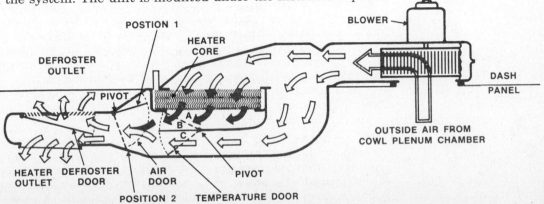

POSTION 1

DEFROSTER OUTLET

HEATER CORE

BLOWER

DASH PANEL

PIVOT

OUTSIDE AIR FROM COWL PLENUM CHAMBER

HEATER OUTLET

DEFROSTER DOOR

AIR DOOR

PIVOT

POSITION 2

TEMPERATURE DOOR

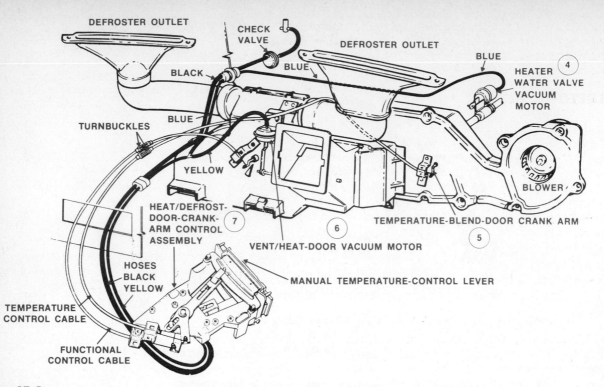

DEFROSTER OUTLET

CHECK VALVE

DEFROSTER OUTLET

BLACK

BLUE

BLUE

HEATER WATER VALVE VACUUM MOTOR

④

BLUE

TURNBUCKLES

BLUE

YELLOW

HEAT/DEFROST-DOOR-CRANK-ARM CONTROL ASSEMBLY

⑦

⑥

⑤

BLOWER

TEMPERATURE-BLEND-DOOR CRANK ARM

VENT/HEAT-DOOR VACUUM MOTOR

HOSES BLACK YELLOW

MANUAL TEMPERATURE-CONTROL LEVER

TEMPERATURE CONTROL CABLE

FUNCTIONAL CONTROL CABLE

Fig. 45-3
A modern heater-control system.

The control assembly is mounted in the instrument panel. It is attached to the main unit by various cables and hoses. Vacuum to operate the vacuum motors is obtained from the engine intake manifold when the engine is running.

Figure 45-4 is a schematic drawing of the heater system. Outside air is drawn into the system through the cool-air intake and flows into the blower housing. From the blower housing, the air flows through the heater case to the temperature-blend door (5 in Fig. 45-4). This door directs air through or around the heater core, depending on the position of the door. The door position is controlled by the temperature-control lever, which is a manual control on the instrument panel (at the top in Fig. 45-4). Setting the control lever at the COOL position causes the door to block off passage of the air through the heater core. The air passes through the system unchanged in temperature. Moving the lever to WARM causes the door to direct all the air through the heater core so that the air is heated. At various positions between COOL and WARM, part of the air goes through the heater core and part bypasses the heater core. The heated and unheated air blend and enter the car. Moving the temperature-control lever moves the temperature-blend door to give the desired amount of heat in the car.

In this system, air can be directed in the following three ways:
- To the floor
- Through registers into the car
- To the defroster vents

The registers are the two louvered outlets mounted at the two extreme ends of the instrument panel. The louvers can be adjusted to aim the flow of air. Also, the heat can be shut off entirely so that untreated outside air flows into the car. When the functional-control lever (see top of Fig. 45-4) is set at VENT, a vacuum motor opens the vent-heat door (6 in Fig. 45-4). At the same time, another vacuum motor closes the water-heater valve (4 in Fig. 45-4) so that the flow of hot coolant to the heater core is cut off.

REFRIGERATION

45-3 REFRIGERATION

Before we discuss air conditioning, let's take a look at refrigeration—the kind of refrigeration you get from the electric refrigerators used in homes. The air conditioner uses a refrigerator to cool and dry the air.

Refrigeration works by the process of evaporation. *Evaporation* happens when a liquid turns into a gas, or vapor. Put a little water on your hand. Blow on your hand, or wave your hand in the air. Your hand feels cold because as the water evaporates, it takes heat from your hand.

The removal of heat by evaporation is the basic principle of refrigeration. For example, heat is removed from food put into the refrigerator by the evaporation of a liquid in the refrigeration system (Fig. 45-5).

The illustration shows a refrigerator containing food, plus a jug of a liquid refrigerant called Freon-12. Freon-12 is a liquid at temperatures below $-22°F$ [$-30°C$]. At temperatures above $-22°F$ [$-30°C$],

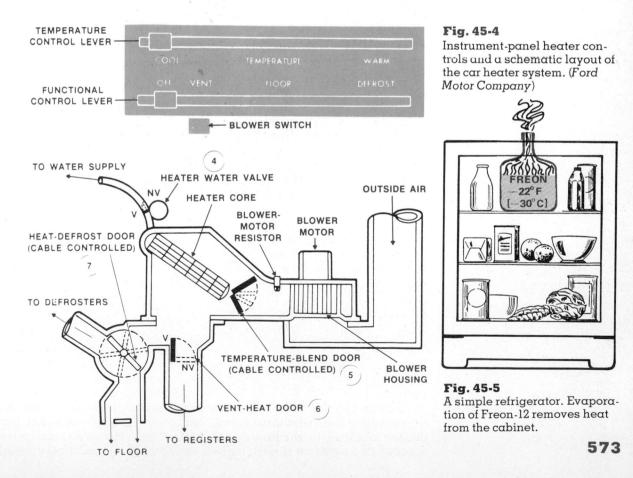

Fig. 45-4
Instrument-panel heater controls and a schematic layout of the car heater system. (*Ford Motor Company*)

Fig. 45-5
A simple refrigerator. Evaporation of Freon-12 removes heat from the cabinet.

573

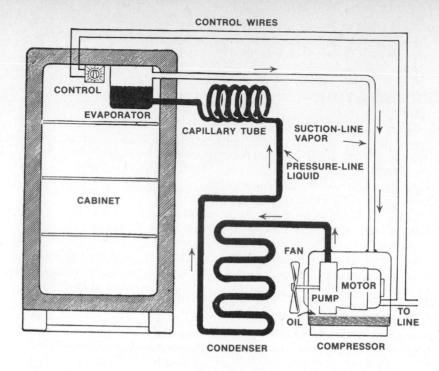

Fig. 45-6
A simplified schematic diagram of an electric refrigerator.

Freon-12 will boil, or turn to vapor. Since the temperature in the refrigerator shown in Fig. 45-5 is well above $-22°F$ [$-30°C$], the Freon-12 boils, or evaporates. As Freon-12 evaporates, it takes heat from the food and therefore cools the refrigerator. The refrigerating action continues as long as there is any Freon-12 left in the jug to evaporate. Because the Freon-12 refrigerates, it is called a "refrigerant."

There are some drawbacks to the system shown in Fig. 45-5. It is wasteful to allow all the refrigerant to escape. Besides, having refrigerant vapor floating around the house could be dangerous. Also, since the refrigerant boils, or evaporates, at $-22°F$ [$-30°C$], it tends to bring everything in the refrigerator down to this temperature. Everything would be frozen.

Two things must be done to improve the system. First, the refrigerant must be recaptured and turned back into a liquid. Second, the refrigerant action must be controlled so that the proper temperature can be maintained in the refrigerator.

45-4 A REFRIGERATOR
Look at Fig. 45-6, which is a simplified diagram of an electric refrigerator. The evaporator serves the same purpose as the Freon-12 in the jug in Fig. 45-5. As the refrigerant evaporates, it is carried through a suction line to the compressor pump. The compressor works something like an engine oil pump, but it is not constructed in the same way. The compressor takes in the vaporized refrigerant and applies a high pressure to it (up to 200 psi [1379 kPa]). The high pressure causes the temperature of the vapor to be increased to above $100°F$ [$38°C$]. The hot vapor, under high pressure, is then sent into the condenser. The condenser is a long tube equipped with fins. The hot vapor, as it passes through the condenser, loses its heat and condenses into liquid again.

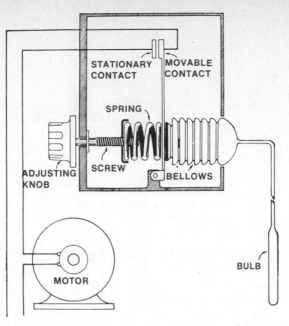

STATIONARY CONTACT

MOVABLE CONTACT

SPRING

ADJUSTING KNOB

SCREW

BELLOWS

MOTOR

BULB

   In this cycle, the refrigerant has carried heat out of the refrigerator. The refrigerant then gets rid of this heat in the condenser. Now, the liquid flows through the capillary tube and back into the evaporator. The capillary tube has a very small diameter. The small diameter restricts the flow of the liquid. The flow of refrigerant must be restricted because there must be a pressure differential between the condenser and the evaporator. The pressure must be high on the pump side, but low on the evaporator side. High pressure is necessary to condense the refrigerant. Low pressure is necessary to allow the refrigerant to evaporate.

45-5 REFRIGERATOR CONTROL

Figure 45-7 is a simplified drawing of a refrigerator control. The bellows and bulb are connected by a tube. The bulb contains a liquid that has a low-temperature boiling point. The bulb is placed in the refrigerator cabinet so that it is subjected to refrigerator temperatures. As the refrigerator temperature goes up, the liquid in the bulb starts to boil. This action creates pressure in the bellows. The pressure expands the bellows, thereby causing the contact points (which can be seen in Fig. 45-7) to close. When the contact points close, the pump motor is turned on and refrigerating action is started.

   The bellows must expand against a spring. The spring tension is controlled by an adjusting knob. When the knob is turned in, more tension is put on the spring. Then the bellows must exert a higher pressure to close the contacts. This means that the pump will not come on until a higher temperature is reached. If the adjusting knob is backed off to relieve spring tension, the bellows pressure needed to close the contacts will be lower. A lower temperature will be maintained in the refrigerator.

CHECK UP ON YOURSELF

Find out how well you understand what you have studied about car heaters and refrigerators by answering the questions that follow.

575

1. Where does the heat for the car heater come from?
2. In the vacuum-motor-operated heating system, there are three doors. What are their names?
3. What is the basic principle of refrigeration?
4. In one part of the refrigerator, refrigerant vaporizes. What is the name of this part?
5. In one part of the refrigerator, the refrigerant changes from a vapor to a liquid. What is this part called?

ANSWERS
1. From the engine cooling system (Sec. 45-1). 2. Temperature-blend door, vent-heat door, heat-defroster door (Sec. 45-2). 3. A liquid evaporates and removes heat from the area requiring cooling (Sec. 45-3). 4. Evaporator (Sec. 45-4). 5. Condenser (Sec. 45-4).

AIR CONDITIONING

45-6 AIR-CONDITIONER ACTION
We explained how the car heater puts heat in the car interior. The air conditioner does just the opposite. It takes heat out of the car interior. The blower that is used for heating is also used for air conditioning. For heating, the blower blows air through the heater core. For cooling, it blows air through the cooler coil, called the *evaporator*.

NOTE

In automotive shop manuals the term "air conditioner" often is shortened to "A/C."

In addition to cooling the air, the evaporator also takes moisture out of the air. This action is the same as the action of moisture condensing on a cold glass. What happens is that as the air flows through the cold evaporator, moisture condenses on the evaporator core. The moisture runs off the evaporator core and drops outside the car. The air conditioner cools the air and dries it. Dry air feels cooler than moist air. The air conditioner helps keep the car interior cool in two ways—by cooling the air and by drying it.

45-7 AUTOMOTIVE AIR CONDITIONER
Figure 45-8 shows the installation of an air conditioner in a car. The assembly includes the same basic parts as the refrigerator we discussed previously. There is a compressor, a condenser, and an evaporator. You cannot see the evaporator in Fig. 45-8. It is in the assembly under the instrument panel. Figure 45-9 is a schematic layout of the assembly. You can see the location of the heater core and of the evaporator core in Fig. 45-9.

Notice that the assembly has several doors. These doors can be opened or closed to direct the flow of air through either the heater core or the evaporator core. Also, the doors can be operated so that the air flowing through the evaporator core can be taken from outside or picked up from inside the car. Air picked up from inside the car is called *recirculated* air. The heated air can also be directed to the defroster outlets or into the dash outlets by operation of other doors.

45-8 AIR-CONDITIONER OPERATION
Figure 45-10 shows the basic air-conditioning system. The compressor takes in the vapor from the evaporator and puts the vapor under

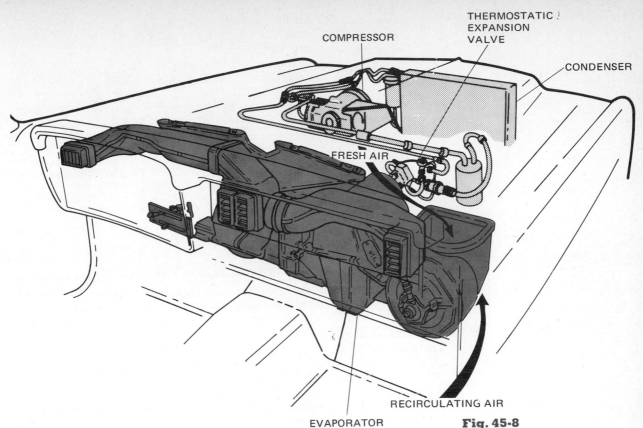

COMPRESSOR

THERMOSTATIC EXPANSION VALVE

CONDENSER

FRESH AIR

RECIRCULATING AIR

EVAPORATOR

Fig. 45-8
The location of major components in a car air conditioner. (*Ford Motor Company*)

pressure. The high-pressure vapor, or gas, is sent to the condenser. In the condenser the vapor loses heat and returns to liquid form. The liquid then flows to the evaporator, where it evaporates. As the liquid turns to vapor, it takes in heat. The vapor then passes back into the compressor. This flow is continuous as long as the air conditioner is operating.

Fig. 45-9
A schematic diagram of an air conditioner for a car. (*American Motors Corporation*)

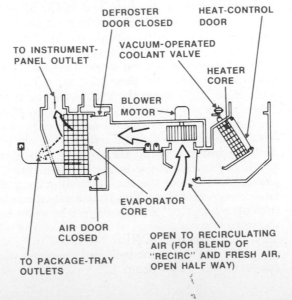

DEFROSTER DOOR CLOSED

HEAT-CONTROL DOOR

TO INSTRUMENT-PANEL OUTLET

VACUUM-OPERATED COOLANT VALVE

HEATER CORE

BLOWER MOTOR

EVAPORATOR CORE

AIR DOOR CLOSED

OPEN TO RECIRCULATING AIR (FOR BLEND OF "RECIRC" AND FRESH AIR, OPEN HALF WAY)

TO PACKAGE-TRAY OUTLETS

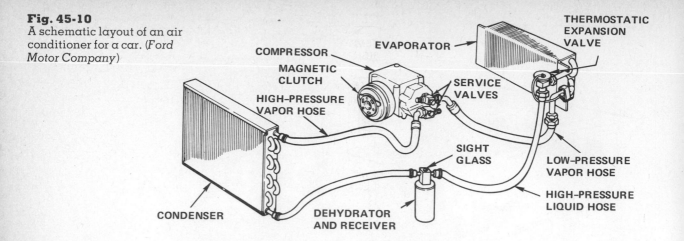

Fig. 45-10
A schematic layout of an air conditioner for a car. (*Ford Motor Company*)

Let's discuss some of the important parts of the automotive air conditioner, such as the receiver, the expansion valve, the suction throttling valve, and the magnetic clutch on the compressor.

45-9 RECEIVER

The purpose of the receiver (Fig. 45-10) is to ensure a supply of liquid refrigerant to the evaporator. The liquid refrigerant flows through an outlet at the bottom of the receiver so that no vapor can mix with the liquid refrigerant. In some systems the outlet is at the top of the receiver, but it is connected to a pipe that goes to the bottom. The liquid refrigerant always settles at the bottom of the receiver so that the outlet always picks up liquid rather than vapor.

The receiver also contains a substance called a *desiccant* that absorbs water. Any moisture in the system is absorbed by the desiccant so that the moisture can do no harm. If moisture were not absorbed, it might freeze in a valve and prevent normal air-conditioner action.

45-10 EXPANSION VALVE

The expansion valve is located in the circuit between the condenser and the evaporator, as shown in Figs. 45-8 and 45-10. The purpose of the expansion valve is to regulate the flow of liquid refrigerant to the evaporator. Figure 45-11 is a sectional view of an expansion valve. A tube is connected to a temperature-sensing bulb located on the top of the evaporator. The bulb is filled with a gas that expands or contracts with changing temperatures. As the temperature in the evaporator goes up, the gas expands. The expansion of the gas exerts pressure on the diaphragm. It overcomes spring tension and forces the valve off its seat. With the valve off its seat, liquid refrigerant is able to flow into the evaporator. Cooling takes place. As the temperature in the evaporator goes down, the gas in the bulb contracts. The pressure on the diaphragm drops, and the spring pushes the valve closed. This stops the flow of liquid refrigerant to the evaporator. Cooling stops. In operation, the valve takes the position needed to provide the right amount of cooling in the car. If cooling needs are low, the valve is almost closed, and only a little cooling is provided. If cooling needs are high, the valve is opened wider so that more liquid refrigerant flows and cooling is increased.

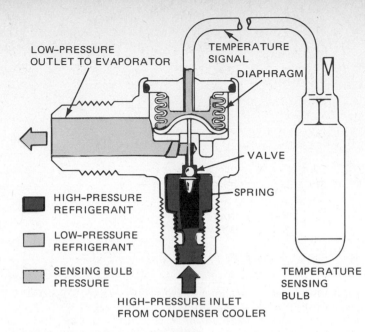

LOW-PRESSURE
OUTLET TO EVAPORATOR

TEMPERATURE
SIGNAL

DIAPHRAGM

VALVE

SPRING

HIGH-PRESSURE
REFRIGERANT

LOW-PRESSURE
REFRIGERANT

SENSING BULB
PRESSURE

TEMPERATURE
SENSING
BULB

HIGH-PRESSURE INLET
FROM CONDENSER COOLER

45-11 SUCTION THROTTLING VALVE

The suction throttling valve is located between the evaporator and the compressor. Its main purpose is to prevent freezing of moisture on the evaporator. If the evaporator temperature goes below 32°F [0°C], any moisture in the air going through the evaporator will freeze. If the evaporator froze, cooling would be reduced. Figure 45-12 is a sectional view of a suction throttling valve. Spring pressure and atmospheric pressure on one side of the valve piston and evaporator pressure on the

Fig. 45-12
A sectional view of a suction throttling valve. (*Pontiac Motor Division of General Motor Corporation*)

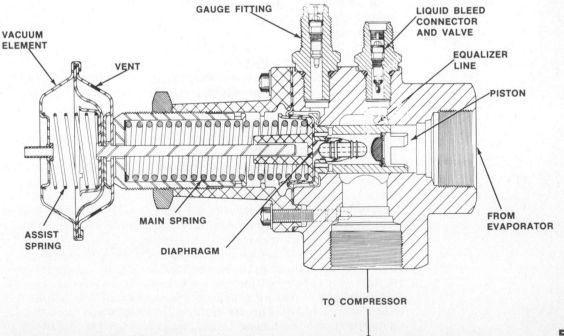

VACUUM
ELEMENT

VENT

GAUGE FITTING

LIQUID BLEED
CONNECTOR
AND VALVE

EQUALIZER
LINE

PISTON

MAIN SPRING

DIAPHRAGM

ASSIST
SPRING

FROM
EVAPORATOR

TO COMPRESSOR

579

Fig. 45-13
Clutch coil and outer-pulley
assembly for a magnetic
clutch. (*Warner Electric Brake
and Clutch Company*)

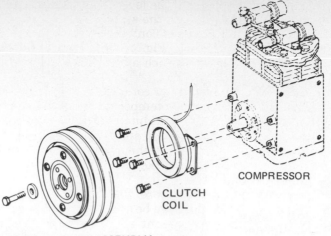

COMPRESSOR

CLUTCH
COIL

ROTOR PULLEY ASSEMBLY

other side control the valve operation. When evaporator pressure exceeds the specific maximum, it pushes the piston back. This action opens the valve so that liquid refrigerant can now flow from the evaporator to the compressor.

The vacuum element comes into operation when the driver turns the control to full cooling. When the driver does this, vacuum from the engine is admitted to the end of the vacuum element. Now, the assist spring is compressed. The compression of the assist spring allows the valve to move farther out so that more refrigerant can flow.

45-12 CONTROLS

The air-conditioning system is controlled by levers or buttons on the instrument panel. Some controls are vacuum-operated, just as in the vacuum-operated heater systems (Sec. 45-2). In one system the levers are set manually and adjusted by the driver for different conditions. In a fully automatic system, the driver simply sets the temperature desired. The system takes over from there. The system will cool when cooling is needed to maintain the temperature set. The system will also heat when heating is needed to maintain the preset temperature.

45-13 MAGNETIC CLUTCH

As part of the control system, the compressor has a magnetic clutch (Fig. 45-13). This clutch is located in the compressor pulley. The pulley is driven by a belt from the crankshaft pulley. When the system calls for cooling, the magnetic clutch is engaged. The compressor is then driven through the magnetic clutch so that cooling is obtained. The purpose of the magnetic clutch is to engage the compressor for cooling and to disengage it when cooling is not needed.

45-14 MANUAL TEMPERATURE-CONTROL SYSTEM

Figure 45-14 shows schematically the manual temperature-control system. Air enters from either outside or inside the car, depending on the positions of doors 1 and 2. These are the outside air door and the recirculating door. The position of these doors is controlled by the movement of the functional-control lever (see Fig. 45-14). When the lever is moved to the left—to MAX A/C—the outside air door is closed, and the recirculating air door is opened. If the lever is set at FRESH A/C, fresh air from outside will be brought into the system.

The speed with which the air moves is controlled by the speed of the blower. The setting of the FAN knob (Fig. 45-14) determines the speed of the blower and the speed with which air is brought into the system.

The air goes first through the evaporator core and may or may not be cooled, depending on the position of the temperature-control lever. If the lever is set at A/C, then the magnetic clutch on the compressor will be actuated. The compressor will operate, and cooling will result. If the lever is set at HEAT or DEF (for defrost), the magnetic clutch will not operate, and no compressor action will take place. There will be no cooling.

After passing through the evaporator core, the air meets the air-restrictor door (3 in Fig. 45-14). This door can be swung up to admit air to the heater core or swung down to prevent air from entering the heater core. The temperature-blend door (5) can be moved varying amounts to control the percentage of heater-core air and evaporator-

Fig. 45-14
A manually controlled air-conditioning and heating system. (*Ford Motor Company*)

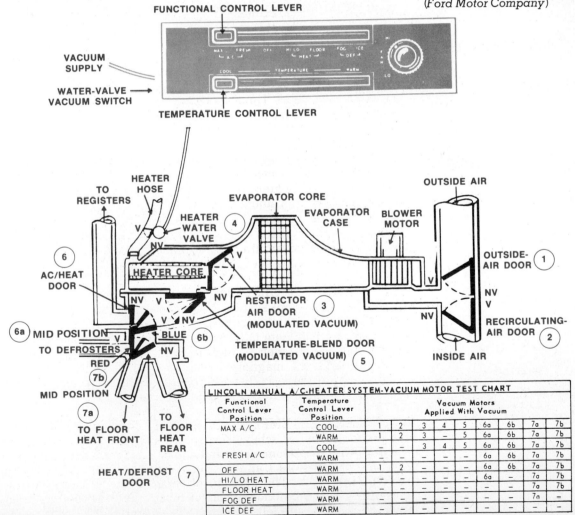

Functional Control Lever Position	Temperature Control Lever Position	Vacuum Motors Applied With Vacuum								
		1	2	3	4	5	6a	6b	7a	7b
MAX A/C	COOL	1	2	3	4	5	6a	6b	7a	7b
	WARM	1	2	3	–	5	6a	6b	7a	7b
FRESH A/C	COOL	–	–	3	4	5	6a	6b	7a	7b
	WARM	–	–	–	–	–	6a	6b	7a	7b
OFF	WARM	1	2	–	–	–	6a	6b	7a	7b
HI/LO HEAT	WARM	–	–	–	–	–	6a	–	7a	7b
FLOOR HEAT	WARM	–	–	–	–	–	–	–	7a	7b
FOG DEF	WARM	–	–	–	–	–	–	–	7a	–
ICE DEF	WARM	–	–	–	–	–	–	–	–	–

LINCOLN MANUAL A/C-HEATER SYSTEM-VACUUM MOTOR TEST CHART

core air that mix at this point. Next, the air meets the air-conditioner-heat door (6), which can be moved one way or the other. In the up position, the passage to the registers is blocked, and the air moves down into the defroster-floor-heat position. Now the air, which has been warmed, can move to the defrosters or to the floor-heat outlets, depending on the position of the heat-defrost door (7).

The system also includes a water-heater valve (4). It shuts off the flow of hot water from the engine cooling system when the air conditioner is running. Both the water valve and the air door are operated by vacuum motors.

45-15 AUTOMATIC TEMPERATURE CONTROL

Figure 45-15 is a schematic layout of the automatic temperature control system. Note that the control panel has two levers. The upper lever can be moved to select the desired temperature (65° to 85°). The lower lever can be moved all the way to the left to get automatic action in high. In this position the blower will operate at the maximum speed until the desired temperature is reached. Then the blower will slow down and operate just fast enough to maintain the desired temperature. If slower action is desired, the driver can set the lever at LOW. If the driver wants only untreated outside air to enter, the driver sets the

Fig. 45-15
The instrument control panel and schematic diagram for a fully automatic heater–air-conditioner system. (*Ford Motor Company*)

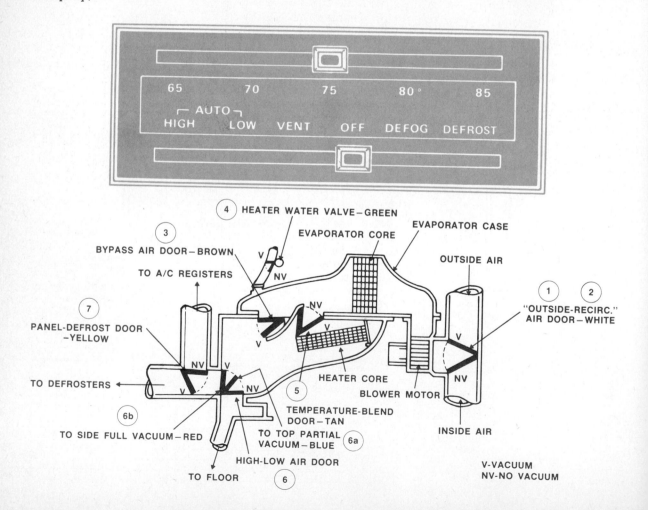

lever at VENT. At this setting the outside-recirculating door (1 and 2 in Fig. 45-15) is moved down so that outside air enters. If the driver wants to defog or defrost the windshield, the driver sets the lever at either of these positions.

The air passes through the evaporator core after it leaves the blower. Whether the air is cooled depends on whether the air conditioner is working. Next, the air either bypasses the heater core or passes through the heater core. If the system calls for heat, then the air conditioner will not be working but the heater core will be hot. This is because hot water from the engine cooling system will be circulating through the heater core. With this operating condition, the water-heater valve (4) will be open. Also, the bypass air door (3) will be closed, and the temperature-blend door (5) will be open. The direction the heated air then takes depends on the positions of the high-low door (6) and the panel-defrost door (7).

If the system calls for cooling, the evaporator core is cold and the air-conditioning system is working. Air passing through the evaporator core is cooled. Then the air goes through the open bypass door and to the air-conditioning registers.

In this system there is a delay circuit in the heating section. This delay circuit prevents the blower from coming on until the water circulating in the heater core is warm. This prevents the circulation of cold air, which would be uncomfortable for the people in the car.

Vacuum motors operate the water heater valve and the air doors, just as in the systems previously covered in the chapter.

CHECK UP ON YOURSELF
You have completed one chapter on heating and air conditioning. Now answer the following questions.

1. What two things does the car air conditioner do?
2. What is the job of the compressor?
3. What is the purpose of the expansion valve?
4. What is the purpose of the suction throttling valve?
5. What is the purpose of the magnetic clutch on the compressor?

ANSWERS
1. Cools and dries the air (Sec. 45-6). 2. To compress the vapor from the evaporator and send it to the condenser under high pressure (Sec. 45-8). 3. To regulate the flow of liquid refrigerant into the evaporator (Sec. 45-10). 4. To prevent freezing of moisture on the outside of the evaporator (Sec. 45-11). 5. To engage the compressor when cooling is needed and to disengage it when cooling is not needed (Sec. 45-13).

CHAPTER FORTY-SIX
HEATER AND AIR-CONDITIONER SERVICE

After studying this chapter, you should be able to:
Explain how to check and service car heating and air-conditioning systems.

The heater is part of the engine cooling system. Manually operated heater systems require little servicing. Air-conditioning systems require more service. In this chapter we will learn how to troubleshoot and service both car heaters and air conditioners.

46-1 SERVICING HEATING SYSTEMS
Heater problems usually result in one of these three complaints: leaks, no heat, or failure of the blower to work.

Leaks usually can be seen and are easily found. They could be caused by leaky hoses or connections, leaks in the radiator core, or leaks in the control valve. No heat could be due to a bad control valve or to clogged hoses or heater core. Failure of the blower to work is probably an electrical problem requiring replacement of the blower, switch, or wiring.

If the system automatically adjusts heating according to the temperature-control setting, failure to heat could be due to several things. A vacuum motor may not be working, the water heater valve may be stuck, the thermostatic control may not be working, or conditions listed in the previous paragraph may be causing the trouble.

The shop manual for the car you are working on will tell you how to completely check and service the system.

46-2 SERVICING AIR CONDITIONERS
You must never work on air conditioners unless you have the proper equipment and know exactly how to use it. This includes attempting to troubleshoot or service an air conditioner. If you use the proper equipment in the right way, there is no special danger in servicing air conditioners. However, if you go at the job the wrong way, you can get hurt! The air-conditioning system contains the refrigerant, which is a high-pressure liquid and vapor. The liquid, if released, can turn to vapor al-

most instantly, freezing anything it touches. This includes skin and eyes! Here are cautions you *must* observe:

- Undercoating. Never apply undercoating to any connections of the refrigerant lines or to the air-conditioning parts.
- Steam-cleaning and welding. Never apply any form of heat to any refrigerant line or to any component of the system. The refrigerant system is under pressure. Heating the refrigerant could increase the pressure excessively and cause an explosion.
- Handling refrigerant. The refrigerant is about the safest refrigerant available, but you can be seriously hurt if you handle it carelessly.

Be sure to use only the refrigerant specified for automotive conditioning systems. The kind used in equipment such as boat air horns or fire-alarm signals is not pure and can ruin an air conditioner.

Refrigerant that escapes into the air can evaporate so quickly that it will freeze anything it touches, including skin and eyes, as we said before. You could be blinded if you get refrigerant in your eyes!

CAUTION
Always wear safety goggles when servicing any part of an air-conditioning system!

Keep a bottle of sterile mineral oil and a bottle of weak boric acid solution handy. If you get refrigerant in your eyes, instantly wash it out with a few drops of mineral oil, followed by the boric acid solution. See a doctor right away! Don't wait, even if the irritation seems to have gone away.

When discharging refrigerant from an air conditioner, discharge it into the garage exhaust system or into the open air. The refrigerant evaporates so quickly that it will displace all the air around the car. This could cause you to suffocate if the immediate area in which you are working is enclosed and without ventilation!

Do not discharge refrigerant in a room where there is an open flame. Refrigerant turns into a poisonous gas when it comes in contact with a flame. The gas is very dangerous if inhaled. This poisonous gas is also produced when you use a flame-type leak detector. But only a small amount of gas is produced, so you don't need to worry as long as you don't inhale it.

Never heat a container of refrigerant when charging an air-conditioner system. The container could explode.

46-3 TROUBLESHOOTING AIR CONDITIONERS
Problems in the refrigerant system are indicated by the temperatures of the refrigerant lines and hoses. Once the system is normalized (after several minutes of operation), feel the temperature of each hose with your hand. The chart in Fig. 46-1 lists the lines and hose in the system and the normal temperature that you should feel for each. The temperatures of the lines and hose are used along with the sight-glass readings to determine if a problem exists in the refrigerant system.

A quick check of the system operation can be made by examining the sight glass with the air conditioner operating. The sight glass is a glass-covered peephole found in the top of most receivers (see Fig. 45-10). All refrigerant leaving the receiver passes under the sight glass.

Line	Should Feel*
Evaporator Inlet	Cold
Evaporator Outlet	Cold
Low-Pressure Hose	Cold
High-Pressure Hose	Hot

* If any line is not as specified to the touch, the refrigerant system has a malfunction.

The appearance of the refrigerant gives some indication of whether the system has the proper charge, or amount of refrigerant in it. With the engine running at about 1500 rpm and the controls set for maximum cooling, watch for bubbles in the sight glass. Typical sight-glass conditions are shown in Fig. 46-2. Here are the conditions that you may see and the procedure to follow for each condition.

- Bubbles in the sight glass. This probably means the system is low on refrigerant. Check the system with a leak detector. Correct the leak, if any. Then evacuate and charge the system. (The procedures on how to evacuate and charge the system are covered in Sec. 46-5.)
- No bubbles, with the sight glass clear. This means the system is either fully charged or empty. Feel the high and low pressure lines at the compressor. Keep your hands away from belts and the engine fan! The high-pressure line should feel warm or hot (Fig. 46-1). The low-pressure, or suction, line should be cold.

Fig. 46-2
Typical sight-glass indications for various conditions in the refrigeration system. (*Sun Electric Corporation*)

OCCASIONAL OR SLOW-MOVING BUBBLES—
REFRIGERANT SLIGHTLY LOW OR RECEIVER-DRIER
SATURATED AND RELEASING MOISTURE

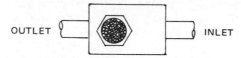

FOAM OR CONTINUOUS FLOW OF BUBBLES—
REFRIGERANT VERY LOW

OIL STREAKS ON GLASS—
COMPLETE ABSENCE OF REFRIGERANT

SIGHT GLASS CLEAR—
NORMAL OPERATION
OF FULLY CHARGED SYSTEM, OR
SYSTEM IS EMPTY.

- Little or no difference in temperature between the lines at the compressor. The system is empty or nearly empty. Turn off the engine. Add about 0.5 pound [230 g] of refrigerant to the system. Check it with a leak detector. Correct the leak. Then evacuate and charge the system.
- Large difference in temperature between the lines at the compressor. The system probably has the proper charge of refrigerant in it. But the system could be overcharged. Too much refrigerant may have been added. This could result in poor cooling, especially at low speeds. Check for overcharging by temporarily disconnecting the compressor clutch while the system is operating. Watch the sight glass. If the refrigerant in the sight glass remains clear for more than 15 seconds (before foaming and then settling away), an overcharge is indicated. The excess refrigerant should be bled off. If the refrigerant in the sight glass foams and then settles away from the sight glass in less than 45 seconds, the system probably has not been overcharged with refrigerant.

Some Ford-built cars do not have a sight glass. Ford states that on some systems using a suction throttling valve the sight glass is not an accurate indicator of refrigerant system condition. If there is no sight glass, install a gauge set to check the system.

46-4 AIR-CONDITIONER PERFORMANCE TEST

To test the air conditioner for performance, you need a gauge set (Fig. 46-3). The gauge set is attached to the refrigerant system to measure the pressures. These pressures tell you where there is trouble. Refer to the car shop manual for details on how to use the gauge set and on what the various results mean.

46-5 EVACUATING AND CHARGING THE SYSTEM

"Evacuating" means removing any air or moisture from the system after it has been opened for service or has leaked. If the system has been opened, air and moisture have entered. All this air and moisture must be removed by applying a vacuum to the system. The vacuum is

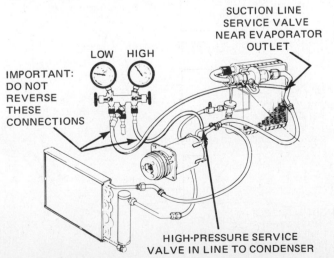

Fig. 46-3
Gauge-set connections for a performance test. (*Ford Motor Company*)

Fig. 46-4
An air-conditioning charging station, which includes a vacuum pump, is used to evacuate and charge the refrigerant system. (*Ford Motor Company*)

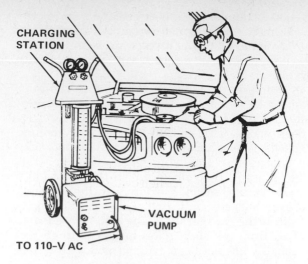

CHARGING
STATION

VACUUM
PUMP

TO 110-V AC

produced by a special vacuum pump used for air-conditioning service work. Figure 46-4 shows a charging station that includes a vacuum pump.

"Charging" the system means to add refrigerant to it. To charge the system, connect a refrigerant container to the charging hose (center hose) of the gauge set. Then open the gauge valve to allow refrigerant to flow into the system (Fig. 46-5). This job is done with the engine running so that the compressor will be in operation.

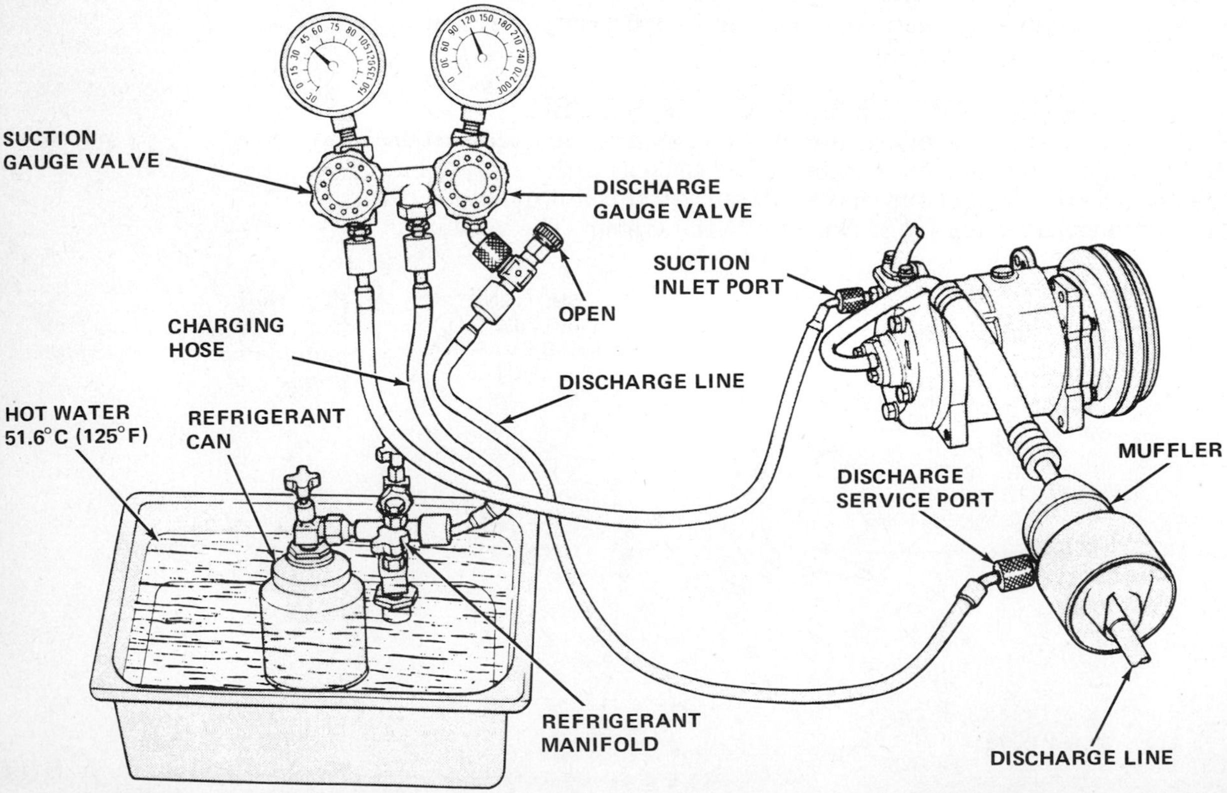

Fig. 46-5
Adding refrigerant to the air conditioner. (*Chrysler Corporation*)

SUCTION
GAUGE VALVE

DISCHARGE
GAUGE VALVE

SUCTION
INLET PORT

OPEN

CHARGING
HOSE

DISCHARGE LINE

HOT WATER
51.6°C (125°F)

REFRIGERANT
CAN

DISCHARGE
SERVICE PORT

MUFFLER

REFRIGERANT
MANIFOLD

DISCHARGE LINE

NOTE

You must have a thorough understanding of air-conditioning service and safety before you attempt to do any work on an air-conditioning system. Also, you should have the proper equipment and the shop manual covering the air conditioner that you are working on.

CHECK UP ON YOURSELF

Servicing air-conditioning systems requires careful work. You must know exactly what you are doing. Review what you have studied by answering the questions that follow.

1. What are the three most common complaints about heater systems?
2. What is the purpose of wearing goggles when working with frigerant?
3. Why shouldn't you discharge refrigerant into a room where there is an open flame?
4. What is the purpose of the sight glass?
5. What is the purpose of the gauge set?

ANSWERS

1. Leaks, no heat, and failure of the blower to work (Sec. 46-1). **2.** To protect your eyes from spraying refrigerant (Sec. 46-2). **3.** When refrigerant hits a flame, a poisonous gas is formed (Sec. 46-2). **4.** To allow you to watch for bubbles in the liquid refrigerant flowing from the condenser (Sec. 46-3). **5.** To check air-conditioner performance by measuring the pressures in the system (Sec. 46-4).

GLOSSARY

A/C Abbreviation for air conditioning

AC or ac Abbreviation for alternating current

Accelerator A foot-operated pedal, linked to the throttle valve in the carburetor; used to control the flow of gasoline to the engine.

Accelerator pump In the carburetor, a pump (linked to the accelerator) which momentarily enriches the air-fuel mixture when the accelerator is depressed at low speed.

Accessories Devices not considered essential to the operation of a vehicle such as the radio, car heater, and electric window lifts.

Additive A substance added to gasoline or oil to improve some property of the gasoline or oil.

Adjust To bring the parts of a component or system to a specified relationship, dimension, or pressure.

Adjustments Necessary or desired changes in clearances, fit, or settings.

Advance The moving ahead of the ignition spark in relation to piston position; produced by centrifugal or vacuum devices in accordance with engine speed and intake-manifold vacuum, or electronically.

AIR Abbreviation for air-injection reactor, part of a system of exhaust-emission control. See Air-injection system.

Air bleed An opening into a gasoline passage through which air can pass, or bleed, into the gasoline as it moves through the passage.

Air cleaner A device, mounted on or connected to the carburetor, for filtering dirt and dust out of the air being drawn into the engine.

Air conditioning An accessory system that conditions passenger-compartment air by cleaning, cooling, and drying it.

Air-cooled engine An engine that is cooled by the passage of air around the cylinders, not by the passage of a liquid through water jackets.

Air filter A filter that removes dirt and dust particles from air passing through it.

Air-fuel mixture The air and fuel traveling to the combustion chamber after being mixed by the carburetor.

Air-fuel ratio The proportions of air and fuel (by weight) supplied for combustion.

Air-injection system An exhaust-emission control system. Air is injected at low pressure into the exhaust manifold or thermal reactor to complete the combustion of unburned hydrocarbons and carbon monoxide in the exhaust gas.

Air pollution Contamination of the air by natural and manufactured pollutants.

Air pressure Atmospheric pressure; also the pressure produced by an air pump or by compression of air in a cylinder.

Air pump Any device for compressing air. In the air-injection system of exhaust-emission control, an engine-driven (belt-driven) pump incorporating a rotor and vanes.

Alignment The act of lining up, or the state of being in a true line.

Alternator In the vehicle electric system, a device that converts mechanical energy into electric energy for charging the battery and operating electrical accessories. Also known as an ac generator.

Ammeter A meter for measuring the amount of current (in amperes) flowing through an electric circuit.

Amperage The amount of current, in amperes.

Ampere A unit of measure for current. One ampere corresponds to a flow of 6.28×10^{18} electrons per second.

Antibackfire valve A valve used in the air-injection system to prevent backfiring in the exhaust system during deceleration.

Antidieseling solenoid See Idle-stop solenoid.

Antifreeze A chemical, usually ethylene glycol, that is added to the engine coolant to raise its boiling point and lower its freezing point.

Antilock system A system installed with the brakes to prevent wheel lockup during braking.

Arcing Name given to the spark that jumps an air gap between two electrical conductors; for example, the arcing of the distributor contact points.

Armature A part moved by magnetism, or a part moved through a magnetic field to produce current.

Aspect ratio The ratio of tire height to width. For example, a G78 tire is 78 percent as high as it is wide. The lower the number, the wider the tire.

Atmospheric pressure The weight of the atmosphere per unit area. Atmospheric pressure at sea level is 14.7 psi absolute [101.35 kPa]; it decreases as altitude increases.

Automatic choke A device that positions the choke valve automatically in accordance with engine temperature or time.

Automatic level control A suspension system which compensates for variations in load in the rear of the car; positions the rear at a predesigned level regardless of load.

Automatic transmission A transmission in which gear ratios are changed automatically, eliminating the necessity of hand-shifting gears.

Axle A theoretical or actual cross bar supporting a vehicle on which one or more wheels turn.

Axle ratio The ratio between the rotational speed (rpm) of the drive shaft and that of the driven wheel; gear reduction in the differential, determined by dividing the number of teeth on the ring gear by the number of teeth on the pinion gear.

Backfiring Preexplosion of the air-fuel mixture so that the explosion passes back around the opened intake valve and through the intake manifold and carburetor; also applied to the loud explosion of overly rich exhaust gas in the exhaust manifold, which exits through the muffler and tail pipe with a loud popping or banging noise.

Backlash In gearing, the clearance between the meshing teeth of two gears.

Ball bearing An antifriction bearing with an inner race and an outer race, and one or more rows of balls between them.

Ball joint A flexible joint consisting of a ball within a socket, used in front-suspension systems and valve-train rocker arms.

Band In an automatic transmission, a hydraulically controlled brake band installed around a metal clutch drum; used to stop or permit drum rotation.

Barrel Term sometimes applied to the cylinders in an engine; used in referring to the number of throttle bores in a carburetor.

Battery An electrochemical device for storing energy in chemical form so that it can be released as electricity; a group of electric cells connected together.

Battery acid The electrolyte used in a battery; a mixture of sulfuric acid and water.

BDC Abbreviation for bottom dead center.

Bead That part of the tire which is shaped to fit the rim; the bead is made of steel wires, wrapped and reinforced by the plies of the tires.

Bearing caps In the engine, caps held in place by bolts or nuts which, in turn, hold bearing halves in place.

Bearing crush The additional height (over a full half) which is purposely manufactured into each bearing half to ensure complete contact of the bearing back with the housing bore when the engine is assembled.

Bearing spin A type of bearing failure in which a lack of lubrication overheats the bearing until it seizes on the shafts, shears its locking lip, and rotates in the housing or block.

Bearing spread A purposely manufactured small extra distance across the parting faces of the bearing half, in excess of the actual diameter of the housing bore.

Belt In a tire, a flat strip of material — glass fiber, rayon, or woven steel — which underlies the tread, all around the circumference of the tire.

Belted-bias tire A tire in which the plies are laid diagonally, crisscrossing one another, with a circumferential belt on top of them. The rubber tread is vulcanized on top of the belt and plies.

Belted-radial tire A tire in which the plies run parallel to one another and perpendicular to the tire bead. Belts running parallel to the tire tread are applied over this radial section.

Belt tension The tightness of a drive belt.

Bevel gear A gear shaped like the lower part of a cone; used to transmit motion through an angle.

Bias-ply tire A conventionally constructed tire in which the plies are laid diagonally, crisscrossing one another at an angle of about 30 to 40°.

Bleeding A process by which air is removed from a hydraulic system (brake or power steering) by draining part of the fluid or operating the system to work out the air.

Block See Cylinder block.

Blowby Leakage of compressed air-fuel mixture and burned gases (from combustion) past the piston rings into the crankcase.

Body On a vehicle, the assembly of sheet-metal sections, together with windows, doors, seats, and other parts, that provides enclosures for the passengers, engine, and luggage compartments.

Boiling Conversion from the liquid to the vapor state, taking place throughout the liquid. The conversion is accompanied by bubbling as vapor rises from below the surface.

Bore An engine cylinder, or any cylindrical hole; also used to describe the process of enlarging or accurately refinishing a hole, as "to bore an engine cylinder." The bore size is the diameter of the hole.

Boring bar An electric-motor-powered cutting tool used to machine, or bore, an engine cylinder, thereby removing metal and enlarging the cylinder diameter.

Bottom dead center The piston position at the lower limit of its travel in the cylinder, such that the cylinder volume is at its maximum.

Brake An energy-conversion device used to slow, stop, or hold a vehicle or mechanism; a device which changes the kinetic energy of motion into useless and wasted heat energy.

Brake drum A metal drum mounted on a car wheel to form the outer shell of the brake; the brake shoes press against the drum to slow or stop drum-and-wheel rotation for braking.

Brake fluid A special non-mineral-oil fluid used in the hydraulic braking system to transmit pressure through a closed system of tubing known as the brake lines.

Brake horsepower Power delivered to the engine and available for driving the vehicle; bhp = torque × rpm/5252.

Brake lining A high-friction material, usually a form of asbestos, attached to the brake shoe by rivets or a bonding process. The lining takes the wear when the shoe is pressed against the brake drum, or rotor.

Brake shoe In drum brakes, arc-shaped metal pieces lined with a high-friction material (the brake lining) which are forced against the revolving drums to produce braking action. In disk brakes, flat metal pieces lined with brake lining which are forced against the rotor face.

Brake system A combination of one or more brakes and their operating and control mechanism.

Brush A block of conducting substance, such as carbon, which rests against a rotating ring or commutator to form a continuous electric circuit.

BTDC Abbreviation for before top dead center; any position of the piston between bottom dead center and top dead center, on the upward stroke.

Bushing A one-piece sleeve placed in a bore to serve as a bearing surface.

Cables Stranded conductors, usually covered with insulating material, used for connections between electric devices.

Calibrate To check or correct the initial setting of a test instrument.

Caliper A tool that can be set to measure the thickness of a block, the diameter of a shaft, or the bore of a hole (inside caliper). In a disk brake, a housing for pistons and brake shoes, connected to the hydraulic system; holds the brake shoes so that they straddle the disk.

Cam A rotating lobe or eccentric which can be used with a cam follower to change rotary motion to reciprocating motion.

Camber The tilt of the top of the wheels from the vertical; when the tilt is outward, the camber is positive. Also, the angle which a front-wheel spindle makes with the horizontal.

Camshaft The shaft in the engine which has a series of cams for operating the valve mechanisms. It is driven by gears or sprockets and a toothed belt or chain from the crankshaft.

Canister A special container, in an evaporative control system, that contains charcoal to trap vapors from the fuel system.

Capacity The ability to perform or to hold.

Carbon (C) A black deposit which is left on engine parts such as pistons, rings, and valves by the combustion of fuel and which inhibits their action.

592

Carbon dioxide (CO_2) A colorless, odorless gas which results from complete combustion; usually considered harmless. The gas absorbed from air by plants in photosynthesis; also used to carbonate beverages.

Carbon monoxide (CO) A colorless, odorless, tasteless, poisonous gas which results from incomplete combustion. A pollutant contained in engine-exhaust gas.

Carburetion The actions that take place in the carburetor; converting liquid fuel to vapor and mixing it with air to form a combustible mixture.

Carburetor The device in an engine fuel system which mixes fuel with air and supplies the combustible mixture to the intake manifold.

Casing The outer part of the tire assembly, made of fabric or cord to which rubber is vulcanized.

Caster Tilting of the steering axis forward or backward to provide directional steering stability. Also, the angle which a front-wheel kingpin makes with the vertical.

Catalyst A substance that can speed or slow a chemical reaction between substances, without itself being consumed by the reaction. In the catalytic converter, platinum and palladium are the active catalysts.

Catalytic converter A mufflerlike device for use in an exhaust system. It converts harmful exhaust gases into harmless gases by promoting a chemical reaction between a catalyst and the pollutants.

Celsius A thermometer scale (formerly called centigrade) on which water boils at $100°$ and freezes at $0°$. The formula $C = \frac{5}{9}(F-32)$ converts Fahrenheit readings to Celsius readings.

Centigrade See Celsius.

Centimeter (cm) A unit of linear measure in the metric system; equal to approximately 0.390 inch.

Centrifugal advance A rotating-weight mechanism in the distributor that advances and retards ignition timing through the centrifugal force resulting from changes in the rotational speed of the distributor shaft.

Charcoal canister A container filled with activated charcoal; used to trap gasoline vapor from the fuel tank and carburetor while the engine is off.

Charge A specific amount of refrigerant or refrigerant oil.

Charging rate The amperage flowing from the alternator into the battery.

Chassis The assembly of mechanisms that make up the major operating part of the vehicle; usually assumed to include everything except the car body.

Check To verify that a component, system, or measurement complies with specifications.

Check valve A valve that opens to permit the passage of air or fluid in one direction only, or operates to prevent (check) some undesirable action.

Chemical reaction The formation of one or more new substances when two or more substances are brought together.

Choke In the carburetor, a device used when starting a cold engine. It "chokes off" the airflow through the air horn, producing a partial vacuum in the air horn for greater fuel delivery and a richer mixture. It operates automatically on most cars.

Chrome-plated ring A piston compression or oil ring with its cylinder-wall face lightly plated with hard chrome.

CID Abbreviation for cubic inch displacement.

Circuit The complete path of an electric current, including the current source. When the path is continuous, the circuit is closed and current flows. When the path is broken, the circuit is open and no current flows. Also used to refer to fluid paths, as in refrigerant and hydraulic systems.

Circuit breaker A protective device that opens an electric circuit to prevent damage when the circuit is overheated by excess current flow. One type contains a thermostatic blade that warps to open the circuit when the maximum safe current is exceeded.

Clearance The space between two moving parts, or between a moving and a stationary part, such as a journal and a bearing. The bearing clearance is filled with lubricating oil when the mechanism is running.

Closed-crankcase ventilation system A system in which the crankcase vapors (blowby gases) are discharged into the engine intake system and pass through to the engine cylinders rather than being discharged into the air.

Clutch A coupling which connects and disconnects a shaft from its drive while the drive mechanism is running. In an automobile power train, the device which engages and disengages the transmission from the engine. In an air-conditioning system, the device which engages and disengages the compressor shaft from its continuously rotating drive-belt pulley.

Clutch disk See Friction disk.

Clutch fork In the clutch, a Y-shaped member into which the throwout bearing is assembled.

Clutch gear See Clutch shaft.

Clutch pedal A pedal in the driver's compartment that operates the clutch.

Clutch shaft The shaft on which the clutch is assembled, with the gear that drives the countershaft in the transmission on one end. On the clutch-gear end, it has external splines that can be used by a synchronizer drum to lock the clutch shaft to the main shaft for direct drive.

Clutch solenoid In automotive air conditioners, a solenoid that operates a clutch on the compressor drive pulley. When the clutch is engaged, the compressor is driven and cooling takes place.

CO See Carbon monoxide.

CO₂ See Carbon dioxide.

Coil In an automobile ignition system, a transformer used to step up the battery voltage (by induction) to the high voltage required to fire the spark plugs.

Coil spring A spring made of an elastic metal such as steel, formed into a wire and wound into a coil.

Coil-spring clutch A clutch using coil springs to hold the pressure plate against the friction disk.

Cold patching A method of repairing a punctured tire or tube by gluing a thin rubber patch over the hole.

Collapsible spare tire A wheel that mounts a special deflated tire. It is furnished with a can of tire-inflation propellant to use when the tire must be inflated and installed.

Collapsible steering column An energy-absorbing steering column designed to collapse if the driver is thrown into it.

Combustion Burning; fire produced by the proper combination of fuel, heat, and oxygen. In the engine, the rapid burning of the air-fuel mixture in the combustion chamber.

Combustion chamber The space between the top of the piston and the cylinder head, in which the air-fuel mixture is burned.

Commutator A series of copper bars at one end of a generator or starting-motor armature, electrically insulated from the armature shaft and insulated from one another by mica. The brushes rub against the bars of the commutator, which form a rotating connector between the armature windings and brushes.

Compact spare tire A special high-pressure spare tire, mounted on a narrow 15 × 4 inch wheel, that can be used on cars without a limited-slip differential.

Compression Reduction in the volume of a gas by squeezing it into a smaller space. Increasing the pressure reduces the volume and increases the density and temperature of the gas.

Compression ignition The ignition of fuel solely by the heat generated when air is compressed in the cylinder; the method of ignition in a diesel engine.

Compression pressure The pressure in the combustion chamber at the end of the compression stroke.

Compression ratio The volume of the cylinder and combustion chamber when the piston is at BDC, divided by the volume when the piston is at TDC.

Compression ring The upper ring or rings on a piston, designed to hold the compression in the combustion chamber and prevent blowby.

Compression stroke The piston movement from BDC to TDC immediately following the intake stroke, during which both the intake and exhaust valves are closed while the air-fuel mixture in the cylinder is compressed.

Compression tester An instrument for testing the amount of pressure, or compression, developed in an engine cylinder during cranking.

Compressor The component of an air-conditioning system that compresses refrigerant vapor to increase its pressure and temperature.

Condensation A change of state during which a gas turns to liquid, usually because of temperature or pressure changes. Also, moisture from the air, deposited on a cool surface.

Condenser In the ignition system, a device that is also called a capacitor; connected across the contact points to reduce arcing by providing a storage place for electricity (electrons) as the contact points open. In an air-conditioning system, the radiatorlike heat exchanger in which refrigerant vapor loses heat and returns to the liquid state.

Conductor Any material or substance that allows current or heat to flow easily.

Connecting rod In the engine, the rod that connects the crank on the crankshaft with the piston. Sometimes called a con rod.

Connecting-rod bearing See Rod bearing.

Connecting-rod cap The part of the connecting-rod assembly that attaches the rod to the crankpin.

Constant-velocity joint Two closely coupled universal joints arranged in such a way that their acceleration-deceleration effects cancel out. This results in an output drive-shaft speed that is always identical with the input drive-shaft speed, regardless of the angle of drive.

Contact points In the conventional ignition system, the stationary and the movable points in the distributor which open and close the ignition primary circuit.

Contaminants Anything other than refrigerant and refrigerant oil in a refrigeration system; includes rust, dirt, moisture, and air.

Control arm A part of the suspension system designed to control wheel movement precisely.

Coolant The liquid mixture of about 50 percent antifreeze and 50 percent water used to carry heat out of the engine.

Cooling system The system that removes heat from the engine by the forced circulation of coolant, and thereby prevents engine overheating. It includes the water jackets, water pump, radiator, and thermostat.

Corrosion Chemical action, usually by an acid, that eats away, or decomposes, a metal.

Countershaft The shaft in the transmission which is driven by the clutch gear; gears on the countershaft drive gears on the main shaft when the latter are shifted into gear.

Crankcase The lower part of the engine in which the crankshaft rotates; including the lower section of the cylinder block and the oil pan.

Crankcase emissions Pollutants emitted into the atmosphere from any portion of the engine-crankcase ventilation or lubrication system.

Crankcase ventilation The circulation of air through the crankcase of a running engine to remove water, blowby, and other vapors; prevents oil dilution, contamination, sludge formation, and pressure buildup.

Cranking motor See Starting motor.

Crankpin The part of a crankshaft to which a connecting rod is attached.

Crankshaft The main rotating member or shaft of the engine, with cranks to which the connecting rods are attached; converts up-and-down (reciprocating) motion into circular (rotary) motion.

Crankshaft gear A gear, or sprocket, mounted on the front of the crankshaft; used to drive the camshaft gear, chain, or toothed belt.

Crank throw One crankpin with its two webs.

Cross-firing Jumping of the high-voltage surge in the ignition secondary circuit to the wrong high-voltage lead, so that the wrong spark plug fires. Usually caused by improper routing of the spark-plug wires, faulty insulation, or a defective distributor cap or rotor.

Cubic centimeter (cu cm or cc) A unit of volume in the metric system; equal to approximately 0.061 cubic inch.

Cubic inch displacement The cylinder volume swept out by the pistons of an engine as they move from BDC to TDC, measured in cubic inches.

Current A flow of electrons, measured in amperes.

Cycle Any series of events which repeat continuously. In the engine, the four (or two) piston strokes that together produce the power.

Cycling-clutch system An air conditioner in which the conditioned-air temperature is controlled by starting and stopping the compressor.

Cylinder A circular, tubelike opening in an engine cylinder block or casting in which a piston moves up and down.

Cylinder block The basic framework of the engine, in and on which the other engine parts are attached. It includes the engine cylinders and the upper part of the crankcase.

Cylinder-compression tester See Compression tester.

Cylinder head The part of the engine that covers and encloses the cylinders. It contains cooling fins or water jackets and, on I-head engines, the valves.

Cylinder hone An expandable rotating tool with abrasive stones turned by an electric motor; used to clean and smooth the inside surface of a cylinder.

Cylinder liner See Cylinder sleeve.

Cylinder sleeve A replaceable sleeve, or liner, set into the cylinder block to form the cylinder bore.

DC or dc Abbreviation for direct current.

Deceleration A decrease in velocity or speed. Also, allowing the car or engine to coast to idle speed from a higher speed with the accelerator at or near the idle position.

Defroster The part of the car heater system designed to melt frost or ice on the inside or outside of the windshield; includes the required duct work.

Degree Part of a circle. One degree is 1/360 of a complete circle.

Desiccant A drying agent. In a refrigeration system, desiccant is placed in the receiver-dehydrator to remove moisture from the system.

Detent A small depression in a shaft, rail, or rod into which a pawl or ball drops when the shaft, rail, or rod is moved; this provides a locking effect.

Detergent A chemical added to engine oil that helps keep internal parts of the engine clean by preventing the accumulation of deposits.

Detonation Commonly referred to as spark knock or ping. In the combustion chamber, an uncontrolled second explosion (after the spark occurs at the spark plug) with spontaneous combustion of the remaining compressed air-fuel mixture, resulting in a pinging noise.

Device A mechanism, tool, or other piece of equipment designed to serve a special purpose or perform a special function.

Diagnosis A procedure followed in locating the cause of a malfunction; the procedure answers the question, What is wrong?

Diaphragm A thin dividing sheet or partition which separates an area into compartments; used in fuel pumps, modulator valves, vacuum-advance units, and other control devices.

Diaphragm-spring clutch A clutch in which a diaphragm spring, rather than a coil spring, applies pressure against the friction disk.

Diesel cycle An engine operating cycle in which air is compressed and fuel oil is injected into the compressed air at the end of the compression stroke. The heat produced by the compression ignites the fuel oil, eliminating the need for spark plugs or a separate ignition system.

Diesel engine An engine operating on the diesel cycle and burning oil instead of gasoline.

Dieseling A condition in which an automobile engine continues to run after the ignition is off; caused by carbon deposits or hot spots in the combustion chamber glowing sufficiently to furnish heat for combustion.

Differential A gear assembly between axles that permits one wheel to turn at a different speed from the other, while transmitting power from the drive shaft to the wheel axles.

Differential case The metal unit that encases the differential pinions and side gears, and to which the ring gear is attached.

Differential side gears The gears inside the differential case which are internally splined to the axle shafts, and which are driven by the differential pinion gears.

Dimmer switch A two-position switch, usually mounted on the car floor, operated by the driver to select the high or low headlight beam.

Diode A solid-state electronic device which allows the passage of an electric current in one direction only. Used in the alternator to convert alternating current to direct current for charging the battery.

Dipstick See Oil-level indicator.

Direct current Electric current that flows in one direction only.

Directional signal A device on the car that flashes lights to indicate the direction in which the driver intends to turn.

Disassemble To take apart.

Discharge To depressurize; to crack a valve to allow refrigerant to escape from an air conditioner; to bleed.

Discharge side In an air conditioner, the portion of the refrigerant system under high pressure; it extends from the compressor outlet to the thermostatic expansion valve.

Disk In a disk brake, the rotor, or revolving piece of metal, against which shoes are pressed to provide braking action.

Disk brake A brake in which brake shoes, on a viselike caliper, grip a revolving disk to stop it.

Dispersant A chemical added to oil to prevent dirt and impurities from clinging together in lumps that could clog the engine lubricating system.

Displacement In an engine, the total volume of air-fuel mixture an engine is theoretically capable of drawing into all cylinders during one operating cycle. Also, the volume swept out by the piston in moving from one end of a stroke to the other.

Distributor Any device that distributes. In the ignition system, the rotary switch that directs high-voltage surges to the engine cylinders in the proper sequence. See Ignition distributor.

Distributor advance See Centrifugal advance, Ignition advance, and Vacuum advance.

Distributor cam The cam on the top end of the distributor shaft which rotates to open and close the contact points.

Distributor timing See Ignition timing.

Diverter valve In the air-injection system of exhaust-emission control, a valve that diverts air-pump output into the air cleaner or the atmosphere during deceleration; prevents backfiring and popping in the exhaust system.

DOHC See Double-overhead-camshaft engine.

Drive line The driving connection between the transmission and the differential; made up of one or more drive shafts.

Driven disk The friction disk in a clutch.

Drive pinion A rotating shaft that transmits torque to another gear; used in the differential. Also called the clutch shaft, in the transmission.

Drive shaft An assembly of one or two universal joints and slip joints connected to a heavy metal tube; used to transmit power from the transmission to the differential. Also called the propeller shaft.

Drop-center wheel The conventional passenger-car wheel which has a well, or drop, in the center for one tire bead to fit into while the other bead is being lifted over the rim flange.

Drum brake A brake in which curved brake shoes press against the inner circumference of a metal drum to produce the braking action.

Dual-brake system A brake system consisting of two separate hydraulic systems; usually, one operates the front brakes, and the other operates the rear brakes.

Dual-displacement engine An engine that can run on either all its cylinders or, for fuel economy, half of its cylinders. For example, a six-cylinder engine that can cut off the flow of air-fuel mixture to three cylinders during idle and part-throttle operation.

Dwell The number of degrees the distributor shaft or cam rotates while the distributor points are closed.

Dwell meter A precision electrical instrument used to measure the cam angle, or dwell, or number of degrees the distributor points are closed while the engine is running.

Dynamic balance The balance of an object when it is in motion (for example, the dynamic balance of a rotating wheel).

Dynamometer A device for measuring the power output, or brake horsepower, of an engine. An engine dynamometer measures the power output at the flywheel; a chassis dynamometer measures the power output at the drive wheels.

Eccentric A disk or offset section (of a shaft, for example) used to convert rotary to reciprocating motion. Sometimes called a cam.

ECU See Electronic control unit.

EGR system Abbreviation for exhaust gas recirculation system.

Electric-assist choke A choke in which a small electric heating element warms the choke spring, causing it to release more quickly. This reduces exhaust emissions during the startup of a cold engine.

Electric current A movement of electrons through a conductor such as a copper wire; measured in amperes.

Electric system In the automobile, the system that electrically cranks the engine for starting; furnishes high-voltage sparks to the engine cylinders to fire the compressed air-fuel charges; lights the lights; and powers the heater motor, radio, and other accessories. Consists, in part, of the starting motor, wiring, battery, alternator, regulator, ignition distributor, and ignition coil.

Electrode In a spark plug, the spark jumps between two electrodes. The wire passing through the insulator is the center electrode. The small piece of metal welded to the spark-plug shell (and to which the spark jumps) is the side, or ground, electrode.

Electrolyte The mixture of sulfuric acid and water used in lead-acid storage batteries. The acid enters into chemical reaction with active material in the plates to produce voltage and current.

Electromagnetic induction The characteristic of a magnetic field that causes an electric current to be created in a conductor if it passes through the field, or if the field builds and collapses around the conductor.

Electron A negatively charged particle that circles the nucleus of an atom. The movement of electrons in an electric current.

Electronic control unit A solid-state device that receives information from sensors and is programmed to operate various circuits and systems based on that information.

Electronic fuel-injection system A system that injects gasoline to a spark-ignition engine and includes an electronic control unit to time and meter the fuel flow.

Electronic ignition system A transistorized ignition system which does not have mechanical contact points in the distributor, but uses the distributor for distributing the secondary voltage to the spark plugs. Also called a solid-state ignition system.

Electronics Electrical assemblies, circuits, and systems that use electron devices such as transistors and diodes.

Element A substance that cannot be further divided into a simpler substance. In a battery, the group of unlike positive and negative plates, separated by insulators, that make up each cell.

Emission control Any device or modification added onto or designed into a motor vehicle for the purpose of reducing air-polluting emissions.

Emission standards Allowable automobile emission levels, set by local, state, and federal legislation.

End play As applied to a crankshaft, the distance that the crankshaft can move forward and back in the cylinder block.

Energy The capacity or ability to do work. Usually measured in work units of pound-feet (kilogram-meters), but also expressed in heat-energy units (Btus [joules]).

Engine A machine that converts heat energy into mechanical energy. A device that burns fuel to produce mechanical power; sometimes referred to as a power plant.

Engine fan See Fan.

Engine tuneup A procedure for inspecting, testing, and adjusting an engine, and replacing any worn parts, to restore the engine to its best performance.

Ethyl See Tetraethyl lead.

Ethylene glycol Chemical name of a widely used type of permanent antifreeze.

Evacuate To use a vacuum pump to pump any air and moisture out of an air-conditioner refrigerant system; required whenever any component in the refrigerant system has been removed and replaced.

Evaporation The transformation of a liquid to the gaseous state.

Evaporation-control system A system which prevents the escape of gasoline vapors from the fuel tank or carburetor to the atmosphere while the engine is off. The vapors are stored in a charcoal canister or in the engine crankcase until the engine is started.

Evaporator The heat exchanger in an air conditioner in which refrigerant changes from a liquid to a gas (evaporates), taking heat from the surrounding air as it does so.

Exhaust emissions Pollutants emitted into the atmosphere through any opening downstream of the exhaust ports of an engine.

Exhaust gas The burned and unburned gases that remain (from the air-fuel mixture) after combustion.

Exhaust-gas analyzer A device for sensing the amounts of air pollutants in the exhaust gas of a motor vehicle. The analyzers used in automotive shops check HC and CO; those used in testing laboratories can also check NO_x.

Exhaust gas recirculation system An NO_x control system that recycles a small part of the inert exhaust gas back through the intake manifold at all throttle positions except idle and wide open, to lower the combustion temperature.

Exhaust manifold A device with several passages through which exhaust gases leave the engine combustion chambers and enter the exhaust piping system.

Exhaust pipe The pipe connecting the exhaust manifold with the muffler.

Exhaust stroke The piston stroke (from BDC to TDC) immediately following the power stroke, during which the exhaust valve opens so that the exhaust gases can escape from the cylinder to the exhaust manifold.

Exhaust system The system through which exhaust gases leave the vehicle. Consists of the exhaust manifold, exhaust pipe, muffler, tail pipe, and resonator (if used).

Exhaust valve The valve that opens during the exhaust stroke to allow burned gases to flow from the cylinder to the exhaust manifold.

Expansion plug A slightly dished plug that is used to seal core passages in the cylinder block and cylinder head. When driven into place, it is flattened and expanded to fit tightly.

Expansion tank A tank at the top of an automobile radiator which provides room for heated coolant to expand and to give off any air that may be trapped in the coolant. Also, a similar device used in some fuel tanks to prevent fuel from spilling out of the tank through expansion.

Expansion valve A metering valve or device located between the condenser and evaporator in an air conditioner; controls the amount of refrigerant sprayed into the evaporator.

Fan The bladed device on the front of the engine that rotates to draw cooling air through the radiator or around the engine cylinders; an air blower, such as the heater fan and the **A/C** blower.

Fast-idle cam A mechanism on the carburetor, connected to the automatic choke, that holds the throttle valve slightly open when the engine is cold; causes the engine to idle at a higher rpm as long as the choke is applies.

Field coil A coil, or winding, in a generator or starting motor which produces a magnetic field as current passes through it.

Field relay A relay that is part of some alternator charging systems; connects the alternator field to the battery when the engine runs and disconnects it when the engine stops.

Filter A device through which air, gases, or liquids are passed to remove impurities.

Fins On a radiator or heat exchanger, thin metal projections over which cooling air flows to remove heat from hot liquid flowing through internal passages. On an air-cooled engine, thin metal projections on the cylinder and head which greatly increase the area of the heat-dissipating surfaces and help cool the engine.

Firing line The high-voltage vertical spike, or line, that appears on the oscilloscope pattern of the ignition-system secondary circuit. The firing line shows when the spark plug begins to fire and the voltage required to fire it.

Firing order The order in which the engine cylinders fire, or deliver their power strokes, beginning with number 1 cylinder.

Fixed-caliper disk brake Disk brake using a caliper which is fixed in position and cannot move; the caliper usually has four pistons, two on each side of the disk.

Flasher An automatic-reset circuit breaker used in the directional-signal and hazard warning circuits.

Flat rate Method of paying mechanics and technicians, by use of a manual which indicates the time normally required to do each service job.

Float bowl In a carburetor, the reservoir from which gasoline is metered into the passing air.

Floating-caliper disk brake Disk brake using a caliper mounted through rubber bushings which permit the caliper to float, or move, when the brakes are applied; there is one large piston in the caliper.

Float level The float position at which the needle valve closes the fuel inlet to the carburetor, to prevent further delivery of fuel.

Float system In the carburetor, the system that controls the entry of fuel and the fuel level in the float bowl.

Flooded Term used to indicate that the engine cylinders received "raw" or liquid gasoline, or an air-fuel mixture too rich to burn.

Fluid Any liquid or gas.

Fluid coupling A device in the power train consisting of two rotating members; transmits power from the engine, through a fluid, to the transmission.

Flush In an air conditioner, to wash out the refrigerant passages with Refrigerant-12 to remove contaminants. In a brake system, to wash out the hydraulic system and the master and wheel cylinders, or calipers, with clean brake fluid to remove dirt or impurities that have gotten into the system.

Flywheel A heavy metal wheel that is attached to the crankshaft and rotates with it; helps smooth out the power surges from the engine power strokes; also serves as part of the clutch and engine cranking system.

Flywheel ring gear A gear, fitted around the flywheel, that is engaged by teeth on the starting-motor drive to crank the engine.

Force Any push or pull exerted on an object; measured in units of weight, such as pounds, ounces, kilograms, or grams.

Four-barrel carburetor A carburetor with four throttle valves. In effect, two two-barrel carburetors in a single assembly.

Four-cycle See Four-stroke cycle.

Four-speed A manual transmission having four forward gears.

Four-stroke cycle The four piston strokes — intake, compression, power, and exhaust — that make up the complete cycle of events in the four-stroke-cycle engine. Also called four-cycle and four-stroke.

Four-wheel drive On a vehicle, driving axles at both front and rear, so that all four wheels can be driven.

Frame The assembly of metal structural parts and channel sections that supports the car engine and body and is supported by the wheels.

Freon-12 Refrigerant used in automobile air conditioners. Also known as Refrigerant-12 and R-12.

Friction The resistance to motion between two bodies in contact with each other.

Friction bearing Bearing in which there is sliding contact between the moving surfaces. Sleeve bearings, such as those used in connecting rods, are friction bearings.

Friction disk In the clutch, a flat disk, faced on both sides with friction material and splined to the clutch shaft. It is positioned between the clutch pressure plate and the engine flywheel. Also called the clutch disk or driven disk.

Front geometry The angular relationship between the front wheels, wheel-attaching parts, and car frame. Includes camber, caster, steering-axis inclination, toe, and turning radius.

Front-wheel drive A vehicle having its drive wheels located on the front axle.

Fuel Any combustible substance. In an automobile engine, the fuel (gasoline) is burned, and the heat of combustion expands the resulting gases, which force the piston downward and rotate the crankshaft.

Fuel filter A device located in the fuel line, ahead of the float bowl; removes dirt and other contaminants from fuel passing through.

Fuel gauge A gauge that indicates the amount of fuel in the fuel tank.

Fuel-injection system A system which delivers fuel under pressure into the combustion chamber, or into the airflow just as it enters each individual cylinder. Replaces the conventional carburetor.

Fuel line The pipe or tubes through which fuel flows from the fuel tank to the carburetor.

Fuel pump The electrical or mechanical device in the fuel system which forces fuel from the fuel tank to the carburetor.

Fuel system In an automobile, the system that delivers the fuel and air to the engine cylinders. Consists of the fuel tank and lines, gauge, fuel pump, carburetor, and intake manifold.

Fuel tank The storage tank for fuel on the vehicle.

Fuel-vapor recovery system See Vapor recovery system.

Full throttle Wide-open throttle position, with the accelerator pressed all the way down to the floorboard.

Fuse A device designed to open an electric circuit when the current is excessive, to protect equipment in the circuit. An open, or "blown," fuse must be replaced after the circuit problem is corrected.

Fuse block A boxlike unit that holds the fuses for the various electric circuits in an automobile.

Fusible link A type of fuse in which a special wire melts to open the circuit when the current is excessive. An open, or "blown," fusible link must be replaced after the circuit problem is corrected.

Gap The air space between two electrodes, as the spark-plug gap or the contact-point gap.

Gas The state of matter in which the matter has neither a definite shape nor a definite volume; air is a mixture of several gases. In an automobile, the discharge from the tail pipe is called the exhaust gas. Also, gas is a slang expression for the liquid fuel gasoline.

Gasket A layer of material, usually made of cork or metal or both, that is placed between two machined surfaces to provide a tight seal.

600

Gasket cement A liquid adhesive material, or sealer, used to install gaskets; in some applications, a layer of gasket cement is used as the gasket.

Gasoline A liquid blend of hydrocarbons, obtained from crude oil; used as the fuel in most automobile engines.

Gassing Hydrogen gas escaping from a battery; the gas is formed during battery charging.

Gauge set One or more instruments attached to a manifold (a pipe fitted with several outlets for connecting pipes) and used for measuring pressure.

Gear lubricant A type of grease or oil designed especially to lubricate gears.

Gear ratio The number of revolutions of a driving gear required to turn a driven gear through one complete revolution. For a pair of gears, the ratio is found by dividing the number of teeth on the driven gear by the number of teeth on the driving gear..

Gears Mechanical devices that transmit power or turning effort from one shaft to another; gears contain teeth that mesh as the gears turn.

Gearshift A linkage-type mechanism by which the gears in an automobile transmission are engaged.

Generator A device that converts mechanical energy into electric energy; can produce either ac or dc electricity. In automotive usage, a dc generator (now seldom used).

Glaze The very smooth, mirrorlike finish that develops on engine-cylinder walls.

Glaze breaker A tool, rotated by an electric motor, used to remove the glaze from engine-cylinder walls.

Grease Lubricating oil to which thickening agents have been added.

Grommet A device, usually made of hard rubber or similar material, used to encircle or support a component. In emission systems, a grommet is located in the valve-cover assembly to support and help seal the PCV valve.

Grounding Connection of an electrical unit to the vehicle engine or frame to provide a return path for electric current.

Ground-return system Common system of electric wiring in which the chassis and frame of a vehicle are used as part of the electric return circuit to the battery or alternator; also known as the single-wire system.

Gulp valve In the air-injection system, a type of antibackfire valve which allows a sudden intake of fresh air through the intake manifold during deceleration; prevents backfiring and popping in the exhaust system.

Harmonic balancer See Vibration damper.

HC Abbreviation for hydrocarbon.

Head See Cylinder head.

Headlights Lights at the front of a vehicle; designed to illuminate the road ahead of the vehicle.

Heat-control valve In the engine, a thermostatically operated valve in the exhaust manifold; diverts heat to the intake manifold to warm it before the engine reaches normal operating temperature.

Heated-air system A system in which a thermostatically controlled air cleaner supplies hot air from a stove around the exhaust manifold to the carburetor during warmup; improves cold-engine operation.

Heat of compression Increase of temperature brought about by the compression of air or air-fuel mixture.

HEI See High-Energy Ignition (HEI) system.

Helical gear A gear in which the teeth are cut at an angle to the center line of the gear.

Heli-Coil A rethreading device used when threads are worn or damaged. The device is installed in a retapped hole to reduce the thread size to the original size.

Hemispherical combustion chamber A combustion chamber resembling a hemisphere, or half a round ball.

High compression Term used to refer to the increased compression ratios of modern automotive engines, as compared with engines built in the past.

High-Energy Ignition (HEI) system A General Motors electronic ignition system without contact points and with all ignition-system components contained in the distributor. Capable of producing 35,000 volts.

High-pressure lines Lines from the air-conditioner compressor outlet to the thermostatic-expansion-valve inlet that carry high-pressure refrigerant. The two longest high-pressure lines are the discharge and liquid lines.

High-speed system In the carburetor, the system that supplies fuel to the engine at speeds above about 25 mph [40 km/h]. Also called the main-metering system.

High-voltage cables The secondary (or spark-plug) cables or wires that carry high voltage from the ignition coil to the spark plugs.

Hone An abrasive stone that is rotated in a bore or bushing to remove material.

Horn An electrical noise-making device on a vehicle, used for signaling.

Horn relay A relay connected between the battery and the horns. When the horn button is pressed, the relay is energized; it then connects the horns to the battery.

Horsepower A measure of mechanical power, or the rate at which work is done. One horsepower equals 33,000 ft-lb (foot-pounds) of work per minute; it is the power necessary to raise 33,000 pounds a distance of one foot in one minute.

Hot patching A method of repairing a tire or tube by using heat to vulcanize a patch onto the damaged surface.

Hub The center part of a wheel.

Hydraulic brakes A braking system that uses hydraulic pressure to force the brake shoes against the brake drums, or rotors, as the brake pedal is depressed.

Hydraulic clutch A clutch that is actuated by hydraulic pressure; used in heavy-duty equipment, and where the engine is some distance from the driver's compartment so it would be difficult to use mechanical linkages.

Hydraulic pressure Pressure exerted through the medium of a liquid.

Hydraulics The use of a liquid under pressure to transfer force or motion, or to increase an applied force.

Hydraulic valve lifter A valve lifter that, by means of oil pressure, maintains zero valve clearance so that valve noise is reduced.

Hydrocarbon(HC) An organic compound containing only carbon and hydrogen, usually derived from fossil fuels such as petroleum, natural gas, and coal; an agent in the formation of photochemical smog. Gasoline is a blend of liquid hydrocarbons refined from crude oil.

Hydrogen (H) A colorless, odorless, highly flammable gas whose combustion produces water; the simplest and lightest element.

Hydrometer A device used to measure specific gravity. In automotive servicing, a device used to measure the specific gravity of battery electrolyte to determine the state of the battery charge; also a device used to measure the specific gravity of coolant to determine its freezing temperature.

Hypoid gear A type of gear used in the differential (drive pinion and ring gear); cut in a spiral form to allow the pinion to be set below the center line of the ring gear, so that the car floor can be designed lower.

IC See Internal-combustion engine.

Idle Engine speed when the accelerator pedal is fully released and there is no load on the engine.

Idle limiter A device that controls the maximum richness of the idle air-fuel mixture in the carburetor; also aids in preventing overly rich idle adjustments. Limiters are of two types: the external plastic-cap type, installed on the head of the idle-mixture adjustment screw, and the internal-needle type, located in the idle passages of the carburetor.

Idle mixture The air-fuel mixture supplied to the engine during idling.

Idle-mixture screw The adjustment screw (on some carburetors) that can be turned in or out to lean out or enrich the idle mixture.

Idler arm In the steering system, a link that supports the tie rod and transmits steering motion to both wheels through the tie-rod ends.

Idle speed The speed, or rpm, at which the engine runs without load when the accelerator pedal is released.

Idle-stop solenoid An electrically operated two-position plunger used to provide a predetermined throttle setting at idle.

Idle system In the carburetor, the passages through which fuel is fed when the engine is idling.

Ignition The action of the spark in starting the burning of the compressed air-fuel mixture in the combustion chamber.

Ignition advance The moving forward, in time, of the ignition spark relative to the piston position. TDC or 1 degree ATDC is considered advanced as compared with 2 degrees ATDC.

Ignition coil The ignition-system component that acts as a transformer to step up (increase) the battery voltage to many thousands of volts;

The high-voltage surge from the coil is transmitted to the spark plug to ignite the compressed air-fuel mixture.

Ignition distributor. The ignition-system component that closes and opens the primary circuit to the ignition coil at the proper times and distributes the resulting high-voltage surges from the ignition coil to the proper spark plugs.

Ignition resistor A resistance connected into the ignition primary circuit to reduce the battery voltage to the coil during engine operation.

Ignition retard The moving back, in time, of the ignition spark relative to the piston position. TDC or 1 degree BTDC is considered retarded as compared with 2 degrees BTDC.

Ignition switch The switch in the ignition system (usually operated with a key) that opens and closes the ignition-coil primary circuit. May also be used to open and close other vehicle electric circuits.

Ignition system In the automobile, the system that furnishes high-voltage sparks to the engine cylinders to fire the compressed air-fuel mixture. Consists of the battery, ignition coil, ignition distributor, ignition switch, wiring, and spark plugs.

Ignition timing The delivery of the spark from the coil to the spark plug at the proper time for the power stroke, relative to the piston position.

I-head engine An overhead-valve (OHV) engine; an engine with the valves in the cylinder head.

Impeller A rotating finned disk; used in centrifugal pumps, such as water pumps, and in torque converters.

Included angle In the front-suspension system, camber angle plus steering-axis-inclination angle.

Independent front suspension The conventional front-suspension system in which each front wheel is independently supported by a spring.

Indicator A device using a light or a dial and pointer to make some condition known; for example, the temperature indicator or oil-pressure indicator.

Induction The action of producing a voltage in a conductor or coil by moving the conductor or coil through a magnetic field, or by moving the field past the conductor or coil.

Inertia The property of an object that causes it to resist any change in its speed or in the direction of its travel.

Infrared analyzer A test instrument used to measure very small quantities of pollutants in exhaust gas. See Exhaust-gas analyzer.

In-line engine An engine in which all the cylinders are located in a single row or line.

In-line steering gear A type of integral power steering; uses a recirculating-ball steering gear to which is added a control valve and an actuating piston.

Inner tube See Tire tube.

Inspect To examine a component or system for surface condition or function.

Install To set up for use on a vehicle any part, accessory, option, or kit.

Insulation Material that stops the travel of electricity (electrical insulation) or heat (heat insulation).

Insulator A poor conductor of electricity or heat.

Intake manifold A device with several passages through which the air-fuel mixture flows from the carburetor to the ports in the cylinder head or cylinder block.

Intake stroke The piston stroke from TDC to BDC immediately following the exhaust stroke, during which the intake valve opens and the cylinder fills with air-fuel mixture from the intake manifold.

Integral Built into, as part of the whole.

Internal-combustion (IC) engine An engine in which the fuel is burned inside the engine itself, rather than in a separate device (as in a steam engine).

Internal gear A gear with teeth pointing inward, toward the hollow center of the gear.

Jet A calibrated passage in the carburetor through which fuel flows.

Journal The part of a rotating shaft which turns in a bearing.

Kickdown In automatic transmissions, a system that produces a downshift when the accelerator is pushed down to the floorboard.

Kilogram (kg) In the metric system, a unit of weight and mass; approximately equal to 2.2 pounds.

Kilometer (km) In the metric system, a unit of linear measure equal to 0.621 mile.

Kilowatt (kW) A unit of power, equal to about 1.34 hp.

Kinetic energy The energy of motion; the energy stored in a moving body through its momentum; for example, the kinetic energy stored in a rotating flywheel.

Kingpin In older cars and trucks, the steel pin on which the steering knuckle pivots; attaches the steering knuckle to the knuckle support or axle.

Kingpin inclination Inward tilt of the kingpin from the vertical. See Steering-axis inclination.

Knock A heavy metallic engine sound which varies with engine speed; usually caused by a loose or worn bearing; name also used for detonation, pinging, and spark knock. See Detonation.

Knuckle A steering knuckle; a front-suspension part that acts as a hinge to support a front wheel and permit it to be turned to steer the car. The knuckle pivots on ball joints or, in earlier models, on kingpins.

Laminated Made up of several thin sheets or layers.

Lash The amount of free motion in a gear train, between gears, or in a mechanical assembly, such as the lash in a valve train.

Lead A cable or conductor that carries electric current (pronounced "leed"). A heavy metal; used in lead-acid storage batteries.

Leaded gasoline Gasoline to which small amounts of tetraethyl lead are added to improve engine performance and to reduce detonation.

Leaf spring A spring made up of a single flat steel plate, or several plates of graduated lengths assembled one on top of another, used on vehicles to absorb road shocks by bending, or flexing, in the middle.

Leak detector Any device used to locate an opening where refrigerant may escape. Common types are flame, electronic, dye, and soap bubbles.

Lean mixture An air-fuel mixture that has a relatively high proportion of air and a relatively low proportion of fuel. An air-fuel ratio of 16:1 is a lean mixture, compared with an air-fuel ratio of 13:1.

Light A gas-filled bulb enclosing a wire that glows brightly when an electric current passes through it; a lamp. Also, any visible radiant energy.

Limited-slip differential A differential designed so that when one wheel is slipping, a major portion of the drive torque is supplied to the wheel with the better traction; also called a nonslip differential.

Linear measurement A measurement taken in a straight line; for example, the measurement of crankshaft end play.

Line boring Using a special boring machine, centered on the original center of the cylinder-block main-bearing bores, to rebore the crankcase into alignment.

Lines of force See Magnetic lines of force.

Lining See Brake lining.

Linkage An assembly of rods, or links, used to transmit motion.

Linkage-type power steering A type of power steering in which the power-steering units (power cylinder and valve) are part of the steering linkage; frequently a bolt-on type of system.

Liquid-cooled engine An engine that is cooled by the circulation of liquid coolant around the cylinders.

Liquid line In an air conditioner, hose that connects the receiver-dehydrator outlet and the thermostatic-expansion-valve inlet. High-pressure liquid refrigerant flows through the line.

Liter (L) In the metric system, a measure of volume; approximately equal to 0.26 gallon (U.S.), or about 61 cubic inches. Used as a metric measure of engine-cylinder displacement.

Lobe A projecting part; for example, the rotor lobe or the cam lobe.

Lower beam A headlight beam used to illuminate the road ahead of the vehicle when the car is meeting or following another vehicle.

Low-lead fuel Gasoline which is low in tetraethyl lead, containing not more than 0.5 g per gallon.

Low-speed system The system in the carburetor that supplies fuel to the air passing through during low-speed, part-throttle operation.

Lubricating system The system in the engine that supplies engine parts with lubricating oil to prevent contact between any two moving metal surfaces.

Machining The process of using a machine to remove metal from a metal part.

Magnetic Having the ability to attract iron. This ability may be permanent, or it may depend on a current flow, as in an electromagnet.

Magnetic clutch A magnetically operated clutch used to engage and disengage the air-conditioner compressor.

Magnetic field The area or field of influence of a magnet, within which it will exhibit magnetic properties; extends from the north pole of the magnet to its south pole. The strength of the field of an electromagnet increases with the number of turns of wire around the iron core and the current flow through the wire.

Magnetic lines of force The imaginary lines by which a magnetic field may be visualized.

Magnetic switch A switch with a winding (a coil of wire); when the winding is energized, the switch is moved to open or close a circuit.

Magnetism The ability, either natural or produced by a flow of electric current, to attract iron.

Mag wheel A magnesium wheel assembly; also frequently used to refer to any chromed, aluminum-offset, or wide-rim wheel of spoke design.

Main bearings In the engine, the bearings that support the crankshaft.

Main jet The fuel nozzle, or jet, in the carburetor that supplies the fuel when the throttle is partially to fully open.

Make A distinctive name applied to a group of vehicles produced by one manufacturer; may be further subdivided into car lines, body types, etc.

Malfunction Improper or incorrect operation.

Manifold A device with several inlet or outlet passageways through which a gas or liquid is gathered or distributed. See Exhaust manifold, Intake manifold, and Manifold gauge set.

Manifold gauge set A high-pressure and a low-pressure gauge mounted together as a set; used for checking pressures in the air-conditioning system.

Manifold heat control See Heat-control valve.

Manifold vacuum The vacuum in the intake manifold that develops as a result of the vacuum in the cylinders on their intake strokes.

Manual low Position of the units in an automatic transmission when the driver moves the shift lever to the low- or first-gear position on the quadrant.

Manufacturer Any person, firm, or corporation engaged in the production or assembly of motor vehicles or other products.

Master cylinder The liquid-filled cylinder in the hydraulic braking system or clutch where hydraulic pressure is developed when the driver depresses a foot pedal.

Matter Anything that has weight and occupies space.

Measuring The act of determining the size, capacity, or quantity of an object.

Mechanism A system of interrelated parts that make up a working assembly.

Meshing The mating, or engaging, of the teeth of two gears.

Meter (m) A unit of linear measure in the metric system, equal to 39.37 inches. Also, the name given to any test instrument that measures a property of a substance passing through it, as an ammeter measures electric current. Also, any device that measures and controls the flow of a substance passing through it, as a carburetor jet meters fuel flow.

Metering rod and jet A device consisting of a small, movable, cone-shaped rod and a jet; used to increase or decrease fuel flow according to engine throttle opening, engine load, or a combination of both.

Metering valve A valve in the disk-brake system which prevents hydraulic pressure to the front brakes until after the rear brakes are applied.

Millimeter (mm) In the metric system, a unit of linear measure approximately equal to 0.039 inch.

MISAR Microprocessed Sensing and Automatic Regulation; a high-energy ignition system in which the centrifugal- and vacuum-advance units are replaced with sensors and an electronic control unit.

Misfire In the engine, a failure to ignite the air-fuel mixture in one or more cylinders. This condition may be intermittent or continuous in one or more cylinders.

Miss See Misfire.

Model year The production period for new motor vehicles or new engines, designated by the calendar year in which the period ends.

Modification An alteration; a change from the original.

Modulator A pressure-regulated governing device; used, for example, in automatic transmissions.

Moisture Humidity, dampness, wetness, or very small drops of water.

Molecule The smallest particle into which a substance can be divided and still retain the properties of that substance.

Monolithic timing Making accurate spark-timing adjustment with an electronic timing device which can be used with the engine running.

Motor A device that converts electric energy into mechanical energy; for example, the starting motor.

Motor vehicle A vehicle propelled by a means other than muscle power, usually mounted on rubber tires, which does not run on rails or tracks.

Mph Abbreviation for miles per hour, a measure of speed.

Muffler In the engine-exhaust system, a device through which the exhaust gases must pass and which reduces the exhaust noise. In an air-conditioning system, a device to minimize pumping sounds from the compressor.

Multiple-displacement engine An engine that can run either on all its cylinders or, for fuel economy, on various numbers of cylinders. For example, a six-cylinder engine that can cut off the flow of air-fuel mixture to three cylinders during idle, and then operate on four, five, or six cylinders as the load and power demands increase.

Multiple-viscosity oil An engine oil which has a low viscosity when cold (for easier cranking) and a higher viscosity when hot (to provide adequate engine lubrication).

Mutual induction The condition in which a voltage is induced in one coil by a changing magnetic field caused by a changing current in another coil. The magnitude of the induced voltage depends on the number of turns in the two coils.

Needle bearing An antifriction bearing of the roller type, in which the rollers are very small in diameter (needle-sized).

Needle valve A small, tapered, needle-pointed valve which can move into or out of a valve seat to close or open the passage through the seat. Used to control the carburetor float-bowl fuel level.

Negative One of the two poles of a magnet, or one of the two terminals of an electrical device.

Negative terminal The terminal from which electrons flow in a complete electric circuit. On a battery, the negative terminal can be identified as the battery post with the smaller diameter; the minus sign (–) is often also used to identify the negative terminal.

Neutral In a transmission, the setting in which all gears are disengaged and the output shaft is disconnected from the drive wheels.

Neutral-start switch A switch wired into the ignition switch to prevent engine cranking unless the transmission shift lever is in NEUTRAL.

Nitrogen (N) A colorless, tasteless, odorless gas that constitutes 78 percent of the atmosphere by volume and is a part of all living tissues.

Nonconductor Same as insulator.

North pole The pole from which the lines of force leave a magnet.

NO_x Abbreviation for nitrogen oxides.

NO_x control system Any device or system used to reduce the amount of NO_x produced by an engine.

Nozzle The opening, or jet, through which fuel passes when it is discharged into the carburetor venturi.

Octane rating A measure of the antiknock properties of a gasoline. The higher the octane rating, the more resistant the gasoline is to spark knock or detonation.

Odometer The meter that indicates the total distance a vehicle has traveled, in miles or kilometers; usually located in the speedometer.

OHC See Overhead-camshaft engine.

Ohm The unit of electrical resistance.

Ohmmeter An instrument used to measure electrical resistance.

OHV See Overhead-valve engine.

Oil A liquid lubricant; made from crude oil and used to produce lubrication between moving parts. In a diesel engine, oil is used for fuel.

Oil cooler A small radiator which lowers the temperature of oil flowing through it.

Oil dilution Thinning of oil in the crankcase; caused by liquid gasoline leaking past the piston rings from the combustion chamber.

Oil filter A filter which removes impurities from crankcase oil passing through it.

Oil-level indicator The indicator that is removed and inspected to check the level of oil in the crankcase of an engine or compressor. Usually called the dipstick.

Oil pan The detachable lower part of the engine, made of sheet metal, which encloses the crankcase and acts as an oil reservoir.

Oil-pressure indicator A gauge that indicates (to the driver) the oil pressure in the engine lubricating system.

Oil pump In the lubricating system, the device that forces oil from the oil pan to the moving engine parts.

Oil pumping Leakage of oil past the piston rings and into the combustion chamber, usually as a result of defective rings or worn cylinder walls.

Oil ring The lower ring or rings of a piston; designed to prevent excessive amounts of oil from working up the cylinder walls and into the combustion chamber. Also called an oil-control ring.

Oil seal A seal placed around a rotating shaft or other moving part to prevent leakage of oil.

One-way clutch See Sprag.

One-wire system On automobiles, use of the car body, engine, and frame as a path for the grounded side of the electric circuits; eliminates the need for a second wire as a return path to the battery or alternator.

Open circuit In an electric circuit, a break, or opening, which prevents the passage of current.

Open system A crankcase emission-control system which draws air through the oil-filler cap, and does not include a tube from the crankcase to the air cleaner.

Orifice A small opening, or hole, into a cavity.

O ring A type of sealing ring made of a special rubberlike material; in use, the O ring is compressed into a groove to provide the sealing action.

Oscillating Moving back and forth, as a swinging pendulum.

Oscilloscope A high-speed voltmeter which visually displays voltage variations on a television-type picture tube. Used to check engine ignition systems; also used to check charging systems and electronic fuel-injection systems.

Output shaft The main shaft of the transmission; the shaft that delivers torque from the transmission to the drive shaft.

Overcharging Continued charging of a battery after it has reached the charged condition. This action damages the battery and shortens its life.

Overdrive Transmission gearing that causes the drive shaft to overdrive, or turn faster than the engine crankshaft.

Overflow Spilling of the excess of a substance; also, to run or spill over the sides of a container, usually because of overfilling.

Overflow tank See Expansion tank.

Overhaul To completely disassemble a unit, clean and inspect all parts, reassemble it with the original or new parts, and make all adjustments necessary for proper operation.

Overhead-camshaft (OHC) engine An engine in which the camshaft is mounted over the cylinder head, instead of inside the cylinder block.

Overhead-valve (OHV) engine An engine in which the valves are mounted in the cylinder head above the combustion chamber, instead of in the cylinder block. In this type of engine, the camshaft is usually mounted in the cylinder block, and the valves are actuated by pushrods.

Overheat To heat excessively; also, to become excessively hot.

Overrunning clutch drive A type of clutch drive which transmits rotary motion in one direction only. When rotary motion attempts to pass through in the other direction, the then driving member overruns and does not pass the motion to the other member. Widely used as the drive mechanism for starting motors.

Oxides of nitrogen See Nitrogen oxides.

Oxygen (O) A colorless, tasteless, odorless, gaseous element which makes up about 21 percent of air. Capable of combining rapidly with all elements except the inert gases in the oxidation process called burning. Combines very slowly with many metals in the oxidation process called rusting.

Pan See Oil pan.

Parade pattern An oscilloscope pattern showing the ignition voltages on one line, from left to right across the scope screen in engine firing order.

Parallel The quality of being the same distance from each other at all points; usually applied to lines and, in automotive work, to machined surfaces.

Parallel circuit The electric circuit formed when two or more electrical devices have their terminals connected, positive to positive and negative to

negative, so that each may operate independently of the others, from the same power source.

Parking brake Mechanically operated brake that is independent of the foot-operated service brakes on the vehicle; set when the vehicle is parked.

Particle A very small piece of metal, dirt, or other impurity which may be contained in the air, fuel, or lubricating oil used in an engine.

Passage A small hole or gallery in an assembly or casting, through which air, coolant, fuel, or oil flows.

Passenger car Any four-wheeled motor vehicle manufactured primarily for use on streets and highways and carrying 10 passengers or fewer.

Pawl An arm pivoted so that its free end can fit into a detent, slot, or groove at certain times to hold a part stationary.

PCV Abbreviation for positive crankcase ventilation.

PCV valve The valve that controls the flow of crankcase vapors in accordance with ventilation requirements for different engine speeds and loads.

Petroleum The crude oil from which gasoline, lubricating oil, and other such products are refined.

Photochemical smog Smog caused by hydrocarbons and nitrogen oxides reacting photochemically in the atmosphere. The reactions take place under low wind velocity, bright sunlight, and an inversion layer in which the air mass is trapped (as between the ocean and mountains in Los Angeles). Can cause eye and lung irritation.

Pickup coil In an electronic ignition system, the coil in which voltage is induced by the reluctor.

Pilot bearing A small bearing, in the center of the flywheel end of the crankshaft, which carries the forward end of the clutch shaft.

Pilot shaft A shaft that is used to align parts, and which is removed before final installation of the parts; a dummy shaft.

Ping Engine spark knock that occurs during acceleration. Usually associated with medium to heavy throttle, acceleration, or lugging at relatively low speeds, especially with a manual transmission. However, it may occur in higher-speed ranges under heavy-load conditions. Caused by too much advance of ignition timing or low-octane fuel.

Pinion gear The smaller of two meshing gears.

Piston A movable part, fitted to a cylinder, which can receive or transmit motion as a result of pressure changes in a fluid. In the engine, the cylindrical part that moves up and down within a cylinder as the crankshaft rotates.

Piston displacement The cylinder volume displaced by the piston as it moves from the bottom to the top of the cylinder during one complete stroke.

Piston pin The cylindrical or tubular metal piece that attaches the piston to the connecting rod. Also called the wrist pin.

Piston rings Rings fitted into grooves in the piston. There are two types: compression rings for sealing the compression pressure in the combustion chamber, and oil rings to scrape excessive oil off the cylinder wall. See Compression ring and Oil ring.

Piston skirt The lower part of the piston, below the piston-pin hole.

Pitman arm In the steering system, the arm that is connected between the steering-gear sector shaft and the steering linkage, or tie rod. It swings back and forth for steering as the steering wheel is turned.

Pivot A pin or shaft upon which another part rests or turns.

Planetary-gear system A gear set consisting of a central sun gear surrounded by two or more planet pinions which are, in turn, meshed with a ring (or internal) gear; used in overdrives and automatic transmissions.

Planet carrier In a planetary-gear system, the carrier or bracket that contains the shaft upon which the planet pinion turns.

Planet pinions In a planetary-gear system, the gears that mesh with, and revolve about, the sun gear; they also mesh with the ring (or internal) gear.

Plastigage A plastic material available in strips of various sizes; used to measure crankshaft main-bearing and connecting-rod-bearing clearances.

Plate In a battery, a rectangular sheet of spongy lead. Sulfuric acid in the electrolyte chemically reacts with the lead to produce an electric current.

Plies The layers of cord in a tire casing; each of these layers is a ply.

Polarity The quality of an electric component or circuit that determines the direction of current flow.

Pollutant Any substance that adds to the pollution of the atmosphere. In a vehicle, any such substance in the exhaust gas from the engine or evaporating from the fuel tank or carburetor.

Pollution Any gas or substance, in the air, which makes the air less fit to breathe. Also, noise pollution is the name applied to excessive noise from machinery or vehicles.

Port In the engine, the opening in which the valve operates and through which air-fuel mixture or burned gases pass; the valve port.

Ported vacuum switch A water-temperature-sensing vacuum-control valve used in distributor and EGR vacuum systems. Sometimes called the vacuum-control valve or coolant override valve.

Positive crankcase ventilation (PCV) A crankcase-ventilation system; uses intake-manifold vacuum to return the crankcase vapors and blowby gases from the crankcase to the intake manifold to be burned, thereby preventing their escape into the atmosphere.

Positive terminal The terminal to which electrons flow in a complete electric circuit. On a battery, the positive terminal can be identified as the battery post with the larger diameter; the plus sign (+) is often also used to identify the positive terminal.

Post A point at which a cable is connected to the battery.

Potential energy Energy stored in a body because of its position. A weight raised to a height has potential energy because it can do work coming down. Likewise, a tensed or compressed spring contains potential energy.

Power The rate at which work is done. A common power unit is the horsepower, which is equal to 33,000 ft-lb/min (foot-pounds per minute).

Power brakes A brake system that uses hydraulic or vacuum and atmospheric pressure to provide most of the effort required for braking.

Power piston In some carburetors, a vacuum-operated piston that allows additional fuel to flow at wide-open throttle; permits delivery of a richer air-fuel mixture to the engine.

Power plant The engine or power source of a vehicle.

Power steering A steering system that uses hydraulic pressure (from a pump) to multiply the driver's steering effort.

Power stroke The piston stroke from TDC to BDC immediately following the compression stroke, during which both valves are closed and the air-fuel mixture burns, expands, and forces the piston down to transmit power to the crankshaft.

Power train The mechanisms that carry the rotary motion developed in the engine to the car wheels; includes the clutch, transmission, drive shaft, differential, and axles.

ppm Abbreviation for parts per million; the unit used in measuring the level of hydrocarbons in exhaust gas with an exhaust-gas analyzer.

PR Abbreviation for ply rating; a measure of the strength of a tire, based on the strength of a single ply of designated construction.

Precombustion chamber In some diesel engines, a separate small combustion chamber into which the fuel is injected and where combustion begins.

Preignition Ignition of the air-fuel mixture in the combustion chamber by some unwanted means, before the ignition spark occurs at the spark plug.

Preload In bearings, the amount of load placed on a bearing before actual operating loads are imposed. Proper preloading requires bearing adjustment and ensures alignment and minimum looseness in the system.

Pressure Force per unit area, or force divided by area. Usually measured in pounds per square inch (psi) and kilopascals (kPa).

Pressure bleeder A piece of shop equipment that uses air pressure to force brake fluid into the brake system for bleeding.

Pressure cap A radiator cap with valves which causes the cooling system to operate under pressure at a higher and more efficient temperature.

Pressure-differential valve The valve in a dual-brake system that turns on a warning light if the pressure drops in one part of the system.

Pressure plate That part of the clutch which exerts pressure against the friction disk; it is mounted on and rotates with the flywheel.

Pressure regulator A device which operates to prevent excessive pressure from developing. In hydraulic systems, a valve that opens to release oil from a line when the oil pressure reaches a specified maximum.

Pressure-relief valve A valve in the oil line that opens to relieve excessive pressure.

609

Pressure tester An instrument that clamps in the radiator filler neck; used to pressure-test the cooling system for leaks.

Pressurize To apply more than atmospheric pressure to a gas or liquid.

Primary The low-voltage circuit of the ignition system.

Primary winding The outer winding of relatively heavy wire in an ignition coil.

Printed circuit An electric circuit made by applying a conductive material to an insulating board in pattern that provides current paths between components mounted on or connected to the board.

Propeller shaft See Drive shaft.

Proportioning valve A valve which admits more braking pressure to the front wheels when high fluid pressures develop during braking.

Prussian blue A blue pigment; in solution, useful in determining the area of contact between two surfaces.

psi Abbreviation for pounds per square inch, a measure of pressure.

Pull The result of an unbalanced condition. For example, uneven braking at the front brakes or unequal front-wheel alignment will cause a car to swerve (pull) to one side when the brakes are applied.

Pulley A metal wheel with a V-shaped groove around the rim; drives, or is driven by, a belt.

Pump A device that transfers gas or liquid from one place to another.

Purge To remove, evacuate, or empty trapped substances from a space. In an air conditioner, to remove moisture and air from the refrigerant system by flushing with nitrogen or Refrigerant-12.

Purge valve A valve used on some charcoal canisters in evaporative emission--control systems; limits the flow of vapor and air to the carburetor during idling.

Pushrod In the I-head engine, the rod between the valve lifter and the rocker arm; transmits cam-lobe lift.

PVS Abbreviation for ported vacuum switch.

Quad carburetor A four-barrel carburetor.

Quadrant A term sometimes used to identify the shift-lever selector mounted on the steering column.

Quick charger A battery charger that produces a high charging current which charges, or boosts, a battery in a short time.

Races The metal rings on which ball or roller bearings rotate.

Rack-and-pinion steering gear A steering gear in which a pinion on the end of the steering shaft meshes with a rack on the major cross member of the steering linkage.

Radial-ply tire A tire in which the plies are placed radially, or perpendicular to the rim, with a circumferential belt on top of them. The rubber tread is vulcanized on top of the belt and plies.

Radiator In the cooling system, the device that removes heat from coolant passing through it; takes hot coolant from the engine and returns the coolant to the engine at a lower temperature.

Radiator pressure cap See Pressure cap.

Raster pattern An oscilloscope pattern showing the the ignition voltages one above the other, from the bottom to the top of the screen in the engine firing order.

Ratio Proportion; the relative amounts of two or more substances in a mixture. Usually expressed as a numerical relationship, as in 2:1.

Rear-end torque The reaction torque that acts on the rear-axle housing when torque is applied to the wheels; tends to turn the axle housing in a direction opposite to wheel rotation.

Reassembly Putting back together of the parts of a device.

Rebore To increase the diameter of a cylinder.

Recapping A form of tire repair in which a cap of new tread material is placed on the old casing and vulcanized into place.

Receiver In a car air conditioner, a metal tank for holding excess refrigerant. Liquid refrigerant is delivered from the condenser to the receiver.

Receiver-dehydrator In a car air conditioner, a container for storing liquid refrigerant from the condenser. A sack of desiccant in this container removes small traces of moisture that may be left in the system after purging and evacuating.

Recharging The action of forcing electric current into a battery in the direction opposite to that in which current normally flows during use. Reverses the chemical reaction between the plates and electrolyte.

Reciprocating motion Motion of an object between two limiting positions; motion in a straight line, back and forth or up and down.

Recirculating-ball-and-nut steering gear A type of steering gear in which a nut, meshing with a gear sector, is assembled on a worm gear; balls circulate between the nut and worm threads.

Rectifier A device which changes alternating current to direct current; in the alternator, a diode.

Refrigerant A substance used to transfer heat in an air conditioner, through a cycle of evaporation and condensation.

Refrigerant-12 The refrigerant used in vehicle air-conditioning systems. It is sold under such trademarks as Freon-12.

Refrigeration Cooling of an object or substance by removal of heat through mechanical means.

Regulator In the charging system, a device that controls alternator output to prevent excessive voltage.

Relay An electrical device that opens or closes a circuit or circuits in response to a voltage signal.

Release bearing See Throwout bearing.

Relief valve A valve that opens when a preset pressure is reached. This relieves or prevents excessive pressures.

Reluctor In an electronic ignition system, the metal rotor (with a series of tips) which replaces the conventional distributorr cam.

Remove and reinstall (R and R) To perform a series of servicing procedures on an original part or assembly; includes removal, inspection, lubrication, all necessary adjustments, and reinstallation.

Replace To remove a used part or assembly and install a new part or assembly in its place; includes cleaning, lubricating, and adjusting as required.

Reserve capacity A battery rating; the number of minutes a battery can deliver a 25-ampere current before the cell voltages drop to 1.75 volts per cell.

Resistance The opposition to a flow of current through a circuit or electrical device; measured in ohms. A voltage of one volt will cause one ampere to flow through a resistance of one ohm. This is known as Ohm's law, which can be written in three ways: amperes = volts/ohms; ohms = volts/amperes; and volts = amperes × ohms.

Resonator A device in the exhaust system that reduces the exhaust noise.

Retard Usually associated with the spark-timing mechanisms of the engine; the opposite of spark advance. Also, to delay the introduction of the spark into the combustion chamber.

Return spring A pull-back spring, often used in brake systems.

Rich mixture An air-fuel mixture that has a relatively high proportion of fuel and a relatively low proportion of air. An air-fuel ratio of 13:1 indicates a rich mixture, compared with an air-fuel ratio of 16:1.

Ring See Compressiion ring and Oil ring.

Ring gap The gap betweeen the ends of the piston ring when the ring is in place in the cylinder.

Ring gear A large gear carried by the differential case; meshes with and is driven by the drive pinion.

Ring grooves Grooves cut in a piston, into which the piston rings are assembled.

Ring ridge The ridge formed at the top of a cylinder as the cylinder wall below is worn away by piston-ring movement.

Road-draft tube A method of removing fumes and pressure from the engine crankcase; used prior to crankcase emission-control systems. The tube, which was connected into the crankcase and suspended slightly above the ground, depended on venturi action to create a partial vacuum as the vehicle moved. The method was ineffective below about 20 mph [32 km/h].

Rocker arm In an I-head engine, a device that rocks on a shaft (or pivots on a stud) as the cam moves the pushrod, causing a valve to open.

Rod bearing In an engine, the bearing in the connecting rod in which a crankpin of the crankshaft rotates. Also called a connecting-rod bearing.

Room temperature 68 to 72 °F [20 to 22 °C].

Rotary Term describing the motion of a part that continually rotates or turns.

Rotary-valve steering gear A type of power-steering gear.

Rotor A revolving part of a machine, such as an alternator rotor, disk-brake rotor, distributor rotor, or Wankel-engine rotor.

rpm Abbreviation for revolutions per minute, a measure of rotational speed.

Run-on See Dieseling.

Runout Wobble.

SA Designation for lubricating oil that is acceptable for use in engines operated under the mildest conditions.

SAE Abbreviation for Society of Automotive Engineers. Used to indicate a grade or weight of oil measured according to Society of Automotive Engineers standards.

SB Designation for lubricating oil that is acceptable for minimum-duty engines operated under mild conditions.

SC Designation for lubricating oil that meets requirements to use in the gasoline engines in 1964 to 1967 passenger cars and trucks.

Schematic A pictorial representation, most often in the form of a line drawing. A systematic positioning of components and their relationship to one another or to the overall function.

Schrader valve A spring-loaded valve through which a connection can be made to a refrigeration system; also used in tires.

Scope Short for oscilloscope.

Scored Scratched or grooved, as a cylinder wall may be scored by abrasive particles moved up and down by the piston rings.

Scraper ring On a piston, an oil-control ring designed to scrape excess oil back down the cylinder and into the crankcase.

Screens Pieces of fine-mesh metal fabric; used to prevent solid particles from circulating through any liquid or vapor system and damaging vital moving parts. In an air conditioner, screens are located in the receiver-dehydrator, thermostatic expansion valve, and compressor.

Scuffing A type of wear in which there is a transfer of material between parts moving against each other; shows up as pits or grooves in the mating surfaces.

SD Designation for lubricating oil that meets requirements for use in the gasoline engines in 1968 to 1971 passenger cars and some trucks.

SE Designation for lubricating oil that meets requirements for use in the gasoline engines in 1972 and later cars and in certain 1971 passenger cars and trucks.

Seal A material, shaped around a shaft, used to close off the operating compartment of the shaft, preventing oil leakage.

Sealed-beam headlight A headlight that contains the filament, reflector, and lens in a single sealed unit.

Sealer A thick, tacky compound, usually spread with a brush, which may be used as a gasket or sealant, to seal small openings or surface irregularities.

Seat The surface upon which another part rests, as a valve seat. Also, to wear into a good fit; for example, new piston rings seat after a few miles of driving.

Secondary circuit The high-voltage circuit of the ignition system; consists of the coil, rotor, distributor cap, spark-plug cables, and spark plugs.

Sector A gear that is not a complete circle; specifically, the gear sector on the pitman shaft, in many steering systems.

Segments The copper bars of a commutator.

Self-adjuster A mechanism used on drum brakes; compensates for shoe wear by automatically keeping the shoe adjusted close to the drum.

Self-discharge Chemical activity in the battery which causes the battery to discharge even though it is furnishing no current.

Self-induction The inducing of a voltage in a current-carrying coil of wire because the current in that wire is changing.

Semiconductor A material that acts as an insulator under some conditions and as a conductor under other conditions.

Semiconductor ignition system See Electronic ignition system.

Sensor Any device that receives and reacts to a signal, such as a change in voltage, temperature, or pressure.

Series circuit An electric circuit in which the devices are connected end to end, positive terminal to negative terminal. The same current flows through all the devices in the circuit.

Service manual A book published annually by each vehicle manufacturer, listing the specifications and service procedures for each make and model of vehicle. Also called a shop manual.

Service rating A designation that indicates the type of service for which an engine lubricating oil is best suited. See SA, SB, SC, SD, and SE.

Servo A device in a hydraulic system that converts hydraulic pressure to mechanical movement. Consists of a piston which moves in a cylinder as hydraulic pressure acts on it.

Shackle The swinging support by which one end of a leaf spring is attached to the car frame.

Shift lever The lever used to change gears in a transmission. Also, the lever on the starting motor which moves the drive pinion into or out of mesh with the flywheel teeth.

Shift valve In an automatic transmission, a valve that moves to produce the shifts from one gear ratio to another.

Shim A slotted strip of metal used as a spacer to adjust the front-end alignment on many cars; also used to make small corrections in the position of body sheet metal and other parts.

Shimmy Rapid oscillation. In wheel shimmy, for example, the front wheel turns in and out alternately and rapidly; this causes the front end of the car to oscillate or shimmy.

Shock absorber A device placed at each vehicle wheel to regulate spring rebound and compression.

Shoe In the brake system, aa metal plate that supports the brake lining and absorbs and transmits braking forces.

Short circuit A defect in an electric circuit which permits current to take a short path, or circuit, instead of following the desired path.

Side clearance The clearance between the sides of movig parts when the sides do not serve as load-carrying surfaces.

Sight glass In a car air conditioner, a viewing glass or window set in the refrigerant line, usually in the top of the receiver-dehydrator; the sight glass allows a visual check of the refrigerant passing from the receiver to the evaporator.

Single-overhead-camshaft (SOHC) engine An engine in which a single camshaft is mounted over each cylinder head, instead of inside the cylinder block.

Skid control A device that operates to prevent wheel locking during braking.

Slip joint In the power train, a variable-length connection that permits the drive shaft to change the effective length.

Slip rings In an alternator, the rings that form a rotating connection between the armature windings and the brushes.

Sludge An accumulation of water, dirt, and oil in the oil pan; sludge is very viscous and tends to reduce lubrication.

Smog A term coined from the words ""smoke" and "fog." First applied to the foglke layer that hangs in the air under the certain atmospheric conditions; now generally used to describe any condition of dirty air and/or fumes or smoke. Smog is compounded from smoke, moisture, and numerous chemicals which are produced by combustion.

Smoke Small gas-borne or air-borne particles, exclusive of water vapor, that result from combustion; such particles emitted by an engine into the atmosphere is sufficient quantity to be observable.

Smoke in exhaust A visible blue or black substance often present in the automotive exhaust. A blue color indicates excessive oil in the combustion chamber; black indicates excessive fuel in the air-fuel mixture.

Snap ring A metal fastener, available in two types: the external snap ring fits into a groove in a shaft; the internal snap ring fits into a groove in a housing. Snap rings must be installed and removed with special snap-ring pliers.

SOHC See Single-overhead-camshaft engine.

Solenoid An electromechanical device which, when connected to an electrical source such as a battery, produces a mechanical movement. This movement can be used to control a valve or to produce other movements.

Solenoid relay A relay that connects a solenoid to a current source when its contacts close; specifically, the starting-motor solenoid relay.

Solenoid switch A switch that is opened and closed electromagnetically, by the movement of a solenoid core. Usually, the core also causes a mechanical action, such as the movement of a drive pinion into mesh with flywheel teeth for cranking.

Solid-state regulator An alternator regulator encapsulated in a plastic material and mounted in the alternator.

Solvent A petroleum product of low volatility used in the cleaning of engine and vehicle parts.

South pole The pole at which magnetic lines of force enter a magnet.

Spark advance See Advance.

Spark duration The length of time a spark is established across a spark gap, or the length of time current flows in a spark gap.

Spark knock See Detonation.

Spark line Part of the oscilloscope pattern of the ignition secondary circuit; the spark line shows the voltage required to sustain the spark at the spark plug, and the number of distributor degrees through which the spark exists.

Spark plug A device that screws into the cylinder head of an engine; provides a spark to ignite the compressed air-fuel mixture in the combustion chamber.

Spark-plug heat range The distance heat must travel from the center electrode to reach the outer shell of the spark plug and enter the cylinder head.

Spark test A quick check of the ignition system; made by holding the metal spark-plug end of a spark-plug cable about $\frac{3}{16}$ inch [5 mm] from the cylinder head, or block; cranking the engine; and checking for a spark.

Specifications Information provided by the manufacturer that describes each automotive system and its components, operation, and clearances. Also, the service procedures that must be followed for a system to operate properly.

Specific gravity The weight per unit volume of a substance as compared with the weight per unit volume of water.

Specs Short for specifications.

Speedometer An instrument that indicates vehicle speed; usually driven from the transmission.

Splines Slots or grooves cut in a shaft or bore. Splines on a shaft are matched to splines in a bore, to ensure that two parts turn together.

Spool valve A rod with indented sections; used to control oil flow in automatic transmissions.

Sprag In an automatic transmission, a one-way clutch; a clutch that can transmit power in one direction, but not in the other.

Spring A device that changes shape under stress or pressure, but returns to its original shape when the stress or pressure is removed; the component of the automotive suspension system that absorbs road shocks by flexing and twisting.

Spring shackle See Shackle.

Sprung weight That part of the car which is supported on springs (includes the engine, frame, and body).

Spur gear A gear in which the teeth are parallel to the center line of the gear.

Stabilizer bar An interconnecting shaft between the two lower suspension arms; reduces body roll on turns.

Stacked pattern See Raster pattern.

Stall test A starting-motor test in which the current draw is measured with the motor stalled.

Starter See Starting motor.

Starting motor The electric motor that cranks the engine, or turns the crankshaft, for starting.

Starting-motor drive The drive mechanism and gear on the end of the starting-motor armature shaft; used to couple the starting motor to, and disengage it from, the flywheel ring-gear teeth.

Static balance The balance of an object while it is not moving.

Stator In the torque converter, a third member (in addition to the turbine and pump) which changes the direction of fluid flow under certain operating conditions (when the stator is stationary). In an alternator, the assembly that includes the stationary conductors.

Steering-and-ignition lock A device that locks the ignition switch in the OFF position and locks the steering wheel so it cannot be turned.

Steering arm The arm attached to the steering knuckle that turns the knuckle and wheel for steering.

Steering axis The center line of the ball joints in a front-suspension system.

Steering-axis inclination The inward tilt of the steering axis from the vertical.

Steering gear That part of the steering system that is located at the lower end of the steering shaft; carries the rotary motion of the steering wheel to the car wheels for steering.

Steering geometry See Toe-out on turns.

Steering kickback Sharp and rapid movements of the steering wheel as the front wheels encounter obstructions in the road; the shocks of these encounters "kick back" to the steering wheel.

Steering knuckle The front-wheel spindle which is supported by upper and lower ball joints and by the wheel, the part on which a front wheel is mounted, and which is turned for steering.

Steering shaft The shaft extending from the steeering gear to the steering wheel.

Steering system The mechanism that enables the driver to turn the wheels for changing the direction of vehicle movement.

Steering wheel The wheel at the top of the steering shaft that is used by the driver to guide, or steer, the car.

Stoplights Lights at the rear of a vehicle which indicate that the driver is applying the brakes.

Stoplight switch The switch that turns the stoplights on and off as the brakes are applied and released.

Storage battery A device that changes chemical energy into electric energy; that part of the electric system which acts as a reservoir for electric energy, storing it in chemical form.

Stratified charge In a gasoline-fueled spark-ignition engine, an air-fuel charge with a small layer of very rich air-fuel mixture; the rich layer is ignited first, after which ignition spreads to the leaner mixture filling the rest of the combustion chamber. The diesel engine is a stratified-charge engine.

Stroke In an engine cylinder, the distance that the piston moves in traveling from BDC to TDC or from TDC to BDC.

Strut A bar that connects the lower control arm to the car frame; used when the lower control arm is attached to the frame at only one point. Also called a brake-reaction rod.

Suction line In an air conditioner, the tube that connects the evaporator outlet and the compressor inlet. Low-pressure refrigerant vapor flows through this line.

Suction pressure The pressure at the air-conditioner compressor inlet; the compressor intake pressure, as indicated by a gauge set.

Suction-throttling valve In an air conditioner, a valve located between the evaporator and the compressor; controls the temperature of the air flowing from the evaporator, to prevent freezing of moisture on the evaporator.

Sulfation The lead sulfate that forms on battery plates as a result of the battery action that produces electric current.

Sulfuric acid See Electrolyte.

Sulfur oxides (SO$_x$) Acids that can form in small amounts as the result of a reaction between hot exhaust gas and the catalyst in a catalytic converter.

Sun gear In a planetary-gear system, the center gear that meshes with the planet pinions.

Supercharger In the intake system of the engine, a pump that pressurizes the ingoing air-fuel mixture. This increases the amount of mixture delivered to the cylinders, which increases the engine output. If the supercharger is driven by the engine exhaust gas, it is called a turbocharger.

Superimposed pattern On an oscilloscope, a pattern showing the ignition voltages one on top of the other, so that only a single trace, and variations from it, can be seen.

Suspension The system of springs and other parts which supports the upper part of a vehicle on its axles and wheels.

Suspension arm In the front suspension, one of the arms pivoted on the frame at one end and on the steering-knuckle support at the other end.

Sway bar See Stabilizer bar.

Switch A device that opens and closes an electric circuit.

Synchromesh transmission A transmission with a built-in device that automatically matches the rotating speeds of the transmission gears, thereby eliminating the need for double-clutching.

Synchronize To make two or more events or operations occur at the same time or at the same speed.

Synchronizer A device in the transmission that synchronizes gears about to be meshed, so that no gear clash will occur.

Synthetic oil An artificial oil that is manufactured; not a natural mineral oil made from petroleum.

Tachometer A device for measuring engine speed, or rpm.

Taillights Steady-burning low-intensity lights used on the rear of a vehicle.

Tank unit The part of the fuel-indicating system that is mounted in the fuel tank.

Taper A gradual reduction in the width of a shaft or hole; in an engine cylinder, uneven wear, more pronounced at the top than at the bottom.

Tappet See Valve lifter.

Temperature The measure of heat intensity, in degrees. Temperature is not a measure of heat quantity.

Temperature gauge A gauge that indicates to the driver the temperature of the coolant in the engine cooling system.

Temperature indicator See Temperature gauge.

Temperature-sending unit A device, in contact with the engine coolant, whose electrical resistance changes as the coolant temperature increases or decreases; these changes control the movement of the indicator needle of the temperature gauge.

Tetraethyl lead A chemical which, when added to engine fuel, increases its octane rating, or reduces its knocking tendency. Also called ethyl.

Thermal Of or pertaining to heat.

Thermistor A heat-sensing device with a negative temperature coefficient of resistance; that is, as its temperature increases, its electrical resistance decreases. Used as the sensing device for engine-temperature indicating instruments.

Thermometer An instrument which measures heat intensity (temperature) via the thermal expansion of a liquid.

Thermostat A device for the automatic regulation of temperature; usually contains a temperature-sensitive element that expands or contracts to open or close off the flow of air, a gas, or a liquid.

Thermostatically controlled air cleaner An air cleaner in which a thermostat controls the preheating of intake air.

Thermostatic clutch An adjustable component used in a cycling-clutch air conditioner. Engages and disengages the compressor to prevent water from freezing on the evaporator core, and controls the temperaturre of air flowing from the evaporator.

Thermostatic expansion valve Component of a refrigeration system that controls the rate of refrigerant flow to the evaporator. Commonly called the expansion valve.

Thermostatic gauge An indicating device (for fuel quantity, oil pressure, engine temperature) that contains a thermostatic blade or blades.

Thermostatic vacuum switch A temperature-sensing device screwed into the coolant system; connects full manifold vacuum to the distributor when its critical temperature is reached. The resultant spark advance causes an increase in engine rpm, which cools the engine.

Threaded insert A threaded coil that is used to restore the original thread size to a hole with damaged threads; the hole is drilled oversize and tapped, and the insert is threaded into the tapped hole.

Throttle A disk valve in the carburetor base that pivots in response to accelerator-pedal position; allows the driver to regulate the volume of air-fuel mixture entering the intake manifold, thereby controlling the engine speed. Also called the throttle plate or throttle valve.

Throttle-return check Same as dashpot.

Throttle valve A round disk valve in the throttle body of the carburetor; can be turned to admit more or less air, thereby controlling engine speed.

Throwout bearing In the clutch, the bearing that can be moved in to the release levers by clutch-pedal action, to cause declutching, or disengaging the engine crankshaft from the transmission.

Thrust bearing In the engine, the main bearing that has thrust faces to prevent excessive end play, or forward and backward movement of the crankshaft.

Tie rods In the steering system, the rods that link the pitman arm to the steering-knuckle arms; small steel components that connect the front wheels to the steering mechanism.

Tilt steering wheel A type of steering wheel that can be tilted at various angles, through a flex joint in the steering shaft.

Timing In an engine, delivery of the ignition spark or operation of the valves (in relation to the piston position) for the power stroke. See Ignition timing and Valve timing.

Timing chain A chain that is driven by a sprocket on the crankshaft and that drives the sprocket on the camshaft.

Timing gear A gear on the crankshaft. It drives the camshaft by meshing with a gear on its end.

Timing light A light that can be connected to the ignition system to flash each time the number 1 spark plug fires; used for adjusting the timing of the ignition spark.

Tire The casing-and-tread assembly (with or without a tube) that is mounted on a car wheel to provide pneumatically cushioned contact and traction with the road.

Tire tread See Tread.

Tire-wear indicator Small strips of rubber molded into the bottom of the tire-tread grooves; they appear as narrow strips of smooth rubber across the tire when the tread depth decreases to $\frac{1}{16}$ inch [1.6 mm].

Toe-in The amount, in inches or millimeters, by which the front of a front wheel points inward.

Toe-out on turns The difference between the angles each of the front wheels makes with the car frame during turns. On a turn, the inner wheel turns, or toes out, more. Also called the turning radius.

616

Top dead center The piston position when the piston has reached the upper limit of its travel in the cylinder and the center line of the connecting rod is parallel to the cylinder walls.

Torque Turning or twisting effort; usually measured in pound-feet or kilogram-meters. Also, a turning force such as that required to tighten a connection.

Torque converter In an automatic transmission, a fluid coupling which incorporates a stator to permit a torque increase.

Torsional vibration Rotary vibration that causes a twist-untwist action on a rotating shaft, so that a part of the shaft repeatedly moves ahead of, or lags behind, the remainder of the shaft; for example, the action of a crankshaft responding to the cylinder firing impulses.

Torsion-bar spring A long, straight bar that is fastened to the vehicle frame at one end and to a suspension part at the other. Spring action is produced by a twisting of the bar.

Tracking Rear wheels following directly behind (in the tracks of) the front wheels.

Transistor An electronic device that can be used as an electric swich; used to replace the contact points in electronic ignition systems.

Transmission An assembly of gears that provides the different gear ratios, as well as neutral and reverse, through which engine power is transmitted to the differential to rotate the drive wheels.

Transmission-controlled spark (TCS) system A General Motors NO_x exhaust-emission control system; makes use of the transmission-gear position to allow distributor vacuum advance in high gear only.

Transmission-oil cooler A small radiator, either mounted separately or as part of the engine radiator, which cools the transmission fluid.

Tread The part of the tire that contacts the road. It is the thickest part of the tire and is cut with grooves to provide traction for driving and stopping.

Trouble diagnosis The detective work necessary to find the cause of a trouble.

Tubeless tire A tire that holds air without the use of a tube.

Tuneup A procedure for inspecting, testing, and adjusting an engine, and replacing any worn parts, to restore engine performance.

Turbocharger A supercharger driven by the engine-exhaust gas.

Turn signal See Directional signal.

Unit An assembly or device that can perform its function only if it is not further divided into its components.

Universal joint In the power train, a jointed connection in the drive shaft that permits the driving angle to change.

Unleaded gasoline Gasoline to which no lead compounds have been intentionally added. Gasoline that contains 0.05 g or less of lead per gallon; required by law to be used in 1975 and later vehicles equipped with catalytic converters.

Upper beam A headlight beam intended primarily for distant illumination, not for use when other vehicles are being met or followed.

Upshift To shift a transmission into a higher gear.

Unsprung weight The weight of that part of the car which is not supported on springs; for example, the wheels and tires.

Vacuum Negative gauge pressure, or a pressure less than atmospheric pressure. Vacuum can be measured in pounds per square inch (psi) but is usually measured in inches or millimeters of mercury (Hg); a reading of 30 inches [762 mm] Hg would indicate a perfect vacuum.

Vacuum advance The advancing (or retarding) of ignition timing by changes in intake-manifold vacuum, reflecting throttle opening and engine load. Also, a mechanism on the ignition distributor that uses intake-manifold vacuum to advance the timing of the spark to the spark plugs.

Vacuum-advance control Any type of NO_x emission-control system designed to allow vacuum advance only during certain modes of engine and vehicle operation.

Vacuum gauge In automotive-engine service, a device that measures intake-manifold vacuum and thereby indicates actions of engine components.

Vacuum modulator In automatic transmissions, a device that modulates, or changes, the main-line hydraulic pressure to meet changing engine loads.

Vacuum motor A small motor, powered by intake-manifold vacuum; used for jobs such as raising and lowering headlight doors.

Vacuum pump A mechanical device used to evacuate a system.

Vacuum switch A switch that closes or opens its contacts in response to changing vacuum conditions.

Valve A device that can be opened or closed to allow or stop the flow of a liquid or gas.

Valve clearance The clearance between the rocker arm and the valve-stem tip in an overhead-valve engine; the clearance in the valve train when the valve is closed.

Valve float A condition in which the engine valves do not close completely or fail to close at the proper time.

Valve grinding Refacing a valve in a valve-refacing machine.

Valve guide A cylindrical part in the cylinder block or head in which a valve is assembled and in which it moves up and down.

Valve-in-head engine See I-head engine.

Valve lash Same as valve clearance.

Valve lifter A cylindrical part of the engine which rests on a cam of the camshaft and is lifted, by cam action, so that the valve is opened. Also called a lifter, tappet, valve tappet, or cam follower.

Valve overlap The number of degrees of crankshaft rotation during which the intake and exhaust valves are open together.

Valve refacer A machine for removing material from the seating face of a valve to true up the face.

Valve seat The surface against which a valve comes to rest to provide a seal against leaking.

Valve-seat inserts Metal rings inserted in cylinder heads to act as valve seats (usually for exhaust valves). They are made of special metals able to withstand very high temperatures.

Valve-seat recession The tendency for valves, in some engines run on unleaded gasoline, to contact the seat in such a way that the seat wears away, or recedes, into the cylinder head. Also known as lash loss.

Valve spool A spool-shaped valve such as in the power-steering unit.

Valve stem The long, thin section of the valve that fits in the valve guide.

Valve-stem seal A device placed on or around the valve stem to reduce the amount of oil that can get on the stem and then work its way down into the combustion chamber.

Valve tappet See Valve lifter.

Valve timing The timing of the opening and closing of the valves in relation to the piston position.

Valve train The valve-operating mechanism of an engine; includes all components from the camshaft to the valve.

Vane A flat, extended surface that is moved around an axis by or in a fluid. Part of the internal revolving portion of an air-supply pump.

Vapor A gas; any substance in the gaseous state, as distinguished from the liquid or solid state.

Vaporization A change of state from liquid to vapor or gas, by evaporation or boiling; a general term including both evaporation and boiling.

Vapor lines Lines that carry refrigerant vapor. See Suction line, Discharge line, and Equalizer line.

Vapor-liquid separator A device in the evaporative emission-control system; prevents liquid gasoline from traveling to the engine through the charcoal-canister vapor line.

Vapor lock A condition in the fuel system in which gasoline vaporizes in the fuel line or fuel pump; bubbles of gasoline vapor restrict or prevent fuel delivery to the carburetor.

Vapor-recovery system An evaporative emission-control system that recovers gasoline vapor escaping from the fuel tank and carburetor float bowl. See Evaporation control system.

Variable-venturi carburetor A carburetor in which the size of the venturi changes according to engine speed and load.

Vent An opening through which air can leave an enclosed chamber.

Venturi In the carburetor, a narrowed passageway or restriction which increases the velocity of air moving through it; produces the vacuum responsible for the discharge of gasoline from the fuel nozzle.

Vibration A rapid back-and-forth motion; an oscillation.

Vibration damper A device attached to the crankshaft of an engine to oppose crankshaft torsional vibration (the twist-untwist actions of the crankshaft caused by the cylinder firing impulses). Also called a harmonic balancer.

618

Viscosity The resistance to flow exhibited by a liquid. A thick oil has greater viscosity than a thin oil.

Viscosity rating An indicator of the viscosity of engine oil. There are separate ratings for winter driving and for summer driving. The winter grades are SAE5W, SAE10W, and SAE20W. The summer grades are SAE20, SAE30, SAE40, and SAE50. Many oils have multiple viscosity ratings, as, for example, SAE20W-30.

Viscous Thick; tending to resist flowing.

Volatile Evaporating readily. For example, Refrigerant-12 is volatile (evaporates quickly) at room temperature.

Volatility A measure of the ease with which a liquid vaporizes. Volatility has a direct relationship to the flammability of a fuel.

Voltage The force which causes electrons to flow in a conductor. The difference in electrical pressure (or potential) between two points in a circuit.

Voltage regulator A device that prevents excessive alternator or generatr votage by alternately inserting and removing a resistance in the field circuit.

Voltmeter A device for measuring the potential difference (voltage) between two points, such as the terminals of a battery or alternator or two points in an electric circuit.

V type engine An engine with two banks or rows of cylinders, set at an angle to form a V.

VV carburetor See Variable-venturi carburetor.

Wankel engine A rotary engine in which a three-lobe rotor turns eccentrically in an oval chamber to produce power.

Water jackets The spaces between the inner and outer shells of the cylinder block or head, through which coolant circulates.

Water pump In the cooling system, the device that circulates coolant between the engine water jackets and the radiator.

Wedge combustion chamber A combustion chamber resembling a wedge in shape.

Wheel alignment A series of tests and adjustments to ensure that wheels and tires are properly positioned on the vehicle.

Wheel balancer A device that checks a wheel-and-tire assembly statically and/or dynamically for balance.

Wheelbase The distance between the center lines of the front and rear axles. For trucks with tandem rear axles, the rear center line is considered to be midway between the two rear axles.

Wheel cylinders In a hydraulic braking system, hydraulic cylinders located in the brake mechanisms at the wheels. Hydraulic pressure from the master cylinder causes the wheel cylinders to move the brake shoes into contact with the brake drums for braking.

Wheel tramp Tendency for a wheel to move up and down so it repeatedly bears down hard, or "tramps," on the road. Sometimes called high-speed shimmy.

Wiring harness A group of individually insulated wires, wrapped together to form a neat, easily installed bundle.

Work The changing of the position of an object against an opposing force; measured in foot-pounds or meter-kilograms. The product of a force and the distance through which it acts.

Worm Type of gear in which the teeth resemble threads; used on the lower end of the steering shaft.

WOT Abbreviation for wide-open throttle.

INDEX

A

Ac (*see* Alternating current)
Adjustments, 16
Air cleaners, 194–196, 316–317, 334–336
  auxiliary air inlet in, 195–196
  servicing of, 334–336
  thermostatic, 194–195, 316–317
Air-conditioning systems, 576–583, 584–589
  action of, 576
  automatic temperature control of, 582–583
  compressor in, 574, 576–577
  controls for, 580
  evacuating and charging, 587–589
  expansion valve in, 578
  magnetic clutch in, 580
  manual temperature control of, 580–582
  operation of, 576–578
  performance test of, 587
  receiver in, 578
  service of, 584–589
  suction throttling valve in, 579–580
  troubleshooting of, 585–587
  (*See also* Refrigeration)
Air-cooled engines, 95, 100, 105
Air-fuel mixture, control of, 316–318
Air-fuel ratios, 198
Air-injection system, 322–344
  servicing of, 329–330
Air tools, 47–48
Alternating current, 234
Alternator, 255–264
  construction of, 257–258
  diodes in, 258–259
  principles of, 255–256
  regulator for, 260
  repair of, 262–263
  rotor in, 257
  service of, 261

  stator in, 258
  troubleshooting of, 261–262
Ammeter, 230–231, 302
Antifreeze solutions, 181–182
Antidieseling solenoid, 206
Antiknock, 184–185
Antilock brake systems, 533–534
Arbor press, 62
Aspect ratio, 555
Automatic chokes, 203–205
  electric, 205
Automatic headlight control, 297–298
Automatic level control, 488–489
Automatic transmissions, 443–458
  (*See also* Transmissions, automatic)
Automobile dealer shops, 3
Automotive components, 5–7
Automotive pollution, sources of, 308–309
  combustion as a source of, 300–309
  leaded gasoline as a source of, 316
Automotive service business, 2–4

B

Ball studs, replacing of, 393
Battery, 238–245, 252, 375–377
  charging of, 243–244
  checking condition of, 241
  cleaning corrosion from, 241
  cold cranking rate, 240
  connection of booster battery, 252
  construction of, 238
  electrolyte in, 238–239, 240
  maintenance of, 240–243
  ratings of, 239–240
  removal of, 244
  reserve capacity, 239–240
  specific gravity of, 241
  tests of, 241–243, 375–377
BDC (bottom dead center), 70

Bearing crush, 403
Bearing spread, 403
Bearings, engine, 129–132, 401–403
  construction of, 132
  failure analysis of, 400–401
  lubrication of, 129–130
  servicing of, 400–403
Belt-tension tester, 368–371
Bias-ply tires, 552–553
Blowby, 140, 309
Bolts, 38–39
Bolt and screw strength, 37–38
Bore, cylinder, 82
Box wrenches, 49
Brake fluid, 523–524
Brake horsepower, 90
Brake lines, 522–523
Brake lining, 524
Brakes, 434–435, 520–549
  antilock systems, 533–534
  bleeding of, 548
  combination valve in, 533
  disk, 527–532
    (*See also* Disk brakes)
  drum, 524–527
    (*See also* Drum brakes)
  dual braking system, 520
  master cylinder in, 521–522
  operation of, 520
  parking, 537–538
  power, 535–537
  pressure-differential valve in, 521, 532
  proportioning valve in, 532
  self-adjusting, 526
  service of, 539–549
  stoplight switch for, 534–535
  warning light for, 532
  wheel cylinder, 525–527

C

Cadmium-tip test, 243
Calipers, 24, 26, 32–33
Camber, 492, 515–517
Camshaft, 79, 144–145, 155, 395